AMERICAN MARRIAGE
RECORDS BEFORE 1699

AMERICAN MARRIAGE RECORDS BEFORE 1699

Edited and Compiled by

WILLIAM MONTGOMERY CLEMENS

Editor of Genealogy Magazine

———

Reprinted with a Supplement

———

CLEARFIELD

Reprinted for
Clearfield Company, Inc. by
Genealogical Publishing Co., Inc.
Baltimore, Maryland
1998, 2004

Originally published: Pompton Lakes, New Jersey, 1926
Reprinted: Genealogical Publishing Co., Inc.
Baltimore, 1967
Reprinted with a Supplement from *Genealogy Magazine:
A Journal of American and British Ancestry,*
Vol. XIV, No. 4 (July 1929) – Vol. XV, No. 3 (July 1930)
Genealogical Publishing Co., Inc.
Baltimore, 1975, 1977, 1979, 1984
Library of Congress Catalogue Card Number 67-30754
International Standard Book Number 0-8063-0075-2
Made in the United States of America

INTRODUCTION

L IKE setting forth to discover a River of Doubt, the compiler of this volume began, a score of years ago, to assemble the thousands of marriage records in this country covering the Colonial period, from the arrival of the first emigrants in James Town, New Netherlands and Plymouth, down to the year of 1700. The task was a long one, and wearisome, but the thought was uppermost that in our humble way we were producing something unique in Americana, adding a valuable chapter to the history of this land of ours, and giving to our fellow citizens a book to aid them in tracing their first emigrant ancestors.

Imagine if you will, what these thousands of marriages meant to the future of the Republic, for from these united husbands and wives were to come descendants now numbering many millions of Americans. The political conditions and the early governing agencies of these colonists are described elsewhere in a chapter on the colonies up to the year 1699. But visualize the domestic conditions under which these marriages were consummated. Marriage then was a sacred, religious ceremony with the thought of divorce as far away as the mirage of the desert. With the constant danger from hostile tribes of savages, these thousands of marriages were celebrated with the Bible and the musket lying in close proximity. The light that was shed at evening nuptials was the blaze of the tallow dip. The wedding feast was the meat of the deer and a pudding of maize. The bridegrooms in knee breeches and jackets of homespun; the brides in silk or linsley-woolsey. These were the simple, God-fearing days of the sacred marriage bond.

Picture the humble daily life and habit of these thousands of Colonial pioneers—these first white Americans, the forefathers of this great republic. It is not for us to alone idolize the fighting heroes of 1776 who made way for liberty—we need pay more devout reverence to those sturdy, brave emigrants of the Colonial period who brought to these shores the true Protestant Christian spirit of manhood and womanhood, which made possible the Revolution of 1776. In cabins of rough hewn timber they lived and loved and worshipped the God of their fathers. Hear the crackling logs on the hearthstone, the whistling of the snowstorm, the fervent words of morning and evening prayer, the nightly reading from the Book of Books, and at early morn the echo of the axe and the gun. After three hundred years we sense the flavor of the smoking venison, and the browned loaf. We hear the bubbling of the kettle in the red glow of the fireplace, and the soft metallic voice of the family pewter. We note the kindly speech and the gentle love and affection of parents, and the quiet, thoughtful children, lending helping hands to ease the burdens of their elders. This was the epoch in our national life when divine love enveloped, encouraged and protected, the founders of Human Liberty. This was the Alpha of the real America.

Ninety per cent of the population of the American colonies in 1699 were persons of English birth or parentage. Counting the Swedes of the Delaware, the Dutch of New York, the handful of Germans in Pennsylvania, and the small group of French Huguenots in New Rochelle, there was still a vast percentage of English, New England and Virginia being populated almost entirely by them. One hundred years later, when the government took its first census, in 1790, we find that out of a total population of two million eight hundred thousand, some one million three hundred thousand were of English birth and parentage. The Scots came next with one hundred and eighty thousand, the Germans with one hundred and fifty-six thousand, the Dutch with fifty-four thousand, the Irish with forty-four thousand and the French with but a scant thirteen thousand. No doubt historians will agree that this has been an English country from its inception down to recent years when the Italian, the Russian Jew, the Pole, the Slav, the Armenian and the Asiatic, has made this nation a babel of many tongues, with its melting pot accompanied by crime, poverty and illiteracy.

Indicative of the character and profession of our earliest colonial ancestors, I have established facts concerning a group of seventy-five original planters in West Jersey who were given deeds by royal grant to property between the years 1670 and 1690. It is interesting to note that of the seventy-five, twenty-seven of the sixty-three came hither from Yorkshire, twenty-three from London, seven from Surrey and six from Sheffield. As to their professions fifteen were merchants, thirteen were yeomen, nine were gentlemen, four were planters, three were carpenters, while there were two tailors, shipwrights, chemists, shoemakers, innkeepers, tanners, weavers, skinners and salesmen. Other trades and professions were represented by a cheesemonger, a milliner, a distiller, a brewer, a haberdasher, a malster and a barber. Here we have a fairly good company fitted in every way to make up the population of a prosperous American village of 1926, rather than a colony in the wilderness of New Jersey nearly three hundred years ago.

Our great men and their ancestors are well represented in the succeeding pages. We have chronicled the marriages of the first Coolidge, the first Lincoln, the first Garfield, the first Grant, the first Cleveland (spelled in the old days Cleaveland), the first Benedict Arnold and a host of names representing the arts and sciences, like the Whittiers and the Emersons, and the Fords and the Wrights. Alas, there are no Woodrow Wilsons, who were very late arrivals, in 1810, from Scotland, or the Hoovers (or Hubers), who came from Berlin, Germany, in 1826.

The passengers on the Mayflower and on the ships arriving the same year and later are well represented in the marriages of the sons and daughters of the Pilgrims and in certain instances of the Pilgrims themselves. The early arrivals from England were largely men of families, and strange to relate, their children who accompanied them numbered more females than males. This may account for the many daughters in one family as compared with the sons. In many cases these daughters married single men who had made the long sailing alone from the other side.

There were three distinct groups of colonists arriving before 1699, first the English in Boston and vicinity, second the Dutch and English in New Amsterdam and the English in Virginia. Of the latter we have little if any records of value. Even history is vague as to the movements and conditions in James Town, which was peopled long before the Pilgrims landed in New England. The tide of migration from Massachusetts was to Maine, New Hampshire and Connecticut. From

Connecticut the New Englanders crossed the sound into Long Island and from thence to Staten Island and to New Jersey. Others of the Connecticut population moved into New York and settled in that section reaching from Westchester to Albany. Some of these early Yankees moved West of the Hudson and into New Jersey and intermarried with the sons and daughters of the Dutch settlers of Bergen.

The Virginians migrated into the Carolinas and in some cases to Maryland and Pennsylvania, where they intermarried with the Dutch and English from New Jersey and the North. But the genuine Virginia movement of population was always Westward, even to this day, first to what was to become Kentucky and Tennessee and thence on to the Missouri River and the Southwest in later periods of time.

Before 1699 only a handful of Celts and Scots made their appearance in the colonies as is proven by a glance at the Macs and the Mcs in the marriage lists. The Welsh came along in small numbers, but nine-tenths of the colonists were absolutely English. The Germans were early in New York and Pennsylvaina, but were missing in the New England sections. The Huguenots were early settlers in Westchester County, New York, obtaining a tract of land which they called New Rochelle.

The Society of Friends, more commonly called Quakers, established churches or what was termed "meetings" early in our colonial history, and to a great extent carefully preserved their marriage records. We are thus enabled to chronicle here the marriages before 1699 in the New Jersey Quaker meetings of Shrewsbury, Burlington and Chesterfield, and in Pennsylvania the marriages recorded at the Philadelphia, Middletown and Falls meetings. In Maryland the marriages are carefully recorded from St. James Episcopal Church in Ann Arundel County, St. George Episcopal Church in Harford County and the church of St. John's Parish in Prince George County. In New Jersey we find many marriage records in the Bergen Dutch Reformed Church in Hackensack, and in the books of St. James Episcopal Church of Piscataway, and the Baptist Church of Middletown.

In New York the records were available from the early Dutch churches of New York City, the church records in Long Island, and in Albany and Kingston. In Pennsylvania the records were obtainable but covering only a brief period from the Moravian Church at Bethlehem.

In the New England Colonies every town (they were called towns and not villages) had its town meeting place. Some of these became eventually established churches and we have still preserved the records of the earlier Boston congregations, the First Church of Charlestown, the First Church of Rowley, the First Church of Roxbury, the churches of Beverly and Newton, and the First Church of Guilford, Conn. Likewise the Baptist Church in Newport, R. I., the First Baptist Church of Northwood, N. H., and many others of the Protestant religions. There was no established place of worship for Roman Catholics in this country until the year 1720.

The genealogist, or the one who may search for a missing ancestor, will be disappointed in not finding enrolled among the marriages some traditional name in the family. The name may appear in an old deed or even the family Bible and yet the official record of the marriage is not to be found. There are many and numerous reasons for these omissions. The church where the marriage was recorded in the original instance may have been destroyed by fire, or as in the case of a Virginian, the record was burned during the Civil War when numerous cities and their court houses and churches were destroyed in battle. Books containing lists of marriages have been lost or mislaid, some have been destroyed by storm and flood, and there are other reasons why they cannot be found.

Hundreds of marriages before 1699 have been discarded in the preparation of this volume, owing to mere guess work as to dates. To list the marriage with the statement that the couple were united "before 1660," or "after 1660," means nothing whatsoever to the true genealogist.

To err is human, and of necessity mistakes have occurred in the compiling of this volume, but such mistakes are no more numerous than those found in the publications of the two largest and oldest genealogical societies in this country, the New England Historical and Genealogical Society and the New York Genealogical and Biographical Society.

In reading over the marriages in this volume the reader will come across, unexpectedly and at times surprisingly, names that are familiar household words, like the Gortons of Rhode Island, suggestive of the first codfish purveyors, or the ancestors of Lydia Pinkham in New Hampshire. In New Jersey and Pennsylvania we find the names of Biddle and Lippincott, the two oldest and perhaps the most distinguished families in the City of Brotherly Love. In New York was the marriage of Captain William Kidd, the alleged notorious pirate, who probably was never in the pirate class. In New York, too, we find the marriage of a Livingston to a Schuyler, both historic names. In Boston there is the record of an Ann Praske, who married in 1661 an Indian of the name of John Wampony, so that the melting pot was beginning to boil a hundred years before the Revolutionary War of 1776. Elizabeth Foster, who was married to Isaac Ver Goose in Boston in 1692, was the original Mother Goose, and when she became a widow, in 1719, published the first edition of her melodies.

Many names found in this volume are now extinct, as for instance, that of Bonython. Captain Richard Bonython settled in Saco, Maine, in 1629. His son, John, a man of ill-temper, was known as the Sagamore of Saco, and on his tomb was written the couplet, which represents John going to the evil spirit of the Indians:

> "Here lies Bonython, the Sagamore of Saco;
> He lived a rogue, and died a knave and went to Hobomocko."

In the spelling of the family name we have followed the records as accurately as possible. If a careless clergyman, or an illiterate sexton, or town clerk, registered a marriage with the names of the contracting parties spelled in an unusual manner, there is no more reason why this compiler should change the spelling, or correct it, than he should change a date or locality. In the case of the name Otis, the original records of Hingham, in Massachusetts, show the name as Otis, Ottis, Otys, Otes, Oates, Oattis and Outis. In our nomenclature we frequently find a Beet, an Onion, a Root or a Corn. In one line there comes to the surface a Turnipseed. But recently was found a record of the marriage of Rhoda Bagger, and she was united to a Cook.

In the early days of the Dutch in New York the names of towns were spelled as they were in Holland, and thus we find Breukelen for Brooklyn, Boswyck for Bushwick, Schanhechtade for Schenectady, Flakbos for Flatbush, and Newwarke for Newark.

In England we find that the learned Dr. Crown, who, in the various books he published in the latter half of the seventeenth century, spelt his name indifferently Cron, Croon, Croun, Crone, Croone, Croune. The modern spelling of any particular name is a pure accident. Before the Elementary Education Act of 1870 a considerable proportion of English people did not spell their names at all. They trusted to the parson and the clerk, who did their best with unfamiliar names. Even now old people in rural districts may find half a dozen orthographic variants of their own names among the sparse documentary records of their lives. And so, dear reader, if you are of the Cousins family and fail in looking over these pages to find the name you are seeking, take a look at Cosins. Gould may be spelled Gold, or Gregg may be Grigg, Hoyt perhaps may occur often as Hoit, and Knowles will be found under Noales.

Naturally, omissions and missing marriage records will come to us in due course. A thousand correspondents will send in authentic records long since lost or hidden. In some obscure garret may be found a missing church record, and as the months pass hundreds of additional marriage records will find their way into our archives. These we promise to publish at a future time either as a supplementary volume or as volume two. But in the present publication we offer the result of our years of labor, applied with no little patience, industry and care, and trust the work will find due appreciation.   W. M. C.

Pompton Lakes, New Jersey, September, 1926.

THE COLONIES BEFORE 1699

THE following pages contain a resume of the beginning and progress of the original plantations, or colonies, in this country, from their first settlement to the year 1699. The exact population of the colonies before 1699 probably will never be known. The first Government census was not taken until a century later, in 1790. There had been attempts at a partial census, especially in Maryland, but in this volume the attempt is made to make a first directory of the colonists, and broadly speaking, this is the first census of the American people.

CONNECTICUT, at the time of the first arrival of the English, was possessed by the Pequot, the Mohegan, the Podunk, and other smaller tribes of Indians. The first grant of Connecticut was made by the Plymouth council in England to the Earl of Warwick in 1630. Attracted by the trade with the Indians, some of the settlers of Plymouth had explored the Connecticut River and fixed upon Windsor for the establishment of a trading house. A company from Dorchester settled at Mattaneaug, which they called Windsor; several people from Watertown commenced a plantation at Pauquiaug, which they called Wethersfield, and others from Newtown established themselves at Hartford.

The planters in Connecticut at first settled under the general government of Massachusetts, but the administration of their affairs was entirely in their own hands. The first court, which exercised all the powers of government, was held April 26, 1636, at Hartford, the plantation between Windsor and Wethersfield.

In the year 1636 a large accession was made to the inhabitants on the Connecticut River. Messrs. Hooker and Stone, the ministers of Newtown, near Boston, with their whole church and congregation, travelled in June through a trackless wilderness, driving 160 cattle and subsisting during the journey on the milk of the cows. They settled at Hartford, having purchased the land of an Indian sachem. At the close of the year there were about 800 persons in the colony. The year 1637 is distinguished by the war with the Pequots. A body of troops was sent out under the command of John Mason, and on May 26 they attacked the enemy in one of their forts near New London and killed 600 of the Iudians. Only two of the English were killed and sixteen wounded. The Pequots were entirely subdued, and the other Indians of New England were inspired with such terror as to restrain them from open hostilities for nearly forty years.

In 1637 a new colony was commenced in Connecticut. John Davenport, accompanied by Theophilus Eaton and Edward Hopkins, and other persons from London, arrived in the summer at Boston, seeking the unmolested enjoyment of civil and religious liberty. Not finding a convenient place in Massachusetts, and being informed of a large bay to the southwest of the Connecticut River, commodious for trade, they applied to their friends in Connecticut to purchase for them of the native proprietors all the lands lying between the rivers of Connecticut and Hudson. This purchase was in part effected. In the autumn Mr. Eaton and some others of the company made a journey to Connecticut to explore the lands and harbors on the sea coast and pitched upon Quinnipiack, afterwards called New Haven, for the place of their settlement.

The foundation of two colonies was now laid, which were called the colonies of Connecticut and New Haven. The original constitution of the former was established by a convention of all the free planters of Windsor, Hartford and Wethersfield, which met at Hartford January 14, 1639. It was ordained that there should be annually two general courts or assemblies.

These two colonies remained distinct until the year 1665, when they were united into one; but though distinct in government yet a union, rendered necessary by common danger, subsisted between them. The apprehension of hostilities from the Indians, and the actual encroachments and violence of the Dutch, induced the colonies of New Haven, Connecticut, Massachusetts and Plymouth to adopt articles of confederation, which were signed at Boston May 19, 1643. This union was of the highest importance to the colonies, particularly to Connecticut and New Haven, which were peculiarly exposed to hostilities from the Dutch. It subsisted more than forty years until the abrogation of the charters of the New England colonies by King James II.

The colonies continued to increase, and new towns, purchased of the Indians, were constantly settled. In 1661 Major John Mason bought of the natives all lands which had not before been purchased by particular towns and made a public surrender of them to the colony in the presence of the general assembly. A petition was now prepared to King Charles II for a charter and John Winthrop, who had been chosen governor of Connecticut, was employed to present it. His majesty issued his letters under the great seal, April 23, 1662, ordaining that there should be annually two general assemblies, consisting of the governor, the deputy governor, and twelve assistants, with two deputies from every town or city. This charter remained the basis of the government of Connecticut until 1818.

The number of men in Connecticut in 1671 was 2,050. In 1672 the union of Connecticut, Massachusetts and Plymouth was renewed and the first code of Connecticut laws was published. The Indian wars in 1675 and 1676 occasioned much suffering in the colony. In 1687 an attempt was made to wrest the charter from Connecticut. A quo warranto against the governor and company had been issued two years before, and in October of this year, when the assembly was sitting, Governor Edmond Andros went to Hartford with sixty regular troops, demanded the charter, and declared the government to be dissolved. The subject was debated in the assembly until evening, when the charter was brought and laid upon the table; but the lights being instantly extinguished, Captain Wadsworth of Hartford seized it and secreted it in the cavity of a large oak tree in front of the house of Samuel Wyllys. Andros assumed the government and the records of the colony were closed. He appointed all officers, civil and military. Notwithstanding the professions of regard to the public good, made by the tyrant, he soon began to infringe the rights of the people. After the seizure of Andros by the daring friends of liberty in Massachusetts the old magistrates of Connecticut were induced again to accept the government, at the request of the freemen, May 9, 1689. In 1691 the old charter was resumed, being acknowledged to be valid.

DELAWARE, was first settled at Cape Henlopen by a colony of Swedes and Finns in 1627. They laid out a small town near Wilmington in 1631, but it was destroyed by the Dutch. They were at first subject to a governor under a commission from the King of Sweden. In 1655 they were subdued by the Dutch from New York and they continued under this government until the Dutch were subdued by the English in 1664, when they passed under the authority of the English governor of New York. In 1682 this colony was united to Pennsylvania under William Penn, and the inhabitants enjoyed all the benefit of the laws of the province. They were from this time to be considered as the same people. The freemen were summoned to attend the assembly in person, but they chose to elect representatives. In the settlement of this country under the government of Penn the lands were purchased and not forcibly taken from the natives. The Dutch had previously adopted a similar practice. In 1692 the government of Pennsylvania and Delaware was assumed by the Crown and was entrusted to Colonel Fletcher, Governor of New York. But in the latter end of 1693 the government was restored to Mr. Penn, who appointed William Markham Lieutenant Governor. During his administration, in 1696, another frame of government was adopted, which continued to be the constitution of Pennsylvania and Delaware during the whole time of their union in legislation. When the next charter was accepted by the province of Pennsylvania in October, 1701, it was totally rejected by the members of the three lower counties of Delaware and separation followed. By the new charter the principles of the first constitution were essentially altered.

MAINE, was discovered by Martin Pring in June, 1603. He ranged the coast from the Penobscot to Massachusetts Bay. The country was called Mawooshen. In 1605 George Weymouth visited the Penobscot River. An attempt was made to form a permanent settlement in Maine in 1607, the same year in which Virginia was settled and thirteen years before the settlement at Plymouth. George Popham and Raleigh Gilbert commanded the "Gift," and the "Mary and John," and arrived with 100 men at the Island of Monhegan, August 11, and landed at the mouth of the Sagadohoc, or Kennebec, on the western shore, near Cape Small Point. There they read their patent and laws and built a fort, called St. George. When the ships returned to England, December 5, they left a colony of forty-five persons. Popham was President and Gilbert, Admiral. During the winter the store house was burnt and Popham died and the colony was much discouraged. The first permanent settlement was made in 1630.

Sir Ferdinando Gorges obtained a charter of the land from Piscataqua to Sagadohoc, called the Province of Maine. The name probably was given from Maine in France, of which the Queen of England was the proprietor. Gorges set up a government. In 1640 the first general court was held at Saco. But this government being feeble the inhabitants submitted themselves to Massachusetts in 1652 and sent deputies to the general court at Boston. In the new charter of Massachusetts, in 1692, Maine was included.

MARYLAND, was granted by King Charles I to Cecilius Calvert, Lord Baltimore, June 20, 1632. It received its name in honor of the Queen Henrietta Maria, daughter of Henry the Great, King of France. It was the first colony which was erected into a province of the British Empire and governed by laws enacted in a provincial legislature. The proprietor arrived in February, 1634, and in March, at the head of about two hundred Roman Catholics, he took possession of the territory, which had been granted him. Lord Baltimore, himself a Roman Catholic, established his province on the basis of perfect freedom in religion and security to property. The land was purchased of the Indians for a consideration, which seemed to be satisfactory. Fifty acres of land were given to every emigrant in absolute fee.

A collection of regulations was prepared by the assembly in 1638. The province was divided into baronies and manors and bills were passed for securing the liberties of the people. A house of assembly, composed of representatives, was established in 1639, and a code of laws passed. All the inhabitants were required to take the oath of allegiance to the King, and the rights of the proprietary were acknowledged. At this period the colony was very inconsiderable in numbers and wealth for a general contribution was thought necessary to erect a watermill for the use of the colony. Slavery seems to have existed at the time of its original settlement. The encroachments of the English awakened the apprehensions of the natives that they should be annihilated as a people, and an Indian War was commenced in 1642, which lasted several years. After a peace was made salutary regulations were adopted, securing to the Indians their rights. A rebellion, in 1645, produced by a few restless men, obliged the Governor to flee into Virginia, but it was suppressed in the following year. The constitution was established in 1646, and it continued with a little interruption till 1776.

MASSACHUSETTS, was formerly divided into the two colonies of Plymouth and of Massachusetts Bay, which were distinct for many years. Roger Williams, who was skillful in the Indian language and anxious to ascertain the import of the names of places, says: "I had learnt that Massachusetts was so called from the Blue Hills," Wachusett, in the Indian language means a hill, and as Eliot in his Bible gives Mahsag as meaning great, the combination of Mahsag Wachusett, meaning Great Hill, would make the word Massachusetts.

Plymouth was first settled in December, 1620, by the Mayflower Pilgrims, who intended to commence a plantation in the territory of the South Virginia company, but who on account of the advanced season of the year were induced to establish themselves where they first landed. They formed a government for themselves and chose Carver for their governor. In 1620 all the land from sea to sea, between the fortieth and forty-eighth degrees of north latitude, was granted to the council at Plymouth, in England. From this company a patent was obtained in 1621. For several years the whole property of the colony was in common. The governor, who was chosen annually, had at first but one assistant; in 1624 he had five; and in 1633 the number was increased to seven. The last patent was obtained in 1630, by which the colonists were allowed to establish their own government. The first House of Representatives was formed in 1639, being rendered necessary by the increase of the inhabitants and the extension of the settlements.

The patent of Massachusetts Bay was obtained in 1628. This colony was bounded on the south by a line three miles distant from the Charles River. In the same year a few people under the government of John Endicott began a settlement at Naumkeak, now Salem. In 1629 a form of government was settled and thirteen persons, resident on the plantation, were entrusted with the sole management of the affairs of the colony. All these were but deputy officers, as they were appointed in England. This state of things, however, lasted but a short time. It was soon determined to transfer the government entirely to New England. Governor Winthrop accordingly sailed, in 1630, taking the charter with him. This instrument vested the whole executive power in the Governor, Deputy Governor, and nineteen assistants, and the legislative power in a general court, composed of the above and of the freemen of the colony. This assembly was authorized to elect their governor and all necessary officers. But the provisions of the charter were not very carefully observed. The emigrants, considering themselves as subject to no laws excepting those of reason, and equity and Scripture, modelled their government according to their own pleasure.

Early in 1631 the general court ordained that the Governor, Deputy Governor, and assistants, should be chosen by the freemen alone; they directed that there should be two courts instead of four in a year; in May, 1634, they created a representative body; they established judicatories of various kinds, and in 1644 the general court was divided into the two houses of deputies and of magistrates. Massachusetts continued to increase till the Indian wars of 1675 and 1676, which occasioned great distress. About 600 of the inhabitants of New England were killed and twelve towns were entirely destroyed, and this colony was the greatest sufferer.

In 1684 the charter of Massachusetts was declared to be forfeited by the high courts of chancery in England in consequence of charges of disrespect to the laws of England. In 1686 Joseph Dudley received his commission of president of New England, though Plymouth was not included, but at the close of the year Andros arrived with a commission, which included that colony. In 1689 this tyrannical governor was deposed and imprisoned by an indignant people and Massachusetts and Plymouth re-established their old government. In 1692 a charter was obtained which constituted Massachusetts a province and added to the colony of Plymouth the province of Maine, the province of Nova Scotia and the Elizabeth Islands and Nantucket and Martha's Vineyard. From this period Massachusetts and Plymouth were blended and under one government.

NEW HAMPSHIRE, was first settled in 1623 by persons sent out by Gorges and Mason under authority of a grant from the council of Plymouth. The settlements went on but slowly for several years. In 1638 three associations for government were formed at Portsmouth, Dover and Exeter. In 1641 and 1642 the inhabitants of these towns voluntarily submitted themselves to the jurisdiction of Massachusetts, securing to themselves the same privileges with the rest of the colony and being exempted from all public charges, except such as arose among themselves. New Hampshire was separated from Massachusetts and a royal government established in 1680, consisting of a president and council appointed by the King and representatives chosen by the people. A change was made in 1686 and all New England was entrusted to a president and council. After the imprisonment of Andros the union with Massachusetts was revived in 1689, but in 1692 the old separate government was re-established.

NEW JERSEY, was first settled by the Swedes, and was formerly a part of New Netherlands, which was divided into Nova Caesarea, or New Jersey, and New York in 1664, when it was conquered by the English. It has its name from the Island of Jersey, the residence of the family of Sir George Carteret, to whom this territory was granted. Philip Carteret was appointed governor in 1665 and took possession of Elizabethtown, the capital, then consisting of four families, just settled in the wilderness. In 1672 he was driven from his government by insurgents who refused the payment of rents under the pretence that they held their possessions by Indian grants and not from the proprietors. In 1673 the Dutch retook New Netherlands, but in the following year it was restored by treaty to the English. In 1676 New Jersey was divided into East and West Jersey. The government of the latter was retained as a dependency of New York, and a confusion of jurisdiction commenced, which long distracted the people, and which at length terminated in the annihilation of the authority of the proprietors. West Jersey was reinstated in its former privileges in 1680. Sir George Carteret, in 1682, transferred his rights in East Jersey to William Penn. At this time there were supposed to be in the province about seven hundred families. In 1688 the Jerseys were added to the jurisdiction of New England. They were united under one government in 1702 and received the single name of New Jersey.

NEW YORK, was discovered in 1608 by Henry Hudson, who passed up the river which bears his name. His right to the country which he had discovered under a commission from King James I he sold to the Dutch. In 1614 the States General granted a patent for an exclusive trade on Hudson's River to a number of merchants, who built a fort near Albany. In the same year the Dutch were visited by Captain Argal from Virginia, and being unable to resist him they submitted for the time to the King of England. The country was granted by the States General to the West India Company in 1621. In June, 1629, Wouter Van Twiller arrived at Fort Amsterdam, now New York, and took upon himself the government. The extension of the English settlements naturally occasioned some disputes respecting the boundaries of the Dutch possessions.

The last Dutch governor was Peter Stuyvesant, who began his administration in 1647. The inroads upon his territory kept him constantly employed. In 1655 he subdued the few Swedes on the west side of Delaware Bay and placed the country under the command of lieutenant governor. But he was himself obliged at last to submit to the English. The country in the possession of the Dutch was given by the King of England to the Duke of York and Albany. An expedition was fitted out and August 27, 1664, Governor Stuyvesant was reduced to the necessity of capitulating to Colonel Nicolls, and the whole of the New Netherlands soon became subject to the English crown. The country was retaken by the Dutch in 1673, but it was restored in the following year. In 1683 the inhabitants of New York first participated in the legislative power. Previously to this period they had been completely subjected to the governor, but in this year they were summoned to choose representatives to meet in an assembly. In 1688 New York was annexed to the jurisdiction of New England. In 1691 a governor arrived from England and the first assembly was held. The population in 1699 was about 18,000.

NORTH CAROLINA, was originally included in the territory called South Virginia, and it was in North Carolina that the first English settlements were made in America. They were, however, broke up, and the first permanent colony was established on the Chesapeake. This State was afterwards included in the grant of Carolina in 1663. It began to be settled about the year 1710 by a few Palatines from Germany.

SOUTH CAROLINA, was first granted to the Earl of Clarendon and others in 1663. A small plantation had for some years been established within the boundaries of the patent. A more ample charter was obtained in 1664 and the government was placed in the hands of the proprietors. This proprietary government continued about fifty years. The Governor was appointed by the crown, and he had a negative on all the bills passed by the assemblies. The English constitution was the model. During the proprietary government the colony was involved in perpetual quarrels.

PENNSYLVANIA, was granted by King Charles II to William Penn March 4, 1681, and in this year a colony commenced a settlement above the confluence of the Schuylkill with the Delaware. In the following year the proprietary published a frame of government and a body of laws. All legislative powers were vested in the Governor and freemen of the province in the provincial council and a general assembly. The Governor had a treble vote in the council, which consisted of seventy-two members chosen by the people, and the assembly at first embraced all the freemen, but as the colony increased it was limited to five hundred. Liberty of conscience was extended to all. A treaty was immediately held with the natives and the purchase of the soil was commenced. The friendly intercourse with the Indians, which was now begun, was not interrupted for more than seventy years. The first settlers of Pennsylvania were chiefly Quakers who had suffered persecution on account of their religion. In 1683 the first assembly was held at Philadelphia, and a new frame of government was adopted, by which the council was reduced and the Governor vested with a negative upon all bills passed in the assembly. Mr. Penn being soon called to England he entrusted the government to five commissioners. In 1688 he appointed a deputy, and in 1701 gave the people the last charter of privileges.

RHODE ISLAND, was first settled from Massachusetts, and its settlement was owing to religious persecution. Roger Williams, in 1636, laid the foundation of the town of Providence. In 1638 John Clark and others purchased of the Indian sachems Aquetneck, or the principal island, which was called Rhode Island, and incorporated themselves into a body politic, making choice of William Coddington as their chief magistrate. In 1644 Roger Williams, who had been sent to England as agent, obtained a patent for the Providence plantations. They were, however, incorporated with Rhode Island under one government, in 1647, in which year the first general assembly was held. The executive power was placed in the hands of a president and four assistants. A charter was given by King Charles II in 1663, which vested the legislative power in an assembly, of which the governor and assistants were members. Nothing but allegiance was reserved to the king.

An act was passed, in 1663, declaring that all men of competent estates and good conduct, who professed Christianity, with the exception of Roman Catholics, should be admitted freemen. In 1665 the government passed an order to outlaw Quakers and seize their estates, because they would not bear arms, but the people would not suffer it to be carried into effect. A quo warranto was issued against the colony in 1685. At the close of the following year Andros assumed the government, but after his imprisonment, in 1689, the charter was resumed.

VIRGINIA, was given by patent to the London company in 1606. For twenty years previously to this time attempts had been made to establish a colony in Virginia under the patronage of Sir Walter Raleigh, but the settlements were broken up and the attempts were unsuccessful. The first permanent colony, sent out by the company already mentioned, arrived in 1607. The adventurers took possession of a peninsula on Powhatan, or James River, May 13, and immediately commenced building a town, which they called James Town. This was the first permanent habitation of the English in America. Before the close of the year the number of the colony amounted to two hundred. In 1608 Captain Smith, in an open barge, with fourteen persons, expored the waters from Cape Henry to the Susquehannah. On his return he was made president of the colony. A second charter with more ample privileges was granted in 1609 and as the number of proprietors was increased the augmented wealth and reputation enabled them to proceed with greater spirit. Seven ships were fitted out with three hundred people for the colony. Soon after their arrival a plot was formed by the Indians for exterminating them, but it being disclosed by Pocahontas, they were providentially saved from destruction.

In 1610 the sufferings of the colony were extreme, both on account of the hostility of the Indians and the want of provisions. Of near five hundred persons left at the departure of Captain Smith sixty only remained at the expiration of six months. The small number in the colony had embarked with the intention of returning to England when the arrival of Lord Delaware prevented them from abandoning the country. He came with three ships and an abundant supply of provisions. He appointed a council to assist him in the administration. Under his care the affairs of the colony were soon re-established. A third charter, granted in 1612, annexed to Virginia all the islands within three hundred miles of that coast. A provincial legislature, in which the colonists were represented, was established in 1619. In the following year the settlement was increased and strengthened by the accession of more than twelve hundred persons. As many of the settlers were destitute of wives, the company sent over one hundred and fifty girls, young and handsome. The price of a wife at first was one hundred pounds of tobacco, but as the number was diminished the price was increased to one hundred and fifty pounds, the value of which in money was three shillings per pound. The first negroes were imported into Virginia in 1620. In the following year Sir Francis Wyatt arrived as governor with seven hundred people. Some changes took place in the government favorable to freedom. The constitution at this period became fixed. The assembly was composed of two burgesses from every plantation, and all matters were to be decided by a majority, reserving a negative to the governor.

The year 1622 is memorable for the massacre of the English. March 27 the Indians carried into effect a preconcerted conspiracy and massacred with indiscriminuate barbarity two hundred and forty-seven of the English who were unresisting and defenceless. A war immediately commenced, and to its evils were added the miseries of famine. A new supply from the parent country soon, however, counter-balanced the losses, which had been sustained. In 1624 the charter of Virginia was vacated and the company was dissolved. King Charles I, in 1625, made Virginia dependent on the crown. In 1636 laws were enacted to preserve uniformity in religion. Sir William Berkeley was appointed governor in 1639, and a regular administration of justice took place. Virginia was the last of the king's dominions which submitted to Cromwell's usurpation and the first that threw it off. After the restoration, in the year 1662, the Church of England was regularly established by the assembly, and all ministers not ordained by some bishop in England were prohibited from preaching on pain of suspension or banishment. The year 1676 is memorable for Bacon's Rebellion.

MARRIAGES BEFORE 1699

A

ABBOTT, Benjamin and Sarah Farnum, 22 April 1685, Andover, Mass.
ABBOTT, Elizabeth and Nathan Stevens, 24 October 1692, Andover, Mass.
ABBOTT, George and Hannah Chandler, 12 December 1646, Roxbury, Mass.
ABBOTT, George and Sarah Farnum, 26 April 1658, Andover, Mass.
ABBOTT, George and Elizabeth Ballard, 13 September 1689, Andover, Mass.
ABBOTT, George and Dorcas Graves, 17 April 1678, Andover, Mass.
ABBOTT, Hannah and John Chandler, 20 December 1676, Andover, Mass.
ABBOTT, Hannah and James Ingalls, 16 April 1695, Andover, Mass.
ABBOTT, Jane and Edward Smout, 16 February 1691, Burlington, N. J.
ABBOTT, John and Ann Meliverer, 7 March 1696, Chesterfield, N. J.
ABBOTT, John and Sarah Barker, 17 November 1673, Andover, Mass.
ABBOTT, Jonathan and Sarah Olmstead, 5 June 1696, Norwalk, Conn.
ABBOTT, Lydia and Henry Chandler, 28 November 1695, Andover, Mass.
ABBOTT, Maria and John Robbins, 4 November 1659, Branford, Conn.
ABBOTT, Mary and Stephen Barker, 13 May 1687, Andover, Mass.
ABBOTT, Nathaniel and Dorcas Hibbert, 22 October 1695, Andover, Mass.
ABBOTT, Nehemiah and Mary How, 14 October 1659, Ipswich, Mass.
ABBOTT, Nehemiah and Abigail Lovejoy, 9 April 1691, Andover, Mass.
ABBOTT, Sarah and Henry Ingalls, Sr., 1 August 1689, Andover, Mass.
ABBOTT, Sarah and Ephriam Stevens, 11 October 1680, Andover, Mass.
ABBOTT, Sarah and John Faulkner, 19 October 1682, Andover, Mass.
ABBOTT, Sarah and Joseph Chandler, 26 November 1691, Andover, Mass.
ABBOTT, Thomas and Sarah Steward, 15 December 1664, Andover, Mass.
ABBOTT, Thomas and Hannah Grey, 7 December 1697, Andover, Mass.
ABBOTT, Timothy and Hannah Graves, 27 December 1689, Andover, Mass.
ABBOTT, William and Elizabeth Geery, 19 June 1682, Andover, Mass.
ABDY, Mathew and Alice Cox, 24 May 1662, Boston, Mass.
ABEL, Elizabeth and Henry Curtis, 13 May 1645, Windsor, Conn.
ABELL, Experience and John Hyde, 3 March, 1698, Norwich, Conn.
ABELL, Joanna and William Hide, 4 June 1667, Rehoboth, Mass.
ABORN, Samuel and Catherine Smith, 1635, Marblehead, Mass.
ABRAHAMS, Annetje and Jan Bommel, 13 May 1662, Brooklyn, N. Y.
ABRAHAMS, Annetje and Jan the Negro, 20 December 1693, Brooklyn, N. Y.
ACKWORTH, Richard and Sarah Hardy, 6 December 1683, Somerset Co., Md.
ACKWORTH, Sarah and William Keen Jr., 14 July 1692, Somerset Co., Md.
ACTON, Benjamin and Christina England, 27 June 1686, Philadelphia, Penn.

ADAMS, Abigail and Edward Higbee, 1684, Huntington, I. L., N. Y.

ADAMS, Abraham and Mary Pettengill, 10 November 1670, Newbury, Mass.

ADAMS, Bertha and John Webb, May 1680, Braintree, Mass.

ADAMS, David and Loves Collins, 15 December 1698, Boston, Mass.

ADAMS, Edward and Elizabeth Buckland, 25 May 1660, Windsor, Conn.

ADAMS, Edward and Abigail Day, 7 October 1678, Dedham, Mass.

ADAMS, Edward and Elizabeth Walley, 19 May 1692, Bristol, R. I.

ADAMS, Elisha and Mehitable Cary, 18 December 1689, Bristol, R. I.

ADAMS, Elizabeth and James Moulton, 10 February 1662, Wenham, Mass.

ADAMS, Elizabeth and Samuel Smith, 14 August 1695, Dedham, Mass.

ADAMS, Elizabeth and John Hollinghead, 1692, Moorestown, N. J.

ADAMS, Fenwick and Anne Watkins, 18 August 1687, Salem Co., N. J.

ADAMS, Geo. and Widow Bradfield, 5 September 1651, Branford, Conn.

ADAMS, Hannah and Francis Muncy, 6 December 1659, Ipswich, Mass.

ADAMS, Hannah and Samuel Savill, 10 February 1673, Braintree, Mass.

ADAMS, Henry and Elizabeth Paine, 17 August 1643, Braintree, Mass.

ADAMS, Henry and Mary Petty, 10 May 1660, Boston, Mass.

ADAMS, Henry and Martha Hewes, 10 January 1694, Boston, Mass.

ADAMS, Isaac and Martha Stocker, 4 January 1699, Boston, Mass.

ADAMS, James and Esther Allen, 2 July 1695, Shrewsbury, N. J.

ADAMS, John and Abigail Smith, 1657, Hartford, Conn.

ADAMS, John and Dorcas DeWitt, 8 May 1677, Ipswich, Mass.

ADAMS, John and Michal Bloyse, 2 April 1685, Medfield, Mass.

ADAMS, John, Jr. and Hannah Treadwell, 22 May 1690, Ipswich, Mass.

ADAMS, John and Hannah Checkley, 19 October 1694, Boston, Mass.

ADAMS, Jonathan and Mary Ellis, 1678, Medfield, Mass.

ADAMS, Jonathan and Alice Mays (widow), 24 May 1686, Philadelphia, Penn.

ADAMS, Jonathan and Tamersen Shofeld, 1 February 1696-7, Dedham, Mass.

ADAMS, Joseph and Abigail Baxter, 2 November 1650, Braintree, Mass.

ADAMS, Joseph and Mary Chapin, 1682, Braintree, Mass.

ADAMS, Joseph and Elizabeth Hewes, 3 May 1694, Boston, Mass.

ADAMS, Lucie and Silvester Harbert, 21 July 1652, Boston, Mass.

ADAMS, Lydia and Joseph Daniels, 27 January 1696-7, Dedham, Mass.

ADAMS, Marah and Samuel Webb, 16 December 1686, Braintree, Mass.

ADAMS, Mary and George Fairbanks, 26 October 1646, Dedham, Mass.

ADAMS, Mary and Thomas French, 29 February 1659, Ipswich, Mass.

ADAMS, Mary and Jeremiah Goodridge, 15 November 1660, Newbury, Mass.

ADAMS, Mary and John Vial, 27 December 1694, Boston, Mass.

ADAMS, Nathaniel and Elizabeth Purmott, 24 September 1652, Boston, Mass.

ADAMS, Nathaniel and Mary Dickinson, 30 June 1668, Ipswich, Mass.

ADAMS, Nathaniel and Abigail Kimball, January 1693, Ipswich, Mass.

ADAMS, Peter and Mary Long, 4 January 1682, Dorchester, Mass.

ADAMS, Philip and Mary Barry, 1 September 1691, Somerset Co., Md.

ADAMS, Rebecca and Joseph Snelling, 19 July 1694, Boston, Mass.

ADAMS, Robert and Sarah Glover, 6 February 1678, Newbury, Mass.

ADAMS, Robert and Rebecca Knight, 1 August 1695, Newbury, Mass.

ADAMS, Ruth and Amos Fisher, 22 December 1691, Dedham, Mass.

ADAMS, Samuel and Mehitable Norton, 20 December 1664, Ipswich, Mass.

ADAMS, Sarah and Edward Counts, 25 February 1663, Malden, Mass.

ADAMS, Sarah and Henry Nock, 10 January 1692, Dover, N. H.

ADAMS, Sarah and Daniel Black, 19 July 1695, Boxford, Mass.

ADAMS, Seamerey and Mary Brett, 28 August 1687, Philadelphia, Penn.

ADAMS, Thomas and Rebeckah Potter, 27 November 1667, New Haven, Conn.

ADAMS, William and Mary Manning, 15 August 1673, Dedham, Mass.

ADAMS, William and Alice Bradford, 27 March 1680, Dedham, Mass.

ADAMS, William and Sarah Nostock, 10 December 1691, Boston, Mass.

ADDIS, Anne and Ambrose Dart, 24 April 1653, Boston, Mass.

ADDIS, Millicent and William Southmayd, 28 November, 1642, Boston, Mass.

ADGATE, Abigail and Daniel Tracey, 9 September 1682, Conn.

ADRIANCE, Annetje and Jacob Jansen, 4 January 1665, Kingston, N. Y.

ADY, William and Hannah Smith, 19 July 1697, Bristol, R. I.

AEALY, Susan and William Pitts, 7 October 1655, Boston, Mass.

AERSTSEN, Grietie and Jacob Van Elmendorp, 28 January 1668, Esopus, N. Y.

AERSTSEN, Neettjie and Cornelis Fynhout, 6 June 1667, Esopus, N. Y.

AINSWORTH, John and Sarah Bridger, 15 July 1678, Richmond Co., Va.

ALBERTSON, Elsje and Benjamin Provoost, 5 November 1671, New York City.

ALBINS, Abigail and John Heiford, 8 April 1679, Braintree, Mass.

ALCOCK, Elizabeth and Joseph Soper, 6 March 1656, Boston, Mass.

ALCOCK, Margery (widow) and John Benham, 16 November 1660, Boston, Mass.

ALCOCK, Mary and James Robinson, 27 July 1664, Dorchester, Mass.

ALDEN, Elizabeth and Benjamin Snow, 12 December 1693, Bridgewater, Mass.

ALDEN, Elizabeth and John Seabury, 1697, New London, Conn.

ALDEN, Isaac and Mehitable Allen, 2 December 1685, Bridgewater, Mass.

ALDEN, Nathaniel and Hepsiba Mountjoy, 1 October 1691, Boston, Mass.

ALDEN, Ruth and John Bass, 3 February 1657, Duxbury, Mass.

ALDEN, William and Mary Drewrey, 21 May 1691, Boston, Mass.

ALDINE, John and Elizabeth Everill, 1 April 1660, Boston, Mass.

ALDIS, Daniel and Sarah Payne, 23 November 1685, Dedham, Mass.

ALDIS, John and Sarah Elliott, 27 July 1650, Dedham, Mass.

ALDIS, John and Mary Winchester, 23 May 1682, Wrentham, Mass.

ALDIS, Mary and Joshua Fisher, 14 January 1643, Dedham, Mass.

ALDIS, Mary and Nathaniel Richards, 21 December 1678, Dedham, Mass.

ALDIS, Sarah and Gershon Hubbard, 26 February 1674, Dedham, Mass.

ALDRICH, Thomas and Elizabeth Prentice, 4 March 1674, Dedham, Mass.

ALDRICH, Thomas and Hannah Colburn, 16 January 1677, Dedham, Mass.

ALDRIDGE, John and Sarah Leach, 31 October 1678, Braintree, Mass.

ALDRIDGE, Joseph and Patience Osborne, 26 December 1661, Braintree, Mass.

ALDRIDGE, Mary and Samuel Judson, 6 August 1646, Dedham, Mass.

ALEXANDER, Abigail and Thomas Webster, 16 June 1663, Northampton, Mass.

ALEXANDER, Francis and Sarah Kirk, 13 March 1699, Boston, Mass.

ALEXANDER, George and Susanna Sage, 18 March 1644, Windsor, Conn.

ALEXANDER, John and Sarah Gaylord, 18 November 1671, Windsor, Conn.

ALEXANDER, Sarah and Samuel Curtis, 23 July 1678, Northfield, Mass.

ALFORD, Elizabeth and Nathaniel Hudson, 1 December 1659, Boston, Mass.

ALFORD, Elizabeth and Jacob Winfrey, 1698, New Kent Co., Va.

ALFORD, Josiah and Hannah Westover, 22 May 1693, Simsbury, Conn.

ALGER, Jane and Robert Davise, 19 February 1693, Boston, Mass.

ALGER, Mary and David Bishop, 25 March 1679, Woodbridge, N. J.

ALGOOD, Lidia and William Bashteen, March 1699, Harford Co., Md.

ALLAINBY, Elynor and Charles Goringe, 27 October 1696, Elizabeth City Co., Va.

ALLEN, Amy and Joseph Hatch, 7 December 1683, Falmouth, Mass.

ALLEN, Andrew and Elizabeth Richardson, 1 January 1681, Andover, Mass.

ALLEN, Ann (widow) and James Jewett, 13 March 1653, Boston, Mass.

ALLEN, Deborah and Theodat Lawson, 6 May 1690, Boston, Mass.

ALLEN, Edward and Martha Waye, 7 March 1652, Boston, Mass.

ALLEN, Edward and Sarah Kimball, 24 November 1658, Ipswich, Mass.

ALLEN, Edward and Mercy Painter, 15 November 1683, Deerfield, Mass.

ALLEN, Elenor and George Emlen, 12 November 1685, Philadelphia, Penn.

ALLEN, Elizabeth and Rev. Samuel Stone, July 1641, Boston, Mass.

ALLEN, Elizabeth and Nathaniel Tompkins, 15 January 1670, Newport, R. I.

ALLEN, Elizabeth and Andrew Waker, 8 August 1689, Boston, Mass.

ALLEN, Elizabeth and Moses Bradford, 8 December 1692, Boston, Mass.

ALLEN, Elizabeth and John Briggs, 27 April 1697, Boston, Mass.

ALLEN, Ephriam and Margaret Wardell, 28 August 1687, Shrewsbury, N. J.

ALLEN, Esther and James Adams, 2 July 1695, Shrewsbury, N. J.

ALLEN, Experience and Benjamin Field, 29 June 1692, Long Island, N. Y.

ALLEN, George and Elizabeth Hulett, 22 February 1694, Shrewsbury, N. J.

ALLEN, Gideon and Mary Wright, 1698, Guilford, Conn.

ALLEN, Hannah and Peter Ayers, 15 November 1659, Haverhill, Mass.

ALLEN, Hannah and James Holt, 12 October 1675, Andover, Mass.

ALLEN, Hannah and Thomas Davise, 12 September 1689, Boston, Mass.

ALLEN, James and Ann Guild, 16 January 1638, Dedham, Mass.

ALLEN, James and Elizabeth Cotton, 1688, Salisbury, Mass.

ALLEN, Jeremiah and Mary Caball, 25 June 1695, Boston, Mass.

ALLEN, John and Elizabeth Bacon, 14 October 1650, Newport, R. I.

ALLEN, John and Abigail Rogers, 20 November 1678, Charlestown, Mass.

ALLEN, John and Catherine Major, 15 November 1678, Richmond Co., Va.

ALLEN, John and Elizabeth Pritchard, 22 February 1681, Suffield, Mass.

ALLEN, John and Marcy Peters, 22 May 1686, Andover, Mass.

ALLEN, Nehemiah and Mary Earlishman, 29 August 1685, Middletown, Penn.

ALLEN, Priscilla and Thomas Smith, 9 November 1682, Philadelphia, Penn.

ALLEN, Rachel and John Twambly, 3 October 1693, Dover, N. H.

ALLEN, Samuel and Sarah Teck, 1660, Beverly, Mass.

ALLEN, John and Elizabeth Edwards, 22 July 1697, Boston, Mass.

ALLEN, Joseph and Rachel Griggs, 29 July 1680, Gloucester, Mass.

ALLEN, Margaret and Robert Hubberd, 2 April 1654, Boston, Mass.

ALLEN, Martha and Wm. Sabin, 22 December 1663, Medfield, Mass.

ALLEN, Martha and Thomas Carrier, 7 May 1664, Billerica, Mass.

ALLEN, Martha and Daniel Pegg, 22 February, 1686, Middletown, Penn.

ALLEN, Mary and Thomas Forman, 27 May 1695, Monmouth Co., N. J.

ALLEN, Mary and Thomas French, Jr., 3 October 1696, Shrewsbury, N. J.

ALLEN, Mathew and Sarah Kirby, 5 June 1657, Sandwich, R. I.

ALLEN, Mehitable and Isaac Alden, 2 December 1685, Bridgewater, Mass.

ALLEN, Samuel, Jr., and Jane Waln, 27 March 1691, Middletown, Penn.
ALLEN, Samuel and Mercy Wright, 15 December 1692, Northampton, Mass.
ALLEN, Sarah and John Baldwin, 19 October 1689, Middletown, Penn.
ALLEN, Silence and Hester Wiswall, 20 January 1692, Dorchester, Mass.
ALLEN, Walter and Elizabeth Middleton, 11 December 1693, Boston, Mass.
ALLEN, William and Elizabeth Wall, March 1695, Salem, Mass.
ALLERTON, Elizabeth and Benjamin Starr, 23 December 1675, Westmoreland Co., Va.
ALLEY, Hugh and Rebecca Hood, 9 December 1681, Lynn, Mass.
ALLIN, Anne and Edward Lane, 4 February 1688, Middletown, Penn.
ALLIN, Ann and Martin Bean, 8 October 1698, Elizabeth City Co., Va.
ALLIN, Isabel and John Hope, 7 June 1693, New York.
ALLIN, John and Mrs. Katharine Dudley, 8 September 1653, Dedham, Mass.
ALLIN, John and Ruth Leader, 30 November 1670, Braintree, Mass.
ALLIN, Leah and Joseph Kenny, 1 December 1699, Dover, N. H.
ALLIN, Mary and Henry Harding, 7 July 1698, Dedham, Mass.
ALLIN, Sarah and John Titchborn, 17 August 1699, Boston, Mass.
ALLINE, Benjamin and Mary Fairbank, 16 April 1696, Dedham, Mass.
ALLING, Abigail and John Punderson, August 1699, New Haven, Conn.
ALLING, Lydia and Benjamin Todd, 23 January 1699, New Haven, Conn.
ALLINGSWORTH, Richard and Margaret Covington, 22 October 1672, Somerset Co., Md.
ALLIS, Hannah and William Scott, 28 January 1670, Hatfield, Mass.
ALLISON, James and Elizabeth Vesey, 28 May 1674, Dorchester, Mass.
ALLISON, Mary and John Welles, 6 May 1667, Hatfield, Mass.
ALLISON, Thomas and Cornelia Johnson, 4 July 1698, New York.
ALLYN, John and Anne Smith, 19 November 1651, Springfield, Mass.
ALLYN, John and Elizabeth Gager, 24 December 1668, New London, Conn.
ALLYN, Mehitable and Samuel Annable, 1 June 1667, Barnstable, Mass.
ALLYN, Sarah and George Geer, 17 February 1658, New London, Conn.
ALLYN, Sarah and Edward Smith, 21 April 1685, Ipswich, Mass.
ALLYN, Susannah and Christopher Price, 15 October 1697, New York.
ALLYN, Thomas and Abigail Wareham, October 1658, Windsor, Conn.
ALSOP, Joseph and Abigail Thompson, 25 November 1672, New Haven, Conn.
ALVORD, Benedictus and Ione Nuton, 26 November 1640, Windsor, Conn.
ALVORD, Alexander and Mary Vore, 29 October 1646, Windsor, Conn.
ALVORD, Elizabeth and Job Drake, 20 March 1671, Windsor, Conn.
ALCORD, Jane and Ambrose Fowler, 6 May 1646, Windsor, Conn.
ALYN, Obediah and Darkis Wright, 29 November 1699, Middletown, Conn.
ALYN, Thomas and Hannah Leek, 4 May 1698, Middletown, Conn.
AMBLER, Joseph and Sarah Jerman, 30 September 1688, Philadelphia, Penn.
AMBROSS, William and Elizabeth Mattock, 6 January 1697, Boston, Mass.
AMES, Hannah and John Hoidon, 6 February 1660, Braintree, Mass.
AMORY, Mary and Benjamin Emmons, 10 September 1694, Boston, Mass.
AMOS, Anna and Henry Walbridge, 25 December 1688, Preston, Conn.
ANDERSON, David and Hannah Philips, 5 January 1699, Boston, Mass.
ANDERSON, George and Elizabeth Stevenson, 26 June 1693, New York.
ANDERSEN, William and Deborah Lyndell, 7 October 1697, New York.
ANDREWS, Abigail and Joseph Blaney, 16 January 1694, Hingham, Mass.

ANDREWS, Christian and John Burchard, 1653, Boston, Mass.
ANDREWS, Edward and Sarah Ong, 8 February 1694, Burlington Co., N. J.
ANDREWS, Elizabeth and James Giddings, 9 February 1681, Chebacco, Mass.
ANDREWS, Elizabeth and James Rayner, 25 October 1692, Boston, Mass.
ANDREWS, Ephriam and Dorcas Smith, 16 November 1671, Barnstable, Mass.
ANDREWS, Esther and George Parker, 5 September 1692, Chesterfield, N. J.
ANDREWS, Jamima and Benjamin Snelling, 29 January 1694, Boston, Mass.
ANDREWS, Joseph and Sarah Ring, 16 February 1680, Chebacco, Mass.
ANDREWS, Mary and Edward Shipton, July 1663, Saybrook, Conn.
ANDREWS, Mary and John Pratt, 10 August 1676, Saybrook, Conn.
ANDREWS, Ralph and Abigail Very, 12 December 1682, Gloucester, Mass.
ANDREWS, Rebecca and Samuel Marble, 26 November 1675, Andover, Mass.
ANDREWS, Rebecca and Samuel Benedict, 7 July 1678, Fairfield, Conn.
ANDREWS, Ruth and Edward Phelps, 9 March 1682, Andover, Mass.
ANDREWS, Thomas, Jr., and Phebe Gourd, 31 October 1667, Dorchester, Mass.
ANDREWS, Thomas and Mary Belcher, 9 February 1681, Ipswich, Mass.
ANDREWS, Thomas and Elizabeth Owen, 25 August 1689, Philadelphia, Penn.
ANDREWS, William and Margaret Woodward, 21 October 1672, Chebacco, Mass.
ANDREWS, William and Hester Dexter (widow), 30 October 1680, Warwick, R. I.
ANDRIES, Ann and Jan Woertman, 17 January 1691, Brooklyn, N. Y.
ANGELS, Charles and Katherine Knox, 6 October 1690, Salem Co., N. J.
ANNABLE, Anthony (2nd marriage) and Ann Clark, 3 March 1644, Barnstable, Mass.
ANNABLE, Mehitable (widow) and Cornelius Briggs, 6 May 1683, Scituate, Mass.
ANNABLE, Samuel and Mehitable Allyn, 1 June 1667, Barnstable, Mass.
ANNIBAL, Anna and Consider Atherton, 19 October 1671, Dorchester, Mass.
ANNIS, Charles and Sarah Chase, 15 May 1666, Newbury, Mass.
ANNIS, Elizabeth and Nathaniel Itle, 3 April 1684, Philadelphia, Penn.
ANTHONY, Elizabeth and James Greene, 3 August 1665, Warwick, R. I.
ANTHONY, John and Elizabeth Geritse, 18 October 1693, New York.
ANTROM, James and Mary Hance, 14 March 1696, Shrewsbury, N. J.
APPLEBY, Richard and Ann Arnold, 4 July 1680, Richmond Co., Va.
APPLEGATE, Barthomew and Hannah Patricke, June 1650, Gravesend, N. Y.
APPLEGATE, Helena and Louis Hulet, 15 August 1646, New York City.
APPLEGATE, Helena and Carl Morgan, 9 February 1648, New York City.
APPLETON, John and Elizabeth Rogers, 23 November 1681, Ipswich, Mass.
APPLETON, Mary and Samuel Smith, 25 November 1685, Burlington, N. J.
ARCHER, John and Sarah Odell, 7 October 1686, New York.
ARCHER, John and Mehitable Shears, 5 June 1692, Bristol, R. I.
ARCHER, Mary and Edward Hill, 15 February 1699, Boston, Mass.
ARCHER, Samuel and Hannah Osgood, 21 May 1660, Andover, Mass.
ARCHER, Sarah and Roger Roberts, 23 November 1693, Anne Arundel Co, Md.
ARENTSE, Huybert and Elizabeth Konning, 11 August 1691, New York City.
ARMISTEAD, Hannah and William Sheldon, 10 December 1698, Elizabeth City Co., Va.
ARMISTEAD, Judah and John West, 15 October 1695, Elizabeth City Co., Va.
ARMITAGE, Johanna and Thomas Gwin, 21 November 1689, Boston, Mass.
ARMSTRONG, Mary and Ebenezer Lamb, 6 May 1690, Norwich, Conn.
ARMSTRONG, Matthew and Margaret Halce, 7 June 1694, Boston, Mass.

ARNOLD, Benedict and Mary Turner, 9 March 1671, Newport, R. I.
ARNOLD, Isaac and Sarah Washbourne, 30 October 1691, New York City.
ARNOLD, Isreal and Elizabeth Smith, 28 February 1698-9, Warwick, R. I.
ARNOLD, Joseph and Rebecca Curtis, 8 June 1648, Braintree, Mass.
ARNOLD, Mary and Thomas Copeland, 17 May 1699, Boston, Mass.
ARNOLD, Phebe and Benjamin Smith, 25 December 1691, Warwick, R. I.
ARNOLD, Richard and Sarah Chamberlin, 19 February 1681, Burlington, N. J.
ARNOLD, Stephen and Sarah Smith, 24 November 1646, Rehoboth, Mass.
ARNOLD, Susanna and John Farnum, 7 February 1654, Boston, Mass.
ARNOTT, Mary and John Barnes, 28 July 1688, Philadelphia, Penn.
ASBURY, John and Eleanor Griffin, 18 October 1699, Boston, Mass.
ASHBURY, Ebenezer and Margaret Deffose (Devos), 19 July 1694, Salem Co.,
N. J.
ASHBY, Sarah and Samuel Utley, 9 April 1691, Stonington, Conn.
ASHFORDBY, Susannah and John Beatty, 7 November 1691, Kingston, N. Y.
ASLETT, John and Mary Osgood, 8 July 1680, Andover, Mass.
ASLETT, Mary and Samuel Fry, 20 November 1671, Andover, Mass.
ASLETT, Rebecca and Timothy Johnson, 15 December 1674, Andover, Mass.
ASHLEY, David and Hannah Glover, 24 November 1663, New Haven, Conn.
ASHLEY, David and Mary Dewey, 11 July 1688, Westfield, Mass.
ASHLEY, Mary and John Root, 18 October 1664, Westfield, Mass.
ASHLEY, Mary and Joseph Wiliston, 2 March 1699, Springfield, Mass.
ASHLY, Thomas and Hannah Broome (widow), 1 January 1661, Boston, Mass.
ASHTON, Rebecca and David Stout, 1688, Freehold, N. J.
ASKIN, William and Jennette Mill, 10 January 1692, Shrewsbury, N. J.
ASPINWALL, Mary and John Gove, 6 October 1658, Boston, Mass.
ASPINWALL, Nathaniel and Abigail Bowen, 11 November 1698, Woodstock, Conn.
ASPINWALL, Peter and Remember Palfrey, 12 February 1661, Boston, Mass.
ASPINWALL, Peter and Elizabeth Leavens, 24 March 1698-9, Woodstock, Conn.
ASTIN, Mehitable and Benjamin Gibson, 4 January 1699, Boston, Mass.
ASTIN, Samuel and Lucy Poor, 11 October 1691, Andover, Mass.
ASTIN, Thomas and Hannah Foster, 15 September 1690, Andover, Mass.
ATHERTON, Consider and Ann Annibal, 19 October 1671, Dorchester, Mass.
ATHERTON, Elizabeth and Isaac Gross, 28 August 1691, Milton, Mass.
ATHERTON, James and Abigail Hudson, 6 June 1684, Lancaster, Mass.
ATHERTON, Jonathan and Mary Gullifer, 17 March 1679, Milton, Mass.
ATHERTON, Mary and Joseph Weeks, 9 February 1667, Dorchester, Mass.
ATHERTON, Patience and Isaac Humfrey, 7 July 1685, Dorchester, Mass.
ATHERTON, Thankful and Thomas Bird, 2 December 1665, Dorchester, Mass.
ATHERTON, Waching and Elizabeth Rigbee, 23 January 1678, Dorchester, Mass.
ATKINS, Josiah and Elizabeth Whetmore, 8 October 1673, Middletown, Conn.
ATKINSON, Elizabeth and John Lawrence, 8 December 1653, Boston, Mass.
ATKINSON, Helen and Joseph Hills, November 1655, Malden, Mass.
ATKINSON, Jane and William Biles, 11 October 1688, Middletown, Penn.
ATKINSON, John and Sarah Myrick, 27 April 1664, Newbury, Mass.
ATKINSON, Sarah and Stephen Coffin, 8 October 1685, Newbury, Mass.
ATKINSON, William and Sarah White, 31 August 1698, Boston, Mass.
ATWATER, Mercy and John Austin, 5 November 1667, New Haven, Conn.
ATWOOD, Anne and Thomas Saxton, 10 January 1651, Boston, Mass.

ATWOOD, Elizabeth and Philip Connell, 1688, Malden, Mass.
ATWOOD, Herman and Ann Copp, 11 June 1646, Boston, Mass.
ATWOOD, John and Mary Smith, 27 October 1690, Boston, Mass.
ATWOOD, Philip and Elizabeth Grover, 7 April 1675, Malden, Mass.
AUGUR, William and Ruth Hill, 7 October 1659, Malden, Mass.
AUKES, Annetje and Direk J. Woertman, 9 April 1691, New York City.
AUSTIN, Isabella and Philip Towle, 19 November 1657, Hampton, N. H.
AUSTIN, John and Mercy Atwater, 5 November 1667, New Haven, Conn.
AUSTIN, John and Elizabeth Brackett, 21 January 1685, New Haven, Conn.
AUSTIN, John and Jane Potts, 11 November 1686, Philadelphia, Penn.
AUSTIN, Joseph and Elizabeth Pitts, 10 November 1692, Charlestown, Mass.
AUSTIN, Mary and Samuel Hoskins, 5 February 1684, Windsor, Conn.
AUSTIN, William and Hannah Trerice, 30 June 1696, Charlestown, Mass.
AVENS, Javacay and William Francis, 2 August 1684, Staten Island, N. Y.
AVERY, Elizabeth and William Bullard, 6 August 1697, Dedham, Mass.
AVERY, Jonathan and Sibbele Sparhauke, 22 May 1679, Dedham, Mass.
AVERY, Hanah and Benjamin Dyar, 22 March 1677, Dedham, Mass.
AVERY, Lydia and Michael Wigglesworth, 23 June 1691, Braintree, Mass.
AVERY, Mary and James Tesdell, 5 November 1666, Dedham, Mass.
AVERY, Mary and Eleazer Fisher, 13 October 1698, Dedham, Mass.
AVERY, Rachel and William Summer, 22 March 1677, Dedham, Mass.
AVERY, Robert and Elizabeth Lane, 3 February 1677, Dedham, Mass.
AVERY, Sarah and Thomas Metcalfe, 24 November 1696, Dedham, Mass.
AVERY, Thomas and Abigail Coombs, 8 October 1697, Dover, N. H.
AVERY, William and Elizabeth White, 29 June 1682, Dedham, Mass.
AVERY, William and Mehitable Worden, 25 August 1698, Boston, Mass.
AVISE, Sarah and Samuel Clark, 8 September 1692, Boston, Mass.
AWBREY, William and Rachel Rawson, 18 November 1652, Boston, Mass.
AXTELL, Mary and John Goodenow, 19 September 1656, Sudbury, Mass.
AYERS, Mary and Samuel Colcord, 1680, Exeter, N. H.
AYERS, Mary and Joseph Calef, 24 March 1693, Boston, Mass.
AYERS, Moses and Bethiah Millet, 3 June 1666, Dorchester, Mass.
AYERS, Peter and Hannah Allen, 15 November 1659, Haverhill, Mass.
AYERS, Robert and Elizabeth Palmer, 27 February 1650, Haverhill, Mass.
AYERS, Susannah and Jonathan Stanhope, 16 April 1656, Charlestown, Mass.
AYERS, Thomas and Elizabeth Hutchins, 1 April 1656, Haverhill, Mass.
AYERS, Timothy and Ruth Johnson, 24 November 1682, Haverhill, Mass.
AYLETT, John and Mary Hawkins, 21 September 1654, Boston, Mass.
AYRES, Ann and John Checkley, 5 January 1652, Boston, Mass.
AYRES, Ann and John Lawson, 28 December 1699, Boston, Mass.
AYRES, Elizabeth and Joseph Lockwood, 19 May 1698, Stamford, Conn.
AYRES, Hannah and John Osgood, 17 October 1681, Andover, Mass.
AYRES, Mary and Emphriam Davis, 19 March 1688, Andover, Mass.
AYRES, Samuel and Abigail Fellows, 16 April 1677, Ipswich, Mass.
AYRES, Zachariah and Elizabeth Chase, 27 June 1678, Andover, Mass.

B

BABAGE, James and Eliza Davise, 9 October 1693, Boston, Mass.
BABBITT, Edward and Sarah Tarne, 7 September 1654, Boston, Mass.
BABBITT, Edward and Elizabeth Thayer, 22 December 1698, Taunton, Mass.
BABBITT, Elkanah and Elizabeth Briggs, 1689, Taunton, Mass.
BABCOCK, Abigail and John Barber, 17 December 1674, Milton, Mass.
BABCOCK, Benjamin and Hannah Daniel, 11 February 1673, Milton, Mass.
BABCOCK, Dorothy and John Daniel, 29 March 1672, Milton, Mass.
BABCOCK, Hannah and Thomas Vose, Jr., 28 May 1695, Milton, Mass.
BABCOCK, Jonathan and Mary Curtis, 1 August 1676, Milton, Mass.
BABCOCK, Nicholas and Ann Cole, 1686, Dover, N. H.
BABCOCK, Return and Sarah Deneson, 1 December 1681, Milton, Mass.
BABCOCK, Samuel and Hanah Emes, 1 July 1674, Milton, Mass.
BABCOCK, Thankful and George Lion, 14 February 1688, Milton, Mass.
BACKUS, Sarah and Edward Culver, Jr., 5 January 1682, Norwich, Conn.
BACON, Alice and Thomas Bancroft, 31 January 1647, Dedham, Mass.
BACON, Daniell and Elizabeth Martin, 21 February 1685, Dedham, Mass.
BACON, Elizabeth and John Allen, 14 October 1650, Newport, R. I.
BACON, John and Lydia Dewing, 15 December 1683, Dedham, Mass.
BACON, John and Lydia Dewing, 15 December 1683, Dedham, Mass.
BACON, John and Elizabeth Smith, 17 October 1688, Salem Co., N. J.
BACON, Joseph and Elizabeth Pancost, 14 August 1693, Salem Co., N. J.
BACON, Lydia and Josiah Wood, 28 October 1657, Charlestown, Mass.
BACON, Mary and Nathaniel Kingsbury, 14 October 1673, Dedham, Mass.
BACON, Michael and Mary Jobs, 31 August 1624, Dedham, Mass.
BACON, Michael and Mary Richardson (widow), 26 October 1655, Woburn, Mass.
BACON, Rebeccah and John Gay, 13 December 1678, Dedham, Mass.
BACON, Samuel and Martha Foxhall, 9 May 1659, Barnstable, Mass.
BACON, Sarah and Anthony Hubard, 14 February 1648, Dedham, Mass.
BACON, Susanah and Jonathan Duein, 7 January 1692, Dedham, Mass.
BACON, Thomas and Abigail Maskill, 12 March 1685, Simsbury, Conn.
BACON, Thomas and Rebeccah Bugbey, 2 November 1688, Milton, Mass.
BACON, Thomas and Hannah Fales, 22 January 1691, Dedham, Mass.
BADGER, Elizabeth and Richard Brown, 16 February 1648, Newbury, Mass.
BAGART, Aertie and Theodorus Polhemus, 14 October 1677, Flatbush, L. I., N. Y.
BAGGLEY, Charles and Elizabeth Stevens, 27 May 1682, Burlington Co., N. J.
BAGLEY, Sarah and John Mack, 5 April 1681, Salisbury, Mass.
BAILEY, John and Sarah White, 25 January 1672, Scituate, Mass.
BAILEY, John and Ruth Clothier, 9 December 1699, Scituate, Mass.
BAILEY, Thomas and Lydia Redfield, 10 January 1655, New London, Conn.
BAILY, Rebecca and Richard More, 11 January 1694, New York.
BAINBRIDGE, John and Sarah Clows, 15 June 1685, Middletown, Penn.
BAKER, Abigall and Nathaniell Kingsbery, 5 December 1695, Dedham, Mass.
BAKER, Ann and Thomas Bayes, 26 October 1639, Dedham, Mass.
BAKER, Ann (widow) and William White, 12 August 1699, Harford Co., Md.

BAKER, Catherine and Henry Kemble, 10 April 1693, New York.
BAKER, Christian and Simon Roberts, 18 May 1654, Boston, Mass.
BAKER, Dorothy and Philip Yarnall, 20 April 1694, Chester Co., Penn.
BAKER, Elizabeth (widow) and Peter Hackley, 31 August 1669, New London, Conn.
BAKER, Elizabeth and Hopestill Humphry, 21 November 1677, Dorchester, Mass.
BAKER, Elizabeth and William Pratt, 26 October 1680, Dorchester, Mass.
BAKER, Hanah and John Wiswel, 5 May 1685, Dorchester, Mass.
BAKER, Hannah and Francis Yarnall, 1686, Chester Co., Penn.
BAKER, Henry and Mary Radcliff, 13 August 1692, Middletown, Penn.
BAKER, Hepsiba and Caleb Pomery, 8 March 1664, Windsor, Conn.
BAKER, Jeffery and Ione Rockwell, 15 November 1642, Windsor, Conn.
BAKER, John and Joan Swift, 5 September 1657, Boston, Mass.
BAKER, John and Thankful Foster, 8 November 1663, Dorchester, Mass.
BAKER, John and Preserved Trott, 11 May 1667, Dorchester, Mass.
BAKER, John and Abigail Fisher, 17 December 1668, Dedham, Mass.
BAKER, John and Mary Peachee, 16 November 1696, Burlington, N. J.
BAKER, Joseph and Ruth Holton, 1663, Northampton, Mass.
BAKER, Joseph and Hanna Cook, 30 January 1676, Windsor, Conn.
BAKER, Mary and Joseph Safford, 6 March 1660, Ipswich, Mass.
BAKER, Mary and Mark Roberts, 1 January 1682, Warwick, R. I.
BAKER, Mary and John Minott, 21 March 1696, Dorchester, Mass.
BAKER, Mary and Thomas Johnson, April 1688, Calvert Co., Md.
BAKER, Moses and Elizabeth Browne, 12 January 1694, Elizabeth City Co., Va.
BAKER, Rachel and Robert Bunting, 27 April 1689, Middletown, Penn.
BAKER, Rebekah and John Wilsford, 4 February 1695, Chesterfield, N. J.
BAKER, Roger and Mary Walkington, 4 September 1693, New York.
BAKER, Sarah and John Gould, 14 October 1660, Ipswich, Mass.
BAKER, Sarah and James White, 22 December 1664, Dorchester, Mass.
BAKER, Sarah and Sebas Jackson, 19 April 1671, Roxbury, Mass.
BAKER, Sarah and Peter Robertson, 27 April 1685, Warwick, R. I.
BAKER, Sarah and Oliver Wiswall, 1 January 1690, Dorchester, Mass.
BAKER, Sarah and Stephen Wilson, 13 August 1692, Middletown, Penn.
BAKER, Samuel and Febee Eglington, 19 December 1699, Boston, Mass.
BAKER, Thomas and Alice Dayton, 20 June 1643, New Haven, Conn.
BAKER, Thomas and Ann Topping, 29 April 1686, East Hampton, N. Y.
BAKER, William and Mary Eddington, 23 July 1651, Boston, Mass.
BAKER, William and Pilgrim Edye, 22 February 1656, Boston, Mass.
BALDEN, Sarah and Daniell Crocker, 30 November 1660, Boston, Mass.
BALDWIN, Daniel and Elizabeth Botsford, 27 June 1665, Milford, Conn.
BALDWIN, John and Mary Bruen, 1653, Milford, Conn.
BALDWIN, John, Sr., and Hannah Bruen, 30 October 1663, Morris Co., N. J.
BALDWIN, John and Catherine Turner, 31 March 1689, Philadelphia, Penn.
BALDWIN, John and Sarah Allen, 19 October 1689, Middletown, Penn.
BALDWIN, Joseph and Elizabeth Grover, 20 June 1691, Malden, Mass.
BALDWIN, Martha and William Parsons, 15 September 1697, Boston, Mass.
BALDWIN, Phoebe and Samuel Richardson, 7 November 1676, Woburn, Mass.
BALDWIN, Sarah and Samuel Royce, 5 June 1690, Wallingford, Conn.
BALDWIN, William and Ruth Brooks, 2 July 1688, Wallingford, Conn.

BALIE, Margaret and Thomas Hill, 4 January 1655, Kent Co., Md.
BALL, Adam and Elizabeth Collins, 31 August 1699, New York.
BALL, Elizabeth and John Smith, 13 August 1685, Burlington, N. J.
BALL, Francis and Abigail Salter, 27 November 1663, Dorchester, Mass.
BALL, John and Elizabeth Fox, 3 October 1665, Concord, Mass.
BALL, John and Sarah Bullard, 17 October 1665, Watertown, Mass.
BALL, Mercy and George Pardee, 10 February 1675, New Haven, Conn.
BALL, Ruth and David Walsbee, 24 July 1656, Braintree, Mass.
BALLENTINE, Sarah and John Wharton, 14 October 1698, Boston, Mass.
BALLINTINE, Susana and Benjamin Webb, 21 November 1692, Boston, Mass.
BALLANTINE, William and Hannah Hollard, 23 May 1652, Boston, Mass.
BALLARD, Ann and John Spaulding, 20 July 1681, Chelmsford, Mass.
BALLARD, Eleanor and John Johnson, 13 September 1689, Andover, Mass.
BALLARD, Elizabeth and William Blunt, 11 November 1668, Chelmsford, Mass.
BALLARD, Elizabeth and George Abbott, 13 September 1689, Andover, Mass.
BALLARD, Esther and James Jenckes, 1655, Lynn, Mass.
BALLARD, Francis and Mary Servant, 25 December 1699, Elizabeth City Co., Va.
BALLARD, Hannah and John Spaulding, 20 July 1681, Chelmsford, Mass.
BALLARD, Isaac and Sarah Jones, 3 November 1654, Boston, Mass.
BALLARD, John and Rebecca Hooper, 16 November 1681, Andover, Mass.
BALLARD, Joseph and Elizabeth Phellps, 28 February 1665, Andover, Mass.
BALLARD, Joseph, Sr., and Rebecca Horn (widow), 15 November 1692, Andover, Mass.
BALLARD, Joseph and Rebecca Johnson, 17 August 1698, Andover, Mass.
BALLARD, Lydia and Joseph Butterfield, 12 February 1697, Chelmsford, Mass.
BALLARD, Mary and Samuel Lynde, 20 October 1674, Boston, Mass.
BALLARD, Nathaniel and Rebecca Hudson, 16 December 1662, Lynn, Mass.
BALLARD, Sarah and Henry Holt, 24 February 1669, Andover, Mass.
BALLARD, William and Hannah Hooper, 20 April 1682, Andover, Mass.
BANCKER, Maria and Cornelis De Peyster, 19 September 1694, New York.
BANCROFT, Anna and John Griffin, 13 May 1647, Windsor, Conn.
BANCROFT, Elizabeth and Martin Saunders, 23 March 1654, Braintree, Mass.
BANCROFT, Ephriam and Sarah Stiles, 1 May 1681, Windsor, Conn.
BANCROFT, John and Hanna Draper, 3 December 1650, Windsor, Conn.
BANCROFT, Nathaniel and Hanna Williams, 26 December 1677, Windsor, Conn.
BANCROFT, Thomas and Alice Bacon, 31 January 1647, Dedham, Mass.
BANCROFT, Thomas and Elizabeth Metcalfe, 15 July 1648, Dedham, Mass.
BANCROFT, Thomas, Jr., and Sarah Poole, 10 April 1673, Reading, Mass.
BANES, William and Ann Phesey, 26 December 1684, Somerset Co., Md.
BANFORD, Hannah and John Dinsdale, 19 September 1694, Boston, Mass.
BANGS, Appiah and John Knowls, 28 December 1679, Eastham, Mass.
BANGS, John and Hanah Smalley, 23 January 1660, Plymouth, Mass.
BANGS, Jonathan and Mary Mayo, 16 July 1664, Brewster, Mass.
BANGS, Joshua and Hanah Scudder, 1 December 1669, Plymouth, Mass.
BANGS, Lydia and Benjamin Higgins, 24 December 1661, Eastham, Mass.
BANGS, Mercy and Stephen Merrick, 28 December 1670, Plymouth, Mass.
BANK, Joseph and Elizabeth Harmon, 28 February 1695, York, Maine.
BANKS, John and Mehitable Mattox, 29 August 1694, Boston, Mass.
BANKS, Phebe and Daniel Kigan, 8 August 1660, Charles City Co., Va.

BANT, Martha and John Grantham, 8 December 1690, Boston, Mass.
BARBAR, George and Elizabeth Clarke, 24 September 1642, Dedham, Mass.
BARBER, Abigail and Samuel Thorn, 17 December 1691, Boston, Mass.
BARBER, Abigail and Ichabod Harding, 15 November 1699, Milton, Mass.
BARBER, Elizabeth and Jabez Beers, 17 May 1694, Boston, Mass.
BARBER, Ellin and James Thomas, 26 May 1689, Philadelphia, Penn.
BARBER, George and Elizabeth Clark, 24 September 1642, Dedham, Mass.
BARBER, Jane and Henry Jaman, 31 August 1696, New York.
BARBER, John and Bethsheba Cozzens, September 1666, Windsor, Conn.
BARBER, John and Abigail Babcock, 17 December 1674, Milton, Mass.
BARBER, John and Abigail Loomis, 22 November 1677, Windsor, Conn.
BARBER, John and Anne Hume, 31 August 1680, Somerset Co., Md.
BARBER, Mary and John Gillet, 8 July 1669, Windsor, Conn.
BARBER, Rebecca and Joseph Pelham, 19 March 1697, Boston, Mass.
BARBER, Samuel and Sarah Mills, 6 July 1676, Dedham, Mass.
BARBER, Sara and Timothy Hall, 26 November 1663, Windsor, Conn.
BARBER, Thomas and Abigail Buell, 25 May 1699, Simsbury, Conn.
BARBOR, Elizabeth and Samuel Howard, 27 December 1699, Dorchester, Mass.
BARBOR, James and Elizabeth Hide, 23 June 1680, Dorchester, Mass.
BARBOUR, Margaret C. and John P. Farnsworth, 25 November 1685, New York.
BARDING, Sarah and Thomas Spencer, 11 September 1645, Hartford, Conn.
BARENTS, Margaret and Joseph Smith, 8 July 1695, New York.
BARENTZ, Lambert and Leentie Dirck, 21 September 1661, Brooklyn, N. Y.
BARKER, Benjamin and Hannah Marstone, 2 January 1688, Andover, Mass.
BARKER, Ebenezer and Abigail Wheeler, 25 May 1686, Andover, Mass.
BARKER, Esther and John Stevens, 10 August 1676, Andover, Mass.
BARKER, Ester and Ambrose Due, 10 December 1651, Boston, Mass.
BARKER, Hannah and Christopher Osgood, 27 May 1680, Andover, Mass.
BARKER, Isaac and Judith Prence, 28 December 1665, Duxbury, Mass.
BARKER, James and Mercy Jones, 6 January 1675, Springfield, Mass.
BARKER, John and Judith Symonds, 9 December 1668, Concord, Mass.
BARKER, John and Mary Stevens, 6 July 1670, Andover, Mass.
BARKER, Mary and John Gillette, 8 July 1669, Windsor, Conn.
BARKER, Mary and Richard Temple, 7 June 1699, Concord, Mass.
BARKER, Richard and Hannah Kimball, 21 April 1682, Andover, Mass.
BARKER, Sarah and John Abbot, 17 November 1673, Andover, Mass.
BARKER, Stephen and Mary Abbott, 13 May 1687, Andover, Mass.
BARKER, William and Mary Dix, 20 February 1676, Andover, Mass.
BARKLY, William and Mary Miriour, 13 January 1697, Boston, Mass.
BARLEIGH, Pasque and Hannah Keene, 21 August 1684, Somerset Co., Md.
BARLOW, Elizabeth (widow of Thomas Barlow) and John Combes, 24 February
    1661, Boston, Mass.
BARLOW, Phebe and James Olmstead, 1 May 1673, Norwalk, Conn.
BARNABE, Elizabeth and William Hinderson, 1 July 1680, Somerset Co., Md.
BARNABE, Mary and Edwin Jones, 1669, Somerset Co., Md.
BARNARD, Dorothy and Richard Currier, 28 August 1695, Amesbury, Mass.
BARNARD, Elizabeth and Alwin Bucher, 15 December 1698, Boston, Mass.
BARNARD, Francis and Hanna Merrell, 1 August 1644, Hartford, Conn.

BARNARD, Hannah and John Stevens, 13 June 1662, Andover, Mass.
BARNARD, Hannah and Thomas Olcott, 11 November 1695, Hartford, Conn.
BARNARD, Hannah and John Marble, 23 April 1695, Andover, Mass.
BARNARD, John and Hannah Hoksey, 21 November 1689, Boston, Mass.
BARNARD, Joseph and Mary Jewell, 1 December 1693, Salisbury, Mass.
BARNARD, Mary and William Barrett, 19 May 1662, Watertown, Mass.
BARNARD, Nathaniel and Mary Lugg, 11 February 1658, Boston, Mass.
BARNARD, Richard and Elizabeth Negus, 2 March 1659, Boston, Mass.
BARNARD, Richard and Katherine Wilson, 3 April 1690, Boston, Mass.
BARNARD, Stephen and Rebecca How, 1 May 1671, Andover, Mass.
BARNARD, Thomas and Elizabeth Price, 14 December 1686, Andover, Mass.
BARNARD, Thomas and Abigail Bull, 28 April 1696, Andover, Mass.
BARNES, Abigail and Daniel Harris, 11 December 1680, Middletown, Conn.
BARNES, Anney and Joseph Pierson, 17 November 1675, Cumberland Co., N. J.
BARNES, Deborah and Samuel Davis, December 1663, Haverhill, Mass.
BARNES, Esther and John Rickard, 31 October 1651, Plymouth, Mass.
BARNES, Hannah and Samuel Harrington, 2 July 1698, Branford, Conn.
BARNES, John and Mercy Betts, 16 November 1669, North Haven, Conn.
BARNES, John and Mary Arnott, 28 July 1688, Philadelphia, Penn.
BARNES, Lawrence and Eleanor Lawrence, 1 May 1690, New York.
BARNES, Lydia and Benjamin Savill, 30 October 1670, Braintree, Mass.
BARNES, Matthew and Elizabeth Hunt (widow), 4 September 1657, Boston, Mass.
BARNES, Richard and Susanna Searle, 1 February 1672, Somerset Co., Md.
BARNES, Ruth and John Frisbie, 20 December 1674, Branford, Conn.
BARNES, Sarah and John Tomline, 26 December 1660, Boston, Mass.
BARNES, William and Martha Bromley, 13 February 1682, Burlington, N. J.
BARNEY, Dorcas and Daniel Throop, 23 August 1689, Bristol, R. I.
BARNEY, John and Mary Throop, 4 November 1686, Bristol, R. I.
BARNS, Ebenezer and Luranda Shattuck, 19 September 1668, North Haven, Conn.
BARNS, Rebecca and Jonathan Livermore, 23 November 1699, Watertown, Mass.
BARRE, Mary and Thermis Titus, 20 December 1677, New York City.
BARREL, John and Sebella Legg, 14 September 1693, Boston, Mass.
BARRELL, Mary (widow) and Daniel Turell, December 1659, Boston, Mass.
BARRETT, Ann and Charles Lee, 3 April 1684, Philadelphia, Penn.
BARRETT, Anna and John Swallow, 3 January 1693, Chelmsford, Mass.
BARRETT, James and Dorcas Greene, 11 January 1672, Malden, Mass.
BARRETT, John and Sarah Eustace, 28 September 1699, Boston, Mass.
BARRETT, Jonathan and Abigail Weston, 26 June 1696, Woburn, Mass.
BARRETT, Jonathan and Abigail Tuttle, 8 December 1698, Boston, Mass.
BARRETT, Joseph and Martha Gould, 17 September 1672, Chelmsford, Mass.
BARRETT, Joseph and Abigail Hildreth, 25 December 1696, Chelmsford, Mass.
BARRETT, Lydia and James Harwood, 11 April 1678, Chelmsford, Mass.
BARRETT, Margaret and Edward Spalding, 22 November 1681, Chelmsford, Mass.
BARRETT, Margaret and Robert Gyles, 17 February 1692, Boston, Mass.
BARRETT, Martha and Henry Sparks, 10 July 1676, Chelmsford, Mass.
BARRETT, Mary and Shadrock Thayer, 11 February 1654, Braintree, Mass.
BARRETT, Mary and George Robbins, 21 January 1686, Chelmsford, Mass.
BARRETT, Mary and Nathaniel Collar, 10 October 1693, Chelmsford, Mass.
BARRETT, Moses and Anna Smith, 10 September 1684, Dorchester, Mass.

BARRETT, Mehitable and Samuel Gould, 17 March 1684, Chelmsford, Mass.
BARRETT, Rebecca and Walter Powers, 16 December 1696, Braintree, Mass.
BARRETT, Thomas and Frances Wolderson, 14 July 1655, Braintree, Mass.
BARRETT, Thomas and Mary Dike, 22 January 1695, Milton, Mass.
BARRETT, Samuel and Sarah Manning, 8 March 1694, Boston, Mass.
BARRETT, Samuel and Sarah Buttrick, 21 February 1683, Concord, Mass.
BARRETT, Sarah and Ambrose Swallow, 8 December 1696, Chelmsford, Mass.
BARRETT, William and Sarah Champney, 19 August 1656, Cambridge, Mass.
BARRETT, William and Mary Barnard, 19 May 1662, Watertown, Mass.
BARRETTE, de Barbara and Genett Van Swearingen, 1659, New Castle, Del.
BARRIMAN, Martha and Peter Cullom, 8 April 1695, New York.
BARRINGER, Mary and James Fogg, 9 January 1695, Hampton, N. H.
BARROW, Deborah and John Bucland, 17 October 1693, Plymouth, Mass.
BARROW, George and Patience Simmons, 14 February 1694-5, Plymouth, Mass.
BARRY, Elizabeth and Richard Davis, 1676, Somerset Co., Md.
BARRY, Mary and Philip Adams, 1 September 1691, Somerset Co., Md.
BARSHAM, Susanna and John Capen, Jr., 19 September 1663, Dorchester, Mass.
BARSLEY, Ann and William Fisher, 1 August 1696, New York.
BARSTOW, Joseph and Susanna Lincoln, 16 May 1666, Scituate, Mass.
BARSTOW, Mary and William Ingram, 14 March 1656, Boston, Mass.
BARSTOW, William and Ann Hubbard, 8 May 1638, Dedham, Mass.
BARTHOLOMEW, Abigail and Joseph Frissell, 11 January 1691-2, Woodstock, Conn.
BARTHOLOMEW, Elizabeth and Samuel Lothrop, 28 November 1644, Barnstable, Mass.
BARTHOLOMEW, Elizabeth and Edmund Chamberlain, 21 November 1699, Woodstock, Conn.
BARTHOLOMEW, Mary and Matthew Whipple, 24 December 1657, Gloucester, Mass.
BARTLETT, Deborah and John Spinning, 16 March 1687, Guilford, Conn.
BARTLETT, Elizabeth and Anthony Sprague, 26 December 1661, Hingham, Mass.
BARTLETT, Ezaya and Abraham Gillet, 3 December 1663, Windsor, Conn.
BARTLETT, George and Mary Cruttenden, 14 September 1650, Guilford, Conn.
BARTLETT, Hepsibah and Samuel Dibble, 21 January 1668, Windsor, Conn.
BARTLETT, Joseph, Sr., and Mary Waite, 27 October 1668, Newton, Mass.
BARTLETT, Mehitable and Joseph Perkins, December 1672, Simsbury, Conn.
BARTLETT, Mercy and John Ivey, 4 January 1669, Plymouth, Mass.
BARTLETT, Sarah and Samuel Rider, 23 December 1656, Plymouth, Mass.
BARTLETT, Sarah and Elisha Holmes, 2 September 1695, Plymouth, Mass.
BARTON, Ann and Mathias Clark, 25 December 1699, Boston, Mass.
BARTON, Benjamin and Susan Gorton, 10 June 1672, Warwick, R. I.
BARTON, Margaret and Robert Calfe, 23 December 1699, Boston, Mass.
BARTON, Mary and Jabez Green, 17 March 1697-8, Warwick, R. I.
BARTON, Phebey and Richard Codner, 23 May 1691, Warwick, R. I.
BARTON, William and Hannah Hull, July 1696, New York.
BASFORD, John and Damares Lynns, 16 June 1696, New York.
BASHTEEN, William and Lidia Algood, March 1699, Harford Co., Md.
BASNETT, Elizabeth and Richard Dell, 11 August 1698, Burlington, N. J.

BASNETT, Richard and Elizabeth Frampton, 30 September 1688, Philadelphia, Penn.

BASS, Deborah and Joseph Webb, 29 November 1699, Boston, Mass.

BASS, Hannah and Stephen Paine, 15 November 1651, Roxbury, Mass.

BASS, John and Ruth Alden, 3 December 1657, Braintree, Mass.

BASS, John and Hannah Sturdevant, 21 July 1675, Braintree, Mass.

BASS, Mary and John Capen, 20 September 1647, Roxbury, Mass.

BASS, Samuel and Rebecca Faxon, 30 July 1678, Braintree, Mass.

BASS, Thomas and Sarah Wood, 4 October 1660, Medford, Mass.

BASS, Thomas and Susanna Blancher, 30 November 1680, Braintree, Mass.

BASSET, Mary and Edward Boston, 27 May 1695, Boston, Mass.

BASSETT, Ruth and John Whitemore, 22 December 1692, Bridgewater, Mass.

BASTER, Susanna and Samuel Gray, 15 April 1695, Boston, Mass.

BATRAP, Eleanor and William Gray, 19 September 1683, Bristol, R. I.

BATCHELAR, Ruth and James Blake, Jr., 8 July 1684, Dorchester, Mass.

BATCHELDER, Agnes and Thomas Bill, 23 November 1699, Boston, Mass.

BATCHELOR, Elizabeth and James Davis, 6 December 1666, Gloucester, Mass.

BATCHELOR, Jane and Richard Tucker, 1 February 1684, Philadelphia, Penn.

BATCHELOR, John and Mary Dennis, 12 July 1661, Salem, Mass.

BATCHELOUR, Sarah and John Warner, 20 April 1665, Essex Co., Mass.

BATEMAN, Elizabeth and Joseph Wright, 7 July 1692, Charlestown, Mass.

BATES, Esther and Richard Cobb, 16 September 1691, Boston, Mass.

BATES, James and Ruth Lyford, 19 April 1643, Hingham, Mass.

BATES, John and Mary Farwell, 22 December 1665, Chelmsford, Mass.

BATES, Joseph and Esther Hilliard, 9 January 1657-8, Hingham, Mass.

BATES, Joshua and Rachel Tower, 15 January 1695, Hingham, Mass.

BATES, Lydia and William Fletcher, 7 October 1645, Concord, Mass.

BATES, Mary and William Hough, 18 August 1685, Saybrook, Conn.

BATES, Rachel and Caleb Lincoln, 8 May 1684, Hingham, Mass.

BATES, Samuel and Lydia Lapham, 20 February 1666, Scituate, Mass.

BATES, Samuel and Mary Chapman, 2 May 1676, Saybrook, Conn.

BATES, Sarah and Simeon Ellis, 1692, Haddonfield, N. J.

BATRAP, Eleanor and William Corbet, 19 September 1683, Bristol, R. I.

BATT, Timothy and Sarah Tudman, 3 August 1699, Boston, Mass.

BATTELLE, Mary and John Bryant, 20 January 1677, Dedham, Mass.

BATTELLE, John and Hannah Holbrook, 18 September 1678, Dedham, Mass.

BATTELLE, Sarah and Silas Titus, 23 August 1679, Dedham, Mass.

BATTELLE, Jonathan and Mary Onion, 15 April 1690, Dedham, Mass.

BATTIS, John and Mary Kelly, 15 June 1693, Boston, Mass.

BAXTER, Abigail and Joseph Adams, 2 November 1650, Braintree, Mass.

BAXTER, Bethiah and Samuel Deering, 1647, Braintree, Mass.

BAXTER, John and Anna White, 24 September 1659, Braintree, Mass.

BAXTER, John and Huldah Hayward, 24 January 1692-3, Milton, Mass.

BAXTER, Mary and Thomas Buttolph, 5 September 1660, Boston, Mass.

BAXTER, Roger and Mary Croutch, 6 December 1655, Kent Co., Md.

BAYARD, Ann Mary and Augustus Jay, 27 October 1697, New York.

BAYES, Thomas and Ann Baker, 26 October 1639, Dedham, Mass.

BAYLEY, Elizabeth and James Harris, 14 February 1692-3, Bridgewater, Mass.

BAYLEY, Rebecca and William Brown, 26 April 1694, Boston, Mass.

BAYLEY, Stephen and Abigail Hooper, 8 August 1673, Southold, L. I., N. Y.
BAYLEY, Susanna and Peter Thatcher, 25 December 1699, Boston, Mass.
BAYLEY, Thomas and Ruth Porter, 19 September 1660, Weymouth, Mass.
BAYLIS, John and Ruth Rusco, 12 March 1665, Queens Co., N. Y.
BAYLOR, John and Lucy T. O'Brien, 1698, Gloucester Co., Va.
BEAKS, Stephen and Elizabeth Biles, 31 August 1688, Middletown, Penn.
BEAL, Joshua and Mary Stowall (widow), 10 October 1689, Hingham, Mass.
BEAL, Sarah and Edward Winn, 10 August 1649, Woburn, Mass.
BEAMAN, Elizabeth and John Chapman, 26 March 1677, Saybrook, Conn.
BEAMAN, Noah and Patience Trescote, 1 January 1684, Dorchester, Mass.
BEAMAN, Sarah and Ebenezer Williams, 28 December 1680, Dorchester, Mas
BEAMENT, William and Lydia Danford, 9 December 1643, Saybrook, Conn.
BEAMONT, Deborah and Thomas Gilbert, 27 September 1681, Saybrook, Conn.
BEAMONT, Mary and John Tully, 3 January 1671, Saybrook, Conn.
BEAMONT, Rebecca and John Clark, 17 December 1684, Saybrook, Conn.
BEAMONT, Sarah and Nathaniel Pratt, 2 May 1688, Saybrook, Conn.
BEAMSLEY, Hannah and Abraham Perkins, 16 October 1661, Boston, Mass.
BEAMSLEY, Mary and Michael Willborne, 17 August 1656, Boston, Mass.
BEAN, Martin and Ann Allin, 8 October 1698, Elizabeth City Co., Va.
BEANS, Elhenah and Thomas Dure, 26 July 1694, Middletown, Penn.
BEAR, Edward and Mary Hale, 19 May 1693, Boston, Mass.
BEARCRAFT, Sarah and William Dadey, 28 January 1694, Bristol, R. I.
BEARD, George and Abiel Buttolph, 17 December 1691, Boston, Mass.
BEARD, Mary and John Hudson, 25 July 1689, Dover, N. H.
BEARD, Mary and John Clough, 12 April 1693, Boston, Mass.
BEARDSLEY, Mary and John Sady, 25 November 1678, Ipswich, Mass.
BEASOR, John and Esther Whitehead, 21 December 1694, Philadelphia, Penn.
BEATTY, John and Susannah Ashfordby, 7 November 1691, Kingston, N. Y.
BEAZER, Elizabeth and William Clayton, 5 February 1685, Chester Co., Penn.
BEAUCHAMP, Edmund and Sarah Dixon, 11 June 1668, Somerset Co., Md.
BEAUCHAMP, Elizabeth and Zachariah Goodell, 30 April 1666, Salem, Mass.
BEAUCHAMP, Thomas and Mary Turpin, 9 October 1692, Somerset Co., Md.
BECK, Isaac, Jr., and Eunice Turner, 24 October 1684, Scituate, Mass.
BECK, Mary and Joseph Green, 30 July 1698, Boston, Mass.
BECKET, Mary and Samuel Browne, 4 August 1691, Middletown, Conn.
BECKLEY, Sarah and John Church, 27 October 1657, Hartford, Conn.
BEDLE, Thomas and Mary Harington, 20 September 1698, Boston, Mass.
BEDFORD, William and Hannah Briant, 22 February 1697, Boston, Mass.
BEDWELL, Anna and James Enno, 18 August 1648, Windsor, Conn.
BEDWELL, Mary and Isaac Webb, 16 April 1678, Richmond Co., Va.
BEDWELL, Samuel and Mary Hodgkinson, 2 December 1653, Boston, Mass.
BEE, Sarah and James English, September 1681, Somerset Co., Md.
BEEBE, Agnes and John Daniels, 3 December 1685, New London, Conn.
BEEBE, Hannah and John Hawke, 16 January 1689, New London, Conn.
BEEBE, James and Mary Boltwood, 24 October 1668, Hadley, Mass.
BEEBE, James and Sarah Benedict, 19 December 1679, Norwalk, Conn.
BEEBE, John and Abigail Yorke, 1659, Stonington, Conn.
BEEBE, Rebecca and Nathaniel Holt, 5 April 1680, New London, Conn.
BEEBE, Samuel and Elizabeth Rogers, 9 February 1681, New London, Conn.

BEEDLE, Nathaniel and Eliza Sharp, 30 January 1694, Boston, Mass.
BEELS, Jeremiah and Sarah Ripley, 26 September 1653, Boston, Mass.
BEER, John and Mary Eades, 21 September 1694, Boston, Mass.
BEERE, John and Mary Fowler, 20 January 1673, Gloucester, Mass.
BEERS, Jabez and Elizabeth Barber, 17 May 1694, Boston, Mass.
BEERS, Sarah and Isaac Stearns, 24 June 1660, Watertown, Mass.
BEIGHTON, Lydia and John Cunniball, 2 November 1694, Boston, Mass.
BELCHER, Abigail and William Wadle, 28 April 1697, Milton, Mass.
BELCHER, Andrew and Hannah Walker, 13 February, 1689, Boston, Mass.
BELCHER, Dorothy and Edmund Gross, 19 February 1693, Boston, Mass.
BELCHER, Edward and Mary Wormwood, 8 November 1655, Boston, Mass.
BELCHER, Gregory and Elizabeth Ruggles, 25 March 1689-90, Milton, Mass.
BELCHER, Jemima and Joseph Sill, 5 December 1660, Lyme, Conn.
BELCHER, Joseph and Hannah Bill, 7 January 1697, Boston, Mass.
BELCHER, Josias and Ranus Ransford, 3 January 1655, Boston, Mass.
BELCHER, Mary and Alexander Nash, 19 October 1655, Braintree, Mass.
BELCHER, Mary and Thomas Andrews, 9 February 1681, Ipswich, Mass.
BELCHER, Mary and Nathaniel Vose, 16 December 1696, Milton, Mass.
BELCHER, Mary and Benjamin Fenno, 16 December 1696, Milton, Mass.
BELCHER, Mary and George Vaughn, 8 December 1698, Boston, Mass.
BELCHER, Mercy and Edward Kettow, 4 December 1691, Boston, Mass.
BELCHER, Moses and Mary Nash, 23 March 1666, Braintree, Mass.
BELCHER, Moses and Hannah Lyon, 19 December 1694, Milton, Mass.
BELCHER, Rebecca and Joseph Fuller, 30 November 1687, Lynn, Mass.
BELCHER, Rebecca and Samuel Miller, 25 June 1690, Milton, Mass.
BELCHER, Samuel and Mary Billings, 15 October 1663, Braintree, Mass.
BELCHER, Sarah and Samuel Irons, 13 September 1677, Braintree, Mass.
BELCHER, Sarah and Abner Dole, 5 January 1698, Boston, Mass.
BELCHER, Theodora and Simon Lee, 9 December 1698, Boston, Mass.
BELDEN, Joseph and Mercy Willard, 1693, Wethersfield, Conn.
BELKNAP, Joseph and Abigail Buttolph, 1 April 1690, Boston, Mass.
BELKNAP, Thomas and Jane Cheeney, 6 March 1694, Boston, Mass.
BELL, Abigail and James Chisholm, 31 August 1678, Somerset Co., Md.
BELL, Ann (widow) and William Mullings, 7 March 1656, Boston, Mass.
BELL, Anthony and Abigail Roatik, 25 December 1687, Somerset Co., Md.
BELL, Deborah and James York, 19 January 1669, Boston, Mass.
BELL, Esther and Richard Marshall, 11 February 1676, Taunton, Mass.
BELL, Mary and Peter Elzey, 11 November 1672, Somerset Co., Md.
BELL, Thomas and Ann Culver, 20 November 1641, Roxbury, Mass.
BELLOWS, Abigail and Isaac Lawrence, 19 April 1682, Norwich, Conn.
BELLOWS, Matthias and Maudlin Wright, 29 November 1696, Philadelphia, Penn.
BEMIS, Rebecca and Benedict Satterlee, 2 August 1682, New London, Conn.
BEMOND, Lidia and Samuel Boyes, 3 February 1667, Saybrook, Conn.
BENBOW, Margaret and Richard Roe, 20 June 1695, Boston, Mass.
BENEDICT, Esther and Joseph Ives, 11 May 1697, Wallingford, Conn.
BENEDICT, John and Phebe Gregory, 11 November 1670, Norwalk, Conn.
BENEDICT, Mary and John Olmstead, 17 July 1673, Norwalk, Conn.
BENEDICT, Samuel and Rebecca Andrews, 7 July 1678, Fairfield, Conn.
BENEDICT, Sarah and James Beebe, 19 December 1679, Norwalk, Conn.

BENHAM, John and Margery Alcock (widow), 16 November 1660, Boston, Mass
BENHAM, Joseph and Winifred King, 15 November 1656, Boston, Mass.
BENJAMIN, Abigail and Samuel Neale, 18 February 1678, Braintree, Mass.
BENJAMINE, Joseph and Jemima Lumbard, 10 June 1661, Boston, Mass.
BENKS, William and Elizabeth Woniloe, 28 January 1690, Philadelphia, Penn.
BENMORE, John and Mary Richards, 16 November 1693, Boston, Mass.
BENNET, Alice and Ralph Hatchinson, 8 June 1656, Boston, Mass.
BENNET, Ambrose and Mary Simons, 15 February 1653, Boston, Mass.
BENNET, Richard and Margaret Gurgefield (widow), 11 May 1655, Boston, Mass
BENNET, Rose and Isaac Willey, 14 December 1697, Lyme, Conn.
BENNET, Susanna and Joshua Cornish, 8 November 1692, Boston, Mass.
BENNETT, Edmund and Elizabeth Potts, 7 October 1685, Philadelphia, Penn.
BENNETT, Elizabeth and Jacob Davis, 20 January 1662, Gloucester, Mass.
BENNETT, James and Ruth Rogers, 12 July 1694, Bristol, R. I.
BENNETT, John and Deborah Grover, 1671, Beverly, Mass.
BENNETT, John and Sarah Furnis, 6 February 1683, Somerset Co., Md.
BENNETT, John and Elizabeth Pack, 8 March 1687, Stonington, Conn.
BENNETT, John and Sarah Harris, 25 October 1699, Boston, Mass.
BENNETT, Mary and John Peckham, 1695, Newport, R. I.
BENNETT, Priscilla and William Carpenter, 5 October 1651, Rehoboth, Mass.
BENNETT, Ruth and Francis Mathews, 23 February 1692, Dover, N. H.
BENNIT, Jan and Aeltje Wynans, 12 April 1690, Brooklyn, N. Y.
BENSE, Mary and John Sargeant, 3 September 1669, Malden, Mass.
BENSON, John and Elizabeth Van Deusen, 26 July 1676, Albany, N. Y.
BENSON, Sarah and Ezekial Buck, 13 January 1698, Farmington, Conn.
BENSSON, George and Anne Roberts, May 1682, Somerset Co., Md.
BENT, Joseph and Rachel Fuller, 27 October 1698, Dedham, Mass.
BENTIE, John and Elizabeth Van Clyff, 1 August 1696, New York.
BENTLY, William and Mary Houghton, 20 January 1673, Dorchester, Mass.
BENTON, Mary and Samuel Thorpe, 6 December 1666, Wallingford, Conn.
BENTON, Sarah and Thomas Wright, 9 December 1673, Guilford, Conn.
BERBEANE, Mary and Jonas Houghton, 15 February 1681, Woburn, Mass.
BERKEIM, Roger and Lucia Jones, 10 December 1681, Somerset Co., Md.
BERRY, Agnes and Giles Cowes, 27 February 1672, Ipswich, Mass.
BERRY, Daniel and Mary Mayer, 8 July 1697, Boston, Mass.
BERRY, Deliverance and Richard Pommery, 14 February 1698, Dover, N. H.
BERRY, Elizabeth and Joseph Townsend, 22 May 1690, Boston, Mass.
BERRY, Elizabeth and Robert Oliver, 14 September 1693, Boston, Mass.
BERRY, Jacobus and Elizabeth Lucas, 22 June 1688, New York City.
BERRY, Jane and Robert Goss, 5 January 1693, Dover, N. H.
BERRY, Margaret and John Leveret, 25 November 1697, Boston, Mass.
BERRY, Nathaniel and Elizabeth Philbrick, 2 July 1691, Dover, N. H.
BERRY, Samuel and Catherine Martens, 28 February 1691, Brooklyn, N. Y.
BERRY, Thomas and Margaret Rogers, 28 December 1682, Boston, Mass.
BERRY, William and Naomy Walley, 9 July 1686, Middletown, Penn.
BERRY, William and Sabrina Locke, 19 December 1689, Dover, N. H.
BETHEL, William and Helena Claypoole, 2 February 1688, Amboy, N. J.
BETTERWORTH, Patience and William Finiconie, 12 September 1695, New York
BETTS, George and Bridget Bozman, 7 November 1669, Somerset Co., Md.

BETTS, Grace and Edward Morris, 20 September 1655, Boston, Mass.
BETTS, Jonathan and Maria Ward, 4 November 1662, Branford, Conn.
BETTS, Mary and Richard Raymond, 10 December 1664, Norwalk, Conn.
BETTS, Mercy and John Barnes, 16 November 1669, North Haven, Conn.
BETTYES, John and Susana Ashfordby, 7 November 1691, New York City.
BEVENS, Rowland and Mary Bewry, 4 August 1672, Somerset Co., Md.
BEVERLEY, Peter and Elizabeth Peyton, 1689, Gloucester Co., Va.
BEWRY, Mary and Rowland Bevens, 4 August 1672, Somerset Co., Md.
BIBB, Thomas and Ruth Kettle, 20 July 1693, Burlington, N. J.
BICKFORD, Eliza and John Wells, 31 October 1698, Boston, Mass.
BICKFORD, John and Elizabeth Tibbetts, 1 December 1692, Dover, N. H.
BICKNER, Hannah and Charles Bueford, 10 February 1692, Boston, Mass.
BIDDLE, William and Lydia Wardell, 1691, Shrewsbury, N. J.
BIDWELL, Hannah and James Eno, 18 August 1648, Windsor, Conn.
BIDWELL, Mary and Isaac Webb, 1678, Richmond Co., Va.
BIGELOW, John and Mary Warren, 30 October 1642, Watertown, Mass.
BIGNELL, Richard and Abigail Lawrence, 2 November 1699, Boston, Mass.
BIGNELL, Zachery and Hannah Smith, 24 November 1692, Boston, Mass.
BIGSBIE, Daniel and Hannah Chandler, 2 December 1674, Andover, Mass.
BILES, William and Jane Atkinson, 11 October 1688, Middletown, Penn.
BILL, Hannah and James Belcher, 7 January 1697, Boston, Mass.
BILL, Martha and Thomas Gyles, 18 January 1699, Boston, Mass.
BILL, Mary and Joseph Hall, 13 July 1693, Boston, Mass.
BILL, Thomas and Agnis Batchelder, 23 November 1699, Boston, Mass.
BILL, Thomas and Elizabeth Nichols (widow), 14 November 1652, Boston, Mass.
BILLE, Mary and Samuel Buckner, 27 October 1692, Boston, Mass.
BILLIAN, Peter and Perkie Hendricke, 19 January 1696, New York.
BILLING, Mary and John Whiting, 25 December 1688, Milton, Mass.
BILLINGE, Roger and Sarah Paine, 22 January 1678, Dorchester, Mass.
BILLINGS, Ebenezer and Sarah Church, 1690, Hadley, Conn.
BILLINGS, Elizabeth and Richard Parks, 14 July 1690, Concord, Mass.
BILLINGS, Hanna and John Peniman, 24 December 1664, Braintree, Mass.
BILLINGS, Hanna and Nathaniel Gulliver, 1 July 1698, Milton, Mass.
BILLINGS, Mary and Samuel Belcher, 15 October 1663, Braintree, Mass.
BILLINGS, Mary and John Whiting, 4 December 1688, Wrentham, Mass.
BILLINGTON, Martha and Samuel Eaoton, 10 January 1660, Plymouth, Mass.
BILLINGTON, Mary and Samuel Sabin, 20 November 1663, Rehoboth, Mass.
BILLINGTON, Miss and Denis McCarthy, 1668, Old Rappahannock Co., Va.
BINGHAM, Bridget and William Walton, 3 September 1687, Chesterfield, N. J.
BINGHAM, Mary and William West, 17 November 1697, New York.
BINGHAM, Thomas and Mary Rudd, 12 December 1666, Norwich, Conn.
BINGLEY, Anna and Samuel White, 6 December 1687, Milton, Mass.
BIRD, Anne and John Clark, 16 April 1697, Dorchester, Mass.
BIRD, Hannah and Nathaniel Morgan, 19 January 1691, Springfield, Mass.
BIRD, Hannah and John Dean, 21 September 1699, Dorchester, Mass.
BIRD, James and Mary George, 6 February 1669, Dorchester, Mass.
BIRD, James and Ann Withington, 13 November 1679, Dorchester, Mass.
BIRD, John and Mary Ryall, 20 September 1696, Dorchester, Mass.
BIRD, Thomas and Thankful Atherton, 2 December 1665, Dorchester, Mass.

BIRD, Thomas and Mary Woodford, 3 July 1693, Farmington, Conn.
BIRDSALE, Judith and Henry Cook, 1 June 1639, Plymouth, Mass.
BISBEE, Martha and Jonathan Turner, 1677, Scituate, R. I.
BISCON, Isaac and Ann Brooks, 20 November 1690, Boston, Mass.
BISCOW, Mary and Samuel Silsbee, 4 July 1676, Lynn, Mass.
BISHOP, Alice (widow) and John Lewis, 22 November 1659, Boston, Mass.
BISHOP, Abigail and John Bonney, 14 June, 1695, Duxborough, Mass.
BISHOP, Benjamin and Susanna Pierson, 6 June 1696, Stamford, Conn.
BISHOP, Damaris and William Sutton, 11 July 1666, Eastham, Mass.
BISHOP, David and Mary Alger, 25 March 1679, Woodbridge, N. J.
BISHOP, Edward and Elizabeth Cash, 9 March 1692, Salem, Mass.
BISHOP, Henry and Elizabeth Wilbore (widow), 20 December 1656, Boston, Mass.
BISHOP, Hannah and Isaac Lobdale, 12 August 1697, Boston, Mass.
BISHOP, James and Elizabeth Moadsley, 16 November 1692, Dorchester, Mass.
BISHOP, Joana and John Pickard, 5 March 1690, Ipswich, Mass.
BISHOP, John and Mary Bowen, 31 December 1672, Somerset Co., Md.
BISHOP, Marie (widow) and Charles Gilman, 9 January 1684, Woodbridge, N. J.
BISHOP, Ruth and John Peirce, 15 February 1656, Boston, Mass.
BISHOP, Samuel and Hannah Yale Talmage, 2 November 1695, New Haven, Conn.
BISHOP, Sarah and Samuel Bucknell, 18 July 1654, Boston, Mass.
BISHOP, Sarah and William Hinderson, 10 August 1685, Somerset Co., Md.
BISSELL, Abigail and James Enno, 26 December 1678, Windsor, Conn.
BISSELL, John and Izrell Mason, 17 June 1658, Windsor, Conn.
BISSELL, John and Abigail Tilly, 26 August 1680, Windsor, Conn.
BISSELL, Joyse and Samuel Pinne, 17 November 1665, Windsor, Conn.
BISSELL, Mary and Jacob Drake, 12 April 1649, Windsor, Conn.
BISSELL, Mary (widow) and Peter Buel, 28 June 1698, Simsbury, Conn.
BISSELL, Nathaniel and Mindwell Moore, 25 September 1662, Windsor, Conn.
BISSELL, Nathaniel and Dorothy Fitch, 4 July 1689, Windsor, Conn.
BISSELL, Samuel and Abigail Holsom, 11 June 1658, Windsor, Conn.
BISSELL, Thomas and Abigail Moore, 11 October 1655, Windsor, Conn.
BLACHLEY, Samuel and Abigail Finch, 6 April 1699, Stamford, Conn.
BLACK, Daniel and Mary Commings, 14 July 1691, Boxford, Mass.
BLACK, Daniel and Sarah Adams, 19 July 1695, Boxford, Mass.
BLACK, Edward and Betty Morey, 26 June 1696, Milton, Mass.
BLACK, Lidia and Isaac Davis, 28 September 1659, Beverly, Mass.
BLACK, Mehitable and William Briggs, 16 June 1696, Milton, Mass.
BLACK, Nathaniel and Martha Moore, 1695, Milton, Mass.
BLACK, Persis and Robert Follett, 29 July 1655, Salem, Mass.
BLACK, Susanah and Nathaneel Wales, 30 August 1688, Milton, Mass.
BLACKEMAN, John and Jane Weekes, 26 March 1685, Dorchester, Mass.
BLACKLEECH, Benjamin and Mary Bucknell, 18 September 1693, Boston, Mass.
BLACKLEECH, Exercise and Richard Raser, 24 August 1660, Boston, Mass.
BLACKMAN, Benjamin and Sarah Scottow, 1 April 1675, Malden, Mass.
BLACKMAN, Hannah and Joseph Hasie, 12 January 1693, Boston, Mass.
BLACKMAN, Joseph and Elizabeth Church, 12 November 1685, Dorchester, Mass.
BLACKSHAW, Phebe and Joseph Kirkbride, 13 January 1688, Middletown, Penn.
BLACKWELL, James and Mary Glenn, 18 April 1699, New Kent Co., Va.

BLACKWELL, Mary and Philip Stanwood, 22 November 1677, Gloucester, Mass.
BLACKWELL, Robert and Mary Manningham, 26 April 1676, New York City.
BLADES, Jane and Thomas Gillet, 17 October 1685, Somerset Co., Md.
BLAGROVE, Nathaniel and Elizabeth Hayman (widow), 18 June 1690, Bristol, R. I.
BLAGUE, Joseph and Martha Kirtland, 10 February 1685, Saybrook, Conn.
BLAKE, Abigall and Obadiah Swift, 31 December 1695, Dorchester, Mass.
BLAKE, Andrew and Sarah Stevens, 14 August 1696, Wrentham, Mass.
BLAKE, Edward and Elizabeth Mory, 26 June 1696, Milton, Mass.
BLAKE, Elizabeth and Joseph Johnson, 25 January 1698, Middletown, Conn.
BLAKE, James and Hannah Macy, 6 December 1682, Dorchester, Mass.
BLAKE, James, Jr., and Ruth Batchelar, 8 July 1684, Dorchester, Mass.
BLAKE, Jane and Thomas Kilton, 25 March 1685, Milton, Mass.
BLAKE, John and Mary Shaw (widow), 16 June 1654, Boston, Mass.
BLAKE, John and Sarah Hall, 1673, Malden, Mass.
BLAKE, John and Joana Whiting, 6 February 1699, Wrentham, Mass.
BLAKE, Jonathan and Elizabeth Candage, 16 February 1699, Boston, Mass.
BLAKE, Mary and Samuel Pitcher, 3 August 1681, Milton, Mass.
BLAKE, Mehitabell and William Briggs, 16 June 1696, Milton, Mass.
BLAKE, Nathaniell and Martha Mory, 9 October 1695, Milton, Mass.
BLAKE, Prudence and Moses Tyler, 6 July 1666, Andover, Mass.
BLAKE, Sarah and John Roberts, 27 December 1693, Middletown, Conn.
BLAKE, Sarah and Amos Tinker, 1 June 1682, Lyme, Conn.
BLAKE, Sarah and Matthew Pool, 29 May 1694, Boston, Mass.
BLAKE, Susanah and Nathaniell Wales, 29 August 1688, Milton, Mass.
BLAKE, William and Hannah Lion, 22 November 1693, Milton, Mass.
BLAKELEY, Esther and John Bond, 25 August 1649, Newbury, Mass.
BLAKLEY, Miriam and Samuel Pond, 3 February 1669, Branford, Conn.
BLAKESLEY, Hannah (widow) and Henry Brooks, 21 December 1676, New Haven, Conn.
BLAKESLEY, Samuel and Hannah Potter, 3 December 1650, New Haven, Conn.
BLAKESLEY, Samuel and Sarah Kimberly, 20 November 1684, New Haven, Conn.
BLAKSTONE, William and Sarah Stephenson (widow), 4 July 1659, Cumberland, R. I.
BLANCHARD, Hannah (widow) and George Manning, 13 January 1655, Boston, Mass.
BLANCHARD, Hannah and Stephen Osgood, 24 May 1699, Andover, Mass.
BLANCHARD, Jonathan and Anna Lovejoy, 26 May 1685, Andover, Mass.
BLANCHARD, John and Joana Gaultier, 28 June 1695, New York.
BLANCHARD, Joseph and Abiah Hassell, 25 May 1696, Cambridge, Mass.
BLANCHARD, Thomas and Tabitha Lepingwell, 13 February 1689, Woburn, Mass.
BLANCHARD, Thomas and Rose Holmes, 22 March 1699, Andover, Mass.
BLANCHER, Susanna and Thomas Bass, 30 November 1680, Braintree, Mass.
BLANEY, Joseph and Abigail Andrews, 16 January 1694, Hingham, Mass.
BLASHFORD, Elizabeth and Thomas Cox, 17 April 1665, Newton, L. I., N. Y.
BLIN, James and Marget Dennison, 6 December 1698, Boston, Mass.
BLINSTON, Mary and John Otter, 29 August 1686, Philadelphia, Penn.
BLISS, Abigail and John Charles, 3 November 1684, New Haven, Conn.

BLISS, Catherine (widow) and Thomas Gilbert, 31 July 1655, Springfield, Mass.
BLISS, Elizabeth and Miles Morgan, 15 February 1670, Springfield, Mass.
BLISS, Experience and Nathaniel Chaffee, 19 August 1669, Swansea, Mass.
BLISS, Lydia and Samuel Letherbee, 15 November 1695, Boston, Mass.
BLISS, Mary and Nicholas Ide, 16 May 1647, Springfield, Mass.
BLISS, Samuel and Mary Leonard, 10 November 1665, Springfield, Mass.
BLITHE, Ann and Robert Chapman, 29 April 1642, Saybrook, Conn.
BLODGETT, Benjamin and Mary Pellat, 14 February 1683, Chelmsford, Mass.
BLODGETT, Samuel and Ruth Eggleton, 13 December 1655, Woburn, Mass.
BLOGGET, Daniel and Mary Butterfield, 15 September 1653, Chelmsford, Mass.
BLOODGOOD, Geertie and Jan Masten, 19 November 1677, Flatbush, N. Y.
BLORE, Elizabeth and James Talbet, 25 December 1699, Boston, Mass.
BLOSS, Dorothy and James Carpenter, 26 June 1690, Rehoboth, Mass.
BLOSSOM, Anne (widow) and Henry Rowley, 17 October 1633, Plymouth, Mass.
BLOSSOM, Elizabeth and Edwin Fittsrandolph, 10 May 1637, Scituate, Mass.
BLOTT, Mary and Thomas Woodford, 4 March 1634, Roxbury, Mass.
BLOTT, Sarah and Edwin Ellis, 6 August 1652, Boston, Mass.
BLOWER, Thomas and Eliza Gridley, 21 September 1693, Boston, Mass.
BLOYES, Judith and Thomas Davis, September 1671, Somerset Co., Md.
BLOYSE, Michal and John Adams, 2 April 1685, Medfield, Mass.
BLUNT, Mary and Henry Gray, 3 May 1699, Andover, Mass.
BLUNT, William and Elizabeth Ballard, 11 November 1668, Chelmsford, Mass.
BLYDENBURGH, Joseph and Mary Smith, 8 July 1692, New York.
BLYDENBURG, Joseph and Catherine Dehart, 19 May 1699, New York.
BOBBET, Edward and Sarah Tarne, 7 July 1654, Boston, Mass.
BOCK, Maria and Johann Friedrich Reichel, 14 May 1699, Bethlehem, Penn.
BODEN, Elizabeth and Daniel Souther, 15 June 1697, Boston, Mass.
BODY, Peter and Frances Cannon, 28 December 1686, Somerset Co., Md.
BOEDANN, Helen and Daniel Letson, 15 February 1696, New York.
BOELEN, Antie and Abraham Ketteltas, 16 December 1692, New York.
BOFFEE, Elizabeth and Robert Harris, 21 June 1642, Roxbury, Mass.
BOGARDUS, Catherine and Cornelius Vielle, 10 April 1693, New York.
BOGART, Margaret and Peter J. Haring, 4 December 1687, New York.
BOGART, Roeluf C. and Gertrude Briant, October 1695, Hackensack, N. J.
BOLEN, James and Elizabeth Godfrey, 14 March 1699, New York.
BOLT, Alice and Simon Dewolfe, 19 January 1693, Boston, Mass.
BOLTON, Elizabeth and Experience Willis, 25 October 1676, Dorchester, Mass.
BOLTWOOD, Mary and James Beebe, 24 October 1668, Hadley, Mass.
BOMMEL, Jan and Annetje Abrahams, 13 May 1662, Brooklyn, N. Y.
BOND, Abigail and Ezra Rolfe, 2 March 1676, Haverhill, Mass.
BOND, Dorothy and William Rowles, 24 April 1690, Middletown, Penn.
BOND, John and Esther Blakeley, 25 August 1649, Newbury, Mass.
BOND, John and Hannah Coolidge, 6 August 1679, Watertown, Mass.
BOND, Jonas and Grace Coolidge, 29 January 1689, Watertown, Mass.
BOND, Joseph and Elizabeth Prentice, 13 November 1699, Boston, Mass.
BOND, Mary and Simon Gross, 23 October 1675, Hingham, Mass.
BOND, Mary and Richard Coolidge, 21 June 1693, Watertown, Mass.
BOND, Stephen and Elizabeth Rogerson, 19 May 1673, Somerset Co., Md.
BONDMAN, Andrew and Eliza Tuesdell, 16 December 1697, Boston, Mass.

BONELL, Robert and Esther Wardell, 4 August 1699, Shrewsbury, N. J.
BONHAM, Elizabeth and Edward Slater, 9 January 1685, Piscataway, N. J.
BONHAM, Hannah and Daniel Lippington, 19 September 1677, Piscataway, N. J.
BONHAM, Mary and (Rev.) Edmund Dunham, 15 July 1681, Piscataway, N. J.
BONHAM, Nicholas and Hannah Fuller, 1 January 1659, Barnstable, Mass.
BONHAM, Sarah and John Fitzrandolph, 1 October 1681, Piscataway, N. J.
BONNELL, Martha and Nathaniel Walton, 10 December 1685, Philadelphia, Penn.
BONNER, John and Persis Wanton, 23 September 1699, Boston, Mass.
BONNEY, John and Abigail Bishop, 14 June 1695, Duxborough, Mass.
BONUE, Elizabeth and Henry Freeman, 16 May 1695, Woodbridge, N. J.
BOODEY, Moses and Ruth Wittum, 29 November 1697, Dover, N. H.
BOONE, Christine and Edmond de Castel, 1 May 1693, Philadelphia, Penn.
BOOTH, Alice and Ebenezer Marsh, 1 November 1699, Salem, Mass.
BOOTH, Deborah and John Town, 28 September 1691, Middletown, Penn.
BOOTH, Elizabeth and Jonathan Pease, 11 October 1693, Enfield, Conn.
BOOTH, Zachariah and Mary Harmon, 26 May 1696, Enfield, Conn.
BORDEN, Benjamin and Abigail Grover, 22 September 1670, Shrewsbury, N. J.
BORDEN, Dinah and John Davies, 23 December 1699, Philadelphia, Penn.
BORDEN, Elizabeth and Benjamin Jones, 18 September 1696, Bristol, R. I.
BORDEN, John and Mary Earl, 25 December 1670, Portsmouth, R. I.
BORDEN, Richard and Jane Vickars, 12 April 1677, Shrewsbury, N. J.
BORDEN, John and Hannah Hough, 11 February 1662, New London, Conn.
BORER, Robert and Eliza Row, 22 November 1698, New Kent Co., Va.
BOSCH, Lambert and Saradde Plancken, 1 January 1663, Brooklyn, N. Y.
BOSTON, Edward and Mary Dasset, 27 May 1695, Boston, Mass.
BOSTON, Henry and Elizabeth Rogerson, 19 May 1673, Somerset Co., Md.
BOSTWICK, Mary and George Dobson, 24 September 1653, Boston, Mass.
BOTSFORD, Elizabeth and Daniel Baldwin, 27 June 1665, Milford, Conn.
BOTTS, Elizabeth and Samuel Brackett, 25 November 1694, Berwick, Maine.
BOTTUM, Daniel and Elizabeth Lamb, 15 February 1692, Norwich, Conn.
BOUDEY, Moses and Ruth Wittum, 29 November 1697, Dover, N. H.
BOULDERSON, James and Joanna Grey, 19 May 1698, Boston, Mass.
BOULT, John and Elizabeth Clemmons, 23 November 1694, Norwalk, Conn.
BOULTON, Edward and Eleanor Jones, 30 January 1694, Philadelphia, Penn.
BOULTON, Elizabeth and Experience Willis, 25 October 1676, Dorchester, Mass.
BOULTON, Ruth and Arthur Hughes, 15 August 1698, Boston, Mass.
BOURN, Eliza and Robert Sample, 12 October 1696, Boston, Mass.
BOURNE, Alice and John Mann, 4 October 1672, Braintree, Mass.
BOURNE, Anne and Nehemiah Smith, 21 January 1639, Mansfield, Mass.
BOURNE, Elizabeth and John Welles, 1647, Stratford, Conn.
BOURNE, Elizabeth and John Wilcoxsen, March 1663, Stratford, Conn.
BOURNE, Elizabeth and Samuel Hall, 7 April 1686, Taunton, Mass.
BOURNE, Martha and Valentine Decrow, 27 February 1678, Braintree, Mass.
BOURNE, Thomas and Elizabeth Rouse, 10 April 1681, Marshfield, Mass.
BOURTHIER, Michael and Mary English, 20 February 1693, New York.
BOUTCHER, Ann and Vincent Runyan, 17 July 1668, Elizabethtown, N. J.
BOUTON, Elizabeth and Edward Waring, 6 October 1698, Norwalk, Conn.
BOWDEN, Mary and James Washburn, 20 December 1693, Bridgewater, Mass.
BOWEN, Abigail and Nathaniel Aspinwall, 11 November 1698, Woodstock, Conn.

BOWEN, Henry and Elizabeth Johnson, 20 December 1658, Woodstock, Conn.
BOWEN, Hannah and Timothy Brooks, 10 November 1685, Swansea, Mass.
BOWEN, John, Jr., and Milcah Claxton, 7 October 1699, Anne Arundel Co., Md.
BOWEN, Margaret and John Weld, 24 December 1647, Roxbury, Mass.
BOWEN, Mary and John Bishop, 31 December 1672, Somerset Co., Md.
BOWNE, Mary and Joseph Thorn, 1679, Woodbridge, N. J.
BOWEN, Ruth and George Kendrick, 23 April 1647, Rehoboth, Mass.
BOWER, Mary and Moses Lewis, 16 September 1695, New York.
BOWERMAN, Tristum and Ann Hooper, 28 July 1685, Bristol, R. I.
BOWERS, John and Hannah Partridge, 22 January 1676, Medfield, Mass.
BOWERS, Silence and Elnathan Dunckly, 14 October 1656, Dedham, Mass.
BOWES, Sarah and Thomas Bowes, 21 June 1697, Boston, Mass.
BOWES, Thomas and Sarah Bowes, 21 June 1697, Boston, Mass.
BOWLAND, Elizabeth and Samuel Lee, 2 June 1655, Boston, Mass.
BOWLING, Martha and Nathaniel Walton, 1 December 1685, Philadelphia, Penn.
BOWLES, John and Sarah Edgecomb, 3 January 1699, Wells, Maine.
BOWLES, Joseph and Mary Howell, 1640, Wells, Maine.
BOWLES, Mary (widow) and Nathaniel Lord, 31 December 1665, Rochester, Mass.
BOWLES, Mary and Samuel Staples, 30 June 1652, Braintree, Mass.
BOWLES, Thomas and Mary Gibbons, 17 November 1686, Philadelphia, Penn.
BOWMAN, Agatha and Cornelius Nevius, 15 April 1683, Flatbush, N. Y.
BOWMAN, Frances and John Bowne, 26 December 1692, Burlington, N. J.
BOWMAN, Isabella and John Langford, 30 October 1686, Burlington, N. J.
BOWNE, Elizabeth and John Haines, 9 November 1687, New York City.
BOWNE, Hannah and Benjamin Field, 30 November 1691, Flushing, N. Y.
BOWNE, James and Mary Stout, 31 December 1664, Monmouth Co., N. J.
BOWNE, John and Hannah Feke, 7 May 1656, Flatbush, N. Y.
BOWNE, John and Frances Bowman, 26 December 1692, Burlington, N. J.
BOYCE, Antipas and Hannah Hill, 24 January 1659, Boston, Mass.
BOYDEN, Mary and Joshua Clap, 22 December 1696-7, Dedham, Mass.
BOYDEN, Thomas and Hannah Mosse (widow), 3 November 1658, Boston, Mass.
BOYEN, Henry and Frances Gill, 17 August 1656, Boston, Mass.
BOYES, Lydia and Alexander Pygan, 15 April 1684, Saybrook, Conn.
BOYES, Samuel and Lidia Bemond, 3 February 1667, Saybrook, Conn.
BOYKIM, Bethia and James Dennison, 25 November 1662, Milford, Conn.
BOYLE, Jane and Andrew Groves, 8 February 1693, New York.
BOYLSTON, Abigail and John Fuller, 30 June 1668, Framingham, Mass.
BOYNTON, Eleanor (widow) and Maximillian Jewett, 30 August 1671, Rowley,
    Mass.
BOZMAN, Bridget and George Betts, 7 November 1669, Somerset Co., Md.
BRABUCK, Joane and Thomas Penny, 17 May 1682, Gloucester, Mass.
BRACKET, Martha and Robert Twelves, 22 September 1655, Boston, Mass.
BRACKETT, Elenor and John Johnson, 26 December 1661, Dover, N. H.
BRACKETT, Elizabeth and John Austin, 21 January 1685, New Haven, Conn.
BRACKETT, Jane and Mathias Haynes, 28 December 1671, Dover, N. H.
BRACKETT, John and Hannah French, 6 July 1661, Braintree, Mass.
BRACKETT, Martha and Robert Twelve, 23 September 1655, Braintree, Mass.
BRACKETT, Peter and Elizabeth Bozworth, 6 July 1661, Braintree, Mass.
BRACKETT, Samuel and Elizabeth Botts, 25 November 1694, Berwick, Maine.

BRACKETT, Sarah and Joseph Crosbee, 1 April 1675, Braintree, Mass.
BRADALL, Martha and John Hall, 16 August 1692, Harford Co. ,Md.
BRADFIELD, Martha and John Whitehead, 9 March 1661, Branford, Conn.
BRADFIELD, Samuel and Sarah Graves, 27 June 1677, Branford, Conn.
BRADFORD, Alice and William Adams, 27 March 1680, Dedham, Mass.
BRADFORD, John and Mercy Warren, 6 January 1674, Plymouth, Mass.
BRADFORD, Moses and Eliza Allen, 8 December 1692, Boston, Mass.
BRADFORD, William (Gov.) and Alice Southworth (widow), 14 August 1623, Plymouth, Mass.
BRADFORD, William and Rachel Raymond, 14 November 1676, Beverly, Mass.
BRADLEY, Isaac and Mary Clement, 25 February 1680, Haverhill, Mass.
BRADLEY, Joshua and Judith Lum, 26 May 1663, Rowley, Mass.
BRADLEY, Martha and Samuel Munson, 28 October 1665, New Haven, Conn.
BRADLEY, Mary and Samuel Todd, 25 November 1668, New Haven, Conn.
BRADLEY, Nathan and Mary Evans, 17 May 1666, Dorchester, Mass.
BRADLEY, Susannah and Edwin Hammon, 5 January 1684, Bristol, R. I.
BRADLEY, William and Alice Pritchard, 1645, North Haven, Conn.
BRADLY, Nathan and Ruth Hause, 2 January 1695-6, Dorchester, Mass.
BRADSHAWE, Elizabeth and John Broughton, 26 February 1684, Somerset Co., Md.
BRADSTREET, Dorothy and Seaborn Cotton, 14 June 1654, Andover, Mass.
BRADSTREET, Dudley and Ann Price, 12 November 1673, Andover, Mass.
BRADSTREET, Hannah and Andrew Wiggin, 3 June 1659, Andover, Mass.
BRADSTREET, Mercy and Nathaniel Wade, 31 October 1672, Andover, Mass.
BRADSTREET, Moses and Elizabeth Harris, 11 March 1665, Ipswich, Mass.
BRADSTREET, Simon and Lucy Woodbridge, 2 October 1667, Newbury, Mass.
BRAGGE, Mary and Joseph Eveleth, 1 January 1668, Gloucester, Mass.
BRAINARD, James and Deborah Indley, 1 April 1696, Saybrook, Conn.
BRAKET, Elizabeth and Daniel Draper, 16 November 1691, Dedham, Mass.
BRANCH, Catherine and Thomas Petit, 26 November 1698, New York.
BRANCH, Peter and Mary Speed, 6 December 1652, Marshfield, Mass.
BRANGEMAN, Alice and John Hill, September 1674, Somerset Co., Md.
BRAND, Thomas and Sarah Larkin, 29 October 1672, Stonington, Conn.
BRANNAN, Philip and Susannah Thomas, February 1699, Harford Co., Md.
BRASIER, Abigail and James Sabin, 18 October 1689, Rehoboth, Mass.
BRASSER, Richard and Elizabeth How, 7 July 1678, Richmond Co., Va.
BRATTLE, Mary and John Mico, 20 August 1689, Boston, Mass.
BRATTLE, William and Eliza Hayman, 3 November 1697, Boston, Mass.
BRAUN, Jan and Marie Hendricks, 14 January 1663, Brooklyn, N. Y.
BRAZIER, Mary and Philip Wilkinsen, 16 September 1697, New York.
BRAY, Hannah and Thomas Paine, 25 August 1659, Boston, Mass.
BRAY, Hannah and John Roberts, 4 February 1678, Gloucester, Mass.
BREADSTEAD, John and Margaret Peters, 10 May 1699, New York.
BREAM, Benjamin and Eliza Clemmy, 28 May 1694, Boston, Mass.
BREAM, Hannah and Robert Bronson, 12 April 1694, Boston, Mass.
BRECK, Edward and Susannah Wiswall, 1 April 1698, Dorchester, Mass.
BRECK, Mrs. Edward (widow) and Anthony Fisher, 14 September 1663, Dorchester, Mass.
BRECK, Elizabeth and John Minot, 11 March 1670, Dorchester, Mass.

BRECK, Elizabeth and Nathaniel Butt, 16 July 1698, Dorchester, Mass.
BRECK, Joanna and Michael Perry, 12 July 1694, Boston, Mass.
BRECK, John and Mehitable Morse, 9 March 1697, Sherborn, Mass.
BRECK, Mary and Samuel Paul, 9 November 1666, Dorchester, Mass.
BRECK, Robert and Sarah Hawkins, 4 November 1653, Boston, Mass.
BRECK, Susanna and John Harris, 20 March 1674, Dorchester, Mass.
BRECK, Susanna and John Toleman, February 1696-7, Dorchester, Mass.
BRECK, Thomas and Mary Hill, 12 February 1657, Dorchester, Mass.
BREDING, James and Hannah Rocke, 9 August 1657, Boston, Mass.
BRENE, Margaret and John Rcylean, 15 March 1661, Boston, Mass.
BRENTON, Elizabeth and John Pole, 28 March 1672, Dorchester, Mass.
BRETT, Mary and Seamerey Adams, 28 August 1687, Philadelphia, Penn.
BRETT, Mary and John Tuder, 9 September 1697, New York.
BREWER, Hannah and Henry Loker, 24 March 1647, Sudbury, Mass.
BREWER, John and Mary Whitmore, 23 August 1647, Ipswich, Mass.
BREWER, John, Jr., and Susanna Warner, January 1674, Ipswich, Mass.
BREWER, Mary and William Lane, 21 June 1656, Boston, Mass.
BREWER, Sarah and Samuel Graves, 12 March 1678, Lynn, Mass.
BREWER, Sarah and Thomas Webster, 29 November 1657, Hampton, N. H.
BREWSTER, Love and Sarah Collier, 25 May 1634, Plymouth, Mass.
BREWSTER, Patience and Thomas Prence, 5 August 1624, Plymouth. Mass.
BREWSTER, Ruth and John Pickett, 14 March 1651, New London, Conn.
BREWSTER, Shackelford and Elizabeth Watkins (widow), April 1655, Surry
    Co., Va.
BRICKNELL, Mary and William Hough, 24 March 1693, Boston, Mass.
BRIDG, Samuel and Sarah Smith, 24 December 1696, Boston, Mass.
BRIDG, Samuel and Christian Peirse, 3 December 1690, Boston, Mass.
BRIDGAR, Elizabeth and Richard Haynie, 10 October 1681, Northumberland
    Co., Va.
BRIDGE, Abigail and Samuel Torry, 29 June 1690, Boston, Mass.
BRIDGE, Anna and Samuel Liverence, 4 June 1668, Watertown, Mass.
BRIDGE, Elizabeth and Benjamin Garfield, 19 January 1678, Watertown, Mass.
BRIDGE, Mary and Samuel Gay, 23 November 1661, Dedham, Mass.
BRIDGE, Samuel and Sarah Leeds Payson, 21 December 1690, Dorchester, Mass.
BRIDGEMAN, James and Sarah Lyman, 1642, Hartford, Conn.
BRIDGEMAN, John and Mary Sheldon, 11 December 1670, Northampton, Mass.
BRIDGEMAN, Martha and Samuel Dickinson, 4 January 1668, Springfield, Mass.
BRIDGES, Charles and Sarah Willett, 2 November 1647, New York.
BRIDGES, Edmund (3rd marriage) and Mary Littlehale, 6 April 1665, Ipswich,
    Mass.
BRIDGES, Elizabeth and Joseph Parker, 7 October 1680, Andover, Mass.
BRIDGES, John and Mary Post (widow), 1 March 1678, Andover, Mass.
BRIDGES, John and Sarah Marstone, 24 May 1672, Andover, Mass.
BRIDGES, Mary and Nathaniel Wheeler, 9 November 1697, Boston, Mass.
BRIDGES, Sarah and Samuel Preston. 2 April 1694, Andover, Mass.
BRIDGMAN, Walter and Blanch Constable, 2 June 1686, Middletown, Penn.
BRIGGS, Cornelius and Mehitable Annable (widow), 6 May 1683, Scituate, Mass.
BRIGGS, Elizabeth and Elkanah Babbitt, 1689, Taunton, Mass.
BRIGGS, Hannah and John Harris, 10 July 1657, Boston, Mass.

BRIGGS, Hannah and Andrew Hetherington, 11 April 1695, Boston, Mass.

BRIGGS, John and Sarah Curtis, 11 January 1697, Boston, Mass.

BRIGGS, John and Elizabeth Allen, 27 April 1697, Boston, Mass.

BRIGGS, William and Abigail Mason, 7 February 1680, Dedham, Mass.

BRIGGS, William and Rebecca Dyer, 10 June 1695, Boston, Mass.

BRIGGS, William and Mehitabell Blake, 16 June 1696, Milton, Mass.

BRIGHAM, Charles and Hannah Renager, 12 July 1685, Philadelphia, Penn.

BRIGHAM, Mercy and Edmund Rice, 1 March 1655, Sudbury, Mass.

BRIGHT, Abigail and Elisha Odlin, August 1659, Watertown, Mass.

BRIMBLECOMBE, John and Barbara Davis, 14 November 1655, Boston, Mass.

BRINKERHOFF, Abraham and Aeltge Stryker, 20 May 1660, Flatbush, N. Y.

BRINSMADE, Mary and Benjamin Leeds, 17 July 1667, Dorchester, Mass.

BRINTON, William, Jr., and Jean Thatcher, 6 October 1690, Chester Co., Penn.

BRISCO, Abigail (widow) and Abraham Busby, 23 September 1659, Boston, Mass.

BRISCO, Joseph and Abigail Compton, 30 November 1651, Boston, Mass.

BRITTEN, Rebecca and Abram Cole, 9 March 1695, New York.

BRITZ, Mary and Giles Cory, 11 April 1664, Salem, Mass.

BROADLY, George and Jane Killinsworth, 6 December 1698, Anne Arundel Co., Md.

BROADWELL, Sarah and Isaac Taylor, 1689, Chester, Penn.

BROCK, Ann and James Vales, 28 March 1655, Dedham, Mass.

BROCK, Elizabeth and Robert Gowing, 31 August 1644, Dedham, Mass.

BROCK, Francis and Mary Butler, 29 July 1698, Boston, Mass.

BROCK, Jane and John Elves, 6 October 1698, Boston, Mass.

BROCK, John and Elizabeth Rowden, 5 June 1684, Philadelphia, Penn.

BROCK, Mary and Henry Phillips, 5 January 1639, Dedham, Mass.

BROCKLEBANK, Samuel and Elizabeth Platts, 22 November 1681, Rowley, Mass.

BROMLEY, Martha and William Barnes, 13 February 1682, Burlington Co., N. J.

BRONSDON, Robert and Hannah Bream, 12 April 1694, Boston, Mass.

BRONSON, John and Rachel Buck, January 1697, Wethersfield, Conn.

BROOKE, Baker and Ann Calvert, 1664, Calvert Co., Md.

BROOKE, Thomas and Eleanor Hatton, 1660, Calvert Co., Md.

BROOKER, Francis and Sarah Hubbert, 9 November 1693, Boston, Mass.

BROOKES, Elizabeth and John Pierce, 24 May 1682, Simsbury, Conn.

BROOKS, Abigail and Levird Preston, 16 October 1695, Swansea, Mass.

BROOKS, Ann and Isaac Biscon, 20 November 1690, Boston, Mass.

BROOKS, Elizabeth and Julian Bullier, 15 January 1665, Saybrook, Conn.

BROOKS, Elizabeth and Thomas Lewis, 10 April 1689, Swansea, Mass.

BROOKS, Gilbert and Sarah Carpenter, 18 January 1688, Rehoboth, Mass.

BROOKS, Hannah and Thomas Fox, 13 October 1647, Concord, Mass.

BROOKS, Hannah and Robert Crossman, 21 July 1679, Taunton, Mass.

BROOKS, Henry and Hannah Blakely, 21 December 1676, Wallingford, Conn.

BROOKS, Hepsibeth and Palatiah Mason, 22 May 1694, Swansea, Mass.

BROOKS, Joana and David Roberts, 2 October 1678, Woburn, Mass.

BROOKS, John and Eunice Mousell, 1 November 1649, Woburn, Mass.

BROOKS, John and Susanna Hanmore, 25 May 1652, Windsor, Conn.

BROOKS, Mary and Richard Norcross, 24 June 1650, Watertown, Mass.

BROOKS, Mary and Mathew Ford, 12 July 1674, Wallingford, Conn.

BROOKS, Mary and John Sharp, 6 September 1697, Boston, Mass.

BROOKS, Rebecca and Melatiah Martin, 6 November 1696, Swansea, Mass.
BROOKS, Ruth and William Baldwin, 2 July 1688, Wallingford, Conn.
BROOKS, Sarah and John Mousall, 13 May 1650, Woburn, Mass.
BROOKS, Sarah and Benjamin Robins, 29 August 1687, Wallingford, Conn.
BROOKS, Timothy and Mary Russell, 2 December 1659, Woburn, Mass.
BROOKS, Timothy and Hannah Bowen, 10 November 1685, Swansea, Mass.
BROOKS, Titus and Eliza Noaks, 20 November 1694, Boston, Mass.
BROOME, Hannah (widow) and Thomas Ashly, 1 January 1661, Boston, Mass.
BROUGHTON, John and Hannah Woodruff, 29 October 1678, Northampton, Mass.
BROUGHTON, John and Elizabeth Bradshaw, 26 February 1684, Somerset
       Co., Md.
BROWN, Abraham and Leah Clayton, 29 July 1692, Middletown, N. J.
BROWN, Agnes and Anthony Morris, 25 August 1689, Philadelphia, Penn.
BROWN, Anna and Hezekiah Willett, 7 January 1675, Rehoboth, Mass.
BROWN, Cornelius and Sarah Lamson, 6 March 1664-5, Reading, Mass.
BROWN, Daniel and Sarah Tucker, 9 June 1698, Anne Arundel Co., Md.
BROWN, Dorothy and James Kent, Jr., 12 November 1690, Rehoboth, Mass.
BROWN, Eleazer and Ann Pendleton, 18 October 1693, Westerly, R. I.
BROWN, Elizabeth and James Kidder, 23 September 1678, Billerica, Mass.
BROWN, George and Annabell Knocks (widow), 13 February 1693, Woodbridge,
       N. J.
BROWN, Gillam and Thomas Milner, 3 September 1696, Chesterfield, N. J.
BROWN, James, Jr., and Margaret Denison, 5 June 1678, Rehoboth, Mass.
BROWN, Jesabell and Anthony Hoskins, 16 July 1656, Windsor, Conn.
BROWN, Joana and Daniel Harris, 1682, Roxbury, Mass.
BROWN, Joana and John Cox, 18 November 1698, Boston, Mass.
BROWN, John and Rebecca Sprague, 24 June 1697, Malden, Mass.
BROWN, John and Sarah Burroughs, 21 April 1698, Boston, Mass.
BROWN, Joseph and Hannah Fitch, 10 November 1680, Rehoboth, Mass.
BROWN, Joshua and Sarah Sawyer, 15 January 1669, Newbury, Mass.
BROWN, Josiah and Mary Fellows, 23 November 1666, Redding, Conn.
BROWN, Lydia adn Thomas Parsons, 28 June 1641, Windsor, Conn.
BROWN, Lydia and William Parker, 6 September 1676, Saybrook, Conn.
BROWN, Martha and John Hamton, 3 January 1687, Middletown, N. J.
BROWN, Mary and John Lewis, 10 April 1650, Malden, Mass.
BROWN, Mary and John Moses, 18 May 1653, Windsor, Conn.
BROWN, Mary (widow) and Henry Walker, 26 September 1662, Gloucester, Mass
BROWN, Mary and Edward Saunders, 1687, Middlesex Co., Va.
BROWN, Mary and John Levensworth, 21 August 1694, Boston, Mass.
BROWN, Mehitable and John Townsend, 23 April 1690, Lynn, Mass.
BROWN, Peter and Mary Gillet, 15 July 1658, Windsor, Conn.
BROWN, Richard and Elizabeth Badger, 16 February 1648, Newbury, Mass.
BROWN, Samuel and Martha Harding, 19 February 1682, Plymouth, Mass.
BROWN, Samuel and Elizabeth Morrell, 3 February 1698, Boston, Mass.
BROWN, Sarah and William Scant, 29 January 1654, Braintree, Mass.
BROWN, Sarah and Joseph Moore, 29 August 1681, Windsor, Conn.
BRAWN, Sarah and Jabez Negus, 9 January 1693, Boston, Mass.
BROWN, Thankful and Joseph Hubbert, 4 August 1698, Boston, Mass.
BROWN, Thomas and Martha Eaton, 7 October 1656, Cambridge, Mass.

BROWN, William and Mary Murdock, 16 July 1649, Plymouth, Mass.
BROWN, William and Rebecca Bayley, 26 April 1694, Boston, Mass.
BROWN, William and Mercy Jacklin, 29 October 1694, Boston, Mass.
BROWN, William and Catharine Williams, 26 March 1699, Philadelphia, Penn.
BROWNE, Abraham and Rebecca Usher, 1 May 1660, Boston, Mass.
BROWNE, Abram and Jane Skipper, 19 June 1653, Boston, Mass.
BROWNE, Anne and John Chamberline, 19 March 1653, Boston, Mass.
BROWNE, Boaz and Mary Richards, 30 September 1695, Dedham, Mass.
BROWNE, Edmond and Elizabeth Oklye, 14 December 1653, Boston, Mass.
BROWNE, Elizabeth and John Robinson, 21 March 1666, Baltimore, Md.
BROWNE, Elizabeth and Moses Baker, 12 January 1694, Elizabeth City Co., Va.
BROWNE, Faith and Daniel Warner, 1 June 1660, Ipswich, Mass.
BROWNE, Hannah and John Parker, 24 May 1687, Andover, Mass.
BROWNE, John and Ester Makepeace, 24 February 1655, Boston, Mass.
BROWNE, John and Elizabeth Osgood, 12 October 1659, Andover, Mass.
BROWNE, Lydia and Andrew Hodges, 27 November 1659, Ipswich, Mass.
BROWNE, Marcy and John Everit, 3 January 1699, Dedham, Mass.
BROWNE, Martha and Edwin Farington, 9 April 1690, Andover, Mass.
BROWNE, Mary and William Haskell, Jr., 3 July 1667, Gloucester, Mass.
BROWNE, Rebecca and James Hudson, 3 December 1652, Boston, Mass.
BROWNE, Samuel and Mary Mattocke, 9 July 1661, Boston, Mass.
BROWNE, Samuel and Mary Becket, 4 August 1691, Middletown, Penn.
BROWNE, Thomas and Ruth Jones (widow), 12 November 1677, Concord, Mass.
BROWNE, William and Elizabeth Ruggles, 24 February 1655, Boston, Mass.
BRUCE, Elizabeth and Ebenezer Swan, 2 March 1698, Woburn, Mass.
BRUCE, George and Elizabeth Clark, 20 December 1659, Woburn, Mass.
BRUCE, John and Rose Wattel, 31 January 1693, Woburn, Mass.
BRUEN, Mary and John Baldwin, Sr., 1653, Milford, Conn.
BRUEN, Hannah and John Baldwin, 30 October 1663, Morris Co., N. J.
BRUNO, Francis and Sarah Vringe, 26 January 1699, Boston, Mass.
BRUNSON, Abigail and Jonathan Winchell, May 1666, Farmington, Conn.
BRUSH, Rebecca and Jeremiah Hobart, 8 February 1682, Huntington, L. I., N. Y.
BRIANT, Antje and Anna de Sill, 20 December 1691, Bergen Co., N. J.
BRIANT, Gertrude and Roeluf C. Bogart, October 1695, Hackensack, N. J.
BRIANT, Hannah and William Bedford, 22 February 1697, Boston, Mass.
BRYAN, Elizabeth and John Durend, 10 November 1698, New York.
BRYANT, Mary and John Finney, 14 June 1693, Plymouth, Mass.
BRYANT, William and Hannah Disiter, 9 June 1692, Boston, Mass.
BRYER, Elisha and Abigail Drew, 4 October 1689, Dover, N. H.
BUCHER, Alwin and Elizabeth Barnard, 15 December 1698, Boston, Mass.
BUCK, Ezekial and Sarah Benson, 13 January 1698, Farmington, Conn.
BUCK, Henry and Elizabeth Churchill, 31 October 1660, Wethersfield, Mass.
BUCK, John and Sarah Doty, 26 April 1692, Scituate, Mass.
BUCK, Martha and James Robinson, 21 December 1653, Boston, Mass.
BUCK, Rachel and John Dwelly, 4 January 1692-3, Scituate, Mass.
BUCKINGHAM, Daniel and Sarah Lee, 24 May 1693, Saybrook, Conn.
BUCKINGHAM, Mary and John Parker, 24 December 1666, Saybrook, Conn.
BUCKINGHAM, Thomas and Hester Hosmer, 20 September 1666, Saybrook, Conn.

BUCKINGHAM, Thomas and Margaret Griswold, 16 December 1691, Saybrook, Conn.

BUCKLAND, Elizabeth and Edward Adams, 25 May 1660, Windsor, Conn.

BUCKLAND, Hanna and Joshua Welles, 14 August 1681, Windsor, Conn.

BUCKLAND, Lydia and William Lord, 13 June 1660, Rehoboth, Mass.

BUCKLANT, Timothy and Abigail Vore, 27 March 1662, Windsor, Conn.

BUCKLEY, Mary and Sylvester Whittredge, 17 November 1684, Essex Co., Mass.

BUCKLEY, Mary and Benjamin Proctor, 18 December 1694, Lynn, Mass.

BUCKLY, David and Hannah Tally, 3 June 1697, Boston, Mass.

BUCKMAN, Joses and Judith Worth, 1 May 1673, Malden, Mass.

BUCKMAN, Mercy and Benjamin Webb, 7 December 1669, Malden, Mass.

BUCKMASTER, Abigail and John Gutterson, 14 January 1688, Andover, Mass.

BUCKMASTER, Dorcas and Clement Corbet, 7 January 1655, Boston, Mass.

BUCKMASTER, Johanna and Edward Garfield, 1 July 1661, Watertown, Mass.

BUCKMASTER, Sarah and John Lawrence, 30 September 1657, Boston, Mass.

BUCKMASTER, Sarah and William Chandler, 28 December 1682, Andover, Mass.

BUCKMASTER, Zachariah and Sarah Webb, 7 January 1655, Boston, Mass.

BUCKMINSTER, Mary and Benjamin Dana, 24 May 1688, Cambridge, Mass.

BUCKMAN, James and Deborah Melen, 22 September 1697, Malden, Mass.

BUCKNAM, Sarah and Richard Dexter, 23 February 1698, Malden, Mass.

BUCKNAM, William and Hannah Wayte, 11 October 1676, Malden, Mass.

BUCKNELL, Mary and Benjamin Blackleech, 18 September 1693, Boston, Mass.

BUCKNELL, Samuel and Sarah Bishop, 18 July 1654, Boston, Mass.

BUCKNER, Samuel and Mary Bille, 27 October 1692, Boston, Mass.

BUCLAND, John and Deborah Barrow, 17 October 1693, Plymouth, Mass.

BUDD, Dorothy and William Daniel, 27 September 1699, Boston, Mass.

BUDD, Joseph and Sarah Underhill, 11 October 1695, Rye, N. Y.

BUDD, Martha and William Shute, 19 May 1690, Boston, Mass.

BUDD, Sarah and John Murray, 26 February 1689, Philadelphia, Penn.

BUDLONG, Francis and Rebecca Howard (widow), 19 May 1668-9, Warwick, R. I.

BUEFORD, Charles and Hannah Bickner, 10 February 1692, Boston, Mass.

BUEL, Martha and Nathan Holcomb, 1 November 1695, Simsbury, Conn.

BUEL, Peter and Mary Bissell (widow), 30 June 1699, Simsbury, Conn.

BUELL, Abigail and Thomas Barber, 25 May 1699, Simsbury, Conn.

BUELL, Hannah and Timothy Palmer, 17 September 1663, Windsor, Conn.

BUELL, Mary and Simon Miller, 20 February 1660, Windsor, Conn.

BUELL, Samuel and Judith Stevens, 1686, Killingworth, Conn.

BUFF, Daniel and Mary Emblem, 12 May 1698, Boston, Mass.

BUGBEE, John and Abigail Corbit(?), 10 July 1696, Woodstock, Conn.

BUGBEE, Mehitable and John Scarbro, 17 October 1695, Woodstock, Conn.

BUGBEY, Rebeccah and Thomas Bacon, 2 November 1688, Milton, Mass.

BUGBY, Elizabeth and Andrew Cload, 29 July 1653, Boston, Mass.

BULKELEY, Gershom and Sarah Chauncy, 26 October 1659, Lancaster, Mass.

BULKLEY, Rebecca and Joanthan Prescott, 18 December 1689, Concord, Mass.

BULL, Abigail and Thomas Barnard, 28 April 1696, Andover, Mass.

BULL, David and Hannah Chapman, 27 December 1677, Saybrook, Conn.

BULL, John and Mary Woodward, 21 April 1692, Boston, Mass.

BULL, Joseph and Sarah Manning, 11 April 1671, Hartford, Conn.

BULL, Isaac and Sarah Parker, 22 April 1653, Boston, Mass.
BULL, Margaret and John Jones, 29 May 1699, Boston, Mass.
BULL, Mary and John Stiler, 9 June 1697, Boston, Mass.
BULL, Mehitable and Windsor Sandey, 12 February 1694, Boston, Mass.
BULL, Phebe and Samuel Chalker, 7 November 1676, Saybrook, Conn.
BULL, Robert and Phebe Jose, 15 December 1649, Saybrook, Conn.
BULLARD, Anne and David Joanes, 18 March 1685, Dorchester, Mass.
BULLARD, Augustine and Hannah Dyer (widow), 12 October 1693, Dover, N. H.
BULLARD, Benjamin and Martha Pidge, 5 February 1659, Dedham, Mass.
BULLARD, Isaac and Ann Wight, 11 February 1655, Dedham, Mass.
BULLARD, Mary and John Farrington, 23 February 1649, Dedham, Mass.
BULLARD, Mary and Jonathan Gay, 29 June 1682, Dedham, Mass.
BULLARD, Mary and Samuell Holmes, 26 December 1696, Dedham, Mass.
BULLARD, Nathaniell and Mary Richards, 15 October 1658, Dedham, Mass.
BULLARD, Samuell and Hanna Thorp, 14 November 1683, Dedham, Mass.
BULLARD, Sarah and John Ball, 17 October 1665, Watertown, Mass.
BULLARD, William and Elizabeth Avery, 6 August 1697, Dedham, Mass.
BULLEN, Anne and Jonathan Stout, 27 August 1685, Monmouth Co., N. J.
BULLEN, Samuel and Mary Morse, 10 June 1641, Dedham, Mass.
BULLIER, Elizabeth and James Fitzgerald, 28 April 1678, Saybrook, Conn.
BULLIER, Julian and Elizabeth Brooks, 15 January 1665, Saybrook, Conn.
BULLIN, Mary and Thomas Harding, 8 April 1686, Philadelphia, Penn.
BULLING, Meletiah and Josiath Fisher, 27 November 1679, Dedham, Mass.
BULLOCK, Mary and Thomas Harding, 5 February 1686, Philadelphia, Penn.
BULMAN, Alexander and Margaret Taylor, 22 December 1690, Boston, Mass.
BUNDICK, Dorothy and James Connier, 18 September 1673, Somerset Co., Md.
BUNKER, John and Hannah Miller, July 1655, Malden, Mass.
BUNKER, Martha and Stephen Hussey, 8 October 1676, Lynn, Mass.
BUNN, Edward and Elizabeth Mason, 20 June 1657, Boston, Mass.
BUNN, Elizabeth and John Shield, 16 January 1696, Harford Co., Md.
BUNNELL, Mary and Eleaser Peck, 31 October 1671, New Haven, Conn.
BUNNELL, Nathaniel and Susan Whitehead, 3 June 1665, New Haven, Conn.
BUNT, Mary and Christian Lawrier, December 1698, New York.
BUNTIN, George and Anne Lee, 27 April 1687, Philadelphia, Penn.
BUNTING, Robert and Rachel Baker, 27 April 1689, Middletown, Penn.
BURBANK, Ebenezer and Rebecca Pritchard (widow), 9 October 1699, Suffield, Conn.
BURBANK, Caleb and Martha Smith, 6 May 1669, Rowley, Mass.
BURBANK, John and Susannah Merrill, 15 October 1663, Newbury, Mass.
BURCH, William and Hanna Robinson, 4 September 1693, New York.
BURCHAM, Frances and Isaac Willy, 8 June 1660, Boston, Mass.
BURCHARD, John and Christian Andrews, April 1653, Boston, Mass.
BURDEN, Sarah and John Mays, 8 July 1683, Roxbury, Mass.
BURDITT, Robert and Hannah Winter, November 1653, Malden, Mass.
BURGE, Daniel and Elizabeth Gayler, 5 October 1641, Windsor, Conn.
BURGE, Daniel and Debra Holcom, 5 November 1668, Windsor, Conn.
BURGE, James and Hanna Watson, 28 March 1678, Windsor, Conn.
BURGE, John and Mary Larned (widow), 9 June 1662, Chelmsford, Mass.
BURGE, John and Grizzell Gurney, 3 July 1667, Chelmsford, Mass.

BURGER, Eva and George Hulgrow, 30 June 1696, New York.
BURGES, Roger and Esther Palmer, 3 August 1698, Boston, Mass.
BURGESS, Elizabeth and Ezra Perry, 12 February 1651, Sandwich, Mass.
BURGESS, John and Mary Worden, 8 September 1657, Yarmouth, Mass.
BURGESS, Mary and Francis Traveres, 27 January 1699, Boston, Mass.
BURGESS, William and Hannah Stinson, 20 May 1684, Cambridge, Mass.
BURGESSE, James and Lydia Meed, 19 August 1652, Boston, Mass.
BURGIS, Sarah and Nathaniel Witherly, 10 December 1699, Boston, Mass.
BURKBIE, Sarah and Samuel Spofford, 5 December 1676, Rowley, Mass.
BURKBIE, Thomas and Sarah Kelly, 15 April 1659, Rowley, Mass.
BURLE, Joshua and Judith Sexton, 5 September 1698, New York.
BURLINGAM, Mary and Amos Stafford, 19 December 1689, Warwick, R. I.
BURNAM, Thomas, Jr., and Naomi Hull, 4 January 1676, Killingworth, Conn.
BURNAP, Elizabeth and Jonathan Eaton, 1683, Reading, Mass.
BURNAP, Isaac and Hannah Antrum, 8 September 1658, Salem, Mass.
BURNETT, John and Mary Rice, 7 April 1634, Charlestown, Mass.
BURNETT, Lois and Robert Collins, 1 December 1689, Hampton, L. I., N. Y.
BURNETT, Mary and William Eaton, 1692, Lynn, Mass.
BURR, Daniel and Abigail Glover, 11 December 1678, New Haven, Conn.
BURR, Elizabeth and John Terry, 27 November 1662, Hartford, Conn.
BURR, Hannah and Andrew Hillyard, September 1681, Simsbury, Conn.
BURR, Mary and Christopher Crow, 15 January 1657, Hartford, Conn.
BURREL, Samuel and Margaret Jarvis, 17 September 1697, Boston, Mass.
BURREL, Theophilus and Lydia Gethercole, 5 July 1694, Boston, Mass.
BURRELL, Lois and Samuel Sprague, 5 June 1695, Boston, Mass.
BURRILL, John and Lois Ivory, 10 May 1666, Boston, Mass.
BURRILL, John and Mercy Alden, June 1688, Taunton, Mass.
BURROUGHS, John and Patience Hinman, 10 January 1694, Stratford, Conn.
BURROUGHS, Mary and Michael Homer, 13 July 1693, Boston, Mass.
BURROUGHS, Sarah and John Brown, 21 April 1698, Boston, Mass.
BURROWS, John and Hannah Culver, 14 December 1670, New London, Conn.
BURROWS, John and Lydia Hubbard, 1694, New London, Conn.
BURSHAM, Ann and William Satterthwaite, 3 October 1685, Chesterfield, N. J.
BURSLEY, Johanna and Shubael Dimmock, April 1663, Barnstable, Mass.
BURSLEY, John and Joana Hull, 28 May 1639, Cape Cod, Mass.
BURT, David and Mary Holton, 18 November 1655, Northampton, Mass.
BURT, David and Mary Reed, 19 October 1673, Richmond Co., Va.
BURT, Mercy and Judah Wright, 17 January 1667, Deerfield, Mass.
BURT, Richard and Margaret Glenn, 18 October 1697, New York.
BURTHEL, Mary and Thomas Butler, 23 January 1696, Harford Co., Md.
BURTON, Elizabeth and Thomas Hedger, 30 October 1674, Warwick, R. I.
BURTON, Mary Ann and Hendrick J. Vanderbergh, 11 October 1694, New York.
BURTON, Robert and Catherine Cotton, 11 February 1676, Accomac Co., Va.
BURTON, Stephen and Elizabeth Winslow, 4 September 1684, Bristol, R. I.
BURTON, Susannah and Samuell Gorton, 11 December 1684, Warwick, R. I.
BURWELL, Samuel and Rebecca Bunnell, 1684, New Haven, Conn.
BUSBY, Abraham and Abigail Brisco (widow), 23 September 1659, Boston, Mass.
BUSCH, Cornelia and Peter Cavaleer, 1 March 1697, New York.
BUSECOTT, Mary and Peeter Spicer, 15 December 1670, Warwick, R. I.

BUSH, John and Hannah Pendleton, 13 January 1679, Sudbury, Mass.

BUSHNELL, Francis and Hannah Seymour, 12 October 1675, Norwalk, Conn.

BUSHNELL, Jane and John Hill, 14 April 1670, Saybrook, Conn.

BUSHNELL, Martha and Jonathan Smith, 1 January 1663, Saybrook, Conn.

BUSHNELL, Mary and George Robinson, 3 August 1657, Boston, Mass.

BUSHNELL, Mary and Samuel Jones, 1 January 1663, Saybrook, Conn.

BUSHNELL, Mary and William Miller, 19 April 1693, Saybrook, Conn.

BUSHNELL, Richard and May Marvin, 11 October 1648, Hartford, Conn.

BUSHNELL, Sarah and Joseph Hingham, 20 June 1655, Saybrook, Conn.

BUSHNELL, Sarah and Thomas Stevens, 9 November 1688, Killingworth, Conn.

BUSHNELL, Samuel and Patience Rodd, 7 October 1675, Saybrook, Conn.

BUSHNELL, Samuel and Ruth Sanford, 17 April 1684, Saybrook, Conn.

BUSKMAN, Ruth and Richard Harrison, 7 February 1686, Chesterfield, N. J.

BUSS, Hannah and William Wheeler, 30 October 1659, Concord, Mass.

BUSSWELL, Robert and Hannah Tyler, 9 December 1697, Andover, Mass.

BUTCHER, John and Mary Deane, 30 January 1661, Boston, Mass.

BUTLER, Elizabeth and Michael Pamer, 2 December 1662, Branford, Conn.

BUTLER, Grace and Andrew Rankin, 5 April 1692, Boston, Mass.

BUTLER, Hannah and James Chadwick, February 1677, Malden, Mass.

BUTLER, James and Grace Newcomb, 1687, Boston, Mass.

BUTLER, John and Hannah Potter, 17 November 1684, Branford, Conn.

BUTLER, John and Mary Clemmons, 23 November 1694, Stamford, Conn.

BUTLER, Lydia and John Minot, 19 May 1647, Dorchester, Mass.

BUTLER, Mary (widow) and John Hinds, 9 February 1681-2, Lancaster, Mass.

BUTLER, Mary and Francis Brock, 29 July 1698, Boston, Mass.

BUTLER, Susannah and Nathaniel Roring, 13 December 1699, Boston, Mass.

BUTLER, Thomas and Mary Burthel, 23 January 1696, Harford Co., Md.

BUTLER, Thomas and Abigail Shepard, 8 August 1691, Hartford, Conn.

BUTTLER, Thomas and Margery Crue, 1 March 1685, New Kent Co., Va.

BUTT, Nathaniel and Elizabeth Breck, 16 July 1698, Dorchester, Mass.

BUTT, Sherebiah and Silence Rigby, 19 November 1697, Dorchester, Mass.

BUTTERFIELD, Benjamin and Hannah Whittemore (widow), 3 June 1663, Chelmsford, Mass.

BUTTERFIELD, Jane and William Phillips, 2 April 1691, Boston, Mass.

BUTTERFIELD, Jonathan and Ruth Wright, 20 March 1693, Woburn, Mass.

BUTTERFIELD, Joseph and Lydia Ballard, 12 February 1674, Chelmsford, Mass.

BUTTERFIELD, Mary and Daniel Blogget, 15 September 1653, Chelmsford, Mass.

BUTTERFIELD, Nathaniel and Deborah Underwood, 25 December 1668, Chelmsford, Mass.

BUTTERFIELD, Nathaniel and Sarah Fletcher, 18 January 1697, Chelmsford, Mass.

BUTTON, Mary and Edwin Yeomans, 2 December 1652, Haverhill, Mass.

BUTTON, Mathias and Elizabeth Duston, 9 June 1663, Haverhill, Mass.

BUTTON, Mathias and Mary Neff, 24 November 1686, Haverhill, Mass.

BUTTOLPH, Abiel and George Beard, 17 December 1691, Boston, Mass.

BUTTOLPH, Abigail and David Saywell, 15 August 1660, Boston, Mass.

BUTTOLPH, Abigail and Joseph Belknap, 1 April 1690, Boston, Mass.

BUTTOLPH, Nicholas and Mary Guttridge, 28 June 1699, Boston, Mass.

BUTTOLPH, Thomas and Mary Baxter, 5 September 1660, Boston, Mass.

BUTTOLPH, Thomas and Abiel Sanders, 3 December 1689, Boston, Mass.
BUTTRICK, Sarah and Samuel Barrett, 21 February 1683, Concord, Mass.
BUXTON, Elizabeth and Robert Hustis, 9 January 1655, Stamford, Conn.
BUYS, Jacob and Maritje Joris, 22 November 1690, Brooklyn, N. Y.
BUZIGUT, Ruth and Thomas Thurber, 23 February 1677, Swansea, Mass.
BYFIELD, Sarah and William Taylor, 2 March 1699, Boston, Mass.

C

CABALL, Mary and Jeremiah Allen, 25 June 1695, Boston, Mass.
CADY, Benjamin and Mary Pease, 16 February 1663, Andover, Mass.
CADY, Jona and Hester Chandler, 12 November 1667, Andover, Mass.
CAIG, Alc and Samuel Pitcher, 30 November 1671, Milton, Mass.
CAIRNESS, John and Eliza Mortimor, 24 June 1697, Boston, Mass.
CALDWELL, John and Sarah Foster, 1 May 1689, Ipswich, Mass.
CALEF, Joseph and Mary Ayer, 24 March 1693, Boston, Mass.
CALFE, Robert and Margaret Barton, 23 December 1699, Boston, Mass.
CALHOUNE, John and Jane Carter, June 1676, Somerset Co., Md.
CALKINS, Elizabeth and Samuel Hyde, 10 December 1690, Lebanon, Conn.
CALL, Elizabeth and Daniel Shepardson, 11 April 1668, Malden, Mass.
CALL, Mercy and Samuel Lee, 4 November 1662, Malden, Mass.
CALL, Thomas and Elidea Shepardson, 22 May 1657, Malden, Mass.
CALLOMER, Mary and Robert Stetson, 12 January 1692-3, Scituate, Mass.
CALLOWAY, Elizabeth and John Vance, June 1697, Middlesex Co., Va.
CALLOWE, Oliver and Judith Clocke (widow), 28 February 1655, Boston, Mass.
CALVERT, Ann and Baker Brooke, 1664, Calvert Co., Md.
CAMDEN, Edward and Ruth Pasco, 25 September 1694, Boston, Mass.
CAMMELL, Elizabeth and Anthony Dixon, 8 January 1684, Salem Co., N. J.
CAMP, Nicholas and Katherine Thompson, 16 July 1652, Milford, Conn.
CAMPBALL, Mercy and James Turberfeeld, 6 December 1699, Boston, Mass.
CAMPBELL, Ebenezer and Hannah Pratt, 29 March 1694, Taunton, Mass.
CAMPBELL, Jane and George Gilbert, 4 May 1698, New York.
CAMPISON, Leonard and Margaret Morgan, 26 December 1677, Somerset Co., Md.
CAMBY, Thomas and Sarah Jervis, 27 August 1693, Philadelphia, Penn.
CANCE, Elizabeth and John Mayson, 27 December 1677, New York City.
CANDAGE, Elizabeth and Jonathan Blake, 16 February 1699, Boston, Mass.
CANN, John and Ester Read, 30 July 1661, Boston, Mass.
CANNEY, Joseph and Mary Clements, 20 October 1670, Dover, N. H.
CANNEY, Mary and John Twambly, 18 April 1687, Dover, N. H.
CANNING, Ann and John Petty, 30 May 1662, Boston, Mass.
CANNON, Andrew and Ann Puppyn, 18 November 1695, New York.
CANNON, Frances and Peter Body, 28 December 1686, Somerset Co., Md.
CANNON, Jan and Maria LeGrand, September 1697, New York City.
CANNON, William and Mary Willing, 18 February 1695, Harford Co., Md.
CANNY, Joseph and Mary Clements, 20 December 1670, Dover, N. H.
CANTWELL, Edward and Jane Chattum, 5 December 1699, Harford Co., Md.
CAPEN, Bernard and Sarah Trot, 2 June 1675, Dorchester, Mass.
CAPEN, Bernard and Joan Purchase, March 1696, Dorchester, Mass.
CAPEN, John and Redegon Clapp, 20 October 1637, Dorchester, Mass.
CAPEN, John and Mary Bass, 20 September 1647, Roxbury, Mass.
CAPEN, John, Jr., and Susanna Barsham, 19 September 1663, Dorchester, Mass
CAPEN, Preserved and Mary Pason, 16 May 1682, Dorchester, Mass.
CAPEN, Samuel and Ann Stone, 16 November 1693, Boston, Mass.

CAPEN, Samuel and Susanna Payson, 9 April 1673, Dorchester, Mass.

CAPER, Mary and Joseph Gilson, 18 November 1660, Chelmsford, Mass.

CAPIN, Mary and James Foster, 22 September 1674, Dorchester, Mass.

CAPRON, Banfield and Elizabeth Challender (daughter of John), December 1680, Rehoboth, Mass.

CARD, John and Elizabeth Winchester (widow), 16 January 1683, York, Maine.

CARD, Thomas and Mary Winchester, 26 July 1694, New York.

CARDER, James and Mary Whyppoll, 6 January 1686-7, Warwick, R. I.

CARDER, John and Mary Houldon, 1 December 1671, Warwick, R. I.

CARDER, Mary and Malachy Roads, 27 May 1675, Warwick, R. I.

CARDER, Sarah and Benjamin Gorton, 5 December 1672, Warwick, R. I.

CARLETON, John and Hannah Osgood, 27 August 1688, Andover, Mass.

CARLETON, John and Abigail Osgood, 2 August 1694, Andover, Mass.

CARLY, Mary and James Spencer, 28 May 1695, New York.

CARMAN, John and Elizabeth Ludlom, 20 January 1683, Staten Island, N. Y.

CARNABY, Nicholas and Jane Downing, 12 December 1694, New York.

CARPENTER, Abraham and Mehitable Read, 30 May 1690, Rehoboth, Mass.

CARPENTER, Hannah and Joseph Carpenter, 21 April 1659, Rehoboth, Mass.

CARPENTER, James and Dorothy Bloss, 26 June 1690, Rehoboth, Mass.

CARPENTER, Joseph and Hannah Carpenter, 21 April 1659, Rehoboth, Mass.

CARPENTER, Mary and Thomas Crockes, 8 April 1697, New London, Conn.

CARPENTER, Nathaniel and Mary Preston, 13 October 1695, Dorchester, Mass.

CARPENTER, Priscilla and Peter Morss, 28 December 1698, Woodstock, Conn.

CARPENTER, Rebecca and Jared Ingraham, 28 May 1662, Boston, Mass.

CARPENTER, Samuel and Sarah Readaway, 25 May 1660, Rehoboth, Mass.

CARPENTER, Samuel and Patience Ide, 8 January 1683, Rehoboth, Mass.

CARPENTER, Sarah and Nathaniel Perry, 17 May 1683, Rehoboth, Mass.

CARPENTER, Sarah and Gilbert Brooks, 18 January 1688, Rehoboth, Mass.

CARPENTER, William and Priscilla Bennett, 5 October 1651, Rehoboth, Mass.

CARPENTER, William and Miriam Searles, 10 December 1663, Rehoboth, Mass.

CAREY, Edwin and Katherine Ferrill, 10 December 1680, Somerset Co., Md.

CAREY, Mathew and Mary Sylvester, 1 August 1693, Bristol, R. I.

CAREY, Mehitable and Elisha Adams, 18 December 1689, Bristol, R. I.

CAREY, Thomas and Elizabeth Hinds, 8 January 1694, Elizabeth City Co., Va.

CARR, Anne and Edwin Hazard, February 1671, Somerset Co., Md.

CARR, Elizabeth and John Covan, 8 March 1680, Somerset Co., Md.

CARR, Elizabeth and John Woodmansey, 1 May 1662, Boston, Mass.

CARR, Joanna and Robert Clemons, 2 April 1667, Dover, N. H.

CARRIER, Richard and Elizabeth Sessions, 18 July 1694, Andover, Mass.

CARRIER, Thomas and Martha Allen, 7 May 1664, Billerica, Mass.

CARRINGTON, Mary and Phineas Sprague, 11 October 1661, Malden, Mass.

CARROLL, Abigail and Isaac Foster, 25 November 1678, Ipswich, Mass.

CARROLL, Thomas, Jr., and Rebecca Walton (widow), 19 October 1686, Somerset Co., Md.

CARTER, Abigail and Stephen Flanders, 28 December 1670, Salisbury, Mass.

CARTER, Anne and William Cotton, 6 November 1699, Boston, Mass.

CARTER, Eunice and John Kendall, 29 March 1681, Woburn, Mass.

CARTER, George and Mary Nichollson, 4 September 1677, Somerset Co., Md.

CARTER, Katherine and Edward Turner, 25 January 1687, Philadelphia, Penn.

CARTER, Jane and John Calhoune, June 1676, Somerset Co., Md.
CARTER, John and Philippe White, 6 November 1699, Boston, Mass.
CARTER, Judith and Samuel Converse, June 1660, Woburn, Mass.
CARTER, Maria and Samuel Ward, 1 January 1658, Branford, Conn.
CARTER, Robert and Hannah Lucas, 19 April 1694, Bristol, R. I.
CARTER, Thomas and Ruth Mountfort, 2 May 1693, Boston, Mass.
CARTER, Timothy and Anna Fisk, 3 May 1680, Lexington, Mass.
CARTER, Zebulon and Heiltie Sloat, 19 December 1693, New York.
CARVER, Eleazer and Experience Sumner, 11 June 1695, Milton, Mass.
CARVER, John and Millicent Ford, 4 November 1658, Duxbury, Mass.
CARVER, Millicent (widow) and Thomas Drake, 9 March 1681, Weymouth, Mass.
CARVER, William and Joan Kinsly, 14 January 1690, Bucks Co., Penn.
CARVER, William and Elizabeth Foster, 18 January 1682, Marshfield, Mass.
CARWITHEN, David and Francis Oldam (widow), 22 September 1660, Boston, Mass.
CARWITHY, Joshua and Elizabeth Farnam, 6 June 1657, Boston, Mass.
CASE, Abigail and John Torbet, 17 November 1698, Dedham, Mass.
CASE, Anne and Thomas Lyon, 1 November 1693, Boston, Mass.
CASE, Barthol and Mary Humphries, 7 December 1699, Simsbury, Conn.
CASE, Ebenezer and Patience Draper, 13 March 1690, Roxbury, Mass.
CASE, John and Mary Olcott, 16 September 1684, Simsbury, Conn.
CASE, John and Joana Johnson, 27 April 1692, Dover, N. H.
CASE, Joseph and Ann Enno, 6 April 1699, Simsbury, Conn.
CASE, Mary and James Hillard, 30 March 1699, Simsbury, Conn.
CASE, Sarah and Joseph Phelps, 9 November 1699, Simsbury, Conn.
CASH, Elizabeth and Edwin Bishop, 9 March 1692, Salem, Mass.
CASTLE, Elizabeth and Henry Dickeson, 25 October 1693, Boston, Mass.
CASWELL, Elizabeth and Uriah Leonard, 1 June 1685, Taunton, Mass.
CASWELL, Francis and Priscilla Tapril, 18 August 1699, Boston, Mass.
CASWELL, Mary and Thomas Stephens, 28 September 1699, Taunton, Mass.
CATLIN, John and Mary Marshall, 27 July 1665, Hartford, Conn.
CAVALEER, Peter and Cornelia Busch, 1 March 1697, New York.
CERGOE, Margery and Edwin Willake, 28 April 1692, New York.
CEYSLER, Hesther and Barnet Reyners, 10 March 1696, New York.
CHADWICK, Elizabeth and Gersham Hills, 11 November 1667, Malden, Mass.
CHADWICK, Elizabeth and Thomas Fox, 24 April 1683, Watertown, Mass.
CHADWICK, James and Hannah Butler, 11 February 1677, Malden, Mass.
CHADWICK, Mary and Dane Robinson, 18 January 1694, Andover, Mass.
CHADWICK, Sarah and Thomas Grover, 23 May 1668, Malden, Mass.
CHAFFEE, Nathaniel and Experience Bliss, 19 August 1669, Swansea, Mass.
CHALKER, Abraham and Hannah Sanford, 16 January 1679, Saybrook, Conn.
CHALKER, Alexander and Catherine Post, September 1649, Saybrook, Conn.
CHALKER, Katherine and John Hill, 23 September 1673, Saybrook, Conn.
CHALKER, Mary and Richard Coozens, 7 March 1678, Saybrook, Conn.
CHALKER, Samuel and Phebe Bull, 7 November 1676, Saybrook, Conn.
CHAMBERLAIN, Edmund and Elizabeth Bartholomew, 21 November 1699, Woodstock, Conn.
CHAMBERLAIN, Jacob and Mary Child, 24 January 1685, Roxbury, Mass.
CHAMBERLAIN, Mary and James Leavens, 21 November 1699, Woodstock, Conn.

CHAMBERLIN, Alexander and Sarah Tinny, 20 April 1699, Boston, Mass.
CHAMBERLIN, Sarah and Richard Arnold, 19 February 1681, Burlington, N. J.
CHAMBERLIN, Susanna and John Tuckerman, 14 November 1693, Boston, Mass.
CHAMBERLINE, John and Anne Browne, 19 March 1653, Boston, Mass.
CHAMBERS, Benjamin and Hannah Smith, 3 March 1686, Philadelphia, Penn.
CHAMBERS, John and Mary Drummond, 17 August 1693, New York.
CHAMBERS, John and Bridget Huet, 4 September 1696, Freehold, N. J.
CHAMBERS, Richard and Mary Ivery, 24 May 1676, Somerset Co., Md.
CHAMPNEY, Henry and Eliza Worthylake, 8 December 1693, Boston, Mass.
CHAMPNEY, Sarah and William Barrett, 19 August 1656, Cambridge, Mass.
CHANCY, Charles and Sarah Wally, 19 October 1699, Boston, Mass.
CHANDLER, Hannah and George Abbott, 12 December 1646, Roxbury, Mass.
CHANDLER, Hannah and Daniel Bigsbie, 2 December 1674, Andover, Mass.
CHANDLER, Henry and Lydia Abbott, 28 November 1695, Andover, Mass.
CHANDLER, Hester and Jona Cady, 12 November 1667, Andover, Mass.
CHANDLER, John and Mary Ramond, 10 November 1692, Woodstock, Conn.
CHANDLER, John and Hannah Abbot, 20 December 1676, Andover, Mass.
CHANDLER, Joseph and Sarah Abbott, 26 November 1691, Andover, Mass.
CHANDLER, Lydia and Richard Higgins, 11 December 1634, Plymouth, Mass.
CHANDLER, Mary and Jonathan Sampson, 16 November 1695, Newbury, Mass.
CHANDLER, Mehitable and John Coit, 25 June 1695, Woodstock, Conn.
CHANDLER, Samuel and Sarah Davis (widow), 21 October 1664, Dorchester, Mass.
CHANDLER, Samuel and Abigail Palmer, 10 April 1684, Dorchester, Mass.
CHANDLER, Sarah and Samuel Phelps, 29 May 1682, Andover, Mass.
CHANDLER, Sarah and William Coit, 7 June 1697, Woodstock, Conn.
CHANDLER, Thomas and Mary Peters, 22 May 1686, Andover, Mass.
CHANDLER, William and Mary Dane, 24 August 1658, Andover, Mass.
CHANDLER, William and Bridget Richardson, 8 October 1679, Andover, Mass.
CHANDLER, William and Sarah Buckmaster, 28 December 1682, Andover, Mass.
CHANDLER, William and Elenor Phelps, 21 April 1687, Andover, Mass.
CHANTRIL, Joseph and Amie Gardner, 13 December 1697, Boston, Mass.
CHANTRIL, Mary and Thomas Marshall, 18 June 1697, Boston, Mass.
CHAPIN, Catherine and Thomas Gilbert, 30 June 1655, Springfield, Mass.
CHAPIN, Hannah and Nathaniel Hitchcock, 27 September 1666, Springfield, Mass.
CHAPIN, Japhet and Abilenah Cooley, 22 July 1664, Milton, Conn.
CHAPIN, Jonah and Lydia Pratt, 26 July 1676, Braintree, Mass.
CHAPIN, Mary and Joseph Adams, 1682, Braintree, Mass.
CHAPIN, Mary and Benjamin Wright, 24 January 1694, Springfield, Mass.
CHAPIN, Mehitable and John Ware, 14 January 1696, Wrentham, Mass.
CHAPIN, Ruth and William Thwing, 26 January 1698, Boston, Mass.
CHAPIN, Samuel and Mary Hobart, May 9, 1688, Milton, Mass.
CHAPIN, Thomas and Sarah Wright, 15 February 1694, Lebanon, Conn.
CHAPLINE, Barbery and Ebenezar Joanes, 2 June 1685, Dorchester, Mass.
CHAPMAN, Hannah and David Bull, 27 December 1677, Saybrook, Conn.
CHAPMAN, John and Jane Saddler, 12 June 1670, Wrightstown, Penn.
CHAPMAN, John and Elizabeth Hally, 7 June 1670, Saybrook, Conn.
CHAPMAN, John and Elizabeth Beamon, 26 March, 1677, Saybrook, Conn.
CHAPMAN, Mary and William Throop, 4 May 1666, Barnstable, Mass.

CHAPMAN, Mary and Samuel Bate, 2 May 1676, Saybrook, Conn.

CHAPMAN, Mrs. and Samuel Cross, 12 July 1677, Windsor, Conn.

CHAPMAN, Nathaniel and Mary Collins, 29 June 1681, Saybrook, Conn.

CHAPMAN, Robert and Ann Blithe, 29 April 1642, Saybrook, Conn.

CHAPMAN, Robert and Sarah Griswold, 27 June 1671, Saybrook, Conn.

CHAPMAN, Robert and Mary Sheather, 29 October 1694, Saybrook, Conn.

CHAPMAN, Samuel and Ruth Ingalls, 20 May 1678, Ipswich, Mass.

CHAPPELL, Francis and Ann Fromansteel, 27 November 1695, New York.

CHAPPELL, George and Alice Waye, 3 October 1676, New London, Conn.

CHAPPELL, Mary and John Daniel, 19 January 1664, New London, Conn.

CHAPPELL, Thomas and Elizabeth Jones, 1670, Charles City Co., Va.

CHARLES, John and Abigail Bliss, 3 November 1684, New Haven, Conn.

CHARLES, Mary and Martin Tichenor, 16 May 1651, New Haven, Conn.

CHARLES, Rebecca and William Hill, 19 June 1691, Milton, Mass.

CHASE, Benjamin and Amy Borden, 21 September 1696, Cumberland, R. I.

CHASE, Elizabeth and Zachariah Eires, 27 June 1678, Andover, Mass.

CHASE, Priscilla and Abel Merrill, 10 February 1671, Newbury, Mass.

CHASE, Thomas and Rebecca Follansbee, 22 November 1677, Newbury, Mass.

CHATFIELD, John and Anna Harger, 5 February 1684, Derby, Conn.

CHATTUM, Jane and Edward Cantwell, 5 December 1699, Harford Co., Md.

CHAUNCY, Sarah and Gershom Bulkeley, 26 October 1659, Lancaster, Mass.

CHECKLEY, Hannah and John Adams, 19 October 1694, Boston, Mass.

CHECKLEY, John and Ann Eires, 5 January 1652, Boston, Mass.

CHEEK, Elizbeth and John Moore, 8 September 1696, New York.

CHEESBROUGH, Samuel and Mary Ingraham, 8 December 1687, Swansea, Mass.

CHEEVER, Elizabeth and Samuel Goldthwaite, 6 September 1666, Charleston, Mass.

CHEEVER, Elizabeth and Stephen Palmer, 19 January 1692, Boston, Mass.

CHEEVER, Ezekial and Ellen Lothrop, 15 November 1652, Ipswich, Mass.

CHEEVER, Ezekial and Abigail Lippingwell, 17 June 1680, Salem, Mass.

CHEEVER, Susanna and Joseph Russell, 5 June 1693, Boston, Mass.

CHENEY, Eliza and Thomas Owen, 10 September 1694, Boston, Mass.

CHENEY, Hannah and Richard Smith, November 1660, Ipswich, Mass.

CHENEY, Jane and Thomas Belknap, 6 March 1694, Boston, Mass.

CHENEY, John, Sr., and Grizell Kidbee, 12 September 1661, Braintree, Mass.

CHENEY, John and Mary Chute, 7 March 1693, Sudbury, Mass.

CHENEY, Martha and William Worcester, 29 January 1690, Rowley, Mass.

CHENEY, Peter and Hannah Noyes, 14 May 1663, Newbury, Mass.

CHENY, Benjamin and Martha Royall, 2 February 1699, Dorchester, Mass.

CHESHIRE, John and Ann Sutton, 14 February 1692, Middletown, N. J.

CHESLEY, Thomas and Elizabeth Thomas, 22 August 1663, Dover, N. H.

CHEW, Joseph and Mary Smith, 17 November 1685, Herring Creek, Md.

CHICKERING, Esther and Daniel Smith, 20 October 1659, Dedham, Mass.

CHICKERING, Francis and Sarah Sibble, 11 April 1650, Dedham, Mass.

CHICKERING, Mary and John Metcalfe, 23 January 1647, Dedham, Mass.

CHICKERING, Nathaniel and Mary Judson, 30 December 1668, Dedham, Mass.

CHICKERING, Ann and Stephen Paine, 3 September 1652, Dedham, Mass.

CHILCOTT, James and Mary Tindale, 1698, Anne Arundel Co., Md.

CHILCOTT, Mary and Paulus Rose, 28 July 1698, Anne Arundel Co., Md.

CHILD, John and Hannah French, 5 September 1693, Boston, Mass.
CHILD, Mary and Jacob Chamberlain, 24 January 1685, Roxbury, Mass.
CHILDERS, Delia and Johanes Groenendyke, 18 September 1694, New York.
CHIPMAN, Mercy and Nathan Skiff, 13 December 1699, Sandwich, Mass.
CHISHOLM, James and Abigail Bell, 31 August 1678, Somerset Co., Md.
CHITTENDEN, Mary and John Leete, 4 October 1670, Guilford, Conn.
CHONOR, Rebecca and Theophilus Philpot, 22 September 1697, Boston, Mass
CHRISTEN, Abial and Sarah Tylestone, 18 January 1699, Boston, Mass.
CHUBB, Pascoe and Hannah Faulkner, 29 May 1689, Andover, Mass.
CHURCH, Abigail and Samuel Piper, 23 April 1694, Dover, N. H.
CHURCH, Caleb and Joana Sprague, 16 December 1667, Hingham, Mass.
CHURCH, Elizabeth and Joseph Blackman, 12 November 1685, Dorchester, Ma
CHURCH, Hepzibah and Sam Spencer, 16 August 1696, Hadley, Conn.
CHURCH, John and Sarah Beckley, 27 October 1657, Hartford, Conn.
CHURCH, John and Mercy Hanson, 1 December 1699, Dover, N. H.
CHURCH, Joseph and Mary Tucker, 13 December 1660, Hingham, Mass.
CHURCH, Mary and Phillip Russell, 25 December 1658, Hadley, Conn.
CHURCH, Naomi and Joseph Rodman, 11 May 1687, Hadley, Conn.
CHURCH, Rebecca and Joseph Seldon, 11 February 1677, Hadley, Conn.
CHURCH, Richard and Anne Marsh, 18 May 1627, Barnstable, Mass.
CHURCH, Richard and Elizabeth Noble, 3 March 1692, Westfield, Mass.
CHURCH, Sarah and Ebenezer Billings, 1690, Hadley, Conn.
CHURCH, Thomas and Sarah Haymon, 21 February 1698, Bristol, R. I.
CHURCHER, Frances and James Creeke, 20 August 1688, Burlington, N. J.
CHURCHILL, Ann and Samuel Royce, 9 January 1667, Wethersfield, Conn.
CHURCHILL, Elizabeth and Henry Buck, 31 October 1660, Wethersfield, Cor
CHUTE, James and Mary Wood, 10 November 1673, Ipswich, Mass.
CHUTE, Mary and John Cheney, 7 March 1693, Sudbury, Mass.
CILLEY, Chas. and Elizabeth Sanders, 6 November 1697, Elizabeth City Co., \
CLAES, Pietertje and Jans Jacobus Joralemon, 12 December 1696, Bergen C
　　　N. J.
CLAP, Abigael and Samuel King, 30 October 1693, Milton, Mass.
CLAP, Desire and Sarah Pond, 21 October 1679, Dorchester, Mass.
CLAP, Elizabeth and Ebenezer Sumner, 14 March 1699, Dorchester, Mass.
CLAP, Ezra and Experience Houghton, 22 May 1684, Dorchester, Mass.
CLAP, Hopestill and Susanna Swift, 18 February 1672, Dorchester, Mass.
CLAP, John and Silence Foster, 26 May 1698, Dorchester, Mass.
CLAP, Joshua and Mary Boyden, 22 December 1696-7, Dedham, Mass.
CLAP, Mary and Nathaniel Pitcher, 8 July 1685, Milton, Mass.
CLAP, Mary and John Evans, 7 January 1694, Boston, Mass.
CLAP, Roger and Joana Ford, 6 November 1633, Dorchester, Mass.
CLAP, Samuel and Elizabeth Smith, 31 January 1668, Dorchester, Mass.
CLAP, Sammuell and Mary Paull, 7 April 1698, Dorchester, Mass.
CLAP, Sarah and Joseph Mathar, 20 June 1689, Dorchester, Mass.
CLAP, Sarah and Thomas Swift, 16 October 1676, Milton, Mass.
CLAP, Thomas and Mary Fisher, 10 September 1662, Dedham, Mass.
CLAPP, Barbara and Joseph Welde, 20 October 1639, Milton, Mass.
CLAPP, Redegon and John Capen, 20 October 1637, Dorchester, Mass.
CLAPP, Sarah and Samuel Howe, 18 September 1685, Sudbury, Mass.

CLARE, Catherine and Jeremy Kittle, 27 October 1686, New York.
CLARK, Abigall and Thomas Lyon, 8 July 1698, Dedham, Mass.
CLARK, Anna and Anthony Annable, 3 March 1645, Scituate, Mass.
CLARK, Charity and Nicholas Lawrence, 24 September 1699, Perth Amboy, N. J.
CLARK, Daniel and Mary Newberry, 13 June 1644, Windsor, Conn.
CLARK, Eliza and David Mason, 12 December 1693, Boston, Mass.
CLARK, Elizabeth and George Bruce, 20 December 1659, Woburn, Mass.
CLARK, Elizabeth and Samuel Tompkins, 1680, York Co., Va.
CLARK, Frances and Thomas Dewey, 22 March 1638, Windsor, Conn.
CLARK, George and Ann Lutterell, 3 February 1690, Boston, Mass.
CLARK, John and Rebecca Parker, 16 October 1650, Saybrook, Conn.
CLARK, John and Rebecca Cooper, 12 July 1677, Northampton, Mass.
CLARK, John and Mary Strong, 16 March 1679, Northampton, Mass.
CLARK, John and Rebecca Beaumont, 17 December 1684, Saybrook, Conn.
CLARK, John and Sarah Shrimpton, 30 April 1691, Boston, Mass.
CLARK, John and Anne Bird, 16 April 1697, Dorchester, Mass.
CLARK, Joseph and Mary Davis, 18 August 1685, Haverhill, Mass.
CLARK, Joseph and Demaris Francis, 19 August 1675, Braintree, Mass.
CLARK, Mary and John Strong, Jr., 26 November 1656, Windsor, Conn.
CLARK, Mary and John Coney, 8 November 1694, Boston, Mass.
CLARK, Mary and Bartholomew Stevenson, 10 October 1680, Dover, N. H.
CLARK, Mathias and Ann Barton, 25 December 1699, Boston, Mass.
CLARK, Matthew and Abigail Maverick, 4 April 1655, Boston, Mass.
CLARK, Melatiah and Timothy Hammant, 19 January 1696, Boston, Mass.
CLARK, Nathaniel and Sarah (Lay) Dewolfe, 3 December 1696, Lyme, Conn.
CLARK, Penelope and Jonathan Everrard, 9 August 1697, Boston, Mass.
CLARK, Rebecca and Isreal Rust, 9 December 1669, Northampton, Mass.
CLARK, Samuel and Sarah Avise, 8 September 1692, Boston, Mass.
CLARK, Samuel and Elizabeth Crafts, 5 May 1696, Boston, Mass.
CLARK, Samuel and Hannah Fairweather, 23 June 1698, Boston, Mass.
CLARK, Samuel and Mary Kirtland, 14 December 1699, Saybrook, Conn.
CLARK, Sarah and Jonathan Laws (dau. of George), 1668, Milford, Conn.
CLARK, Sarah and Renold Mason, 27 November 1663, Milford, Conn.
CLARK, Sarah and Thomas Cornwall, 14 November 1671, Middletown, Conn.
CLARK, Sarah and Samuel Willard, 6 June 1683, Saybrook, Conn.
CLARK, Sarah and Nicholas Gilman, 10 June 1697, Newbury, N. H.
CLARK, Solomon and Mary White, 24 October 1698, Dedham, Mass.
CLARK, Susanna and Barnabas Lothrop, 3 November 1658, Plymouth, Mass.
CLARK, Thomas and Rebecca Miller, 12 February 1681, Marshfield, Mass.
CLARK, Thomas and Rebecca Smith, 30 April 1691, Boston, Mass.
CLARKE, Ann and Samuel Jackson, 22 October 1672, Somerset Co., Md.
CLARKE, Edward and Dorothy Reynells, 14 December 1678, New York.
CLARKE, Elizabeth and George Barber, 24 September 1642, Dedham, Mass.
CLARKE, Elizabeth and John Freake, 28 May 1661, Boston, Mass.
CLARKE, Elizabeth and William Perkins, 24 October 1669, Topsfield, Mass.
CLARKE, Faith and Edward Doty, 6 January 1634, Plymouth, Mass.
CLARKE, Jemima and Robert Drue, 6 September 1656, Boston, Mass.
CLARKE, Lydia and Charles Gott, 25 December 1665, Lynn, Mass.
CLARKE, Margaret and Samuel Ruck, 22 May 1656, Boston, Mass.

CLARKE, Mary and Benjamin Smith, 10 June 1641, Dedham, Mass.
CLARKE, Prissilla and Nathaniell Coleborne, 25 May 1639, Dedham, Mass.
CLARKE, Regdon and Peter Wittoms, 17 April 1652, Boston, Mass.
CLARKE, Sarah and George Hisket, 11 June 1662, Boston, Mass.
CLARKE, Sarah and Thomas Reynolds, 11 October 1683, Newport, R. I.
CLARKE, Sarah and Ephriam Little, 29 November 1698, Plymouth, Mass.
CLARKE, William and Martha Farr, 18 September 1661, Boston, Mass.
CLARKSON, Mathew and Catherine Van Schaick, 19 January 1692, Albany, N. Y
CLARY, Sarah and John Perry, 13 December 1667, Watertown, Mass.
CLAXTON, Milcah and John Bowen, Jr., 7 October 1699, Anne Arundel Co., Mt
CLAY, Ann and Samuel Sarson, 3 January 1694, Boston, Mass.
CLAY, Mary and Richard Smith, 9 February 1699, Boston, Mass.
CLAY, Rebecca and Nicholas Green, 22 March 1697, Boston, Mass.
CLAYPOOL, Helena and William Bethell, 2 February 1688, Amboy, N. J.
CLAYPOOLE, George and Mary Righton, 23 December 1699, Philadelphia, Pen
CLAYPOOLE, Mary and Francis Cooke, 11 October 1688, Philadelphia, Penn.
CLAYTON, Leah and Abraham Brown, Jr., 29 July 1692, Middletown, N. J.
CLAYTON, Sibella and James Harpin, 28 June 1699, Burlington, N. J.
CLAYTON, William and Elizabeth Berger, 5 February 1685, Chester Co., Penn.
CLEAR, William and Bethiah(?) Greenleaf, 21 December 1699, Boston, Mas
CLEARE, George and Martha Ward, 26 November 1648, Dedham, Mass.
CLEARK, Agnes and Thomas Penny, 15 June 1668, Gloucester, Mass.
CLEAVERY, John and Sarah Steevins, 18 January 1664, Braintree, Mass.
CLEAVES, John and Mercy Eaton, 26 January 1699, Beverly, Mass.
CLEMANS, Rebecca and Daniel Collings, 13 December 1693, Boston, Mass.
CLEMENCE, Elizabeth and James Mathewson, 5 April 1696, Providence, R. I.
CLEMENCE, Hannah and Caleb Knapp, 23 November 1694, Stamford, Conn.
CLEMENS, James and Martha Deane, 28 December 1674, Marshfield, Mass.
CLEMENS, Judith and Jeremiah Whitney, 29 September 1659, Plymouth, Mas
CLEMENS, Robert and Elizabeth Fawne, 8 December 1652, Ipswich, Mass.
CLEMENT, Fawne and Sarah Hoyt, 21 November 1688, Haverhill, Mass.
CLEMENT, James and Sarah Hinchman, 2 July 1696, New York.
CLEMENT, John and Elizabeth Fawne, 22 February 1676, Haverhill, Mass.
CLEMENT, Lydia and John Johnson, Jr., 19 February 1689, Haverhill, Mass.
CLEMENT, Mary and John Osgood, 15 November 1653, Haverhill, Mass.
CLEMENT, Mary and Isaac Bradley, 25 February 1680, Haverhill, Mass.
CLEMENT, Robert and Deliverence Oddihorne, 18 December 1695, Great Islan
    N. H.
CLEMENT, Samuel and Hannah Ings, 2 May 1657, Boston, Mass.
CLEMENT, Samuel and Rebecca Collins, 1696, Haddonfield, N. J.
CLEMENT, Sarah and Abraham Morrill, 10 June 1645, Haverhill, Mass.
CLEMENT, Sarah and Thomas Mudgett, 8 October 1665, Haverhill, Mass.
CLEMENTS, Abigail and Moses Pingree, 13 February 1666, Haverhill, Mass.
CLEMENTS, Job and Abigail Heard, 28 February 1688, Dover, N. H.
CLEMENTS, John and Sarah Osgood (daughter of John), 1 June 1648, Have
    hill, Mass.
COGGSHALL, Joshua and Rebecca Russell, 21 June 1677, Middletown, N. J.
COGSWELL, Hannah and Josiah Dibell, 20 January 1692, Saybrook, Conn.
COGSWELL, Samuel and Susana Hearn, 27 October 1668, Saybrook, Conn.

COIT, John and Mehitable Chandler, 25 June 1695, Woodstock, Conn.

COIT, William and Sarah Chandler, 7 June 1697, Woodstock, Conn.

COLBORNE, Priscilla and James Morse, 12 November 1668, Dedham, Mass.

COLBORNE, Deborah and Joseph Wite, 15 November 1679, Dedham, Mass.

COLBURN, Deborah and William Lyon, 8 November 1699, Woodstock, Conn.

COLBURN, Hannah and Thomas Aldrich, 16 January 1677, Dedham, Mass.

COLBURN, Hannah and Joseph Farwell, 23 January 1696, Chelmsford, Mass.

COLBURN, Mary and Elisha Odlen, 30 December 1697, Boston, Mass.

COLBURN, Thomas and Hannah Rolfe, 6 August 1672, Chelmsford, Mass.

COLCORD, Samuel and Mary Ayer, 1680, Exeter, N. H.

COLDUM, Elizabeth and Francis Norwood, 15 October 1663, Gloucester, Mass.

COLE, Abigail and John Stevens, 28 April 1684, Wallingford, Conn.

COLE, Abraham and Ann Townsend, 30 September 1697, Boston, Mass.

COLE, Abraham and Rebecca Britten, 9 March 1695, New York.

COLE, Ann and Nicholas Babcock, 1686, Dover, N. H.

COLE, Elizabeth and Thomas Pierce, 6 May 1635, Woburn, Mass.

COLE, Elizabeth and Elkanah Cushman, 10 February 1677, Plymouth, Mass.

COLE, Israel and Mary Rogers (widow), 24 April 1679, Eastham, Mass.

COLE, James and Mary Foxwell, 8 January 1654, Barnstable, Mass.

COLE, John and Susanna Hutchinson, 30 October 1651, Boston, Mass.

COLE, Lydia and Peter Masett, 6 April 1695, New York.

COLE, Mary and Joshua Hopkins, 26 May 1681, Eastham, Mass.

COLE, Mary and William Ogborne, 17 November 1698, Burlington, N. J.

COLE, Nathaniel and Martha Parkeson, 30 August 1667, Warwick, R. I.

COLE, William and Hannah Snow, 2 December 1688, Eastham, Mass.

COLEBORNE, Mary and John Richards, 1 August 1672, Dedham, Mass.

COLEBORNE, Nathaniell and Prissilla Clarke, 25 May 1639, Dedham, Mass.

COLEBORNE, Nathaniel and Mary Brooks, 19 November 1669, Dedham, Mass.

COLEMAN, Hannah and Thomas Nash, August 1685, Hadley, Mass.

COLEMAN, Hanry and Mary Meade, December 1691, New York City.

COLEMAN, Henry and Elenor Hunt, 27 July 1698, New York.

COLMAN, John and Judith Hobbey, 19 July 1694, Boston, Mass.

COLEMAN, John and Hannah Wright, 24 April 1695, Wethersfield, Conn.

COLEMAN, Mary (widow) and Peter Montague, 16 September 1680, Hadley, Mass.

COLEMAN, Noah and Mary Crow, 27 December 1666, Hadley, Mass.

COLEMAN, William and Bridget Roe (widow), 14 November 1662, Gloucester, Mass.

COLMAN, William and Margaret Haywood, 30 June 1692, Boston, Mass.

COLES, Ussillah and Wigleworth Switser, 2 February 1699, Boston, Mass.

COLLAR, Nathaniel and Mary Barrett, 10 October 1693, Chelmsford, Mass.

COLLEE, Thomas and Anne Fann, 13 July 1673, Richmond Co., Va.

COLLIER, Elizabeth and Constant Southworth, 2 November 1637, Duxbury, Mass.

COLLIER, Margaret and Thomas Leeds, 6 August 1678, Burlington, N. J.

COLLIER, Richard and Mary Jarvis, 25 January 1699, Boston, Mass.

COLLIER, Robert and Elizabeth Dashiell, 2 March 1675, Somerset Co., Md.

COLLIER, Sarah and Love Brewster, 25 May 1634, Plymouth, Mass.

COLLINGS, Daniel and Rebecca Clemans, 13 December 1693, Boston, Mass.

COLLINS, Abigail and Andrew Townshend, 18 July 1678, Lynn, Mass.

COLLINS, Elizabeth and Samuel Gorton, 9 May 1695, Warwick, R. I.
COLLINS, Elizabeth and Adam Ball, 31 August 1699, New York.
COLLINS, James and Elizabeth Kennedy, 17 April 1692, New York.
COLLINS, Joane and Robert Scamp, 25 December 1661, Gloucester, Mass.
COLLINS, John and Ann Leete, 23 July 1691, Guilford, Conn.
COLLINS, John and Jane Loyd, 22 April 1697, Boston, Mass.
COLLINS, John and Dorcas Tainter (widow), 6 March 1699, Branford, Conn.
COLLINS, Joseph and Ruth Knowles, 20 March 1671, Eastham, Mass.
COLLINS, Joseph and Catherine Huddleston, 1698, Burlington Co., N. J.
COLLINS, Loves and David Adams, 15 December 1698, Boston, Mass.
COLLINS, Mary and Samuel Johnson, 22 January 1664, Lynn, Mass.
COLLINS, Mercy and Nathaniel Chapman, 29 June 1681, Saybrook, Conn.
COLLINS, Martha and William Harris, 8 January 1690, Middletown, Conn.
COLLINS, Rebecca and Samuel Clement, 1696, Haddonfield, N. J.
COLLINS, Robert and Lois Barnett, 1 December 1689, Hampton, L. I., N. Y.
CLEMENTS, John and Mehitable Miller, 20 September 1688, Springfield, Mass.
CLEMENTS, Mary and Joseph Canney, 20 October 1670, Dover, N. H.
CLEMMONS, Elizabeth and John Boult, 23 November 1694, Norwalk, Conn.
CLEMMONS, Mary and John Butler, 23 November 1694, Stamford, Conn.
CLEMMY, Eliza and Benjamin Bream, 28 May 1694, Boston, Mass.
CLEMONS, Margaret and Polus Luneras, 1 May 1652, Boston, Mass.
CLEMONS, Robert and Joanna Carr, 2 April 1667, Dover, N. H.
CLERK, Joseph and Sarah Wells, 11 December 1693, Boston, Mass.
CLERKE, Charity and Richard Lawrence, 24 September 1699, New York.
CLEVELAND, Moses and Ann Winn, 26 September 1648, Woburn, Mass.
CLEVERLY, Hannah and Joshua Tucker, 2 November 1697, Boston, Mass.
CLEVERLY, John and Sarah Cowel, 17 October 1695, Boston, Mass.
CLEVERLY, John and Elizabeth Glover, 5 November 1696, Boston, Mass.
CLIFFORD, Israel and Ann Smith, 15 March 1680, Hampton, N. H.
CLOAD, Andrew and Elizabeth Bugby, 29 July 1653, Boston, Mass.
CLOCKE, Judith (widow) and Oliver Callowe, 28 February 1655, Boston, Mass.
CLOMP, Huybert and Janette Williams, 25 July 1662, Brooklyn, N. Y.
CLOTHIER, Ruth and John Bailey, 9 December 1699, Scituate, Mass.
CLOTWORTHY, John and Mary Leeson, 10 May 1694, New York.
CLOUGH, Ebenezer and Martha Goodwin, 28 March 1693, Boston, Mass.
CLOUGH, John and Mary Beard, 12 April 1693, Boston, Mass.
CLOUGH, Mary and Benjamin Lawrence, 4 July 1689, Boston, Mass.
CLOUGH, Sarah and Daniel Merrill, 14 May 1667, Newbury, Mass.
CLOUTMAN, Edward and Sara Tuttle, 22 April 1698, Dover, N. H.
CLOWES, Margery and Richard Hough, 17 January 1684, Bucks Co., Penn. (First
    marriage in Bucks Co.)
CLOWES, Samuel and Katherine Douw, 18 July 1698, New York.
CLOWS, Rebecca and John Lambert, 13 October 1687, Middletown, Penn.
CLOWS, Sarah and John Bainbridge, 15 June 1685, Middletown, Penn.
COALBURNE, Benjamin and Abia Fisher, 5 March 1684-5, Dedham, Mass.
COALBURNE, Samuel and Mary Pateridg, 12 January 1682-3, Dedham, Mass.
COALE, Sammuell and Anne Keayne (widow), 16 October 1660, Boston, Mass.
COARS, Micah and Rachel Short, 7 July 1699, Boston, Mass.
COATE, Thomas and Beulah Jacocs, 25 July 1696, Philadelphia, Penn.

COATES, Abigail and Samuel Rhodes, 16 January 1682, Lynn, Mass.
COATS, Edward and Sarah Thornson, January 1694, New York.
COBB, Elizabeth and Samuel Knapp, 26 May 1687, Taunton, Mass.
COBB, James and Sarah Lewis, 26 December 1663, Barnstable, Mass.
COBB, John and Martha Nelson, 17 June 1632, Plymouth, Mass.
COBB, Richard and Esther Bates, 16 September 1691, Boston, Mass.
COBB, Sarah Lewis (widow) and Jonathan Sparrow, 23 November 1698, Barnstable, Mass.
COBBITT, Ann and Samuel Henry, 21 January 1686, New York.
CORBITT, Lydia and Thomas Wright, 28 August 1696, New York.
COBRON, Martha and Daniel Riggs, 29 October 1689, Philadelphia, Penn.
COCK, Elizabeth and Edward Proctor, 24 November 1691, Boston, Mass.
COCK, Mary and John Mountfort, 17 January 1693, Boston, Mass.
COCKE, Joseph and Susanna Upshall, 10 November 1659, Boston, Mass.
COCKER, Thomas and Sarah Waldren, 3 May 1697, Boston, Mass.
COCKIN, Mary and Randolph Spikeman, 29 August 1697, Philadelphia, Penn.
COCKS, Abraham and Sarah Woolfe, 26 October 1686, Bucks Co., Penn.
CODDINGTON, Emma (widow) and John Jephson, 7 March 1656, Boston, Mass.
CODNER, Rachel and John Darbey, 9 October 1690, Boston, Mass.
CODNER, Richard and Phebey Barton, 23 May 1671, Warwick, R. I.
CODNER, William and Sarah Young, 21 November 1697, Boston, Mass.
COE, John and Sarah Pabodie, 10 November 1681, Duxbury, Mass.
COE, John and Mary Hawley, 20 December 1682, Stratford, Conn.
COFFIN, Abigail and David Davidson, 16 December 1673, Ipswich, Mass.
COFFIN, Deborah and Joseph Knight, 31 October 1677, Newbury, Mass.
COFFIN, Elizabeth and Stephen Greenleaf, 13 November 1651, Newbury, Mass.
COFFIN, Stephen and Sarah Atkinson, 8 October 1685, Newbury, Mass.
COFFIN, Tristram and Judith Greenleaf, 2 March 1653, Newbury, Mass.
COGAN, Ruth and Samuel Taylor, 24 June 1675, Springfield, Mass.
COGGAN, John and Martha Winthrop, 10 January 1651, Boston, Mass.
COGGIN, John and Mary Long, 22 December 1664, Charlestown, Mass.
COGGESHALL, Joshua and Rebecca Russell, 21 June 1677, Tiverton, R. I.
COGGSHALL, Elizabeth and John Warner, Jr., 27 November 1694, Warwick, R. I.
COGGSHALL, Joshua and Joan West, 22 December 1652, Shrewsbury, N. J.
COLLINS, Samuel and Susannah Henchman, 1693, Boston, Mass.
COLLINS, Samuel and Margaret Hodson, 3 September 1680, Somerset Co., Md.
COLLINS, Sarah (widow) and John Potter, 7 January 1684-5, Warwick, R. I.
COLLINS, Sarah and Joseph Eliot, 29 July 1697, Boston, Mass.
COLLINS, Susanna and Thomas Walker, 25 March 1662, Boston, Mass.
COLLINS, Thomas and Abigail House, 17 February 1692, Warwick, R. I.
COLLYE, Martha and William Throop, 20 March 1698, Bristol, R. I.
COLTON, George and Deboriah Gardner, 1640 Hartford, Conn.
COLVER, Edward and Ann Ellice, 19 July 1639, Dedham, Mass.
COLVER, Samuel and Elizabeth Spencer, 23 December 1663, Farmington, Conn.
COLWELL, John and Elizabeth Tucker, 5 January 1698, Elizabeth City Co., Va.
COMBES, John and Elizabeth Barlow (widow of Thomas), 24 February 1661, Boston, Mass.
COMER, John and Mary Pitton, 9 February 1698, Boston, Mass.
COMER, Ruth and Edward Gipson, 11 January 1699, Boston, Mass.

COMER, Sarah and John Dolbear, 9 June 1698, Boston, Mass.
COMLEY, Joan and Joseph English, 26 February 1685, Middletown, Penn.
COMPTON, Abigail and Joseph Briscoe, 30 November 1651, Boston, Mass.
COMPTON, Sarah and John Drake, 9 December 1697, Woodbridge, N. J.
COMSTOCK, Elizabeth and Edward Shipman, 1 January 1651, Saybrook, Conn.
COMSTOCK, William and Neomy Nyles, 10 September 1695, Lyme, Conn.
CONANT, Joshua and Christine More, 31 August 1676, Salem, Mass.
CONANT, Martha and Luke Perkins, 31 May 1688, Salem, Mass.
CONDAGE, Mary and Samuel Earle, 13 December 1698, Boston, Mass.
CONDEY, Eliza and Andrew Dolbery, 31 December 1689, Boston, Mass.
CONEY, John and Mary Clark, 8 November 1694, Boston, Mass.
CONEY, Rebecca and Joylieffe Price, 7 December 1692, Boston, Mass.
CONGER, Hannah and Joseph Fitzrandolph, 16 January 1688, Woodbridge, N. J.
CONKLIN, John and Sarah Solomon, 2 December 1653, Southold, L. I., N. Y.
CONKLING, Joseph and Sarah Horton, 1657, Southold, L. I., N. Y.
CONKLING, Joseph and Abigail Tuthill, November 1690, Southold, N. Y.
CONNARD, Philip and Mary Dann, 17 December 1677, Somerset Co., Md.
CONNEL, Philip and Elizabeth Atwood, 1688, Malden, Mass.
CONNER, Winifred and John King, 21 October 1695, Elizabeth City Co., Va.
CONNEY, John and Elizabeth Nash, 20 April 1654, Boston, Mass.
CONNIER, James and Dorothy Bundick, 18 September 1673, Somerset Co., Md.
CONSTABLE, Blanch and Walter Bridgman, 2 June 1686, Middletown, Penn.
CONVERSE, Mary and Simon Thompson, 19 December 1643, Woburn, Mass.
CONVERSE, Samuel and Judith Carter, June 1660, Woburn, Mass.
CONWAY, Edwin and Elizabeth Thompson, 1695, Lancaster Co., Va.
COOK, Anna and Mark Snow, 18 January 1654, Abington, Mass.
COOK, Elizabeth and Daniel Wilcox, 28 November 1661, Portsmouth, R. I.
COOK, Francis and Mary Claypoole, 24 April 1687, Philadelphia, Penn.
COOK, Henry and Judith Birdsall, June 1639, Plymouth, Mass.
COOK, John and Ruth Greenliefe, 16 December 1689, Boston, Mass.
COOK, John and Mary Downs, 25 November 1686, Dover, N. H.
COOK, Nathaniel and Lidia Vore, 29 June 1649, Windsor, Conn.
COOK, Rachel and William Vinson, 17 October 1660, Gloucester, Mass.
COOK, Rachel and Elisha Kibbe, 7 May 1667, Salem, Mass.
COOK, Robert and Submit Weeks, 26 October 1693, Boston, Mass.
COOK, Sara and Richard Sexton, 16 April 1646, Windsor, Conn.
COOK, Samuel and Mehetabel Jones, 2 June 1668, Dedham, Mass.
COOK, Samuel and Lydia Wright, 27 April 1681, Medfield, Mass.
COOK, Samuel and Mary Roberts (widow), 14 July 1690, New Haven, Conn.
COOKE, Aaron, Jr., and Sarah Westwood, 20 May 1661, Hadley, Mass.
COOKE, Elizabeth and John Harrude, 24 December 1666, Warwick, R. I.
COOKE, Frances and Thomas Greene, 5 July 1659, Malden, Mass.
COOKE, Jacob and Lidia Miller, 29 December 1681, Marshfield, Mass.
COOKE, John and Mary Ellwell, 2 February 1680, Gloucester, Mass.
COOKE, Judith and John Putney, 18 November 1662, Salem, Mass.
COOKE, Mary and John Tomson, 5 January 1646, Plymouth, Mass.
COOKE, Penelope and John Verin, 30 August 1683, Seaconnet, R. I.
COOKE, Samuel and Hope Parker, 2 May 1667, New Haven, Conn.
COOKE, Samuel and Hannah Ives, 3 March 1692, New Haven, Conn.

COOLEY, Abelina and Japhet Chapin, 22 July 1664, Springfield, Mass.
COOLEY, Joseph and Mary Griswold, 22 January 1684, Longmeadow, Mass.
COOLIDGE, Grace and Col. Jonas Bond, 29 January 1689, Watertown, Mass.
COOLIDGE, Hannah and John Bond, 6 August 1679, Watertown, Mass.
COOLIDGE, John and Hannah Livermore, 14 February 1655-6, Watertown, Mass.
COOLIDGE, Mary and Daniel Livermore, 28 May 1697, Watertown, Mass.
COOLIDGE, Sarah and Nathan Fiske, 14 October 1696, Watertown, Mass.
COOLIDGE, Richard and Mary Bond, 21 June 1693, Watertown, Mass.
COOMBS, Abigail (widow) and Thomas Avery, 8 October 1697, Dover, N. H.
COOMBS, Anthony and Dorcas Wooden, 5 September 1688, York Co., Maine.
COOMBS, Elizabeth and George Scotson, 24 July 1686, Philadelphia, Penn.
COOMBS, Mary and John Harris, 19 January 1693, Marblehead, Mass.
COOPER, Benjamin and Helena Wilkins, 7 April 1694, New York.
COOPER, Deborah and Timothy Pratt, 9 November 1659, Boston, Mass.
COOPER, Elizabeth and Timothy Ide, 20 December 1687, Rehoboth, Mass.
COOPER, John and Sara Lord, 13 December 1692, Dover, N. H.
COOPER, Josiah and Wayte-a-while Makepeace, 13 September 1661, Boston, Mass.
COOPER, Mary and Abraham Dickerman, 10 February 1658, Dorchester, Mass.
COOPER, Rebecca and John Clark, 12 July 1677, Northampton, Mass.
COOPER, Sarah and Thomas Day, 27 October 1659, Springfield, Mass.
COOPER, Tacy and Samuel Hubbard, 4 January 1636, Windsor, Conn.
COOPER, Thomas and Ann Bosworth (widow), 17 August 1656, Boston, Mass.
COOPER, Thomas and Mehitable Minot, 6 March 1683, Boston, Mass.
COPE, David and Obedience Topliffe, 20 February 1659, Boston, Mass.
COPELAND, Lawrence and Lydia Townsend, 12 October 1654, Braintree, Mass.
COPELAND, Thomas and Mary Arnold, 17 May 1699, Boston, Mass.
COPLEY, Elizabeth and Nathaniel Phelps, September 1650, Windsor, Conn.
COPP, Aaron and Mary Heath, 30 December 1698, Haverhill, Mass.
COPP, Ann and Herman Atwood, 11 June 1646, Boston, Mass.
COPP, David and Patience Short, 27 December 1694, Boston, Mass.
COPP, William and Ann Ruck, 24 May 1692, Boston, Mass.
CORBEE, Samuel and Mary Crippen, 28 January 1692, Haddam, Conn.
CORBET, Clement and Dorcas Buckmaster, 7 January 1655, Boston, Mass.
CORBET, Mary and John Peirce, 9 November 1698, Boston, Mass.
CORBETT, John and Christina Milton, 6 May 1699, New York.
CORBETT, William and Eleanor Batrop, 19 September 1683, Bristol, R. I.
CORBIN, James and Hannah Eastman, 7 April 1697, Woodstock, Conn.
CORBIN, Margaret and Matho Davis, 27 February 1690-1, Woodstock, Conn.
CORBIN, Mary and Nathaniel Wiet, 13 December 1688, Milton, Mass.
CORBIT, Abigail and John Bugbee, 10 July 1696, Woodstock, Conn.
CORD, Thomas and Hannah Matthews, 4 August 1698, Harford Co., Md.
COREMAN, Daniel and Anna M. Plevier, 30 June 1698, New York.
CORISH, Scissilla and William Hunter, 30 January 1656, Boston, Mass.
CORLEIS, George and Jeborah Hance, 23 September 1699, Shrewsbury, N. J.
CORLIES, George and Exercise Shattock, 10 December 1680, Shrewsbury, N. J.
CORLISS, George and Joanna Davis, 26 October 1645, Haverhill, Mass.
CORLISS, John and Mary Wilford, 17 December 1684, Haverhill, Mass.
CORLISS, Martha and Joseph Greeley, 5 February 1695, Haverhill, Mass.
CORLISS, Mary and William Neff, 23 June 1665, Haverhill, Mass.

CORLISS, John and Mary Wilford, 18 November 1667, Haverhill, Mass.
CORNELL, Sara and Thomas Willett, 1 September 1643, New York City.
CORNISH, Joshua and Susanna Bennet, 8 November 1692, Boston, Mass.
CORNWALL, Hannah and Daniel Doolittle, 3 May 1698, Wallingford, Conn.
CORNWALL, Thomas and Sarah Clark, 14 November 1671, Middletown, Conn.
CORNWALL, William and Esther Ward, 22 January 1692, Middletown, Conn.
CORNWELL, George and Ann Merchant, 14 August 1699, New York.
CORTAS, Joseph and Mary Elline, 18 November 1687, Milton, Mass.
CORTLANDT, John and Anna Mary Van Schaick, 20 June 1695, New York.
CORY, Giles and Mary Britz, 11 April 1664, Salem, Mass.
COSINS, Barne and Grace Sanford, 28 April 1697, New York.
COTTEN, Elizabeth and Robert Gover, 5 December 1695, Anne Arundel Co., Md
COTTINGHAM, Thomas and Mary Dixon, 8 July 1666, Somerset Co., Md.
COTTON, Catherine and Robert Burton, 11 February 1676, Accomac Co., Va.
COTTON, Elizabeth and Jeremiah Eggington, 12 August 1655, Boston, Mass.
COTTON, Elizabeth and (Rev.) James Allen, 1688, Salisbury, Mass.
COTTON, John and Joanna Rossiter, 7 November 1660, Wethersfield, Conn.
COTTON, Mary and John Matson, 7 March 1659, Boston, Mass.
COTTON, Sarah and Rev. Richard Mather, 26 June 1656, Boston, Mass.
COTTON, Seaborn and Dorothy Bradstreet, 14 June 1654, Andover, Mass.
COTTON, William and Ana Carter, 6 November 1699, Boston, Mass.
COULBOURNE, William (Capt.) and Anne Revell, 15 June 1678, Somerse
    Co., Md.
COULYLIE, Margaret and Henry Roof, 9 August 1699, New York.
COUNTS, Edward and Sarah Adams, 25 February 1663, Malden, Mass.
COURSER, Sarah and Anthony Thoring, 3 November 1693, Boston, Mass.
COURTNEY, George and Dorcas Selly, 2 June 1698, Boston, Mass.
COUSSINS, Edmond and Margaret Bird, November 1656, Boston, Mass.
COUSSINS, Isaac and Ann Hunt, July 1657, Boston, Mass.
COUZENS, Richard and Mary Chalker, 7 March 1678, Saybrook, Conn.
COVAN, John and Elizabeth Carr, 8 March 1680, Somerset Co., Md.
COVEL, Joseph and Alice Palmer, 27 February 1685, Charlestown, Mass.
COVERT, Altje and William Post, 14 May 1679, New York City.
COVINGTON, Margaret and Richard Allingsworth, 22 October 1672, Somerse
    Co., Md.
COVINGTON, Nehemiah and Miss Ingram, July 1667, Somerset Co., Md.
COVINGTON, Nehemiah and Rebecca Denwood, 15 November 1679, Somerse
    Co., Md.
COWEL, Joseph and Eliza Williams, 6 August 1696, Boston, Mass.
COWEL, Sarah and John Cleverly, 17 October 1695, Boston, Mass.
COWELL, John and Elizabeth Tucker, 5 January 1698, Elizabeth City Co., Va.
COWELL, Margaret and John Johnson, 2 August 1693, Boston, Mass.
COWEN, Rebecca and Obadiah Haws, 19 December 1693, Boston, Mass.
COWGELL, John and Bridget Crosdell, 19 August 1693, Middletown, Penn.
COWGILL, Jane and Stephen Sands, 25 August 1685, Middletown, Penn.
COWLES, Samuel and Abigail Stanley, 14 February 1660, Hartford, Conn.
COX, Abraham and Sarah Wolf, 26 September 1686, Middletown, Penn.
COX, Alice and Mathew Abdy, 24 May 1662, Boston, Mass.

COX, Elizabeth (widow) and Thomas Ingraham, 9 September 1681, Monmouth Co., N. J.

COX, Jacobus and Catherine Davids, 31 December 1694, New York.

COX, John and Hannah Hill (widow), 22 May 1694, Dover, N. H.

COX, John and Joanna Brown, 18 November 1698, Boston, Mass.

COX, Leah and James Perkins, 13 December 1681, Hampton, N. H.

COX, Mary and Charles Turner, 12 August 1695, New Kent Co., Va.

COX, Mary and Thomas Grover, 29 July 1697, Malden, Mass.

COX, Mary and Benjamin Stapils, 26 May 1699, Boston, Mass.

COX, Moses and Prudence Swain (widow), 16 June 1658, Salem, Mass.

COX, Thomas and Elizabeth Blashford, 17 April 1665, Newtown, L. I., N. Y.

COY, Matthew and Elizabeth Roberts, 29 June 1654, Boston, Mass.

COYTE, Abigail and Isaac Eveleth, 13 November 1677, Gloucester, Mass.

COYTE, Mary (widow) and John Fitch, 3 October 1667, Gloucester, Mass.

COYTE, Mary and William Ellery, 13 June 1676, Gloucester, Mass.

COZZENS, Bethsheba and John Barber, September 1666, Windsor, Conn.

CRAB, Henry and Hannah Emmons, 1 November 1657, Boston, Mass.

CRABTREE, Alice (widow of John) and Joshua Hewes, 11 December 1656, Boston, Mass.

CRACKER, Agnes and Thomas Degresha, 16 March 1699, Boston, Mass.

CRAFORD, Mary and James Wiborn, 11 January 1699, Boston, Mass.

CRAFT, Griffin and Widow Robinson, 15 May 1673, Dorchester, Mass.

CRAFT, Griffin and Hannah Reed, 15 May 1699, Chelmsford, Mass.

CRAFT, Samuel and Elizabeth Sharp, 25 December 1693, Roxbury, Mass.

CRAFTS, Elizabeth and Samuel Clark, 5 May 1696, Boston, Mass.

CRAGE, David and Deborah Man, 3 July 1698, Boston, Mass.

CRAIGE, Ursula and Elisha Parker, 27 September 1697, Woodbridge, N. J.

CRAM, John and Mary Wadleigh, March 1690, Exeter, N. H.

CRAMPTON, Hannah and Benjamin Scribner, 5 March 1680, Norwalk, Conn.

CRAN, Harry, Jr., and Elizabeth Vose, 18 October 1683, Milton, Mass.

CRANDALL, John and Elizabeth Gorton, 10 June 1672, Warwick, R. I.

CRANE, Ebenezer and Mary Tolman, 13 December 1689, Milton, Mass.

CRANE, Jonathan and Deborah Griswold, 7 March 1678, Saybrook, Conn.

CRANE, Martha and (Capt.) Samuel Terry, 4 January 1698, Wethersfield, Conn.

CRANE, Stephen and Mary Denison, 2 July 1676, Milton, Mass.

CRARY, Peter and Christobel Gallup, 31 December 1677, New London, Conn.

CRAVATH, Elizabeth and Samuel Weaver, 27 March 1697, Boston, Mass.

CRAVATH, Ezekial and Elizabeth Hooks, 14 June 1698, Boston, Mass.

CRAVEN, Ann and Isaac Warner, 30 October 1692, Philadelphia, Penn.

CRAVEN, James and Rebecca Stilwell, 23 March 1644, Guilford, Conn.

CRAWFORD, Elizabeth and John Stout, 12 January 1671, Monmouth Co., N. J.

CRAWFORD, Mongo and Susanna Kennet, 29 January 1694, Boston, Mass.

CRAWFORD, Recuba and Samuel Sprague, 23 June 1655, Boston, Mass.

CREEKE, James and Frances Churcher, 20 August 1688, Burlington, N. J.

CREGO, Richard and Sarah Stilwell, 29 June 1696, New York.

CREHORE, Mary and Henry Glover, 31 March 1696, Milton, Mass.

CREHORE, Mary and Matthias Puffer, 14 May 1697, Milton, Mass.

CREHORE, Rebeccah and Robert Pelton, 2 September 1697, Milton, Mass.

CREHORE, Timothy and Ruth Riol, 10 February 1688, Milton, Mass.

CRESWELL, William and Ann Allen, 18 June 1677, Richmond Co., Va.
CREESE, Thomas and Rookby Greenleaf, 30 June 1697, Boston, Mass.
CRIPPIN, Mary and Samuel Corbee, 28 January 1692, Haddam, Conn.
CRIPPS, Nathan and Grace Whitten, 9 January 1694, Burlington, N. J.
CRISP, Sarah and William Harris, 11 April 1695, Boston, Mass.
CROASDALE, Alice and David Potts, 26 November 1693, Philadelphia, Penn.
CROASDELL, Mary and William Smith, 20 September 1690, Middletown, Penn.
CROASDILL, Ezra and Ana Peacock, 6 February 1687, Middletown, Penn.
CROASDILL, John and Marah Chapman, 28 February 1697, Middletown, Penn.
CROASDILL, William and Elizabeth Hayhurst, 10 February 1690, Middletown, Penn.
CROCKER, Daniell and Sarah Balden, 30 November 1660, Boston, Mass.
CROCKER, Sarah and Thomas Hudson, 24 October 1697, Boston, Mass.
CROCKER, Thomas and Mary Carpenter, 8 April 1697, New London, Conn.
CROOKE, Bathya and Thomas Gray, 1 October 1699, Elizabeth City Co., Va.
CROOKE, Elizabeth and John Guild, 24 April 1645, Dedham, Mass.
CROOKE, Ruth and William Read, 20 January 1654, Boston, Mass.
CROSBEE, Joseph and Sarah Brackett, 1 April 1675, Braintree, Mass.
CROSBY, Anthony and Prudence Wade, 28 December 1659, Rowley, Mass.
CROSBY, Dorothy and William Pillsbury, June 1641, Dorchester, Mass.
CROSBY, Jane and John Pickard, 29 November 1644, Rowley, Mass.
CROSBY, Rachel and Ephriam Kidder, 4 August 1685, Billerica, Mass.
CROSBY, Simon and Rachel Brackett, 15 May 1659, Braintree, Mass.
CROSDELL, Bridget and John Cowgill, 19 August 1693, Middletown, Penn.
CROSS, Edmund and Martha Dammon, 21 April 1699, Boston, Mass.
CROSS, Faith and Mark Pilkinton, 18 November 1691, Boston, Mass.
CROSS, Martha and William Durkee, 20 December 1664, Ipswich, Mass.
CROSS, Mary and Ephriam Herrick, 3 July 1661, Salem, Mass.
CROSS, Mercy and Joseph Shaw, 22 February 1699, Boston, Mass.
CROSS, Robert and Martha Treadwell, 19 February 1665, Ipswich, Mass.
CROSS, Samuel and Widow Chapman, 12 July 1677, Windsor, Conn.
CROSS, Stephen and Mary Lawrence, 23 January 1692, Boston, Mass.
CROSSDEL, Alice and David Potts, 22 January 1693, Middletown, Penn.
CROSSE, Mary and Roger Hill, 1 November 1658, Wells, Maine.
CROSSE, Mary and James Penniman, 10 May 1659, Boston, Mass.
CROSSMAN, Robert and Sarah Kingsbury, 25 May 1652, Dedham, Mass.
CROSSMAN, Robert and Hannah Brooks, 21 July 1679, Taunton, Mass.
CROSSMAN, Sarah and John Woodward, 11 November 1675, Rehoboth, Mass.
CROUSEN, Gerritt and Neeltie Jans, 30 October 1661, Brooklyn, N. Y.
CROUTCH, Mary and Roger Baxter, 6 December 1655, Kent Co., Md.
CROW, Christopher and Mary Burr, 15 January 1657, Hartford, Conn.
CROW, Mary and Noah Coleman, 27 December 1666, Hadley, Mass.
CROW, Sarah and Robert Sanderson, 21 December 1693, Boston, Mass.
CROW, William and Eliza Sergent, 10 December 1691, Boston, Mass.
CROWELL, Edward and Mary Lothrop, 16 January 1673, Barnstable, Mass.
CROWELL, John and Bethiah Sears, 27 May 1684, Eastham, Mass.
CROWELL, Mary (widow) and Samuel Dennes, 14 April 1689, Woodbridge, N. J.
CRUE, Margery and Thomas Buttler, 1 March 1685, New Kent Co., Va.
CRUMWELL, Elizabeth and Richard Price, 18 August 1659, Boston, Mass.

CRUNDALL, Deborah and Thomas Lyndall, 7 September 1691, New York City.

CRUTTENDEN, Mary and George Bartlett, 14 September 1650, Guilford, Conn·

CRUTTERTON, Hannah and Joseph Hotchkiss, April 1699, New Haven, Conn.

CUBBY, Patience and James Wakerwithy, 20 February 1670, Dedham, Mass.

CUDDEBACK, Jacob and Margriet Provoost, 21 October 1695, Minisink, N. Y.

CULLEN, George and Avis Grottin, 1 October 1673, Somerset Co., Md.

CULLEN, John and Mary, 12 October 1694, Somerset Co., Md.

CULLICK, Hannah and Pelatiah Glover, 20 May 1660, Boston, Mass.

CULLIMORE, Isaac and Margery Page, 22 November 1651, Boston, Mass.

CULLOM, Peter and Martha Barriman, 8 April 1695, New York.

CULPEPER, Susanna and Francis Linsley, 6 July 1655, Branford, Conn.

CULVER, Ann and Thomas Bell, 20 November 1641, Roxbury, Mass.

CULVER, Edward and Ann Ellis, 19 September 1638, Dedham, Mass.

CULVER, Edward, Jr., and Sarah Backus, 5 January 1682, Norwich, Conn.

CULVER, Hannah and John Burrows, 14 December 1670, New London, Conn.

CULVER, Joshua and Elizabeth Ford, 23 December 1672, New Haven, Conn.

CUMBY, Humphrey and Sarah, 1649, Boston, Mass.

CUMINGS, Elizabeth and John Gould, 2 July 1686, Chelmsford, Mass.

CUMMINGS, Ann and John Pease, 8 October 1669, Enfield, Conn.

CUMMINGS, Mary and Daniel Black, 14 July 1691, Topsfield, Mass·

CUMMINGS, Thomas and Priscilla Warner, 19 December 1688, Ipswich, Mass.

CUNLIFFE, John and Jane Mountain, 7 August 1660, Charles City Co., Va.

CUNNIBALL, John and Lydia Beighton, 2 November 1694, Boston, Mass.

CURNEY, John and Abigail Skilling, 18 November 1670, Gloucester, Mass.

CURRIER, Richard and Dorothy Barnard, 28 August 1695, Amesbury, Mass.

CURTICE, Lydia and James Thornbury, 14 September 1699, Boston, Mass.

CURTICE, Mehitable and Ebenezer Liscombe, 18 October 1694, Boston, Mass.

CURTIS, Abigail and John Paine, 8 August 1699, Burlington, N. J.

CURTIS, Abigail (nee Thompson) and Samuel Sherman, Jr., 1 August 1695, Stratford, Conn.

CURTIS, David and Rachel Wright, 2 July 1697, Chesterfield, N. J.

CURTIS, Elizabeth and Thomas Faulke, Jr., 7 December 1688, Chesterfield, N. J.

CURTIS, Elizabeth and Robert Dudley, 1691, Middlesex Co., Va.

CURTIS, Henry and Elizabeth Abel, 13 May 1645, Windsor, Conn.

CURTIS, James and Sarah Hall, 2 February 1685, Somerset Co., Md·

CURTIS, John and Rebecca Wheeler, 26 December 1661, Boston, Mass.

CURTIS, John and Dorcas Peake, 1678, Roxbury, Mass.

CURTIS, John and Sarah Locke, 4 December 1672, Topsfield, Mass.

CURTIS, Mary and Jonathan Babcock, 1 August 1676, Milton, Mass.

CURTIS, Rebecca and Joseph Arnold, 8 June 1649, Braintree, Mass.

CURTIS, Samuel and Sarah Alexander, 23 July 1678, Northfield, Mass.

CURTIS, Sarah and James Scales, 7 November 1677, Rowley, Mass.

CURTIS, Sarah and John Briggs, 11 January 1697, Boston, Mass.

CURTIS, Solomon and Mary Greene, 1 July 1666, Somerset Co., Md.

CURTIS, Solomon and Prudence Gatlive, 11 April 1673, Braintree, Mass.

CURTIS, Teophilus and Hannah Payn, 7 January 1673, Dorchester, Mass.

CURTIS, Thomas and Mary Merriman, 9 June 1674, New Haven, Conn.

CUSHING, Deborah and Thomas Loring, 19 April 1699, Boston, Mass.

CUSHING, Jeremiah and Judeth Parminter, 29 March 1693, Boston, Mass.

CUSHING, Thomas and Deborah Thaxter, 17 October 1687, Boston, Mass.

CUSHMAN, Elizabeth and John Hawkes, 11 April 1661, Saugus, Mass.

CUSHMAN, Elkanah and Elizabeth Cole, 10 February 1677, Plymouth, Mass.

CUSHMAN, Rev. Isaac and Rebecca Pickard, 1675, Plymouth, Mass.

CUSHMAN, Thomas and Ruth Howland, 7 November 1664, Plymouth, Mass.

CUTLER, Dorothy and Josiah Treadway, 3 February 1697, Charlestown, Mass.

CUTLER, Jane and John Taylor, 11 May 1685, Bucks Co., Pa.

CUTLER, Lydia and John Stanwood, 9 December 1680, Gloucester, Mass.

CUTLER, Margaret and Joseph Walker, 27 January 1694, Philadelphia, Penn.

CUTLER, Nathan and Mary Gould, 29 September 1655, Charlestown, Mass.

CUTT, John and Hannah Starr, 30 July 1662, Dover, N. H.

CUTTIN, Susan and Peter Nucome, 26 April 1672, Braintree, Mass.

CUTTING, Mary and Nicholas Noyes, 1640, Newbury, Mass.

CUTTING, Mary and Samuel Moody, 30 November 1657, Newbury, Mass.

CUTTS, Robert and Dorcas Hammond, 18 August 1698, York Co., Maine.

CUYLER, Rachel and Meyndert Schuyler, 23 October 1693, New York.

D

DABBS, John and Nan Eates, October 1655, Kent Co., Md.

DADEY, William and Sarah Bancroft, 28 January 1694, Bristol, R. I.

DAGGETT, John, Jr., and Anna Sutton, 23 September 1651, Rehoboth, Mass.

DAGGETT, Joseph and Mary Palmer, 14 February 1689, Rehoboth, Mass.

DAGGETT, Thomas and Elizabeth Hawes, 22 January 1683, Bristol, R. I.

DALE, Robert and Joana Farrar, 30 November 1680, Woburn, Mass.

DALLISON, Gilbert and Margaret Story, 24 October 1661, Boston, Mass.

DAM, John and Elizabeth Furber, 9 November 1664, Dover, N. H.

DAM, Judith and William Tibbetts, 6 July 1684, Dover, N. H.

DAMAN, John and Katherine Merritt, 16 June 1644, Scituate, Mass.

DAMARILL, Sarah (widow) and John Hawkins, 15 September 1654, Boston, Mass.

DAME, Abigail and Thomas Starbord, 4 January 1687, Dover, N. H.

DAMEN, Aeltje and Samuel Flipsen, 29 October 1695, Brooklyn, N. Y.

DAMMON, Martha and Edmund Cross, 21 April 1699, Boston, Mass.

DAMON, Joseph and Elizabeth Kingsbery, 12 December 1686, Dedham, Mass.

DANA, Benjamin and Mary Buckminster, 24 May 1688, Cambridge, Mass.

DANA, Elizabeth and Daniel Woodward, 14 January 1679, Watertown, Mass.

DANE, Abigail and Francis Faulkner, 12 October 1675, Andover, Mass.

DANE, Elizabeth and Stephen Johnson, 5 November 1661, Andover, Mass.

DANE, John and Abigail Warner, 27 December 1671, Essex Co., Mass.

DANE, Mary and William Chandler, 24 August 1658, Andover, Mass.

DANE, Mary and Thomas Pellet, 5 March 1659, Concord, Mass.

DANE, Phebe and James Robinson, 30 May 1671, Andover, Mass.

DANE, Sarah and Daniel Warner, 23 September 1668, Essex Co., Mass.

DANFORD, Lydia and William Beament, 9 December 1643, Saybrook, Conn.

DANFORTH, Jonathan and Elizabeth Powter, 22 September 1654, Boston, Mass.

DANFORTH, John and Elizabeth Minott, 21 November 1682, Dorchester, Mass.

DANSON, Eliza and Thomas Okes, 2 February 1692, Boston, Mass.

DANIEL, Elizabeth and Samuel Spear, 5 June 1694, Milton, Mass.

DANIEL, Hannah and Benjamin Badcock, 11 February 1673, Dorchester, Mass.

DANIEL, John and Mary Chappell, 19 January 1684, New London, Conn.

DANIEL, John and Dorothy Badcock, 29 March 1672, Milton, Mass.

DANIEL, Mary and Jonathan Wood, 26 May 1674, Dorchester, Mass.

DANIEL, Mary and Edward Evans, 22 May 1676, Somerset Co., Md.

DANIEL, Samuel and Deborah Ford, 14 March 1694, Boston, Mass.

DANIELL, Mary and Benjamin Scot, 31 May 1699, Milton, Mass.

DANIELL, Susana and John Kinsly, 25 June 1669, Milton, Mass.

DANIELS, John and Agnes Beebey, 3 December 1685, New London, Conn.

DANIELS, Joseph and Lydia Adams, 27 January 1696-7, Dedham, Mass.

DANIL, William and Dorothy Bud, 27 September 1699, Boston, Mass.

DARBY, Edward and Susanna Hooke, 25 January 1659, Boston, Mass.

DARBEY, John and Rachel Codner, 9 October 1690, Boston, Mass.

DARE, Sara and Thomas Parsons, Jr., 24 December 1668, Windsor, Conn.

DARK, Samuel and Ann Knight, 17 April 1683, Bucks Co., Penn.
DARK, Samuel and Martha Worial, 6 December 1685, Middletown, Penn.
DARKINS, Lydia and Jacobus Rolloquin, 25 May 1698, New York.
DARLEY, Dennis and Hannah Francis, 3 November 1662, Braintree, Mass.
DARLIN, John and Elizabeth Downam, 13 March 1664, Braintree, Mass.
DARLING, John and Ann Rocket, 2 January 1687, Boston, Mass.
DART, Ambrose and Anne Adis, 24 April 1653, Boston, Mass.
DARVALL, Katherine and Frederick Phillips, 1 December 1692, New York City.
DARWIN, Ephriam and Elizabeth Goodrich, 10 June 1678, Guilford, Conn.
DASHIELL, Elizabeth and Robert Collier, 2 March 1675, Somerset Co., Md.
DASSET, Sarah and Henry Mountfort, 27 September 1694, Boston, Mass.
DASSITT, John and Hannah Flint, 15 September 1662, Braintree, Mass.
DAUNFORTH, Abiel and Thomas Fitch, 12 April 1694, Boston, Mass.
DAVENPORT, Francis and Rebecca Destow, 1 July 1692, Chesterfield, N. J.
DAVENPORT, Jonathan and Hannah Maner, 1 December 1680, Dorchester, Mass.
DAVENPORT, John and Abigail Pierson, 27 November 1662, Cranford, Conn.
DAVENPORT, John and Bridget Watkins, 1 September 1667, Dorchester, Mass.
DAVENPORT, Margaret and James Gooding, Jr., 23 January 1695, Boston, Mass.
DAVENPORT, Rebecca and George Walker, 5 October 1699, Boston, Mass.
DAVIDS, Catherine and Jacobus Cox, 31 December 1694, New York.
DAVIDSON, David and Abigail Coffin, 16 December 1673, Ipswich, Mass.
DAVIES, Engeltie and Thomas Giles, 6 July 1696, New York.
DAVIES, Elizabeth and William Owen, 29 July 1650, Braintree, Mass.
DAVIES, John and Dinah Borden, 23 December 1699, Philadelphia, Penn.
DAVIS, Abigail and Nathaniell Lovel, 8 June 1696, Dedham, Mass.
DAVIS, Barbara and John Brimblecombe, 14 November 1655, Boston, Mass.
DAVIS, Bridget and Thomas King, 26 December 1655, Sudbury, Mass.
DAVIS, Edward and Hannah Gridley, 16 July 1657, Boston, Mass.
DAVIS, Edward and Mary Paxon, 15 November 1677, Richmond Co., Va.
DAVIS, Ephriam and Mary Johnson, 29 December 1660, Andover, Mass.
DAVIS, Elizabeth and Robert Hastings, 31 October 1676, Haverhill, Mass.
DAVIS, Elizabeth and Thomas Mayo, 4 May 1699, Roxbury, Mass.
DAVIS, Hester and John Finch, 25 March 1693, New York.
DAVIS, Isaac and Lydia Black, 28 September 1659, Beverly, Mass.
DAVIS, Jacob and Elizabeth Bennett, 20 January 1662, Gloucester, Mass.
DAVIS, James and Elizabeth Eaton, 1 December 1648, Haverhill, Mass.
DAVIS, James and Elizabeth Bacheler, 6 December 1666, Gloucester, Mass.
DAVIS, Jane and William Wilson, 16 September 1698, Elizabeth City Co., Va.
DAVIS, Joanna and George Corliss, 26 October 1645, Haverhill, Mass.
DAVIS, John and Jane Peaslee, December 1646, Haverhill, Mass.
DAVIS, John and Returne Gridley, 9 February 1656, Boston, Mass.
DAVIS, John and Marie Torrey, 14 January 1673, Dorchester, Mass.
DAVIS, Joseph and Elizabeth Saywell, 7 May 1662, Boston, Mass.
DAVIS, Joseph and Rebecca Patton, 18 June 1691, Billerica, Mass.
DAVIS, Judith and Samuel Gile, 1 September 1647, Haverhill, Mass.
DAVIS, Judith and Samuel Emerson, 14 February 1687, Haverhill, Mass.
DAVIS, Martha and Charles Hall, Jr., 31 October 1693, Somerset Co., Md.
DAVIS, Matho and Margaret Corbin, 27 February 1690-91, Woodstock, Conn.
DAVIS, Mary and Thomas Ivory, 17 May 1660, Lynn, Mass.

DAVIS, Mary and Philip Gifford, 30 June 1684, Lynn, Mass.
DAVIS, Mary and Joseph Clark, 18 August 1685, Haverhill, Mass.
DAVIS, Mary and John Hutchins, 30 October 1692, Philadelphia, Penn.
DAVIS, Mary and Michael Greenham, 14 April 1693, New York.
DAVIS, Mary and John Lowery, 13 November 1699, Boston, Mass.
DAVIS, Mary and John Thorp, 15 May 1699, Fairfield, Conn.
DAVIS, Naomi and Walter Horldsworthy, 11 October 1660, Charles City Co., Va.
DAVIS, Ephriam and Mary Eires, 19 March 1688, Andover, Mass.
DAVIS, Richard and Elizabeth Barry, 1676, Somerset Co., Md.
DAVIS, Ruth and Stephen Hall, 3 December 1663, Concord, Mass.
DAVIS, Samuel and Sarah Thayer, 20 May 1651, Boston, Mass.
DAVIS, Samuel and Deborah Barnes, December 1663, Haverhill, Mass.
DAVIS, Sarah (widow) and Samuel Chandler, 21 October 1664, Dorchester, Mass.
DAVIS, Sarah and John Miles, 14 March 1689, Bristol, R. I.
DAVIS, Sarah and John Page, 18 June 1683, Haverhill, Mass.
DAVIS, Sarah and Ebenezar Morriss, 1 September 1692, Woodstock, Conn.
DAVIS, Sarah and Joseph Rayner, 3 February 1696, Boston, Mass.
DAVIS, Simeon and Ann Low, 24 September 1685, Bristol, R. I.
DAVIS, Thomas and Judith Bloyer, September 1671, Somerset Co., Md.
DAVIS, Thomas and Abigail Wadsworth, 25 November 1689, Milton, Mass.
DAVIS, Thomas and Sarah Guy, 7 March 1687, Somerset Co., Md.
DAVIS, Thomas and Grace Hult, 27 January 1697, Boston, Mass.
DAVIS, William and Alice Thorpe, 21 October 1658, Roxbury, Mass.
DAVIS, William and Anne Hooper, August 1667, Somerset Co., Md.
DAVIS, William and Elizabeth Thrift, 27 April 1677, Richmond Co., Va.
DAVIS, William and Rebecca Skiner, 5 April 1698, Elizabeth City Co., Va.
DAVISE, Eliza and James Babage, 9 October 1693, Boston, Mass.
DAVISE, Hannah and Joseph Skeath, 18 April 1692, Boston, Mass.
DAVISE, Robert and Jane Alger, 19 February 1693, Boston, Mass.
DAVISE, Thomas and Hannah Allen, 12 September 1689, Boston, Mass.
DAVISON, Daniel and Sarah Dodge, 28 June 1685, Ipswich, Mass.
DAVISON, Thomas and Hannah Tracey, 28 November 1695, Norwich, Conn.
DAVISON, William and Eleanor Goff, 25 February 1699, New York.
DAWES, Hannah and Richard Gridley, 27 February 1694, Boston, Mass.
DAWNING, Jane and Nicholas Carnaby, 12 December 1694, New York.
DAY, Abigail and John Smith, 21 October 1677, Dedham, Mass.
DAY, Abigail and Edward Adams, 7 October 1678, Dedham, Mass.
DAY, Edward and Jane Walker, 2 April 1681, Somerset Co., Md.
DAY, George and Eleanor Virly, 10 June 1669, Somerset Co., Md.
DAY, John and Abigail Pond, 22 March 1678, Dedham, Mass.
DAY, Mary and John Pain, 7 December 1676, Dedham, Mass.
DAY, Ralph and Suzan Fairebanck, 12 August 1647, Dedham, Mass.
DAY, Ralph and Abigail Rugles, 15 September 1659, Dedham, Mass.
DAY, Ralph and Sarah Fuller, 6 October 1682, Dedham, Mass.
DAY, Sarah and Thomas Miller, 8 July 1698, Boston, Mass.
DAY, Thomas and Sarah Cooper, 27 October 1659, Springfield, Mass.
DAY, Thomas and Mary Laughton, 30 December 1673, Gloucester, Mass.
DAYTON, Alice and Thomas Baker, 20 June 1643, New Haven, Conn.
DEAN, Hannah and Benjamin Phips, 10 October 1693, New York.

DEAN, John and Hannah Bird, 21 September 1699, Dorchester, Mass.
DEAN, Thomas and Catherine Stephens, 5 January 1669, Taunton, Mass.
DEAN, Thomas and Mary Kinsley, 7 January 1696, Milton, Mass.
DEAN, William and Mehitable Wood, 13 October 1677, Dedham, Mass.
DEANE, Francis and Mary Thomas, 21 November 1677, Andover, Mass.
DEANE, Francis and Hannah Poor, 16 November 1681, Andover, Mass.
DEANE, Martha and James Clemens, 28 December 1674, Marshfield, Mass.
DEANE, Mary and John Butcher, 30 January 1661, Boston, Mass.
DEANE, Nathaniel and Deliverance Hazeltine, 12 December 1672, Andover, Mass.
DEARBORN, John and Hannah Dow, 10 January 1695, Hampton, N. H.
DEARING, Samuel and Bethia Baxter, 1647, Braintree, Mass.
DEARLOVE, Peter and Jane Mullikin, 27 October 1697, Boston, Mass.
DEBELL, Mary and John Enns, 10 May 1681, Windsor, Conn.
DEBELL, Thomas, Jr., and Mary Tucker, 10 October 1676, Windsor, Conn.
DEBOW, Catherine and William Beekman, 5 September 1649, New York City.
DE CASTEL, Edmond and Christine Boone, 1 May 1693, Philadelphia, Penn.
DECKER, Gerrit and Magdalen Schut, April 1684, Kingston, N. Y.
DECOSTER, Isaac and Mary Temple, 2 November 1699, Boston, Mass.
DECOW, Elizabeth and Richard Dell, 5 June 1695, Burlington, N. J.
DECOW, Jacob and Elizabeth Newbold, 21 December 1699, Burlington, N. J.
DECROW, Valentine and Martha Bourne, 27 February 1678, Braintree, Mass.
DEE, Henry and Hannah Hillard, 30 September 1697, Boston, Mass.
DEERIN, Samuel and Hannah Farebanks, 26 June 1688, Milton, Mass.
DEERING, Mary and George Speere, 27 February 1675, Braintree, Mass.
DEERING, Rachel and Ebenezer Speere, 16 July 1679, Braintree, Mass.
DEERING, Sarah and John Hawse, 27 March 1683, Dedham, Mass.
DEERING, Samuel and Mary Ray, 5 September 1651, Braintree, Mass.
DEERINGE, Samuel and Mary Nucome, 10 September 1657, Braintree, Mass.
DEFFOSE, Margaret and Ebenezer Ashbury, 19 July 1694, Salem Co., N. J.
DEGRESHA, Thomas and Agnes Cracker, 16 March 1699, Boston, Mass.
DEHANCE, Jan and Margaret S. Uthuse, 9 October 1697, New York.
DEHART, Catherine and Joseph Blydenburgh, 19 May 1699, New York.
DEHART, Katherine and James Larkin, 22 August 1691, New York City.
DEHART, Matthew and Jeannett Mauritz, 27 June 1695, New York.
DEHONNEUR, Johanes and Johanna Maynard, 12 April 1694, New York.
DEKEY, Jacobus and Sarah Willett, 9 May 1694, New York.
DE LA MATER, Jacobus and Gertrude Ysselsteyn, 1688 Claverack, N. Y.
DELANO, Jonathan and Hannah Doten, 12 January 1699, Duxbury, Mass.
DELANO, Philip and Hester Dewsbury, 19 December 1634, Duxbury, Mass.
DELANOY, Peter and Mary Edsall, 21 February 1696, New York.
DE LA PLAINE, Marie and Jean Lechevelier, 27 June 1692, New York City.
DELL, Richard and Elizabeth Decow, 5 June 1695, Burlington, N. J.
DELL, Richard and Elizabeth Basnett, 11 August 1698, Burlington, N. J.
DEMAUZADAY, Philip and Margaret Glansha, 22 November 1682, Dorchester,
   Mass.
DEMEYER, Agnetre and William Jenoway, 11 August 1696, New York.
DE MORRIS, Nicholas and Elanor Williams, 20 January 1686, New York.
DENNESON, Mary and Steven Crane, 2 July 1676, Milton, Mass.
DENNESON, Sarah and Return Babcocke, 1 December 1681, Milton, Mass.

DENHAM, David and Mary Elsley, 18 August 1699, New York.
DENISON, Borodel and Samuel Stanton, 15 June 1680, Stonington, Conn.
DENISON, Robert and Joanna Stanton, 1696, Stonington, Conn.
DENKIN, Margaret and Adam Read, 11 January 1699, Boston, Mass.
DENNES, Samuel and Mary Crowell (widow), 14 April 1689, Woodbridge, N. J.
DENNIS, Ebenezer and Damaris Robinson, 3 May 1699, Boston, Mass.
DENNIS, Elizabeth and John Manning, 4 April 1693, Woodbridge, N. J.
DENNIS, Mary and John Batchelor, 12 July 1661, Salem, Mass.
DENNIS, Robert and Sarah Howland, 19 November 1672, Portsmouth, R. I.
DENNIS, Sarah (widow) and Abner Ordway, 15 June 1656, Boston, Mass.
DENNIS, Sarah and Benjamin FitzRandolph, July 1689, New Brunswick, N. J.
DENNISON, James and Bethia Boykin, 25 November 1662, Milford, Conn.
DENNISON, John and Phoebe Lay, 26 November 1667, Saybrook, Conn.
DENNISON, Margaret and James Blin, 6 December 1698, Boston, Mass.
DENNISON, William and Mary Parker, 27 October 1659, Boston, Mass.
DENSEY, John and Sarah Hollyman, 28 October 1688, Philadelphia, Penn.
DENSLOW, John and Mary Eggleston, 7 June 1655, Windsor, Conn.
DENSLOW, Mary and Thomas Rowley, 5 May 1669, Windsor, Conn.
DENSLOW, Susanna and John Hodge, 1 August 1666, Windsor, Conn.
DENT, Margaret and Edmund Howard, 26 May 1681, Somerset Co., Md.
DENTON, Abigail and Benjamin Stebbins, 9 October 1682, Springfield, Mass.
DENTON, Phebe and Richard Thorne, 29 August 1699, New York.
DENTON, Richard and Ruth Tilleston, 10 November 1657, Dorchester, Mass.
DENTON, Ruth and Timothy Foster, 13 October 1663, Dorchester, Mass.
DENWOOD, Elizabeth and Henry Hooper, 4 July 1669, Somerset Co., Md.
DENWOOD, Rebecca and Nehemiah Covington, 15 November 1679, Somerset Co., Md.
DEPEYSTER, Cornelia and Alexander Stuart, 18 August 1699, New York.
DEPEYSTER, Cornilus and Maria Bancker, 19 September 1694, New York.
DEPOST, Marten and Tammeson Holt, 16 January 1697, Harford Co., Md.
DEPUY, Jean and Margaret Jano, 28 May 1655, Bushwick, L. I., N. Y.
DE SILL, Anna and Antje Briant, 20 December 1691, Bergen Co., N. J.
DE SILLE, Anna and Hendrick Kip, 29 February 1660, New York City.
DESTOW, Rebecca and Francis Davenport, 1 July 1692, Chesterfield, N. J.
DEVEREAUX, Susanna and Stephen Parker, 10 January 1695, Andover, Mass.
DEVIN, Andrew and An Donstall, 10 September 1652, Dedham, Mass.
DEVOE, Frederick and Hester Tourneur, 24 June 1677, Harlem, N. Y.
DEVOTION, Elizabeth and Joseph Weld, 2 September 1674, Roxbury, Mass.
DEWER, David and Jannet Neal, 29 July 1697, Boston, Mass.
DEWEY, Mary and David Ashley, 11 July 1688, Westfield, Mass.
DEWEY, Thomas and Frances Clark, 22 March 1638, Windsor, Conn.
DEWEY, Thomas and Constance Hawes, 1 April 1663, Dorchester, Mass.
DEWIND, Levin and Ariantie Moll, 26 May 1698, New York.
DEWING, Lydia and John Bacon, 15 December 1683, Dedham, Mass.
DEWITT, Dorcas and John Adams, 8 May 1677, Ipswich, Mass.
DEWITT, Jan and Gertryde Van Wyngarden, 1 May 1662, Brooklyn, N. Y.
DEWITT, Sarah and Christopher Hodglandt, 15 February 1696, New York.
DEWITT, Sophie and Humphrey Seward, 31 May 1687, New York.
DEWITT, Tjerk and Barbara Andriessen, 24 April 1656, New York City.

DEWOLFE, Sarah L. (widow) and Nathaniel Clark, 3 December 1696, Lyme, Conn.

DEWOLFE, Simon and Sarah Lay, 12 November 1682, Lyme, Conn.

DEWOLFE, Simon and Alice Bolt, 19 January 1693, Boston, Mass.

DEWSBURY, Hester and Phillip Delano, 19 December 1684, Duxbury, Mass.

DEXTER, Hester and William Andreue, 30 October 1680, Warwick, R. I.

DEXTER, Richard and Sarah Buckman, 23 February 1698, Malden, Mass.

DEYO, Elizabeth and Simon LeFevre, April 1676, Hurley, N. Y.

DEYO, Marie and Abraham Hasbrouck, 17 November 1675, Hurley, N. Y.

DEYO, Margaret and Abraham Du Bois, 6 March 1681, Kingston, N. Y.

DIAS, Thomas and Jane Pelingham, September 1674, Somerset Co., Md.

DIBBLE, Eben and Mary Wakefield, 27 October 1663, Windsor, Conn.

DIBBLE, Isreal and Elizabeth Hull, 28 November 1661, Windsor, Conn.

DIBBLE, Samuel and Hepsibah Bartlett, 21 January 1668, Windsor, Conn.

DIBELL, Josiah and Hanna Cogswell, 20 January 1692, Saybrook, Conn.

DICKEMAN, Abraham and Mary Cooper, 10 February 1658, Dorchester, Mass.

DICKENSON, Martha and William Quarles, 9 December 1669, Ipswich, Mass.

DICKERSON, Henry and Eliza Castle, 25 October 1693, Boston, Mass.

DICKINSON, Hannah and Isaac Gibbs, April 1696, Oyster Bay, N. Y.

DICKINSON, Joseph and Rose Townsend, 1680, Oyster Bay, N. Y.

DICKINSON, Mary and Nathaniel Adams, 30 June 1668, Ipswich, Mass.

DICKINSON, Samuel and Martha Bridgeman, 4 January 1668, Springfield, Mass.

DICKISON, Mary and John Roe, 27 September 1663, Gloucester, Mass.

DIGGENS, John and Rebecca Man, 19 January 1695, Boston, Mass.

DIKE, Mary and Thomas Barret, 22 January 1695, Milton, Mass.

DIKE, Richard and Rebecca Dolliver, 7 August 1667, Gloucester, Mass.

DILL, Abigail (widow) and John Hanniford, 8 September 1655, Boston, Mass.

DILL, Mary and Robert Robbins, 27 March 1697, Chelmsford, Mass.

DILLINGHAM, Edward and Abigail Nye, 18 April 1678, Sandwich, Mass.

DIMMOCK, Joseph and Lydia Fuller, 12 May 1699, Barnstable, Mass.

DIMMOCK, Shuball and Johanna Bursley, April 1663, Barnstable, Mass.

DIMMOCK, Shuball and Tabitha Lothrop, 4 May 1699, Barnstable, Mass.

DINELY, Mary and Benjamin Gold, 5 May 1698, Boston, Mass.

DINNIS, Mary and Thomas Jacobs, 21 March 1695, Boston, Mass.

DINSDALE, John and Hannah Banford, 19 September 1694, Boston, Mass.

DINSDELL, Mary and Benjamin Loyd, 17 January 1699, Boston, Mass.

DIRCK, Leentie and Lambert Barentz, 21 September 1661, Brooklyn, N. Y.

DISCHINGTON, Cornelia and Andrew Law, 10 April 1695, New York.

DISHINGTON, Cornelia and Alexander Streard, 18 August 1699, New York.

DISITER, Hannah and William Bryant, 9 June 1692, Boston, Mass.

DIX, Mary and William Barker, 20 February 1676, Andover, Mass.

DIXEY, Sarah and Thomas Gwin, November 1691, Boston, Mass.

DIXON, Elizabeth and Robert Dukes, April 1674, Somerset Co., Md.

DIXON, Mary and Thomas Cottingham, 8 July 1666, Somerset Co., Md.

DIXON, Sarah and Edmund Beauchamp, 11 June 1668, Somerset Co., Md.

DIXON, Thomas and Christina Potter (or Porter), 12 August 1672, Somerset Co., Md.

DOANE, Anne and David Young, 20 January 1687, Eastham, Mass.

DOANE, Rebecca and Elisha Paine, 20 January 1685, Eastham, Mass.

DOBSON, George and Mary Bostwicke, 24 September 1653, Boston, Mass.
DODD, Stephen and Sarah Stevens, 18 May 1678, Killingworth, Conn.
DODGE, Richard and Mary Eaton, 23 February 1668, Watertown, Mass.
DODGE, Sarah and Daniel Davison, 28 June 1685, Ipswich, Mass.
DODRIG, Philip and Frances Moore, 15 October 1696, New York.
DOLBEAR, John and Sarah Comer, 9 June 1698, Boston, Mass.
DOLBERY, Andrew and Eliza Condey, 31 December 1689, Boston, Mass.
DOLBERRY, Elizabeth and Nathaniel Thomas, 5 October 1696, Marshfield, Mass.
DOLE, Abner and Sarah Belcher, 5 January 1698, Boston, Mass.
DOLE, Sarah and Andrew Griscom, 7 February 1685, Philadelphia, Penn.
DOLING, Mary and Walter Merry, 18 June 1653, Boston, Mass.
DOLLIVER, Rebecca and Richard Dike, 7 August 1667, Gloucester, Mass.
DOLMAN, Elizabeth and John Fyler, 17 October 1672, Windsor, Conn.
DOLPHIN, Thomas and Elizabeth Edwards, 1698, Anne Arundel Co., Md.
DONALDSON, John and Elizabeth Harmon, 23 March 1690-1, New York City.
DONIER, Mary and Joseph Kingsbury, 7 September 1681, Wrentham, Mass.
DONSTALL, An and Andrew Devin, 10 September 1652, Dedham, Mass.
DOOLITTLE, Daniel and Hannah Cornwall, 3 May 1698, Wallingford, Conn.
DOOR, Mary and James Houston, 23 December 1692, Dover, N. H.
DORCHESTER, Anthony and Martha Kitcherell (widow), 2 January 1651, Hartford, Conn.
DORMAN, Hannah and George Johnson, 4 January 1694, Stratford, Conn.
DORMAN, John and Sarah Percell, 31 December 1672, Somerset Co., Md.
DORMAN, Mathew and Phillipa Gilman, 19 August 1672, Somerset Co., Md.
DORMAN, Thomas and Judith Wood, 16 March 1662, Topsfield, Mass.
DORMAN, Timothy and Elizabeth Knowlton, 16 November 1688, Ipswich, Mass.
DOTEN, Hannah and Jonathan Delano, 12 January 1699, Duxbury, Mass.
DOTEY, Sarah and John Buck, 26 April 1693, Scituate, Mass.
DOTY, Edward and Faith Clarke, 6 January 1634, Plymouth, Mass.
DOTEY, John, Sr., and Sarah Jones, 22 November 1694, Plymouth, Mass.
DOTY, John, Jr., and Mehitable Nelson, 2 February 1692-3, Plymouth, Mass.
DOUGHERTY, Nathaniel and Alce Ward, 14 September 1679, Somerset Co., Md.
DOUGHTY, James and Lydia Turner, 15 August 1649, Scituate, Mass.
DOUGLAS, Ann and Elliphalet Het, 1 September 1660, Boston, Mass.
DOUGLASS, Robert and Mary Hempstead, 28 September 1665, New London, Conn.
DOUS, Relief and Timothy Foster, 9 March 1681, Dorchester, Mass.
DOUW, Catherine and Samuel Clowes, 18 July 1698, New York.
DOWSE, Elizabeth and Samuel Miles, 16 October 1659, Boston, Mass.
DOW, Hannah and John Dearborn, 10 January 1695, Hampton, N. H.
DOW, Hendrick and Neeltie Meynderts, 23 September 1697, New York.
DOW, Margaret (widow) and Richard Kimball, 23 October 1661, Ipswich, Mass.
DOW, Mary and William Richards, 23 August 1694, Dover, N. H.
DOW, Stephen and Mary Hutchins, 14 December 1697, Haverhill, Mass
DOWDING, Joseph and Ann Sands, 21 September 1694, Boston, Mass.
DOWELL, James and Eliza Wing, 27 April 1693, Boston, Mass.
DOWN, John and Ruth Badcock, 30 August 1696, Boston, Mass.
DOWNAM, Elizabeth and John Darlin, 13 March 1664, Braintree, Mass.
DOWNE, Mary A. and John Johnson, 15 December 1667, Warwick, R. I.

DOWNING, James and Sarah Evans, 6 November 1694, New York.
DOWNING, Jane and Edward Lambert, 11 November 1696, New York.
DOWNING, John and Hannah Ridgaway, 27 September 1698, Boston, Mass.
DOWNS, Mary and John Cook, 25 November 1686, Dover, N. H.
DOWNS, Thomas and Abigail Hall (widow), 24 October 1698, Dover, N. H.
DRAKE, Abigail and Andrew Hillyard, 17 November 1687, Simsbury, Conn.
DRAKE, Elizabeth and William Gaylord, 17 November 1653, Windsor, Conn.
DRAKE, Elizabeth and Ezekial Hamlen, 8 June 1654, Boston, Mass.
DRAKE, Elizabeth and Hugh Dunn, Sr., 19 December 1670, Piscataway, N. J.
DRAKE, Enoch and Sarah Porter, 11 November 1680, Windsor, Conn.
DRAKE, Francis, Jr., and Patience Walker, 10 November 1698, Piscataway, N. J.
DRAKE, George and Mary Oliver, 13 November 1677, Elizabethtown, N. J.
DRAKE, Hester and Thomas Griswold, 11 August 1681, Windsor, Conn.
DRAKE, Jacob and Mary Bissell, 12 April 1649, Windsor, Conn.
DRAKE, Job and Mary Wolcott, 25 June 1646, Windsor, Conn.
DRAKE, Job and Elizabeth Alvord, 20 March 1671, Windsor, Conn.
DRAKE, John and Rebecca Trotter, 7 July 1677, Elizabethtown, N. J.
DRAKE, John and Sarah King, 12 December 1687, Milton, Mass.
DRAKE, John and Sarah Compton, 9 December 1697, Woodbridge, N. J.
DRAKE, Lydia and Joseph Loomis, 10 April 1681, Windsor, Conn.
DRAKE, Thomas and Millicent Carver (widow), 9 March 1681, Weymouth, Mass.
DRAPER, Daniel and Elizabeth Braket, 16 November 1691, Dedham, Mass.
DRAPER, Hannah and John Bancroft, 3 December 1650, Lynn, Mass.
DRAPER, John and Abigail Mason, 3 September 1686, Dedham, Mass.
DRAPER, Moses and Mary Thatcher, 3 November 1692, Boston, Mass.
DRAPER, Patience and Ebenezer Case, 13 March 1690, Roxbury, Mass.
DRAPER, Richard and Elizabeth Mann, 12 September 1680, Richmond, Va.
DRAPER, Richard and Sarah Kilby, 22 October 1689, Boston, Mass.
DREW, Abigail and Electa Bryer, 4 October 1689, Dover, N. H.
DREW, Ann and Benjamin Watson, 15 September 1694, Boston, Mass.
DREWREY, Mary and William Alden, 21 May 1691, Boston, Mass.
DRINCAL, Thomas and Ann Watson, 17 April 1699, New York.
DRINKER, Edward and Mary Emmons, 6 March 1694, Boston, Mass.
DRIVER, Anne and Henry Tradway, 8 November 1685, Burlington, N. J.
DRIVER, Ruth and Robert Potter, 25 January 1660, Salem, Mass.
DRUE, Robert and Jemima Clarke, 6 September 1656, Boston, Mass.
DRUMMOND, John and Lydia Hallet (widow), 27 November 1661, Boston, Mass.
DRUMMOND, Mary and John Chambers, 17 August 1693, New York.
DRY, Ann and Timothy Mackhew, 15 May 1699, Boston, Mass.
DUBBLEDEE, Elijah and Sarah Pain, 23 January 1697, Boston, Mass.
DUBOIES, Anne and Peter C Dupin, 14 March 1699, New York.
DUBOIS, Abraham and Margaret Deyo, 6 March 1681, Kingston, N. Y.
DUBOIS, Isaac and Maria Hasbrook, June 1683, Kingston, N. Y.
DUBOIS, Louis and Catherine Blancon, 10 October 1655, New Paltz, N. Y.
DUBOIS, Louis and Hester Grosset, 28 August 1696, New York.
DUBOY, Anna and Benjamin Funelle, July 1699, New York.
DUCKETT, Thomas and Ruth Wood (widow), 28 January 1687, Philadelphia, Penn.
DUDLEY, Abigail and John Kent, 9 May 1680, Suffield, Conn.

DUDLEY, Deborah and James Brainard, 1 April 1696, Saybrook, Conn.
DUDLEY, Dorothy and Moses Leavitt, October 1681, Exeter, N. H.
DUDLEY, Elizabeth and James Parker, 1678, Middlesex Co., Va.
DUDLEY, Francis and Sarah Wheeler, 26 October 1665, Concord, Mass.
DUDLEY, James and Mary Welch, 1679, Gloucester Co., Va.
DUDLEY, Joseph and Ann Robinson, 16 October 1670, Guilford, Conn.
DUDLEY, Margery and Ebenezer Wilson, 17 September 1687, New York.
DUDLEY, Mary and Nicholas Mason, 11 March 1686, Saybrook, Conn.
DUDLEY, Robert and Elizabeth Curtis, 1691, Middlesex Co., Va.
DUDLEY, Ruth and John Whittlesey, 20 June 1664, Saybrook, Conn.
DUDLEY, William and Mary Roe, 4 November 1661, Saybrook, Conn.
DUDSON, Abigail and Roger Kilcup, 4 July 1695, Boston, Mass.
DUDSON, Abigail and Barnabas Lathrop, 15 November 1698, Boston, Mass.
DUE, Ambrose and Ester Barker, 10 December 1651, Boston, Mass.
DUEIN, Jonathan and Susannah Bacon, 7 January 1692, Dedham, Mass.
DUEIN, Lydia and John Bacon, 15 October 1683, Dedham, Mass.
DUEING, Andrew and Dority Hide, 27 October 1682, Dedham, Mass.
DUEING, Annah and Daniel Wight, 17 December 1686, Dedham, Mass.
DUGLES, John and Sarah Mason (widow), 16 September 1687, Dover, N. H.
DUKES, Robert and Elizabeth Dixon, April 1674, Somerset Co., Md.
DUMBLETON, Hannah and Thomas Merrick, 18 December 1690, Springfield, Mass.
DUMBLETON, John and Lydia Leonard, 18 March 1675, Springfield, Mass.
DUMMER, Margaret and Job Clemens, 25 December 1644, Haverhill, Mass.
DUMMER, Robert and Martha Weaver, 22 June 1699, Burlington, N. J.
DUNAWIN, Tellen and Edmund Gradde, 10 March 1697, Harford Co., Md.
DUNBAR, Joshua and Hannah Hatch, 21 September 1699, Hingham, Mass.
DUNCAN, Mary and William Sergent, 21 June 1678, Gloucester, Mass.
DUNCKLY, Elnathan and Silence Bowers, 14 October 1656, Dedham, Mass.
DUNHAM, Edmund and Mary Bonham, 15 July 1681, Piscataway, N. J.
DUNHAM, Hannah and Giles Rickard, 31 October 1651, Plymouth, Mass.
DUNHAM, John and Mary Smith, 1 March 1680, Barnstable, Mass.
DUNHAM, Jonathan and Rebecca Trotter, 7 July 1677, Elizabethtown, N. J.
DUNHAM, Samuel and Sarah Watson (widow), 15 January 1693-4, Plymouth, Mass.
DUNK, Thomas and Elizabeth Stedman, 10 July 1677, Saybrook, Conn.
DUNKAN, Alexander and Elizabeth Turnerr, 6 July 1698, Boston, Mass.
DUNN, Elizabeth and John Runyan, 1692, New Jersey.
DUNN, Hugh, Sr., and Elizabeth Drake, 19 December 1670, Piscataway, N. J.
DUNN, Pascho and Hannah Powers, 8 April 1695, Elizabeth City Co., Va.
DUNSCOMB, Daniel and Helena Swann, 8 July 1696, New York.
DUPER, Hannah and John Bancroft, 3 December 1650, Windsor, Conn.
DUPIN, Peter C and Anne Dubois, 14 March 1699, New York.
DUPLONVIS, John and Whanky Taney, 29 February 1687, Philadelphia, Penn.
DU PLOUNY, Jan and Weyntie Van Janen, 3 May 1687, Philadelphia, Penn.
DU PUIS, Francois and Greetje Williams, 26 December 1661, Brooklyn, N. Y.
DURE, Thomas and Elhenah Beans, 26 July 1694, Middletown, Penn.
DUREND, John and Elizabeth Bryan, 10 November 1698, New York.
DURHAM, Samuel and Eliza Reed, 6 July 1691, Boston, Mass.

DURKEE, William and Martha Cross, 20 December 1664, Ipswich, Mass.
DUSTON, Elizabeth and Mathias Button, 9 June 1663, Haverhill, Mass.
DUTCH, Esther and Samuel Elwell, 7 June 1658, Gloucester, Mass.
DUTCH, Mary and Joseph Elwell, 22 June 1669, Gloucester, Mass.
DUTTON, John and Sarah Shed, 20 September 1681, Billerica, Mass.
DUTTON, Sarah and Samuel Lewis, 3 April 1683, Billerica, Mass.
DWELLY, John and Rachel Buck, 4 January 1692-3, Scituate, Mass.
DWIGHT, Elizabeth and Joseph Gallop, 1 March 1694, Boston, Mass.
DWIGHT, Hannah and Nathaniel Whiting, 4 November 1643, Dedham, Mass.
DWIGHT, John and Elizabeth Harding, 8 December 1696, Dedham, Mass.
DWIGHT, Sarah and Nathaniel Renolds, 30 October 1657, Boston, Mass.
DWIGHT, Timothy and Sarah Pennan, 11 September 1651, Dedham, Mass.
DWIGHT, Timothy and Sarah Powell, 3 March 1653, Dedham, Mass.
DWIGHT, Timothy and Anna Flint, 9 November 1664, Dedham, Mass.
DWIGHT, Timothy and Mary Edwind, 7 November 1685, Dedham, Mass.
DWIGHT, Timothy and Bethia Morse, 1 February 1691-2, Dedham, Mass.
DWIGHT, Timothy and Easter Fisher, 31 July 1690, Dedham, Mass.
DYAR, Benjamin and Hanah Avery, 22 March 1677, Dedham, Mass.
DYER, Benjamin and Hannah Odlin, 10 December 1691, Boston, Mass.
DYER, Barret and Hannah Stewart, 29 June 1699, Boston, Mass.
DYER, Eliza and George Rayson, 21 May 1689, Boston, Mass.
DYER, Hannah (widow) and Augustine Bullard, 12 October 1693, Dover, N. H.
DYER, John and Hannah Morton, 6 June 1694, Boston, Mass.
DYER, Rebecca and William Briggs, 10 June 1695, Boston, Mass.
DYKEMAN, Mary and James Hewett, 16 September 1695, New York.
DYMAND, Israel and Abeball Prouse, 5 January 1690, Amesbury, Mass.
DYMOND, Rachel and John Morgan, 16 November 1665, Preston, Conn.

E

EADES, Mary and John Beer, 21 September 1694, Boston, Mass.

EAME, William and Mary Balston, 12 July 1693, Boston, Mass.

EAMES, Anna and Thomas Wilder, 1640, Charlestown, Mass.

EARL, Roger and Lydia Travise, 25 October 1694, Boston, Mass.

EARL, Samuel and Lydia Flood, 20 April 1694, Boston, Mass.

EARLE, Samuel and Mary Condage, 13 December 1698, Boston, Mass.

EARLISHMAN, Mary and Nehemiah Allen, 29 August 1685, Middletown, Penn.

EAST, Eliza and John Parminter, 1 November 1694, Boston, Mass.

EAST, Hannah and Daniel Street, 16 January 1687, Philadelphia, Penn.

EASTBOURN, John and Margaret Jones, 27 February 1694, Philadelphia, Penn.

EASTMAN, Hannah and James Corbin, 7 April 1697, Woodstock, Conn.

EASTMEAD, Arthur and Mary Hix, 4 August 1693, Boston, Mass.

EAMES, Anthony and Mercy Sawyer, 2 December 1686, Marshfield, Mass.

EARL, Mary and John Borden, 25 December 1670, Portsmouth, R. I.

EATES, Nan and John Dabbs, October 1655, Kent Co., Md.

EATON, Abigail and Robert Mason, 10 September 1659, Dedham, Mass.

EATON, Benjamin and Sarah Hoskins, 4 December 1660, Plymouth, Mass.

EATON, Elizabeth and James Davis, 1 December 1648, Haverhill, Mass.

EATON, Grace (widow) and Henry Sillisby, 18 November 1680, Lynn, Mass.

EATON, Jabez and Experience Mead, 4 October 1663, Dorchester, Mass.

EATON, John and Elizabeth Kendall, 8 March 1658, Watertown, Mass.

EATON, John and Dorcas Green, 26 November 1674, Reading, Mass.

EATON, Jonathan and Elizabeth Burnap, 1683, Reading, Mass.

EATON, Martha and Thomas Brown, 7 October 1656, Cambridge, Mass.

EATON, Mary and John Mason, 5 March 1651, Dedham, Mass.

EATON, Mary and John Gilbert, 5 March 1653, Boston, Mass.

EATON, Mary and Richard Dodge, 23 February 1668, Watertown, Mass.

EATON, Mercy and Samuel Fuller, 7 January 1685, Plymouth, Mass.

EATON, Mercy and John Cleaver, 26 January 1699, Beverly, Mass.

EATON, Rebecca and James Richardson, 1698, Reading, Mass.

EATON, Rebecca and Josiah Rickard, 21 November 1699, Plymouth, Mass.

EATON, Samuel and Martha Billington, 10 January 1660, Plymouth, Mass.

EATON, Samuel and Elizabeth Fuller, 24 May 1694, Middleborough, Mass.

EATON, Thomas and Unity Smylolary, 6 January 1658, Andover, Mass.

EATON, Thomas and Lydia Gay, 5 October 1697, Dedham, Mass.

EATON, William and Mary Burnett, 1692, Lynn, Mass.

EBELL, Alice and William Trotter, 28 September 1667, New York City.

EDDINGTON, Mary and William Baker, 23 July 1651, Boston, Mass.

EDDY, Bennet and Israel Woodward, 28 December 1698, Taunton, Mass.

EDDY, Hannah and Eliezar Fisher, 24 December 1696, Norton, Mass.

EDDY, Samuel and Sarah Mead, 31 September 1664, Dorchester, Mass.

EDGAR, Jane and Thomas Horsman, 19 September 1681, Somerset Co., Md.

EDGECOMB, John and Sarah Stallion, 9 November 1673, New London, Conn.

EDGECOMB, John and Hannah Hempstead, 29 February 1699, New London, Conn.

EDGERLY, Thomas and Rebecca Halwell, 28 September 1665, Dover, N. H.

EDGERLY, Thomas and Jane Whedon, 3 December 1691, Oyster River, N. H.

EDGERTON, Richard and Mary Sylvester, 17 April 1653, Saybrook, Conn.

EDGERTON, Sarah and Joseph Reynolds, 10 January 1688, Norwich, Conn.

EDMONS, Mary and Joseph Hutchins, 1 July 1657, Boston, Mass.

EDMUNDS, Robert and Rebecca Pasmore, 26 March 1695, Boston, Mass.

EDMUNDS, William and Ann Martine (widow), 1 July 1657, Boston, Mass.

EDSALL, Mary and Peter DeLanoy, 21 February 1696, New York.

EDWARDS, Alexander and Sarah Searle (widow), 28 April 1642, Springfield, Mass.

EDWARDS, Ann and Daniel I. Pond, 18 July 1661, Dedham, Mass.

EDWARDS, Benjamin and Martha Gaines, 14 May 1687, Wenham, Mass.

EDWARDS, Elizabeth and John Allen, 22 July 1697, Boston, Mass.

EDWARDS, Elizabeth and Thomas Dolphin, 1698, Anne Arundel Co., Md.

EDWARDS, Johanna (widow) and Henry Raynor, 9 June 1662, Boston, Mass.

EDWARDS, John and Mary Stanborough, 1666, East Hampton, L. I., N. Y.

EDWARDS, John and Amey Warren, 2 March 1693, Boston, Mass.

EDWARDS, John and Sibella Newman, 29 October 1694, Boston, Mass.

EDWARDS, John and Anna Dodge, 1 April 1698, Wenham, Mass.

EDWARDS, Robert and Judith Mosston, 13 January 1698, New York.

EDWARDS, Susanna and John Noyes, 16 March 1699, Boston, Mass.

EDWIND, Mary and Timothy Dwight, 7 November 1685, Dedham, Mass.

EDZALL, Thomas and Elizabeth Ferman, 16 July 1652, Boston, Mass.

EDYE, Pilgrim and William Baker, 22 February 1656, Boston, Mass.

EEDEY, Asadiah and Lamuel Samson, 29 May 1695, Duxborough, Mass.

EGELSTON, Sarah and John Pettibone, 16 February 1664, Windsor, Conn.

EGGINGTON, Jeremiah and Elizabeth Cotton, 12 August 1655, Boston, Mass.

EGGLETON, Ruth and Samuel Blodgett, 13 December 1655, Woburn, Mass.

EGGLETON, Sarah and John Nutting, 28 August 1650, Woburn, Mass.

EGGLESTON, Mary and John Denslow, 7 June 1655, Windsor, Conn.

EGLESTON, Edward and Phebee Holman, 27 July 1693, Boston, Mass.

EGLETON, William and Dorcas Greetian, 28 September 1698, Boston, Mass.

EGLINGTON, Phebe and Samuel Baker, 19 December 1699, Boston, Mass.

ELCOCK, Mary and Jonathan Perkins, 14 June 1682, New Haven, Conn.

ELDER, Daniel and Lydia Holmes, 12 January 1667, Dorchester, Mass.

ELDREDG, Elizabeth and Joseph Halsey, 29 January 1697, Boston, Mass.

ELDRIDGE, Eliza and Elias Heath, 13 May 1699, Boston, Mass.

ELDRIDGE, Eliza and John Tully, 20 January 1696, Boston, Mass.

ELDRIDGE, Elizabeth and Samuel Russell, November 1682, Marblehead, Mass.

ELENOR, Andrew and Anica Hanson, 5 March 1656, Kent Co., Md.

ELICE, John and Elizabeth Fisher, 10 January 1686, Dedham, Mass.

ELICE, Thomas and Mary Wright, 21 May 1657, Medfield, Mass.

ELIOT, Abigail and Thomas Wiborne, 16 October 1657, Boston, Mass.

ELIOT, Elizabeth and Isaac Royall, 1 July 1697, Boston, Mass.

ELIOT, Hannah and Stephen Willis, 3 June 1670, Braintree, Mass.

ELIOT, Miss and Edmond Quincy, 8 December 1680, Braintree, Mass.

ELIOT, Joseph and Sarah Collins, 29 July 1697, Boston, Mass.

ELITHROP, Abigail (widow) and Thomas Jones, 25 June 1657, Boston, Mass.

ELKINS, Hester (widow) and Abraham Lee, 21 June 1686, Dover, N. H.

ELKINS, Robert and Patience Evans (widow), 9 November 1686, Dover, N. H.

ELLERY, William and Hannah Vinson, 8 October 1663, Gloucester, Mass.

ELLERY, William and Mary Coyte, 13 June 1676, Gloucester, Mass.

ELLES, Abigail and Ebenezer Fisher, 7 February 1695, Wrentham, Mass.

ELLES, Joanna and Nathaniel Rocket, 7 December 1698, Wrentham, Mass.

ELLICE, Ann and Edward Colver, 19 July 1638, Dedham, Mass.

ELLICE, Eleazer and Mahitabell Thurston, 27 May 1690, Dedham, Mass.

ELLICE, John and Suzan Lumber, 10 September 1641, Dedham, Mass.

ELLICE, Joseph and Dorithy Spaldin, 18 May 1690, Dedham, Mass.

ELLICE, Mary and Amos Fisher, 12 January 1678, Dedham, Mass.

ELLICE, Richard and Elizabeth French, 19 July 1650, Dedham, Mass.

ELLIN, Nicholas and Mary Pond, 3 May 1663, Dorchester, Mass.

ELLINE, Mary and Joseph Cortas, 18 November 1687, Milton, Mass.

ELLIOTT, Jacob and Mary Wilcock (widow), 9 November 1654, Boston, Mass.

ELLIOTT, Hannah and Theophilus Frery, 4 April 1653, Boston, Mass.

ELLIOTT, Hannah and Habbakuke Glover, 4 March 1653, Boston, Mass.

ELLIOTT, Sarah and John Aldis, 27 July 1650, Dedham, Mass.

ELLIS, Edward and Sarah Blott, 6 August 1652, Boston, Mass.

ELLIS, Elizabeth and William C. Currier, June 1683, Somerset Co., Md.

ELLIS, John and Mary Herring, 1 February 1678, Medfield, Mass.

ELLIS, John, Jr., and Mary Shilletto, September 1686, Somerset Co., Md.

ELLIS, John and Mary Hill, 7 April 1698, Boston, Mass.

ELLIS, Joseph and Mary Graves, 25 October 1688, Dedham, Mass.

ELLIS, Mary and Jonathan Adams, 1678, Medfield, Mass.

ELLIS, Mary and William Ruicks, 29 March 1694, Boston, Mass.

ELLIS, Mary and William Corson, 27 June 1699, Boston, Mass.

ELLIS, Mathias and Mary Burgess, 1678, Sandwich, Mass.

ELLIS, Rebecca and John Fisher, 15 April 1681, Dedham, Mass.

ELLIS, Robert and Elizabeth Pemberton, 4 June 1698, Boston, Mass.

ELLIS, Simeon and Sarah Bates, 1692, Haddonfield, N. J.

ELLISE, Joanna and Nathaniel Kettle, 5 October 1692, Boston, Mass.

ELLISTON, Jonathan and Eliza Wesendonck, 27 June 1695, Boston, Mass.

ELLSWORTH, Elizabeth and Nathaniel Loomis, 23 December 1680, Windsor, Conn.

ELLSWORTH, Johanes and Anna Peters, 3 June 1696, New York.

ELLSWORTH, Josiah and Elizabeth Holcomb, 16 November 1654, Windsor, Conn.

ELLSWORTH, Josias and Martha Taylor, 30 October 1679, Windsor, Conn.

ELLSWORTH, Mary and Daniel Loomis, 23 December 1680, Windsor, Conn.

ELLWELL, Mary and John Cooke, 2 February 1680, Gloucester, Mass.

ELMES, Jonathan and Patience Spur, 24 May 1693, Milton, Mass.

ELMORE, Francis and Anne Allen, 2 December 1677, Richmond Co., Va.

ELSLEY, Mary and David Denham, 18 August 1699, New York.

ELSON, Margaret and John Harris, 22 May 1695, Lynn, Mass.

ELSSE, Hannah and John Willis, 11 November 1654, Boston, Mass.

ELTON, Mary and Thomas Kendall, 25 December 1684, Burlington, N. J.

ELUM, Ann and Simon Young, 10 May 1695, New York.

ELVES, John and Jane Brock, 6 October 1698, Boston, Mass.

ELWELL, Joseph and Mary Dutch, 22 June 1669, Gloucester, Mass.
ELWELL, Robert and Alice Leach, 29 May 1676, Gloucester, Mass.
ELWELL, Samuel and Esther Dutch, 7 June 1658, Gloucester, Mass.
ELWELL, Thomas and Sarah Bassett, 23 November 1675, Gloucester, Mass.
ELWOOD, Grace and William Thompson, 1680 Middlesex Co., Va.
ELY, Jane and Anthony Hubbard, 5 November 1652, Dedham, Mass.
ELY, Joshua and Rachel Lee, 9 November 1699, Burlington, N. J.
ELY, Ruth and Jeremiah Horton, 3 August 1661, Springfield, Mass.
ELY, William and Elizabeth Smith, 12 May 1681, Lyme, Conn.
ELZEY, Arnold and Mazer Waller, October 1682, Somerset Co., Md.
ELZEY, Peter and Mary Bell, 11 November 1672, Somerset Co., Md.
EMANS, Abraham and Rebecca Stilwell, 20 October 1693, New York.
EMARY, James and Elizabeth Pidge, 28 December 1695, Dedham, Mass.
EMBLEM, Mary and Daniel Buff, 12 May 1698, Boston, Mass.
EMERIE, Joseph and Elizabeth Merritt, 2 October 1693, Andover, Mass.
EMERSON, Elizabeth and John Fuller, 31 May 1652, Ipswich, Mass.
EMERSON, John and Elizabeth Leech, 27 December 1693, Bridgewater, Mass.
EMERSON, Mary and Robert Nokes, 17 August 1699, Boston, Mass.
EMERSON, Samuel and Judith Davis, 14 February 1687, Haverhill, Mass.
EMERTON, John and Mary Harrington, 21 January 1698, Anne Arundel Co., Md.
EMERY, Daniel and Margaret Gowan (Smith), 17 March 1695, Berwick, Maine.
EMERY, Elizabeth and John Kelly, 6 November 1696, Newbury, Mass.
EMERY, John and Mary Webster, 2 October 1648, Newbury, Mass.
EMERY, John and Mary Sawyer, 12 June 1683, Newbury, Mass.
EMERY, Mary and Samuel Sawyer, 13 March 1670, Newbury, Mass.
EMERY, Stephen and Ruth Jaques, 1692, Newbury, Mass.
EMERY, Zachariah and Elizabeth Goodwin, 9 December 1686, Kittery, Maine.
EMLEN, George and Ellener Allen, 12 November 1685, Philadelphia, Penn.
EMLEN, George and Hannah Garrett, 25 March 1694, Philadelphia, Penn.
EMMONS, Benjamin and Mary Amory, 10 September 1694, Boston, Mass.
EMMONS, Elizabeth and John Hincksman, 10 August 1660, Boston, Mass.
EMMONS, Hannah and Henry Crab, 1 November 1657, Boston, Mass.
EMMONS, Mary and Edward Drinker, 6 March 1694, Boston, Mass.
EMMONS, Samuell and Mary Scott, 16 August 1660, Boston, Mass.
EMONS, Nathaniel and Mary Warmal, 15 September 1698, Boston, Mass.
EMONS, Obadiah and Judith Hubberd, 7 November 1699, Boston, Mass.
EMPSON, Cornelius and Sarah Wilson, 1 April 1693, Chesterfield, N. J.
ENDICOTT, John and Elizabeth Houchin, 9 September 1653, Boston, Mass.
ENGLAND, Christina and Benjamin Acton, 27 June 1686, Philadelphia, Penn.
ENGLAND, Francis and Edward Hiscox, 20 May 1656, Branford, Conn.
ENGLAND, Ellen and Jeremy Westcott, 27 February 1665, Warwick, R. I.
ENGLISH, James and Joanna Farnum, 7 November 1657, Boston, Mass.
ENGLISH, James and Sarah Bee, September 1681, Somerset Co., Md.
ENGLISH, Joseph and Joan Comley, 26 February 1685, Middletown, Penn.
ENGLISH, Mary and Michael Bourthier, 20 February 1693, New York.
ENGOLLS, Henry and Mary Osgood, 6 July 1653, Andover, Mass.
ENNES, Daniel and Lydia Wheeler, 25 April 1683, Andover, Mass.
ENNO, Ann and Joseph Case, 6 April 1699, Simsbury, Conn.
ENNO, James and Anna Bedwell, 18 August 1648, Windsor, Conn.

ENNO, James and Abigail Bissell, 26 December 1678, Windsor, Conn.
ENNO, John and Mary Debell, 10 May 1681, Windsor, Conn.
ENO, James and Hannah Bidwell, 18 August 1648, Windsor, Conn.
ENSDELL, Elizabeth and James Rising, 7 May 1657, Boston, Mass.
ENSIGN, Hannah and Thomas Shepard, 19 September 1658, Malden, Mass.
ENSIGN, Sarah and John Rockwell, 6 May 1651, Windsor, Conn.
ENSIGN, Thomas and Hannah Shepard, 1 December 1692, Hartford, Conn.
ENSINGNE, David and Mahitable Gunn, 22 October 1663, Hartford, Conn.
ESTERBROOK, Thomas and Sarah Temple, 11 May 1683, Concord, Mass.
EUELEY, Margaret and Nathaniel Gallop, 11 April 1652, Boston, Mass.
EUSTACE, Sarah and John Barrett, 28 September 1699, Boston, Mass.
EUSTICE, Jonathan and Sarah Scholly, 16 November 1699, Boston, Mass.
EVANS, Barbery and William Pittman, 29 September 1653, Boston, Mass.
EVANS, Edward and Mary Daniel, 22 May 1676, Somerset Co., Md.
EVANS, Elinor and John Sweeting, 7 February 1694, Boston, Mass.
EVANS, Hannah and Samuel Hicks, 27 July 1665, Dorchester, Mass.
EVANS, John and Catherine Macgregere, 10 September 1694, New York.
EVANS, John and Mary Clap, 7 January 1694, Boston, Mass.
EVANS, Mathias and Patience Mead, 28 February 1669, Boston, Mass.
EVANS, Mary and Nathan Bradley, 17 May 1666, Dorchester, Mass.
EVANS, Patience (widow) and Robert Elkins, 9 November 1686, Dover, N. H.
EVANS, Rebeckah and Robert Searle, 4 December 1695, Dorchester, Mass.
EVANS, Sarah and James Downing, 6 November 1694, New York.
EVANS, Thomas and Hannah Glover, 10 March 1686, Dorchester, Mass.
EVARTS, Hannah and Thomas Stevens, 9 June 1686, Killingworth, Conn.
EVELETH, Hannah and Nathaniel Kettall, June 1669, Boston, Mass.
EVELETH, Isaac and Abigail Coyte, 13 November 1677, Gloucester, Mass.
EVELETH, Joseph and Mary Bragge, 1 January 1668, Gloucester, Mass.
EVELETH, Sylvaster and Bridget Parkman, 6 September 1672, Gloucester, Mass.
EVERARD, Abigail and Mathias Puffer, 11 February 1677, Dedham, Mass.
EVERETT, Judith and Samuel Rogers, 12 December 1657, Ipswich, Mass.
EVERETT, Mary and James Macarory, November 1662, Dedham, Mass.
EVERETT, Ruth and Richard Puffer, 23 March 1681, Dorchester, Mass.
EVERETT, Samuel and Mary Pepper, 28 August 1669, Dedham, Mass.
EVERID, John and Elizabeth Pepper, 13 March 1662, Dedham, Mass.
EVERILL, Abiel and Elizabeth Phillips, 6 May 1655, Boston, Mass.
EVERILL, Elizabeth and John Aldine, 1 April 1660, Boston, Mass.
EVERINDEN, Robert and Ann Smith, 11 July 1698, New York.
EVERIT, John and Marcy Browne, 3 January 1699, Dedham, Mass.
EVERITT, Abigail (widow) and William Jones, 18 October 1687, Watertown,
Mass.
EVERITT, Sarah and Cornelius Fisher, 25 July 1665, Dedham, Mass.
EVERRARD, Jonathan and Penelope Clark, 9 August 1697, Boston, Mass.
EVERTON, Thomas and Anne Wood, April 1686, Somerset Co., Md.
EWEN, Mary and Nathan Stanbury, 31 January 1699, Philadelphia, Penn.
EZGATE, Eleazer and Joyce Goodwin, 24 April 1675, Braintree, Mass.

F

FAIREBANCK, John and Sarah Fiske, 16 January 1641, Dedham, Mass.

FAIREBANCK, Suzan and Ralph Day, 12 August 1647, Dedham, Mass.

FAIREBANK, Mary and Richard Trusdell, 24 February 1696-7, Dedham, Mass.

FAIRBANK, Mary and Benjamin Alline, 16 April 1696, Dedham, Mass.

FAIRBANKE, Mary and Michael Metcalfe, 2 February 1644, Dedham, Mass.

FAIRBANKS, Constance and Samuel Mattock, 30 January 1653, Boston, Mass.

FAIRBANKS, George and Mary Adams, 16 October 1646, Dedham, Mass.

FAIRBANKS, Hesadiah and John Moore, 1 January 1698, Concord, Mass.

FAIRBANKS, John and Mary Whiting, 1 January 1672, Dedham, Mass.

FAIRBANKS, Jeremiah and Mary Penfield, 19 April 1698, Bristol, R. I.

FAIRBANKS, Jonas and Lydia Prescott, 28 May 1658, Lancaster, Mass.

FAIREWEATHER, John and Sarah Turner, 15 November 1660, Boston, Mass.

FAIREFIELD, Mary and John Parker, 20 August 1660, Boston, Mass.

FAIREFIELD, Elizabeth and William Goddard, 29 October 1697, Boston, Mass.

FAIRFIELD, Elizabeth and James Souther, 22 August 1657, Boston, Mass.

FAIRFIELD, John and Sarah Geary, 26 March 1666, Wenham, Mass.

FAIRFIELD, John and Eliza Badson, 18 April 1693, Boston, Mass.

FAIRFIELD, Walter and Sarah Skipper, 28 December 1654, Reading, Mass.

FAIRWEATHER, Hannah and Samuel Clark, 23 June 1698, Boston, Mass.

FAIRWETHER, John and Mary Hewes, 17 November 1692, Boston, Mass.

FALE, Hannah and Thomas Bacon, 22 January 1691, Wrentham, Mass.

FALES, James and Deborath Fisher, 28 August 1679, Dedham, Mass.

FALES, Timothy and Deborah Fisher, 20 August 1679, Dedham, Mass.

FALL, Jane and George Siry, 16 March 1697, Boston, Mass.

FALLOWELL, Ann and Thomas Pope, 28 January 1637, Plymouth, Mass.

FANN, William and Alicia Sanford, 23 January 1675, Richmond Co., Va.

FAREBANKS, Hannah and Samuel Deerin, 26 June 1688, Milton, Mass.

FARNAM, Elizabeth and Joshua Carwithy, 6 June 1657, Boston, Mass.

FARNAM, Tabitha and John Frye, 1 November 1694, Andover, Mass.

FARNELIE, Marie and Jan Schout, 10 June 1663, Brooklyn, N. Y.

FARNSWORTH, Rachel and Mathias Poffer, 18 January 1662, Braintree, Mass.

FARNSWORTH, Rebecca and John Ruggles, 18 January 1662, Braintree, Mass.

FARNUM, Elizabeth and George Holt, 10 May 1698, Andover, Mass.

FARNUM, Hannah and Samuel Holt, 28 March 1693, Andover, Mass.

FARNUM, Joanna and James English, 7 November 1657, Boston, Mass.

FARNUM, John and Susanna Arnold, 7 February 1654, Boston, Mass.

FARNUM, John and Rebecca Kent, 12 November 1667, Andover, Mass.

FARNUM, John and Elizabeth Parker, 10 April 1684, Andover, Mass.

FARNUM, John and Mary Tyler, 30 June 1693, Andover, Mass.

FARNUM, John and Deborah Mean, 16 September 1687, Boston, Mass.

FARNUM, Martha and John Fry, 1 November 1694, Andover, Mass.

FARNUM, Mary and Daniel Pore, 20 October 1650, Boston, Mass.

FARNUM, Mary and William Lovejoy, 29 November 1680, Andover, Mass.

FARNUM, Mehitable and Peter Johnson, 29 October 1693, Andover, Mass.

FARNUM, Ralph and Sarah Sterling, 9 October 1685, Andover, Mass.
FARNUM, Ralph and Elizabeth Holt, 26 October 1658, Andover, Mass.
FARNUM, Samuel and Hannah Holt, 4 January 1698, Andover, Mass.
FARNUM, Sarah and George Abbot, 26 April 1658, Andover, Mass.
FARNUM, Sarah and Benjamin Abbott, 22 April 1685, Andover, Mass.
FARNUM, Thomas and Elizabeth Sibborns, 8 July 1660, Andover, Mass.
FARNUM, Thomas and Hannah Hutchinson, 14 May 1693, Andover, Mass.
FARNWORTH, Benjamin and Mary Prescott, April 1695, Groton, Mass.
FARR, Elizabeth and Nicholas Huchin, 4 April 1666, Lynn, Mass.
FARR, Martha and William Clarke, 18 September 1661, Boston, Mass.
FARR, Mary and John Mycall, 11 October 1657, Braintree, Mass.
FARR, Stephen and Mary Taylor, 25 May 1674, Concord, Mass.
FARRAR, Ann and John Houghton, 10 May 1676, Lancaster, Mass.
FARRAR, George and Ann Whitmore, 16 November 1643, Ipswich, Mass.
FARRAR, Joana and Robert Dale, 30 November 1680, Woburn, Mass.
FARRAR, Sarah and Melatiah Lathrop, 20 May 1667, Lynn, Mass.
FARRE, Mary (widow) and Samuel Jinkins, 6 July 1670, Dorchester, Mass.
FARINGTON, Edward and Martha Browne, 9 April 1690, Andover, Mass.
FARRINGDON, John and Mary Janes, 24 July 1677, Dedham, Mass.
FARRINGTON, Daniel and Abigail Fisher, 5 October 1691, Wrentham, Mass.
FARRINGTON, Elizabeth and Mark Graves, 14 November 1667, Andover, Mass.
FARRINGTON, John and Mary Bullard, 23 February 1649, Dedham, Mass.
FARRINGTON, Mary and John Pidge, 27 April 1667, Dedham, Mass.
FARRINGTON, Sarah and John Goddard, 1697, Lynn, Mass.
FARROW, Hannah and Joseph Josselyn, 17 March 1687, Hingham, Mass.
FARROW, Mary and Samuel Stowell, 25 October 1649, Hingham, Mass.
FARWELL, Hannah and Samuel Woods, 30 December 1685, Chelmsford, Mass.
FARWELL, Joseph and Hannah Colburn, 23 January 1696, Chelmsford, Mass.
FARWELL, Mary and John Bates, 27 December 1665, Chelmsford, Mass.
FARWELL, Thomas and Hannah Rolfe, 6 August 1672, Chelmsford, Mass.
FAULKNER, Hannah and Pascoe Chubb, 29 May 1689, Andover, Mass.
FAULKNER, John and Sarah Abbott, 19 October 1682, Andover, Mass.
FAWKNER, Edward and Dorothy Robinson, 4 February 1647, Salem, Mass.
FAWKNER, Francis and Abigail Dane, 12 October 1675, Andover, Mass.
FAWKNER, Mary and John Marble, 30 May 1671, Andover, Mass.
FAWN, Elizabeth and Robert Clemens, 8 December 1652, Ipswich, Mass.
FAWRE, Eliazer and Mary Preston, 28 May 1662, Boston, Mass.
FAXIN, Johanna and Anthony Fisher, 7 July 1647, Dedham, Mass.
FAXON, Deborah and William Savell, 1 January 1679, Braintree, Mass.
FAXON, Rebecca and Samuel Bass, 30 July 1678, Braintree, Mass.
FAXON, Thomas, Jr., and Deborah Thayer, 11 April 1653, Braintree, Mass.
FAY, Bathsheba and Joshua Pratt, 1630, Plymouth, Mass.
FEKE, Hannah and John Bowne, 7 May 1656, Flatbush, N. Y.
FELLOWS, Abigail and Samuel Ayers, 16 April 1677, Ipswich, Mass.
FELLOWS, Isaac and Joana Boardman, 24 January 1672, Ipswich, Mass.
FELLOWS, May and Josiah Brown, 23 November 1666, Redding, Conn.
FELLOWS, Samuel and Deborah Sanborn, 15 November 1698, Ipswich, Mass.
FELT, Mary and James Nicholls, February 1660, Malden, Mass.
FELT, Phillippa and Samuel Platts, 19 December 1681, Rowley, Mass.

FEN, Robert and Mary Hawkins (widow), 26 April 1654, Boston, Mass.
FENN, Edward and Mary Thorpe, 15 November 1688, Wallingford, Conn.
FENN, Mary (widow) and Henry Shrimpton, 27 February 1661, Boston, Mass.
FENNO, Benjamin and Mary Belsher, 23 September 1696, Milton, Mass.
FENNO, John, Jr., and Rachel Newcombe, 25 June 1690, Milton, Mass.
FENWICK, Jeremiah and Elizabeth Steadford, 3 January 1699, Boston, Mass.
FENNO, Rebeccah and Dependance French, 27 April 1688, Milton, Mass.
FERGUSON, Bathia and Josiah Hunt, Jr., 20 December 1697, New York.
FERGUSON, Mary and Thomas Lawrence, 9 November 1692, New York City.
FERMAN, Elizabeth and Thomas Edzall, 16 July 1652, Boston, Mass.
FERNALD, Lydia and Moses Dennett, 18 February 1674, York Co., Maine.
FERNALD, Samuel and Hannah Spinney, December 1698, Portsmouth, N. H.
FERNALD, Samuel and Susannah Paul, 12 October 1699, York Co., Maine.
FERNALD, William and Elizabeth Langdon, 16 November 1671, Portsmouth, N. H.
FERRILL, Catherine and Edward Carey, 10 December 1680, Somerset Co., Md.
FERRIS, Hannah and John Knapp, 10 June 1692, Stamford, Conn.
FERRIS, John and Abigail Hoight, 13 February 1695, Greenwich, Conn.
FERRIS, Mary and Thomas Merritt, 3 February 1696, Wethersfield, Conn.
FIELD, Abigail and Daniel Jacobs, 24 October 1697, Dover, N. H.
FIELD, Benjamin and Hannah Bowne, 30 November 1691, Flushing, N. Y.
FIELD, Elizabeth and Stephen Jones, 28 January 1663, Dover, N. H.
FIELD, Joseph and Abigail Pillsbury, 29 October 1645, York Co., Maine.
FIELD, Mary and John Woodman, 15 July 1656, Oyster River, N. H.
FIELD, Mary and Thomas Jefferson, 20 October 1698, Henrico Co., Va.
FIELD, Robert and Mary Jennery, 11 October 1680, Braintree, Mass.
FIELD, Sarah and Jonathan Whitehead, 23 July 1696, New York.
FIELDING, Nicholas and Deborah Cooley, 9 August 1694, New York.
FIFIELD, Mary and Samuel Haines, 17 January 1673, Hampton, N. H.
FILLEY, Anne and Samuel Grant, 6 December 1683, Windsor, Conn.
FILLEY, Elizabeth and Davis Winchell, 17 November 1669, Windsor, Conn.
FILLEY, Jonathan and Deborah Loomis, January 1679, Windsor, Conn.
FILLEY, Mary and Joseph Skinner, 5 April 1666, Windsor, Conn.
FILLEY, Samuel and Anna Gillet, 29 October 1663, Windsor, Conn.
FILLEY, William and Margaret, 2 September 1642, Simsbury, Conn.
FILLY, Abigail and John Bissell, 26 August 1680, Windsor, Conn.
FINCH, Abigail and Samuel Blachley, 6 April 1699, Stamford, Conn.
FINCH, John and Hester Davis, 25 March 1693, New York.
FINCHER, Mary and Christopher Sibthorpe, 26 February 1689, Philadelphia, Penn.
FINICONIE, William and Patience Betterworth, 12 September 1695, New York.
FINLISON, John and Mary Lookingglasse, 22 April 1692, New York City.
FINNEY, John and Mary Bryant, 14 June 1693, Plymouth, Mass.
FINNEY, Jonathan and Joana Kinnecut, 18 October 1682, Bristol, R. I.
FINNEY, Joshua and Mercy Watts, 31 May 1688, Bristol, R. I.
FINNEY, Jeremiah and Esther Lewis, 7 January 1684, Bristol, R. I.
FIRMAN, Rachel and Timothy Hancock, 1684, Burlington Co., N. J.
FISEN, Ann and Joshua Rogers, 12 August 1653, Boston, Mass.
FISHER, Abia and Benjamin Coalburne, 5 March 1684-5, Dedham, Mass.

FISHER, Abigail and John Houlton, 1 March 1667, Dedham, Mass.

FISHER, Abigail and John Baker, 17 December 1668, Dedham, Mass.

FISHER, Abigail and Daniel Farrington, 5 October 1691, Wrentham, Mass.

FISHER, Amos and Mary Ellice, 12 January 1678-9, Dedham, Mass.

FISHER, Amos and Ruth Adams, 22 December 1691, Dedham, Mass.

FISHER, Anthony and Johanna Faxin, 7 July 1647, Dedham, Mass.

FISHER, Anthony and Mrs. Edward Breck (widow), 14 September 1663, Dorchester, Mass.

FISHER, Bethia and John Pepper, 25 August 1669, Dedham, Mass.

FISHER, Cornelius and Leah Heaton, 22 December 1652, Dedham, Mass.

FISHER, Cornelius and Sarah Everitt, 25 July 1665, Dedham, Mass.

FISHER, Daniel and Abigail Marriott, 17 September 1641, Dedham, Mass.

FISHER, Daniel and Mary Fuller, 19 November 1673, Dedham, Mass.

FISHER, Deborath and James Fales, 28 August 1679, Dedham, Mass.

FISHER, Easter and Timothy Dwight, 31 July 1690, Dedham, Mass.

FISHER, Ebenezer and Abigail Elles, 7 February 1695, Wrentham, Mass.

FISHER, Eleazer and Hannah Lenard, 21 March 1688, Wrentham, Mass.

FISHER, Eleazer and Mary Avery, 13 October 1698, Dedham, Mass.

FISHER, Eleazer and Hannah Eddy, 24 December 1696, Norton, Mass.

FISHER, Elizabeth and John Elles, March 1686, Wrentham, Mass.

FISHER, Elizabeth and Jonathan Wight, 19 April 1687, Suffolk Co., Mass.

FISHER, Esther and Thomas Fuller, Jr., 25 April 1688, Milton, Mass.

FISHER, John and Rebecca Ellis, 15 April 1681, Dedham, Mass.

FISHER, John and Barbary Morton, 1 June 1695, New York.

FISHER, Joshua and Mary Aldis, 15 January 1643, Dedham, Mass.

FISHER, Joshua and Liddia Oliver, 16 December 1653, Dedham, Mass.

FISHER, Josiah and Joanna Morse, 1 September 1693, Dedham, Mass.

FISHER, Josiath and Meletiah Bulling, 27 November 1679, Dedham, Mass.

FISHER, Lydia and Nathaniel Chickering, 3 October 1673, Dedham, Mass.

FISHER, Mary and Thomas Battaly, 5 July 1648, Dedham, Mass.

FISHER, Mary and Thomas Clap, 10 September 1662, Dedham, Mass.

FISHER, Mary and John Gay, 24 May 1692, Dedham, Mass.

FISHER, Mary and John Huntting, 23 February 1697-8, Dedham, Mass.

FISHER, Meletiah and Eleazer Medcalf, 9 April 1684, Wrentham, Mass.

FISHER, Nathaniell and Easter Hunting, 26 October 1649, Dedham, Mass.

FISHER, Rebecca and Edward Gay, 25 March 1688, Wrentham, Mass.

FISHER, Ruth and John Potter, 2 June 1664, Warwick, R. I.

FISHER, Sammuell and Millatiah Snow, 22 January 1659, Dedham, Mass.

FISHER, Samuel and Milcha Snow, 22 March 1659, Boston, Mass.

FISHER, Samuel and Abigail Heath, 9 April 1684, Wrentham, Mass.

FISHER, Sarah and John Guild, 22 March 1677, Dedham, Mass.

FISHER, Sarah and Benjamin Hall, 9 January 1691, Wrentham, Mass.

FISHER, Susannah and Joseph Smith, 17 August 1698, Dedham, Mass.

FISHER, Thomas and Rebecca Woodward, 11 December 1666, Dedham, Mass.

FISHER, Vigalence and Hannah Lyon, 14 April 1696, Dorchester, Mass.

FISHER, Vigilance and Rebeccah Partridge, 27 September 1678, Dedham, Mass.

FISHER, William and Bridget Hodgkins, 7 February 1687, Philadelphia, Penn.

FISHER, William and Ann Barsley, 1 August 1696, New York.

FISK, Anna and Timothy Carter, 3 May 1680, Lexington, Mass.

FISK, Joseph and Elizabeth Haman, 22 May 1677, Lynn, Mass.

FISK, Nathan and Elizabeth Fry, 26 February 1665, Dorchester, Mass.

FISK, William and Sarah Kilham, 15 January 1662, Wenham, Mass.

FISKE, Bridget (widow) and Thomas Rix, November 1661, Salem, Mass.

FISKE, David, Jr., and Seeborn Wilson, 6 September 1655, Ipswich, Mass.

FISKE, Moses and Sarah Symmes, 7 September 1672, Braintree, Mass.

FISKE, Nathan and Sarah Coolidge, 14 October 1696, Watertown, Mass.

FISKE, Sarah and John Fairebanck, 16 January 1641, Dedham, Mass.

FISKE, William and Bridget Muskett, 1643, Salem, Mass.

FITCH, Benjamin and Mary Hett, 2 March 1693, Boston, Mass.

FITCH, Bridget and Jonathan Poole, 1691, Reading, Mass.

FITCH, Daneil and Mary Sherwood, March 1698, Fairfield, Conn.

FITCH, Dorothy and Nathaniel Bissell, 4 July 1689, Windsor, Conn.

FITCH, Hannah and Rev. Edward Taylor, 5 September 1674, Westfield, Mass.

FITCH, Hannah and Joseph Brown, 10 November 1680, Rehoboth, Mass.

FITCH, James (Rev.) and Priscilla Mason, October 1664, Windham, Mass.

FITCH, John and Abigail Whitfield, 1 October 1648, Saybrook, Conn.

FITCH, John (Capt.) and Elizabeth Waterman, 10 July 1695, Windham, Conn.

FITCH, John and Mary Coyte (widow), 3 October 1667, Gloucester, Mass.

FITCH, John and Rebecca Lindall, 3 December 1674, Norwalk, Conn.

FITCH, Jeremiah and Martha Messenger, 5 September 1689, Boston, Mass.

FITCH, Joseph and Anne Kibbe, 29 June 1688, Reading, Mass.

FITCH, Sarah and John Stoughton, 23 January 1689, Hartford, Conn.

FITCH, Sarah and Thomas Warren, 14 December 1694, Boston, Mass.

FITCH, Thomas and Abiel Daunforth, 12 April 1694, Boston, Mass.

FITCHUE, Robert and Hannah Man, 4 April 1695, Boston, Mass.

FITTSRANDOLPHE, Edward and Elizabeth Blossom, 10 May 1637, Scituate, Mass.

FITZGERALD, James and Elizabeth Bullier, 28 April 1678, Saybrook, Conn.

FITZRANDOLPH, Benjamin and Sarah Dennis, July 1689, New Brunswick, N. J.

FITZRANDOLPH, Edward and Mary Holley, November 1662, Woodbridge, N. J.

FITZRANDOLPH, Elizabeth and Andrew Wooden, 22 August 1676, Piscataway, N. J.

FITZRANDOLPH, Elizabeth (widow) and John Pike, 30 June 1685, Woodbridge, N. J.

FITZRANDOLPH, John and Sarah Bonham, 1 October 1681, Piscataway, N. J.

FITZRANDOLPH, Joseph and Hannah Conger, 16 January 1688, Woodbridge, N. J.

FITZRANDOLPH, Nathaniel and Grace Hill, 23 April 1692, Woodbridge, N. J.

FITZRANDOLPH, Ruth and Stephen Tuttle, 12 September 1695, New Haven, Conn.

FITZRANDOLPH, Samuel and Mary Jones, 8 June 1693, Woodbridge, N. J.

FITZWATER, Thomas and Elizabeth Palmer, 3 April 1684, Philadelphia, Penn.

FIZE, Daniel and Sarah Lambert, 6 November 1699, Boston, Mass.

FLACK, John and Mary Varney, 23 December 1693, Boston, Mass.

FLAGG, Gershom and Hannah Leffingwell, 15 April 1668, Woburn, Mass.

FLANDERS, Stephen and Abigail Carter, 28 December 1670, Salisbury, Mass.

FLETCHER, Francis and Elizabeth Wheeler, 11 October 1656, Concord, Mass.

FLETCHER, Joseph and Mary Dudley, 17 June 1688, Concord, Mass.

FLETCHER, Mary and Thomas Stevens, 1650, Milford, Conn.

FLETCHER, Robert and Susanna Worthileg, 13 January 1697, Boston, Mass.

FLETCHER, Sarah and Nathaniel Butterfield, 18 January 1697, Chelmsford, Mass.

FLETCHER, William and Lydia Bates, 11 November 1645, Concord, Mass.

FLINT, Anna and Timothy Dwight, 9 November 1664, Dedham, Mass.

FLINT, Hannah and John Dassitt, 15 September 1662, Braintree, Mass.

FLINT, John and Mary Oakes, 12 November 1667, Concord, Mass.

FLINTBURG, John and Margaret Rodoffsen, 16 May 1687, New York.

FLIPSEN, Samuel and Aeltje Damen, 29 October 1695, Brooklyn, N. Y.

FLOOD, Joseph and Joanna Mitchill, 10 March 1698, Boston, Mass.

FLOOD, Lydia (widow) and Joseph Gridley, 9 June 1654, Boston, Mass.

FLOOD, Lydia and Samuel Earl, 20 April 1694, Boston, Mass.

FLOOD, Richard and Eliza Harmon, 1 December 1691, Boston, Mass.

FLOWER, Hannah and Thomas Fuller, 22 September 1643, Dedham, Mass.

FLOYD, Daniel and Mary Hallewel, 18 January 1697, Boston, Mass.

FLOYD, Jannettie and Gilbert Marriner, 31 March 1694, New York.

FLUSTER, Jane and Richard Haskins, 2 August 1686, Taunton, Mass.

FLYNT, Dorothy and Samuel Shepperd, 30 February 1666, Braintree, Mass.

FLYNT, Joana and Noah Numan, 30 October 1669, Braintree, Mass.

FOGG, Daniel and Hannah Libbey, 1684, Scarborough, Maine.

FOGG, James and Mary Barringer, 9 January 1695, Hampton, N. H.

FOGG, Samuel and Anne Shaw, 12 November 1652, York Co., Maine.

FOGG, Samuel and Mary Page, 1662, Hampton, N. H.

FOGG, Samuel and Hannah Marston, 19 November 1676, York Co., Maine.

FOLKES, Hannah and Anthony Woodward, 3 December 1686, Chesterfield, N. J.

FOLLANSBEE, Rebecca and Thomas Chase, 22 November 1677, Newbury, Mass.

FOLLE, Ann and Paul Saunders, 30 April 1699, Philadelphia, Penn.

FOLLET, Abigail and Andrew Wiggin, 2 September 1697, Dover, N. H.

FOLLETT, Robert and Persis Black, 29 July 1655, Salem, Mass.

FONDA, Geertie and Tennis Slingerland, 9 April 1684, Albany, N. Y.

FONDA, Jellis A. and Hester Wynne, 1695, Albany, N. Y.

FONES, Mary and James Greene, Jr., 29 January 1688-9, Warwick, R. I.

FORBEE, John and Penelope Leigh, 4 December 1699, Boston, Mass.

FORCE, Elizabeth and Samuel Smith, 8 January 1692, Woodbridge, N. J.

FORCE, Mark and Deborah Maccane, 13 October 1698, Wrentham, Mass.

FORCE, Mathew and Elizabeth Palmer, April 1667, Gravesend, N. Y.

FORD, Ann and Thomas Newberry, 12 March 1676, Windsor, Conn.

FORD, Deborah and Samuel Daniel, 14 March 1694, Boston, Mass.

FORD, Elizabeth and Joshua Culver, 23 December 1672, New Haven, Conn.

FORD, Joana and Roger Clap, 6 November 1633, Dorchester, Mass.

FORD, Joana and John Rockwood, 15 July 1662, Braintree, Mass.

FORD, Martin and Lydia Griffing, 5 March 1684, Bradford, Mass.

FORD, Mary and Nathaniel Thorpe, 20 November 1662, New Haven, Conn.

FORD, Mathew and Mary Brooks, 12 July 1674, Wallingford, Conn.

FORD, Millicent and John Carver, 4 November 1658, Duxbury, Mass.

FORDHAM, Joseph and Mary Maltby, 5 December 1689, Southampton, L. I., N. Y.

FORLISSON, John and Anne Mool, 5 July 1699, New York.

FORMAN, Thomas and Mary Allen, 27 May 1695, Monmouth Co., N. J.
FORSYTHE, Mathew and Rebecca Odling, 5 September 1696, Chesterfield, N. J.
FORT, Abram and Hannah Hutchinson (widow), 18 November 1655, Boston, Mass.
FOSDICK, John and Anna Shapley, 1648, Charlestown, Mass.
FOSDICK, Samuel and Mercy Pickett, 1 November 1682, New London, Conn.
FOSTER, Abraham and Ester Foster, 13 July 1681, Andover, Mass.
FOSTER, Andrew and Mary Ruse, 7 June 1662, Andover, Mass.
FOSTER, Bartholomew and Hannah Very, 9 November 1669, Gloucester, Mass.
FOSTER, Eliza and Christopher Killiowe, 28 May 1694, Boston, Mass.
FOSTER, Elizabeth and William Carver, 18 January 1682, Marshfield, Mass.
FOSTER, Elizabeth and Isaac Virgoose, 5 July 1692, Boston, Mass.
FOSTER, Elisha and Sarah Payson, 10 April 1678, Dorchester, Mass.
FOSTER, Esther and Abraham Foster, 13 July 1681, Andover, Mass.
FOSTER, Hannah and Hugh Stone, 15 October 1667, Andover, Mass.
FOSTER, Hannah and Thomas Astin, 15 September 1690, Andover, Mass.
FOSTER, Isaac and Abigail Carroll, 25 November 1678, Ipswich, Mass.
FOSTER, James and Mary Capin, 22 September 1674, Dorchester, Mass.
FOSTER, James and Anna Lane, 7 October 1680, Dorchester, Mass.
FOSTER, John and Martha Tompkins, 1648, Salem, Mass.
FOSTER, John and Mary Stuard, 18 March 1672, Salem, Mass.
FOSTER, John and Abigail Kellond, 28 November 1689, Boston, Mass.
FOSTER, John and Mary Pomeroy, 12 July 1692, Salem, Mass.
FOSTER, Mary and Lawrence Lay, 5 August 1673, Andover, Mass.
FOSTER, Mary and Samuel Kilburn, 20 November 1682, Rowley, Mass.
FOSTER, Mary and Ebenezer Lovejoy, 11 July 1693, Andover, Mass.
FOSTER, Mary and Timothy Nash, 2 April 1694, Boston, Mass.
FOSTER, Reginald and Sarah Martin, September 1665, Ipswich, Mass.
FOSTER, Relefe and Henrie Leadbetter, 9 March 1691-2, Dorchester, Mass.
FOSTER, Samuel and Easter Kemp, 15 September 1648, Dedham, Mass.
FOSTER, Sarah and Ebenezar Wiswel, 26 March 1685, Dorchester, Mass.
FOSTER, Sarah and John Caldwell, 1 May 1689, Ipswich, Mass.
FOSTER, Silence and John Clap, 26 May 1698, Dorchester, Mass.
FOSTER, Timothy and Ruth Denton, 13 October 1663, Dorchester, Mass.
FOSTER, Thankful and John Baker, 8 November 1663, Dorchester, Mass.
FOSTER, Timothy and Relief Dous, 9 March 1681, Dorchester, Mass.
FOSTER, William and Mary Jackson, 15 May 1661, Ipswich, Mass.
FOTHERGILL, Mary and Christopher Wetherill, 8 April 1687, Burlington, N. J.
FOULGER, Abiah and Josiah Franklin, 25 November 1689, Boston, Mass.
FOULKE, Thomas, Jr., and Elizabeth Curtis, 7 December 1688, Chesterfield, N. J.
FOUL, Mary and Job Hilliard, 4 July 1693, Boston, Mass.
FOWLE, Catherine and Timothy Kimball, 18 August 1699, Boston, Mass.
FOWLE, John and Elizabeth Prescott, 27 September 1678, Concord, Mass.
FOWLER, Ambrose and Jane Alvord, 6 May 1646, Windsor, Conn.
FOWLER, Mary and John Beere, 20 January 1673, Gloucester, Mass.
FOWLER, Mary and John Sherbutt, 14 September 1697, Anne Arundel Co., Md.
FOWLER, Patience and John Harker, 14 December 1680, Boston, Mass.
FOWLER, Phillip and Mary Norton, 27 February 1659, Ipswich, Mass.
FOWLER, Sarah and John Griffin, 3 August 1695, Anne Arundel Co., Md.
FOWLER, Thomas and Hannah Jordan, 23 April 1660, Ipswich, Mass.

FOWLES, Dorothy and Francis Parnell, 15 August 1692, Boston, Mass.
FOX, David and Lydia Jaquith, 10 January 1678, Woburn, Mass.
FOX, Eliphalet and Mary Wheeler, 26 October 1665, Concord, Mass.
FOX, Eliphalet and Mary Stone Hunt (widow), 30 April 1681, Sudbury, Mass.
FOX, Elizabeth and John Ball, 3 October 1665, Concord, Mass.
FOX, Elizabeth and George Newby, 7 February 1693, Charlestown, Mass.
FOX, Hanna and Thomas Loomis, 1 November 1653, Windsor, Conn.
FOX, Isaac and Abigail Osborn, 18 May 1678, Billerica, Mass.
FOX, James, Jr., and Ann Wills, 31 January 1699, Philadelphia, Penn.
FOX, Samuel and Ruth Knight, 13 June 1693, Concord, Mass.
FOX, Thomas and Hannah Brooks, 13 October 1647, Concord, Mass.
FOX, Thomas and Ellen Green (widow), 24 May 1650, Cambridge, Mass.
FOX, Thomas and Elizabeth Chadwick, 24 April 1683, Watertown, Mass.
FOX, Thomas and Rebecca Wythe (widow), 16 December 1685, Cambridge, Mass.
FOX, Thomas and Esther Jarvise, 21 March 1690, Boston, Mass.
FOXHALL, Martha and Samuel Bacon, 9 May 1659, Barnstable, Mass.
FOXWELL, Mary and James Cole, 8 January 1654, Barnstable, Mass.
FOY, John and Sarah Lynde, 16 November 1699, Boston, Mass.
FRAMPTON, Elizabeth and Richard Basnett, 30 September 1688, Philadelphia, Penn.
FRANCIS, Demaris and Joseph Clark, 19 August 1675, Braintree, Mass.
FRANCIS, Hannah and Dennis Darling, 3 November 1662, Braintree, Mass.
FRANCIS, John and Mary Savoy, 19 December 1698, Elizabeth City Co., Va.
FRANCIS, William and Janacay Avens, 2 August 1684, Staten Island, N. Y.
FRANCIS, William and Triphena Yelling, 29 April 1699, Boston, Mass.
FRANCKLINE, Elizabeth and George May, 6 August 1656, Boston, Mass.
FRANKLIN, Josiah and Abiah Faulger, 25 November 1689, Boston, Mass.
FRANKLIN, Martha and William Phillips, Jr., 24 August 1650, Boston, Mass.
FRANKLIN, Richard and Abigail Stanbury, 29 September 1697, Boston, Mass.
FRANKLIN, Sarah and William Horn, 28 October 1697, Anne Arundel Co., Md.
FRANKS, Sarah and Abigail Sherman, 12 July 1694, Boston, Mass.
FRAREY, Theophilus and Mary Greenwood, 12 June 1690, Boston, Mass.
FRERY, Theophilus and Hannah Elliott, 4 April 1653, Boston, Mass.
FREAKE, John and Elizabeth Clarke, 28 May 1661, Boston, Mass.
FREEK, Mary and Josiah Wilcot, 1 May 1694, Boston, Mass.
FREAKS, Henry and Mary, August 1691, Somerset Co., Md.
FREDRICKSEN, Katherine and John Wicken, 28 April 1693, New York.
FREEMAN, Henry and Elizabeth Bonue, 16 May 1695, Woodbridge, N. J.
FREEMAN, John and Rachel Moody, 7 July 1671, Somerset Co., Md.
FREEMAN, Joseph and Mary Robbins, 14 February 1673, Somerset Co., Md.
FREEMAN, Nathaniel and Alice Penuel, 18 January 1699, Boston, Mass.
FREEMAN, Ralph and Katharine Lion, 21 October 1652, Dedham, Mass.
FREEMAN, Sarah and Thomas Judd, 1668, Milford, Conn.
FRENCH, Dependance and Rebeccah Fenno, 27 April 1688, Milton, Mass.
FRENCH, Dorcas and Christopher Peake, 3 January 1636, Roxbury, Mass.
FRENCH, Elizabeth and Richard Ellice, 19 July 1650, Dedham, Mass.
FRENCH, Hannah and John Brackett, 6 July 1661, Braintree, Mass.
FRENCH, Hannah and Thomas Philbrick, 22 July 1669, Hampton, N. H.
FRENCH, Hannah and John Child, 5 September 1693, Boston, Mass.

FRENCH, John and Mary Palmer, 27 November 1678, Rehoboth, Mass.
FRENCH, John and Mary White, 30 August 1694, Shrewsbury, N. J.
FRENCH, Nathanial and Mary Tisdale, 9 January 1677, Taunton, Mass.
FRENCH, Thomas and Mary Adams, 29 February 1659, Ipswich, Mass.
FRENCH, Thomas and Elizabeth Stanton, 25 July 1696, Philadelphia, Penn.
FRENCH, Thomas, Jr., and Mary Allen, 3 October 1696, Shrewsbury, N. J.
FRETWELL, Better and Elizabeth Wright, 6 September 1687, Chesterfield, N. J.
FRETWELL, Rebecca and John Warren, May 1688, Chesterfield, N. J.
FRINK, Hannah and William Parke, 3 December 1684, Preston, Conn.
FRINK, Judith and Daniel Young, 12 January 1699, New London, Conn.
FRISBEE, John and Ruth Barnes, 20 December 1674, Branford, Conn.
FRISSEL, John and Dorothy Parnel, 22 July 1698, Boston, Mass.
FRISSELL, Joseph and Abigail Bartholomew, 11 January 1691-2, Woodstock, Conn.
FRISTOW, Robert and Jane Sherman, 1 August 1675, Richmond Co., Va.
FRIZELL, Mary and John Jordon, 4 October 1699, Boston, Mass.
FROMANTEEL, Ann and Francis Chappell, 27 November 1695, New York.
FROST, Charles and Mary Bowles, 1666, Wells, Maine.
FROST, Charles and Sarah Wainwright, 7 February 1698-9, Haverhill, Mass.
FROST, Hannah and John Thorpe, 1684, Fairfield, Conn.
FROST, Jasper and Elizabeth Wakefield, 20 August 1660, Boston, Mass.
FROST, Kathrine and William Leighton, June 1656, Kittery, Maine.
FROST, Mary and John Hendirckson, 12 September 1692, New York City.
FROST, Mary and John Hill, 12 December 1694, York Co., Maine.
FROST, Mehetable and Thomas Linkoln, 3 August 1689, Boston, Mass.
FROST, Mehitable and Thomas Pearce, 5 January 1698, York Co., Maine.
FRY, Benjamin and Mary Parker, 23 May 1678, Andover, Mass.
FRY, Elizabeth and Robert Stilman, 4 October 1660, Andover, Mass.
FRY, Elizabeth and Nathan Fisk, 26 February 1665, Dorchester, Mass.
FRY, John and Elizabeth Hummery, 18 June 1695, Bristol, R. I.
FRY, James and Lydia Osgood, 20 January 1679, Andover, Mass.
FRY, John and Eunice Potter, 4 October 1660, Andover, Mass.
FRY, John and Martha Farnum, 1 November 1694, Andover, Mass.
FRY, Mary and Joseph Stevens, 22 December 1696, Andover, Mass.
FRY, Phoebe and Samuel Peters, 15 December 1696, Andover, Mass.
FRY, Samuel and Mary Aslett, 20 November 1671, Andover, Mass.
FRY, Thomas and Welthian Greene, 1 February 1688, East Greenwich, R. I.
FRYBY, John and Mary Tucker, 5 June 1699, Elizabeth City Co., Va.
FULLER, Abner and Mary H. Crofut, 16 July 1667, Berlin, Conn.
FULLER, Amos and Catherine Smith, 26 June 1694, Guilderland, N. Y.
FULLER, Elizabeth and John Kingsbury, 29 November 1666, Dedham, Mass.
FULLER, Elizabeth and James King, 23 March 1674, Ipswich, Mass.
FULLER, Elizabeth and Samuel Eaton, 24 May 1694, Middleborough, Mass.
FULLER, Experience and James Wood, 12 April 1693, Middleborough, Mass.
FULLER, Hannah and Nicholas Bonham, 1 January 1659, Barnstable, Mass.
FULLER, John and Deborah Ring, 7 February 1622, Plymouth, Mass.
FULLER, John and Elizabeth Emerson, 31 May 1652, Ipswich, Mass.
FULLER, John and Abigail Boylston, 30 June 1668, Framingham, Mass.
FULLER, John and Judith Gay, 8 November 1672, Dedham, Mass.

FULLER, John and Sarah Mills, 27 June 1678, Dedham, Mass.

FULLER, Joseph and Rebecca Belcher, 30 November 1687, Lynn, Mass.

FULLER, Lydia and Joseph Dimmock, 12 May 1699, Barnstable, Mass.

FULLER, Margaret and James King, 10 March 1674, Ipswich, Mass.

FULLER, Mary and Daniel Fisher, 19 November 1673, Dedham, Mass.

FULLER, Rachel and Joseph Bent, 27 October 1698, Dedham, Mass.

FULLER, Samuel and Jane Lathrop, 8 April 1635, Scituate, Mass.

FULLER, Samuel and Mary Ide, 12 December 1673, Rehoboth, Mass.

FULLER, Samuel and Mercy Eaton, 7 January 1685, Plymouth, Mass.

FULLER, Sarah and Ralph Day, 6 October 1682, Dedham, Mass.

FULLER, Susanne and William Story, 25 October 1671, Ipswich, Mass.

FULLER, Thomas and Elizabeth Tidd, 13 June 1643, Woburn, Mass.

FULLER, Thomas and Hannah Flower, 22 September 1643, Dedham, Mass.

FULLER, Thomas and Sarah Wyman, 25 August 1684, Woburn, Mass.

FULLER, Thomas, Jr., and Esther Fisher, 25 April 1688, Milton, Mass.

FUNEILE, Benjamin and Anna Du Boy, July 1699, New York.

FURBER, Elizabeth and John Dam, Jr. (second wife), 9 November 1664, Dover, N. H.

FURBER, William and Elizabeth Nute (widow), 13 August 1694, Dover, N. H.

FURNALD, Sarah and Allen Lyde, 3 December 1661, Dover, N. H.

FURNEL, Olive and John Smallpeice, 7 April 1699, Boston, Mass.

FURNELL, Elinor (widow) and Michaell Lambert, October 1659, Boston, Mass.

FURNIS, Sarah and John Bennett, 6 February 1683, Somerset Co., Md.

FURS, John and Jane Wilson, 21 September 1698, Boston, Mass.

FUTCHER, William and Mary King, 16 November 1672, Somerset Co., Md.

FYLER, John and Elizabeth Dolman, 17 October 1672, Windsor, Conn.

FYLER, Zernabel and Experience Strong, 27 May 1669, Windsor, Conn.

FYNHOUT, Cornelis and Neettjie Aerstsen, 6 June 1667, Esopus, N. Y.

G

GAGE, Naomi and Stephen Bedford, 15 February 1693, Bristol, R. I.

GAGER, Elizabeth and John Allyn, 24 December 1668, New London, Conn.

GAINES, John and Mary Treadwell, 1659, Ipswich, Mass.

GAINES, Martha and Benjamin Edwards, 14 May 1687, Wenham, Mass.

GAINES, Samuel and Ann Wright, 7 April 1665, Lynn, Mass.

GAITHER, Ruth and John Warfield, 16 February 1690, South River, Md.

GALE, Alce and James Marsh, 14 July 1699, Anne Arundel Co., Md.

GALE, Aliza and William Porter, 31 January 1694, Boston, Mass.

GALLAIS, Mary and Stephen Vallou, 19 November 1692, New York.

GALLEY, Mary and John Ross, 9 May 1661, Ipswich, Mass.

GALLOP, Benjamin and Hannah Sharp, 1 November 1694, Boston, Mass.

GALLOP, John, Jr., and Hannah Lake, 1643, Boston, Mass.

GALLOP, Joseph and Elizabeth Dwight, 1 March 1694, Boston, Mass.

GALLOP, Nathaniel and Margaret Eueley, 11 April 1652, Boston, Mass.

GALLOP, Samuel and Mary Phillips, 20 December 1650, Boston, Mass.

GALLOWAY, Benjamin and Elizabeth Hodgdon, 31 January 1699, York Co., Maine.

GALLUP, Samuel and Elizabeth Southworth, 12 May 1685, Bristol, R. I.

GAMMON, Grace and John Stevens, 6 June 1694, Boston, Mass.

GANNET, Sarah and William Savill, 9 June 1655, Braintree, Mass.

GANSON, Elizabeth and Nathaniel Prisbury, 16 February 1698, Boston, Mass.

GARDENER, Samuel and Eliza Goodwin, 11 May 1693, Boston, Mass.

GARDINER, Elizabeth and James Parshall, 1678, Easthampton, N. Y.

GARDNER, Annie and Joseph Cantrill, 13 December 1697, Boston, Mass.

GARDNER, Deborah and George Colton, 1640, Hartford, Conn.

GARDNER, James and Elizabeth Vinson, 19 January 1662, Gloucester, Mass.

GARDNER, John and Priscella Sanders, 20 February 1654, Salem, Mass.

GARDNER, John and Elizabeth Walter, 3 April 1684, Philadelphia, Penn.

GARDNER, Margaret and Obadiah Procter, 24 August 1699, Boston, Mass.

GARFIELD, Edward and Johanna Buckmaster, 1 July 1661, Watertown, Mass.

GARFIELD, Benjamin and Elizabeth Bridge, 19 January 1678, Watertown, Mass.

GARMINE, Elizabeth and Joseph Randall, 20 October 1692, Dover, N. H.

GARNER, George and Tabitha Tiffe, 13 February 1670, Warwick, R. I.

GARNET, John and Mary Stowell, 25 February 1683, Hingham, Mass.

GARRESON, Edward and Joan Pullen, 29 August 1660, Boston, Mass.

GARRET, Hannah and John Wiatt, 7 February 1694, Boston, Mass.

GARRETSON, John and Alice Willey, 5 December 1659, Boston, Mass.

GARRETT, Hannah and George Emlen, 25 March 1694, Philadelphia, Penn.

GARWOOD, Martin and Priscilla Sherman, 25 March 1658, Dedham, Mass.

GARWOOD, Priscilla (widow) and William Smith, 11 September 1683, Dedham, Mass.

GARWOOD, Thomas, Jr., and Jane White, 28 July 1693, Shrewsbury, N. J.

GARY, Nathaniel and Ann Douglass, 14 October 1658, Roxbury, Mass.

GARY, Nathaniel and Mary Rice, 12 November 1684, Roxbury, Mass.

GATCHEL, Elizabeth and Israel Woodcock, 5 September 1682, Dedham, Mass.
GATES, Thomas and Margaret Geer, December 1695, Preston, Conn.
GATLIVE, Prudence and Solomon Curtis, 11 April 1673, Braintree, Mass.
GAULTIER, Joanna and John Blanchard, 28 June 1695, New York.
GAURD, Maria and William Gayer, 4 July 1690, Boston, Mass.
GAWDREN, Mary (widow) and Edmond Jackson, 7 November 1652, Boston Mass.
GAY, Abiel and Daniel Haws, 23 November 1677, Dedham, Mass.
GAY, Edward and Rebecca Fisher, 25 March 1688, Wrentham, Mass.
GAY, Elizabeth and Richard Martine, July 1660, Boston, Mass.
GAY, Johanna and Nathaniel Whiting, 29 March 1664, Dedham, Mass.
GAY, John and Rebecca Bacon, 13 February 1678, Dedham, Mass.
GAY, John and Mary Fisher, 24 May 1692, Dedham, Mass.
GAY, Jonathan and Mary Bullard, 29 June 1682, Dedham, Mass.
GAY, Judith and John Fuller, 8 November 1672, Dedham, Mass.
GAY, Lydia and Thomas Eaton, 5 October 1697, Dedham, Mass.
GAY, Mary and Jabez Pond, 11 January 1698-9, Dedham, Mass.
GAY, Samuell and Mary Bridge, 23 November 1661, Dedham, Mass.
GAYER, William and Maria Gaurd, 4 July 1690, Boston, Mass.
GAYLAR, Anne and Isaac Phelps, 11 March 1664, Windsor, Conn.
GAYLAR, Joana and John Porter, Jr., 16 December 1669, Windsor, Conn.
GAYLER, Elizabeth and Daniel Birg, 5 October 1641, Windsor, Conn.
GAYLORD, Ann and George Phelps, 11 May 1663, Windsor, Conn.
GAYLORD, Sarah and John Alexander, 18 November 1671, Windsor, Conn.
GAYLORD, William and Anne Porter, 24 February 1641, Windsor, Conn.
GAYLORD, William and Elizabeth Drake, 17 November 1653, Windsor, Conn.
GEE, Joshua and Eliza Harrise, 25 September 1688, Boston, Mass.
GEARS, Joseph and Sarah Howard, 7 January 1692, Preston, Conn.
GEARY, Sarah and John Fairfield, 26 March 1666, Wenham, Mass.
GEER, George and Sarah Allyn, 17 February 1658, New London, Conn.
GEER, Margaret and Thomas Gates, December 1695, New London, Conn.
GEERY, Elizabeth and William Abbott, 19 June 1682, Andover, Mass.
GEERY, Sarah and John Holt, 3 July 1685, Andover, Mass.
GENERY, Lambert and Thamasen Hews, 14 March 1658, Dedham, Mass.
GENNES, Hannah and Thomas Martyn, 22 December 1662, Brooklyn, N. Y.
GENOUR, Jan and Grietje Sueden, 13 August 1664, Harlem, N. Y.
GENT, Mary and Tobias Green, 17 November 1699, Boston, Mass.
GEORGE, John and Hannah Grover, 22 August 1699, Boston, Mass.
GEORGE, John and Frances Servant, 16 June 1696, Elizabeth City Co., Va.
GEORGE, Mary and James Bird, 6 February 1669, Dorchester, Mass.
GEORGE, Mary and Ebenezer Holmes, 5 August 1697, Dorchester, Mass.
GEORGE, Nicholas and Mary Wales, 4 June 1684, Dorchester, Mass.
GEORGE, Richard and Mary Pell, 1 September 1655, Boston, Mass.
GERRISH, Elizabeth and John Wade, 3 September 1696, Dover, N. H.
GERRISH, John and Lydia Watts, 19 April 1692, Boston, Mass.
GERITSE, Elizabeth and John Anthony, 18 October 1693, New York.
GERREARDY, Mary and Jeremiah Smith, 2 January 1672, Warwick, R. I.
GERRITSE, Hannah and John Peterson, 20 June 1693, New York.
GETHERCOLE, Lydia and Theophilus Burrell, 5 July 1694, Boston, Mass.

GIBB, Andrew and Hannah Smith, 13 April 1696, New York.

GIBBINS, Ruth and William Lawrence, 24 June 1686, Middletown, N. J.

GIBBONS, Anna and Samuel Sellers, 13 August 1684, Darby, Penn.

GIBBONS, Mary and Thomas Bowles, 17 November 1686, Philadelphia, Penn.

GIBBS, Abigail and Jireh Swift, 26 November 1697, Sandwich, Mass.

GIBBS, Ann and John Holstone, 7 August 1684, Philadelphia, Penn.

GIBBS, Catherine and William Trotter, 9 December 1652, Newbury, Mass.

GIBBS, Henry and Mercy Greenough, 9 June 1692, Boston, Mass.

GIBBS, Isaac and Hannah Dickinson, April 1696, Oyster Bay, N. Y.

GIBBS, Robert and Elizabeth Sheaffe, 7 September 1660, Boston, Mass.

GIBBS, Robert and Mary Shrimpton, 19 May 1692, Boston, Mass.

GIBSON, Benjamin and Mehitable Astin, 4 January 1699, Boston, Mass.

GIBSON, John and Joana Prentiss, 24 July 1662, Cambridge, Mass.

GIBSON, John and Hannah Underwood, 14 October 1680, Watertown, Mass.

GIBSON, Samuel and Elizabeth Stedman, 14 June 1679, Roxbury, Mass.

GIDDINGS, James and Elizabeth Andrews, 9 February 1681, Chebacco, Mass.

GIDINGS, Samuel and Elizabeth Sample, 8 November 1699, Boston, Mass.

GIFFORD, Phillip and Mary Davis, 30 June 1684, Lynn, Mass.

GILBERT, George and Jane Campell, 4 May 1698, New York.

GILBERT, Hannah and Joseph Parker, 3 June 1673, Saybrook, Conn.

GILBERT, John and Mary Eaton, 5 March 1653, Boston, Mass.

GILBERT, John and Elizabeth Kilham, 12 September 1677, Ipswich, Mass.

GILBERT, Mary and Jeremiah Horton, 5 May 1664, New Haven, Conn.

GILBERT, Thomas and Catherine Bliss (widow), 31 July 1655, Springfield, Mass.

GILBERT, Thomas and Catherine Chapin, 30 June 1655, Springfield, Mass.

GILBERT, Thomas and Abilene Marshfield, 15 August 1680, Springfield, Mass.

GILBERT, Thomas and Deborah Beamont, 27 September 1681, Saybrook, Conn.

GILBORD, Jan and Samuel Gullifer, 15 November 1675, Milton, Mass.

GILBOURNE, Francis and Mary Wickes, 9 June 1671, Warwick, R. I.

GILE, Samuel and Judith Davis, 1 September 1647, Haverhill, Mass.

GILES, John and Sarah Welsh, 1 October 1695, Anne Arundel Co., Md.

GILES, Thomas and Engeltie Davies, 6 July 1696, New York.

GILKISON, Mary and Peter Webster, 30 November 1695, Middletown, Penn.

GILL, Frances and Henry Boyen, 17 August 1656, Boston, Mass.

GILL, John and Elizabeth Parsons, 1 June 1698, Boston, Mass.

GILL, Samuel and Sarah Worth, 5 November 1678, Salisbury, Mass.

GILL, William and Eliza Scarlet, 3 May 1692, Boston, Mass.

GILLAM, Benjamine and Hannah Savage, 26 October 1660, Boston, Mass.

GILLAM, Zechariah and William Phillips, 26 July 1659, Boston, Mass.

GILLET, Abraham and Ezaya Bartlett, 3 December 1663, Windsor, Conn.

GILLET, Anna and Samuel Filley, 29 October 1663, Windsor, Conn.

GILLET, John and Elizabeth Perry (widow), 22 October 1653, Boston, Mass.

GILLET, John and Mary Barber, 8 July 1669, Windsor, Conn.

GILLET, Jonathan and Mary Kelsey, 23 April 1661, Windsor, Conn.

GILLET, Joseph and Elizabeth Hawkes, 1664, Windsor, Conn.

GILLET, Josiah and Johana Taintor, 30 June 1676, Windsor, Conn.

GILLET, Mary and Peter Brown, 15 July 1658, Windsor, Conn.

GILLET, Thomas and Jane Blades, 17 October 1685, Somerset Co., Md.

GILLETT, Joan and Josiah Strong, 6 January 1699, Windsor, Conn.

GILLETT, Mary and Joseph Moore, 15 July 1658, Windsor, Conn.
GILLETT, William and Susanna Mills, November 1674, Somerset Co., Md.
GILLETT, William and Mary Saxton, 14 September 1699, Simsbury, Conn.
GILLETT, Sarah and Elezer Hill, 29 December 1679, Simsbury, Conn.
GILLETTE, Mary and John Ives, 6 December 1693, Wallingford, Conn.
GILLING, Edward and Mary Thortes, 25 December 1696, Boston, Mass.
GILLOW, John and Sarah Keaser, 7 April 1666, Lynn, Mass.
GILMAN, Charles and Marie Bishop (widow), 9 January 1684, Woodbridge, N. J.
GILMAN, Marie (widow) and Benjamin Jones, 20 May 1692, Piscataway, N. J.
GILMAN, Nicholas and Sarah Clark, 10 June 1697, Newbury, N. H.
GILMAN, Philippa and Mathew Dorman, 19 August 1672, Somerset Co., Md.
GILMAN, Sarah and Richard Glidden, 1687, Gilmanton, N. H.
GILSON, Joseph and Mary Coper, 18 November 1660, Chelmsford, Mass.
GINOM, Jan and Grietie Snedinx, 12 August 1662, Brooklyn, N. Y.
GIPSON, Edward and Ruth Comer, 11 January 1699, Boston, Mass.
GIPSON, Jeremiah and Mary Hunter, 13 April 1698, Boston, Mass.
GISBERTZ, Theus and Thijntje Jans, 10 October 1655, New York.
GLADDING, John and Elizabeth Rogers, 17 July 1666, Newbury, Mass.
GLADDING, John and Alice Warden, 31 October 1693, Bristol, R. I.
GLANSHA, Margaret and Philip Demauzaday, 22 November 1682, Dorchester, Mass.
GLEAVE, Richard and Hana Philips, 15 August 1699, New York.
GLENN, Margaret and Richard Burt, 18 October 1697, New York.
GLENN, Maria and Albert Vedder, 17 December 1699, Schenectady, N. Y.
GLENN, Mary and James Blackwell, 18 April 1699, New Kent Co., Va.
GLIDDEN, Richard and Sarah Gilman, 1687, Gilmanton, N. H.
GLOVER, Elinor and Daniel Burr, 11 December 1678, New Haven, Conn.
GLOVER, Elizabeth and John Cleverly, 5 November 1696, Boston, Mass.
GLOVER, Habbacuke and Hannah Eliott, 4 March 1653, Boston, Mass.
GLOVER, Hannah and Thomas Evens, 10 March 1686, Dorchester, Mass.
GLOVER, Hannah and David Ashley, 24 November 1663, New Haven, Conn.
GLOVER, Hannah and Nathaniel Leonard, 9 January 1694, Middletown, N. J.
GLOVER, Henry and Mary Crehore, 31 March 1696, Milton, Mass.
GLOVER, Mary and Jeremiah King, 12 December 1698, New York.
GLOVER, Pelatiah and Hannah Cullick, 20 May 1660, Boston, Mass.
GLOVER, Sarah and Henry Short, 1648, Newbury, Mass.
GLOVER, Sarah and Robert Adams, 6 February 1678, Newbury, Mass.
GLOVER, Stephen and Ruth Stevens, 7 October 1663, Gloucester, Mass.
GODDARD, George and Judith Goodin, 14 July 1679, Somerset Co., Md.
GODDARD, John and Sarah Farrington, 1697, Lynn, Mass.
GODDARD, William and Eliza Fayrefield, 29 October 1697, Boston, Mass.
GODFREY, Elizabeth and James Bolen, 14 March 1699, New York.
GOFF, Eleanor and William Davison, 25 February 1699, New York.
GOFFE, Abia and Henry Wolcot, Jr., 12 October 1664, Windsor, Conn.
GOFFE, Abigail and Samuel Wentworth, 28 October 1699, Boston, Mass.
GOFFE, Hannah and John Moore, 21 September 1664, Windsor, Conn.
GOFFE, Sarah and John Foss, 25 January 1686, York Co., Maine.
GOFFE, Lydia and John Sprague, 2 May 1651, Malden, Mass.
GOFFE, Lydia and Edward Sprague, 11 April 1693, Malden, Mass.

GOLD, Benjamin and Mary Dinely, 5 May 1698, Boston, Mass.
GOLD, William and Mercy Harris, 16 April 1699, Boston, Mass.
GOLDEN, Winsor and Eliza Ingolsby, 14 May 1698, Boston, Mass.
GOLDSMITH, George and Ellen Harrison, 29 November 1696, Philadelphia, Penn.
GOLDSMITH, Martha and John Hall, 18 July 1693, Harford Co., Md.
GOLDTHWAITE, Samuel and Elizabeth Cheever, 6 September 1666, Charlestown, Mass.
GOODALE, Thomas and Sarah Horrell, 2 December 1698, Beverly, Mass.
GOODELL, Zachariah and Elizabeth Beauchamp, 30 April 1666, Salem, Mass.
GOODEN, Sarah and George Smedley, 24 April 1687, Philadelphia, Penn.
GOODENOW, John and Mary Axtell, 19 September 1656, Sudbury, Mass.
GOODENOW, Mary and James Ross, 5 December 1638, Sudbury, Mass.
GOODIN, Judith and George Goddard, 14 July 1679, Somerset Co., Md.
GOODING, James and Margaret Davenport, 23 January 1695, Boston, Mass.
GOODNOW, Elizabeth and Josiah Hayden, 6 March 1691, Sudbury, Mass.
GOODRICH, Elizabeth and Ephriam Darwin, 10 June 1678, Guilford, Conn.
GOODRIDGE, Jeremiah and Mary Adams, 15 November 1660, Newbury, Mass.
GOODRIDGE, Mary and Edward Woodman, 20 December 1653, Newbury, Mass.
GOODSELL, Thomas and Sarah Hemmingway, 4 June 1684, New Haven, Conn.
GOODWIN, Daniel, Jr., and Anne Thompson, 17 October 1682, York Co., Maine.
GOODWIN, Elizabeth and Zachariah Emery, 9 December 1686, Kittery, Maine.
GOODWIN, Elizabeth and Samuel Gardener, 11 May 1693, Boston, Mass.
GOODWIN, James and Sarah Thompson, 11 December 1686, York Co., Maine.
GOODWIN, Martha and Ebenezer Clough, 28 March 1693, Boston, Mass.
GOODWIN, Philip and Eliza Luxford, 14 June 1694, Boston, Mass.
GOOKIN, Sarah and Francis Yardley, 20 November 1647, Norfolk Co., Va.
GOOLD, Thomas and Frances Robinson, 10 July 1656, Boston, Mass.
GOOSE, John and Sarah Trerice, 10 August 1666, Charlestown, Mass.
GORE, Dorothy and Richard Yaresly, 23 October 1694, New York.
GORHAM, Desire and (Capt.) John Hawes, 7 October 1661, Yarmouth, Mass.
GORHAM, Lydia and John Thatcher, 1 January 1683, Yarmouth, Mass.
GORINGE, Charles and Elenor Allainby, 27 October 1696, Elizabeth City Co., Va.
GORTON, Anna and John Warner, 4 August 1670, Warwick, R. I.
GORTON, Benjamin and Sarah Carder, 5 December 1672, Warwick, R. I.
GORTON, Elizabeth and John Crandall, Jr., 10 June 1672, Warwick, R. I.
GORTON, John and Margrett Wooten, 20 January 1668, Warwick, R. I.
GORTON, John and Patience Hopkins, 2 February 1699, Warwick, R. I.
GORTON, Mary and Samuell Greene, 24 January 1694-5, Warwick, R. I.
GORTON, Samuell and Susannah Burton, 11 December 1684, Warwick, R. I.
GORTON, Samuel and Elizabeth Collins, 9 May 1695, Warwick, R. I.
GORTON, Sarah and John Wickes, 15 December 1698, Warwick, R. I.
GORTON, Susan and Benjamin Barton, 10 June 1672, Warwick, R. I.
GOSS, Mary and John Houghton, Jr., 20 November 1698, Concord, Mass.
GOSS, hillip and Mary Prescott, 29 March 1690, Lancaster, Mass.
GOSS, Robert and Jane Barry, 5 January 1693, Dover, N. H.
GOSSUTCH, Richard and Elizabeth Martin, 3 December 1696, Talbot Co., Md.
GOTT, Alice and William Smith, 2 February 1696, Anne Arundel Co., Md.
GOTT, Charles and Lydia Clarke, 25 December 1665, Lynn, Mass.
GOTTSCHICK, George and Elizabeth Oliver, 25 April 1697, Philadelphia, Penn.

GOUGH, William and Alice Thacker, 31 May 1688, Middlesex Co., Va.
GOULD, Henry and Sarah Ward, 30 September 1675, Ipswich, Mass.
GOULD, John and Elizabeth Cumings, 2 July 1686, Chelmsford, Mass.
GOULD, John and Sarah Baker, 14 October 1660, Ipswich, Mass.
GOULD, Leah and Jonathan Squire, 29 August 1681, Chelmsford, Mass.
GOULD, Mary and Nathan Cutler, 29 September 1655, Charlestown, Mass.
GOULD, Mary and John Waddell, 25 December 1665, Braintree, Mass.
GOULD, Martha and Joseph Barrett, 17 September 1672, Braintree, Mass.
GOULD, Samuel and Mehitable Barrett, 17 March 1684, Chelmsford, Mass.
GOULDING, William and Margaret Lake, 2 April 1676, Westchester Co., N. Y.
GOURD, Phebe and Thomas Andrews, Jr., 31 October 1667, Dorchester, Mass.
GOURDEN, Abram and Abigail Towers, 5 January 1692, Boston, Mass.
GOURDEN, Abraham and Sarah Hodder, 12 May 1698, Boston, Mass.
GOVE, John and Mary Aspinwall, 6 October 1658, Boston, Mass.
GOVER, Robert and Elizabeth Cotten, 5 December 1695, Anne Arundel Co., Md.
GOVERNEUR, Abraham and Mary Milborne, 16 May 1699, New York.
GOWAN (Smith), Margaret and Daniel Emery, 17 March 1695, Berwick, Maine.
GOWING, Robert and Elizabeth Brock, 31 August 1644, Dedham, Mass.
GOZZARD, Elizabeth and Samuel Neal, 2 August 1699, Simsbury, Conn.
GRADDE, Edmund and Tellen Dunawin, 10 March 1697, Harford Co., Md.
GRAFTON, Elizabeth and William Hewes, 25 November 1689, Boston, Mass.
GRAFTON, Priscilla and John Sanders, 1636, Salem, Mass.
GRAFTON, Priscilla and Thomas Jackson, 15 October 1690, Boston, Mass.
GRAHAM, Alse and Thomas Powell, 25 August 1676, Windsor, Conn.
GRAHAM, Isabella and Lewis Morris, 3 November 1691, New York City.
GRAHAM, James and Elizabeth Windebank, 18 July 1684, Staten Island, N. Y.
GRANGER, John and Martha Poor, 9 February 1679, Andover, Mass.
GRANT, Elizabeth (widow), and Joshua Willes, 12 May 1697, Tolland, Conn.
GRANT, James and Sarah Othea, 28 January 1664, Dedham, Mass.
GRANT, James and Margaret Wood, 5 October 1676, Dedham, Mass.
GRANT, James and Mary Nason, 6 October 1693, York Co., Maine.
GRANT, John and Mary Hull, 2 August 1666, Windsor, Conn.
GRANT, Mary and John Hallaway, 2 February 1692, Boston, Mass.
GRANT, Peter and Sarah Scarlet, 25 July 1694, Boston, Mass.
GRANT, Samuel and Mary Porter, 27 May 1658, Windsor, Conn.
GRANT, Samuel and Annie Filley, 6 December 1683, Windsor, Conn.
GRANT, Toban and Hanna Palmer, 22 January 1662, Windsor, Conn.
GRANT, William and Martha Nason, 26 December 1695, York Co., Maine.
GRANT, William and Jane Warren, 4 August 1690, Dover, N. H.
GRANTHAM, John and Martha Bant, 8 December 1690, Boston, Mass.
GRASSET, Hester and Louis Dubois, 28 August 1696, New York.
GRAVES, Abraham and Anna Hayward, 28 June 1677, Concord, Mass.
GRAVES, Deliverance and Walter Taylor, 24 September 1697, New York.
GRAVES, Dorcas and George Abbot, Jr., 17 April 1678, Andover, Mass.
GRAVES, Francis and Amy Puddington (widow), 27 August 1689, Dover, N. H.
GRAVES, George and Elizabeth Stilwell, 26 November 1657, Guilford, Conn.
GRAVES, Hannah and John Mayo, 1654, Roxbury, Mass.
GRAVES, Hannah and Timothy Abbott, 27 December 1689, Andover, Mass.
GRAVES, Hannah and Christopher Pottle, 12 March 1694, Ipswich, Mass.

GRAVES, Jane and Mauris Leiston, 8 June 1685, Middletown, Penn.
GRAVES, Mark and Elizabeth Farrington, 14 November 1667, Andover, Mass.
GRAVES, Mary and Joseph Haskell, 2 December 1675, Gloucester, Mass.
GRAVES, Ruth and Henry Keskeyes, 7 June 1656, Boston, Mass.
GRAVES, Sarah and Samuel Bradfield, 27 June 1677, Branford, Conn.
GRAVES, Samuel and Sarah Brewer, 12 March 1678, Lynn, Mass.
GRAY, Edward and Susanna Harrison, 11 August 1699, Boston, Mass.
GRAY, Henry and Mary Blunt, 3 May 1699, Andover, Mass.
GRAY, John and Joanna Morton, 9 December 1686, Kingston, Mass.
GRAY, Mary and Benjamin Rider, 10 June 1680, Yarmouth, Nova Scotia.
GRAY, Thomas and Anna Little, 3 July 1694, Boston, Mass.
GRAY, Samuel and Susanna Baster, 15 April 1695, Boston, Mass.
GRAY, Thomas and Bathya Crooke, October 1699, Elizabeth City Co., Va.
GREELEY, Joseph and Martha Corliss, 5 February 1695, Haverhill, Mass.
GREELY, Andrew and Sarah Brown, 12 June 1673, Salisbury, Mass.
GREEN, Anna and Nathaniel Hinchman, 1694, Worcester, Mass.
GREEN, Benjamin and Susannah Holden, 25 January 1689, Warwick, R. I.
GREEN, Dorcas and John Eaton, 26 November 1674, Reading, Mass.
GREEN, Elizabeth and John Lynde, 25 August 1691, Malden, Mass.
GREEN, Elizabeth and Peter King, 29 October 1697, New York.
GREEN, Ellen and Thomas Fox, 24 May 1650, Cambridge, Mass.
GREEN, Esther and Samuel Moody, 4 April 1695, Boston, Mass.
GREEN, Hannah and Nathaniel Henchman, 11 January 1693, Boston, Mass.
GREEN, Jabez and Mary Barton, 17 March 1697-8, Warwick, R. I.
GREEN, James and Elizabeth Anthony, 3 August 1665, Warwick, R. I.
GREEN, John and Dorothy Benjamin, 24 August 1673, Richmond Co., Va.
GREEN, John and Bethiah Messenger, 17 January 1692, Boston, Mass.
GREEN, John and Mary Green, 23 February 1698, Malden, Mass.
GREEN, Joseph and Mary Beck, 30 July 1698, Boston, Mass.
GREEN, Lydia and Thomas Hatherly, 1 August 1693, Boston, Mass.
GREEN, Nicholas and Rebecca Clay, 22 March 1697, Boston, Mass.
GREEN, Philitia and Abraham Hooper, 3 March 1687, Philadelphia, Penn.
GREEN, Priscilla and Samuel Grice, 14 July 1691, Boston, Mass.
GREEN, Richard and Hannah Sherrar, 1 June 1692, Boston, Mass.
GREEN, Rebecca and Thomas Hayne, 9 January 1699, Boston, Mass.
GREEN, Sarah and Nathaniel Keene, 2 November 1688, York Co., Maine.
GREEN, Tobias and Mary Gent, 17 November 1699, Boston, Mass.
GREEN, William and Elizabeth Wheeler, 13 July 1659, Malden, Mass.
GREENE, Dorcas and James Barrett, 11 January 1672, Malden, Mass.
GREENE, Elizabeth and Timothy Harney, 26 December 1682, Somerset Co., Md.
GREENE, Hannah and John Vinten, 16 August 1677, Malden, Mass.
GREENE, Henry and Hester Hasse, 11 January 1672, Malden, Mass.
GREENE, James and Rebecca Jones, 19 November 1661, Boston, Mass.
GREENE, James, Jr., and Mary Jones, 29 January 1688-9, Warwick, R. I.
GREENE, Job and Phebe Sayles, 22 January 1684-5, Warwick, R. I.
GREENE, John and Sarah Wheeler, 18 October 1660, Malden, Mass.
GREENE, John and Mary Jenkins, 12 September 1666, Dover, N. H.
GREENE, Mary (widow of William) and John Holmes, 12 October 1680, Warwick, R. I.

GREENE, Mary and James Renals, 16 February 1681-5, Warwick, R. I.
GREENE, Mary and John Green, 23 February 1698, Malden, Mass.
GREENE, Mary and Daniel Curtis, 1 July 1666, Somerset Co., Md.
GREENE, Nathaniel and Mary Houchine, 22 April 1656, Boston, Mass.
GREENE, Peter and Elizabeth Slocum, 12 February 1695-6, Warwick, R. I.
GREENE, Richard and Ellin Sailes, 16 February 1692-3, Warwick, R. I.
GREENE, Samuel and Mary Wheeler, 4 May 1694, Malden, Mass.
GREENE, Samuell and Mary Gorton, 24 January 1694-5, Warwick, R. I.
GREENE, Thomas and Mary Weeks, 22 March 1676, Malden, Mass.
GREENE, Thomas and Elizabeth Webb, 19 August 1667, Malden, Mass.
GREENE, Thomas and Frances Cooke, 5 July 1659, Malden, Mass.
GREENE, Welthian and Thomas Fry, 1 February 1688, East Greenwich, R. I.
GREENE, William and Elizabeth Manlove (widow), 2 February 1666, Somerset Co., Md.
GREENE, William and Mary Sayles, 17 December 1674, Warwick, R. I.
GREENFIELD, Ann and Richard Leekey, 4 July 1687, Boston, Mass.
GREENFIELD, Sanuel and Susannah Wise (widow), 26 March 1639, Ipswich, Mass.
GREENHAM, Michael and Mary Davis, 14 April 1693, New York.
GREENHILL, Rebecca and John Shepard, 4 October 1649, Cambridge, Mass.
GREENLEAF, Bethy and William Clear, 21 December 1699, Boston, Mass.
GREENLEAF, Edmond and Abigail Somerby, 2 July 1691, Hampton, N. H.
GREENLEAF, John and Hanna Veasy, 26 August 1665, Braintree, Mass.
GREENLEAF, Judith and Tristram Coffin, 2 March 1653, Newbury, Mass.
GREENLEAF, Rooksby and Thomas Creese, 30 June 1697, Boston, Mass.
GREENLEAF, Ruth and John Cook, 16 December 1689, Boston, Mass.
GREENLEAF, Stephen and Elizabeth Coffin, 13 November 1651, Newbury, Mass.
GREENLEAF, Stephen and Hester Swett (widow of Benjamin), 31 March 1678, Newbury, Mass.
GREENLEAF, Tristram and Margret Pipes, 12 November 1689, Hampton, N. H.
GREENOUGH, John and Eliza Gross, 18 October 1693, Boston, Mass.
GREENOUGH, Mercy and Henry Gibbs, 9 June 1692, Boston, Mass.
GREENOUGH, William and Elizabeth Upshall, 4 July 1652, Boston, Mass.
GREENOW, William and Ruth Swift, 10 October 1660, Boston, Mass.
GREENWOOD, Alice and Robert Portis, 3 November 1659, Boston, Mass.
GREENWOOD, Mary and Theophilus Frarey, 12 June 1690, Boston, Mass.
GREENWOOD, Nathaniel and Mary Allen, 24 January 1656, Weymouth, Mass.
GREENWOOD, Samuel and Elizabeth Bronson, 1687, Roxbury, Mass.
GREETIAN, Dorcas and William Egleton, 28 September 1698, Boston, Mass.
GREG, Robert and Leena Mourits, 13 December 1694, New York.
GREGGS, Humphrey and Grizel Jewell, 1 September 1655, Braintree, Mass.
GREGORY, Judah and Hannah Hoyt, 20 October 1664, Norwalk, Conn.
GREGORY, Phebe and John Benedict, 11 November 1670, Norwalk, Conn.
GREY, Hannah and Thomas Abbott, 7 December 1697, Andover, Mass.
GREY, Joanna and James Boulderson, 19 May 1698, Boston, Mass.
GRICE, Samuel and Priscilla Green, 14 July 1691, Boston, Mass.
GRIDLEY, Eliza and Thomas Blower, 21 September 1693, Boston, Mass.
GRIDLEY, Hannah and Edward Davis, 16 July 1657, Boston, Mass.
GRIDLEY, Joseph and Lydia Flood (widow), 9 June 1654, Boston, Mass.

GREADLY, Joseph and Elizabeth Hickman, 24 June 1675, Dorchester, Mass.
GRIDLEY, Returne and John Davis, 9 February 1656, Boston, Mass.
GRIDLEY, Richard and Hannah Dawes, 27 February 1694, Boston, Mass.
GRIFFEN, Hannah and Isaac Pond, 20 May 1667, Windsor, Conn.
GRIFFEN, Mary and Samuel Wilson, 1 May 1672, Windsor, Conn.
GRIFFIN, Abigail and Richard Segar, 21 March 1682, Simsbury, Conn.
GRIFFIN, David and Catharine Howard, 14 June 1697, Boston, Mass.
GRIFFIN, Eleanor and John Asbury, 18 October 1699, Boston, Mass.
GRIFFIN, Elizabeth and Edwin Deare, 3 March 1660, Ipswich, Mass.
GRIFFIN, John and Ann Bancroft, 13 May 1647, Windsor, Conn.
GRIFFIN, John and Sarah Fowler, 3 August 1695, Anne Arundel Co., Md.
GRIFFIN, Nathaniel and Elizabeth Ping, 26 August 1671, Andover, Mass.
GRIFFIN, Robert and Mary Ruddock, 1 February 1693, Boston, Mass.
GRIFFINE, John and Susanna Price, 27 February 1655, Boston, Mass.
GRIFFING, Jasper and Hannah, 1675, Manchester, Mass.
GRIFFING, Lydia and Martin Ford, 5 March 1684, Bradford, Mass.
GRIFFITH, Thomas and Elizabeth Knowles, 23 December 1699, Philadelphia, Penn.
GRIGGS, John and Mary Patton, 1 November 1652, Roxbury, Mass.
GRIGGS, Joseph and Hannah Davis, 8 November 1654, Roxbury, Mass.
GRIGGS, Margorie (widow) and William Hay, 20 September 1655, York Co., Va.
GRIGGS, Mary and Thomas Stow, 4 December 1639, Roxbury, Mass.
GRIGGS, Rachel and Joseph Allen, 29 July 1680, Gloucester, Mass.
GRIGGS, Thomas and Mary Green, 26 August 1640, Roxbury, Mass.
GRINFELD, Anne and Robert Hooper, 4 December 1684, Marblehead, Mass.
GRISCOM, Andrew and Sarah Dole, 7 February 1685, Philadelphia, Penn.
GRISSELL, Elizabeth and Jonah Palmer, 3 May 1665, Charlestown, Mass.
GRISWOLD, Deborah and Jonathan Crane, 7 March 1678, Saybrook, Conn.
GRISWOLD, Hannah and John Kent, 21 March 1662, Dedham, Mass.
GRISWOLD, Hannah and William Clark, 7 March 1678, Saybrook, Conn.
GRISWOLD, Mary and Timothy Phelps, 19 May 1661, Windsor, Conn.
GRISWOLD, Mary and Jonathan Tracy, 11 July 1672, Saybrook, Conn.
GRISWOLD, Mary and Joseph Cooley, 22 January 1684, Longmeadow, Mass.
GRISWOLD, Margaret and Thomas Buckingham, 16 December 1691, Saybrook, Conn.
GRISWOLD, Samuel and Susannah Huntington, 10 December 1685, Saybrook, Conn.
GRISWOLD, Sarah and Robert Chapman, 27 June 1671, Saybrook, Conn.
GRISWOLD, Thomas and Hester Drake, 11 August 1681, Windsor, Conn.
GROENENDYKE, Johannes and Della Childers, 18 September 1694, New York.
GROESBECK, Willem Claase and Gertruy Schuyler, March 1684, Albany, N. Y.
GROSS, Anna and Walter Gutridge, 12 November 1696, Boston, Mass.
GROSS, Edmund and Dorothy Belcher, 19 February 1693, Boston, Mass.
GROSS, Elizabeth and John Greenough, 18 October 1693, Boston, Mass.
GROSS, Elizabeth and Richard Tally, 27 January 1697, Boston, Mass.
GROSS, Hannah and Nathaniel Halsie, 22 June 1693, Boston, Mass.
GROSS, Isaac and Elizabeth Atherton, 28 August 1691, Milton, Mass.
GROSS, Simon and Mary Bond, 23 October 1675, Hingham, Mass.
GROSSE, Ann (widow) and Samuel Sheeres, 15 June 1658, Boston, Mass.

GROSSE, Matthew and Mary Trott, 5 August 1652, Boston, Mass.
GROTTIN, Avis and George Cullen, 1 October 1673, Somerset Co., Md.
GROVE, Ann and John Lippett (the younger), 9 February 1664, Warwick, R. I.
GROVES, Andrew and Jane Boyle, 8 February 1693, New York.
GROVER, Abigail and Benjamin Borden, 22 September 1670, Shrewsbury, N. J.
GROVER, Andrew and Hannah Hills, 7 February 1674, Malden, Mass.
GROVER, Deborah and John Bennett, 1671, Beverly, Mass.
GROVER, Elizabeth and Philip Atwood, 7 April 1675, Malden, Mass.
GROVER, Hannah and John George, 22 August 1699, Boston, Mass.
GROVER, Elizabeth and Joseph Baldwin, 26 June 1691, Malden, Mass.
GROVER, Lydia and John Scolly, 22 December 1690, Boston, Mass.
GROVER, Thomas and Sarah Chadwick, 23 May 1668, Malden, Mass.
GROVER, Thomas and Mary Cox, 29 July 1697, Malden, Mass.
GRUBB, Henry and Mary Perkins, 24 March 1683, Burlington, N. J.
GRUBB, Mary and Seth Hill, 8 May 1685, Burlington, N. J.
GUEST, Elizabeth and Arthur Holton, 29 September 1695, Philadelphia, Penn.
GUILD, Ann and James Allen, 16 January 1648, Dedham, Mass.
GUILD, Elizabeth and George Robinson, 17 November 1680, Rehoboth, Mass.
GUILD, John and Elizabeth Crooke, 24 April 1645, Dedham, Mass.
GUILD, John and Sarah Fisher, 22 March 1677, Dedham, Mass.
GUILD, Samuel and Mary Woodcock, 29 September 1676, Dedham, Mass.
GUILFORD, Susanna and Thomas Jewell, 18 October 1672, Amesbury, Mass.
GULIVER, Hannah and Ephriam Tucker, 27 September 1688, Milton, Mass.
GULIVER, Jonathan and Mary Roberson, 17 January 1686, Milton, Mass.
GULL, Richard and Rebecca Hill, 24 January 1694, Boston, Mass.
GULLIFER, Mary and Jonathan Atherton, 17 March 1679, Milton, Mass.
GULLIFER, Samuel and Jan Gilbord, 15 November 1675, Milton, Mass.
GULLISON, Elisha and Margaret Trickey, 10 November 1674, Dover, N. H.
GULLIVER, Nathaniell and Hanna Billing, 1 July 1698, Milton, Mass.
GUNN, Debro and Timothy Trall, 10 November 1659, Windsor, Conn.
GUNN, Mehitable and David Ensingne, 22 October 1663, Hartford, Conn.
GUNN, Sarah and Samuel Kellogg, 24 November 1664, Hartford, Conn.
GUNS, Mary and Thomas Woodward, 7 March 1659, Boston, Mass.
GURGEFIELD, Margaret (widow) and Richard Bennet, 11 May 1655, Boston, Mass.
GURNEY, Grizzell and John Burge, 3 July 1667, Chelmsford, Mass.
GURNEY, Samuel and Sarah Shapley, 26 October 1693, Boston, Mass.
GUSTEEN, Mary and Richard Ward, 22 October 1697, Boston, Mass.
GUTRIDG, Robert and Margaret Ireland, 25 October 1656, Braintree, Mass.
GUTRIDGE, Walter and Anna Cross, 12 November 1696, Boston, Mass.
GUTSILL, Thomas and Sarah Heminway, 4 June 1684, Branford, Conn.
GUTTERIDGE, Mary and Thomas Spaule, 18 June 1653, Boston, Mass.
GUTTERSON, John and Abigail Buckmaster, 14 January 1688, Andover, Mass.
GUTTERSON, Susanna and Samuel Preston, 27 May 1672, Andover, Mass.
GUTTRIDGE, Mary and Nicholas Buttolph, 28 June 1699, Boston, Mass.
GUY, Sarah and Thomas Davis, 7 March 1687, Somerset Co., Md.
GWIN, Thomas and Johanna Armitage, 21 November 1689, Boston, Mass.
GWIN, Thomas and Sarah Dixey, November 1691, Boston, Mass.
GYLES, Robert and Margaret Barret, 17 February 1692, Boston, Mass.
GYLES, Thomas and Martha Bill, 18 January 1699, Boston, Mass.

H

HABERFIELD, Mary and Thomas Salter, 4 May 1693, Boston, Mass.

HABOUR, John, Jr. and Joel Thayre, 17 January 1654, Braintree, Mass.

HACK, William and Susannah Kingley, 13 November 1694, Milton, Mass.

HACKHORN, Hannah and Samuel Hunting, 24 October 1662, Dedham, Mass.

HACKLEY, Peter and Elizabeth Baker (widow), 31 August 1669, New London, Conn.

HACKLY, Ann and John Rice, 27 September 1649, Dedham, Mass.

HADLOCK, Nathaniel and Remember Joanes, 1 May 1673, Gloucester, Mass.

HADLOCKE, Deborah and Abraham Temple, 4 December 1673, Concord, Mass.

HAGBOURNE, Elizabeth and James Toung, 8 July 1654, Boston, Mass.

HAGGERT, Hannah and Philip Welch, 20 February 1666, Wenham, Mass.

HAGGETT, Moses and Joana Johnson, 23 October 1671, Andover, Mass.

HAINES, Eleanor and Samuel Weeks, 23 August 1695, Greenland, N. H.

HAINES, Hannah and John Heath, 16 December 1697, Haverhill, Mass.

HAINES, Jane (widow) and Isaac Marston, 28 December 1671, Falmouth, Maine.

HAINES, John and Elizabeth Bowne, 9 November 1687, New York City.

HAINES, Ruth and Eleazer Hawes, 28 December 1669, Dorchester, Mass.

HAINES, Samuel and Mary Fifield, 17 January 1673, Hampton, N. H.

HALCE, Margaret and Matthew Armstrong, 7 June 1694, Boston, Mass.

HALE, Abigail and Henry Poore, 12 September 1679, Rowley, Mass.

HALE, Hannah and John Spaulding, May 1658, Concord, Mass.

HALE, Mary and Edward Bear, 19 May 1693, Boston, Mass.

HALE, Samuel and Martha Palmer, 3 November 1698, Rowley, Mass.

HALE, Thomas and Mary Hutchinson, 26 May 1657, Salem, Mass.

HALL, Abigail (widow) and Thomas Downs, 24 October 1698, Dover, N. H.

HALL, Benjamin and Sarah Fisher, 9 January 1691, Wrentham, Mass.

HALL, Charles, Jr. and Martha Davis, 31 October 1693, Somerset Co., Md.

HALL, Christopher and Mary Homer, 5 February 1699, Cambridge, Mass.

HALL, Elizabeth and Isaac Pearson, 9 November 1685, Philadelphia, Penn.

HALL, Elizabeth (widow) and Thomas Packer, 7 August 1687, Dover, N. H.

HALL, Elizabeth and Joshua Peirce, 24 January 1695, Portsmouth, N. H.

HALL, John, Jr. and Abigail Roberts, 8 November 1671, Dover, N. H.

HALL, John and Martha Bradall, 16 August 1692, Harford Co., Md.

HALL, John and Martha Goldsmith, 18 July 1693, Harford Co., Md.

HALL, John and Margery Miller, 30 April 1694, Marshfield, Mass.

HALL, John and Ann Hollis, 6 May 1697, Harford Co., Md.

HALL, Jonathan and Margaret Seward, 21 June 1698, Boston, Mass.

HALL, Joseph and Elizabeth Rand, 3 March 1674, Lynn, Mass.

HALL, Joseph and Hannah Miller, 12 February 1689, Marshfield, Mass.

HALL, Joseph and Mary Bill, 13 July 1693, Boston, Mass.

HALL, Martha and Ebenezer Williams, 18 September 1674, Dorchester, Mass.

HALL, Rebecca and John Bacon, 17 December 1651, Dedham, Mass.

HALL, Richard and Jane (widow of Obadiah) Judkins, 6 August 1699, Talbot Co., Md.

HALL, Robert and Elizabeth Mackeniff, 18 October 1682, Somerset Co., Md.
HALL, Samuel and Bashua Hinckley, 6 June 1681, Dorchester, Mass.
HALL, Samuel and Elizabeth Bourne, 7 April 1686, Taunton, Mass.
HALL, Sarah and James Curtis, 2 February 1685, Somerset Co., Md.
HALL, Stephen and Ruth Davis, 3 December 1663, Concord, Mass.
HALL, Thomas and Abigail Martin, 25 February 1690, Dedham, Mass.
HALL, Thomas and Hannah Paine, 15 February 1694, Boston, Mass.
HALL, Timothy and Sara Barber, 26 November 1663, Windsor, Conn.
HALLAWELL, Benjamin and Mary Stocker, 12 May 1692, Boston, Mass.
HALLEWELL, Mary and Daniel Floyd, 18 January 1697, Boston, Mass.
HALLET, Lydia (widow) and John Drummond, 27 November 1661, Boston, Mass.
HALLY, Elizabeth and John Chapman, 7 June 1670, Saybrook, Conn.
HALSEY, Joseph and Elizabeth Eldredg, 29 January 1697, Boston, Mass.
HALSEY, Nathaniel and Anne Stausbrough, 15 December 1697, Southampton, N. Y.
HALSEY, Priscilla and Ezekial Needham, 10 March 1696, Boston, Mass.
HALSIE, Nathaniel and Hannah Gross, 22 June 1693, Boston, Mass.
HAMBLETON, William and Mary Richardson, 7 June 1654, Boston, Mass.
HAMBY, Catherine and Edward Hutchinson, 13 October 1636, Boston, Mass.
HAM, John and Mary Hurd, 6 May 1668, Dover, N. H.
HAMILTON, David and Annah Jackson, 14 July 1662, Biddeford, Maine.
HAMLEN, Ezekiel and Elizabeth Drake, 8 June 1654, Boston, Mass.
HAMLIN, Mary and Noahdiah Russell, 20 February 1689, Middletown, Conn.
HAMM, John and Elizabeth Knight, 14 March 1698, Dover, N. H.
HAMMANT, Timothy and Melatiah Clark, 19 January 1696, Boston, Mass.
HAMMOND, Dorcas and Robert Cutts, 18 April 1698, York Co., Maine.
HAMMON, Edward and Susannah Bradley, 5 January 1684, Bristol, R. I.
HAMMOND, Joseph and Hannah Storer, 19 September 1699, Wells, Maine.
HAMMOND, Thomas and Mehitabel Veray, 15 June 1693, Boston, Mass.
HAMMOND, Thomas and Mary Heath, 30 July 1694, Baltimore Co., Md.
HAMPTON, Jennett and Robert Ray, 9 November 1689, Shrewsbury, N. J.
HAMTON, John and Martha Brown, 3 January 1687, Middletown, N. J.
HANBURY, Hannah and Francis Johnson, 24 August 1656, Boston, Mass.
HANCE, Elizabeth and John Worthly, 12 January 1676, Shrewsbury, N. J.
HANCE, Jeborah and George Corleis, 23 September 1699, Shrewsbury, N. J.
HANCE, Mary and James Antrom, 14 March 1696, Shrewsbury, N. J.
HANCHETT, John and Esther Pritchett, 6 September 1677, Suffield, Conn.
HANCOCK, Anna and Thomas Shaw, 20 April 1692, New York City.
HANCOCK, Elizabeth and Benjamin Wyman, 25 August 1674, Cambridge, Mass.
HANCOCK, John and Jane Wills, 8 December 1698, New York.
HANCOCK, Judith and Gilbert Murrell, 1691, Burlington Co., N. J.
HANCOCK, Mary and William Matlack, 1682, Burlington Co., N. J.
HANCOCK, Nathaniel and Mary Prentice, 8 March 1664, Cambridge, Mass.
HANCOCK, Timothy and Rachel Firman, 1684, Burlington Co., N. J.
HANCOKE, Anthony and Sarah Wilson, 17 April 1678, Dorchester, Mass.
HAND, Alice and William Shipman, 25 November 1690, Saybrook, Conn.
HAND, Joseph and Jane Wright, 1664, Guilford, Conn.
HANDS, Mehitable and John Savill, 20 August 1668, Braintree, Mass.
HANDY, Samuel and Mary Sewell, 31 March 1679, Somerset Co., Md.

HANET, Ann and William Thornton, 17 August 1697, Boston, Mass.
HANMER, Sarah and Gabriel Ludlow, 5 April 1697, New York.
HANMORE, Susanna and John Brooks, 25 May 1652, Windsor, Conn.
HANNAH, Robert and Hannah Matson, 2 May 1695, Boston, Mass.
HANNES, Miles and Elizabeth Kelleboth, November 1698, Harford Co., Md.
HANNIFORD, John and Abigail Dill (widow), 8 September 1655, Boston, Mass.
HANSON, Anica and Andrew Elenor, 5 March 1656, Kent Co., Md.
HANSON, Catherine and Hendrick Jansen, 14 December 1672, Esopus, N. Y.
HANSON, Mercy and John Church, 1 December 1699, Dover, N. H.
HANSON, Tobias and Ann Lord, 28 August 1698, Dover, N. H.
HARBERT, Silvester and Lucie Adams, 21 July 1652, Boston, Mass.
HARBITTLE, Dorothy and Thomas Lamb, 16 July 1640, Roxbury, Mass.
HARBOUR, John and Joell Thayer, 17 March 1654, Braintree, Mass.
HARDENBERGH, Johannes and Hilenah Meyer, 10 July 1696, New York.
HARDENBERGH, Johannus and Cathrine Ruthse, 12 September 1699, New York.
HARDENBERGH, Mary and William Pead, 4 June 1694, New York.
HARDENBROOK, Mary and David Jamison, 7 May 1692, New York City.
HARDIER, Liddia and Martin Saunders, 1 February 1651, Braintree, Mass.
HARDING, Amaziah and Thomas Rogers, 1671, Eastham, Mass.
HARDING, Elizabeth and John Dwight, 3 December 1696, Dedham, Mass.
HARDING, Henry and Mary Aline, 7 July 1698, Dedham, Mass.
HARDING, Ichabod and Abigail Barber, 15 November 1699, Milton, Mass.
HARDING, John and Widow Tybott, 22 February 1652, Plymouth, Mass.
HARDING, John and Hanna Wood, 28 November 1665, Watertown, Mass.
HARDING, Martha and Samuel Brown, 19 February 1682, Plymouth, Mass.
HARDING, Philip and Susanna Haviland (widow), 23 August 1659, Boston, Mass.
HARDING, Thomas and Mary Bullock, 5 February 1686, Philadelphia, Penn.
HARDY, Elizabeth and John Mifflin, 1 February 1684, Philadelphia, Penn.
HARDY, Ruth and John Mead, 27 October 1681, Greenwich, Conn.
HARDY, Samuel and Rebecca Hobby, 18 November 1686, Stamford, Conn.
HARDY, Sarah and Richard Ackworth, 6 December 1683, Somerset Co., Md.
HARGER, Anna and John Chatfield, 5 February 1684, Derby, Conn.
HARICE, Mary and Nicholas Laurence, 3 November 1681, Dorchester, Mass.
HARING, Peter and Margaret Bogart, 4 December 1687, New York City.
HARINGTON, Mary and Thomas Bedle, 20 September 1698, Boston, Mass.
HARKER, John and Dorothy Mills (widow), 30 June 1647, York Co., Maine.
HARKER, John and Patience Fowler, 14 December 1680, Boston, Mass.
HARMON, Ann and John McCarthy, 9 July 1684, Staten Island, N. Y.
HARMON, Elizabeth and John Donaldson, 23 March 1690-1, New York City.
HARMON, Elizabeth and Richard Flood, 1 December 1691, Boston, Mass.
HARMON, Elizabeth and Joseph Bank, 28 February 1695, York, Maine.
HARMON, Mary and Zachariah Booth, 26 May 1696, Enfield, Conn.
HARMON, Nathaniel and Mary Skinner, 19 November 1685, Suffield, Conn.
MARNETT, Edward and Mary Marsh, 11 October 1671, New York City.
HARNEY, Timothy and Elizabeth Greene, 26 December 1682, Somerset Co., Md.
HARPER, Christian and William Hicks, 27 November 1699, Boston, Mass.
HARPER, Dorcas and Isaac Woody, 20 January 1656, Boston, Mass.
HARPER, Edward and Lydia Huttson, 13 May 1682, Somerset Co., Md.

HARPER, Experience and Joseph Hull, October 1676, Barnstable, Mass.
HARPIN, James and Sibella Clayton, 28 June 1699, Burlington, N. J.
HARODEN, Mary and George Manning, 15 May 1653, Boston, Mass.
HARRADEN, Elizabeth and Thomas Prince, 27 September 1676, Gloucester, Mass.
HARRADEN, Mary and Abraham Robinson, 7 July 1668, Gloucester, Mass.
HARRINGTON, Mary and John Emerton, 21 January 1698, Anne Arundel Co., Md.
HARRINGTON, Samuel and Hannah Barnes, 2 July 1698, Branford, Conn.
HARRIS, Daniel and Abigail Barnes, 11 December 1680, Middletown, Conn.
HARRIS, Daniel and Joana Brown, June 1682, Roxbury, Mass.
HARRIS, Elizabeth and Moses Bradstreet, 11 March 1665, Ipswich, Mass.
HARRIS, Elizabeth and Zachariah Sawtell, April 1668, Malden, Mass.
HARRIS, Elizabeth and William Weaver, 27 December 1693, East Greenwich, R. I.
HARRIS, John and Hannah Briggs, 10 July 1657, Boston, Mass.
HARRIS, John and Susannah Breck, 20 March 1674, Dorchester, Mass.
HARRIS, John and Agnes Way, 14 May 1679, New London, Conn.
HARRIS, John and Grace Searle, 8 January 1685, Ipswich, Mass.
HARRIS, John and Elizabeth Waller, 1687, Berkeley, N. Car.
HARRIS, James and Elizabeth Bayley, 14 February 1692, Bridgewater, Mass.
HARRIS, John and Mary Coombs, 19 January 1693, Marblehead, Mass.
HARRIS, John and Margaret Elson, 22 May 1695, Lynn, Mass.
HARRIS, Margaret and Clement Sumner, 18 May 1698, Boston, Mass.
HARRIS, Mary and John Ward, 18 April 1664, Middletown, Conn.
HARRIS, Mary and Isaac Johnson, December 1669, Boston, Mass.
HARRIS, Mercy and William Gold, 16 April 1699, Boston, Mass.
HARRIS, Rebecca and Walter Rost, 29 December 1698, Boston, Mass.
HARRIS, Richard and Susanna Richardson, 17 January 1682, Somerset Co., Md.
HARRIS, Robert and Elizabeth Boffee, 21 June 1642, Roxbury, Mass.
HARRIS, Robert and Elizabeth Turner, October 1699, New Kent Co., Va.
HARRIS, Samuel and Agnes Way, 14 May 1689, New London, Conn.
HARRIS, Sarah and Stephen White, 25 September 1695, Boston, Mass.
HARRIS, Sarah and John Bennet, 25 October 1699, Boston, Mass.
HARRIS, Thomas and Martha Lake, 15 November 1647, Ipswich, Mass.
HARRIS, William and Alce Roberts, 1 March 1676, Somerset Co., Md.
HARRIS, William and Martha Collins, 8 January 1690, Middletown, Conn.
HARRISON, Ellen and John Thompson, 25 October 1650, Milford, Conn.
HARRISON, Ellen and George Goldsmith, 29 November 1696, Philadelphia, Penn.
HARRISON, Erasmus and Mary Rouse, 3 January 1694, Boston, Mass.
HARRISON, Hannah and Philip Ludwell, 11 November 1697, Surrey Co., Va.
HARRISON, John and Judith Godfrey, 18 February 1670, Somerset Co., Md.
HARRISON, Maria and Thomas Pierson, 27 November 1662, Branford, Conn.
HARRISON, Richard and Ruth Buskman, 7 February 1686, Chesterfield, N. J.
HARRISON, Susanna and Edward Gray, 11 August 1699, Boston, Mass.
HARRISE, Elizabeth and Joshua Gee, 25 September 1689, Boston, Mass.
HARRISE, William and Sarah Crisp, 11 April 1695, Boston, Mass.
HARROD, Richard and Mary Jones, 30 October 1698, New York.
HARRUDE, John and Elizabeth Cooke, 24 December 1666, Warwick, R. I.

HARRY, Sarah and Francis West, 10 November 1696, Anne Arundel Co., Md.

HART, Elizabeth and John Winbourne, 11 April 1667, Malden, Mass.

HARTWELL, Ebenezer and Sarah Smedley, 27 March 1690, Concord, Mass.

HARTWELL, John and Priscilla Wright, 1 June 1664, Bedford, Mass.

HARTWELL, Marie and Joseph Wickes, 7 May 1656, Kent Co., Md.

HARVEY, Elizabeth and Elihu Plaisted, 11 October 1689, Dover, N. H.

HARVEY, Mary and Mark Hunkins, 29 June 1697, Dover, N. H.

HARVIE, Thomas and Widow Hendrick, 2 October 1696, Elizabeth City Co., Va.

HARVY, Martha (widow) and Henry Tewsbery, 10 November 1659, Boston, Mass.

HARWOOD, George and Miss Willemke, 19 August 1695, New York.

HARWOOD, James and Lydia Barrett, 11 April 1678, Chelmsford, Mass.

HARWOOD, Mehitabel and Thomas Savage, 5 February 1690, Boston, Mass.

HARWOOD, Thomas and Rachel Woodward (widow), 7 May 1654, Boston, Mass.

HARWOOD, Thomas and Ann Wythe, Sr., 7 September 1695, Elizabeth City Co., Va.

HARWOOD, William and Esther Perry, 11 May 1692, Dunstable, Mass.

HASBROUCK, Abraham and Marie Deys, 17 November 1675, Hurley, N. Y.

HASBROUCK, Maria and Isaac Du Bois, June 1683, Kingston, N. Y.

HASCALL, John, Jr., and Mary Squire, 2 March 1699, Cambridge, Mass.

HASELTINE, David and Mary Jewett, 26 November 1668, Bradford, Mass.

HASELTON, John and Mary Nelson, 16 July 1682, Haverhill, Mass.

HASFORT, George and Clemens Kerne, 8 October 1674, Somerset Co., Md.

HASEY, Joseph and Hannah Buckman, 12 January 1694, Boston, Mass.

HASEY, William and Judith Poole, 16 May 1681, Hull, Mass.

HASKALL, Benjamin and Mary Riggs, 21 November 1677, Gloucester, Mass.

HASKELL, John and Patience Soule, January 1666, Middleboro, Mass.

HASKELL, Joseph and Mary Graves, 2 December 1675, Gloucester, Mass.

HASKELL, William and Mary Tybott, 6 November 1643, Gloucester, Mass.

HASKELL, William and Mary Browne, 3 July 1667, Gloucester, Mass.

HASKINS, Richard and Jane Fluster, 2 August 1686, Taunton, Mass.

HASSE, Hester and Henry Greene, 11 January 1672, Malden, Mass.

HASSE, Sarah and Phineas Sprague, 5 January 1670, Malden, Mass.

HASSELL, Abiah and Joseph Blanchard, 25 May 1696, Cambridge, Mass.

HASSELL, Elizabeth and Joseph Wright, 1 November 1661, Charlestown, Mass.

HASTE, Daniel and Sarah Rodgers, 2 August 1680, Somerset Co., Md.

HASTINGS, Robert and Elizabeth Davis, 31 October 1676, Haverhill, Mass.

HATCH, Hannah and Joshua Dunbar, 21 September 1699, Hingham, Mass.

HATCH, Joseph and Amy Allen, 7 December 1683, Falmouth, Mass.

HATCH, Ruth and Samuel Swift, 9 April 1686, Watertown, Mass.

HATHAWAY, Hannah and John Symonds, 14 December 1697, Taunton, Mass.

HATHERLY, Thomas and Lydia Green, 1 August 1693, Boston, Mass.

HATTON, Eleanor and Thomas Brooke, 1660, Calvert Co., Md.

HAUGH, Atherton and Mercy Winthrop, 11 July 1699, Boston, Mass.

HAUGH, Samuel and Margaret Johnson, 30 September 1697, Boston, Mass.

HAUSE, Ruth and Nathan Bradly, 2 January 1695-6, Dorchester, Mass.

HAVILAND, Susanna (widow) and Philip Harding, 23 August 1659, Boston, Mass.

HAWARD, Abigail and John Upham, 31 October 1688, Malden, Mass.

HAWARD, Jonathan and Elizabeth Lee, 24 May 1690, Malden, Mass.

HAWES, Constance and Thomas Dewey, 1 April 1663, Dorchester, Mass.
HAWES, Deborah and Ephraim Pond, 6 January 1685, Wrentham, Mass.
HAWES, Edward and Elicony Lombard, 15 February 1648, Dedham, Mass.
HAWES, Eleazer and Ruth Haines, 28 December 1669, Dorchester, Mass.
HAWES, Elizabeth and Nathaniel Potter, 1 April 1675, New Haven, Conn.
HAWES, Elizabeth and Thomas Daggett, 22 January 1683, Bristol, R. I.
HAWES, Elizabeth and Jonathan Wight, 19 August 1687, Wrentham, Mass.
HAWES, Hannah and John Mason, 5 November 1676, Dedham, Mass.
HAWES, John (Capt.) and Desire Gorham, 7 October 1661, Yarmouth, Mass.
HAWKE, John and Hannah Beebe, 16 January 1689, New London, Conn.
HAWKES, Elizabeth and Joseph Gillet, 1664, Windsor, Conn.
HAWKES, John and Rebecca Maverick, 3 June 1658, Lynn, Mass.
HAWKES, John and Elizabeth Cushman, 11 April 1661, Saugus, Mass.
HAWKES, Sarah and Samuel Wardle, 9 January 1672, Andover, Mass.
HAWKES, Sarah and Francis Johnson, 1 February 1693, Andover, Mass.
HAWKINS, Abigail and Samuell Moore, 13 May 1660, Boston, Mass.
HAWKINS, Anthony and Ann Welles, 16 July 1656, Farmington, Conn.
HAWKINS, Elizabeth and Benjamin Turner, 16 April 1692, Scituate, Mass.
HAWKINS, Hannah and Edward Howard, 7 June 1661, Boston, Mass.
HAWKINS, Jeffery and Ellin Pierson, 21 September 1687, Middletown, Penn.
HAWKINS, John and Sarah Damarill (widow), 15 September 1654, Boston, Mass.
HAWKINS, Mary (widow) and Robert Fenn, 26 April 1654, Boston, Mass.
HAWKINS, Mary and John Aylett, 21 September 1654, Boston, Mass.
HAWKINS, Robert and Esther Hughs, 7 June 1694, Boston, Mass.
HAWKINS, Sarah and Robert Breck, 4 November 1653, Boston, Mass.
HAWLEY, Ebenezer and Esther Ward (widow), February 1678, Stratford, Conn.
HAWLEY, Mary and John Coe, 20 December 1682, Stratford, Conn.
HAWS, Daniel and Abiel Gay, 23 November 1677, Dedham, Mass.
HAWS, Obadiah and Rebecca Cowen, 19 December 1693, Boston, Mass.
HAWSE, John and Sarah Deering, 27 March 1683, Dedham, Mass.
HAWTHORNE, Sarah and John Mason, 30 March 1684-5, Dedham, Mass.
HAY, Mary and James Webster, 14 February 1658, Boston, Mass.
HAY, William and Marjorie Griggs (widow), 20 September 1655, York Co., Va.
HAYDEN, Jonathan and Elizabeth Lee, 20 February 1669, Braintree, Mass.
HAYDEN, John and Hannah Maynard, June 1669, Boston, Mass.
HAYDEN, Josiah and Elizabeth Goodnow, 6 March 1691, Sudbury, Mass.
HEYDEN, Samuel and Ruth Miver, 23 January 1679, Somerset Co., Md.
HAYDEN, Sarah and John Wilde, 1 June 1689, Braintree, Mass.
HAYDEN, Susanna and John Jackson, 19 May 1699, Boston, Mass.
HAYES, Richard and Elizabeth Lewis, April 1697, Radnor, Penn.
HAYHURST, Elizabeth and William Croadsdill, 10 February 1690, Middletown, Penn.
HAYMAN, Eliza and William Brattle, 3 November 1697, Boston, Mass.
HAYMAN, Elizabeth and Joseph Fisk, 22 May 1677, Lynn, Mass.
HAYMAN, Elizabeth and Nathaniel Blagrove, 18 June 1690, Bristol, R. I.
HAYMAN, Henry, Jr. and Matheme Standridge, 24 August 1687, Somerset Co., Md.
HAYMON, Sarah and John Wekes, 4 November 1674, Dorchester, Mass.
HAYNE, Thomas and Rebecca Green, 9 January 1699, Boston, Mass.

HAYNES, Mathias and Jane Brackett, 28 December 1671, Dover, N. H.
HAYNES, Samuel and Mary Fifield, 9 January 1672, Dover, N. H.
HAYNIE, Richard and Elizabeth Bridgar, 10 October 1681, Northumberland Co., Va.
HAYWARD, Huldah and Farthandro Thayre, 14 January 1653, Braintree, Mass.
HAYWARD, Huldah and John Baxter, 24 January 1692-3, Milton, Mass.
HAYWARD, Jonathan and Sarah Thayre, 6 March 1663, Braintree, Mass.
HAYWARD, Judith and William Simonds, 8 January 1644, Woburn, Mass.
HAYWARD, William and Hannah Newcomb, 22 November 1693, Quincey, Mass.
HAYWOOD, Margaret and William Colman, 30 June 1692, Boston, Mass.
HAYWOOD, Persis and Jacob Kendall, 2 January 1683, Woburn, Mass.
HAZARD, Edwin and Anne Carr, February 1671, Somerset Co., Md.
HAZELTINE, Ann and Caleb Kimball, 7 November 1660, Rowley, Mass.
HAZELTINE, Deliverence and Nathaniel Deane, 12 December 1672, Andover, Mass.
HAZEN, Isabell and John Wood, 26 January 1680, Rowley, Mass.
HAZEN, Samuel and Jane Pickard, 6 November 1684, Rowley, Mass.
HEADER, Sarah (widow) and Thomas Langston, 28 August 1686, Philadelphia, Penn.
HEALD, John and Sarah Dane, 10 June 1661, Concord, Mass.
HEALD, John and Mary Chandler, 18 December 1690, Concord, Mass.
HEALY, Sarah and John Leonard, 12 October 1640, Springfield, Mass.
HEARD, Abigail and Job Clements, 28 February 1688, Dover, N. H.
HEARD, Edmond and Elizabeth Warner, 26 September 1672, Essex Co., Mass.
HEARD, John and Phebe Littlefield, 27 April 1690, Dover, N. H.
HEARING, Thomas and Mary Pearce, 15 February 1650, Dedham, Mass.
HEARN, Susana and Samuel Cogswell, 27 October 1668, Saybrook, Conn.
HERNE, William and Katherine Maltis, 31 December 1672, Somerset Co., Md.
HEATH, Abigail and Samuel Fisher, 9 April 1684, Wrentham, Mass.
HEATH, Anna (widow) and Francis Younger, 2 December 1685, Dedham, Mass.
HEATH, Elias and Eliza Eldridge, 13 May 1699, Boston, Mass.
HEATH, Elizabeth and Samuel Shears, 27 October 1683, Wrentham, Mass.
HEATH, John and Hannah Haines, 16 December 1697, Haverhill, Mass.
HEATH, Mary and Aaron Copp, 30 December 1698, Haverhill, Mass.
HEATH, Mehitable and Seth Smith, 10 January 1693, Boston, Mass.
HEATON, Grace and Thomas Stackhouse, 27 July 1688, Middletown, Penn.
HEATON, James and Sarah Street, 20 November 1662, New Haven, Conn.
HEATON, Leah and Cornelius Fisher, 22 December 1652, Dedham, Mass.
HEDGE, Henry and Mary Parker, November 1699, Harford Co., Md.
HEDGE, Mary and Samuel Sturgis, 1667, Yarmouth, Maine.
HEDGE, William and Blanche Hall, April 1655, Yarmouth, Maine.
HEDGER, Thomas and Elizabeth Burton, 30 October 1674, Warwick, R. I.
HEDGES, Tristram and Ann Nickerson, 20 October 1657, Boston, Mass.
HEIDON, Hannah and Nathaniel Thayer, 27 May 1679, Braintree, Mass.
HEIFERNAN, Joanna and Christopher Vale, 21 September 1692, Boston, Mass.
HEIFORD, John and Abigail Albins, 8 April 1679, Braintree, Mass.
HEIRS, Moses and Elizabeth Toalman, 28 October 1692, Dorchester, Mass.
HELY, Judieth and Joseph Wood, 20 October 1697, Boston, Mass.
HEMAN, John and Mary Somes, 17 October 1660, Gloucester, Mass.

HEMINGWAY, Elizabeth and John Holbrook, 24 September 1663, Dorchester, Mass.

HEMINGWAY, Sarah and Thomas Goodsell, Jr., 4 June 1684, Branford, Conn.

HEMPSTEAD, Hannah and John Edgecomb, 29 February 1699, New London, Conn.

HEMPSTEAD, Mary and Robert Douglas, 28 September 1665, New London, Conn.

HENBERY, Arthur and Lydia Hill, 5 May 1670, Simsbury, Conn.

HENCHMAN, Daniel and Mary Poole, 26 February 1672, Dorchester, Mass.

HENCHMAN, Nathaniel and Hannah Green, 11 January 1693, Boston, Mass.

HENCHMAN, Richard and Esther Webster, 24 December 1697, Boston, Mass.

HENCHMAN, Susannah and Samuel Collins, 1693, Boston, Mass.

HENDRICK, Sarah and Samuel Ingalls, 4 June 1682, Andover, Mass.

HENDRICK, Widow and Thomas Harvie, 2 October 1696, Elizabeth City Co., Va.

HENDRICKE, Perkie and Peter Billian, 19 January 1696, New York.

HENDRICKS, Marie and Jan Braun, 14 January 1663, Brooklyn, N. Y.

HENDRICKSEN, Volckert and Elizabeth Paulus, 4 June 1695, New York.

HENDRICKSON, John and Mary Frost, 12 September 1692, New York City.

HENEWAY, John and Mary Trescott, 6 August 1665, Dorchester, Mass.

HENLEY, Terrence and Eliza Weeks, 2 April 1694, Boston, Mass.

HENLY, Elias and Sarah Thompson, 4 September 1657, Boston, Mass.

HENRICKE, Daniell and Mary Stockbridge (widow), 8 April 1660, Boston, Mass.

HENRY, Ann and Joseph Wright, 1 January 1694, New York.

HENRY, Elizabeth and David Vyland, 17 February 1696, New York.

HENRY, Samuell and Ann Cobbitt, 21 January 1686-7, New York.

HENSHA, Thankfull and Nathaniel Leman, 27 January 1699, Dorchester, Mass.

HEPWORTH, William and Mary Lock, 3 January 1697, Boston, Mass.

HERD, Hannah and Thomas Masters, 2 September 1685, Philadelphia, Penn.

HERNDEN, Sarah and David Whipple, 15 May 1675, Hingham, Mass.

HERRICK, Ephraim and Mary Cross, 3 July 1661, Salem, Mass.

HERRING, Hannah and Ephraim Ware, 13 July 1685, Dedham, Mass.

HERRING, James and Sarah Steadman, 16 February 1685, Dedham, Mass.

HERRING, Martha and Ebenezer Ware, 18 March 1690, Dedham, Mass.

HERRING, Mary and John Ellis, 1 February 1678, Medfield, Mass.

HERSEY, William and Sarah May (widow), 2 October 1691, Abington, Mass.

HET, Eliphalet and Ann Douglas, 1 September 1660, Boston, Mass.

HETCHBONE, Ruth and William Pasco, 20 October 1690, Boston, Mass.

HETHRINGTON, Andrew and Hannah Briggs, 11 April 1695, Boston, Mass.

HETT, Mary and Benjamin Fitch, 2 March 1693, Boston, Mass.

HEWEN, Martha and Henry Adams, 10 January 1694, Boston, Mass.

HEWENS, Hannah and Israel Lyon, 25 March 1690, Dorchester, Mass.

HEWES, Elizabeth and Joseph Adams, 3 May 1694, Boston, Mass.

HEWES, Joshua and Alice Crabtree (widow of John), 11 December 1656, Boston, Mass.

HEWES, Mary and Capt. John Fairwether, 17 November 1692, Boston, Mass.

HEWES, William and Eliza Grafton, 25 November 1689, Boston, Mass.

HEWETT, James and Mary Dykeman, 16 September 1695, New York.

HEWINS, Elizabeth and Nicholas Ide, 27 December 1677, Dorchester, Mass.

HEWINS, Joseph and Mehitable Lyon, 29 January 1690, Dorchester, Mass.
HEWITT, Mary and Thomas Strong, 5 December 1660, Northampton, Mass.
HEWLINGS, William and Mary Lovett, 23 July 1693, Burlington, N. J.
HEWS, Thanasen and Lambert Genery, 14 March 1658, Dedham, Mass.
HEWSON, John and Susanna Norden, 17 August 1693, Boston, Mass.
HIATT, Elizabeth (widow) and Cornelius Jones, 6 October 1657, Stamford, Conn.
HIBBERT, Dorcas and Nathaniel Abbott, 22 October 1695, Andover, Mass.
HICK, Thomas and Mary Doughty, 6 July 1677, New York.
HICKS, Eliza and Francis Thresher, 9 August 1694, Boston, Mass.
HICKS, Elizabeth and John Needham, 10 October 1679, Cambridge, Mass.
HICKS, Ephraim and Elizabeth Howland, 13 September 1649, Barnstable, Mass.
HICKS, Lydia and Robert Young, 22 March 1694, Eastham, Mass.
HICKS, Samuel and Hannah Evans, 27 July 1665, Dorchester, Mass.
HICKS, Williams and Christian Harper, 27 November 1699, Boston, Mass.
HICKMAN, Elizabeth and Joseph Greadly, 24 June 1675, Dorchester, Mass.
HICKMAN, Thomas and Martha Thacker, 18 December 1683, Middlesex Co., Va.
HIDDEN, Andrew and Sarah Houstin, 17 April 1654, Rowley, Mass.
HIDE, Ann and Daniel Weld, 30 May 1647, Braintree, Mass.
HIDE, Dority and Andrew Dueing, 27 October 1682, Dedham, Mass.
HIDE, Elizabeth and James Barbor, 23 June 1680, Dorchester, Mass.
HIDE, Hannah and John Woodward, 11 April 1698, Boston, Mass.
HIDE, Hester and John Post, March 1652, Saybrook, Conn.
HIDE, Sarah and John Osland, 14 October 1697, Boston, Mass.
HIDE, William and Joanna Abel, 4 June 1667, Rehoboth, Mass.
HIGBEE, Edward and Abigail Adams, 1684, Huntington, L. I., N. Y.
HIGGINS, Benjamin and Lydia Bangs, 24 December 1661, Eastham, Mass.
HIGGINS, Jodia and Mary Newbold, 12 May 1684, Burlington, N. J.
HIGGINS, Rebecca and Thomas Martin, 28 April 1683, Piscataway, N. J.
HIGGINS, Richard and Lydia Chandler, 23 November 1634, Plymouth, Mass.
HIGGINS, Richard and Mary Yates, October 1651, Eastham, Mass.
HIGGINS, Robert and Susanna Westoe, 2 September 1654, Boston, Mass.
HIGGINS, Zerah and Elizabeth Oliver, 1680, Piscataway, N. J.
HILAND, Sarah and Thomas Turner, 6 January 1652, Scituate, Mass.
HILDRETH, Abigail and Joseph Barrett, 25 December 1696, Chelmsford, Mass.
HILDRETH, Dorothy and John Robbins, 30 November 1698, Chelmsford, Mass.
HILDRETH, Ephraim and Anne Moore, 8 October 1686, Stow, Mass.
HILDRETH, James and Margaret Ward, 1 June 1659, Chelmsford, Mass.
HILDRETH, Joseph and Abigail Wilson, 25 February 1683, Chelmsford, Mass.
HILL, Charles and Ruth Pickett (widow), 2 July 1686, New London, Conn.
HILL, Edward and Mary Archer, 15 February 1699, Boston, Mass.
HILL, Elezer and Sarah Gillett, 29 December 1679, Simsbury, Conn.
HILL, Elizabeth and Thomas Thompson, 1682, Middlesex Co., Va.
HILL, Elizabeth and William Randoll, 10 December 1691, Boston, Mass.
HILL, Grace and Nathaniel Fitzrandolph, 23 April 1692, Woodbridge, N. J.
HILL, Hannah and Antipas Boyce, 24 January 1659, Boston, Mass.
HILL, Hannah and Joseph Storer, September 1691, Saco, Maine.
HILL, Hannah (widow) and John Cox, 22 May 1694, Dover, N. H.
HILL, James and Hannah Hincksman, 10 April 1662, Boston, Mass.
HILL, John and Elizabeth Strong, 16 November 1656, Boston, Mass.

HILL, John and Jane Bushnell, 14 April 1670, Saybrook, Conn.
HILL, John and Katern Chalker, 23 September 1673, Saybrook, Conn.
HILL, John and Alice Brangeman, September 1674, Somerset Co., Md.
HILL, John and Mary Frost, 12 December 1676, York, Maine.
HILL, Joseph and Elizabeth Peck, 22 December 1698, Boston, Mass.
HILL, Lydia and Arthur Henbery, 5 May 1670, Simsbury, Conn.
HILL, Martha and Charles Redman, 10 February 1688, Milton, Mass.
HILL, Mary and Thomas Breck, 12 February 1657, Dorchester, Mass.
HILL, Mary and John Saxton, 30 July 1677, Windsor, Conn.
HILL, Mary and Thomas Moorhouse, 3 April 1690, Boston, Mass.
HILL, Mary and John Ellis, 7 April 1698, Boston, Mass.
HILL, Nathaniel and Elizabeth Holmes, 21 June 1667, Cambridge, Mass.
HILL, Prudence and William Sherman, 23 January 1638, Plymouth, Mass.
HILL, Rebecca and Richard Gull, 24 January 1694, Boston, Mass.
HILL, Roger and Mary Crosse, 1 November 1658, Wells, Maine.
HILL, Ruth and William Augur, 7 October 1659, Malden, Mass.
HILL, Ruth and Roger Willis, 19 May 1664, Dorchester, Mass.
HILL, Samuel and Phebe Leonard, 6 November 1694, Duxbury, Mass.
HILL, Sarah and Joseph Loomis, 17 September 1646, Windsor, Conn.
HILL, Sarah (widow) and Nathaniel Sowther, 5 November 1653, Boston, Mass.
HILL, Seth and Mary Grubb, 8 May 1685, Burlington, N. J.
HILL, Thomas and Margaret Balie, 4 January 1655, Kent Co., Md.
HILL, Thankful and Thomas Lambe, 10 February 1688, Milton, Mass.
HILL, William and Rebecca Charles, 19 June 1691, Milton, Mass.
HILLARD, Hannah and Henry Dee, 30 September 1697, Boston, Mass.
HILLBORN, Thomas and Elizabeth Hutton, 12 October 1688, Shrewsbury, N. J.
HILLIARD, James and Mary Case, 30 March 1699, Simsbury, Conn.
HILLIARD, Job and Mary Fowl, 4 July 1693, Boston, Mass.
HILLS, Abram and Hannah Stower, October 1666, Malden, Mass.
HILLS, Gersham and Elizabeth Chadwick, 11 November 1667, Malden, Mass.
HILLS, Hannah and Andrew Grover, 7 February 1674, Malden, Mass.
HILLS, Isaac and Hannah Howard, June 1666, Malden, Mass.
HILLS, Joseph and Hannah Mellows, 24 June 1651, Malden, Mass.
HILLS, Joseph and Hannah Smith, November 1653, Malden, Mass.
HILLS, Joseph and Anne Lunt (widow of Henry), 8 March 1665, Newbury, Mass.
HILLS, Joseph and Helen Adkinson, November 1655, Malden, Mass.
HILLS, Samuel and Abigail Wheeler, 20 May 1679, Newbury, Mass.
HILLYARD, Andrew and Hannah Burr, September 1681, Simsbury, Conn.
HILLYARD, Andrew and Abigail Drake (2nd marriage), 17 November 1687, Simsbury, Conn.
HILLYER, Lydia and Daniel Wear, 31 October 1698, Boston, Mass.
HILTON, Hannah and Jonathan Woodman, 2 July 1668, Newbury, Mass.
HILTON, Mary and Thomas Sears, 11 December 1656, Newbury, Mass.
HINCHMAN, Sarah and Thomas Willet, 24 August 1695, New York.
HINCKLEY, Bashua and Samuel Hall, 6 June 1681, Dorchester, Mass.
HINCKLEY, Samuel and Martha Lathrop, 29 September 1699, Boston, Mass.
HINCKLEY, Susanna and Stephen Smith, 1643, Machias, Maine.
HINCKLEY, Thomas and Mary Richards, 4 December 1641, Barnstable, Mass.

HINCKLEY, Thomas and Mary Smith, 15 March 1660, Barnstable, Mass.
HINCKSMAN, Hannah and James Hill, 10 April 1662, Boston, Mass.
HINCKSMAN, John and Elizabeth Emmons, 10 August 1660, Boston, Mass.
HINCKSMAN, William and Mary Philberd, 20 November 1652, Boston, Mass.
HINDE, Hannah (widow) and Pasho Dunn, 1695, Elizabeth City Co., Va.
HINDERSON, William and Sarah Bishop, 1 July 1680, Somerset Co., Md.
HINDERSON, John and Elizabeth Barnabe, 1 July 1680, Somerset Co., Md.
HINDS, Judith and Alexander Swan, 15 November 1678, Richmond Co., Va.
HINDS, Elizabeth and Thomas Carey, 8 January 1694, Elizabeth City Co., Va.
HINGHAM, Joseph and Sarah Bushnell, 20 June 1655, Saybrook, Conn.
HINKSMAN, Elnatham and Eliab Turner, 22 November 1694, Scituate, Mass.
HINMAN, Benjamin and Elizabeth Lum, 12 July 1684, Woodbury, Conn.
HINMAN, Patience and John Burroughs, 10 January 1694, Stratford, Conn.
HINTON, John and Jane Niles, 20 November 1683, Bristol, R. I.
HISCOCK, Edward and Frances England, 20 May 1656, Branford, Conn.
HISKET, George and Sarah Clarke, 11 June 1662, Boston, Mass.
HITCHCOCK, Mary and Ralph Russell, 12 October 1663, New Haven, Conn.
HITCHCOCK, Nathaniel and Hannah Chapin, 27 September 1666, Springfield, Mass.
HITCHIL, Barbary and Philip Slow, 24 February 1697, Boston, Mass.
HIX, Mary and Arthur Eastmead, 4 August 1693, Boston, Mass.
HIXSON, Richard and Margaret Wadkins, 14 September 1686, Milton, Mass.
HOAR, Benjamin and Rebecca Smith, 10 April 1699, Bristol, R. I.
HOAR, Elizabeth and Jonathan Prescott, 23 December 1675, Concord, Mass.
HOARE, Joane and Edmond Quincy, 26 May 1648, Braintree, Mass.
HOARE, Johanna and Ezra Morse, 18 February 1670, Dedham, Mass.
HOARE, Mercy and John Spurr, 26 December 1676, Dorchester, Mass.
HOBART, Aaron and Rebecca Sumner, 27 January 1697, Milton, Mass.
HOBART, Benjamin and Susanna Newcomb, 5 April 1699, Boston, Mass.
HOBART, Jeremiah and Rebecca Brush, 8 February 1682, Huntington, L. I., N. Y.
HOBART, Mary and Samuel Chapin, 9 May 1688, Milton, Mass.
HOBBS, Mehitable and Joseph Towle, 14 December 1692, Hampton, N. H.
HOBBS, Morris and Sarah Swett, 13 June 1678, Hampton, N. H.
HOBBS, Sarah and John Lovett, 30 December 1691, Dover, N. H.
HOBBY, Elizabeth and Thomas Lilly, 2 June 1698, Boston, Mass.
HOBBY, Judith and John Colman, 19 July 1694, Boston, Mass.
HOBBY, Rebecca and Samuel Hardy, 18 November 1686, Stamford, Conn.
HOBDAY, Mary and William Howard, 4 January 1673, Somerset Co., Md.
HODDER, Sarah and Abraham Gourden, 12 May 1698, Boston, Mass.
HODEY, John and Mary Redden, 21 June 1675, Dover, N. H.
HODGE, Bethia and John Pain, 5 July 1698, Boston, Mass.
HODGE, Hannah and Thomas Lamere, 11 August 1699, Boston, Mass.
HODGE, John and Susanna Denslow, 1 August 1666, Windsor, Conn.
HODGES, Andrew and Lydia Browne, 27 November 1659, Ipswich, Mass.
HODGES, Jane and Joseph Wheeler, 1 July 1695, Boston, Mass.
HODGKIN, John and Mary Hull, 10 March 1697, Guilford, Conn.
HODGKINS, Bridget and William Fisher, 28 November 1686, Philadelphia, Penn.
HODGKINS, Hannah and John Somers, 2 January 1685, Somerton, Penn.
HODGKINS, Thomas and Abigail Hovey, 12 December 1689, Ipswich, Mass.

HODGKINS, William and Anne Hynes, 21 December 1638, Plymouth, Mass.
HODGKINSON, Mary and Samuel Bidwell, 2 December 1653, Boston, Mass.
HODGSON, Alice and Phineas Pemberton, 18 March 1699, Falls, Penn.
HODGSON, Daniel and Hannah Holme, 4 April 1689, Philadelphia Co., Penn.
HODSON, Daniel and Sarah Sherman, 20 October 1696, Boston, Mass.
HODSON, Margaret and Samuel Collins, 3 September 1680, Somerset Co., Md.
HOFFMAN, Martinus and Emerentze DeWitt, May 1664, Hoffmantown, N. Y.
HOG, John and Eliza Lewis, 22 February 1699, Boston, Mass.
HOIDON, John and Hannah Ames, 6 February 1660, Braintree, Mass.
HOIDON, Samuel and Hannah Thayre, 28 August 1664, Braintree, Mass.
HOIGHT, Abigail and John Ferris, 13 February 1695, Greenwich, Conn.
HOIT, Naomi and John Lovejoy, 23 March 1678, Andover, Mass.
HOKSEY, Hannah and John Barnard, 21 November 1689, Boston, Mass.
HOLBROOK, Eleazer and Sarah Pond, 14 June 1698, Dedham, Mass.
HOLBROOK, Hannah and John Battelle, 18 September 1678, Dedham, Mass.
HOLBROOK, Hopestill and Samuel Read, 10 May 1668, Uxbridge, Mass.
HOLBROOK, John and Elizabeth Hemmingway, 24 September 1663, Dorchester, Mass.
HOLBROOK, Patience and Hopestill Leland, 2 February 1691, Sherborn, Mass.
HOLCOM, Abigail and Samuel Bissell, 11 June 1658, Windsor, Conn.
HOLCOM, Debra and Daniel Birg, 5 November 1668, Windsor, Conn.
HOLCOM, Joshua and Ruth Sherwood, 4 June 1663, Windsor, Conn.
HOLCOMB, Elizabeth and Josiah Ellsworth, 16 November 1654, Windsor, Conn.
HOLCOMB, Nathan and Martha Buel, 1 November 1695, Simsbury, Conn.
HOLDEN, Barbara and Samuel Wickham, 4 June 1691, Warwick, R. I.
HOLDEN, Ellen and Richard Roberts, 28 May 1686, Philadelphia, Penn.
HOLDEN, Susannah and Benjamin Green, 25 January 1689-90, Warwick, R. I.
HOLDRIDGE, John and Elizabeth Perry, 16 September 1663, Dedham, Mass.
HOLDRIDGE, William and Lydia Quimby, 10 April 1674, Amesbury, Mass.
HOLEBROOK, Mary and John Puffer, 17 October 1695, Dorchester, Mass.
HOLEMAN, Mary and Samuell Mason, 29 May 1662, Boston, Mass.
HOLGRAVE, Theoda and Samuel Williams, 2 March 1653, Roxbury, Mass.
HOLIDAY, William and Katherine Russell, 2 June 1694, Anne Arundel Co., Md.
HOLLAND, Thomas and Joyce Johnson, 2 August 1675, Richmond Co., Va.
HOLLARD, Hannah and William Ballantine, 23 May 1652, Boston, Mass.
HOLLINGWORTH, Richard and Elizabeth Powell, 23 August 1659, Boston, Mass.
HOLLIOCKE, Susanna and Michael Martine, 12 July 1656, Boston, Mass.
HOLLIS, Ann and John Hall, 6 May 1697, Harford Co., Md.
HALLAWAY, John and Mary Grant, 2 February 1692, Boston, Mass.
HOLLEY, Mary and Edward Fitzrandolph, November 1662, Woodbridge, N. J.
HOLLOWAY, Grace and Josiah Reed, November 1666, Marshfield, Mass.
HOLLY, Lydia and Abel Platts, 8 May 1672, Rowley, Mass.
HOLLYMAN, Mary and William Rodney, 25 November 1688, Philadelphia, Penn.
HOLLYMAN, Sarah and John Densey, 28 October 1688, Philadelphia, Penn.
HOLMAN, Abigail and Standfast Foster, 3 October 1688, Milton, Mass.
HOLMAN, Phebee and Edward Egleston, 27 July 1693, Boston, Mass.
HOLMAN, Rachel and Josiah Sanders, 4 December 1693, Boston, Mass.
HOLMAN, Thomas and Abigail Rigby, 19 December 1663, Dorchester, Mass.
HOLME, Hannah and Dr. Daniel Hodgson, 4 April 1689, Philadelphia Co., Penn.

118   MARRIAGE RECORDS BEFORE 1699

HOLME, John and Mary More, 3 January 1688, Philadelphia Co., Pa.
HOLMES, Alice (widow) and William Osborn, 1680, Long Island, N. Y.
HOLMES, Ann and John Sandy, 7 May 1653, Boston, Mass.
HOLMES, Ebenezer and Mary George, 5 August 1697, Dorchester, Mass.
HOLMES, Elisha and Sarah Bartlett, 2 September 1695, Plymouth, Mass.
HOLMES, Elizabeth and Nathaniel Hill, 21 June 1667, Cambridge, Mass.
HOLMES, Francis and Rebecca Wharfe, 15 February 1693, Boston, Mass.
HOLMES, Israel and Anna Rouse, April 1678, Marshfield, Mass.
HOLMES, John and Frances Houldon, 1 December 1671, Warwick, R. I.
HOLMES, John and Mary Greene (widow of William), 12 October 1680, War-
    wick, R. I.
HOLMES, John and Hannah Newell, 9 April 1690, Woodstock, Conn.
HOLMES, Joshua and Fear Sturgis, 1698, Yarmouth, Mass.
HOLMES, Katherine and George Revedly, 28 August 1696, New York.
HOLMES, Lydia and Daniel Elder, 12 January 1667, Dorchester, Mass.
HOLMES, Nathaniel and Patience Topliffe, 27 March 1667, Roxbury, Mass.
HOLMES, Nathaniel and Sarah Thaxter, 1 October 1691, Boston, Mass.
HOLMES, Rely and John Simson, 4 June 1695, Boston, Mass.
HOLMES, Rose and Thomas Blanchard, 22 March 1699, Andover, Mass.
HOLMES, Samuel and Alice Stilwell, 26 October 1665, Long Island, N. Y.
HOLMES, Samuell and Mary Bullard, 26 December 1696, Dedham, Mass.
HOLMS, Ebenezer and Sarah Withington (widow), 2 February 1692, Dorchester,
    Mass.
HOLST, Hannah and Richard Pateshal, 20 April 1694, New York.
HOLSTONE, John and Ann Gibbs, 7 August 1684, Philadelphia, Penn.
HOLSWORTH, Joshua and Sarah Rawlins, 10 May 1669, Lynn, Mass.
HOLT, Elizabeth and Ralph Farnum, 26 October 1658, Andover, Mass.
HOLT, Elizabeth and John Potter, Jr., 23 February 1691-2, New Haven, Conn.
HOLT, George and Elizabeth Farnum, 10 May 1698, Andover, Mass.
HOLT, Henry and Sarah Bullard, 24 February 1669, Andover, Mass.
HOLT, Hannah and Samuel Farnum, 4 January 1698, Andover, Mass.
HOLT, James and Hannah Allen, 12 October 1675, Andover, Mass.
HOLT, John and Sarah Geery, 3 July 1685, Andover, Mass.
HOLT, Mary and Thomas Johnson, 5 July 1657, Andover, Mass.
HOLT, Nathaniel and Rebecca Beebe, 5 April 1680, New London, Conn.
HOLT, Nicholas and Hannah Pope (widow), 12 June 1658, Andover, Mass.
HOLT, Nicholas and Widow Preston, 21 May 1666, Andover, Mass.
HOLT, Nicholas and Mary Russell, 8 January 1679, Andover, Mass.
HOLT, Oliver and Hannah Russell, 9 March 1698, Andover, Mass.
HOLT, Richard and Lidia Wormwood, 10 May 1693, Bridgewater, Mass.
HOLT, Samuel and Hannah Farnum, 28 March 1693, Andover, Mass.
HOLT, Tammeson and Marten Depost, 16 January 1696, Harford Co., Va.
HOLTON, Arthur and Elizabeth Guest, 29 September 1695, Philadelphia, Penn.
HOLTON, John and Abigail Fisher, 1 March 1667, Dedham, Mass.
HOLTON, Mary and David Burt, 18 November 1655, Northampton, Mass.
HOLTON, Rachel and Thomas Strong, 10 October 1671, Guilford, Conn.
HOLTON, Ruth and Joseph Baker, 1663, Northampton, Mass.
HOLTON, Samuel and Mary Rossiter (widow), 21 June 1673, Northampton, Mass.
HOLTON, Sarah and John King, 18 November 1656, Northampton, Mass.

HOLTON, William and Sarah Marshfield, 22 November 1676, Springfield, Mass.
HOLYOKE, Ann and Thomas Putman, 7 October 1643, Lynn, Mass.
HOLYOKE, Mary and John Tuttell, 10 February 1646, Boston, Mass.
HOMAN, Joana and Edwin Sargent, 3 June 1695, Dover, N. H.
HOMAN, Sarah and Samuell Parker, 9 February 1657, Dedham, Mass.
HOMER, John and Margery Stephens, 13 July 1693, Boston, Mass.
HOMER, Mary and Christopher Hall, 5 February 1699, Cambridge, Mass.
HOMER, Michael and Mary Burroughs, 13 July 1693, Boston, Mass.
HOMES, Jeremiah and Sarah Walker, 22 September 1689, Dover, N. H.
HONAN, Daniel and Sarah Jones, 6 October 1694, New York.
HONEY, Ann and Samuel Lipis, 7 February 1688, New York.
HOOD, Jaspar and Kathrine Anderson, 2 June 1696, New York.
HOOD, Rebecca and Hugh Alley, 9 December 1681, Lynn, Mass.
HOOGLANT, Stoppel and Katherine Kregiers, 23 June 1661, New York.
HOOGLANDT, Christopher and Sarah DeWitt, 15 February 1696, New York.
HOOKE, Francis and Mary Palsgrave (widow), 20 September 1660, Boston, Mass.
HOOKE, Susanna and Edward Darby, 25 January 1659, Boston, Mass.
HOOKER, John and Abigail Standley, 24 November 1687, Farmington, Conn.
HOOKER, Mary and Stephen Osgood, 24 October 1663, Andover, Mass.
HOOKS, Elizabeth and Ezekiel Cravath, 14 June 1698, Boston, Mass.
HOOPER, Abigail and Stephen Bayley, 8 August 1673, Southold, L. I., N. Y.
HOOPER, Abraham and Philitia Green, 3 March 1687, Philadelphia, Penn.
HOOPER, Ann and Tristram Bowerman, 28 July 1685, Bristol, R. I.
HOOPER, Anne and William Davis, August 1667, Somerset Co., Md.
HOOPER, Hannah and William Ballard, 20 April 1682, Andover, Mass.
HOOPER, Henry and Elizabeth Denwood, 4 July 1669, Somerset Co., Md.
HOOPER, Isabel and Robert Jackson, 24 August 1699, Harford Co., Md.
HOOPER, John and Mary Litchfeeld, 27 January 1690, Boston, Mass.
HOOPER, Rebecca and John Ballard, 16 November 1681, Andover, Mass.
HOOPER, Robert and Anne Grinfeld, 4 December 1684, Marblehead, Mass.
HOOPER, Samuel and Mary White, 16 February 1693, Boston, Mass.
HOOPER, William and Abigail Mansfield, 9 December 1697, Salem, Mass.
HOOPS, Daniel and Jane Worrilow, 10 October 1696, Middletown, Penn.
HOOPS, Joshua and Eleanor Downal, 20 October 1693, Middletown, Penn.
HOOTEN, Thomas and Mary Lippincott, 28 August 1697, Shrewsbury, N. J.
HOOTON, Thomas and Elizabeth Stanley, 30 November 1686, Philadelphia, Penn.
HOPE, John and Isabel Allin, 7 June 1693, New York.
HOPKINS, Ann and Henry Roberts, 10 December 1699, Anne Arundel Co., Md.
HOPKINS, Bethiah and Edward Stocking, 27 May 1652, Hartford, Conn.
HOPKINS, Dorcas and Jonathan Webster, 11 May 1681, Hartford, Conn.
HOPKINS, Ebenezer and Mary Butler, 21 January 1691, Hartford, Conn.
HOPKINS, Elizabeth and James Walcom, 27 May 1695, Boston, Mass.
HOPKINS, Lady Frances and Monsieur Belvele, 9 April 1656, Boston, Mass.
HOPKINS, Joseph and Ruth Long, 1 December 1686, Charlestown, Mass.
HOPKINS, Joseph and Hannah Peck, 27 April 1699, Hartford, Conn.
HOPKINS, Joshua and Mary Cole, 26 May 1681, Eastham, Mass.
HOPKINS, Mary and Samuel Smith, 3 March 1667, Hingham, Mass.
HOPKINS, Mary and Daniel Sherwood, 26 December 1689, Talbot Co., Md.
HOPKINS, Thomas and Mary Smith, 1 April 1678, Providence, R. I.

HOPKINS, Stephen and Sarah Judd, 17 November 1686, Hartford, Conn.
HOPKINS, Stephen and Sarah Howes, 19 May 1692, Harwich, Mass.
HOPPEN, Hannah and John Jackson, 16 July 1679, Dorchester, Mass.
HOPPER, John and Margaret Tindell, 5 July 1698, New York.
HOPSON, Eliza and Samuel Wentworth, 12 November 1691, Boston, Mass.
HORE, Mary and Duncan Makcum, 2 December 1698, Boston, Mass.
HORLDSWORTHY, Walter and Naome Davis, 11 October 1660, Charles City Co., Va.
HORNE, Ann and William Pruden, 10 November 1696, New York.
HORN, Mary (widow) and John Waldron, 29 August 1698, Dover, N. H.
HORN, Rebecca and Joseph Ballard, Sr., 15 November 1692, Andover, Mass.
HORN, Thomas and Judith Riccar, 14 April 1699, Dover, N. H.
HORN, William and Sarah Franklin, 28 October 1697, Anne Arundel Co., Md.
HORNER, Isaac and Lydia Wright, March 1684, Oyster Bay, N. Y.
HORRELL, Humphrey and Eliza Smith, 10 January 1687, Beverly, Mass.
HORRELL, Sarah and Thomas Goodale, 2 December 1698, Beverly, Mass.
HORSEY, Isaac and Sarah, 7 August 1688, Somerset Co., Md.
HORSMAN, Thomas and Jane Edgar, 19 September 1681, Somerset Co., Md.
HORTON, Barnabas and Sarah Hines, April 1686, Southold, N. Y.
HORTON, Hopestill and Ebenezer Snow, 22 December 1698, Eastham, Mass.
HORTON, Jeremiah and Ruth Ely, 3 August 1661, Springfield, Mass.
HORTON, Jeremiah and Mary Gilbert, 5 May 1664, New Haven, Conn.
HORTON, Rachel and Thomas Strong, 10 October 1671, Northampton, Mass.
HORTON, Sarah and John Conklin, 1675, Southold, L. I., N. Y.
HORTON, Thomas and Susannah Keney, 25 December 1693, Milton, Mass.
HOSFORD, John and Phillipa Thrall, 5 November 1657, Windsor, Conn.
HOSFORD, Sara and Stephen Tayler, 1 November 1642, Windsor, Conn.
HOSFORD, Susana and Roland Ould, December 1668, Windsor, Conn.
HOSKINS, Anthony and Jesabell Brown, 16 July 1656, Windsor, Conn.
HOSKINS, Sarah and Benjamin Eaton, 4 December 1666, Plymouth, Mass.
HOSKINS, Samuel and Mary Austin, 5 February 1684, Windsor, Conn.
HOSLEY, James and Martha Parker, 10 March 1674, Dorchester, Mass.
HOSMER, Hester and Thomas Buckingham, 20 September 1666, Saybrook, Conn.
HOSMER, Sarah and Thomas Howe, 8 June 1681, Concord, Mass.
HOTCHKISS, John and Elizabeth Peck, 5 December 1672, New Haven, Conn.
HOTCHKISS, Joseph and Hannah Crutterton, April 1699, New Haven, Conn.
HOTCHKISS, Samuel and Sarah Talmadge, 18 March 1679, New Haven, Conn.
HOUCHIN, Elizabeth and John Endicott, 9 September 1653, Boston, Mass.
HOUCHINE, Mary and Nathaniel Greene, 22 April 1656, Boston, Mass.
HOUGH, Elizabeth and James Pitts, 10 March 1691, Boston, Mass.
HOUGH, Hannah and John Bordon, 11 February 1662, New London, Conn.
HOUGH, Richard and Margery Clows, 17 January 1683, Bucks Co., Penn.
HOUGH, Samuel and Susanna Wrotham, 25 November 1679, Farmington, Conn.
HOUGH, Sarah and Ephriam Savage, 12 April 1688, Charlestown, Mass.
HOUGH, William and Mary Bate, 18 August 1685, Saybrook, Conn.
HOUGH, William and Mary Bricknell, 24 March 1693, Boston, Mass.
HOUGHTON, Experience and Ezra Clap, 22 May 1684, Dorchester, Mass.
HOUGHTON, John and Ann Farrar, 10 May 1676, Lancaster, Mass.
HOUGHTON, John, Jr., and Mary Goss, 20 November 1698, Concord, Mass.

HOUGHTON, Jonas and Mary Berbeane, 15 February 1681, Woburn, Mass.

HOUGHTON, Joseph and Jane Vose, 31 October 1693, Milton, Mass.

HOUGHTON, Mary and William Bently, 20 January 1675, Dorchester, Mass.

HOUGHTON, Sarah and Caleb Sawyer, 28 December 1687, Lancaster, Mass.

HOULDON, Elizabeth and John Risse, 16 July 1674, Warwick, R. I.

HOULDON, Frances and John Holmes, 1 December 1671, Warwick, R. I.

HOULDON, Mary and John Carder, 1 December 1671, Warwick, R. I.

HOULDRIDE, Rebecca and Richard Margun, 21 May 1660, Andover, Mass.

HOULSTON, Martha and David Ogden, 12 January 1686, Chester Co., Penn.

HOUSE, Abigail and Thomas Collins, 17 February 1692, Warwick, R. I.

HOUSE, Samuel and Rebecca Nichols, 1664, Scituate, Mass.

HOUSTIN, Sarah and Andrew Hidden, 17 April 1654, Rowley, Mass.

HOUSTON, James and Mary Duer, 23 December 1692, Dover, N. H.

HOVEY, Abigail and Thomas Hodgkins, 12 December 1689, Ipswich, Mass.

HOVEY, Daniel and Esther Treadwell, 8 October 1665, Ipswich, Mass.

HOVEY, Elizabeth and Thomas Upham, 21 April 1693, Topsfield, Mass.

HOVEY, Priscilla and Samuel Smith, 23 November 1699, Malden, Mass.

HOW, Deborah and Joseph Skilton, 25 February 1673, Dorchester, Mass.

HOW, Elizabeth and James Redfield, May 1669, New Haven, Conn.

HOW, Elizabeth and John Wilkins, 27 April 1697, Boston, Mass.

HOW, Mary and Nehemiah Abbott, 14 December 1659, Ipswich, Mass.

HOW, Mary and Joseph Underwood, 26 February 1665, Dorchester, Mass.

HOW, Nicholas and Mary Summer, 19 November 1671, Dorchester, Mass.

HOW, Rebecca and Stephen Barnard, 1 May 1671, Andover, Mass.

HOWARD, Ann (widow) and Thomas Judkins, 25 November 1665, Gloucester, Mass.

HOWARD, Benjamin and Mary Paine, 15 April 1687, Philadelphia, Penn.

HOWARD, Catherine and David Griffin, 14 June 1697, Boston, Mass.

HOWARD, Edward and Hannah Hawkins, 7 June 1661, Boston, Mass.

HOWARD, Edward and Martha Row, 22 August 1689, Dover, N. H.

HOWARD, Edmund and Margaret Dent, 26 May 1681, Somerset Co., Md.

HOWARD, Hannah and Isaac Hills, June 1666, Malden, Mass.

HOWARD, Hannah and John Sergent, 24 December 1679, Gloucester, Mass.

HOWARD, Joseph and Rebecca Lippett, 2 February 1664, Warwick, R. I.

HOWARD, Judith and Samuel Walker, 1 June 1688, Concord, Mass.

HOWARD, Mary and Thomas Phillips, 1 March 1692, Boston, Mass.

HOWARD, Rebecca (widow of Joseph) and Francis Budlong, 19 May 1668-9, Warwick, R. I.

HOWARD, Samuel and Elizabeth Sweetser, 1661, Malden, Mass.

HOWARD, Samuel and Susanna Wilkinson, March 1671, Malden, Mass.

HOWARD, Samuel and Elizabeth Barbor, 27 December 1699, Dorchester, Mass.

HOWARD, Sarah and Joseph Gears, 7 January 1692, Preston, Conn.

HOWARD, Thomas and Ruth Joanes, 15 November 1667, Lynn, Mass.

HOWARD, William and Mary Hobday, 4 January 1673, Somerset Co., Md.

HOWARTON, William and Katherine Ridge, 19 January 1695, Anne Arundel Co., Md.

HOWD, Abraham and Elizabeth Maltbie, 14 March 1697, Branford, Conn.

HOWD, Elizabeth and John Nash, 22 August 1677, Branford, Conn.

HOWE, Joseph and Frances Willey, 16 May 1652, Boston, Mass.

HOWE, Samuel and Sarah Clapp, 18 September 1685, Sudbury, Mass.

HOWE, Thomas and Sarah Hosmer, 8 June 1681, Concord, Mass.

HOWELL, Anne and Walter Reeve, 11 December 1682, Burlington, N. J.

HOWELL, Daniel and Hannah Lakin, 4 September 1686, Philadelphia, Penn.

HOWELL, Elizabeth and Solomon Walker, 29 October 1699, Philadelphia, Penn.

HOWELL, Mary and Joseph Bolles, 1640, Wells, Maine.

HOWELL, Philip and Jane Tuffe, 3 March 1686, Philadelphia, Penn.

HOWELL, Sarah and William Walton, 20 April 1689, Byberry, Penn.

HOWEN, Mary and William Lay, 11 January 1689, Boston, Mass.

HOWES, Sarah and Stephen Hopkins, 19 May 1692, Harwich, Mass.

HOWLAND, Elizabeth and Ephriam Hicks, 13 September 1649, Barnstable, Mass.

HOWLAND, John and Elizabeth Tilley, 1624, Yarmouth, Maine.

HOWLAND, Ruth and Thomas Cushman, 7 November 1664, Plymouth, Mass.

HOWLAND, Sarah and Robert Dennis, 19 November 1672, Portsmouth, R. I.

HOWLE, Mary and Thomas Wood, 3 November 1685, Burlington Co., N. J.

HOXWORTH, Peter and Elizabeth Stephens, 27 February 1699, Boston, Mass.

HOYT, Benjamin and Hannah Weed, 5 January 1670, Stamford, Conn.

HOYT, Dorothy and Nathaniel Lovejoy, 21 March 1694, Andover, Mass.

HOYT, Hannah and Judah Gregory, 20 October 1664, Norwalk, Conn.

HOYT, Joshua and Mary Pickett, 16 March 1698, Stamford, Conn.

HOYT, Mary and Luke Hill, 6 May 1651, Windsor, Conn.

HUBARD, Anthony and Sarah Bacon, 14 February 1648, Dedham, Mass.

HUBBARD, Abigail and Humphrey Spinning, Jr., 14 October 1657, Guilford, Conn.

HUBBARD, Ann and William Barstow, 8 May 1638, Dedham, Mass.

HUBBARD, Anthony and Jane Ely, 5 November 1652, Dedham, Mass.

HUBBARD, Comfort and Joshua Weeks, 7 November 1699, Greenland, N. H.

HUBBARD, Edward and Martha Turner, 2 March 1670, New York.

HUBBARD, Gershon and Sarah Aldis, 26 February 1674, Dedham, Mass.

HUBBARD, Jeremiah and Rebecca Brush, 21 January 1682, Huntington, N. Y.

HUBBARD, John and Mary Merriam, 1648, Wethersfield, Conn.

HUBBARD, Jonathan and Hannah Rice, 15 January 1681, Concord, Mass.

HUBBARD, Lydia and John Burrows, 1694, New London, Conn.

HUBBARD, Mary and Tobias Langdon, 17 November 1686, Dover, N. H.

HUBBARD, Samuel and Tacy Cooper, 4 January 1636, Windsor, Conn.

HUBBART, Aaron and Rebecca Sumner, 27 January 1697, Milton, Mass.

HUBBART, Mary and Ichabod Sayre, 31 March 1697, New London, Conn.

HUBBERD, Comfort and Joshua Week, 7 November 1699, Boston, Mass.

HUBBERD, Judith and Obadiah Emons, 7 November 1699, Boston, Mass.

HUBBERD, Robert and Margaret Allen, 2 April 1654, Boston, Mass.

HUBBERT, Caleb and Eilzabeth Jackson (widow), 15 November 1675, Braintree, Mass.

HUBBERT, Joseph and Thankful Brown, 4 August 1698, Boston, Mass.

HUBBERT, Nathaniel and Mary Stowel, 31 May 1695, Boston, Mass.

HUBBERT, Sarah and Francis Brooker, 9 November 1693, Boston, Mass.

HUCKINS, Elizabeth and John Lewis, 4 January 1695, Barnstable, Mass.

HUDDLESTON, Catherine and Joseph Collins, 1698, Burlington Co,. N. J.

HUDNALL, Mary (widow) and Edward Saunders, May 1660, Northumberland Co., Va.

HUDSON, Ann and Samuel Woodhouse, 22 January 1694, Salem Co., N. J.
HUDSON, Elizabeth and John Fairfield, 18 April 1693, Boston, Mass.
HUDSON, Hannah and John Leverett, 13 May 1640, Boston, Mass.
HUDSON, Hannah and Benjamin Richards, 10 October 1661, Boston, Mass.
HUDSON, James and Rebecca Browne, 3 December 1652, Boston, Mass.
HUDSON, John and Mary Beard, 25 July 1689, Dover, N. H.
HUDSON, John and Susanna Norden, 17 August 1693, Boston, Mass.
HUDSON, Nathaniel and Elizabeth Alford, 1 December 1659, Boston, Mass.
HUDSON, Rebecca and Nathaniel Ballard, 16 December 1662, Lynn, Mass.
HUDSON, Thomas and Sarah Crocker, 24 October 1697, Boston, Mass.
HUDSON, William and Ann Ways, 12 August 1686, Philadelphia, Penn.
HUENS, Jacob and Martha Trescot, 24 February 1680, Dorchester, Mass.
HUESTIS, Abigail and Josiah Hunt, Jr., 24 December 1695, New York.
HUET, Bridget and John Chambers, 4 September 1696, Freehold, N. J.
HUETT, Sarah and John Lippincott, 7 May 1692, Shrewsbury, N. J.
HUGHES, Arthur and Ruth Boulton, 15 August 1698, Boston, Mass.
HUGHES, John and Deliverance Pallard, 15 September 1698, Boston, Mass.
HUGHS, Esther and Robert Hawkins, 7 June 1694, Boston, Mass.
HUGHS, Gwen and William Laycock, 27 May 1694, Philadelphia, Penn.
HULET, Jennet and Adam Maet (Mott), 28 July 1647, New York City.
HULETT, Elizabeth and George Allen, 22 February 1694, Shrewsbury, N. J.
HULETT, Louis and Helena Applegate, 15 August 1646, New York City.
HULGROW, George and Eva Burger, 30 June 1696, New York.
HULIN, Francis and Susanna Nicholas, 12 June 1696, New York.
HULL, Edward and Elinor Newman, 20 November 1652, Boston, Mass.
HULL, Elizabeth and Israel Dibble, 28 November 1661, Windsor, Conn.
HULL, Hannah and William Barton, July 1696, New York.
HULL, Hopewell and Mary Martin, 1669, Woodbridge, N. J.
HULL, Joana and John Bursley, 28 May 1639, Cape Cod, Mass.
HULL, John and Mary Jones, 19 October 1671, Wallingford, Conn.
HULL, Joseph and Experience Harper, October 1676, Barnstable, Mass.
HULL, Josias and Elizabeth Loomis, 20 May 1641, Windsor, Conn.
HULL, Mary and John Grant, 2 August 1666, Windsor, Conn.
HULL, Mary and Vincent Runyan, 1691, Elizabethtown, N. J.
HULL, Mary and John Hodgkins, 10 March 1697, Guilford, Conn.
HULL, Naomi and Thomas Burnam, Jr., 4 January 1676, Killingworth, Conn.
HULL, Samuel and Mary Manning, 16 November 1677, Piscataway, N. J.
HULL, Thomas and Hannah Townsend, 3 April 1657, Boston, Mass.
HULT, Grace and Thomas Davis, 27 January 1697, Boston, Mass.
HUME, Anne and John Barber, 31 August 1680, Somerset Co., Md.
HUMFREY, Isaac and Patience Atherton, 7 July 1685, Dorchester, Mass.
HUMMER, Frances and William Landford, 31 March 1684, Bucks Co., Penn.
HUMMERY, Elizabeth and John Fry, 18 June 1695, Bristol, R. I.
HUMPHREY, Thomas and Hannah Lane, 24 December 1665, Hingham, Mass.
HUMPHREY, Thomas and Mary King, 20 April 1674, Somerset Co., Md.
HUMPHRI, John and Sarah Pittibon, 6 July 1699, Simsbury, Conn.
HUMPHRIES, Martha and John Shipman, 5 May 1686, Saybrook, Conn.
HUMPHRIES, Mary and Barthol Case, 7 December 1699, Simsbury, Conn.
HUMPHRIS, Benhemoth and Elizabeth Whitimore, 11 March 1699, Dedham, Mass.

HUMPHRIS, Elizabeth and Nicholas Ireland, 25 September 1692, Philadelphia, Penn.

HUMPHRY, John and Kate Johnson, 2 June 1698, Boston, Mass.

HUMPHRY, Joseph and Sarah Smith, 28 October 1697, Boston, Mass.

HUMPHRY, Hopestill and Elizabeth Baker, 21 November 1677, Dorchester, Mass.

HUMPHRY, Isac and Ruth Leadbetter, 6 October 1692, Dorchester, Mass.

HUMPHRYES, James and Thankful White, 4 November 1697, Boston, Mass.

HUN, Harmen and Catalina Berck, June 1661, Albany, N. Y.

HUN, Priscilla and Thomas Walton, 28 December 1689, Philadelphia, Penn.

HUN, Thomas and Mayeke Jansen, 1692, Albany, N. Y.

HUNKINS, Mark and Mary Harvey, 29 June 1697, Dover, N. H.

HUNKINS, William and Sarah Partridge, 12 May 1692, Dover, N. H.

HUNLOCK, Mary and Jonathan Williams, 12 July 1697, Boston, Mass.

HUNN, Anna (widow) and Walter Philpot, 16 October 1651, Boston, Mass.

HUNT, Ann and Isaac Coussins, July 1657, Boston, Mass.

HUNT, Christine and Richard More, 20 October 1636, Plymouth, Mass.

HUNT, Eleanor and Henry Coleman, 27 July 1698, New York.

HUNT, Josiah and Abigail Hustis, 29 December 1695, West Chester, N. Y.

HUNT, Josiah, Jr., and Batthia Ferguson, 20 December 1697, New York.

HUNT, Mary and Matthew Pugsley, 22 November 1683, New York.

HUNT, Naomi and George Lawton, 17 January 1677, Portsmouth, R. I.

HUNT, Sarah and John Smith, 1647, Lancaster, Mass.

HUNT, Thomas and Susanna Saxton, 21 June 1694, Boston, Mass.

HUNTER, Mary and Jeremiah Gipson, 13 April 1698, Boston, Mass.

HUNTER, William and Scissilla Corish, 30 January 1656, Boston, Mass.

HUNTING, Ann and Henry Phillips, 1 March 1641, Dedham, Mass.

HUNTING, John and Elizabeth Paine, 18 April 1671, Dedham, Mass.

HUNTING, Mary and William Jaye, January 1653, Boston, Mass.

HUNTING, Samuel and Hannah Hackborn, 24 October 1662, Dedham, Mass.

HUNTING, Susan and Edward Richards, 10 July 1638, Dedham, Mass.

HUNTINGE, Margaret and Robert Ware, 24 March 1644-5, Dedham, Mass.

HUNTTING, John and Mary Fisher, 23 February 1697-8, Dedham, Mass.

HUNTINGTON, Susannah and Samuel Griswold, 10 December 1685, Saybrook, Conn.

HUNTLEY, Elizabeth and John Lewis, 24 May 1677, New London, Conn.

HUNTRESS, Mary and Henry Lewer, 20 June 1694, Dover, N. H.

HURD, Hanna and Thomas Masters, 7 December 1685, Philadelphia, Penn.

HURD, John and Eliza Webb, 16 March 1691, Boston, Mass.

HURD, Mary and John Ham, 6 May 1668, Dover, N. H.

HURST, Sarah and Richard Wilson, 7 February 1654, Boston, Mass.

HURTLY, Richard and Mary Naylor (widow), 10 December 1698, Elizabeth City Co., Va.

HUSE, Abel and Mary Hilton Sears (widow), 25 May 1663, Newbury, Mass.

HUSE, William and Ann Russell, 17 August 1699, Boston, Mass.

HUSSEY, John and Rebecca Perkins, 21 September 1659, Hampton, N. H.

HUSSEY, Stephen and Martha Bunker, 8 October 1676, Lynn, Mass.

HUST, Als and Joshuah Story, 7 September 1692, Dorchester, Mass.

HUSTIS, Abigail and Josiah Hunt, 29 December 1695, West Chester, N. Y.

HUSTIS, Robert and Elizabeth Buxton, 9 January 1655, Stamford, Conn.

HUTCHINS, Elizabeth and Thomas Ayer, 1 April 1656, Haverhill, Mass.
HUTCHINS, Enoch and Mary Stevenson, 5 April 1667, Dover, N. H.
HUTCHINS, John and Mary Davis, 30 October 1692, Philadelphia, Penn.
HUTCHINS, Joseph and Mary Edmons, 1 July 1657, Boston, Mass.
HUTCHINS, Mary and Samuel Thomas, 15 May 1688, Calvert Co., Md.
HUTCHINS, Mary and Stephen Dow, 14 December 1697, Haverhill, Mass.
HUTCHINS, Nicholas and Elizabeth Farr, 4 April 1666, Haverhill, Mass.
HUTCHINS, Samuel and Hannah Johnson, 24 June 1662, Andover, Mass.
HUTCHINS, William and Mary Edmunds, 1 September 1657, Bradford, Mass.
HUTCHINSON, Abigail and Thomas Palmer, 29 January 1696, Boston, Mass.
HUTCHINSON, Edward and Catherine Hamby, 13 October 1636, Boston, Mass.
HUTCHINSON, Elizabeth and Edward Winslow, 8 February 1668, Plymouth, Mass.
HUTCHINSON, Hannah (widow) and Abram Fort, 18 November 1655, Boston, Mass.
HUTCHINSON, Hannah and Thomas Farnum, 14 May 1693, Andover, Mass.
HUTCHINSON, Hannah and John Ruch, 29 April 1697, Boston, Mass.
HUTCHINSON, Mary and Thomas Hale, 26 May 1657, Salem, Mass.
HUTCHINSON, Mary and James Stanfield, 27 April 1690, Philadelphia, Penn.
HUTCHINSON, Ralph and Alice Bennet, 8 June 1656, Boston, Mass.
HUTCHINSON, Samuel and Elizabeth Parker, 26 April 1686, Andover, Mass.
HUTCHINSON, Susanna and John Cole, 30 October 1651, Boston, Mass.
HUTSON, Hannah and Isreal Ward, 29 October 1697, New York.
HUTTON, Elizabeth and Thomas Hillborn, 12 October 1688, Shrewsbury, N .J.
HUTTON, John and Katrine Strangnish, 28 October 1695, New York.
HUTTSON, Lydia and Edward Harper, 13 May 1682, Somerset Co., Md.
HUYBERTS, Cathalina and Carl Morgan, 15 December 1652, New York City.
HUYKEN, Mattelje and Coules Van Duyneo, 3 January 1691, Brooklyn, N. Y.
HYDE, John and Experience Abell, 3 March 1698, Norwich, Conn.
HYDE, Jonathan and Dorothy Kidder, 6 May 1673, Billerica, Mass.
HYDE, Samuel and Jane Lee, June 1657, Norwich, Conn.
HYDE, Samuel and Elizabeth Calkins, 10 December 1690, Lebanon, Conn.
HYNES, Anne and William Hodgkins, 21 December 1638, Plymouth, Mass.

I

IDE, Jane and George Kendrick, 1 April 1691, Rehoboth, Mass.
IDE, Martha and Philip Walker, 11 November 1681, Rehoboth, Mass.
IDE, Mary and Samuel Fuller, 12 December 1673, Rehoboth, Mass.
IDE, Nicholas and Mary Bliss, 16 May 1647, Springfield, Mass.
IDE, Nicholas and Mary Ormsbee, 27 December 1677, Rehoboth, Mass.
IDE, Patience and Samuel Carpenter, 8 January 1683, Rehoboth, Mass.
IDE, Timothy and Elizabeth Cooper, 20 December 1687, Rehoboth, Mass.
IGGEDEN, Elizabeth (widow) and Joseph Patchen, 10 April 1642, Roxbury, Mass.
IGGLEDEN, Richard and Ann Prince, 19 July 1660, Boston, Mass.
INGALLS, Henry, Sr., and Sarah Abbott, 1 August 1689, Andover, Mass.
INGALLS, James and Hannah Abbott, 16 April 1695, Andover, Mass.
INGALLS, John and Sarah Russell, 10 June 1696, Andover, Mass.
INGALLS, Mary and Joseph Stevens, 28 May 1679, Andover, Mass.
INGALLS, Ruth and Samuel Chapman, 20 May 1678, Ipswich, Mass.
INGALLS, Samuel and Sarah Hendrick, 4 June 1682, Andover, Mass.
INGERSALL, Dorothy and Jacob Phelps, 2 May 1672, Hartford, Conn.
INGERSOLL, John and Dorothy Lord, April 1651, Hartford, Conn.
INGOLSBY, Eliza and Winsor Golden, 14 May 1698, Boston, Mass.
INGHAM, Samuel and Rebekah Williams, 3 November 1686, Saybrook, Conn.
INGRAHAM, Jared and Rebecca Carpenter, 28 May 1662, Boston, Mass.
INGRAHAM, Jarrett and Elizabeth Searles, 28 May 1662, Boston, Mass.
INGRAHAM, Mary and Samuel Cheesbrough, 8 December 1687, Swansea, Mass.
INGRAHAM, Thomas and Elizabeth Cox (widow), 9 September 1681, Monmouth Co., N. J.
INGRAM, Miss and Nehemiah Covington, July 1667, Somerset Co., Md.
INGRAM, William and Mary Bairstow, 14 March 1656, Boston, Mass.
INGS, Hannah and Samuel Clement, 2 May 1657, Boston, Mass.
IRELAND, Deborah and Joseph Rud, 19 May 1698, Boston, Mass.
IRELAND, Joan and Richard Lattin, 24 August 1671, Hempstead, N. Y.
IRELAND, Margaret and Robert Gutridg, 25 October 1656, Braintree, Mass.
IRELAND, Nicholas and Elizabeth Humphris, 25 September 1692, Philadelphia, Penn.
IRONMONGER, John and Sarah Lakin, 4 February 1687, Philadelphia, Penn.
IRONS, Samuel and Sarah Belcher, 13 September 1677, Braintree, Mass.
ISHAM, John and Jane Parker, 16 December 1667, Barnstable, Mass.
ISHAM, Mary and William Randolph, 1680, Henrico Co., Va.
ITLE, Nathaniel and Elizabeth Annis, 3 April 1684, Philadelphia, Penn.
IVERY, Mary and Richard Chambers, 24 May 1676, Somerset Co., Md.
IVES, Hannah and Samuel Cooke, 3 March 1692, New Haven, Conn.
IVES, John and Hannah Merriman, 12 November 1668, Wallingford, Conn.
IVES, John and Mary Gillette, 6 December 1693, Wallingford, Conn.
IVES, Joseph and Mary Yale, 3 January 1672, New Haven, Conn.
IVES, Joseph and Esther Benedict, 11 May 1697, Wallingford, Conn.

IVET, Mary and Nathaniel Orrise, 11 September 1690, Boston, Mass.
IVEY, John and Mercy Bartlett, 4 January 1669, Plymouth, Mass.
IVORY, Lois and John Burrill, 10 May 1666, Boston, Mass.
IVORY, Thomas and Mary Davis, 17 May 1660, Lynn, Mass.

J

JACKLIN, Hannah and William Turner, 28 August 1689, Boston, Mass.
JACKLIN, Mercy and William Brown, 29 October 1694, Boston, Mass.
JACKLIN, Rosamond and William Monsey, 10 January 1699, Dover, N. H.
JACKSON, Abraham and Remember Morton, 18 November 1657, Salem, Mass.
JACKSON, Daniel and Elizabeth Johnson, 2 April 1697, Boston, Mass.
JACKSON, Elizabeth and Caleb Hubbert, 15 November 1675, Braintree, Mass.
JACKSON, Elizabeth and Thomas Morris, 14 July 1698, Harford Co., Md.
JACKSON, Edmund and Mary Gawdren (widow), 7 November 1652, Boston, Mass.
JACKSON, Edmund and Elizabeth Pilkenton, 27 October 1660, Boston, Mass.
JACKSON, John and Jane Thomas, 14 September 1657, Boston, Mass.
JACKSON, John and Hannah Hoppen, 16 July 1679, Dorchester, Mass.
JACKSON, John and Susanna Hayden, 19 May 1699, Boston, Mass.
JACKSON, Mary and William Foster, 15 May 1661, Ipswich, Mass.
JACKSON, Mary and George Walker, 25 December 1689, Dover, N. H.
JACKSON, Margaret Nathaniel Shaw, 12 July 1698, Boston, Mass.
JACKSON, Robert and Isabel Hooper, 24 August 1699, Harford Co., Md.
JACKSON, Samuel and Ann Clarke, 22 October 1672, Somerset Co., Md.
JACKSON, Samuel and Mary Melcher, 12 October 1693, Dover, N. H.
JACKSON, Samuel and Hannah Mare, 7 December 1698, Boston, Mass.
JACKSON, Samuel and Sarah Matthews, 11 December 1698, Harford Co., Md.
JACKSON, Sebas and Sarah Baker, 19 April 1671, Roxbury, Mass.
JACKSON, Thomas and Deborah Thayre, 29 January 1654, Braintree, Mass.
JACKSON, Thomas and Sarah Savill (widow), 5 July 1670, Braintree, Mass.
JACKSON, Thomas and Priscilla Grafton, 15 October 1690, Boston, Mass.
JACOB, Elizabeth and Elisha Turner, 6 June 1687, Scituate, Mass.
JACOBS, Anna and Thomas Lynch, 6 November 1695, New York.
JACOBS, Daniel and Abigail Field, 24 October 1697, Dover, N. H.
JACOBS, Elizabeth and Samuel Lincoln, 2 June 1692, Windham, Conn.
JACOBS, Jannetie and Caspar Springsten, 24 July 1695, New York.
JACOBS, John and Mary Carey, 8 November 1680, Richmond Co., Va.
JACOBS, Joseph and Mary Storrs, 6 December 1666, Ipswich, Mass.
JACOBS, Thomas and Mary Dinnis, 21 March 1695, Boston, Mass.
JACOBSON, Rebecca and William Mansell, 29 June 1694, Boston, Mass.
JACOCS, Beulah and Thomas Coate, 25 July 1696, Philadelphia, Penn.
JAGGERS, Elizabeth and Robert Usher, 13 May 1659, Middlesex Co., Mass.
JAMAN, Henry and Jane Barber, 31 August 1696, New York.
JAMES, Ann and John Turner, Jr., 24 April 1649, Scituate, Mass.
JAMES, Constance and Digory Sargent, 13 October 1693, Boston, Mass.
JAMES, Edmund and Mary Michell, 23 June 1669, Bradford, Mass.
JAMES, Mary and Legoe Tracey, 5 November 1694, Anne Arundel Co., Md.
JAMISON, David and Mary Hardenbrook, 7 May 1692, New York City.
JAN, the Negro, and Annetje Abrahans, 20 December 1693, Brooklyn, N. Y.
JANES, Mary and John Farrington, 24 July 1677, Dedham, Mass.
JANS, Dievert and John Masten, 27 October 1650, New York City.

JANS, Margaret and Jean DePuy, 28 May 1655, Bushwick, L. I., N. Y.

JANS, Neeltie and Gerritt Crousen, 30 October 1661, Brooklyn, N. Y.

JANS, Thijntje and Theus Gishertz, 10 October 1655, New York.

JANSEN, Hendrick and Catherine Hanson, 14 December 1672, Esopus, N. Y.

JANSEN, Jacob and Annetje Adriance, 4 January 1665, Kingston, N. Y.

JANSEN, Jan and Jannetje Roosa, 1690, Kingston, N. Y.

JAQUES, Henry and Anne Knight, 1648, Newbury, Mass.

JAQUES, Ruth and Stephen Emery, 1692, Newbury, Mass.

JARVIS, Elizabeth and Solomon Townsend, 20 June 1698, Boston, Mass.

JARVIS, Isaac and Abigail Voden, 19 January 1698, Boston, Mass.

JARVIS, John and Rebecca Parkman, 18 September 1661, Boston, Mass.

JARVIS, Margaret and Samuel Burrell, 17 September 1697, Boston, Mass.

JARVIS, Mary and Richard Collier, 25 January 1699, Boston, Mass.

JARVISE, Esther and Thomas Fox, 21 March 1690, Boston, Mass.

JARVISE, James and Penelopee Waters, 18 July 1694, Boston, Mass.

JARVISE, Nathaniel and Eliza Salter, 28 September 1691, Boston, Mass.

JAY, Augustus and Ann Mary Bayard, 27 October 1697, New York.

JAY, Mary and John Stodder, 14 November 1699, Boston, Mass.

JAYE, William and Mary Hunting, January 1653, Boston, Mass.

JEFF, William and Ruth Marthens, 12 August 1697, Harford Co., Md.

JEFFERSON, Thomas and Mary Field, 20 October 1698, Henrico Co., Va.

JEFFREY, Francis and Ann Worth, 2 December 1680, Shrewsbury, N. J.

JEFFERYES, George and Hannah Porter, 28 November 1694, Boston, Mass.

JELLET, Elizabeth (widow) and William Wardell, 5 October 1656, Boston, Mass.

JENKINS, Francis and Henri Weedons (widow), 12 April 1672, Somerset Co., Md.

JENKINS, Hannah and Thomas Turner, 9 February 1695, Scituate, Mass.

JENKINS, Lemuel and Elizabeth Oakes, 12 July 1670, Malden, Mass.

JENKINS, Lydia and John Paul, 3 March 1657, Malden, Mass.

JENKINS, Mary and John Greene, 12 September 1666, Dover, N. H.

JENKINS, Obadiah and Mary Lewis, 11 January 1677, Malden, Mass.

JENKINS, William and Ann Stadley, 25 August 1674, Somerset Co., Md.

JENNER, Thomas and Rebecca Trevice, 22 May 1655, Charlestown, Mass.

JENNERY, Mary and Robert Field, 11 October 1680, Braintree, Mass.

JENNEY, Sarah and Thomas Pope (2nd marriage), 19 May 1646, Plymouth, Mass.

JENOWAY, William and Mrs. Agnetie DeMeyer, 11 August 1696, New York.

JEPHSON, John and Emma Coddington (widow), 7 March 1656, Boston, Mass.

JERMAN, Sarah and Joseph Ambler, 30 September 1688, Philadelphia, Penn.

JERVIS, Sarah and Thomas Canby, 27 August 1693, Philadelphia, Penn.

JEWELL, Hannah and John Parish, 30 June 1664, Braintree, Mass.

JEWELL, George and Susanna Pangburne, 17 April 1688, New York.

JEWELL, Grizel and Humphrey Greggs, 1 September 1655, Braintree, Mass.

JEWELL, Mary and Joseph Barnard, 1 December 1693, Salisbury, Mass.

JEWELL, Thomas and Susanna Guilford, 18 October 1672, Amesbury, Mass.

JEWETT, Deborah and Nathaniel Knowlton, 8 May 1682, Ipswich, Mass.

JEWETT, Ellen and William Warner, 1 June 1686, Rowley, Mass.

JEWITT, Joseph and Ann Allen (widow of Capt. Bozon Allen), 13 March 1653, Boston, Mass.

JEWETT, Mary and David Haseltine, 26 November 1668, Bradford, Mass.

JEWETT, Nehemiah and Experience Pearse, 19 October 1668, Lynn, Mass.

JEWETT, Maximillian and Eleanor Boynton (widow), 30 August 1671, Rowley, Mass.

JEWIT, Jemima and John Staaple, 6 July 1693, Milton, Mass.

JINKINS, Samuel and Mary Farre (widow), 6 July 1670, Dorchester, Mass.

JOANES, David and Anne Bullard, 18 March 1685, Dorchester, Mass.

JOANES, Ebenezer and Barbary Chapline, 2 June 1685, Dorchester, Mass.

JOANES, Remember and Nathaniel Hadlock, 1 May 1673, Gloucester, Mass.

JOANES, Ruth and Thomas Howard, 15 November 1667, Lynn, Mass.

JOANES, Samuel and Mary Tucker, 25 July 1681, Dorchester, Mass.

JOBO, Mary and Michael Bacon, 31 August 1624, Dedham, Mass.

JOHNES, Edward and Annie Griggs, 1640, Charlestown, Mass.

JOHNS, Hannah and Richard S. Smith, 19 October 1669, Warwick, R. I.

JOHNSON, Ann and William Makepeace, 23 May 1661, Boston, Mass.

JOHNSON, Christian and Thomas Walley, 22 September 1692, Boston, Mass.

JOHNSON, Cornelia and Thomas Allison, 4 July 1698, New York.

JOHNSON, Eliza and George Nowell, 13 October 1693, Boston, Mass.

JOHNSON, Elizabeth and Henry Bowen, 20 December 1658, Woodstock, Conn.

JOHNSON, Elizabeth and Thomas Tolman, 4 November 1664, Lynn, Mass.

JOHNSON, Elizabeth and Thomas Walker, 1695, Elizabeth City Co., Va.

JOHNSON, Elizabeth and Daniel Jackson, 2 April 1697, Boston, Mass.

JOHNSON, Francis and Hannah and Hanbury, 24 August 1656, Boston, Mass.

JOHNSON, Francis and Sarah Hawkes, 1 February 1693, Andover, Mass.

JOHNSON, George and Hannah Dorman, 4 January 1694, Stratford, Conn.

JOHNSON, Hannah and Samuel Hutchins, 24 June 1662, Andover, Mass.

JOHNSON, Isaac and Elizabeth Porter, 20 January 1637, Boston, Mass.

JOHNSON, Isaac and Mary Harris, December 1669, Boston, Mass.

JOHNSON, Joana and Moses Haggett, 23 October 1671, Andover, Mass.

JOHNSON, Joana and John Case, 27 April 1692, Dover, N. H.

JOHNSON, James and Elizabeth Peters, 26 April 1692, Andover, Mass.

JOHNSON, John and Hannah Parmlee, 30 September 1651, Guilford, Conn.

JOHNSON, John and Bertha Reed, 28 April 1657, Lexington, Mass.

JOHNSON, John and Eleanor Brackett, 26 December 1661, Greenland, N. H.

JOHNSON, John and Mary A. Downe, 15 December 1667, Warwick, R. I.

JOHNSON, John and Eleanor Bullard, 13 September 1689, Andover, Mass.

JOHNSON, John and Margaret Cowell, 2 August 1693, Boston, Mass.

JOHNSON, Joseph and Sarah Daniel, 26 March 1675, York Co., Maine.

JOHNSON, Joseph and Elizabeth Blake, 25 January 1698, Middletown, Conn.

JOHNSON, Kate and John Humphrey, 2 June 1698, Boston, Mass.

JOHNSON, Margaret and Samuel Haugh, 30 September 1697, Boston, Mass.

JOHNSON, Mary and Ephriam Davis, 31 December 1659, Haverhill, Mass.

JOHNSON, Mary and Robert Puffer, 1664, Boston, Mass.

JOHNSON, Mary and Return Johnson, 7 September 1673, Andover, Mass.

JOHNSON, Mary and William Sutton, 31 January 1694, Boston, Mass.

JOHNSON, Mary and Benjamin Miller, 18 September 1695, Woodstock, Conn.

JOHNSON, Peter and Mehitable Farnum, 29 October 1693, Andover, Mass.

JOHNSON, Philip and Jane Trawell (widow), 15 October 1699, Elizabeth City Co., Va.

JOHNSON, Rebecca and Joseph Ballard, 17 August 1698, Andover, Mass.

JOHNSON, Return and Mary Johnson, 7 September 1673, Andover, Mass.

IOHNSON, Ruth and Timothy Ayer, 24 November 1682, Haverhill, Mass.
IOHNSON, Samuel and Mary Collins, 22 January 1664, Lynn, Mass.
IOHNSON, Samuel and Mary Stevens, 20 December 1698, Boston, Mass.
IOHNSON, Sarah and Peter Virgue, 21 January 1690, Boston, Mass.
IOHNSON, Stephen and Elizabeth Dane, 5 November 1661, Andover, Mass.
IOHNSON, Susanna and Walter Wright, 26 February 1667, Andover, Mass.
IOHNSON, Thomas and Mary Holt, 5 July 1657, Andover, Mass.
IOHNSON, Thomas and Mary Baker, April 1688, Calvert Co., Md.
IOHNSON, Timothy and Rebecca Aslett, 15 December 1674, Andover, Mass.
JOHNSON, William and Sarah Lovejoy, 23 May 1678, Andover, Mass.
JONES, Ann and Paul White, 14 March 1665, Newbury, Mass.
JONES, Ann and John Lyseum, 2 August 1692, Bristol, R. I.
JONES, Benjamin and Marie Gilman (widow), 20 May 1692, Piscataway, N. J.
JONES, Benjamin and Elizabeth Borden, 18 September 1696, Bristol, R. I.
JONES, Cornelius and Elizabeth Hiatt (widow), 6 October 1657, Stamford, Conn.
JONES, Ebenezer and Lydia Norcot, 17 May 1694, Boston, Mass.
JONES, Edward and Mary Barnabee, 1669, Somerset Co., Md.
JONES, Edward and Alicia Lunn, 27 August 1679, Richmond Co., Va.
JONES, Eleanor and Edward Boulton, 30 January 1694, Philadelphia, Penn.
JONES, Elizabeth and Thomas Chappell, 1670, Charles City Co., Va.
JONES, Ellis and Jane Jones, 28 November 1686, Philadelphia, Penn.
JONES, Ephriam and Ruth Wheeler, 7 May 1673, Concord, Mass.
JONES, Hannah and Robert Weare, 3 March 1676, Dedham, Mass.
JONES, Hannah and Mathew Ransom, 7 March 1683, Saybrook, Conn.
JONES, Henry and Rachel Warner (widow), 8 March 1687, Philadelphia, Penn.
JONES, Isaac and Deborah Clark, 21 November 1692, New Haven, Conn.
JONES, James and Joanna Williams, 2 April 1697, Boston, Mass.
JONES, Jane and Thomas Morris, 3 June 1685, Philadelphia, Penn.
JONES, Jane and Ellis Jones, 28 November 1686, Philadelphia, Penn.
JONES, John and Martha Lovell, 8 July 1695, Harford Co., Md.
JONES, John and Margaret Bull, 29 May 1699, Boston, Mass.
JONES, Josiah and Lydia Treadway, 2 October 1667, Watertown, Mass.
JONES, Katherine and Robert Roberts, 5 May 1696, Philadelphia, Penn.
JONES, Lucia and Roger Berkeim, 10 December 1681, Somerset Co., Md.
JONES, Mary and John Hull, 19 October 1671, Wallingford, Conn.
JONES, Mary and John Parker, 11 December 1690, Saybrook, Conn.
JONES, Mary and Jonathan Tilletson, 10 January 1683, Saybrook, Conn.
JONES, Mary and Richard Harrod, 30 October 1698, New York.
JONES, Mary and Samuel Fitzrandolph, 8 June 1693, Woodbridge, N. J.
JONES, Margaret and John Eastbourn, 27 February 1694, Philadelphia, Penn.
JONES, Mehetabel and Samuel Cook, 2 June 1668, Dedham, Mass.
JONES, Mercy and James Barker, 6 January 1675, Springfield, Mass.
JONES, Rebecca and James Greene, 19 November 1661, Boston, Mass.
JONES, Ruth (widow) and Thomas Browne, 12 November 1677, Concord, Mass.
JONES, Samuel and Mary Bushnell, 1 January 1663, Saybrook, Conn.
JONES, Sarah and Isaac Ballard, 3 November 1654, Boston, Mass.
JONES, Sarah and John Pratt, 8 June 1665, Saybrook, Conn.
JONES, Sarah and Philip Oxford, 8 December 1686, Moyamensen, Penn.
JONES, Sarah and Andrew Morrison, Sr., 21 October 1687, New Haven, Conn.

JONES, Sarah and Daniel Honan, 6 October 1694, New York.
JONES, Sarah and John Dotey, Sr., 22 November 1694, Plymouth, Mass.
JONES, Stephen and Elizabeth Field, 28 January 1663, Dover, N. H.
JONES, Thomas and Lydia Sanderson, 13 October 1654, Boston, Mass.
JONES, Thomas and Abigail Elithrop (widow), 25 June 1657, Boston, Mass.
JONES, William and Abigail Everitt (widow), 18 October 1687, Watertown, Mass.
JORALEMON, Jacobus Jans and Pietertje Claes, 12 December 1696, Bergen Co., N. J.
JORDAN, Hannah and Thomas Fowler, 23 April 1660, Ipswich, Mass.
JORDANIE, Henry and Elizabeth Koodrofe, 20 October 1691, New York City.
JORDON, Francis and Jane Wilson, 6 September 1635, Ipswich, Mass.
JORDON, John and Mary Frizell, 4 October 1699, Boston, Mass.
JORIS, Annetje and Marten Reyerzen, 14 May 1663, Brooklyn, N. Y.
JORIS, Maritje and Jacob Buys, 22 November 1690, Brooklyn, N. Y.
JOSE, Phebe and Robert Bull, 15 December 1649, Saybrook, Conn.
JOSLYN, Elizabeth and Edward Yeomans, 12 June 1652, Boston, Mass.
JOSSELYN, Joseph and Hannah Farrow, 17 March 1687, Hingham, Mass.
JOY, Thomas and Elizabeth Stoddard, 6 March 1695, Boston, Mass.
JOYCE, William and Sarah Cleverly, 24 September 1691, Boston, Mass.
JOYLIFFE, John and Ann Knight (widow), 28 November 1656, Boston, Mass.
JUDD, Thomas and Sarah Freeman, 1668, Milford, Conn.
JUDKINS, Sarah and Joseph Pratt, 7 May 1662, Weymouth, Mass.
JUDKINS, Thomas and Ann Howard (widow), 25 November 1665, Gloucester, Mass.
JUDSON, Esther and Eleazer Kingsbury, 30 August 1676, Dedham, Mass.
JUDSON, Mary and Nathaniel Chickering, 30 December 1668, Dedham, Mass.
JUDSON, Samuell and Bridgett Warne, 2 February 1644, Dedham, Mass.
JUDSON, Samuell and Mary Aldridge, 6 August 1646, Dedham, Mass.
JUPE, Mary and John Moss, 24 October 1652, Boston, Mass.
JURRIAESE, Rynbregh and Tuenesen Quick, 7 December 1672, Esopus, N. Y.

K

KEAN, Nathaniel and Sarah Greene, 2 November 1688, York Co., Maine.

KEASER, Sarah and John Gillow, 7 April 1666, Lynn, Mass.

KEAYNE, Anne (widow) and Samuell Coale, 16 October 1660, Boston, Mass.

KEAYNE, Hannah and Edward Lane, 11 October 1657, Boston, Mass.

KEEFE, Mary and Henry Tomson, 8 August 1693, Boston, Mass.

KEELING, Samuel and Elizabeth Oliver, 14 September 1699, Boston, Mass.

KEEN, William, Jr., and Sarah Ackworth, 14 July 1692, Somerset Co., Md.

KEENE, Hannah and Pasque Barleigh, 21 August 1684, Somerset Co., Md.

KELLEBOTH, Elizabeth and Miles Hannes, November 1698, Harford Co., Md.

KELLEY, Charles and Joana Fernald, 25 May 1698, York Co., Maine.

KELLEY, Mary and John Battis, 15 June 1693, Boston, Mass.

KELLEY, Sarah and Thomas Burkbie, 15 April 1659, Rowley, Mass.

KELLING, James and Hannah Trerice (widow), 12 December 1679, Charlestown, Mass.

KELLOGG, Jacob and Sarah Merrill, 22 September 1687, Hartford, Conn.

KELLOGG, Prudence and Abraham Merrill, 16 April 1699, West Hartford, Conn.

KELLOGG, Samuel and Sarah Gunn, 24 November 1664, Hartford, Conn.

KELLOND, Abigail and John Foster, 28 November 1689, Boston, Mass.

KELLY, John and Elizabeth Emery, 6 November 1696, Newbury, Mass.

KELSEY, Joseph and Hannah Hayden, 23 March 1699, Killingworth, Conn.

KELSEY, Mary and Jonathan Gillet, 23 April 1661, Windsor, Conn.

KELSEY, Stephen and Hannah Ingersoll, 15 November 1672, Hartford, Conn.

KEMBLE, Henry and Catharine Baker, 10 April 1693, New York.

KEMP, Easter and Samuell Foster, 15 September 1648, Dedham, Mass.

KEMP, Eliza and Rev. Thomas Thacher, 11 May 1643, Duxbury, Mass.

KEMP, Patience and Samuel Seabury, 16 November 1660, Duxbury, Mass.

KENDALL, Abigail and John Nichols, 1651, Reading, Mass.

KENDALL, Elizabeth and John Eaton, 8 March 1658, Watertown, Mass.

KENDALL, Francis and Mary Tidd, 24 December 1664, Woburn, Mass.

KENDALL, Jacob and Persis Haywood, 2 January 1683, Woburn, Mass.

KENDALL, Jacob and Alice Temple, 10 January 1694, Woburn, Mass.

KENDALL, John and Eunice Carter, 29 March 1681, Woburn, Mass.

KENDALL, Mary and Hancock Lee, 1675, Northampton Co., Va.

KENDALL, Samuel and Rebecca Mixer, 13 November 1683, Woburn, Mass.

KENDALL, Samuel and Mary Locke, 30 March 1692, Woburn, Mass.

KENDALL, Thomas and Mary Elton, 25 December 1684, Burlington, N. J.

KENDRICK, George and Ruth Bowen, 23 April 1647, Rehoboth, Mass.

KENDRICK, George and Jane Ide, 1 April 1691, Rehoboth, Mass.

KENEY, Susannah and Thomas Horton, 25 December 1693, Milton, Mass.

KENICOT, Roger and Joana Sheperdson, November 1661, Malden, Mass.

KENNEDY, Elizabeth and David Thomas, 1683, Middleboro, Mass.

KENNEDY, Elizabeth and James Collins, 17 April 1692, New York City.

KENNET, Susanna and Mongo Crawford, 29 January 1694, Boston, Mass.

KENNEY, Richard and Deborah Stokes, 15 August 1687, Dover, N. H.

KENNEY, Samuel and Sarah Rankin (widow), 15 March 1699, Dover, N. H.

KENNY, Joseph and Leah Allin, 1 December 1699, Dover, N. H.

KENNY, Martha and Benjamin Nason, 30 June 1687, Dover, N. H.

KENNY, Moses and Margaret Letherland, 24 July 1691, Boston, Mass.

KENT, Hannah and Isaac Toppan, 29 September 1669, Haverhill, Mass.

KENT, John and Hannah Griswold, 21 March 1662, Denham, Mass.

KENT, John and Abigail Dudley, 9 May 1680, Suffield, Conn.

KENT, Joseph, Jr., and Dorothy Brown, 12 November 1690, Rehoboth, Mass.

KENT, Joshua and Agnes Okeman, 4 November 1697, Boston, Mass.

KENT, Margaret and John Maddock, 28 January 1690, Philadelphia, Penn.

KENT (or LENT), Penelope and Richard Stout (widow of Von Printzen), 1634-5, Gravesend, L. I., N. Y.

KENT, Rebecca and John Farnum, 12 November 1667, Andover, Mass.

KENT, Robert and Margaret Thompson (widow), 5 August 1686, Philadelphia, Penn.

KENT, Stephen, Jr., and Jane Scott, 25 December 1683, Woodbridge, N. J.

KENT, Thomas and Joane Penny, 28 March 1659, Gloucester, Mass.

KERLEY, Henry and Elizabeth White, 2 November 1654, Sudbury, Mass.

KERNE, Clemens and George Hasfort, 8 October 1674, Somerset Co., Md.

KESKEYES, Henry and Ruth Graves, 7 June 1656, Boston, Mass.

KETCHAM, Edward and Bethia Richardson, 26 February 1677, Westchester Co., N. Y.

KETCHUM, Joseph and Mery Lindall, 3 April 1679, Norwalk, Conn.

KETTALL, Nathaniel and Hannah Eveleth, June 1669, Boston, Mass.

KETTELTAS, Abraham and Antie Boelen, 16 December 1692, New York.

KETTLE, Nathaniel and Joanna Ellise, 5 October 1692, Boston, Mass.

KETTLE, Ruth and Thomas Bibb, 20 July 1693, Burlington, N. J.

KETTOW, Edward and Mercy Belcher, 4 December 1691, Boston, Mass.

KEURLIS, Martha and Thomas Potts, 20 Octomber 1699, Germantown, Penn.

KIBBE, Anne and Joseph Fitch, 29 June 1688, Reading, Mass.

KIBBE, Elisha and Rachel Cook, 7 May 1667, Salem, Mass.

KIBBEE, Elizabeth and Andrew Patterson, 1697, Charlestown, Mass.

KIDBEE, Grizell and John Cheney, Sr., 12 September 1661, Braintree, Mass.

KIDD, William (Captain) and Sarah Oort, 16 May 1691, New York City.

KIDDER, Dorothy and Jonathan Hyde, 6 May 1673, Billerica, Mass.

KIDDER, Ephriam and Rachel Crosby, 4 August 1685, Billerica, Mass.

KIDDER, James and Elizabeth Brown, 23 September 1678, Billerica, Mass.

KIDDER, John and Lydia Parker, 3 December 1684, Chelmsford, Mass.

KIERSTEAD, Ariaentie and Dirck Adolph, 27 September 1693, New York.

KIGAN, Daniel and Phebe Banks, 8 August 1660, Charles City Co., Va.

KILBEY, Christopher and Sarah Simkins, 20 May 1691, Boston, Mass.

KILBEY, Sarah and Richard Draper, 22 October 1689, Boston, Mass.

KILBURN, Samuel and Mary Foster, 20 November 1682, Rowley, Mass.

KILBY, Edward and Elizabeth Yeomans (widow), 9 May 1662, Boston, Mass.

KILCUP, Roger and Abigail Dudson, 4 July 1695, Boston, Mass.

KILHAM, Abigail and Abraham Masters, 18 May 1691, Manchester, Mass.

KILHAM, Ann and Samuel Masters, 25 December 1698, Manchester, Mass.

KILHAM, Elizabeth and John Gilbert, 12 September 1677, Ipswich, Mass.

KILHAM, Sarah and William Fisk, 15 January 1662, Wenham, Mass.

KILLINSWORTH, Jane and George Broadly, 6 December 1698, Anne Arundel Co., Md.

KILLIOWE, Christopher and Eliza Foster, 28 May 1694, Boston, Mass.

KILTON, Thomas and Jane Blake, 25 March 1685, Milton, Mass.

KIM, Elizabeth (widow) and Benjamin Tubbs, 12 January 1699, Dover, N. H.

KIMBALL, Abigail and Philip Voden, 22 December 1692, Boston, Mass.

KIMBALL, Abigail and Nathaniel Adams, January 1693, Ipswich, Mass.

KIMBALL, Caleb and Anna Haseltine, 7 November 1660, Ipswich, Mass.

KIMBALL, Hannah and Richard Barker, 21 April 1682, Andover, Mass.

KIMBALL, Richard and Margaret Dow (widow), 23 October 1661, Ipswich, Mass.

KIMBALL, Sarah and Edward Allen, 24 November 1658, Ipswich, Mass.

KIMBALL, Thomas and Deborah Pemberton, 22 December 1686, Malden, Mass.

KIMBALL, Timothy and Catharine Fowle, 18 August 1698, Boston, Mass.

KIMBERLY, Sarah and Samuel Blakesley, 20 November 1684, New Haven, Conn.

KING, Deborah and Robert Smith, 12 July 1694, Boston, Mass.

KING, Elenezer and Mary Twells, 4 September 1676, Braintree, Mass.

KING, Elizabeth and Samuel Rice, 7 November 1655, Sudbury, Mass.

KING, James and Elizabeth Fuller, 23 March 1674, Ipswich, Mass.

KING, Jeremiah and Mary Glover, 12 December 1698, New York.

KING, John and Sarah Holton, 18 November 1658, Northampton, Mass.

KING, John and Winfred Conner, 21 October 1695, Elizabeth City Co., Va.

KING, Mary and William Futcher, 16 November 1672, Somerset Co., Md.

KING, Mary and Thomas Humphrey, 20 April 1674, Somerset Co., Md.

KING, Peter and Elizabeth Green, 29 October 1697, New York.

KING, Philipa and Tego Ockonell, 1 May 1662, Boston, Mass.

KING, Ralph and Mary E. Walker, March 1663, Lynn, Mass.

KING, Rhoda and John Rogers, 8 August 1656, Boston, Mass.

KING, Samuel and Abigail Clap, 30 October 1693, Milton, Mass.

KING, Sarah and John Drake, 12 December 1687, Milton, Mass.

KING, Thomas and Bridget Davis, 26 December 1655, Sudbury, Mass.

KING, Winifred and Joseph Benham, 15 November 1656, Boston, Mass.

KINGLEY, Susannah and William Hack, 13 November 1694, Milton, Mass.

KINGMAN, Deliverance and Jacob Mitchell, 1 January 1696, Bridgewater, Mass.

KINGMAN, Samuel and Mary Mitchell, 1 January 1696, Bridgewater, Mass.

KINGSBERY, Elizabeth and Joseph Damon, 12 December 1686, Dedham, Mass.

KINGSBERRY, Nathaniell and Abigail Baker, 5 December 1695, Dedham, Mass.

KINGSBURY, Eleazer and Esther Judson, 30 August 1676, Dedham, Mass.

KINGSBURY, Eliazur and Sarah Maccane, 14 April 1696, Wrentham, Mass.

KINGSBURY, Elizabeth and Michael Metcalf, 19 July 1672, Dedham, Mass.

KINGSBURY, John and Elizabeth Fuller, 29 November 1666, Dedham, Mass.

KINGSBURY, Joseph and Mary Donier, 7 September 1681, Wrentham, Mass.

KINGSBURY, Nathaniel and Mary Bacon, 14 October 1673, Dedham, Mass.

KINGSBURY, Sarah and Robert Crossman, 25 May 1652, Dedham, Mass.

KINGSLEY, Hannah and Samuel Richardson, 20 September 1674, Woburn, Mass.

KININGTON, Thomas and Hannah Trego, 15 June 1695, Harford Co., Md.

KINNE, Thomas and Elizabeth Knight, 23 May 1677, Salem, Mass.

KINNEY, Joana and Nathaniel Merrill, 15 October 1661, Newbury, Mass.

KINNECUT, Joana and Jonathan Finney, 18 October 1682, Bristol, R. I.

KINSEY, Joan and William Carver, 14 January 1690, Bucks Co., Penn.

KINSLEY, Mary and Thomas Dean, 7 January 1696, Milton, Mass.
KINSLY, John and Susana Daniell, 25 June 1669, Milton, Mass.
KINSMAN, Joanna and Nathaniel Rust, 22 February 1684, Chebacco, Mass.
KINSMAN, Sarah and Samuel Younglove, 1 August 1660, Ipswich, Mass.
KIP, Abraham and Kathalina Van Vlecq, 26 January 1697, New York.
KIP, Hendrick and Anna DeSille, 29 February 1660, New York City.
KIP, Henricus and Magdalen Van Vlecque, 8 June 1696, New York.
KIPPE, Jesse and Mary Stevens, 30 September 1695, New York.
KIRBY, Jane and Thomas Landers, 2 July 1651, Sandwich, Mass.
KIRBY, Mary and Richard Smith, 6 October 1647, Sudbury, Mass.
KIRBY, Sarah and Mathew Allen, 5 June 1657, Sandwich, R. I.
KIRK, Elinor and John Libbey, 29 December 1692, Dover, N. H.
KIRK, Sarah and Francis Alexander, 13 March 1699, Boston, Mass.
KIRKBRIDE, Joseph and Phebe Blackshaw, 13 January 1688, Middletown, Penn.
KIRTLAND, Hannah and William Pratt, 20 February 1678, Saybrook, Conn.
KIRTLAND, John and Lydia Pratt, 18 November 1679, Saybrook, Conn.
KIRTLAND, Martha and Joseph Blague, 10 February 1685, Saybrook, Conn.
KIRTLAND, Mary and Henry Burchstead, 24 April 1690, Lynn, Mass.
KIRTLAND, Mary and Samuel Clark, 14 December 1699, Saybrook, Conn.
KISSAM, John and Susannah Thorne, 10 July 1667, Jamaica, N. Y.
KITCHELL, Hannah and Rev. Jeremiah Peck, 12 November 1656, Guilford, Conn.
KITCHELL, Samuel and Elizabeth Wakeman, 11 March 1657, Newark, N. J.
KITCHEN, Mary and James White, 28 August 1698, Philadelphia, Penn.
KITCHEN, Thomas and Mary Mace, 7 October 1685, Philadelphia, Penn.
KITCHEREL, Martha and Abel Wright, 1 December 1659, Hartford, Conn.
KITSON, Alice and William Reynolds, 30 August 1638, Plymouth, Mass.
KITT, John and Margaret Murrel, 23 September 1697, Boston, Mass.
KITTLE, Jeremy and Katherine Clare, both of Ulster Co., 27 October 1686, New York.
KNAPP, Caleb and Hannah Clemmons, 23 November 1694, Stamford, Conn.
KNAPP, John and Hannah Ferris, 10 June 1692, Stamford, Conn.
KNAPP, Joshua and Elizabeth Reynolds, 16 March 1687, Greenwich, Conn.
KNAPP, Moses and Abigail Wescott, 1669, Stamford, Conn.
KNAPP, Samuel and Elizabeth Cobb, 26 May 1687, Taunton, Mass.
KNAPP, Timothy and Elizabeth Seaman, 16 March 1699, Greenwich, Conn.
KNIGHT, Abigail and Benjamin Leeds, 11 June 1696, Dorchester, Mass.
KNIGHT, Ann and Samuel Dark, 17 April 1683, Bucks Co., Penn.
KNIGHT, Ann (widow) and John Joyliffe, 28 November 1656, Boston, Mass.
KNIGHT, Anne and Henry Jaques, 1648, Newbury, Mass.
KNIGHT, Elizabeth and Cutting Noyes, 25 February 1673, Newbury, Mass.
KNIGHT, Elizabeth and Joseph Kinne, 23 May 1677, Salem, Mass.
KNIGHT, Elizabeth and John Hamm, 14 March 1698, Dover, N. H.
KNIGHT, Hannah and Richard Way, 13 August 1689, Boston, Mass.
KNIGHT, Joseph and Deborah Coffin, 31 October 1677, Newbury, Mass.
KNIGHT, Rebecca and Robert Adams, 1 August 1695, Newbury, Mass.
KNIGHT, Ruth and Samuel Fox, 13 June 1693, Concord, Mass.
KNIGHT, Sarah and Moses Whitney, 30 September 1686, Stow, Mass.
KNOWLES, Elizabeth and Thomas Griffith, 23 December 1699, Philadelphia, Penn.
KNOWLES, Hannah and William Locke, 23 November 1699, Hampton, N. H.

KNOWLES, Mary and Moses Lippett, 19 November 1667, Warwick, R. I.
KNOWLES, Richard and Ruth Bower, 1639, Plymouth, Mass.
KNOWLES, Ruth and Joseph Collins, 20 March 1672, Eastham, Mass.
KNOWLS, John and Appiah Bangs, 28 December 1670, Eastham, Mass.
KNOWLTON, Elizabeth and Timothy Dorman, 16 November 1688, Ipswich, Mass.
KNOWLTON, Nathaniel and Deborah Jewett, 8 May 1682, Ipswich, Mass.
KNOX, Annable (widow) and George Brown, 13 February 1698, Woodbridge, N. J.
KNOX, Katherine and Charles Angels, 6 October 1690, Salem Co., N. J.
KONNING, Elizabeth and Huybert Arentse, 11 August 1691, New York City.
KREGIERS, Katherine and Stoffel Hooglant, 23 June 1661, New York.
KUTLAND, Hannah and William Pratt, 20 February 1678, Saybrook, Conn.
KUTLAND, John and Lydia Pratt, 18 November 1679, Saybrook, Conn.

L

LABIN, Henry and Anne Lea (widow), 9 March 1687, Philadelphia, Penn.

LADD, Martha and John Whitehart, 6 June 1695, Boston, Mass.

LADD, William and Elizabeth Tompkins, 17 February 1696, Newport, R. I.

LAFORT, Marcus and Hester Richards, 18 January 1693, New York.

LAIN, Dorothy and Edward Sprague, 24 November 1693, Malden, Mass.

LAKE, Anna and Major Richards, 17 August 1686, Hampton, N. H.

LAKE, Hannah and John Gallop, Jr., 1643, Boston, Mass.

LAKE, Henry and Priscilla Wilds, 9 March 1681, Topsfield, Mass.

LAKE, Margaret and William Goulding, 2 April 1676, Westchester Co., N. Y.

LAKE, Martha and Thomas Harris, 15 November 1647, Ipswich, Mass.

LAKE, William and Ann Stratton, 1661, Salem, Mass.

LAKIN, Hannah and Daniel Howell, 4 September 1686, Philadelphia, Penn.

LAKIN, Mary and Henry Willard, 18 July 1674, Groton, Mass.

LAKIN, Sarah and John Ironmonger, 4 February 1687, Philadelphia, Penn.

LAMB, Abiel and Hannah Tailor, 4 December 1699, Framingham, Mass.

LAMB, Decline and Stephen Smith, 7 December 1663, Charlestown, Mass.

LAMB, Ebenezer and Mary Armstrong, 6 May 1690, Norwich, Conn.

LAMB, Elizabeth and Daniel Longbottom, 15 February 1692, Norwich, Conn.

LAMB, Elizabeth (widow) and Robert Old, 23 January 1696-7, Springfield, Mass.

LAMB, Mary and Daniel Walton, 21 June 1688, Byberry, Penn.

LAMB, Sarah and Stephen Scott, 27 May 1664, Braintree, Mass.

LAMB, Thomas and Dorothy Harbittle, 16 July 1640, Roxbury, Mass.

LAMBE, Thomas and Thankful Hill, 10 February 1688, Milton, Mass.

LAMBERT, Edward and Jane Downing, 11 November 1696, New York.

LAMBERT, Hannah and John Scott, 4 February 1695, Chesterfield, N. J.

LAMBERT, John and Mary Lewis, 15 January 1667, Saybrook, Conn.

LAMBERT, John and Rebecca Clows, 13 October 1687, Middletown, Penn.

LAMBERT, Martinus and Catrina Van Newenhuysen, 19 June 1695, New York.

LAMBERT, Michaell and Elinor Furnell (widow), October 1659, Boston, Mass.

LAMBERT, Sarah and Daniel Fize, 6 November 1699, Boston, Mass.

LAMBERT, Thomas and Margaret Scott, 7 January 1695, Chesterfield, N. J.

LAMBETH, Philip and Susana Lear, 14 October 1697, Dover, N. H.

LAMERE, Thomas and Hannah Hodge, 11 August 1699, Boston, Mass.

LAMPRELL, Henry and Elizabeth Mitchell, 24 July 1686, Dover, N. H.

LAMSON, Azubah and Joshua Willes, 5 May 1670, Windsor, Conn.

LAMSON, Mary and Thomas Payne, 20 August 1689, Dedham, Mass.

LAMSON, Sarah and Cornelius Brown, 6 March 1664-5, Reading, Mass.

LANCE, Elizabeth and John Mayson, 29 December 1699, New York.

LANDER, Thomas and Jane Kirby, 2 July 1651, Sandwich, Mass.

LANE, Anna and James Foster, 7 October 1680, Dorchester, Mass.

LANE, Edward and Hannah Keayne, 11 October 1657, Boston, Mass.

LANE, Edward and Anne Allen, 4 February 1688, Middletown, Penn.

LANE, Elizabeth and Robert Avery, 3 February 1677, Dedham, Mass.

LANE, George and Elizabeth Stowell, 14 December 1699, Hingham, Mass.

LANE, Hannah and Thomas Humphrey, 2+ December 1665, Hingham, Mass.

LANE, Job and Anna Reyner, 2 July 1660, Malden, Mass.

LANE, Rebecca and George Pardee, 29 December 1662, New Haven, Conn.

LANE, William and Mary Brewer, 21 June 1656, Boston, Mass.

LANE, William and Sarah Webster, 21 June 1680, Boston, Mass.

LANGDON, Elizabeth and William Fernald, 16 November 1671, Portsmouth, N. H.

LANGDON, Tobias and Mary Hubbard, 17 November 1686, Dover, N. H.

LANGFORD, John and Isabella Bowman, 30 October 1686, Burlington, N. J.

LANGTON, Rachel and Hugh Roe, 10 June 1667, Gloucester, Mass.

LANGSTON, Thomas and Sarah Header (widow), 28 August 1686, Philadelphia, Penn.

LAPHAM, Lydia and Samuel Bates, 20 February 1666, Scituate, Mass.

LARKIN, Edward and Mary Walker (daughter of John), 1 November 1688, Charlestown, Mass.

LARKIN, James and Katherine DeHart, 22 August 1691, New York City.

LARKIN, Katharine and Lancaster Simms, 2 November 1694, New York.

LARKIN, Sarah and Thomas Brand, 29 October 1672, Stonington, Conn.

LARNED, Isaac and Sarah Bigelow, 23 July 1679, Sherborne, Mass.

LARNED, Mary (widow) and John Burge, 9 June 1662, Chelmsford, Mass.

LARRABEE, William and Elizabeth Felt, June 1655, Malden, Mass.

LASH, Joanna and John Manning, 9 May 1695, Boston, Mass.

LATHAM, Joseph and Jane Singleton, 7 February 1698, New York.

LATHROP, Barnabas and Abigail Dudson, 15 November 1698, Boston, Mass.

LATHROP, Elizabeth and Hope Lathrop, 15 November 1696, Barnstable, Mass.

LATHROP, Hope and Elizabeth Lathrop, 15 November 1696, Barnstable, Mass.

LATHROP, Jane and Samuel Fuller, 8 April 1635, Scituate, Mass.

LATHROP, John and Joanna Prince, 21 January 1697, Boston, Mass.

LATHROP, Martha and Samuel Hinckley, 29 September 1699, Boston, Mass.

LATHROP, Melatiah and Sarah Farrar, 20 May 1667, Lynn, Mass.

LATTIN, Richard and Joan Ireland, 24 August 1671, Hempstead, N. Y.

LAUGHTON, John and Johannah Mullings (widow), 21 September 1659, Boston, Mass.

LAUGHTON, Mary and Thomas Day, 30 December 1673, Gloucester, Mass.

LAURENCE, Nicolas and Mary Harice, 3 November 1681, Dorchester, Mass.

LAW, Andrew and Cornelia Dischington, 10 April 1695, New York.

LAWRENCE, Abigail and Richard Bignall, 2 November 1699, Boston, Mass.

LAWRENCE, Benjamin and Mary Clough, 4 July 1689, Boston, Mass.

LAWRENCE, Eleanor and Lawrence Barnes, 1 May 1690, New York.

LAWRENCE, Elizabeth and William Smead, 31 October 1658, Dorchester, Mass.

LAWRENCE, Isaac and Abigail Bellows, 19 April 1682, Norwich, Conn.

LAWRENCE, John and Elizabeth Adkinson, 8 December 1653, Boston, Mass.

LAWRENCE, John and Sarah Buckmaster, 30 September 1657, Boston, Mass.

LAWRENCE, John, Jr., and Sara (Willett) Bridges, 20 November 1682, Jamaica, N. Y.

LAWRENCE, John and Janetie Stevenson, 6 April 1696, Perth Amboy, N. J.

LAWRENCE, Mary and Thomas Modesley, 28 August 1658, Dorchester, Mass.

LAWRENCE, Mary and Stephen Cross, 23 January 1692, Boston, Mass.

LAWRENCE, Nicholas and Charity Clark, 24 September 1699, Perth Amboy, N. J.

LAWRENCE, Thomas and Mary Ferguson, 9 November 1692, New York City.

LAWRENCE, William and Elizabeth Smith, 4 March 1664, Smithtown, L. I., N. Y.

LAWRENCE, William and Deborah Smith, 1 June 1680, Long Island, N. Y.

LAWRENCE, William and Ruth Gibbins, 24 June 1686, Middletown, N. J.

LAWRESON, Thomas and Eliner Loe, 26 August 1691, Boston, Mass.

LAWRIER, Christian and Mary Bunt, December 1699, New York.

LAWS, Jonathan and Sarah Clark (daughter of George), 1663, Milford, Conn.

LAWSON, John and Ann Eyres, 28 December 1699, Boston, Mass.

LAWSON, Theodat and Deborah Allen, 6 May 1690, Boston, Mass.

LAWTON, George and Naomi Hunt, 17 January 1677, Portsmouth, R. I.

LAWTON, Sarah and George Sisson, 1 August 1667, Portsmouth, R. I.

LAY, Lawrence and Mary Foster, 5 August 1673, Andover, Mass.

LAY, Phoebe and John Dennison, 26 November 1667, Saybrook, Conn.

LAY, Robert and Mary Stanton, 22 January 1679, Saybrook, Conn.

LAY, Sarah and Simon DeWolfe, 12 November 1682, Lyme, Conn.

LAY, Sarah and Nathaniel Clark, 3 December 1696, Lyme, Conn.

LAY, William and Mary Howen, 11 January 1689, Boston, Mass.

LAYCOCK, William and Gwen Hughs, 27 May 1684, Philadelphia, Penn.

LAYTON, Sarah and Joseph Williams, 9 December 1698, Boston, Mass.

LAZALL, Sarah and Peter Ripley, 27 April 1693, Hingham, Mass.

LEA, Anne (widow) and Henry Labin, 9 March 1687, Philadelphia, Penn.

LEACH, Alice and Robert Elwell, 29 May 1676, Gloucester, Mass.

LEACH, Sarah and John Willett, 3 July 1663, Gloucester, Mass.

LEACH, Sarah and John Aldridge, 31 October 1678, Braintree, Mass.

LEADBETTER, Deliverance and Joseph Withington, 29 March 1693, Boston, Mass.

LEADBETTER, Henrie and Relefe Foster, 9 March 1691-2, Dorchester, Mass.

LEADBETTER, Katareen and Ephriam Pason, 12 June 1684, Dorchester, Mass.

LEADBETTER, Ruth and Isac Humphry, 6 October 1692, Dorchester, Mass.

LEADBETTER, Sarah and Henry Withington, 29 May 1684, Dorchester, Mass.

LEADER, Ruth and John Allin, 30 November 1670, Braintree, Mass.

LEAR, Susannah and Philip Lambeth, 14 October 1697, Dover, N. H.

LEATHERLAND, Deborah and John Tyler, 2 November 1699, Boston, Mass.

LEAVENS, Elizabeth and Peter Aspinwall, 24 March 1698-9, Woodstock, Conn.

LEAVENS, James and Mary Chamberlain, 21 November 1699, Woodstock, Conn.

LEAVITT, Moses and Dorothy Dudley, October 1681, Exeter, N. H.

LECHEVELIER, Jean and Marie De La Plaine, 27 June 1692, New York City.

LEE, Abraham and Hester Elkins (widow), 21 June 1686, Dover, N. H.

LEE, Anne and George Buntin, 27 April 1687, Philadelphia, Penn.

LEE, Charles and Ann Barrett, 3 April 1684, Philadelphia, Penn.

LEE, Edward and Elizabeth Wright, 7 November 1676, Guilford, Conn.

LEE, Elizabeth and Jonathan Howard, 24 May 1690, Malden, Mass.

LEE, Elizabeth and Benjamin Maplin, 4 June 1695, Burlington, N. J.

LEE, Hancock and Mary Kendall, 1675, Northampton Co., Va.

LEE, Mercy and Richard Wicks, 2 December 1686, Malden, Mass.

LEE, Rachel and Joshua Ely, 9 November 1699, Burlington, N. J.

LEE, Samuel and Elizabeth Bowland, 2 June 1655, Boston, Mass.

LEE, Samuel and Mercy Call, 4 November 1662, Malden, Mass.

LEE, Sarah and Daniel Buckingham, 24 May 1693, Saybrook, Conn.

LEE, Simon and Theodora Belcher, 9 December 1698, Boston, Mass.

LEE, Stephen and Elizabeth Royce, 2 October 1690, New London Co., Conn.
LEECH, Elizabeth and John Emerson, 27 December 1693, Bridgewater, Mass.
LEEDS, Benjamin and Mary Brinsmade, 17 July 1667, Dorchester, Mass.
LEEDS, Benjamin and Abigail Knight, 11 June 1696, Dorchester, Mass.
LEEDS, Daniel and Ann Stacy, February 1681, Springfield, N. J.
LEEDS, Daniel and Dorothy Young, March 1683, Springfield, N. J.
LEEDS, Thomas and Margaret Collier, 6 August 1678, Burlington, N. J.
LEEK, Hannah and Thomas Alyn, 4 May 1698, Middletown, Conn.
LEEKE, Alyce and Jonathan Smith, 25 December 1695, Saybrook, Conn.
LEEKEY, Richard and Ann Greenfield, 4 July 1687, Boston, Mass.
LEESON, Mary and John Clatworthy, 10 May 1694, New York.
LEETE, Ann and John Collins, 23 July 1691, Guilford, Conn.
LEETE, John and Mary Chittenden, 4 October 1670, Guilford, Conn.
LE FEVRE, Simon and Elizabeth Deyo, April 1676, Hurley, N. J.
LEFFINGWELL, Hannah and Gershom Flagg, 15 April 1668, Woburn, Mass.
LEFFINGWELL, Hannah and Israel Walker, 10 December 1696, Woburn, Mass.
LEFFINGWELL, Mary and Joseph Bushnell, 10 December 1654, Norwich, Mass.
LEGG, Sebella and John Barrel, 14 September 1693, Boston, Mass.
LEGRAND, Maria and Jan Cannon, September 1697, New York City.
LEIGH, Penelope and John Forbee, 4 December 1699, Boston, Mass.
LEIGHTON, John and Oner Langdon, 13 June 1686, York Co., Maine.
LEIGHTON, William (Capt.) and Kathrine Frost, June 1656, Kittery, Maine.
LEISLAER, Sussannah and Michaell Vaughton, 24 June 1687, New York.
LEISLER, Frances and Thomas Lewis, 26 November 1694, New York.
LEISTON, Mauris and Jane Graves, 8 June 1685, Middletown, Penn.
LELAND, Hopestill and Patience Holbrook, 2 February 1691, Sherborn, Mass.
LELAND, Mercy and James Travis, 1698, Sherborn, Mass.
LELONOR, Isaah and Judith Waldron, 16 December 1699, New York.
LEMAN, Nathaniel and Thankfull Hensha, 27 January 1699, Dorchester, Mass.
LENARD, Hannah and Eleazer Fisher, 21 March 1688, Wrentham, Mass.
LEONARD, Elizabeth and Vincent Shatleworth, 18 December 1677, Dedham, Mass.
LEONARD, John and Sarah Healy, 12 October 1640, Springfield, Mass.
LEONARD, Joseph and Elizabeth Livermore, 29 March 1683, Springfield, Mass.
LEONARD, Lydia and John Dumbleton, 18 March 1675, Springfield, Mass.
LEONARD, Mary and Samuel Bliss, 10 November 1665, Springfield, Mass.
LEONARD, Nathaniel and Hannah Glover, 9 January 1694, Middletown, N. J.
LEONARD, Phebe and Samuel Hill, 6 November 1694, Duxborough, Mass.
LEONARD, Thomas and Mary Watson, 21 August 1662, Plymouth, Mass.
LEONARD, Uriah and Elizabeth Caswell, 1 June 1685, Taunton, Mass.
LEPINGWELL, Tabitha and Thomas Blanchard, 13 February 1689, Woburn, Mass.
LESTER, Ann and Nathaniel Willett, 3 May 1670, Gloucester, Mass.
LETSON, Daniel and Helena Boedann, 15 February 1696, New York.
LETHERBEE, Samuel and Lydia Bliss, 15 November 1695, Boston, Mass.
LETHERLAND, Margaret and Moses Kenny, 24 July 1691, Boston, Mass.
LEUWIS, Moses and Mary Bayer, 16 September 1695, New York.
LEVENSWORTH, John and Mary Brown, 21 August 1694, Boston, Mass.
LEVERET, John and Margaret Berry, 25 November 1697, Boston, Mass.
LEVERET, Rebecca and James Loyd, 3 November 1691, Boston, Mass.

LEVERETT, John and Hannah Hudson, 13 May 1640, Boston, Mass.
LEVERETT, John and Margaret Rogers, 25 November 1697, Boston, Mass.
LEWES, Sarah and Thomas Lincoln, 6 January 1685, Hingham, Mass.
LEWIS, Eliza and John Hogg, 22 February 1699, Boston, Mass.
LEWIS, Esther and Jeremiah Finney, 7 January 1684, Bristol, R. I.
LEWIS, Hannah and George Mowry, 22 January 1683, Bristol, R. I.
LEWIS, Johanna and John Van Strydt, 22 June 1694, New York.
LEWIS, John and Mary Brown, 10 April 1650, Malden, Mass.
LEWIS, John and Alice Bishop (widow), 22 November 1659, Boston, Mass.
LEWIS, John and Elizabeth Huntley, 24 May 1677, New London, Conn.
LEWIS, John and Elizabeth Huckins, 4 January 1695, Barnstable, Mass.
LEWIS, Mary and Obadiah Jenkins, 11 January 1677, Malden, Mass.
LEWIS, Mary and Samuel Penfield, 30 November 1675, Lynn, Mass.
LEWIS, Mary and Robert Scofield, 14 October 1697, Anne Arundel Co., Md.
LEWIS, Samuel and Sarah Dutton, 3 April 1683, Billerica, Mass.
LEWIS, Sarah and James Cobb, 26 December 1663, Barnstable, Mass.
LEWIS, Thomas and Elizabeth Brooks, 10 April 1689, Swanzey, Mass.
LEWIS, Thomas and Frances Leisler, 26 November 1694, New York.
LEWS, Mary and John Lambert, 15 January 1667, Saybrook, Conn.
LIBBEY, John and Elinor Kirk, 29 December 1692, Dover, N. H.
LIGHTFOOTT, Anna and John Tasher, 6 January 1691, New York City.
LILLY, George and Abigail Smith, 1659, Reading, Mass.
LILLY, Thomas and Elizabeth Hobby, 2 June 1698, Boston, Mass.
LINCFORD, Edward and Hannah Plumly, 16 March 1667, Braintree, Mass.
LINCOLN, Benjamin and Mary Lewes, 17 January 1694, Hingham, Mass.
LINCOLN, Daniel and Sarah Nichols, 16 April 1687, Scituate, Mass.
LINCOLN, Hannah and James Lewis, 17 November 1682, Hingham, Mass.
LINCOLN, Hannah and Samuel Staples, 9 February 1693, Taunton, Mass.
LINCOLN, Joshua and Deborah Hobart, 20 April 1666, Hingham, Mass.
LINCOLN, Prudence and Samuel Payson, 31 March 1677, Roxbury, Mass.
LINCOLN, Rachel and Thomas Randell, 20 January 1697, Taunton, Mass.
LINCOLN, Samuel and Deborah Hearsey, 29 April 1687, Hingham, Mass.
LINCOLN, Samuel and Elizabeth Jacobs, 2 June 1692, Windham, Conn.
LINCOLN, Susanna and Joseph Barstow, 16 May 1666, Scituate, Mass.
LINCOLN, Thomas and Sarah Lewes, 6 January 1685, Hingham, Mass.
LINDALL, Elizabeth and John Pitts, 10 September 1697, Boston, Mass.
LINDALL, Rebecca and John Fitch, 3 December 1674, Norwalk, Conn.
LINDSEY, John and Elizabeth Munro, 29 August 1694, Bristol, R. I.
LINKOLN, Thomas and Mehetable Frost, 3 August 1689, Boston, Mass.
LINKOLN, Joshua and Hannah Palmer, 12 February 1693, Boston, Mass.
LINN, Johanna and William Williams, 19 July 1660, Boston, Mass.
LINSLEY, Francis and Susanna Culpeper, 6 July 1655, Branford, Conn.
LINSLEY, John and Sarah Pond, 2 June 1656, Branford, Conn.
LINSLEY, Thomas and Hannah Nettleton, 10 July 1656, Branford, Conn.
LION, George and Thankfull Badcock, 14 February 1688, Milton, Mass.
LION, Hannah and William Blake, 22 November 1693, Milton, Mass.
LION, Hannah and Moses Belcher, 19 December 1694, Milton, Mass.
LION, Katharine and Ralph Freeman, 21 October 1652, Dedham, Mass.
LIPET, Moses and Sarah Throgmartin, 8 December 1697, New York.

LIPIS, Samuel and Ann Honey, 7 February 1698, New York.

LIPPETT, Ann (widow) and Edward Searle, 21 February 1670, Warwick, R. I.

LIPPETT, John (the younger) and Ann Grove, 9 February 1664, Warwick, R. I.

LIPPETT, Moses and Mary Knowles, 19 November 1667, Warwick, R. I.

LIPPETT, Moses and Sarah Throckmorton, 8 December 1697, Monmouth Co., N. J.

LIPPETT, Rebecca and Joseph Howard, 2 February 1664, Warwick, R. I.

LIPPINCOTT, Elizabeth and Joseph Parker, 2 April 1699, Shrewsbury, N. J.

LIPPINCOTT, John and Sarah Huett, 7 May 1692, Shrewsbury, N. J.

LIPPINCOTT, Mary and Thomas Hooten, 28 August 1697, Shrewsbury, N. J.

LIPPINCOTT, Restore and Hannah Shattock, 6 November 1674, Shrewsbury, N. J.

LIPPINCOTT, Richard and Mary White, 12 October 1695, Shrewsbury, N. J.

LIPPINGTON, Daniel and Hannah Bonham, 19 September 1677, Piscataway, N. J.

LIPPINGWELL, Abigail and Ezekial Cheever, 17 June 1680, Salem, Mass.

LISCOMB, John and Ann Jones, 2 August 1692, Boston, Mass.

LISCOMBE, Ebenezer and Mehitable Curtice, 18 October 1694, Boston, Mass.

LITCHFEELD, Mary and John Hooper, 27 January 1690, Boston, Mass.

LITTLE, Anna and Thomas Gray, 3 July 1694, Boston, Mass.

LITTLE, Ephriam and Sarah Clarke, 29 November 1698, Plymouth, Mass.

LITTLE, Thomas and Mary Mayhew, 5 December 1698, Plymouth, Mass.

LITTLEFIELD, John and Mary Mere, 9 March 1650, Dedham, Mass.

LITTLEFIELD, Mary and John Kittredge, 1 November 1664, Woburn, Mass.

LITTLEFIELD, Mary and John French, 16 January 1678, Billerica, Mass.

LITTLEFIELD, Phebe and John Heard, 27 April 1690, Dover, N. H.

LITTLEFIELD, Sarah and William Sawyer, June 1677, Wells, Maine.

LITTLEHALE, Mary and Edmund Bridges (3rd marriage), 6 April 1665, Ipswich, Mass.

LITTLETON, Esther and John Robins, 9 January 1662, Northampton Co., Va.

LIVERMORE, Daniel and Mary Coolidge, 28 May 1697, Watertown, Mass.

LIVERMORE, Elizabeth and Joseph Leonard, 29 March 1683, Springfield, Mass.

LIVERMORE, Hannah and John Coolidge, 14 February 1655-6, Watertown, Mass.

LIVERMORE, Jonathan and Rebecca Barns, 23 November 1699, Watertown, Mass.

LIVERMORE, Martha and Abraham Parker, 15 July 1682, Chelmsford, Mass.

LIVERMORE, Samuel and Anna Bridge, 4 June 1668, Watertown, Mass.

LIVINGSTONE, Robert, Jr., and Margaret Schuyler, 26 July 1696, New York.

LLOYD, Jane and John Collins, 22 April 1697, Boston, Mass.

LLOYD, Kathrine and George Williams, 30 December 1697, New York.

LOBDALE, Isaac and Hannah Bishop, 12 August 1697, Boston, Mass.

LOBDALE, Joseph and Eliza Townsend, 1 September 1692, Boston, Mass.

LOBDELL, Anna and Samuel Terry, 3 January 1660, Boston, Mass.

LOCK, Mary and William Hepworth, 3 January 1697, Boston, Mass.

LOCKE, Mary and Samuel Kendall, 30 March 1692, Woburn, Mass.

LOCKE, Sabinna and William Berry, 19 December 1689, Dover, N. H.

LOCKE, Sarah and John Curtis, 4 December 1672, Topsfield, Mass.

LOCKE, William and Hannah Knowles, 23 November 1699, Hampton, N. H.

LOCKER, Mary and Jonas Prescott, 14 December 1672, Sudbury, Mass.

LOCKER, Sarah (daughter of Thomas Lockyer) and John Talburs (from Ports-

mouth, England), 2 February 1696, Prince George Co., Md.
LOCKHART, Jane and John Merritt, 17 September 1686, New York City, N. Y.
LOCKWOOD, Joseph and Elizabeth Ayres, 19 May 1698, Stamford, Conn.
LOE, Eliner and Thomas Lawreson, 26 August 1691, Boston, Mass.
LOFT, Eliza and John Pasco, 25 May 1691, Boston, Mass.
LOGAN, Lydia and Thomas Thaxter, 26 November 1696, Boston, Mass.
LOKER, Henry and Hannah Brewer, 24 March 1647, Sudbury, Mass.
LOMBARD, Benjamin and Jane Warren, 19 September 1672, Barnstable, Mass.
LOMBARD, Benjamin and Sarah Walker, 19 November 1685, Barnstable, Mass.
LOMBARD, Benjamin and Hannah Whetstone (widow), 24 May 1694, Barnstable, Mass.
LOMBARD, Elicony and Edward Hawes, 15 February 1648, Dedham, Mass.
LOMBARD, Jedediah and Hannah Wing, 20 May 1668, Barnstable, Mass.
LOMBARD, Jedediah and Hannah Lewis, 8 November 1699, Barnstable, Mass.
LONG, Deborah and William Phillips, 13 November 1689, Boston, Mass.
LONG, Hannah and Clement Weaver, 1 January 1691, E. Greenwich, R. I.
LONG, Margaret and Thomas Pope, 18 November 1681, Dorchester, Mass.
LONG, Mary and John Coggin, 22 December 1664, Charlestown, Mass.
LONG, Mary and Peter Adams, 4 January 1682, Dorchester, Mass.
LONG, Ruth and Joseph Hopkins, 1 December 1686, Charlestown, Mass.
LONG, William and Jane Proby, 4 March 1694, Elizabeth City Co., Va.
LONGBOTTOM, Daniel and Elizabeth Lamb, 15 February 1692, Norwich, Conn.
LOOK, Experience and Samuel Tarbox, 16 October 1678, Lynn, Mass.
LOOK, Mary and John Curtis, 4 December 1672, Topsfield, Mass.
LOOKEN, Ann and Benjamin Wade, 1670, Long Island, N. Y.
LOOKINGGLASSE, Mary and John Finlison, 22 April 1692, New York City.
LOOMIS, Abigail and John Barber, 22 November 1677, Windsor, Conn.
LOOMIS, Daniel and Mary Ellsworth, 23 December 1680, Windsor, Conn.
LOOMIS, Deborah and Jonathan Filley, January 1679, Windsor, Conn.
LOOMIS, Elizabeth and Josias Hull, 20 May 1641, Windsor, Conn.
LOOMIS, John and Elizabeth Scott, 6 February 1648, Windsor, Conn.
LOOMIS, Joseph and Sarah Hill, 17 September 1646, Windsor, Conn.
LOOMIS, Joseph and Lydia Drake, 10 April 1681, Windsor, Conn.
LOOMIS, Nathaniel and Elizabeth Ellsworth, 23 December 1680, Windsor, Conn.
LOOMIS, Thomas and Hannah Fox, 1 November 1653, Windsor, Conn.
LOOMIS, Timothy and Rebecca Porter, 20 March 1689, Windsor, Conn.
LORD, Ann and Thomas Stanton, 1637, Hartford, Conn.
LORD, Ann and Tobias Hanson, 28 August 1698, Dover, N. H.
LORD, Benjamin and Elizabeth Pratt, 13 April 1693, Guilford, Conn.
LORD, Dorothy and John Ingersoll, 1651, Hartford, Conn.
LORD, Dorothy (widow) and William Rackley, 18 October 1689, Dover, N. H.
LORD, Hannah and John Maltby, August 1696, Saybrook, Conn.
LORD, John and Elizabeth Clarke, 9 December 1695, Ipswich, Mass.
LORD, Judith and Richard Tozer, 22 November 1678, York Co., Maine.
LORD, Mary and Thomas Carhart, 22 November 1691, New York City.
LORD, Nathaniel and Mary Bolles (widow), 31 December 1665, Rochester, Mass.
LORD, Richard and Abigail Warren, 14 January 1672, Hartford, Conn.
LORD, Sarah and John Cooper, 13 December 1692, Dover, N. H.
LORD, Sarah and Joseph Wilson, 24 April 1678, Andover, Mass.

LORD, Thomas and Hannah Thurston, 23 July 1652, Boston, Mass.
LORD, Thomas and Alice Rand, 27 June 1660, Ipswich, Mass.
LORD, William and Lydia Buckland, 3 June 1660, Rehoboth, Mass.
LOREING, Isaac and Sarah Young, 5 August 1691, Boston, Mass.
LORESON, Cornelius and Abiel Paig, 4 November 1697, Boston, Mass.
LORESON, Elinor and Thomas Temple, 17 April 1698, Harford Co., Md.
LORING, Daniel and Priscilla Man, 2 February 1698, Boston, Mass.
LORING, John and Katherine Van Clyff, 16 April 1694, New York.
LORING, Thomas and Deborah Cushing, 19 April 1699, Boston, Mass.
LOTHROP, Barnabas and Susanna Clark, 3 Novemer 1658, Plymouth, Mass.
LOTHROP, Ellen and Ezekial Cheever, 15 November 1652, Ipswich, Mass.
LOTHROP, John and Ruth Royce, 15 December 1669, New London, Conn.
LOTHROP, Mary and Edward Crowell, 16 January 1673, Barnstable, Mass.
LOTHROP, Samuel and Elizabeth Bartholomew, 28 November 1644, Barnstable, Mass.
LOTHROP, Tabitha and Shubael Dimmock, 4 May 1699, Barnstable, Mass.
LOVE, Mary and Samuel Wyllys, 28 November 1688, Berwick, Maine.
LOVE, Thomas and Hannah Thurston, 23 July 1652, Boston, Mass.
LOVEJOY, Abigail and Nehemiah Abbott, 9 April 1691, Andover, Mass.
LOVEJOY, Anna and Jonathan Blanchard, 26 May 1685, Andover, Mass.
LOVEJOY, Christopher and Sarah Russ, 26 May 1685, Andover, Mass.
LOVEJOY, Ebenezer and Mary Foster, 11 July 1693, Andover, Mass.
LOVEJOY, John and Mary Osgood, 1 June 1651, Ipswich, Mass.
LOVEJOY, John and Hannah Prichard, 12 November 1676, Andover, Mass.
LOVEJOY, John and Naomi Hoit, 23 March 1678, Andover, Mass.
LOVEJOY, Joseph and Sarah Prichard, 26 May 1685, Andover, Mass.
LOVEJOY, Mary and Joseph Wilson, 4 July 1670, Andover, Mass.
LOVEJOY, Nathaniel and Dorothy Hoyt, 21 March 1694, Andover, Mass.
LOVEJOY, Sarah and William Johnson, 23 May 1678, Andover, Mass.
LOVEJOY, William and Mary Farnum, 29 November 1690, Andover, Mass.
LOVEL, Nathaniell and Abigall Davis, 8 June 1696, Dedham, Mass.
LOVELL, Martha and John Jones, 8 July 1695, Harford Co., Md.
LOVETT, John and Sarah Hobbs, 30 December 1691, Dover, N. H.
LOVETT, Mary and William Hewlings, 23 July 1693, Burlington, N. J.
LOW, Ann and Simeon Davis, 24 September 1685, Bristol, R. I.
LOW, Cornelius and Margaret Van Bursum, 1 July 1695, New York.
LOW, John and Mary Roads, 3 March 1674, Warwick, R. I.
LOW, Matthias and Janitye Van Heyninge, 22 August 1698, New York.
LOW, Thomas and Martha Borman, 4 July 1660, Ipswich, Mass.
LOWDEN, Anthony and Sarah Osborn, 16 September 1696, Dover, N. H.
LOWEL, Samuel and Rachel Williams, 22 July 1698, Boston, Mass.
LOWELL, Joseph and Abigail Procter, 8 March 1660, Boston, Mass.
LOWERY, John and Mary Davis, 13 November 1699, Boston, Mess.
LOWLE, Ebenezer and Elizabeth Shaler, 30 January 1694, Boston, Mass.
LOWLE, John and Hannah Proctor, 3 January 1653, Boston, Mass.
LOYD, Benjamin and Mary Dinsdell, 17 January 1699, Boston, Mass.
LOYD, Edward and Mary Wheelewright, 4 December 1660, Boston, Mass.
LOYD, James and Rebecca Leveret, 3 November 1691, Boston, Mass.
LUCAS, Bethia and Joseph Sundye, 18 October 1682, Bristol, R. I.

LUCAS, Elizabeth and Nathaniel Poole, 23 September 1692, Middletown, Penn.
LUCAS, Elizabeth (widow of Jan Stephense) and Jacobus Berry, 22 June 1688, New York City.
LUCAS, Hannah and Robert Carter, 19 April 1694, Bristol, R. I.
LUDDINGTON, Widow and John Rose, 1663, New Haven, Conn.
LUDDINGTON, William and Mary Whitehead, 2 June 1690, Branford, Conn.
LUDLOM, Elizabeth and Col. John Carman, 20 January 1683, Staten Island, N. Y.
LUDLOW, Gabriel and Sarah Hanmer, 5 April 1697, New York.
LUDWELL, Philip and Hannah Harrison, 11 November 1697, Surry Co., Va.
LUFF, Jane and Philip Howell, 5 May 1686, Philadelphia, Penn.
LUGG, Mary and Nathaniel Barnard, 11 February 1658, Boston, Mass.
LUM, Judith and Joshua Bradley, 26 May 1663, Rowley, Mass.
LUM, Elizabeth and Benjamin Hinman, 12 July 1684, Woodbury, Conn.
LUMBARD, Jemima and Joseph Benjamine, 10 June 1661, Boston, Mass.
LUMBER, Eliony and Edward Hawes, 15 February 1648, Dedham, Mass.
LUMBER, Susan and John Ellis, 10 November 1641, Medfield, Mass.
LUNERUS, Polus and Margaret Clemons (widow), 1 May 1652, Boston, Mass.
LUNT, Anne (widow of Henry) and Joseph Hills, 8 March 1665, Newbury, Mass.
LUNT, Mary and Nathaniel Goodwin, 19 December 1655, Reading, Mass.
LUTTERELL, Ann and George Clark, 3 February 1699, Boston, Mass.
LUWERSEN, Alkie and Webley Rasby, 16 June 1696, New York.
LUXFORD, Elizabeth and Philip Goodwin, 14 June 1694, Boston, Mass.
LYDE, Allen and Sarah Furnald, 3 December 1661, Dover, N. H.
LYMAN, John and Dorcas Plum, 12 January 1654, Branford, Conn.
LYMAN, Sarah and James Bridgeman, 1642, Hartford, Conn.
LYMAN, Sarah and John Marsh, 1666, Northampton, Mass.
LYNCH, Thomas and Anna Jacobs, 6 November 1695, New York.
LYNCK, Mary and James Townsend, 7 November 1693, Boston, Mass.
LYNDALL, Deborah and William Andersen, 7 October 1697, New York.
LYNDALL, Thomas and Deborah Crundall, 7 September 1691, New York City.
LYNDE, Dorothy and Edward Sprague, 24 November 1693, Malden, Mass.
LYNDE, Hannah and John Trerice, 3 September 1663, Charlestown, Mass.
LYNDE, John and Elizabeth Green, 25 August 1691, Malden, Mass.
LYNDE, Nicholas and Dorothy Stanton, 9 May 1696, Stonington, Conn.
LYNDE, Selah and John Foy, 16 November 1699, Boston, Mass.
LYNDE, Samuel and Mary Richardson, 15 September 1698, Boston, Mass.
LYNDE, Samuel and Mary Ballard, 20 October 1674, Boston, Mass.
LYNDE, Simon and Hannah Newgate, 22 December 1652, Boston, Mass.
LYNNS, Damares and John Basford, 16 June 1696, New York.
LYON, Hannah and Vigalence Fisher, 14 April 1696, Dorchester, Mass.
LYON, Israel and Hannah Hewens, 25 March 1690, Dorchester, Mass.
LYON, Jane and Richard Lundy, 24 April 1691, Middletown, Penn.
LYON, Mehitable and Joseph Hewins, 29 January 1690, Dorchester, Mass.
LYON, Mary and Josiah Winchester, 10 December 1678, Dorchester, Mass.
LYON, Thomas and Johanah Payson, 23 October 1690, Dorchester, Mass.
LYON, Thomas and Anne Case, 1 November 1693, Boston, Mass.
LYON, Thomas and Abigall Clark, 8 July 1698, Dedham, Mass.
LYON, William and Sarah Ruggles, 17 June 1646, Roxbury, Mass.
LYON, William and Deborah Colburn, 8 November 1699, Woodstock, Conn.
LYSEUM, John and Ann Jones, 2 August 1692, Bristol, R. I.

M

McCARTHY, Denis and Miss Billington, 1668, Old Rappahannock Co., Va.

McCARTY, John and Ann Harmon, 9 July 1684, Staten Island, N. Y.

McCOOMB, John and Elizabeth Middleton, 21 June 1688, Philadelphia, Penn.

McKENNY, Robert and Rebecca Sparks (widow), 1 December 1692, Dover, N. H.

McROCKY, James and Mary Everett, 1 November 1662, Dedham, Mass.

MACANE, Deborah and Mark Force, 13 October 1698, Wrentham, Mass.

MACARTIE, Florene and Sarah Newwork, 24 August 1697, Boston, Mass.

MacCANE, Sarah and Eliazer Kingsbury, 14 April 1696, Wrentham, Mass.

MACE, Mary and Thomas Kitchen, 7 October 1685, Philadelphia, Penn.

MACEY, Deborah and Daniel Throop, 5 January 1697, Bristol, R. I.

MacGREGERE, Catherine and John Evans, 10 September 1694, New York.

MACK, John and Sarah Bagley, 5 April 1681, Salisbury, Mass.

MackFARLAND, Mary and John Perkins, 11 December 1697, Boston, Mass.

MackHEW, Timothy and Ann Dry, 15 May 1699, Boston, Mass.

MackINTOSH, John and Rebecca Metcalfe, 5 February 1659, Dedham, Mass.

MACKY, John and Jane Persons, 22 March 1693, New York.

MACY, Hannah and James Blake, 6 December 1682, Dorchester, Mass.

MADDOCK, John and Margaret Kent, 28 January 1690, Philadelphia, Penn.

MADOCKS, Edmund and Rebecca Munings, 14 November 1651, Boston, Mass.

MADOCKS, Sarah (widow) and Thomas Rawlins, 2 March 1656, Boston, Mass.

MAET (MOTT), Adam and Jennet Hulet, 28 July 1647, New York City.

MACKASET, Sarah and Arthur Power, 17 January 1693, Boston, Mass.

MAKCUM, Duncan and Mary Hore, 2 December 1698, Boston, Mass.

MAKEPEACE, Ester and John Browne, 24 February 1655, Boston, Mass.

MAKEPEACE, Mary and Lawrence Willis, 5 July 1656, Boston, Mass.

MAKEPEACE, Wayte-a-while and Josiah Cooper, 13 September 1661, Boston, Mass.

MAKEPEACE, William and Ann Johnson, 23 May 1661, Boston, Mass.

MAKEPEACE, William and Abigail Tisdale, 2 December 1685, Taunton, Mass.

MAKERWITHY, James and Patience Cubby, 20 February 1670, Dedham, Mass

MACKINAB, John and Sarah Roper, 18 April 1669, Dedham, Mass.

MALLORY, Mary and Samuel Cook, 14 July 1690, New Haven, Conn.

MALLYEAR, Sarah and John Perrey, 9 December 1697, New York.

MALTBIE, Elizabeth and Abraham Howd, 14 March 1697, Branford, Conn.

MALTBY, John and Hannah Lord, August 1696, Saybrook, Conn.

MALTBY, Mary and Joseph Fordham, 5 December 1689, Southampton, L. I., N. Y.

MALTIS, Catherine and William Herne, 31 December 1672, Somerset Co., Md.

MAN, Deborah and David Crage, 3 July 1698, Boston, Mass.

MAN, John and Alice Bourne, 4 October 1672, Braintree, Mass.

MAN, Priscilla and Daniel Loring, 2 February 1698, Boston, Mass.

MAN, Samuel and Esther Ware, 13 May 1673, Dedham, Mass.

MANER, Hannah and Jonathan Davenport, 1 December 1680, Dorchester, Mass.

MANN, Hannah and Robert Fitchue, 4 April 1695, Boston, Mass.

MANN, Rebecca and John Diggens, 19 January 1696, Boston, Mass.

MANNING, George and Mary Haroden, 15 May 1653, Boston, Mass.

MANNING, George and Hannah Blanchard (widow), 13 January 1655, Boston, Mass.

MANNING, John and Elizabeth Dennis, 4 April 1693, Woodbridge, N. J.

MANNING, John and Joanna Lash, 9 May 1695, Boston, Mass.

MANNING, Mary and William Adams, 15 August 1673, Dedham, Mass.

MANNING, Mary and Samuel Hull, 16 November 1677, Piscataway, N. J.

MANNING, Samuel and Elizabeth Stearns, 13 April 1664, Cambridge, Mass.

MANNING, Samuel and Abiel Wight, 6 May 1673, Billerica, Mass.

MANNING, Sarah and Joseph Bull, 11 April 1671, Hartford, Conn.

MANNING, Sarah and Samuel Barrett, 12 March 1694, Boston, Mass.

MANSELL, William and Rebecca Jacobson, 29 June 1694, Boston, Mass.

MANSFIELD, Abigail and William Hooper, 9 December 1697, Salem, Mass.

MANSFIELD, Martha and Richard Sperry, 16 December 1680, New Haven, Conn.

MANSFIELD, Samuel and Elizabeth Townshend, 22 December 1669, Lynn, Mass.

MAPLIN, Benjamin and Elizabeth Lee, 4 June 1695, Burlington, N. J.

MARBLE, John and Mary Faulkner, 30 May 1671, Andover, Mass.

MARBLE, John and Hannah Barnard, 23 April 1695, Andover, Mass.

MARBLE, Samuel and Rebecca Andrew, 26 November 1675, Andover, Mass.

MARDIN, James and Abigail Webster, 23 October 1695, New Castle, Maine.

MARE, Hannah and Samuel Jackson, 7 December 1698, Boston, Mass.

MARGUN, Richard and Rebecca Houldride, 21 May 1660, Andover, Mass.

MARLTON, William and Sarah Whaly, 1 January 1696, Boston, Mass.

MARRIOTT, Abigail and Danniell Fisher, 17 September 1641, Dedham, Mass.

MARSH, Ann and Richard Church, 18 May 1627, Barnstable, Mass.

MARSH, Ebenezer and Alice Booth, 1 November 1699, Salem, Mass.

MARSH, James and Alce Gale, 14 July 1699, Anne Arundel Co., Md.

MARSH, John and Hepsibah Lyman, 1 October 1664, Hartford, Conn.

MARSH, John and Sarah Youngs, 22 March 1662, Salem, Mass.

MARSH, Joseph and Ann Thurogood, 2 March 1692, Boston, Mass.

MARSH, Sarah and John Merrill, 29 September 1694, West Hartford, Conn.

MARSH, Zachery and Mary Sillsbee, 15 August 1664, Salem, Mass.

MARSHALL, Garviss and Elianer Pey, 27 December 1692, New York City.

MARSHALL, John and Sarah Webb, 26 May 1699, Boston, Mass.

MARSHALL, John and Mary Mills, 12 May 1690, Braintree, Mass.

MARSHALL, Joseph and Mercy Short, 29 July 1694, Boston, Mass.

MARSHALL, Mary and Robert Russell, 6 July 1659, Andover, Mass.

MARSHALL, Mary and John Catlin, 27 July 1665, Hartford, Conn.

MARSHALL, Rebecca and Eliezur Morton, 11 April 1693, Boston, Mass.

MARSHALL, Naomi and Thomas Wells, 1655, Boston, Mass.

MARSHALL, Richard and Esther Bell, 11 February 1676, Taunton, Mass.

MARSHALL, Thomas and Abigail Palmer, 4 February 1686, Dover, N. H.

MARSHALL, Thomas and Mary Chantril, 18 June 1697, Boston, Mass.

MARSHFIELD, Abilene and Thomas Gilbert, 15 August 1680, Springfield, Mass.

MARSHFIELD, Sarah and William Holton, 22 November 1676, Springfield, Mass.

MARSTON, Hannah and Samuel Fogg, Jr., 19 October 1676, Hampton, N. H.

MARSTON, Isaac and Jane Haines (widow), 28 December 1671, Falmouth, Maine.

MARSTONE, Hannah and Benjamin Barker, 2 January 1688, Andover, Mass.

MARSTONE, Jacob and Elizabeth Poor, 7 April 1686, Andover, Mass.
MARSTONE, John and Mary Osgood, 28 May 1689, Andover, Mass.
MARSTONE, Mary and Stephen Parker, 1 December 1680, Andover, Mass.
MARTEN, John and Elizabeth Simms, 17 December 1685, Pennsylvania License.
MARTENS, Catherine and Samuel Berry, 28 February 1691, Brooklyn, N. Y.
MARTHENS, Ruth and William Jeff, 12 August 1697, Harford, Md.
MARTIN, Abigail and Thomas Hall, 25 February 1690, Dedham, Mass.
MARTIN, Elizabeth and Daniell Bacon, 21 February 1685, Dedham, Mass.
MARTIN, Elizabeth and Richard Gossuth, 3 December 1696, Talbot Co., Md.
MARTIN, George and Susanna North, 11 August 1646, Salisbury, Mass.
MARTIN, Grace and Nathaniel Phelps, 11 August 1676, Windsor, Conn.
MARTIN, Hannah and Ezekial Worthen, 4 December 1661, Amesbury, Mass.
MARTIN, Joseph and Sarah Trotter, 25 November 1679, Middlesex Co., N. J.
MARTIN, Mary and Hopewell Hull, 1669, Woodbridge, N. J.
MARTIN, Melatiah and Rebecca Brooks, 6 November 1696, Swansea, Mass.
MARTIN, Samuel and Abigail Norton, 30 March 1676, Andover, Mass.
MARTIN, Sarah and Reginald Foster, September 1665, Ipswich, Mass.
MARTIN, Soloman and Mary Pindar, 1643, Gloucester, Mass.
MARTIN, Thomas and Rebecca Higgins, 28 April 1683, Piscataway, N. J.
MARTINE, Ann (widow) and William Edmunds, 1 July 1657, Boston, Mass.
MARTINE, Michael and Susanna Holliocke, 12 July 1656, Boston, Mass.
MARTINE, Rebecca and Charles Pretorious, 17 September 1653, Boston, Mass.
MARTINE, Richard and Sarah Tuttle, 1 December 1653, Boston, Mass.
MARTINE, Richard and Elizabeth Gay, July 1660, Boston, Mass.
MARTINS, Juda and William Cox, 30 March 1687, New York.
MARTINU, John and Mary Mudge, March 1671, Malden, Mass.
MARTYN, Thomas and Hannah Gennes, 22 December 1662, Brooklyn, N. Y.
MARVIN, May and Richard Bushnell, 11 October 1648, Hartford, Conn.
MASETT, Peter and Lydia Coel, 6 April 1695, New York.
MASH, Alexander and Mary Belcher, 19 October 1655, Braintree, Mass.
MASH, Mary and Joseph Parmenter, 17 September 1675, Braintree, Mass.
MASH, Sarah and Edmond Sheffield, 5 July 1662, Braintree, Mass.
MASKILL, Abigail and Thomas Bacon, 12 March 1685, Simsbury, Conn.
MASON, Abigail and John Draper, 3 September 1686, Dedham, Mass.
MASON, Abigale and William Briggs, 7 February 1680, Dedham, Mass.
MASON, Alice and Samuel Shipard, 14 July 1698, Boston, Mass.
MASON, Arthur and Joanna Parker, 5 May 1655, Boston, Mass.
MASON, Bethiah and John Wood, 23 May 1688, Swansea, Mass.
MASON, Daniel and Rebecca Hobart, 10 October 1679, Norwich, Conn.
MASON, David and Eliza Clark, 12 December 1693, Boston, Mass.
MASON, Elizabeth and Edward Bunn, 20 June 1657, Boston, Mass.
MASON, Elizabeth and Thomas Norton, 8 May 1671, Saybrook, Conn.
MASON, Hannah and Jonathan Waldo, 28 November 1692, Boston, Mass.
MASON, Izrell and John Bissell, 17 June 1658, Windsor, Conn.
MASON, John and Anne Peck, July 1639, Norwich, Conn.
MASON, John and Mary Eaton, 5 March 1651, Dedham, Mass.
MASON, John and Hannah Hawes, 5 November 1676, Dedham, Mass.
MASON, John and Content Wales, 15 October 1679, Dorchester, Mass.
MASON, John and Sarah Harthorne, 30 March 1684-5, Dedham, Mass.

MASON, Mary and Richard Thomas, 16 July 1695, Boston, Mass.
MASON, Nicholas and Mary Dudley, 11 March 1686, Saybrook, Conn.
MASON, Pelatiah and Hepsibeth Brooks, 22 May 1694, Swansea, Mass.
MASON, Priscilla and (Rev) James Fitch, October 1664, Windham, Mass.
MASON, Rebeca and Thomas Ockinton, 5 December 1682-3, Dedham, Mass.
MASON, Reynold and Sarah Clark, 27 November 1663, Milford, Conn.
MASON, Richard and Sarah Messinger, 20 November 1660, Boston, Mass.
MASON, Robert and Abigail Eaton, 10 September 1659, Dedham, Mass.
MASON, Robert and Mariot Redman, 30 January 1693, Boston, Mass.
MASON, Samuell and Mary Holeman, 29 May 1662, Boston, Mass.
MASON, Susanna and William Norton, 14 December 1659, Boston, Mass.
MASTEN, Elizabeth and Reynier Van Quackenbosh, 2 March 1674, New York
    City.
MASTEN, Jan and Geertie Bloodgood, 19 November 1677, Flatbush, N. Y.
MASTEN, John and Dievert Jans, 27 October 1650, New York City.
MASTERS, Abraham and Abigail Kilham, 18 May 1691, Manchester, Mass.
MASTERS, Samuel and Ann Kilham, 25 December 1698, Manchester, Mass.
MASTERS, Thomas and Hannah Herd, 2 September 1685, Philadelphia, Penn.
MATHAR, Joseph and Sarah Clap, 20 June 1689, Dorchester, Mass.
MATHER, Hannah and John Oliver, 28 January 1697, Boston, Mass.
MATHER, Richard and Katharine Wise, 1 July 1680, Dorchester, Mass.
MATHER, Timothy and Elizabeth Weekes, 20 March 1678, Dorchester, Mass.
MATHEWSON, James and Elizabeth Clemence, 5 April 1696, Providence, R. I.
MATLACK, William and Mary Hancock, 1682, Burlington Co., N. J.
MATSON, Hannah and Robert Hannah, 2 May 1695, Boston, Mass.
MATSON, John and Mary Cotton, 7 March 1659, Boston, Mass.
MATSON, Thomas and Mary Read (widow), 14 August 1660, Boston. Mass.
MATTHEWS, Francis and Ruth Bennett, 23 February 1692, Dover, N. H.
MATTHEWS, Hannah and Thomas Cord, 4 August 1698, Harford Co., Md.
MATTHEWS, Margaret and Emanuel Walker, 30 April 1699, Philadelphia, Penn.
MATTHEWS, Sarah and Samuel Jackson, 11 December 1698, Harford Co. ,Md.
MATTOCK, Henry and Diana Souther, 3 March 1698, Boston, Mass.
MATTOCK, Samuel and Ann Marsh, 12 February 1688, Charlestown, Mass.
MATTOCKE, Mary and Samuell Browne, 9 July 1661, Boston, Mass.
MATTOCKE, Samuel and Constance Fairebanks, 30 January 1653, Boston, Mass.
MATTOX, Mehitable and John Banks, 29 August 1694, Boston, Mass.
MAURITZ, Jannetie and Matthew de Hart, 27 June 1695, New York.
MAVERICK, Abigail and Matthew Clark, 4 April 1655, Boston, Mass.
MAVERICK, Elias and Sarah Smith, 3 February 1695, Boston, Mass.
MAVERICK, Margaret and John Prat, 29 July 1691, Boston, Mass.
MAVERICK, Rebecca and John Hawkes, 3 June 1658, Lynn, Mass.
MAVERICK, Sarah and George Robinson, 7 April 1698, Boston, Mass.
MAVERICKE, John and Catharine Skipper, 9 February 1656, Boston, Mass.
MAVERICKE, Mary and John Palsgrave, 8 December 1655, Boston, Mass.
MAVERICKE, Moses and Eunice Roberts (widow of Thomas), 22 August 1656,
    Boston, Mass.
MAVERICKE, Samuell and Rebecca Wheelwright, December 1660, Boston, Mass.
MEYBI, Cathrina and John Van Hoorn, 20 March 1693, New York.
MAXFELD, Samuell and Cristian Pootter, 11 December 1691, Dorchester, Mass.

MAY, George and Elizabeth Franckline, 6 August 1656, Boston, Mass.
MAY, Sarah and John Williams, 14 February 1679, Roxbury, Mass.
MAY, Sarah and William Hersey, 2 October 1691, Abington, Mass.
MAYCOME, Duncan and Mary Smith, 18 April 1695, Boston, Mass.
MAYER, Mary and Daniel Berry, 8 July 1697, Boston, Mass.
MAYHEW, Matthew and Mary, 1 March 1674, Chilmark, Mass.
MAYHEW, Mary and Thomas Little, 5 December 1698, Plymouth, Mass.
MAYHEW, Pain and Mary Rankin, 8 December 1699, Chilmark, Mass.
MAYHOONE, Margaret (widow) and Bryan Morfrey, 20 July 1661, Boston, Mass.
MAYN, John and Mary Peacok, 24 July 1690, Boston, Mass.
MAYNARD, Hannah and John Hayden, 1669, Boston, Mass.
MAYNARD, Johanna and Johannes d'Honneur, 12 April 1694, New York.
MAYNARD, John and Mary Starr, 16 May 1640, Duxbury, Mass.
MAYO, Elizabeth and Jacob Preig, 27 June 1687, Philadelphia, Penn.
MAYO, John and Hannah Freeman, 14 April 1681, Harwich, Mass.
MAYO, John and Hannah Graves, 1654, Roxbury, Mass.
MAYO, John and Sarah Burden, 8 July 1683, Roxbury, Mass.
MAYO, Mary and Jonathan Bangs, 16 July 1664, Eastham, Mass.
MAYO, Mehitable and Thomas Thurston, 23 July 1695, Wrentham, Mass.
MAYO, Nathaniel and Hannah Prence, 13 February 1650, Boston, Mass.
MAYO, Thomas and Elizabeth Davis, 4 May 1699, Roxbury, Mass.
MAYS, Alice (widow) and Jonathan Adams, 24 May 1686, Philadelphia, Penn.
MAYSON, John and Elizabeth Lance, 29 December 1699, New York.
MEACH, John and Hannah Yeomans, 26 August 1691, Preston, Conn.
MEAD, Experience and Jabez Eaton, 4 October 1663, Dorchester, Mass.
MEAD, John and Ruth Hardy, 27 October 1681, Greenwich, Conn.
MEAD, Patience and Matthias Evans, 28 February 1669, Dorchester, Mass.
MEAD, Sarah and Samuel Eddy, 31 September 1664, Dorchester, Mass.
MEADS, Mary and Henry Coleman, December 1691, New York City.
MEAN, Deborah and John Farnum, 16 September 1687, Boston, Mass.
MEARS, Mary and Francis Voyseen, 28 September 1699, Anne Arundel Co., Md.
MEDCALF, Eleazer and Meletiah Fisher, 9 April 1684, Wrentham, Mass.
MEDCALFE, Thomas and Ann Payne, 2 October 1679, Dedham, Mass.
MEED, Lydia and James Burgesse, 19 September 1652, Boston ,Mass.
MEEK, Elizabeth and James Wheeler, 13 January 1696, New York.
MEGDANIELL, John and Elizabeth Smith, 17 May 1658, Boston, Mass.
MEIGS, Janna and Hannah Willard, 18 May 1696, Wethersfield, Conn.
MELCHER, Mary and Samuel Jackson, 12 October 1693, Dover, N. H.
MELEN, Deborah and James Buckman, 22 September 1697, Malden, Mass.
MELIVERER, Ann and John Abbott, 7 March 1696, Chesterfield, N. J.
MELLENS, Thomas and Mary Thredneedle, 28 September 1693, Boston, Mass.
MELLOUS, Thomas and Sarah Mumfort, 3 November 1697, Boston, Mass.
MELLOWES, Martha and Joseph Waters, 13 July 1655, Boston, Mass.
MELLOWES, Mary and Emanuel Springfield, 13 July 1655, Boston, Mass.
MELLOWS, Hannah (widow) and Joseph Hills, 24 June 1651, Malden, Mass.
MELYN, Susannah and John Winans, 1664, New Haven, Conn.
MENDALL, Hannah and Thomas Tilden, 20 December 1692, Marshfield, Mass.
MERCHANT, Ann and George Cornwell, 14 August 1699, New York.
MERE, Mary and John Littlefield, 9 March 1650, Dedham, Mass.

MERICK, John and Elizabeth Wyborne, 3 February 1655, Boston, Mass.
MERRELL, Hannah and Francis Barnard, 1 August 1644, Hartford, Conn.
MERRIAM, John and Mary Cooper, 1663, Concord, Mass.
MERRIAM, Mary and John Hubbard, 1648, Wethersfield, Conn.
MERRICK, Thomas and Hannah Dumbleton, 18 December 1690, Springfield, Mass.
MERRIFIELD, Joseph and Mary Rogers, 6 April 1699, Boston, Mass.
MERRILL, Abel and Priscilla Chase, 10 February 1671, Newbury, Mass.
MERRILL, Abraham and Abigail Webster, 18 January 1681, Newbury, Mass.
MERRILL, Abraham and Prudence Kellogg, 16 April 1699, West Hartford, Conn.
MERRILL, Daniel and Sarah Clough, 14 May 1667, Newbury, Mass.
MERRILL, Hannah and Stephen Swett, 24 May 1647, Newbury, Mass.
MERRILL, John and Sarah Watson, July 1658, Hartford, Conn.
MERRILL, John and Sarah Marsh, 29 September 1694, West Hartford, Conn.
MERRILL, Mary and Edward Taylor, 19 February 1663, Barnstable, Mass.
MERRILL, Nathaniel and Joana Kinney, 15 October 1661, Newbury, Mass.
MERRILL, Nathaniel and Susannah Pratt, 18 January 1698, West Hartford, Conn.
MERRILL, Sarah and Jacob Kellogg, 22 September 1687, Hartford, Conn.
MERRILL, Susannah and John Burbank, 15 October 1663, Newbury, Mass.
MERRIMAN, Hannah and John Ives, 12 November 1668, Wallingford, Conn.
MERRIMAN, Mary and Thomas Curtis, 9 June 1674, New Haven, Conn.
MERRITT, Elizabeth and Joseph Emerie, 2 October 1693, Andover, Mass.
MERRITT, John and Jane Lockhart, 17 September 1686, New York City.
MERRITT, Katharine and John Daman, 16 June 1644, Scituate, Mass.
MERRITT, Thomas and Lucy Ward, 12 September 1695, Boston, Mass.
MERRITT, Thomas and Mary Ferris, 3 February 1696, Wethersfield, Conn.
MERRY, Mary and Robert Thornton, 13 September 1657, Boston, Mass.
MERRY, Walter and Mary Doling, 18 June 1653, Boston, Mass.
MESERVEY, Elizabeth and Michael Whidden, 6 June 1694, Dover, N. H.
MESSENGER, Bethiah and John Green, 17 January 1692, Boston, Mass.
MESSENGER, Martha and Jeremiah Fitch, 5 September 1689, Boston, Mass.
MESSENGER, Mary and William Painter, 28 May 1691, Boston, Mass.
MESSINGER, Sarah and Richard Mason, 20 November 1660, Boston, Mass.
METCALF, Elizabeth and Thomas Bancroft, 15 September 1648, Dedham, Mass.
METCALF, Jane and Philip Walker, 1654, Rehoboth, Mass.
METCALF, Mary and Henry Wilson, 24 September 1642, Dedham, Mass.
METCALF, Sarah and Daniel Whiting, 23 September 1676, Dedham, Mass.
METCALF, Sarah and Robert Ware, 4 June 1677, Dedham, Mass.
METCALFE, John and Mary Chickering, 23 January 1647, Dedham, Mass.
METCALFE, Mary (or Martha) and Christopher Smith, 2 June 1654, Dedham, Mass.
METCALFE, Mary and John Ware, 10 December 1668, Dedham, Mass.
METCALFE, Mary and Jeremiah Woodcock, 5 January 1698-9, Dedham, Mass.
METCALFE, Michael and Mary Fairebanke, 2 February 1644, Dedham, Mass.
METCALFE, Michell and Mary Pidge, 13 June 1645, Dedham, Mass.
METCALFE, Michell and Elizabeth Kinsbury, 19 July 1672, Dedham, Mass.
METCALFE, Rebecca and John Mackintock, 5 February 1659, Dedham, Mass.
METCALFE, Thomas and Sarah Paige, 12 July 1656, Dedham, Mass.
METCALFE, Thomas and Sarah Avery, 24 November 1696, Dedham, Mass.
MEYER, Helenah and Johannes Hardenbergh, 10 July 1696, New York.

MEYER, Katharine and Zachariah Weeks, 8 August 1696, New York.
MEYERS, Elsey and Barnardus Smith, 25 October 1698, New York.
MICALL, Rebecca and Richard Thayer, 16 July 1679, Braintree, Mass.
MICHAEL, Archibald and Sarah Watts, 25 December 1686, Philadelphia, Penn.
MICHEL, Thomas and Mary Molton, September 1655, Malden, Mass.
MICHELL, Mary and Edmund James, 23 June 1669, Bradford, Mass.
MICHELSEN, Cather and Jacob Van Winkle, 15 March 1671, Hudson, N. J.
MICKSCH, Dorothea and Massa Warner, 31 May 1681, Bethlehem, Penn.
MICO, John and Mary Brattle, 20 August 1689, Boston, Mass.
MIDDER, Anna (widow) and William Underwood, 17 March 1685, Chelmsford, Mass.
MIDDLETON, Elizabeth and John McCoomb, 21 June 1688, Philadelphia, Penn.
MIDDLETON, Elizabeth and Walter Allen, 11 December 1693 ,Boston, Mass.
MIFFLIN, John and Elizabeth Hardy, 1 February 1684, Philadelphia, Penn .
MILBORNE, Mary and Abraham Governeur, 16 May 1699, New York.
MILES, John and Sarah Davis, 14 March 1689, Bristol, R. I.
MILES, Martha and George Pardee, 20 October 1650, New Haven, Conn.
MILES, Mary and Lawrence Taylor, 5 February 1699, Harford Co., Md.
MILES, Samuel and Elizabeth Dowse, 16 October 1659, Boston, Mass.
MILES, Samuell and Mary Twitchell, 3 February 1684, Dedham, Mass.
MILFORD, Mary and John Corliss, 17 December 1684, Haverhill, Mass.
MILL, Jennett and William Askin, 10 January 1692, Shrewsbury, N. J.
MILLER, Apphya and Francis Rogers, 15 October 1698, Elizabeth City Co., Va.
MILLER, Benjamin and Mary Johnson, 18 September 1695, Woodstock, Conn.
MILLER, Daniel and Elizabeth Bucklan, 11 December 1699, East Hampton, N. Y.
MILLER, Elizabeth and John Park, 5 April 1694, Watertown, Mass.
MILLER, Hannah and John Bunker, July 1655, Malden, Mass.
MILLER, Hannah and Joseph Hall, 12 February 1689, Marshfield, Mass.
MILLER, John and Margaret Winslow, 24 December 1659, Marshfield, Mass.
MILLER, Jonathan and Sarah Holmes, 25 February 1691, Bedford, N. Y.
MILLER, Lidia and Jacob Cooke, 29 December 1681, Marshfield, Mass.
MILLER, Margery and John Hall, 30 April 1694, Marshfield, Mass.
MILLER, Mary and Samuel Perry, 12 December 1678, Sandwich, Mass.
MILLER, Mary and Thomas Peacher, 3 September 1690, New Jersey License.
MILLER, Mercy and John Nicols, 18 December 1695, Boston, Mass.
MILLER, Paul and Antie van der Heyden, 31 January 1695, New York.
MILLER, Rebecca and Thomas Clark, 12 February 1681, Marshfield, Mass.
MILLER, Robert and Elizabeth Sabin, 24 October 1662, Rehoboth, Mass.
MILLER, Robert and Charity Turber, 14 February 1690, Swansea, Mass.
MILLER, Robert and Susannah Way, 25 August 1696, Boston, Mass.
MILLER, Samuel and Rebecca Belcher, 25 June 1690, Milton, Mass.
MILLER, Sarah and John Titus, 3 July 1677, Rehoboth, Mass.
MILLER, Simon and Mary Buell, 20 February 1660, Windsor, Conn.
MILLER, Thomas and Sarah Day, 8 August 1698, Boston, Mass.
MILLER, William and Mary Bushnell, 19 April 1693, Saybrook, Conn.
MILLET, Mary and Thomas Riggs, 7 June 1658, Gloucester, Mass.
MILLET, Sarah and Morris Smith, 4 November 1681, Gloucester, Mass.
MILLETT, John and Sarah Leach, 3 July 1663, Gloucester, Mass.
MILLETT, Nathaniel and Ann Lester, 3 May 1670, Gloucester, Mass.

MILLETT, Thomas and Elizabeth Racheller, 18 June 1696, Gloucester, Mass.
MILLS, Benjamin and Mary Thorne, 1 May 1673, Dedham, Mass.
MILLS, Dorothy and John Harker, 30 June 1647, York Co., Maine .
MILLS, John, Jr., and Elizabeth Shove, 26 February 1653, Braintree, Mass.
MILLS, Mary and John Marshall, 12 May 1690, Braintree, Mass.
MILLS, Mary and Daniel Willard, 19 June 1691, Milton, Mass.
MILLS, Peter and Jane Warren, 10 December 1691, Hartford, Conn.
MILLS, Phebe and Lot Burnett, 20 October 1675, Easthampton, L. I., N. Y.
MILLS, Rebeca and Samuell Rice, 5 October 1682, Dedham, Mass.
MILLS, Samuell and Frances Pimbrook, 11 January 1645, Dedham, Mass.
MILLS, Sarah and Sam Barber, 6 July 1676, Dedham, Mass.
MILLS, Sarah and John Fuller, 27 June 1678, Dedham, Mass.
MILLS, Simon and Mary Buel, 23 February 1659, Simsbury, Conn.
MILLS, Susanna and William Dawes, 1641, Braintree, Mass.
MILLS, Susanna and William Gillett, November 1674, Somerset Co., Md.
MILLWOOD, Elizabeth and Daniel Pierce, 5 December 1660, Newbury, Mass.
MILNER, Joseph and Pleasant Powlin, 10 May 1690, Middletown, Penn.
MILNER, Thomas and Gillan Brown, 3 September 1696, Chesterfield, N. J.
MILTON, Christian and John Corbitt, 6 May 1699, New York.
MILWARD, Ann and Daniel Peirce, 26 December 1654, Newbury, Mass.
MILWARD, Rebecca and Thomas Thorp, 27 May 1656, Boston, Mass.
MINER, Thomas and Grace Palmer, 23 April 1634, Charlestown, Mass.
MINOR, Clement and Frances Willey, 1662, New London, Conn.
MINOT, John and Lydia Butler, 19 May 1647, Dorchester, Mass.
MINOT, John and Elizabeth Breck, 11 March 1670, Dorchester, Mass.
MINOT, Mehitable and Thomas Cooper, 6 March 1683, Boston, Mass.
MINOTT, Elizabeth and John Danforth, 21 November 1682, Dorchester, Mass.
MINOTT, Elizabeth and Nathananiel Sunderland, 7 December 1695, Dorchester, Mass.
MINOTT, John and Mary Baker, 21 March 1696, Dorchester, Mass.
MINSON, William and Paster Perrin, 4 August 1697, Elizabeth City Co., Va.
MIRICK, Mary and John Monsir, 24 April 1695, Boston, Mass.
MIRICK, Sarah and John Atkinson, 27 April 1664, Newbury, Mass.
MIRIOUR, Mary and William Barkly, 13 January 1697, Boston, Mass.
MITCHELL, Elizabeth and John Washburn, 6 December 1645, Plymouth, Mass.
MITCHELL, Elizabeth and Henry Lamprell, 24 July 1686, Dover, N. H.
MITCHELL, Hannah and Edmund Goffe, 7 May 1696, Boston, Mass.
MITCHELL, Jacob and Susana Pope, 7 November 1666, Plymouth, Mass.
MITCHELL, Jacob and Deliverance Kingman, 1 January 1696, Bridgewater, Mass.
MITCHELL, Joanna and Joseph Flood, 10 March 1698, Boston, Mass.
MITCHELL, John and Hanna Spafford, 20 May 1680, Newbury, Mass.
MITCHELL, John and Constance Moorers, 15 November 1697, Newbury, Mass.
MITCHELL, Jonathan and Margaret Shepard (widow), 19 November 1650, Cambridge, Mass.
MITCHELL, Mary and Robert Savory, 8 December 1656, Newbury, Mass.
MITCHELL, Mary and William Ellis, 1675, Charlestown, Mass.
MITCHELL, Mary and Samuel Kingman, 1 January 1696, Bridgewater, Mass.
MIXER, Rebecca and Samuel Kendall, 13 November 1683, Woburn, Mass.
MYHAM, Paul and Eliza Tay, 17 December 1689, Boston, Mass.

MYRICK, Sarah and Theodore Atkinson, 27 April 1664, Newbury, Mass.

MODESLEY, Thomas and Mary Lawrence, 28 August 1658, Dorchester, Mass.

MOLL, Ariaentie and Lewin Dewind, 26 May 1698, New York.

MOLYNEUX, Mary and Josiah Quimby, 17 June 1689, Westchester Co., N. Y.

MONSEY, William and Rosamond Jacklin, 10 January 1699, Dover, N. H.

MONSIR, John and Mary Mirick, 24 April 1695, Boston, Mass.

MONTAGUE, Abigail and Mark Warner, 8 November 1671, Hadley, Mass.

MONTAGUE, Cicely and Peter Montague, 1633, Nansemond Co., Va.

MONTAGUE, Ellen and William Thompson, 1684, Lancaster Co., Va.

MONTAGUE, Peter and Mary Crow Coleman (widow), 16 September 1680, Hadley, Mass.

MONTAGUE, Peter and Cicely Montague, 1633, Nansemond Co., Va.

MONTGOMERY, William and Isabel Burnet, 8 January 1684, Eglinton, N. J.

MONTTAGUE, Peter and Elizabeth Morris, 1633, Middlesex Co., Va.

MONY, John and Jane Pope, 2 April 1698, Dorchester, Mass.

MOODEY, Samuel and Esther Green, 4 April 1695, Boston, Mass.

MOODY, Caleb and Sarah Peirce, 24 August 1659, Newbury, Mass.

MOODY, Caleb and Judith Bradbury, 9 November 1665, Newbury, Mass.

MOODY, Cutting and Judith Little, 25 March 1696, Newbury, Mass.

MOODY, Daniel and Elizabeth Somerby, 29 March 1683, Salisbury, Mass.

MOODY, Rachel and John Freeman, 7 July 1671, Somerset Co., Md.

MOODY, Samuel and Mary Cutting, 30 November 1657, Newbury, Mass.

MOODY, Sarah and John Pike, 5 May 1681, Boston, Mass.

MOODY, Sarah and Silvanus Plummer, January 1681, Newbury, Mass.

MOOL, Anne and John Fforlisson, 5 July 1699, New York.

MOON, John and Martha Will, 23 May 1686, Philadelphia, Penn.

MOON, Martha and James Shaddock, 25 August 1689, Philadelphia, Penn.

MOORE, Abigail and Thomas Bissell, 11 October 1655, Windsor, Conn.

MOORE, Abraham and Priscilla Poor, 14 December 1687, Andover, Mass.

MOORE, Anne and Ephriam Hildreth, 8 October 1686, Stow, Mass.

MOORE, Frances and Philip Dodridg, 15 October 1696, New York.

MOORE, James and Mary, 6 December 1656, Boston, Mass.

MOORE, John and Anne Smith, 16 November 1654, Sudbury, Mass.

MOORE, John and Hannah Goffe, 21 September 1664, Windsor, Conn.

MOORE, John and Elizabeth Cheek, 8 September 1696, New York.

MOORE, John and Hesadiah Fairbanks, 1 January 1698, Concord, Mass.

MOORE, Joseph and Ruth Starr, 21 March 1656, Boston, Mass.

MOORE, Joseph and Mary Gillett, 15 July 1658, Windsor, Conn.

MOORE, Joseph and Sarah Brown, 29 August 1681, Windsor, Conn.

MOORE, Martha and Nathaniel Black, 1695, Milton, Mass.

MOORE, Mindwell and Nathaniel Bissell, 25 September 1662, Windsor, Conn.

MOORE, Miriam and John Willey, 18 March 1668, New London, Conn.

MOORE, Samuell and Abigail Hawkins, 13 May 1660, Boston, Mass.

MOORERS, Constance and John Mitchell, 15 November 1697, Newbury, Mass.

MOORHOUSE, Thomas and Mary Hill, 3 April 1690, Boston, Mass.

MORE, Christine and Joshua Conant, 31 August 1676, Salem, Mass.

MORE, Mary and John Holme, 3 January 1688, Philadelphia Co., Penn.

MORE, Richard and Christine Hunt, 20 October 1636, Plymouth, Mass.

MORE, Richard and Rebecca Baily, 11 January 1694, New York City, N. Y.

MORE, Thomas and Susan Newell, 3 October 1673, Dorchester, Mass.
MOREY, Betty and Edward Black, 26 June 1696, Milton, Mass.
MORFREY, Bryan and Margaret Mayhoone (widow), 20 July 1661, Boston, Mass.
MORGAN, Catharine (widow) and Nicholas Stilwell, 6 February 1671, Staten Island, N. Y.
MORGAN, Carl and Helena Applegate, 9 February 1648, New York City.
MORGAN, Carl and Cathalina Huyberts, 15 December 1652, New York City.
MORGAN, Elizabeth and William Walker, 25 August 1689, Philadelphia, Penn.
MORGAN, Elizabeth and Jonathan Star, 12 January 1699, New London, Conn.
MORGAN, George and Elizabeth Smith, 10 February 1699, Harford Co., Md.
MORGAN, Hannah and Nehemiah Royce, 20 November 1660, Wallingford, Conn.
MORGAN, John and Rachel Dymond, 16 November 1665, Preston, Conn.
MORGAN, Margaret and Leonard Campison, 26 December 1677, Somerset Co., Md.
MORGAN, Miles and Elizabeth Bliss, 15 February 1670, Springfield, Mass.
MORGAN, Nathaniel and Hannah Bird, 19 January 1691, Springfield, Mass.
MORLEY, John and Constant Starr, 20 February 1647, Braintree, Mass.
MORLEY, Thomas and Martha Wright, 8 December 1681, Springfield, Mass.
MORRELL, Elizabeth and Samuel Brown, 3 February 1698, Boston, Mass.
MORRELL, John and Lysbell Morrell, 31 August 1659, Boston, Mass.
MORRELL, Lysbell and John Morrell, 31 August 1659, Boston, Mass.
MORRILL, Abraham and Sarah Clement, 10 June 1645, Roxbury, Mass.
MORRILL, Jacob and Susanna Whittier, 15 July 1674, Roxbury, Mass.
MOADSLEY, Elizabeth and James Bishop, 16 November 1692, Dorchester, Mass.
MOADSLIE, Thomas and Susanah Rigbie, 24 October 1690, Dorchester, Mass.
MORRIS, Anthony and Agnes Brown, 25 August 1689, Philadelphia, Penn.
MORRIS, Anthony and Mary Jones, 30 January 1676, Burlington Co., N. J.
MORRIS, David and Mary Philpin, 4 March 1685, Philadelphia, Penn.
MORRIS, Edward and Grace Bett, 20 September 1655, Boston, Mass.
MORRIS, Edward and Elizabeth Bowen, 24 May 1683, Roxbury, Mass.
MORRIS, Elizabeth and Peter Montague, 1633, Middlesex Co., Va .
MORRIS, Lewis and Isabella Graham, 3 November 1691, New York.
MORRIS, Mary and John Tilletson, 25 November 1680, Saybrook, Conn.
MORRIS, Thomas and Jane Jones, 3 June 1685, Philadelphia, Penn.
MORRIS, Thomas and Elizabeth Jackson, 14 July 1698, Harford Co., Md.
MORRISON, Andrew, Sr., and Sarah Jones, 21 October 1687, New Haven, Conn.
MORRISS, Ebenezar and Sarah Davis, 1 September 1692, Woodstock, Conn.
MORS, Joshua and Elizabeth Penman, 15 November 1699, Dedham, Mass.
MORSE, Benjamin and Elizabeth Bullard, 8 November 1648, Dedham, Mass.
MORSE, Benjamin and Ruth Sawyer, 27 August 1667, Newbury, Mass.
MORSE, Bethia and Timothy Dwight, 1 February 1691-2, Dedham, Mass.
MORSE, Christopher and Prudence Woodward, July 1661, Boston, Mass.
MORSE, Ezra and Johanna Hoare, 18 February 1670, Dedham, Mass.
MORSE, Joanna and Josiah Fisher, 1 September 1693, Dedham, Mass.
MORSE, Joseph and Hanah Phillips, 1 July 1638, Dedham, Mass.
MORSE, Joseph and Priscella Colburn, 12 November 1669, Dedham, Mass.
MORSE, Mary and Samuel Bullen, 10 June 1641, Dedham, Mass.
MORSE, Mehitable and John Breck, 9 March 1697, Sherborn, Mass.
MORSE, Sarah and Benjamin Stickney, 24 June 1663, Newbury, Mass.
MORSS, Elizabeth and Theodore Percivah, 12 January 1698, Boston, Mass.

MORSS, John and Hannah Williams, 10 May 1697, Woodstock, Conn.

MORSS, Peter and Priscilla Carpenter, 28 December 1698, Woodstock, Conn.

MORTON, Barbary and John Fisher, 1 June 1695, New York.

MORTON, Eliezur and Rebecca Marshall, 11 April 1693, Boston, Mass.

MORTON, Hannah and John Dyer, 6 June 1694, Boston, Mass.

MORTON, Joanna and John Gray, 9 December 1686, Kingston, Mass .

MORTON, Mary (widow) and Hugh Cole, 30 January 1693-4, Plymouth, Mass.

MORTON, Patience and John Nelson, 4 May 1693, Plymouth, Mass.

MORTON, Remember and Abraham Jackson, 18 November 1657, Salem, Mass.

MORY, Elizabeth and Edward Blake, 26 June 1696, Milton, Mass.

MORY, Martha and Nathaniell Blake, 9 October 1695, Milton, Mass.

MOSELEY, Mary and William Webster, 25 November 1696, Boston, Mass.

MOSELY, Rebecca and James Townsend, 22 January 1694, Boston, Mass.

MOSES, John and Mary Brown, 18 May 1653, Windsor, Conn.

MOSES, John and Deborah Thrall, 14 July 1680, Simsbury, Conn.

MOSS, Hannah (widow) and Thomas Boyden, 3 November 1658, Boston, Mass.

MOSS, Mary and Richard Sanders, 17 June 1697, Dover, N. H.

MOSSE, Christopher and Prudence Woodward, July 1661, Boston, Mass.

MOSSE, John and Mary Jupe, 24 October 1652, Boston, Mass.

MOSSTON, Judith and Robert Edwards, 13 January 1698, New York .

MOTT, Adam and Mary Stilwell, 1678, 9 July 1678, Gravesend, N. Y.

MOTT, James and Mary Redman, 5 September 1670, New York City.

MOTT, Nathaniel and Hannah Shooter, 25 October 1656, Braintree, Mass.

MOTT, Richbell and Elizabeth Thorne, 14 October 1695, Hempstead, N. Y.

MOULD, Susannah and Daniel White, March 1683, New London, Conn.

MOULTON, Hannah and Reuben Sanborn, 25 August 1681, Hampton, N. H.

MOULTON, James and Elizabeth Adams, 10 February 1662, Wenham, Mass.

MOULTON, Mary and Thomas Michel, September 1655, Malden, Mass.

MOULTON, Robert and Lucy Smith, 29 May 1689, Hampton, N. H.

MOULTON, Sarah and John Winslow, 5 May 1652, Malden, Mass.

MOULTON, Susanna and Benjamin Thaxter, 4 December 1693, Boston, Mass.

MOUNTAIN, Jane and John Cunliffe, 7 August 1660, Charles City Co., Va.

MOUNTFORT, Henry and Sarah Dasset, 27 September 1694, Boston, Mass.

MOUNTFORT, John and Mary Cock, 17 January 1693, Boston, Mass.

MOUNTFORT, Ruth and Thomas Carter, 2 May 1693, Boston, Mass.

MOUNTJOY, Hepsiba and Nathaniel Alden, 1 October 1691, Boston, Mass.

MOURITS, Leena and Robert Greg, 13 December 1694, New York.

MOUSALL, Eunice and John Brooks, 1 November 1649, Woburn, Mass.

MOUSALL, John and Sarah Brooks, 13 May 1650, Woburn, Mass.

MOWRY, George and Hannah Lewis, 22 January 1683, Bristol, R. I.

MOYON, William and Mary Pordrian, 6 September 1692, New York.

MUDGE, Mary and John Martinu, March 1671, Malden, Mass.

MUDGE, Moses and Elizabeth Wood, 17 December 1668, Warwick, R. I.

MULLIKIN, Jone and Peter Dearlove, 27 October 1697, Boston, Mass.

MULLINGS, Joana (widow) and John Laughton, 21 September 1659, Boston, Mass.

MULLINGS, William and Ann Bell (widow), 7 March 1656, Boston, Mass.

MUMFORD, Stephen and Mary Timberlake, 30 August 1697, Boston, Mass.

MUMFORT, Sarah and Thomas Mellous, 3 November 1697, Boston, Mass.

MUNSON, Ann and John Stebbins, 14 March 1646, Springfield, Mass.

MUNSON, Hannah and Joseph Tuttle, 2 May 1667, New Haven, Conn.

MUNSON, Sanuel and Martha Bradley, 28 October 1665, New Haven, Conn.

MUNCY, Francis and Hannah Adans, 6 December 1659, Ipswich, Mass.

MUNDEN, Elizabeth and John Pickering, 7 July 1688, Dover, N. H.

MUNGY, Mary and John Sanders, 9 August 1650, Braintree, Mass.

MUNINGS, Rebecca and Edmond Madocks, 14 November 1651, Boston, Mass.

MUNRO, Elizabeth and John Lindsey, 29 August 1694, Bristol, R. I.

MUNT, Faith and Clement Short, 21 November 1660, Boston, Mass.

MURDOCK, Mary and William Brown, 16 July 1649, Plymouth, Mass.

MURDOCK, Robert and Hannah Stedman, 28 April 1692, Roxbury, Mass.

MURFIN, Mary and Daniel Smith, 7 April 1695, Chesterfield, N. J.

MURRAY, John and Sarah Budd, 26 February 1689, Philadelphia, Penn.

MURREL, Margaret and John Kitt, 23 September 1697, Boston, Mass.

MURRELL, Gilbert and Judith Hancock, 1691, Burlington Co., N. J.

MUSKETT, Bridgett and William Fiske, 1643, Salem, Mass.

MYCALL, John and Mary Farr, 11 October 1657, Braintree, Mass.

MYCALL, Mary and Joseph Niles, 15 September 1661, Braintree, Mass.

MYGANT, Joseph and Sarah Webster, 15 November 1677, Hartford, Conn.

MYNARD, Sarah and John Brown, 16 September 1668, Somerset Co., Md.

MUZZY, Mary and John Senter, 27 January 1656, Boston, Mass.

MUZZY, Sarah and John Wayte, 12 June 1674, Malden, Mass.

N

NALER, John and Jane Cutler, 11 May 1685, Middletown, Penn.
NASH, Elizabeth and John Conney, 20 April 1654, Boston, Mass.
NASH, John and Elizabeth Howd, 22 August 1677, Branford, Conn.
NASH, Joshua and Elizabeth Porter, 23 February 1658, Boston, Mass.
NASH, Mary and Moses Belcher, 23 March 1666, Braintree, Mass.
NASH, Thomas and Hannah Coleman, August 1685, Hadley, Mass.
NASH, Timothy and Mary Foster, 2 April 1694, Boston, Mass.
NASON, Benjamin and Martha Kenny, 30 June 1687, Dover, N. H.
NASON, John and Hannah Hurd, 6 November 1674, Dover, N. H.
NAYLOR, Mary and Richard Hurtley, 10 December 1698, Elizabeth City Co., Va.
NEAL, Jennet and David Dewer, 29 July 1697, Boston, Mass.
NEAL, Mary and William Philbrick, 10 October 1689, Greenland, N. H.
NEAL, Samuel and Elizabeth Gozzard, 2 August 1699, Simsbury, Conn.
NEALE, Abigail and Peter Scot, 22 January 1673, Dorchester, Mass.
NEALE, Henry and Hannah Pray, 14 December 1655, Braintree, Mass.
NEALE, Samuel and Abigail Benjamin, 18 February 1678, Braintree, Mass.
NEALE, Samuel and Elizabeth Exeter, 29 June 1699, Elizabeth City Co., Va.
NEALL, Benjamine and Lidea Payne, 22 January 1688, Milton, Mass.
NEALL, Deborah and John Paine, 22 January 1688, Milton, Mass.
NEEDAM, John and Hannah Savill, March 1669, Braintree, Mass.
NEEDHAM, Ezekial and Priscilla Halsey, 10 March 1696, Boston, Mass.
NEEDHAM, John and Elizabeth Hicks, 10 October 1679, Cambridge, Mass.
NEFF, Mary and Mathias Button, 24 November 1686, Haverhill, Mass.
NEFF, William and Mary Corliss, 23 June 1665, Haverhill, Mass.
NEGUS, Elizabeth and Richard Barnard, 2 March 1659, Boston, Mass.
NEGUS, Jabez and Sarah Brown, 9 January 1698, Boston, Mass.
NELSON, Hanna and Stephen Tobey, 29 November 1688, Dover, N. H.
NELSON, John and Patience Morton, 4 May 1693, Plymouth, Mass.
NELSON, Martha and William Grant, 26 December 1695, York Co., Maine.
NELSON, Mary and John Heselton, 16 July 1682, Haverhill, Mass.
NELSON, Mehitable and John Doty, Jr., 2 February 1692-3, Plymouth, Mass.
NEVIUS, Cornelius and Agatha Bowman, 15 April 1683, Flatbush, N. Y.
NEVIUS, Johanes and Jan Stryker, 30 April 1679, New York City.
NEWBERRY, Mary and Daniel Clark, 13 June 1644, Windsor, Conn.
NEWBERRY, Sara and Henry Wolcot, 8 November 1640, Windsor, Conn.
NEWBERRY, Thomas and Ann Ford, 12 March 1676, Windsor, Conn.
NEWBOLD, Elizabeth and Jacob DeCow, 21 December 1699, Burlington, N. J.
NEWBOLD, James and Elizabeth Powell, 10 January 1695, Burlington, N. J.
NEWBOLD, Mary and Jodia Higgins, 12 May 1684, Burlington, N. J.
NEWBY, George and Elizabeth Fox, 7 February 1693, Charlestown, Mass.
NEWCOMB, Elizabeth and John Pidge, 3 May 1677, Dedham, Mass.
NEWCOMB, Grace and James Butler, 1687, Boston, Mass.
NEWCOMB, Hannah and James Thorp, 8 November 1657, Dedham, Mass.
NEWCOMB, Hannah and William Hayward, 22 November 1693, Quincy, Mass.

NEWCOMB, Rachel and John Fenno, Jr., 1690-93, Milton, Mass.

NEWCOMB, Susanna and Benjamin Hobart, 5 April 1699, Boston, Mass.

NEWELL, Abraham and Susanna Rand, 8 February 1652, Charlestown, Mass.

NEWELL, Hannah and John Holmes, 9 April 1690, Woodstock, Conn.

NEWELL, Susanna and Thomas More, 3 October 1673, Dorchester, Mass.

NEWGATE, Hannah and Simon Lynde, 22 December 1652, Boston, Mass.

NEWHALL, Thomas and Elizabeth Potter, 29 December 1652, Lynn, Mass.

NEWMAN, Elinor and Edward Hull, 20 November 1652, Boston, Mass.

NEWMAN, Sibella and John Edwards, 29 October 1694, Boston, Mass.

NEWMARCH, John and Mary Hunking (widow), 5 December 1699, York Co., Maine.

NEWTON, Abigail and James Puffer, 3 December 1695, Milton, Mass.

NEWTON, Hanna and Joseph Phelps, 20 September 1660, Windsor, Conn.

NEWWORK, Sarah and Florene Macartie, 24 August 1697, Boston, Mass.

NICHOLAS, Susanna and Francis Hulin, 12 June 1696, New York.

NICHOLS, Elizabeth (widow) and Thomas Bill, 14 November 1652, Boston, Mass.

NICHOLS, Francis and Ann Wines, December 1645, Southold, N. Y.

NICHOLS, Israel and Mary Sumner, 10 January 1688, Milton, Mass.

NICHOLS, John and Hannah Whittemore, 18 November 1686, Malden, Mass.

NICHOLS, John and Abigail Kendall, 1651, Reading, Mass.

NICHOLS, Rachel and Ebenezer Wood, 5 April 1695, Rowley, Mass.

NICHOLS, Rebecca and Samuel House, 1664, Scituate, Mass.

NICHOLS, Sarah and Daniel Lincoln, 16 April 1687, Scituate, Mass.

NICHOLLS, James and Mary Felt, February 1660, Malden, Mass.

NICHOLLS, Mary and Jonathan Stanwood, 27 December 1688, West Amesbury, Mass.

NICHOLSON, Hannah and Samuel Ruck, 4 April 1693, Boston, Mass.

NICHOLLSON, Mary and George Carter, 4 September 1677, Somerset Co., Md.

NICK, Elizabeth and Peter Till, 26 December 1651, Boston, Mass.

NICKERSON, Ann and Tristram Hedges, 20 October 1657, Boston, Mass.

NICOLS, John and Mercy Miller, 18 December 1695, Boston, Mass.

NICOLLS, Margarett and Josiah Robinson, 21 November 1696, New York.

NILES, Increase and Mary Purchase, 4 October 1677, Braintree, Mass.

NILES, Jane and John Hinton, 20 March 1683, Bristol, R. I.

NILES, Joseph and Mary Mycall, 15 September 1661, Braintree, Mass.

NINNY, Joana and Nathaniel Merrill, 15 October 1661, Newbury, Mass.

NOAKS, Eliza and Titus Brooks, 20 November 1694, Boston, Mass.

NOBLE, Elizabeth and Richard Church, 3 March 1692, Westfield, Mass.

NOCK, Henry and Sarah Adams, 10 January 1692, Dover, N. H.

NOCK, Silas and Elizabeth Emery, 20 April 1677, Dover, N. H.

NOKES, Robert and Mary Emerson, 17 August 1699, Boston, Mass.

NORCOT, Lydia and Ebenezer Jones, 17 May 1694, Boston, Mass.

NORCROSS, Richard and Mary Brooks, 24 June 1650, Watertown, Mass.

NORCROSS, Richard, Jr., and Hannah Sanders, 6 August 1695, Watertown, Mass.

NORDEN, Samuel and Elizabeth Pormott, January 1656, Boston, Mass.

NORDEN, Susanna and John Hudson, 17 August 1693, Boston, Mass.

NORTHRUP, Joseph and Mary Norton, April 1646, Milford, Conn.

NORTON, Abigail and Ananias Trians, 6 August 1667, Saybrook, Conn.

NORTON, Abigail and Samuel Martin, 30 March 1676, Andover, Mass.

NORTON, Ann and John Warner, 28 June 1649, Guilford, Conn.

NORTON, Grace and William Seward, 2 April 1651, Guilford, Conn.

NORTON, Mary and Joseph Northrup, April 1646, Milford, Conn.

NORTON, Mary and Philip Fowler, 27 February 1659, Ipswich, Mass.

NORTON, Mary and Samuel Rockwell, 7 April 1660, Windsor, Conn.

NORTON, Mehitable and Samuel Adams, 20 December 1664, Ipswich, Mass.

NORTON, Thomas and Elizabeth Mason, 8 May 1671, Saybrook, Conn.

NORTON, William and Susanna Mason, 14 December 1659, Boston, Mass.

NORWOOD, Benjamin and Cornelia Van Clyff, 20 February 1693, New York.

NORWOOD, Francis and Elizabeth Coldum, 15 October 1663, Gloucester, Mass.

NOSTOCK, Sarah and William Adams, 10 December 1691, Boston, Mass.

NOWELL, Mary and Isaac Winslow, 14 August 1666, Plymouth, Mass.

NOWELL, George and Eliza Johnson, 13 October 1693, Boston, Mass.

NOYES, Cutting and Elizabeth Knight, 25 February 1673, Newbury, Mass.

NOYES, Hannah and Peter Cheney, 14 May 1663, Newbury, Mass.

NOYES, John and Mary Poore, 23 November 1668, Andover, Mass.

NOYES, John and Susanna Edwards, 16 March 1699, Boston, Mass.

NOYES, Nicholas and Mary Cutting, 1640, Newbury, Mass.

NOYES, Thomas and Martha Peirce, 28 December 1669, Newbury, Mass.

NUCOME, Mary and Samuel Deeringe, 10 September 1657, Braintree, Mass.

NUCOME, Peter and Susan Cutting, 26 April 1672, Braintree, Mass.

NUMAN, Noah and Joana Flynt, 30 October 1669, Braintree, Mass.

NUMSTEED, Hannah and Thomas Shearer, 18 April 1659, Boston, Mass.

NUTON, Ione and Benedictus Alvord, 26 November 1640, Windsor, Conn.

NUTTING, John and Sarah Eggleton, 28 August 1650, Woburn, Mass.

NYE, Abigail and Edward Dillinham, 18 April 1678, Sandwich, Mass.

NYE, Benjamin and Katherine Tupper, 19 October 1640, Sandwich, Mass.

NYLES, Neomy and William Comstock, 10 September 1695, Lyme, Conn.

O

OAK, Nathaniel and Mehitable Rediat, 14 December 1686, Sudbury, Mass.

OAKE, Samuel and Joanna Phillips, 4 October 1693, Boston, Mass.

OAKES, Elizabeth and Lemuel Jenkins, 12 July 1670, Malden, Mass.

OAKES, Hannah and Joseph Wayte, 7 August 1672, Malden, Mass.

OAKES, Mary and John Flint, 12 November 1667, Concord, Mass.

OAKLEY, Miles and Mary Wilmot, 1669, Great Neck, L. I., N. Y.

OATES, Stephen and Mary Pittman, 16 April 1674, Dover, N. H.

OBRIEN, Lucy T. and John Baylor, 1698, Gloucester Co., Va.

OCKINGTON, Thomas and Rebeca Mason, 5 December 1682-3, Dedham, Mass.

OCKONELL, Tego and Philipa King, 1 May 1662, Boston, Mass.

ODDIHORNE, Deliverance and Robert Clement, 18 December 1690, Great Island, N. H.

ODELL, Sarah and John Archer of Westchester, 7 October 1686, New York.

ODLIN, Elisha and Abigail Bright, August 1659, Watertown, Mass.

ODLEN, Elisha and Mary Colburn, 30 December 1697, Boston, Mass.

ODLIN, Hannah and Benjamin Dyer, 10 December 1691, Boston, Mass.

ODLING, Rebecca and Mathew Forsythe, 5 September 1696, Chesterfield, N. J.

OGBORNE, William and Mary Cole, 17 November 1698, Burlington, N. J.

OGDEN, David and Martha Houlston, 12 January 1686, Chester Co., Penn.

OKEMAN, Agnes and Joshua Kent, 4 November 1697, Boston, Mass.

OKES, Thomas and Eliza Danson, 2 February 1692, Boston, Mass.

OKLYE, Elizabeth and Edmond Browne, 14 December 1653, Boston, Mass.

OLCOTT, Mary and John Case, 16 September 1684, Simsbury, Conn.

OLCOTT, Thomas and Hannah Barnard, 11 November 1695, Hartford, Conn.

OLDAM, Francis (widow) and David Carwithen, 22 September 1660, Boston, Mass.

OLD, Robert and Elisabeth Lamb (widow), 23 January 1696-7, Springfield, Mass.

OLIVER, Elizabeth and Enoch Wiswell, 25 September 1657, Dorchester, Mass.

OLIVER, Elizabeth and George Gottschick, 25 April 1697, Philadelphia, Penn.

OLIVER, Elizabeth and Zerah Higgins, 1680, Piscataway, N. J.

OLIVER, Elizabeth and Samuel Keeling, 14 September 1699, Boston, Mass.

OLIVER, John and Hannah Mather, 28 January 1697, Boston, Mass.

OLIVER, Liddia and Joshua Fisher, 16 December 1653, Dedham, Mass.

OLIVER, Mary and George Drake, 13 November 1677, Elizabethtown, N. J.

OLIVER, Robert and Elizabeth Burey, 14 September 1693, Boston, Mass.

OLMSTEAD, James and Phebe Barlow, 1 May 1673, Norwalk, Conn.

OLMSTEAD, John and Mary Benedict, 17 July 1673, Norwalk, Conn.

OLMSTEAD, Mary and Thomas Reed, 9 May 1694, Norwalk, Conn.

OLMSTEAD, Sarah and John Abbott, 5 June 1696, Norwalk, Conn.

OLPHERTS, Suert and Hilleke Pieters, 17 September 1697, New York.

OLSTRA, Elizabeth and Christopher Penny, 8 January 1694, Bristol, R. I.

ONEAL, Daniel and Elizabeth Hading, 10 May 1674, Richmond Co., Va.

ONG, Sarah and Edward Andrews, 8 February 1694, Burlington Co., N. J.

ONIAN, Benjamin and Debora Woodcock, 24 March 1683, Dedham, Mass.

ONION, Mary and Jonathan Battelle, 15 April 1690, Dedham, Mass.

ONION, Robert and Grace Ebrew, 3 October 1643, Dedham, Mass.
OORSON, William and Mary Ellis, 27 June 1699, Boston, Mass.
OORT, Sarah and Capt. William Kidd, 16 May 1691, New York City.
ORCHARD, Mary and John Pim, 5 February 1690, Boston, Mass.
ORCHARD, Mehitable and Francis Pumery, 7 February 1694, Boston, Mass.
ORDWAY, Abner and Sarah Dennis (widow), 15 June 1656, Boston, Mass.
ORMES, Richard and Mary Tidder, 3 April 1686, Philadelphia, Penn.
ORMSBEE, Mary and Nicholas Ide, 27 December 1677, Rehoboth, Mass.
ORRIS, Sarah and Elias Purrington, 7 July 1694, Boston, Mass.
ORRISE, Nathaniel and Mary Ivet, 11 September 1690, Boston, Mass.
OSBON, Ann and Humphrey Prior, 12 November 1663, Windsor, Conn.
OSBORN, Abigail and Isaac Fox, 18 May 1678, Billerica, Mass.
OSBORN, Alice (widow) and Daniel Lake, 1683, Long Island, N. Y.
OSBORN, William and Alice Lowden, 16 September 1696, Dover, N. H.
OSBORN, William and Alice Holmes (widow), 1680, Long Island, N. Y.
OSBORN, William and Elizabeth Way, 12 December 1698, New York.
OSBORNE, Mary and John Rosse, 7 May 1659, Boston, Mass.
OSBORNE, Patience and Joseph Aldridge, 26 December 1661, Braintree, Mass.
OSBURNE, Elizabeth and Jacob Ware, 3 October 1692, New York City.
OSGOOD, Abigail and John Carleton, 2 August 1694, Andover, Mass.
OSGOOD, Christopher and Hannah Barker, 27 May 1680, Andover, Mass.
OSGOOD, Deborah and John Ruse, 28 August 1663, Andover, Mass.
OSGOOD, Elizabeth and Robert Quimby, 7 January 1653, Salisbury, Mass.
OSGOOD, Elizabeth and John Browne, 12 October 1659, Andover, Mass.
OSGOOD, Hanna and Samuel Archer, 21 May 1660, Andover, Mass.
OSGOOD, Hannah and John Carleton, 27 August 1688, Andover, Mass.
OSGOOD, Hooker and Dorothy Wood, 13 April 1692, Andover, Mass.
OSGOOD, John and Mary Clemance, 15 November 1633, Haverhill, Mass.
OSGOOD, John and Hannah Eires, 17 October 1681, Andover, Mass.
OSGOOD, Lydia and James Frye, 20 January 1679, Andover, Mass.
OSGOOD, Mary and John Lovejoy, 1 June 1651, Ipswich, Mass.
OSGOOD, Mary and Henry Engolls, 6 July 1653, Andover, Mass.
OSGOOD, Mary and John Aslett, 8 July 1680, Andover, Mass.
OSGOOD, Mary and John Marstone, 28 May 1689, Andover, Mass.
OSGOOD, Stephen and Mary Hooker, 24 October 1663, Andover, Mass.
OSGOOD, Stephen and Hannah Blanchard, 24 May 1699, Andover, Mass.
OSGOOD, Timothy and Deborah Poor, 29 May 1689, Andover, Mass.
OSLAND, John and Sarah Hide, 14 October 1697, Boston, Mass.
OTHEA, Sarah and James Grant, 28 January 1664, Dedham, Mass.
OTIS, Joseph and Dorothy Thomas, 20 November 1688, Scituate, Mass.
OTIS, Stephen and Mary Pittman, 16 April 1674, Dover, Mass.
OTTER, John and Mary Blinston, 29 August 1686, Philadelphia, Penn.
OULD, Robard and Susanna Hosford, December 1668, Windsor, Conn.
OWEN, Elizabeth and Thomas Andrews, 25 August 1689, Philadelphia, Penn.
OWEN, John and Rebecca Wade, 3 October 1650, Windsor, Conn.
OWEN, Thomas and Eliza Chinny, 10 September 1694, Boston, Mass.
OWEN, William and Elizabeth Davies, 29 July 1650, Braintree, Mass.
OWEN, William and Sarah Vitterell, 28 April 1693, Boston, Mass.
OXFORD, Philip and Sarah Jones, 8 December 1686, Mayamensen, Penn.

P

PABODIE, Mary and Edward Southworth, 2 June 1669, Duxbury, Mass.

PABODIE, Mercy and John Simmons, 16 November 1669, Duxbury, Mass.

PABODIE, Priscilla and Ichabod Wiswell, December 1677, Duxbury, Mass.

PABODIE, Rebecca and William Southworth, 1680, Duxbury, Mass.

PABODIE, Sarah and John Coe, 10 November 1681, Duxbury, Mass.

PACA, Aquila and Martha Phillips, 11 September 1699, Harford Co., Md.

PACEN, Prudence and Benjamin Thomson, 13 December 1698, Dedham, Mass.

PACK, Elizabeth and John Bennett, 8 March 1687, Stonington, Conn.

PACKARD, John and Judith Windslow, 12 April 1688, Taunton, Mass.

PACKER, Thomas and Elizabeth Hall (widow), 7 August 1687, Dover, N. H.

PADDY, William and Mary Paiton (widow), 3 October 1651, Boston, Mass.

PAGE, Elizabeth and John Simkins, 28 December 1698, Boston, Mass.

PAGE, Francis and Meribah Smith, 5 December 1669, Hampton, N. H.

PAGE, Isaac and Damaris Shattock, 30 July 1653, Boston, Mass.

PAGE, John and Sarah Davis, 18 June 1683, Haverhill, Mass.

PAGE, Margery and Isaac Cullimore, 22 December 1651, Boston, Mass.

PAGE, Mary and Samuel Fogg (2nd marriage), 1662, Hampton, N. H.

PAGE, Sarah and James Sanders, 14 January 1669, Haverhill, Mass.

PAIG, Abiel and Cornelius Loreson, 4 November 1697, Boston, Mass.

PAIGE, Sarah and Thomas Metcalfe, 12 July 1656, Dedham, Mass.

PAIN, Eleanor and Nathaniel Sikes, 7 April 1686, Philadelphia, Penn.

PAIN, John and Mary Day, 7 December 1676, Dedham, Mass.

PAIN, John and Bethia Hodge, 5 July 1698, Boston, Mass.

PAIN, Sarah and Elijah Dubbledee, 23 January 1697, Boston, Mass.

PAINE, Elisha and Rebecca Doane, 5 January 1685, Eastham, Mass.

PAINE, Elizabeth and Henry Adams, 17 August 1643, Braintree, Mass.

PAINE, Elizabeth and John Hunting, 18 April 1671, Dedham, Mass.

PAINE, Hannah and Thomas Hall, 15 February 1694, Boston, Mass.

PAINE, John and Deborah Neall, 22 January 1688, Milton, Mass.

PAINE, John and Abigail Curtis, 8 August 1699, Burlington, N. J.

PAINE, Mary and James Rogers, 11 January 1670, Eastham, Mass.

PAINE, Rebecca and Thomas Patten, 1 February 1662, Dedham, Mass.

PAINE, Samuel and Mary Peniman, 4 April 1678, Braintree, Mass.

PAINE, Sarah and Roger Billinge, 22 January 1678, Dorchester, Mass.

PAINE, Stephen and An Chickering, 3 September 1652, Dedham, Mass.

PAINE, Steven and Ellen Veasy, 20 February 1681, Braintree, Mass.

PAINE, Thomas and Hannah Bray, 25 August 1659, Boston, Mass.

PAINE, Thomas and Rebecca Peck, 25 April 1671, Dedham, Mass.

PAINTER, Mercy and Edward Allen, 15 November 1683, Deerfield, Mass.

PAINTER, William and Mary Messenger, 28 May 1691, Boston, Mass.

PAITON, Mary (widow) and William Paddy, 3 October 1651, Boston, Mass.

PALFREY, Remember and Peter Aspinwall, 12 February 1661, Boston, Mass.

PALLARD, Deliverance and John Hughes, 15 September 1698, Boston, Mass.

PALMER, Abigail and Samuel Chandler, 10 April 1684, Dorchester, Mass.

PALMER, Abigail and Thomas Marshall, 4 February 1686, Dover, N. H.

PALMER, Alice and Joseph Covel, 27 February 1685, Charlestown, Mass.

PALMER, Elizabeth and Robert Ayers, 27 February 1650, Haverhill, Mass.

PALMER, Elizabeth and Matthew Force, April 1667, Gravesend, L. I., N. Y.

PALMER, Elizabeth and Thomas Fitzwater, 3 April 1684, Philadelphia, Penn.

PALMER, Elizabeth and Isaac Ricketts, 29 February 1687, Philadelphia, Penn.

PALMER, Esther and Roger Burges, 3 August 1698, Boston, Mass.

PALMER, Grace and Thomas Miner, 23 April 1634, Charlestown, Mass.

PALMER, Hanna and Toban Grant, 22 January 1662, Windsor, Conn.

PALMER, Hannah and Joshua Linkoln, 12 February 1693, Boston, Mass.

PALMER, Jonah and Elizabeth Grissell, 3 May 1655, Charlestown, Mass.

PALMER, Jonah and Abigail Titus, 11 February 1692, Rehoboth, Mass.

PALMER, Martha and Samuel Hale, 3 November 1698, Rowley, Mass.

PALMER, Mary and John French, 27 November 1678, Rehoboth, Mass.

PALMER, Mary and James Pendleton, 22 October 1647, Westerly, R. I.

PALMER, Mary and Joseph Daggett, 14 February 1689, Rehoboth, Mass.

PALMER, Samuel and Mary Pearson, 20 December 1671, Rowley, Mass.

PALMER, Stephen and Eliza Cheever, 19 January 1692, Boston, Mass.

PALMER, Timothy and Hanna Buell, 17 September 1663, Windsor, Conn.

PALMER, Thomas and Abigail Hutchinson, 29 January 1696, Boston, Mass.

PALSGROVE, John and Mary Mavericke, 8 December 1655, Boston, Mass.

PALSGROVE, Mary (widow) and Francis Hooke, 20 September 1660, Boston, Mass.

PAMER, Michal and Elizabeth Butler, 2 December 1662, Branford, Conn.

PANCOAST, William and Hannah Scattergood, 1 July 1695, Burlington Co., N. J.

PANCOST, Elizabeth and Joseph Bacon, 11 August 1693, Salem Co., N. J.

PANGBURNE, Susanna and George Jewell of New York, 17 April 1688, New York.

PANTRY, John and Elizabeth Plinco, 16 April 1698, New York.

PARDEE, George and Martha Miles, 20 October 1650, New Haven, Conn.

PARDEE, George and Rebecca Lane, 29 December 1662, New Haven, Conn.

PARDEE, George and Mercy Ball, 10 February 1675, New Haven, Conn.

PARDEE, Joseph and Elizabeth Yale, 31 January 1688, New Haven, Conn.

PARISH, John and Hannah Jewell, 30 June 1664, Braintree, Mass.

PARK, John and Elizabeth Miller, 5 April 1694, Watertown, Mass.

PARKE, William and Hannah Frink, 3 December 1684, Preston, Conn.

PARKER, Abraham and Rose Whitlock, 18 November 1644, Woburn, Mass.

PARKER, Abraham and Martha Livermore, 15 July 1682, Chelmsford, Mass.

PARKER, Anne and Thomas Winslow, 15 August 1694, Essex Co., Va.

PARKER, Ebenezer and Mary Smith, 3 September 1694, Saybrook, Conn.

PARKER, Elisha and Ursula Crage, 27 September 1697, Woodbridge, N. J.

PARKER, Elizabeth and John Farnum, 10 April 1684, Andover, Mass.

PARKER, Elizabeth and Samuel Hutchinson, 26 April 1686, Andover, Mass.

PARKER, George and Esther Andrews, 5 September 1692, Chesterfield, N. J.

PARKER, Hannah and John Tyler, 14 September 1682, Andover, Mass.

PARKER, Hope and Samuel Cooke, 2 May 1667, New Haven, Conn.

PARKER, James and Elizabeth Long, 23 May 1643, Charlestown, Mass.

PARKER, James and Elizabeth Dudley, 1678, Middlesex Co., Va.

PARKER, James, Jr., and Mary Parker, 11 December 1678, Chelmsford, Mass.

PARKER, Jane (widow) and Richard Thayer, July 1646, Boston, Mass.
PARKER, Jane and John Isham, 16 December 1667, Barnstable, Mass.
PARKER, Joana and John Sterns, 22 April 1696, Malden, Mass.
PARKER, Joanna and Arthur Mason, 5 May 1655, Boston, Mass.
PARKER, John and Mary Fairefield, 20 August 1660, Boston, Mass.
PARKER, John and Mary Buckingham, 24 December 1666, Saybrook, Conn.
PARKER, John and Mary Jones, 11 December 1690, Saybrook, Conn.
PARKER, John and Hanah Broune, 24 May 1687, Andover, Mass.
PARKER, John and Isabella Smith (widow), 12 September 1699, Harford Co., Va.
PARKER, Joseph and Hannah Gilbert, 3 June 1673, Saybrook, Conn.
PARKER, Joseph and Elizabeth Bridges, 7 October 1680, Andover, Mass.
PARKER, Joseph and Elizabeth Lippincott, 2 April 1699, Shrewsbury, N. J.
PARKER, Lydia and John Kidder, 3 December 1684, Chelmsford, Mass.
PARKER, Margaret (widow) and Samuel Stratton, 27 June 1657, Boston, Mass.
PARKER, Martha and James Hosley, 10 March 1674, Dorchester, Mass.
PARKER, Mary and William Dennison, 27 October 1659, Boston, Mass.
PARKER, Mary and Benjamin Fry, 23 May 1678, Andover, Mass.
PARKER, Mary and Daniel Robbins, 27 November 1691, Woodbridge, N. J.
PARKER, Moses and Abigail Hildreth, 19 June 1684, Woburn, Mass.
PARKER, Philip and Hanna Sessions, 10 November 1685, Penn. License.
PARKER, Rebecca and John Clark, 16 October 1650, Saybrook, Conn.
PARKER, Samuell and Sarah Homan, 9 February 1657, Dedham, Mass.
PARKER, Sarah and Isaac Bull, 22 April 1653, Boston, Mass.
PARKER, Sarah and John Wayte, 4 August 1675, Malden, Mass.
PARKER, Stephen and Mary Marstone, 1 December 1680, Andover, Mass.
PARKER, Stephen and Susana Devereaux, 10 January 1695, Andover, Mass.
PARKER, William and Mary Turner, 13 November 1651, Scituate, Mass.
PARKER, William and Lydia Brown, 6 September 1676, Saybrook, Conn.
PARKESON, Martha and Nathaniel Cole, 30 August 1667, Warwick, R. I.
PARKHURST, Joseph and Rebecca Reed, 26 June 1656, Chelmsford, Mass.
PARKMAN, Bridget and Sylvester Eveleth, 6 September 1672, Gloucester, Mass.
PARKMAN, Rebecca and John Jarvis, 18 September 1661, Boston, Mass.
PARKS, Richard and Elizabeth Billings, 14 July 1690, Concord, Mass.
PARMENTER, Joseph and Mary Mash, 17 September 1675, Braintree, Mass.
PARMINTER, Judeth and Jeremiah Cushing, 29 March 1693, Boston, Mass.
PARMENTER, Hannah and Samuel Thompson, Jr., 25 October 1684, Braintree, Mass.
PARMETTER, Robert and Leah Wheatley, 13 February 1648, Braintree, Mass.
PARMITER, Thomas and Margaret Smith, 14 August 1697, New York.
PARMITER, Elizabeth and Samuel Pennyman, 6 January 1673, Dorchester, Mass.
PARMILEE, Hannah and John Johnson, 30 September 1651, Guilford, Conn.
PARNEL, Dorothy and John Frissel, 22 July 1698, Boston, Mass.
PARNELL, Francis and Dorothy Fowles, 15 August 1692, Boston, Mass.
PARROTT, Elizabeth and Samuel Worcester, 29 November 1659, Rowley, Mass.
PARSHALL, James and Elizabeth Gardiner, 1678, Easthampton, N. Y.
PARSONS, Elizabeth and John Gill, 1 June 1698, Boston, Mass.
PARSONS, Jeffrey and Sarah Vinson, 11 November 1657, Gloucester, Mass.
PARSONS, Thomas and Lydia Brown, 28 June 1641, Windsor, Conn.
PARSONS, Thomas, Jr., and Sara Dare, 24 December 1668, Windsor, Conn.

PARSONS, William and Martha Baldwin, 15 September 1697, Boston, Mass.
PARTERAGE (or Parteridg), Priscilla and Joseph Plimpton, 22 August 1699, Boston, Mass.
PARTRIDGE, Ann and William Pitts, 29 July 1664, Charlestown, Mass.
PARTRIDGE, Hannah and John Bowers, 22 January 1676, Medfield, Mass.
PARTRIDGE, John and Frances Creswell, 6 April 1678, Richmond Co., Va.
PARTRIDGE, Nathaniel and Lydia Wight, 24 November 1686, Medfield, Mass.
PARTRIDGE, Rebecca and Vigilance Fisher, 27 September 1678, Dedham, Mass.
PARTRIDGE, Samuel and Mehitable Crow, 24 September 1668, Hartford, Conn.
PARTRIDGE, Sarah and William Hunkins, 12 May 1692, Dover, N. H.
PARTRIDGE, William and Sarah Price, 23 November 1654, Dedham, Mass.
PARTRIDGE, William and Mary Smith, 12 December 1644, Hartford, Conn.
PASCO, John and Eliza Loft, 25 May 1691, Boston, Mass.
PASCO, Ruth and Edward Camden, 25 September 1694, Boston, Mass.
PASCO, William and Ruth Hetchbone, 20 October 1690, Boston, Mass.
PASMORE, Rebecca and Robert Edmonds, 26 March 1695, Boston, Mass.
PASON, Ephriam and Katareen Leadbetter, 12 June 1684, Dorchester, Mass.
PASON, Mary and Preserved Capen, 16 May 1682, Dorchester, Mass.
PATCHEN, Joseph and Elizabeth Iggeden (widow), 10 April 1642, Roxbury, Mass.
PATERIDG, Mary and Samuel Coalburne, 12 January 1682-3, Dedham, Mass.
PATERSON, Peter and Elizabeth Rithway, 11 June 1678, Saybrook, Conn.
PATESHAL, Richard and Hannah Holst, 20 April 1694, New York.
PATTEN, Thomas and Rebecca Paine, 1 February 1662, Dedham, Mass.
PATTERSON, Andrew and Elizabeth Kibbee, 1697, Charlestown, Mass.
PATTERSON, James and Rebecca Stinson, 29 May 1662, Cambridge, Mass.
PATTERSON, Mary and Peter Proctor, 30 January 1689, Chelmsford, Mass.
PATTON, Rebecca and Joseph Davis, 18 June 1691, Billerica, Mass.
PATTON, Sarah (widow) and Thomas Richardson, 29 December 1690, Billerica, Mass.
PAUL, Eliza and Henry Roads, 27 February 1694, Boston, Mass.
PAUL, John and Lydia Jenkins, 3 March 1657, Malden, Mass.
PAUL, Mary and Samuell Clap, 7 April 1698, Dorchester, Mass.
PAUL, Mary (widow) and John Toalman, 15 June 1692, Dorchester, Mass.
PAUL, Samuel and Mary Breck, 9 November 1666, Dorchester, Mass.
PAUL, Susanna and Samuel Fernald, 12 October 1699, York Co., Maine.
PAULDING, John and Catherine Duyts, 16 March 1688, Westchester Co., N. Y.
PAULING, Matthew and Susanna Walker 15 June 1698, Boston, Mass.
PAULSGRAVE, Anna and Nicholas Woodbury, 1657, Charlestown, Mass.
PAULUS, Elizabeth and Volckert Hendricksen, 4 June 1695, New York.
PAXSON, William, Jr., and Abigail Pownal, 20 Decmeber 1695, Middletown, Penn.
PAXTON, Henry and Margerie Plumly, 13 June 1684, Middletown, Penn.
PAYN, Hannah and Theophilus Curtis, 7 January 1673, Dorchester, Mass.
PAYN, Jane and Edward Taylor, 4 August 1692, Boston, Mass.
PAYN, William and Mary Taylor, 11 October 1694, Boston, Mass.
PAYNE, Ann and Thomas Medcalfe, 2 October 1679, Dedham, Mass.
PAYNE, Elizabeth and Henry Thacker, Jr., June 1690, Middlesex Co., Va.
PAYNE, John and Miss Monroe, 3 February 1699, Lancaster Co., Va.
PAYNE, Lidea and Benjamine Neall, 22 January 1688, Milton, Mass.

PAYNE, Marie and Jeremiah Vale, 24 May 1660, Southold, N. Y.
PAYNE, Sarah and Daniel Aldis, 23 November 1685, Dedham, Mass.
PAYNE, Steven and Hannah Bass, 15 September 1651, Braintree, Mass.
PAYNE, Thomas and Mary Lamson, 20 August 1689, Dedham, Mass.
PAYSON, Johanah and Thomas Lyon, 23 October 1690, Dorchester, Mass.
PAYSON, Samuel and Prudence Lincoln, 31 March 1677, Roxbury, Mass.
PAYSON, Sarah and Elisha Foster, 10 April 1678, Dorchester, Mass.
PAYSON, Susanna and Samuel Capen, 9 April 1673, Dorchester, Mass.
PEABODY, Jane and Jonathan Smith, 16 March 1682, Watertown, Mass.
PEACHEE, Mary and John Baker, 16 November 1696, Burlington, N. J.
PEACHEE, Thomas and Mary Miller, 3 September 1690, New Jersey License.
PEACOCK, Anna and Ezra Croasdill, 6 February 1687, Middletown, Penn.
PEACOCK, Mary and Samuel Shears, 29 July 1663, Dedham, Mass.
PEACOCK, William and Mary Willis, 12 April 1653, Roxbury, Mass.
PEACOCKE, Richard and Margery Shove (widow), 17 June 1654, Boston, Mass.
PEACOK, Mary and John Mayn, 24 July 1690, Boston, Mass.
PEAD, William and Mary Hardenbergh, 4 June 1694, New York.
PEAKE, Christopher and Dorcas French, 3 January 1636, Roxbury, Mass.
PEAKE, Dorcas and John Curtis, 1678, Roxbury, Mass.
PEARCE, Experience and Nehemiah Jewett, 19 October 1668, Lynn, Mass.
PEARCE, John and Abiagell Thompson, 5 January 1692-3, Dorchester, Mass.
PEARCE, Marcy and James Travis, 8 April 1667, Gloucester, Mass.
PEARCE, Mary and Thomas Hearing, 15 February 1650, Dedham, Mass.
PEARCY, John and Jane Stanwood, 17 July 1673, Gloucester, Mass.
PEARD, Margret and Samuel Swetman, 26 October 1693, Boston, Mass.
PEARL, Nicholas and Elizabeth Bosworth, 26 October 1686, Ipswich, Mass.
PEARS, Abiah and Jeremiah Rogers, 1650, Dorchester, Mass.
PEARSE, George and Mary Woodhouse, September 1659, Boston, Mass.
PEARSON, Benjamin and Hannah Thurston, 1680, Newburyport, Mass.
PEARSON, Isaac and Elizabeth Hall, 2 September 1685, Philadelphia, Penn.
PEARSON, James and Hepzibah Swain, 1698, Lynn, Mass.
PEARSON, Mary and Samuel Palmer, 20 December 1671, Rowley, Mass.
PEART, Thomas and Anna Wilson, 2 February 1688, Philadelphia, Penn.
PEASE, John and Ann Cummings, 8 October 1669, Enfield, Conn.
PEASE, Jonathan and Elizabeth Booth, 11 October 1693, Enfield, Conn.
PEASE, Mary and Benjamin Cody, 16 February 1663, Andover, Mass.
PEASLEE, Jane and John Davis, December 1646, Haverhill, Mass.
PEATHER, Ann and Jeremiah Smith, 21 December 1699, Boston, Mass.
PECK, Eleaser and Mary Bunnell, 31 October 1671, New Haven, Conn.
PECK, Elizabeth and Joseph Hill, 22 December 1698, Boston, Mass.
PECK, Elizabeth and John Hotchkiss, 5 December 1672, New Haven, Conn.
PECK, Hanna and Joseph Hopkins, 27 April 1699, Hartford, Conn.
PECK, Jeremiah and Hannah Kitchell, 12 November 1656, Guilford, Conn.
PECK, Jonathan and Elizabeth Throop, 31 March 1695, Bristol, R. I.
PECK, Mary and John Wells, 18 February 1697, Boston, Mass.
PECK, Rebecca and Thomas Paine, 25 April 1671, Dedham, Mass.
PECKHAM, John and Mary Bennett, 1695, Newport, R. I.
PEGG, Daniel and Martha Allen, 22 February 1686, Middletown, Penn.
PEIRCE, Ann and Francis Whitmore, 7 December 1699, Boston, Mass.

PEIRCE, Daniel and Ann Milward, 26 December 1654, Newbury, Mass.

PEIRCE, John and Rebecca Wheeler (widow), 10 June 1654, Boston, Mass.

PEIRCE, John and Ruth Bishop, 15 February 1656, Boston, Mass.

PEIRCE, John and Mary Corbet, 9 November 1698, Boston, Mass.

PEIRCE, Joshua and Elizabeth Hall, 24 January 1695, Portsmouth, N. H.

PEIRCE, Martha and Col. Thomas Noyes, 28 December 1669, Newbury, Mass.

PEIRCE, Sarah and Caleb Moody, 24 August 1659, Newbury, Mass.

PEIRSE, Christian and Samuel Bridg, 3 December 1690, Boston, Mass.

PELHAM, Joseph and Rebecca Barber, 19 March 1697, Boston, Mass.

PELINGHAM, Jane and Thomas Dias, September 1674, Somerset Co., Md.

PELL, Elizabeth and Joseph Wheeler, 14 December 1697, Boston, Mass.

PELL, Mary and Richard George, 1 September 1655, Boston, Mass.

PELL, William and Elizabeth Van Teuyl, 23 November 1694, New York.

PELLAT, Mary and Benjamin Blodgett, 14 February 1683, Chelmsford, Mass.

PELLET, Thomas and Mary Dane, 5 March 1659, Concord, Mass.

PELTON, Robert and Rebeccah Crehore, 2 September 1697, Milton, Mass.

PELTON, Samuel and Mary Smith, 16 May 1673, Dorchester, Mass.

PEMBERTON, Deborah and Thomas Kimball, 22 December 1686, Malden, Mass.

PEMBERTON, Elizabeth and Robert Ellis, 4 June 1698, Boston, Mass.

PEMBERTON, Phineas and Alice Hodgson, 18 March 1699, Falls, Penn.

PEMBROOK, Frances and Samuel Mills, 11 January 1645, Dedham, Mass.

PENDLETON, Ann and Eleazer Brown, 18 October 1693, Westerly, R. I.

PENDLETON, Hannah and John Bush, 13 January 1679, Sudbury, Mass.

PENDLETON, James and Mary Palmer, 22 October 1647, Westerly, R. I.

PENDLETON, Joseph and Deborah Miner, 8 July 1696, Westerly, R. I.

PENEWELL, Martha and William Perram, 16 November 1693, Boston, Mass.

PENFIELD, Samuel and Mary Lewis, 30 November 1675, Lynn, Mass.

PENFIELD, Mary and Jeremiah Fairbanks, 19 April 1698, Bristol, R. I.

PENIMAN, John and Hanna Billings, 24 December 1664, Braintree, Mass.

PENIMAN, John and Waytinge Robinson, 25 July 1666, Braintree, Mass.

PENIMAN, Mary and Samuel Paine, 4 April 1678, Braintree, Mass.

PENMAN, Elizabeth and Joshua Mors, 15 November 1699, Dedham, Mass.

PENNIMAN, James and Mary Crosse, 10 May 1659, Boston, Mass.

PENNAN, Sarah and Tymothy Dwight, 11 September 1651, Dedham, Mass.

PENNOCK, Sarah and William Salway, 28 July 1688, Philadelphia, Penn.

PENNY, Christopher and Elizabeth Olstra, 8 January 1694, Bristol, R. I.

PENNY, Ellene and Thomas Redding, 20 July 1639, Plymouth, Mass.

PENNY, Joane and Thomas Kent, 28 March 1659, Gloucester, Mass.

PENNY, Thomas and Agnes Cleark, 15 June 1668, Gloucester, Mass.

PENNY, Thomas and Joane Brabrick, 17 May 1682, Gloucester, Mass.

PENNYMAN, Samuel and Elizabeth Parmiter, 6 January 1673, Dorchester, Mass.

PENNIMAN, Sarah and Increase Robinson, 19 November 1663, Dorchester, Mass.

PENQUITE, John and Agnes Sharpe, 14 April 1690, Middletown, Penn.

PENUEL, Alice and Nathaniel Freeman, 18 January 1699, Boston, Mass.

PEPPER, Elizabeth and John Everid, 13 March 1662, Dedham, Mass.

PEPPER, John and Bethia Fisher, 25 August 1669, Dedham, Mass.

PEPPER, Mary and Samuel Everett, 28 August 1669, Dedham, Mass.

PEPPIATT, Barbara and Benjamin Wright, 23 December 1699, Philadelphia, Penn.

PERCELL, Sarah and John Dorman, 31 December 1672, Somerset Co., Md.
PERCIVAH, Theodere and Elizabeth Morss, 12 January 1698, Boston, Mass.
PEREGOE, Marah and Henry Peterson, 15 April 1683, Lyme, Conn.
PERKINS, Abraham and Hannah Beamsley, 16 October 1661, Boston, Mass.
PERKINS, James and Leah Cox, 13 December 1681, Hampton, N. H.
PERKINS, John and Mary Mackfarland, 11 December 1697, Boston, Mass.
PERKINS, Jonathan and Mary Elcock, 14 June 1682, New Haven, Conn.
PERKINS, Joseph and Mehitable Bartlett, December 1672, Simsbury, Conn.
PERKINS, Luke and Marthan Conant, 31 May 1688, Salem, Mass.
PERKINS, Mary and Henery Grubb, 24 March 1683, Burlington, N. J.
PERKINS, Thomas and Remember Woodman, 26 July 1694, Boston, Mass.
PERKINS, William and Elizabeth Wooton, 30 August 1636, Roxbury, Mass.
PERKINS, William and Elizabeth Clarke, 24 October 1669, Topsfield, Mass.
PERKIS, Sarah and Nathaniel Rogers, 26 October 1699, Boston, Mass.
PERRAM, William and Martha Penewell, 16 November 1693, Boston, Mass.
PERREY, John and Sarah Mallyear, 9 December 1697, New York.
PERRIN, Abraham and Sarah Walker, 27 December 1677, Rehoboth, Mass.
PERRIN, Daniel and Maria Thorel, 12 February 1665, Elizabethown, N. J.
PERRIN, Mehitable and Zachariah Richardson, 14 February 1699, Woburn, Mass.
PERRIN, Paster and William Minson, 4 August 1697, Elizabeth City Co., Va.
PERRY, Elizabeth (widow) and John Gillet, 22 October 1653, Boston, Mass.
PERRY, Elizabeth and John Holdridge, 16 September 1663, Dedham, Mass.
PERRY, Esther and William Harwood, 11 May 1692, Dunstable, Mass.
PERRY, Ezra and Elizabeth Burgess, 12 February 1651, Sandwich, Mass.
PERRY, John and Bethia Morse, 23 May 1665, Medfield, Mass.
PERRY, John and Sarah Clary, 13 December 1667, Watertown, Mass.
PERRY, Jonah and Susanna Shaw, 9 June 1698, Boston, Mass.
PERRY, Mary and Samuel Wheeler, 10 November 1673, Stratford, Conn.
PERRY, Mary and William Smith, 8 January 1699, Boston, Mass.
PERRY, Michael and Joanna Breck, 12 July 1694, Boston, Mass.
PERRY, Nathaniel and Sarah Carpenter, 17 May 1683, Rehoboth, Mass.
PERRY, Samuel and Mary Miller, 12 December 1678, Sandwich, Mass.
PERRY, Samuel and Mary Tucker, 9 May 1690, Sandwich, Mass.
PERRY, Thomas and Ruth Ripley, 29 January 1699, Boston, Mass.
PERSON, William and Miss Carrionton, 21 October 1692, Simsbury, Conn.
PERSONS, Jane and John Macky, 22 March 1693, New York.
PETERS, Anna and Johannes Ellsworth, 3 June 1696, New York.
PETERS, Elizabeth and John Sady, 25 November 1678, Ipswich, Mass.
PETERS, Elizabeth and Walter Wright, 9 September 1684, Andover, Mass.
PETERS, Elizabeth and James Johnson, 26 April 1692, Andover, Mass.
PETERS, Margaret and John Breadstead, 10 May 1699, New York.
PETERS, Mary and Thomas Chandler, 22 May 1686, Andover, Mass.
PETERS, Mercy and John Allen, 22 May 1686, Andover, Mass.
PETERS, Samuel and Phobe Fry, 15 December 1696, Andover, Mass.
PETERSON, Benjamin and Hannah Wadsworth, 9 February 1698, Duxbury, Mass.
PETERSON, Henry and Marah Peregoe, 15 April 1683, Lyme, Conn.
PETERSON, John and Mary Soule, 1664, Duxbury, Mass.
PETERSON, John and Hannah Gerritse, 20 June 1693, New York.
PETTENGILL, Mary and Abraham Adams, 10 November 1670, Newbury, Mass.

PETTIBON, Sarah and John Humphri, 6 July 1699, Simsbury, Conn.

PETTIBONE, John and Sara Egelston, 16 February 1664, Windsor, Conn.

PETTIT, Thomas and Cathrine Branch, 26 November 1698, New York.

PETTY, John and Ann Canning, 30 May 1662, Boston, Mass.

PEY, Elianer and Garviss Marshall, 27 September 1692, New York City.

PHELPS, Abraham and Mary Pinne, 6 July 1663, Windsor, Conn.

PHELPS, Edward and Ruth Andrews, 9 March 1682, Andover, Mass.

PHELPS, Eleanor and William Chandler, 21 April 1687, Andover, Mass.

PHELPS, Elizabeth and Joseph Ballard, 28 February 1665, Andover, Mass.

PHELPS, George and Phillury Randall, 1637, Windsor, Conn.

PHELPS, George and Ann Gaylord, 11 May 1663, Windsor, Conn.

PHELPS, Isaac and Ann Gaylord, 10 March 1664, Windsor, Conn.

PHELPS, Jacob and Dorothy Ingersoll, 2 May 1672, Hartford, Conn.

PHELPS, Joseph and Hanna Newton, 20 September 1660, Windsor, Conn.

PHELPS, Joseph and Mary Porter, 26 June 1673, Windsor, Conn.

PHELPS, Joseph and Sarah Case, 9 November 1699, Simsbury, Conn.

PHELPS, Nathaniel and Elizabeth Copley (widow), September 1650, Windsor, Conn.

PHELPS, Nathaniel and Grace Martin, 11 August 1676, Windsor, Conn.

PHELPS, Samuel and Sarah Chandler, 29 May 1682, Andover, Mass.

PHELPS, Timothy and Mary Griswold, 19 May 1661, Windsor, Conn.

PHELPS, Walter and Sarah Skipper, 28 December 1654, Reading, Mass.

PHELPS, William and Sara Pinne, 20 December 1676, Windsor, Conn.

PHENIX, Ann and John Winter, 2 April 1697, Boston, Mass.

PHESEY, Ann and William Banes, 26 December 1684, Somerset Co., Md.

PHILBERD, Mary and William Hinckesman, 20 December 1652, Boston, Mass.

PHILBRICK, Elizabeth and Nathaniel Berry, 2 July 1691, Dover, N. H.

PHILBRICK, William and Mary Neal, 10 October 1689, Greenland, N. H.

PHILIPS, Frederick and Katherine Darwall, 1 December 1692, New York City.

PHILIPS, Hannah and Richard Gleave, 15 August 1693, New York.

PHILLIPS, Elizabeth and Abiel Everill, 6 May 1655, Boston, Mass.

PHILLIPS, Evah and Jacobus Van Courtland, 7 May 1691, New York City.

PHILLIPS, Hannah and Ebenezer White, 1671, Weymouth, Mass.

PHILLIPS, Hanah and Joseph Morse, 1 July 1638, Dedham, Mass.

PHILLIPS, Hannah and David Anderson, 5 January 1699, Boston, Mass.

PHILLIPS, Henry and Mary Brock, 5 January 1639, Dedham, Mass.

PHILLIPS, Henry and An Hunting, 1 March 1641, Dedham, Mass.

PHILLIPS, Jeremiah and Anne Brooks, 3 June 1678, Richmond Co., Va.

PHILLIPS, Joanna and Samuel Oake, 4 October 1693, Boston, Mass.

PHILLIPS, Martha and Aquilla Paca, 11 September 1699, Harford Co., Md.

PHILLIPS, Mary and Samuel Gallop, 20 December 1650, Boston, Mass.

PHILLIPS, Nicholas and Hannah Salter, 4 October 1651, Boston, Mass.

PHILLIPS, Sarah and Thomas Scudder, 4 November 1689, Boston, Mass.

PHILLIPS, Thomas and Mary Howard, 1 March 1692, Boston, Mass.

PHILLIPS, William, Jr., and Martha Franklin, 24 August 1650, Boston, Mass.

PHILLIPS, William and Zechariah Gillman, 26 July 1659, Boston, Mass.

PHILLIPS, William and Deborah Long, 13 November 1689, Boston, Mass.

PHILLPS, William and Jane Butterfeeld, 2 April 1691, Boston, Mass.

PHILPIN, Mary and David Morris, 4 March 1685, Philadelphia, Penn.

PHILPOT, Theophilus and Rebecca Chonor, 22 September 1697, Boston, Mass.

PHILPOT, Walter and Anna Hunn (widow), 16 October 1651, Boston, Mass.

PHILPS, Elizabeth and Joseph Ballard, 28 February 1665, Andover, Mass.

PHIPPEN, Ann and William Weeler, 16 May 1686, Boston, Mass.

PHIPS, Benjamin and Hannah Dean, 10 October 1693, New York.

PHIPS, Hannah and John Smith, 17 September 1697, New York.

PICKARD, Jane and Samuel Hazen, 6 November 1684, Rowley, Mass.

PICKARD, John and Jane Crosby, 29 November 1644, Rowley, Mass.

PICKARD, John and Sarah Smith, 1 February 1679, Rowley, Mass.

PICKARD, John and Joana Bishop, 5 March 1690, Ipswich, Mass.

PICKERING, John and Elizabeth Munden, 17 July 1688, Dover, N. H.

PICKETT, John and Ruth Brewster, 14 March 1651, New London, Conn.

PICKETT, Mary and Joshua Hoyt, 16 March 1698, Stamford, Conn.

PICKETT, Mercy and Samuel Fosdick, 1 November 1682, New London, Conn.

PICKETT, Ruth and Charles Hill, 2 July 1686, New London, Conn.

PICKLES, Nathan and Meriam Turner, 3 August 1687, Scituate, Mass.

PIDGE, Elizebeth and James Emary, 28 December 1695, Dedham, Mass.

PIDGE, John and Mary Farrington, 27 April 1667, Dedham, Mass.

PIDGE, John and Elizabeth Newcomb, 3 May 1677, Dedham, Mass.

PIDGE, Martha and Benjamin Bullard, 5 February 1659, Dedham, Mass.

PIDGE, Mary and Michell Metcalfe, 13 June 1645, Dedham, Mass.

PIERCE, Elizabeth and Samuel Smith, 8 June 1692, Woodbridge, N. J.

PIERCE, John and Elizabeth Brookes, 24 May 1682, Simsbury, Conn.

PIERCE, Judith and Francis Wyman, 30 January 1645, 30 January 1645, Woburn, Mass.

PIERCE, Mary and Ralph Reed, 31 March 1654, Woburn, Mass.

PIERCE, Mary and John Walker, 14 October 1672, Woburn, Mass.

PIERCE, Thomas and Elizabeth Cole, 6 May 1635, Woburn, Mass.

PIERCE, Timothy and Lydia Spaulding, 27 March 1696, Plainfield, Conn.

PIERSON, Abigail and John Davenport, 27 November 1662, Branford, Conn.

PIERSON, Ellin and Jeffery Hawkins, 21 September 1687, Middletown, Penn.

PIERSON, Joseph and Ann Barnes, 17 November 1675, Cumberland Co., N. J.

PIERSON, Susanna and Benjamin Bishop, 6 June 1696, Stamford, Conn.

PIERSON, Thomas and Maria Harrison, 27 November 1662, Branford, Conn.

PIETERS, Hilleke and Suert Olpherts, 17 September 1697, New York.

PIKE, John and Sarah Stout, 2 February 1675, Monmouth Co., N. J.

PIKE, John and Sarah Moody, 5 May 1681, Boston, Mass.

PIKE, John and Elizabeth Fitz Randolph (widow), 30 June 1685, Woodbridge, N. J.

PIKE, Mary and Richard Worth, 11 September 1667, Newbury, Mass.

PILKENTON, Elizabeth and Edmund Jackson, 27 October 1660, Boston, Mass.

PILKINTON, Mark and Faith Cross, 18 November 1691, Boston, Mass.

PILLSBURY, Moses and Susannah Worth, March 1668, Newbury, Mass.

PILLSBURY, William and Dorothy Crosby, June 1641, Dorchester, Mass.

PIM, John and Mary Orchard, 5 February 1690, Boston, Mass.

PIMBROOK, Frances and Samuell Mills, 11 January 1645, Dedham, Mass.

PINCIN, Thomas and Elizabeth White, April 1662, Scituate, Mass.

PINDAR, Joana and Valentine Rowell, February 1643, Salisbury, Mass.

PINDAR, Mary and Solomon Martin, 1643, Gloucester, Mass.

PING, Elizabeth and Nathaniel Griffin, 26 August 1671, Andover, Mass.
PINKHAM, Thomas and Mary Allin, 2 December 1699, Dover, N. H.
PINNE, Mary and Abraham Phelps, 6 July 1663, Windsor, Conn.
PINNE, Samuel and Joyce Bissell, 17 November 1665, Windsor, Conn.
PINNE, Sara and William Phelps, 20 December 1676, Windsor, Conn.
PINSON, Thomas and Sarah Turner, 26 December 1693, Scituate, Mass.
PINTARD, Anthony and Katherine Stale, 14 May 1692, New York City.
PIPER, Margaret and Tristram Greenleaf, 12 November 1689, Hampton, N. H.
PIPER, Samuel and Abigail Church, 23 April 1694, Dover, N. H.
PITCHER, Nathanill and Mary Clap, 8 July 1685, Milton, Mass.
PITCHER, Samuel and Ale Gaig, 30 November 1671, Milton, Mass.
PITCHER, Samuel and Mary Blake, 3 August 1681, Milton, Mass.
PITKEN, Martha and Simon Wolcot, 17 October 1661, Windsor, Conn.
PITTMAN, Mary and Stephen Oates, 16 April 1674, Dover, N. H.
PITTMAN, William and Barbary Evons, 29 September 1653, Boston, Mass.
PITTOM, Mary and John Comer, 9 February 1698, Boston, Mass.
PITTS, Elizabeth and Joseph Austin, 10 November 1692, Charlestown, Mass.
PITTS, James and Elizabeth Hough, 10 March 1691, Boston, Mass.
PITTS, John and Elizabeth Lindall, 10 September 1697, Boston, Mass.
PITTS, William and Susan Aealy (widow of Philip), 7 October 1655, Boston, Mass.
PITTS, William and Ann Partridge, 29 July 1664, Charlestown, Mass.
PITTY, Mary and Henry Adams, 10 May 1660, Boston, Mass.
PLAISTED, Elihu and Elizabeth Harvey, 11 October 1689, Dover, N. H.
PLAISTED, John and Sarah Worthilake, 25 March 1698, Boston, Mass.
PLANCKEN, Sara De and Lambert Bosch, 1 January 1663, Brooklyn, N. Y.
PLATT, Isaac and Phoebe Smith, 12 March 1640, Milford, Conn.
PLATT, Mary and John Woodruff, 22 December 1698, Milford, Conn.
PLATTS, Abel and Lydia Holly, 8 May 1672, Rowley, Mass.
PLATTS, Elizabeth and Samuel Brocklebank, 22 November 1681, Rowley, Mass.
PLATTS, Samuel and Phillippa Felt, 19 December 1681, Rowley, Mass.
PLEASANTS, John and Jane Tucker (widow), February 1670, Henrico Co., Va.
PLEVIER, Anna Maria and Daniel Peterse Coreman, 30 June 1698, New York.
PLIMPTON, John and Jane Dummin, 13 January 1644, Dedham, Mass.
PLIMPTON, Joseph and Priscilla Parterage (or Parteridg), 22 August 1699, Boston, Mass.
PLIMPTON, John and Sarah Turner, 28 February 1696, Dedham, Mass.
PLINCO, Elizabeth and John Pantry, 16 April 1698, New York.
PLUM, Dorcas and John Lyman, 12 January 1654, Branford, Conn.
PLUM, Mary and Matthew Woodruff, 16 June 1668, Milford, Conn.
PLUMLY, Margerie and Henry Paxton, 13 June 1684, Middletown, Penn.
PLUMLY, Hannah and Edward Lincford, 16 March 1667, Braintree, Mass.
PLUMLY, Hester and Timothy Winter, 16 October 1670, Braintree, Mass.
PLUMLY, William and Elizabeth Thompson, 7 January 1688, Middletown, Penn.
PLUMMER, Silvanus and Sarah Moody, January 1681, Newbury, Mass.
POFFER, James and Mary Swalden, 14 December 1655, Braintree, Mass.
POFFER, Mathias and Rachel Farnsworth, 18 January 1662, Braintree, Mass.
POLE, John and Elizabeth Brenton, 28 March 1672, Dorchester, Mass.
POLHEMUS, Daniel and Neeltje Vandeveer, 13 August 1685, Flatbush, N. Y.
POLHEMUS, Theodorus and Aertie Bogart, 14 October 1677, Flatbush, L. I., N. Y.

POLLEY, Joseph and Joan Ken, 4 May 1677, Richmond Co., Va.
POLLING, Simon and Jean Wade, 19 October 1673, Richmond Co., Va.
POLLORD, Jonathan and Mary Winslow, 26 December 1693, Boston, Mass.
POLLY, John and Jane Walker (widow), 2 June 1684, Roxbury, Mass.
POMEROY, Mary and John Foster, 12 July 1692, Salem, Mass.
POMEROY, Medad and Experience Woodward, 21 November 1661, Dorchester, Mass.
POMERY, Caleb and Hepsiba Baker, 8 March 1664, Windsor, Conn.
POMMERY, Richard and Deliverance Berry, 14 February 1698, Dover, N. H.
POND, Abigail and John Day, 22 March 1678, Dedham, Mass.
POND, Daniell and Ann Edwards, 18 July 1661, Dedham, Mass.
POND, Ephriam and Deborah Hawes, 6 January 1685, Wrentham, Mass.
POND, Isaac and Hannah Griffen, 20 May 1667, Windsor, Conn.
POND, Jabez and Mary Gay, 11 January 1698-9, Dedham, Mass.
POND, Mary and Nicholas Ellin, 3 May 1663, Dorchester, Mass.
POND, Rachell and Martha Stone, May 1681, Dedham, Mass.
POND, Samuel and Miriam Blatchley, 3 February 1669, Branford, Conn.
POND, Sarah and Eleazer Holbrook, 14 June 1698, Dedham, Mass.
POND, Sarah and Desire Clap, 21 October 1679, Dorchester, Mass.
POND, Thankfull and Philip Withington, 17 November 1682, Dorchester, Mass.
POOL, Elizabeth and John Sparhawk, 22 June 1699, Boston, Mass.
POOL, Mary and Thomas Thair, 28 October 1687, Milton, Mass.
POOL, Matthew and Sarah Blake, 29 May 1694, Boston, Mass.
POOLE, John and Elizabeth Sheppard (widow), 10 October 1699, Elizabeth City Co., Va.
POOLE, Jonathan and Bridget Fitch, 1691, Reading, Mass.
POOLE, Judith and William Hasey, 16 May 1681, Hull, Mass.
POOLE, Mary and Daniel Henchman, 26 February 1672, Dorchester, Mass.
POOLE, Nathaniel and Elizabeth Lucas, 23 September 1692, Middletown, Penn.
POOLE, Sarah and Thomas Bancroft, Jr., 10 April 1673, Reading, Mass.
POOP, Thankfull and Smith Woodward, 29 July 1691, Dorchester, Mass.
POOR, Deborah and Timothy Osgood, 29 May 1689, Andover, Mass.
POOR, Elizabeth and Jacob Marstone, 7 April 1686, Andover, Mass.
POOR, Hannah and Francis Deane, 16 November 1681, Andover, Mass.
POOR, Lucy and Samuel Astin, 11 October 1691, Andover, Mass.
POOR, Martha and John Granger, 9 February 1679, Andover, Mass.
POOR, Priscilla and Abraham Moore, 14 December 1687, Andover, Mass.
POOR, Ruth and John Stevens, 20 December 1689, Andover, Mass.
POORE, Daniel and Mary Farnum, 20 October 1650, Boston, Mass.
POORE, Henry and Abigail Hale, 12 September 1679, Rowley, Mass.
POORE, Mary and John Noyes, 23 November 1668, Andover, Mass.
POPE, Elizabeth and Christopher Wetherill, 10 November 1690, Burlington Co., N. J.
POPE, Hannah and Nicholas Holt, 12 June 1658, Andover, Mass.
POPE, Jane and John Mony, 2 April 1698, Dorchester, Mass.
POPE, Susana and Jacob Mitchell, 7 November 1666, Plymouth, Mass.
POPE, Thomas (second marriage) and Sarah Jenney, 19 May 1646, Plymouth, Mass. (second marriage).
POPE, Thomas and Ann Fallowell, 28 January 1637, Plymouth, Mass.

POPE, Thomas and Margaret Long, 18 November 1681, Dorchester, Mass.

PORDRIAN, Mary and William Moyon, 6 September 1692, New York City.

PORE, Daniel and Mary Farnum, 20 October 1650, Boston, Mass.

PORMOTT, Elizabeth and Samuel Norden, January 1656, Boston, Mass.

PORTER, Anne and William Gaylord, 24 February 1641, Windsor, Conn.

PORTER, Elizabeth and Isaac Johnson, 20 January 1637, Boston, Mass.

PORTER, Elizabeth and Joshua Nash, 23 February 1658, Boston, Mass.

PORTER, Hannah and George Jefferyes, 28 November 1694, Boston, Mass.

PORTER, James and Sara Tudor, 15 January 1679, Windsor, Conn.

PORTER, John, Jr., and Joana Gaylor, 16 December 1669, Windsor, Conn.

PORTER, Mary and Samuel Grant, 27 May 1658, Windsor, Conn.

PORTER, Mary and Joseph Phelps, 26 June 1673, Windsor, Conn.

PORTER, Mary and Joseph Royce, 1 October 1684, Wallingford, Conn.

PORTER, Ruth and Thomas Bayley, 17 September 1660, Weymouth, Mass.

PORTER, Sara and Nathaniel Winchell, 4 April 1663, Windsor, Conn.

PORTER, Sarah and Enoch Drake, 11 November 1680, Windsor, Conn.

PORTER, William and Eliza Gale, 31 January 1694, Boston, Mass.

PORTEUS, Robert and Alice Greenwood, 3 November 1659, Boston, Mass.

POST, John and Hester Hide, March 1652, Saybrook, Conn.

POST, Kateren and Alexander Chalker, 29 September 1649, Saybrook, Conn.

POST, Mary (widow) and John Bridges, 1 March 1678, Andover, Mass.

POST, William and Altje Covert, 14 May 1679, New York City.

POTTER, Abell and Rachell Warner, 16 November 1669, Warwick, R. I.

POTTER, Bethiah and Thomas Witt, 26 February 1685, Salem, Mass.

POTTER, Christian and Samuell Maxfeld, 11 December 1691, Dorchester, Mass.

POTTER, Christina and Thomas Dixon, 12 August 1672, Somerset Co., Md.

POTTER, Eunice and John Fry, 4 October 1660, Andover, Mass.

POTTER, Hannah and Samuel Blakesley, 3 December 1650, New Haven, Conn.

POTTER, Hannah and John Butler, 17 November 1684, Branford, Conn.

POTTER, Hope and Daniel Robinson, 3 February 1663, New Haven, Conn.

POTTER, John and Ruth Fisher, 2 June 1664, Warwick, R. I.

POTTER, John and Mary Russell, 29 December 1679, New Haven, Conn.

POTTER, John, Jr., and Elizabeth Holt, 23 February 1691-2, New Haven, Conn.

POTTER, John and Sarah Collins (widow), 7 January 1684-5, Warwick, R. I.

POTTER, Nathaniel and Elizabeth Hawes, 1 April 1675, New Haven, Conn.

POTTER, Phebe (widow) and John Rose, Jr., August 1670, New Haven, Conn.

POTTER, Rebeckah and Thomas Adams, 27 November 1667, New Haven, Conn.

POTTER, Richard and Katharine Reay, 18 September 1693, New York.

POTTER, Robert and Ruth Driver, 25 January 1660, Salem, Mass.

POTTER, Samuel and Annah Russell, 21 November 1670, New Haven, Conn.

POTTER, Samuel and Ruth Dunton, 18 April 1692, Ipswich, Mass.

POTTER, Samuel and Sarah Wright, 8 January 1673, Woburn, Mass.

POTTER, Sarah (widow) and John Sanford, 19 December 1656, Boston, Mass.

POTTER, Sarah (widow) and Joshua Saire, 2 January 1677, Concord, Mass.

POTTLE, Christopher and Hannah Graves, 12 March 1694, Ipswich, Mass.

POTTS, David and Alice Crossdel, 22 January 1693, Middletown, Penn.

POTTS, Elizabeth and Edmond Bennet, 22 October 1685, Middletown, Penn.

POTTS, Jane and John Austin, 11 November 1686, Philadelphia, Penn.

POTTS, Thomas and Martha Keurlis, 20 October 1699, Germantown, Penn.

POTTS, Thomas and Mary Records, 20 June 1698, Burlington, N. J.

POWELL, Ann and Joseph Wilcox, 25 January 1687, Philadelphia, Penn.

POWELL, Elizabeth and James Newbold, 10 January 1695, Burlington, N. J.

POWELL, Elizabeth and Richard Hollingworth, 23 August 1659, Boston, Mass.

POWELL, Hannah and Thomas Tuttle, 21 May 1661, New Haven, Conn.

POWELL, Mary and Edward Wright, 27 March 1657, Boston, Mass.

POWELL, Priscilla and John Thompson, 22 May 1667, New Haven, Conn.

POWELL, Sarah and Timothy Dwight, 3 March 1653, Dedham, Mass.

POWELL, Thomas and Alse Graham, 25 August 1676, Windsor, Conn.

POWER, Arthur and Sarah Makaset, 17 January 1693, Boston, Mass.

POWER, Walter and Trial Shepard, 11 January 1660, Malden, Mass.

POWERS, Hannah and Pascho Dunn, 8 April 1695, Elizabeth City Co., Va.

POWLIN, Pleasant and Joseph Milner, 10 May 1690, Middletown, Penn.

POWNAL, Abigail and William Paxton, Jr., 20 December 1695, Middletown, Penn.

POWNAL, Eleanor and Joshua Hoops, 20 December 1693, Middletown, Penn.

POWTER, Elizabeth and Jonathan Danforth, 22 September 1654, Boston, Mass.

PRASKE, Anne and John Wampony (an Indian), 21 May 1661, Boston, Mass.

PRAT, John and Margaret Maverick, 29 July 1691, Boston, Mass.

PRAT, Richard and Mercy, 16 March 1692, Boston, Mass.

PRATT, Elizabeth and Benjamin Lord, 13 April 1693, Guilford, Conn.

PRATT, Hannah and Jonathan Robbins, 11 January 1693-4, Plymouth, Mass.

PRATT, Hannah and Ebenezer Campbell, 29 March 1694, Taunton, Mass.

PRATT, John and Sarah Jones, 8 June 1665, Saybrook, Conn.

PRATT, John and Mary Andrews, 10 August 1676, Saybrook, Conn.

PRATT, John and Martha Pratt, 18 November 1686, Malden, Mass.

PRATT, John and Hannah Williams, 10 November 1697, Saybrook, Conn.

PRATT, Joseph and Sarah Judkins, 7 May 1662, Weymouth, Mass.

PRATT, Joshua and Bathsheba Fay, 1630, Plymouth, Mass.

PRATT, Lydia and Josiah Chapin, 26 July 1676, Braintree, Mass.

PRATT, Lydia and John Kutland, 18 November 1679, Saybrook, Conn.

PRATT, Martha and John Pratt, 18 November 1686, Malden, Mass.

PRATT, Nathaniel and Sarah Beamont, 2 May 1688, Saybrook, Conn.

PRATT, Susannah and Nathaniel Merrill, 18 January 1698, West Hartford, Conn.

PRATT, Timothy and Deborah Cooper, 9 November 1659, Boston, Mass.

PRATT, William and Elizabeth Baker, 26 October 1680, Dorchester, Mass.

PRATT, William and Hannah Kutland, 20 February 1678, Saybrook, Conn.

PRAY, Dorothy and Richard Thayre, 24 October 1651, Braintree, Mass.

PRAY, Hannah and Henry Neale, 14 December 1655, Braintree, Mass.

PREIG, Jacob and Elizabeth Mayo, 27 June 1687, Philadelphia, Penn.

PRENCE, Judith and Isaac Barker, 28 December 1665, Duxbury, Mass.

PRENCE, Thomas and Patience Brewster, 5 August 1624, Plymouth, Mass.

PRENTICE, Elizabeth and Thomas Aldrich, 4 March 1675, Dedham, Mass.

PRENTICE, Elizabeth and Joseph Bond, 13 November 1699, Boston, Mass.

PRENTICE, Mary and Nathaniel Hancock, 8 March 1664, Cambridge, Mass.

PRENTISS, Joana and John Gibson, 24 July 1662, Cambridge, Mass.

PRESBURY, Nathaniel and Elizabeth Ganson, 16 February 1698, Boston, Mass.

PRESCOTT, Elizabeth and John Fowle, 27 September 1678, Concord, Mass.

PRESCOTT, Hannah and John Rugg, 4 March 1660, Lancaster, Mass.

PRESCOTT, Jonas and Mary Locker, 14 December 1672, Sudbury, Mass.

PRESCOTT, Jonas and Thankful Wheeler, 15 October 1699, Concord, Mass.
PRESCOTT, Jonathan and Elizabeth Hoar, 23 December 1675, Concord, Mass.
PRESCOTT, Jonathan and Rebecca Bulkley, 18 December 1689, Concord, Mass.
PRESCOTT, Lydia and Jonas Fairbanks, 28 May 1658, Lancaster, Mass.
PRESCOTT, Mary and Phillip Goss, 29 March 1690, Lancaster, Mass.
PRESCOTT, Mary and Benjamin Farnworth, April 1695, Groton, Mass.
PRESCOTT, Rebecca and Nathaniel Sanborn, 3 December 1691, Dover, N. H.
PRESCOTT, Samuel and Esther Wheeler, 5 May 1698, Acton, Mass.
PRESCOTT, Sarah and Richard Wheeler, 2 August 1658, Lancaster, Mass.
PRESTON, Abigail and Daniel Smith, 23 June 1696, Dorchester, Mass.
PRESTON, John and Susanna Read (widow), 28 May 1661, Boston, Mass.
PRESTON, Mary and Eliazer Fawne, 28 May 1662, Boston, Mass.
PRESTON, Mary and Nathaniel Carpenter, 13 October 1695, Dorchester, Mass.
PRESTON, Levi and Abigail Brooks, 16 October 1695, Swansea, Mass.
PRESTON, Samuel and Susana Gutterson, 27 May 1672, Andover, Mass.
PRESTON, Samuel and Sarah Bridges, 2 April 1694, Andover, Mass.
PRESTON, Widow and Nicholas Holt, 21 May 1666, Andover, Mass.
PRETORIOUS, Charles and Rebecca Martine, 17 September 1653, Boston, Mass.
PRICE, Ann and Dudley Bradstreet, 12 November 1673, Andover, Mass.
PRICE, Christopher and Susannah Allyn, 15 October 1697, New York.
PRICE, Elizabeth and Thomas Barnard, 14 December 1686, Andover, Mass.
PRICE, Joylieffe and Rebecca Coney, 7 December 1692, Boston, Mass.
PRICE, Richard and Elizabeth Crumwell, 18 August 1659, Boston, Mass.
PRICE, Richard and Grace Waite, 6 May 1662, Boston, Mass.
PRICE, Sarah and William Partridge, 23 November 1654, Dedham, Mass.
PRICE, Susanna and John Griffine, 27 February 1655, Boston, Mass.
PRICE, Theodore and Ann Wood, 1 August 1667, Salem, Mass.
PRICHARD, Hannah and John Lovejoy, 22 November 1676, Andover, Mass.
PRICHARD, Sarah and Joseph Lovejoy, 26 May 1685, Andover, Mass.
PRINCE, Ann and Richard Iggleden, 19 July 1660, Boston, Mass.
PRINCE, Joanna and John Lathrop, 21 January 1697, Boston, Mass.
PRINCE, Mary and Hugh Roe, 16 September 1675, Gloucester, Mass.
PRINCE, Thomas and Elizabeth Harraden, 27 September 1676, Gloucester, Mass.
PRINCE, Thomas and Ruth Turner, 23 December 1685, Scituate, Mass.
PRINGLE, Abraham and Isabel Witherspoon, 11 March 1687, Watertown, Mass.
PRIOR, Humphrey and Ann Osbon, 12 November 1663, Windsor, Conn.
PRIOR, Susanna and Robert Watson, 13 February 1690, Boston, Mass.
PRITCHARD, Alice and William Bradley, 1645, North Haven, Conn.
PRITCHARD, Elizabeth and John Allen, 22 February 1681, Suffield, Mass.
PRITCHARD, Rebecca (widow) and Ebenezer Burbank, 9 October 1699, Suffield, Conn.
PRITCHETT, Esther and John Hanchett, 6 September 1677, Suffield, Conn.
PROBY, Jane and William Long, 4 March 1694, Elizabeth City Co., Va.
PROCTER, Abigail and Joseph Lowell, 8 March 1660, Boston, Mass.
PROCTER, Obadiah and Margaret Gardner, 24 August 1699, Boston, Mass.
PROCTOR, Benjamin and Mary Buckley, 18 December 1694, Lynn, Mass.
PROCTOR, Edward and Elizabeth Cock, 24 November 1691, Boston, Mass.
PROCTOR, Hannah and John Lowle, 3 January 1653, Boston, Mass.
PROCTOR, Peter and Mary Patterson, 30 January 1689, Chelmsford, Mass.

PROCTOR, Robert and Jane Hildreth, 31 December 1645, Concord, Mass.
PROUSE, Abehall and Israel Dymand, 5 January 1690, Amesbury, Mass.
PROVOOST, Altie and Gerryt Van Hoorn, 14 June 1693, New York City.
PROVOOST, Benjamin and Elje Albertson, 5 November 1671, New York City.
PROVOOST, Margaret and Johannes Van Brugen, 6 July 1696, New York.
PRUDEN, William and Ann Hoorne, 10 November 1696, New York.
PRYOR, Thomas and Lydia Sinart, 28 February 1699, Philadelphia, Penn.
PUDDINGTON, Thomas and Rachel Williams, 20 September 1689, Dover, N. H.
PUFFER, Esther and William Summer, 2 June 1697, Milton, Mass.
PUFFER, James and Abigail Newton, 3 December 1695, Milton, Mass.
PUFFER, John and Mary Holebrook, 17 October 1695, Dorchester, Mass.
PUFFER, Mathias and Abigail Everard, 11 February 1677, Dedham, Mass.
PUFFER, Matthias and Mary Crehore, 14 May 1697, Milton, Mass.
PUFFER, Richard and Ruth Everet, 23 March 1681, Dorchester, Mass.
PUFFER, Robert and Mary Johnson, 1664, Boston, Mass.
PUGSLEY, Kathrine and Richard Wilson, 27 April 1698, New York.
PUGSLEY, Matthew and Mary Hunt, 22 November 1683, New York.
PULLEN, Joan and Edward Garreson, 29 August 1660, Boston, Mass.
PUMERY, Francis and Mehitabel Orchard, 7 February 1694, Boston, Mass.
PUNDERSON, John and Abigail Alling, August 1699, New Haven, Conn.
PUPPYN, Ann and Andrew Cannon, 18 November 1695, New York.
PURCHASE, Joan and Bernard Capen, March 1696, Dorchester, Mass.
PURCHASE, Mary and Increase Niles, 4 December 1677, Braintree, Mass.
PURMOTT, Elizabeth and Nathaniel Adams, 24 September 1652, Boston, Mass.
PURRINGTON, Elias and Sarah Orris, 7 July 1694, Boston, Mass.
PURRINGTON, Sarah and Charles Sleigh, 27 June 1693, New York.
PUTNAM, Thomas and Ann Holyoke, 7 October 1643, Lynn, Mass.
PUTNEY, John and Judith Cooke, 18 November 1662, Salem, Mass.
PYGAN, Alexander and Lydia Boyer, 15 April 1684, Saybrook, Conn.

Q

QUARLES, Joanna and Richard Smith, 2 August 1654, Boston, Mass.

QUARLES, William and Martha Dickenson, 9 December 1669, Ipswich, Mass.

QUICK, Tuenesen and Rynbregh Jurriaese, 7 December 1672, Esopus, N. Y.

QUILTER, Mary and Myhill Cresie, 6 April 1660, Ipswich, Mass.

QUIMBY, Deborah and William Goulding, 18 June 1688, Westchester Co., N. Y.

QUIMBY, Josiah and Mary Molyneux, 17 June 1689, Westchester Co., N. Y.

QUIMBY, Lydia and William Holdredge, 10 April 1674, Westchester Co., N. Y.

QUIMBY, Robert and Elizabeth Osgood, 7 January 1653, Salisbury, Mass.

QUINCY, Edward and Joane Hoare, 26 May 1648, Braintree, Mass.

QUINCY, Edmond and Miss Eliot, 8 December 1680, Braintree, Mass.

R

RACHELL, Judith and Thomas Reape, 30 November 1660, Boston, Mass.

RACKLEY, William and Dorothy Lord (widow), 18 October 1689, Dover, N. H.

RADCLIFF, Mary and Henry Baker, 13 August 1692, Middletown, Penn.

RAINE, Mary and Nathaniel Stairns, 25 October 1687, Milton, Mass.

RAKESTRAW, Grace and Nathaniel Zane, 27 June 1697, Philadelphia, Penn.

RAMOND, Mary and John Chandler, 10 November 1692, Woodstock, Conn.

RAMSDELL, Elizabeth and John Shaw, 12 August 1674, Malden, Mass.

RAMSDELL, Mary and Ephriam Smith, 6 September 1694, Boxford, Mass.

RAND, Alice and Thomas Lord, 27 June 1660, Ipswich, Mass.

RAND, Elizabeth and Joseph Hall, 3 March 1674, Lynn, Mass.

RAND, Susanna and Abraham Newell, 8 February 1652, Charlestown, Mass.

RANDALL, Hannah and Daniel Turner, 20 June 1665, Scituate, Mass.

RANDALL, Hannah and John Warfield, 26 December 1671, Taunton, Mass.

RANDALL, Mary and Abraham Staples, 17 September 1660, Weymouth, Mass.

RANDALL, Phillury and George Phelps, 1637, Windsor, Conn.

RANDELL, Thomas and Rachel Lincoln, 20 January 1697, Taunton, Mass.

RANDLETT, Charles and Mary Smith, 10 November 1675, Exeter, N. H.

RANDLETT, James and Elizabeth Robinson, 21 November 1699, Stratham, N. H.

RANDOL, William and Elizabeth Skerry, 21 December 1699, Boston, Mass.

RANDOLL, William and Elizabeth Hill, 10 December 1691, Boston, Mass.

RANDOLPH, William and Mary Isham, 1680, Henrico Co., Va.

RANKIN, Andrew and Grace Butler, 5 April 1692, Boston, Mass.

RANKIN, Mary and Pain Mayhew, 8 December 1699, Chilmark, Mass.

RANKIN, Sarah (widow) and Samuel Kenney, 15 March 1699, Dover, N. H.

RANSFORD, Jonathan and Mary Sunderland, 29 September 1656, Boston, Mass.

RANSFORD, Ranus and Josias Belcher, 3 January 1655, Boston, Mass.

RANSOM, Mathew and Hannah Jones, 7 March 1683, Saybrook, Conn.

RANSOM, Mercy and Samuel Waterman, 26 July 1692, Taunton, Mass.

RASBY, Webley and Alkie Luwersen, 16 June 1696, New York.

RAWLE, Francis and Martha Turner, 27 July 1689, Philadelphia, Penn.

RAWLINS, Abigail and Joseph Richards, 12 August 1697, Dover, N. H.

RAWLINS, Sarah and Joshua Holsworth, 10 May 1669, Lynn, Mass.

RAWLINS, Thomas and Sarah Madocks (widow), 2 March 1656, Boston, Mass.

RAWLINSON, William and Jane Sparrow, 16 September 1660, Charles City Co., Va.

RAWSON, Mary and Samuel Torrey, 15 March 1657, Boston, Mass.

RAWSON, Rachel and William Aubrey, 18 November 1652, Boston, Mass.

RAY, Mary and Samuel Deering, 5 September 1651, Braintree, Mass.

RAY, Robert and Jennett Hampton, 9 November 1689, Shrewsbury, N. J.

RAYMOND, Rachel and William Bradford, 14 November 1676, Beverly, Mass.

RAYMOND, Richard and Mary Betts, 10 December 1664, Norwalk, Conn.

RAYNOR, Henry and Johanna Edwards (widow), 9 June 1662, Boston, Mass.

RAYNER, James and Elizabeth Andrews, 25 October 1692, Boston, Mass.

RAYNER, Joseph and Sarah Davis, 3 February 1696, Boston, Mass.

RAYSON, George and Eliza Dyer, 21 May 1689, Boston, Mass.

REA, John and Anna Mary Powell (widow), 8 August 1699, St. James Parish, Anne Arundel Co., Md.

READ, Abigail and Judith Pierce, 2 October 1650, Woburn, Mass.

READ, Adam and Margaret Denkin, 11 January 1699, Boston, Mass.

READ, Ester and John Cann, 30 July 1661, Boston, Mass.

READ, Hannah and John Sowther, 11 January 1660, Boston, Mass.

READ, Isaac and Joan Stone, 10 March 1673, Salem, Mass.

READ, Mehitable and Abraham Carpenter, 30 May 1690, Rehoboth, Mass.

READ, Margaret and Richard Stabbs, 3 March 1659, Boston, Mass.

READ, Mary (widow) and Thomas Matson, 14 August 1660, Boston, Mass.

READ, Samuel and Hopestill Holbrook, 10 May 1668, Uxbridge, Mass.

READ, Susanna and Samuel Smith, 13 December 1659, Boston, Mass.

READ, Susanna (widow) and John Preston, 28 May 1661, Boston, Mass.

READ, William and Ruth Crooke, 20 January 1654, Boston, Mass.

READAWAY, Sarah and Samuel Carpenter, 25 May 1660, Rehoboth, Mass.

READE, Charles and Annie Stanton, 23 July 1690, Middletown, Penn.

READE, Mary and William Vesey, 1 March 1698, New York.

REALOW, John and Mary Rencho, 31 October 1697, Philadelphia, Penn.

REAPE, Thomas and Judith Rachell, 30 November 1660, Boston, Mass.

REAPE, Samuel and Joan Rhodes, 11 January 1666, Providence, R. I.

REAY, Kathrine and Richard Potter, 18 September 1693, New York.

RECORDS, Mary and Thomas Potts, 20 June 1698, Burlington, N. J.

REDDEN, Mary and John Hodey, 21 June 1675, Dover, N. H.

REDDING, John and Mary Bassett, 1676, Sandwich, Mass.

REDDING, Thomas and Ellene Penny, 20 July 1639, Plymouth, Mass.

REDFIELD, James and Elizabeth How, May 1669, New Haven, Conn.

REDFIELD, Lydia and Thomas Bailey, 10 January 1655, New London, Conn.

REDIAT, Mehitable and Nathaniel Oak, 14 December 1686, Sudbury, Mass.

REDMAN, Charles and Martha Hill, 10 February 1688, Milton, Mass.

REDMAN, Mariot and Robert Mason, 30 January 1693, Boston, Mass.

REDMAN, Mary and James Mott, 5 September 1670, New York City.

REED, Bertha and John Johnson, 28 April 1657, Lexington, Mass.

REED, Elizabeth and Samuel Durham, 6 July 1691, Boston, Mass.

REED, Hannah and Griffin Crafts, 15 May 1699, Chelmsford, Mass.

REED, Josiah and Grace Holloway, November 1666, Marshfield, Mass.

REED, Obadiah and Anna Swift, 19 June 1664, Dorchester, Mass.

REED, Ralph and Mary Pierce, 31 March 1654, Woburn, Mass.

REED, Rebecca and Joseph Parkhurst, 26 June 1656, Chelmsford, Mass.

REED, Sarah and Samuel Walker, 10 September 1662, Woburn, Mass.

REED, Sarah and Joshua Towle, 2 December 1686, Hampton, N. H.

REED, Thomas and Mary Wood, 7 March 1678, Sudbury, Mass.

REED, Thomas and Arabella Thong, 29 December 1689, Sudbury, Mass.

REED, Thomas and Mary Olmstead, 9 May 1694, Norwalk, Conn.

REEDMAN, Marey and Richard Smyth, 13 January 1676, Milton, Mass.

REEVE, Mary and Thomas Terrell, 5 September 1665, Southold, L. I., N. Y.

REEVE, Walter and Anne Howell, 11 December 1682, Burlington, N. J.

REEVES, Ann and John Savary, 27 June 1699, Harford Co., Md.

REEVES, Margaret and Francis West, 27 February 1639, Duxbury, Mass.

RÉMINGTON, Thomas and Remember Stowell, 16 March 1688, Hingham, Mass.
REMMINGTON, William and Mary Woodhouse, 13 April 1693, Salem Co., N. J.
RENAGER, Hannah and Charles Brigham, 12 July 1685, Philadelphia, Penn.
RENALS, James and Mary Greene, 16 February 1684-5, Warwick, R. I.
RENCHO, Mary and John Realow, 31 October 1697, Philadelphia, Penn.
REVEDLY, George and Katherine Holmes, 28 August 1696, New York.
REVELL, Ann and Capt. William Coulbourne, 15 June 1678, Somerset Co., Md.
REYERZEN, Marten and Annetje Joris, 14 May 1663, Brooklyn, N. Y.
REYLEAN, John and Margaret Brene, 15 March 1661, Boston, Mass.
REYNER, Anna and Job Lane, July 1660, Malden, Mass.
REYNERS, Barnet and Hesther Ceysler, 10 March 1696, New York.
REYNELLS, Dorothy and Edward Clarke, 14 December 1678, New York.
REYNOLDS, Sarah and Joseph Sill, 12 February 1677, Lyme, Conn.
REYNOLDS, Elizabeth and Joshua Knapp, 16 March 1687, Greenwich, Conn.
REYNOLDS, John and Sarah Grimes, 5 August 1674, Richmond Co., Va.
REYNOLDS, Jonathan and Neülle Ride, 7 December 1682, Greenwich, Conn.
REYNOLDS, Joseph and Sarah Edgerton, 10 January 1688, Norwich, Conn.
REYNOLDS, Mary and John Woodberry, 18 May 1694, Bristol, R. I.
REYNOLDS, Nathaniel and Sarah Dwite, 30 October 1657, Boston, Mass.
REYNOLDS, Thomas (son of John of Stonington) and Sarah Clarke, 11 October
    1683, Newport, R. I.
REYNOLDS, William and Alice Kitson, 30 August 1638, Plymouth, Mass.
RHOADES, Samuel and Abigail Coates, 16 January 1682, Lynn, Mass.
RHOADS, John and Hannah Wilcox, 28 August 1692, Philadelphia, Penn.
RHODES, Joan and Samuel Reape, 11 January 1666, Providence, R. I.
RHODES, Maliki and Dorothy Whipple, 8 March 1699, Providence, R. I.
RHODES, Rebecca and Nicholas Power, 2 February 1671, Providence, R. I.
RICCAR, Judith and Thomas Horn, 14 April 1699, Dover, N. H.
RICE, Dorcas and John Walden, 22 July 1680, Wenham, Mass.
RICE, Ebenezer and Bethyah Williames, 17 May 1698, Dorchester, Mass.
RICE, Edmund and Mercy Brigham (widow), 1 March 1655, Sudbury, Mass.
RICE, Elizabeth and Samuell Ware, 21 July 1690, Dedham, Mass.
RICE, Hannah and Jonathan Hubbard, 15 January 1681, Concord, Mass.
RICE, John and An Hackly, 27 September 1649, Dedham, Mass.
RICE, John and Elizabeth Wilson, 4 October 1684, Dedham, Mass.
RICE, John and Elnathan Whyppoll, 25 July 1695, Warwick, R. I.
RICE, Jonathan and Elizabeth Wheeler, 12 February 1691, Sudbury, Mass.
RICE, Joseph and Sarah Wheeler, 22 December 1677, Dedham, Mass.
RICE, Mary and John Burnett, 7 April 1634, Charlestown, Mass.
RICE, Mary and Nathaniel Gary, 12 November 1684, Roxbury, Mass.
RICE, Samuel and Elizabeth King, 8 November 1655, Sudbury, Mass.
RICE, Samuell and Rebeca Mills, 5 October 1682, Dedham, Mass.
RICE, Sarah and Benedict Webber, 14 May 1694, Boston, Mass.
RICHARDS, Bathsheba and Ezra Whitmarsh, 20 January 1693, Boston, Mass.
RICHARDS, Benjamin and Hannah Hudson, 10 October 1661, Boston, Mass.
RICHARDS, Edward and Susan Hunting, 10 July 1638, Dedham, Mass.
RICHARDS, Esther and Ephriam Warner, 16 August 1692, Waterbury, Conn.
RICHARDS, Hester and Marcus Lafort, 18 January 1693, New York.
RICHARDS, John and Elizabeth Winthrop (widow), 3 March 1654, Boston, Mass.

RICHARDS, John and Mary Coleborne, 1 August 1672, Dedham, Mass.
RICHARDS, John and Mary Brewer, 18 November 1674, Lynn, Mass.
RICHARDS, Joseph and Abigal Rawlins, 12 August 1697, Dover, N. H.
RICHARDS, Major and Anna Lake, 17 August 1686, Hampton, N. H.
RICHARDS, Mary and Nathaniell Bullard, 15 October 1658, Dedham, Mass.
RICHARDS, Mary and Thomas Smith, 11 October 1687, Milton, Mass.
RICHARDS, Mary and John Benmore, 16 November 1693, Boston, Mass.
RICHARDS, Mary and Boaz Browne, 30 September 1695, Dedham, Mass.
RICHARDS, Nathanaeel and Mary Aldis, 21 December 1678, Dedham, Mass.
RICHARDS, Stephen and Mary Van Brughen, 20 July 1696, New York.
RICHARDS, William and Mary Dow, 23 August 1694, Dover, N. H.
RICHARDSON, Bethia and Edward Ketcham, 26 February 1677, Westchester Co., N. Y.
RICHARDSON, Bridget and William Chandler, 8 October 1679, Andover, Mass.
RICHARDSON, Elizabeth and Andrew Allen, 1 January 1681, Andover, Mass.
RICHARDSON, Esther and Benjamin Shaw, 25 May 1663, Hampton, N. H.
RICHARDSON, Israel and Hannah Woodruff, 5 December 1697, Farmington, Conn.
RICHARDSON, James and Rebecca Eaton, 1698, Reading, Mass.
RICHARDSON, John and Margaret Woodmansey, 22 June 1699, Boston, Mass.
RICHARDSON, Katherine and Pilgrim Sympkins, 27 November 1661, Boston, Mass.
RICHARDSON, Mary and Thomas Wyman, 5 May 1696, Yarmouth, Maine.
RICHARDSON, Mary and William Hambleton, 7 June 1654, Boston, Mass.
RICHARDSON, Mary (widow) and Michael Bacon, 26 October 1655, Woburn, Mass.
RICHARDSON, Mary and Samuel Lynde, 15 September 1698, Boston, Mass.
RICHARDSON, Samuel and Hannah Kingsley, 20 September 1674, Woburn, Mass
RICHARDSON, Samuel and Phoebe Baldwin, 7 November 1676, Woburn, Mass.
RICHARDSON, Susanna and Richard Harris, 17 January 1682, Somerset Co., Md.
RICHARDSON, Thomas and Mary Stimson, 5 January 1670, Cambridge, Mass.
RICHARDSON, Thomas and Sarah Patton (widow), 29 December 1690, Billerica, Mass.
RICHARDSON, William and Elizabeth Lonsdale, 31 March 1694, Bucks Co., Penn.
RICHARDSON, William and Elizabeth Wiseman, 22 August 1654, Newbury, Mass.
RICHARDSON, Zachariah and Mehitable Perrin, 14 February 1699, Woburn, Mass.
RICKARD, Giles and Hannah Dunham, 31 October 1651, Plymouth, Mass.
RICKARD, Giles and Joan Tilson, 20 May 1662, Plymouth, Mass.
RICKARD, John and Esther Barnes, 31 October 1651, Plymouth, Mass.
RICKARD, Josiah and Rebecca Eaton, 21 November 1699, Plymouth, Mass.
RICKETTS, Isaac and Elizabeth Palmer, 29 February 1687, Philadelphia, Penn.
RIDE, Neülle and Jonathan Reynolds, 7 December 1682, Greenwich, Conn.
RIDER, Benjamin and Mary Gray, 10 June 1680, Yarmouth, Mass.
RIDER, Hannah and Thomas Wood, Jr., 1 May 1690, Swansea, Mass.
RIDER, Samuel and Sarah Bartlett, 23 December 1656, Plymouth, Mass.

RIDER, Samuel and Lydia Tilden, 14 June 1680, Taunton, Mass.
RIDER, Mary and Ebenezer Warren, 2 June 1697, Milton, Mass.
RIDGE, Katherine and William Howarton, 19 January 1695, Anne Arundel Co., Md.
RIDGEWAY, Hannah and John Downing, 27 September 1698, Boston, Mass.
RIDGEWAY, Solomon and Bethia Wit, 25 April 1698, Boston, Mass.
RIDMAN, Mary and Robert Mason, 31 January 1693, Boston, Mass.
RIGBEE, Elizabeth and Waching Atherton, 23 January 1678, Dorchester, Mass.
RIGBIE, Susanah and Thomas Moadslie, 24 October 1690, Dorchester, Mass.
RIGBY, Abigail and Thomas Holman, 19 December 1663, Dorchester, Mass.
RIGBY, Mehitable and Nathaniel Turner, 29 January 1665, Dorchester, Mass.
RIGBY, Mehitable and John Trott, 3 February 1696, Dorchester, Mass.
RIGBY, Silence and Sherebiah Butt, 19 November 1697, Dorchester, Mass.
RIGGS, Daniel and Martha Cobron, 29 October 1689, Philadelphia, Penn.
RIGGS, Mary and Benjamin Haskall, 21 November 1677, Gloucester, Mass.
RIGGS, Sarah and John Tucker, 9 May 1681, Gloucester, Mass.
RIGGS, Thomas and Mary Millet, 7 June 1658, Gloucester, Mass.
RIGHTON, John and Frances Tuder, 27 November 1696, New York.
RIGHTON, Mary and George Claypoole, 23 December 1699, Philadelphia, Penn.
RILAND, Johanna and Clement Salmon, 13 June 1660, Boston, Mass.
RINDGE, Roger and Rebecca Shatswell, 9 June 1684, Ipswich, Mass.
RING, Deborah and John Fuller, 7 February 1622, Plymouth, Mass.
RING, John and Mary Bray, 18 November 1664, Ipswich, Mass.
RING, Sarah and Joseph Andrews, 16 February 1680, Chebacco, Mass.
RING, William and Hannah Sherman, 1693, Plymouth, Mass.
RIOL, Ruth and Timothy Crehore, 10 February 1688, Milton, Mass.
RIPLEY, Peter and Sarah Lazall, 27 April 1693, Hingham, Mass.
RIPLEY, Ruth and Thomas Perry, 29 January 1699, Boston, Mass.
RIPLEY, Sarah and Jeremiah Beels, 26 September 1653, Boston, Mass.
RIPPLE, Esther and John Wiborn, 10 May 1694, Boston, Mass.
RISEING, James and Elizabeth Endsell, 7 May 1657, Boston, Mass.
RISSE, John and Elizabeth Houldon, 16 July 1674, Warwick, R. I.
RITHWAY, Elizabeth and Peter Paterson, 11 June 1678, Saybrook, Conn.
RIX, Abigail (widow) and Joshua Willes, 1696, Wethersfield, Conn.
RIX, Thomas and Bridget Fiske (widow), November 1661, Salem, Mass.
ROACH, Lydia and William Tubbs, 27 September 1698, New London, Conn.
ROADES, John and Wait Waterman, 12 February 1684-5, Warwick, R. I.
ROADS, Henry and Elizabeth Paul, 27 February 1694, Boston, Mass.
ROADS, Mary and John Low, 3 March 1674, Warwick, R. I.
ROATIK, Abigail and Anthony Bell, 25 December 1687, Somerset Co., Md.
ROBBINS, Daniel and Mary Parker, 27 November 1691, Woodbridge, N. J.
ROBBINS, George and Mary Barrett, 21 January 1686, Chelmsford, Mass.
ROBBINS, Hannah and William Warner, 1 November 1667, Wethersfield, Conn.
ROBBINS, John and Maria Abbott, 4 November 1659, Branford, Conn.
ROBBINS, John and Jane Tilleson, 23 June 1670, Branford, Conn.
ROBBINS, John and Dorothy Hildreth, 30 November 1698, Chelmsford, Mass.
ROBBINS, Jonathan and Hannah Pratt, 11 January 1693-4, Plymouth, Mass.
ROBBINS, Mary and Joseph Freeman, 14 February 1673, Somerset Co., Md.
ROBBINS, Robert and Mary Dill, 27 March 1697, Chelmsford, Mass.

ROBBINS, Sanah and Nathaniel Thorpe, 16 December 1692, New Haven, Conn.
ROBERTS, Alce and William Harris, 1 March 1676, Somerset Co., Md.
ROBERTS, Anne and George Bensson, May 1682, Somerset Co., Md.
ROBERTS, David and Joana Brooks, 2 October 1678, Woburn, Mass.
ROBERTS, Elizabeth and Watthew Coy, 29 June 1654, Boston, Mass.
ROBERTS, Eunice (widow, of Thomas) and Moses Mavericke, 22 August 1656, Boston, Mass.
ROBERTS, Henry and Ann Hopkins, 10 December 1699, Anne Arundel Co., Md.
ROBERTS, Johanna and Thomas Potts, 24 March 1690, Dover, N. H.
ROBERTS, John and Sarah Blake, 27 December 1693, Middletown, Conn.
ROBERTS, John and Hannah Bray, 4 February 1678, Gloucester, Mass.
ROBERTS, John and Patience Saxton, 1686, Windsor, Conn.
ROBERTS, Mark and Mary Baker, 1 January 1682, Warwick, R. I.
ROBERTS, Mary (widow) and Samuel Cook, 14 July 1690, New Haven, Conn.
ROBERTS, Richard and Ellen Holden, 28 May 1686, Philadelphia, Penn.
ROBERTS, Robert and Katherine Jones, 5 May 1696, Philadelphia, Penn.
ROBERTS, Roger and Sarah Archer, 23 November 1693, Ann Arundel Co., Md.
ROBERTS, Simon and Christian Baker, 18 May 1654, Boston, Mass.
ROBERTSON, Mary and Jonathan Gouliver, 17 January 1686, Milton, Mass.
ROBERTSON, Peter and Sarah Baker, 27 April 1685, Warwick, R. I.
ROBINS, Benjamin and Sarah Brooks, 29 August 1687, Wallingford, Conn.
ROBINS, John and Esther Littleton, 9 January 1662, Northampton Co., Va.
ROBINS, Obedience and Grace Waters, 1634, Accomac Co., Va.
ROBINSON, Abraham and Mary Harraden, 7 July 1668, Gloucester, Mass.
ROBINSON, Ann and Joseph Dudley, 16 October 1670, Guilford, Conn.
ROBINSON, Damaris and Ebenezer Dennis, 3 May 1699, Boston, Mass.
ROBINSON, Dane and Mary Chadwick, 18 January 1694, Andover, Mass.
ROBINSON, Daniel and Hope Potter, 3 February 1663, New Haven, Conn.
ROBINSON, Dorothy and Edward Falkner, 4 February 1647, Salem, Mass.
ROBINSON, Frances and Thomas Goold, 10 July 1656, Boston, Mass.
ROBINSON, George and Mary Bushnell, 3 August 1657, Boston, Mass.
ROBINSON, George and Elizabeth Guild, 17 November 1680, Rehoboth, Mass.
ROBINSON, George and Sarah Maverick, 7 April 1698, Boston, Mass.
ROBINSON, Hanna and William Burch, 4 September 1693, New York.
ROBINSON, Increase and Sarah Penniman, 19 November 1663, Dorchester, Mass.
ROBINSON, Increase and Mehitable Williams, 11 February 1695, Taunton, Mass.
ROBINSON, James and Martha Buck, 21 December 1653, Boston, Mass.
ROBINSON, James and Mary Alcock, 27 July 1664, Dorchester, Mass.
ROBINSON, John and Elizabeth Browne, 21 March 1666, Baltimore, Md.
ROBINSON, John and Elizabeth Weeks, 1 May 1667, Falmouth, Mass.
ROBINSON, Joseph and Phebe Dane, 30 May 1671, Andover, Mass.
ROBINSON, Josiah and Margarett Nicholls, 21 November 1696, New York.
ROBINSON, Mary and Thomas Wilmarth, 7 June 1674, Rehoboth, Mass.
ROBINSON, Susanna and Richard Stockton, 8 September 1691, Chesterfield, N. J.
ROBINSON, Thomas and Mary Woodey (widow), 10 November 1652, Boston, Mass.
ROBINSON, Thomas and Susanna Witham, 1 March 1690, Chesterfield, N. J.
ROBINSON, Thomas and Rachell Rosell, 29 December 1697, New York.
ROBINSON, Waytinge and John Peniman, 25 July 1666, Braintree, Mass.

ROBINSON, Widow and Griffin Craft, 15 May 1673, Dorchester, Mass.

ROCKE, Hannah and James Breding, 9 August 1657, Boston, Mass.

ROCKET, Ann and John Darling, 2 January 1687, Boston, Mass.

ROCKET, Nathaniel and Joana Elles, 7 December 1698, Wrentham, Mass.

ROCKETT, Joseph and Mary Wilmarth, 5 January 1681, Rehoboth, Mass.

ROCKWELL, Ione and Jeffrey Baker, 15 November 1642, Windsor, Conn.

ROCKWELL, John and Sarah Ensign, 6 May 1651, Windsor, Conn.

ROCKWELL, Mary and Robert Watson, 16 December 1646, Windsor, Conn.

ROCKWELL, Samuel and Mary Norton, 7 April 1660, Windsor, Conn.

ROCKWOOD, Abigaell and Joshua Wight, 30 November 1696, Dedham, Mass.

ROCKWOOD, John and Joana Ford, 15 July 1662, Braintree, Mass.

RODES, Elizabeth and Nathaniel Whitman, 5 November 1695, Boston, Mass.

RODGERS, Sarah and Daniel Haste, 2 August 1680, Somerset Co., Md.

RODMAN, Joseph and Naomi Church, 11 May 1687, Hadley, Conn.

RODNEY, William and Mary Hollyman, 25 November 1688, Philadelphia, Penn.

ROE, Bridget (widow) and William Coleman, 14 November 1662, Gloucester Mass.

ROE, Hugh and Rachel Langton, 10 June 1667, Gloucester, Mass.

ROE, Hugh and Mary Prince, 16 September 1675, Gloucester, Mass.

ROE, John and Mary Dickison, 27 September 1663, Gloucester, Mass.

ROE, Mary and William Dudley, 4 November 1661, Saybrook, Conn.

ROE, Richard and Margery Benbow, 20 June 1695, Boston, Mass.

ROELOFFSEN, Margarett and John Fflintsburgh, 16 May 1687, New York.

ROGERS, Abiel and William Warren, 1 November 1690, Boston, Mass.

ROGERS, Abigail and John Allen, 20 November 1678, Charlestown, Mass.

ROGERS, Elizabeth and John Gladding, 17 July 1666, Newbury, Mass.

ROGERS, Elizabeth and Nathaniel Williams, 17 November 1668, Duxbury, Mass.

ROGERS, Elizabeth and Samuel Beebe, 9 February 1681, New London, Conn.

ROGERS, Elizabeth and John Appleton, 23 November 1681, Ipswich, Mass.

ROGERS, Francis and Apphya Miller, 15 October 1698, Elizabeth City Co., Va.

ROGERS, Hannah and John Tisdale, 23 November 1664, Duxbury, Mass.

ROGERS, James and Mary Paine, 11 January 1670, Eastham, Mass.

ROGERS, James and Susannah Tracey, 17 February 1697, Eastham, Mass.

ROGERS, Jeremiah and Abiah Pears, 1650, Dorchester, Mass.

ROGERS, John and Rhoda King, 8 August 1656, Boston, Mass.

ROGERS, John and Elizabeth Dennison, 14 November 1660, Ipswich, Mass.

ROGERS, Joshua and Ann Fisen, 12 August 1653, Boston, Mass.

ROGERS, Lydia and Joseph White, 19 September 1660, Mendon, Mass.

ROGERS, Margaret and Thomas Berry, 28 December 1682, Boston, Mass.

ROGERS, Margaret (2d marriage) and John Leverett, 25 November 1697, Boston, Mass.

ROGERS, Mary and Joseph Merrifield, 6 April 1699, Boston, Mass.

ROGERS, Nathaniel and Sarah Wade, 13 November 1661, Ipswich, Mass.

ROGERS, Nathaniel and Sarah Perkis, 26 October 1699, Boston, Mass.

ROGERS, Noah and Elizabeth Taintor, 8 April 1673, Branford, Conn.

ROGERS, Ruth and James Bennett, 12 July 1694, Bristol, R. I.

ROGERS, Samuel and Judith Everett, 12 December 1651, Ipswich, Mass.

ROGERS, Samuel (2d marriage) and Sarah Wade, 13 November 1661, Ipswich, Mass.

ROGERS, Thomas and Awaziah Harding, 1671, Eastham, Mass.
ROGERSON, Elizabeth and Henry Boston, 19 May 1673, Somerset Co., Md.
ROLFE, Ezra and Abigail Bond, 2 March 1676, Haverhill, Mass.
ROLFE, Hannah and Thomas Colburn, 6 August 1672, Chelmsford, Mass.
ROLLOQUIN, Jacobus and Lydia Darkins, 25 May 1698, New York.
ROLLS, William and Margaret Reeves, 8 June 1674, Richmond Co., Va.
ROOF, Henry and Margret Coulylie, 9 August 1699, New York.
ROOME, Peter W. and Hester Van Gelder, 26 November 1684, New York City.
ROOT, John and Mary Ashley, 18 October 1664, Westfield, Mass.
ROOT, Joseph and Hannah Haines, 30 December 1660, Springfield, Mass.
ROPER, Sarah and John Mackinab, 18 April 1669, Dedham, Mass.
RORING, Nathaniel and Susannah Butler, 13 December 1699, Boston, Mass.
ROSE, Dorothy and Daniel Swain, 26 January 1653, Branford, Conn.
ROSE, John and Widow Luddington, 1663, New Haven, Conn.
ROSE, John, Jr., and Phebe Potter (widow), August 1670, New Haven, Conn.
ROSE, Jonathan and Charity Ward, 5 January 1669, Branford, Conn.
ROSE, Paulus and Mary Chilcott, 28 July 1698, Anne Arundel Co., Md.
ROSE, Rebecca and Obadiah Stevens, 18 December 1678, Stamford, Conn
ROSELL, Rachell and Thomas Robinson, 29 December 1697, New York.
ROSEVEST, Janitje and Johannus Vanderhuel, 9 November 1699, New York.
ROSS, Hannah and John Russ, 6 May 1695, Andover, Mass.
ROSS, James and Mary Goodenow, 5 December 1638, Sudbury, Mass.
ROSS, James and Sarah Forgison, 19 December 1695, York Co., Maine.
ROSS, John and Mary Osborne, 7 May 1659, Boston, Mass.
ROSS, John and Mary Galley, 9 May 1661, Ipswich, Mass.
ROSS, Susan and Jacob Wilson, 20 May 1696, Malden, Mass.
ROSSITER, Joanna and John Cotton, 7 November 1660, Wethersfield, Conn.
ROSSITER, Mary and Samuel Holton, 21 June 1673, Northampton, Mass.
ROST, Walter and Rebecca Harris, 29 December 1698, Boston, Mass.
ROUSE, Anna and Israel Holmes, April 1678, Marshfield, Mass.
ROUSE, Elizabeth and Thomas Bourne, 10 April 1681, Marshfield, Mass.
ROUSE, Mary and Erasmus Harrison, 3 January 1694, Boston, Mass.
ROUSE, Thomas and Rebecca Rummeril (widow), 2 September 1689, Dover, N. H.
ROW, Eliza and Robert Borer, 22 November 1698, New Kent Co., Va.
ROW, Martha and Edward Howard, 22 August 1689, Dover, N. H.
ROWDEN, Abigail and Isaac Jarvis, 19 January 1698, Boston, Mass.
ROWDEN, Elizabeth and John Brock, 5 June 1684, Philadelphia, Penn
ROWELL, Thomas and Sarah Barnes, 8 September 1670, Amesbury, Mass.
ROWELL, Valentine and Joanna Pindar, 1643, Salisbury, Mass.
ROWLAND, Elizabeth and Samuel Lee, 2 August 1655, Boston, Mass.
ROWLEY, Henry and Anne Blossom (widow), 17 October 1633, Plymouth, Mass.
ROWLEY, Thomas and Mary Denslow, 5 May 1669, Windsor, Conn.
ROWLES, William and Dorothy Bond, 24 April 1690, Middletown, Penn.
ROYALL, Isaac and Elizabeth Elliot, 1 July 1697, Boston, Mass.
ROYALL, Martha and Benjamin Cheny, 2 February 1699, Dorchester, Mass.
ROYCE, Abigail and Robert Wade, 11 March 1691, Norwich, Conn.
ROYCE, Joseph and Mary Porter, 1 October 1684, Wallingford, Conn.
ROYCE, Nehemiah and Hannah Morgan, 20 November 1660, New London, Conn.
ROYCE, Ruth and John Lothrop, 15 December 1669, New London, Conn.

ROYCE, Samuel and Ann Churchill, 9 January 1667, Wethersfield, Conn.
ROYCE, Samuel and Sarah Baldwin, 5 June 1690, Wallingford, Conn.
RUCH, John and Hannah Hutchinson, 29 April 1697, Boston, Mass.
RUCK, Ann and William Copp, 24 May 1692, Boston, Mass.
RUCK, Samuel and Margaret Clarke, 22 May 1656, Boston, Mass.
RUCK, Samuel and Hannah Nicholson, 4 April 1693, Boston, Mass.
RUD, Joseph and Deborah Areland, 19 May 1698, Boston, Mass.
RUDD, Mary and Thomas Bingham, 12 December 1666, Norwich, Conn.
RUDD, Patience and Samuel Bushnell, 7 October 1675, Saybrook, Conn.
RUDDOCK, Mary and Robert Griffin, 1 February 1693, Boston, Mass.
RUGG, John and Hannah Prescott, 4 March 1660, Lancaster, Mass.
RUGLES, Abigall and Ralph Day, 15 September 1659, Dedham, Mass.
RUGGLES, Elizabeth and William Browne, 24 February 1655, Boston, Mass.
RUGGLES, Elizabeth and Gregory Belcher, 25 March 1689, Milton, Mass.
RUGGLES, John and Rebecca Farnsworth, 18 January 1662, Braintree, Mass.
RUGGLES, Sarah and William Lyon, 17 June 1646, Roxbury, Mass.
RUICKS, William and Mary Ellise, 29 March 1694, Boston, Mass.
RUMBALL, Bethia and Robert Stewart, 13 June 1661, Stratford, Conn.
HUMFORD, John and Mary Scaife, 27 July 1699, Middletown, Penn.
RUMMERIL, Clement and Rebecca Pomeroy (widow), 6 September 1687, Dover,
    N. H.
RUNNALS, Sarah and John Young, 16 March 1698, Northwood, N. H.
RUNNEGAR, Hannah and Charles Bingham, 17 September 1685, Philadelphia, Pa.
RUNYAN, John and Elizabeth Dunn, 1692, New Jersey License.
RUNYAN, Vincent and Ann Boutcher, 17 July 1668, Elizabethtown, N. J.
RUSCO, Ruth and John Baylis, 12 March 1665, Queens Co., N. Y.
RUSE, John and Deborah Osgood, 28 August 1663, Andover, Mass.
RUSE, Mary and Andrew Foster, 7 June 1662, Andover, Mass.
RUSS, John and Hannah Ross, 6 May 1695, Andover, Mass.
RUSS, Mary and John Stone, 14 November 1690, Andover, Mass.
RUSS, Sarah and Christopher Lovejoy, 26 May 1685, Andover, Mass.
RUSSEL, John and Mary Woodward, 5 December 1683, Philadelphia, Penn.
RUSSELL, Ann and William Huse, 17 August 1699, Boston, Mass.
RUSSELL, Annah and Samuel Potter, 21 November 1670, New Haven, Conn.
RUSSELL, Hannah and Oliver Holt, 9 March 1698, Andover, Mass.
RUSSELL, John and Alicia Billington, 11 September 1673, Richmond Co., Va.
RUSSELL, Joseph and Susanna Cheever, 5 June 1693, Boston, Mass.
RUSSELL, Mary and Timothy Brooks, 2 December 1659, Woburn, Mass.
RUSSELL, Mary and Nicholas Holt, 8 January 1679, Andover, Mass.
RUSSELL, Mary and John Potter, 29 December 1679, New Haven, Conn.
RUSSELL, Noahdiah and Mary Hamlin, 20 February 1689, Middletown, Conn.
RUSSELL, Phillip and Mary Church, 25 December 1658, Hadley, Conn.
RUSSELL, Ralph and Mary Hitchcock, 12 October 1663, New Haven, Conn.
RUSSELL, Rebecca and Joshua Coggshall (2nd marriage), 21 June 1677, Middle-
    town, N. J.
RUSSELL, Robert and Mary Marshall, 6 July 1659, Andover, Mass.
RUSSELL, Samuel and Elizabeth Eldridge, November 1682, Marblehead, Mass.
RUSSELL, Sarah and John Ingalls, 10 June 1696, Andover, Mass.
RUSSELL, William and Alice Sparrow (widow), 7 July 1653, Boston, Mass.

RUST, Elizabeth and Richard White, 4 January 1699, Boston, Mass.

RUST, Israel and Rebecca Clark, 9 December 1669, Northampton, Mass.

RUST, Nathaniel and Joanna Kinsman, 22 February 1684, Chebacco, Mass.

RUTHERSE, Anthony and Hendrycke Vandewater, 23 December 1698, New York.

RUTHSE, Cathrine and Johannus Hardenbergh, 12 September 1699, New York.

RUTTER, Thomas and Rebecca Staples, 11 November 1685, Bucks Co., Pa.

RUTTY, Edwin and Rebecca Stevens, 6 May 1678, Killingworth, Conn.

RYALL, Mary and John Bird, 20 September 1696, Dorchester, Mass.

RYDER, Mary and Ebenezer Warren, 2 June 1697, Milton, Mass.

RYSTON, Edward and Margaret Singly, 7 December 1698, Anne Arundel Co., Md.

S

SABIN, Elizabeth and Robert Miller, 24 October 1662, Rehoboth, Mass.
SABIN, James and Abigail Brasier, 18 October 1689, Rehoboth, Mass.
SABIN, Mehitable and Samuel Warren, 2 January 1694-5, Woodstock, Conn.
SABIN, Samuel and Mary Billington, 20 November 1663, Rehoboth, Mass.
SABIN, William and Martha Allen, 22 December 1663, Medfield, Mass.
SACKETT, Richard and Majory L. Sleade, 11 May 1699, New York City.
SADIR, Elizabeth and Walter Wright, 9 September 1684, Andover, Mass.
SADY, John and Mary Beardsley, 25 November 1678, Ipswich, Mass.
SAFFORD, Joseph and Mary Baker, 6 March 1660, Ipswich, Mass.
SAGE, Susanna and George Alexander, 18 March 1644, Windsor, Conn.
SAILES, Ellin and Richard Greene, 16 February 1692-3, Warwick, R. I.
SALE, Mary and Samuel Ward, 10 December 1691, Boston, Mass.
SALISBURY, Sarah and James Williams, 7 August 1694, Boston, Mass.
SALMON, Clement and Johanna Riland, 13 June 1660, Boston, Mass.
SALSBURY, Abegal and John Williston, 9 June 1676, Milton, Mass.
SALTER, Abigail and Francis Ball, 27 November 1663, Dorchester, Mass.
SALTER, Elizabeth and Nathaniel Jarvise, 28 September 1691, Boston, Mass.
SALTER, Hannah and Nicholas Phillips, 4 December 1651, Boston, Mass.
SALTER, Thomas and Mary Habberfeeld, 4 May 1693, Boston, Mass.
SALWAY, William and Sarah Pennock, 28 July 1688, Philadelphia, Penn.
SAMPLE, Elizabeth and Samuel Gidings, 8 November 1699, Boston, Mass.
SAMPLE, Robert and Eliza Bourn, 12 October 1696, Boston, Mass.
SAMPSON, Jonathan and Mary Chandler, 16 November 1695, Newbury, Mass.
SAMS, Sarah and Nicholas Sparry, 20 August 1694, Boston, Mass.
SAMSON, Mary and Richard Waste, 26 October 1693, Duxborough, Mass.
SAMSON, Samuel and Asabiah Eadey, 29 May 1695, Duxborough, Mass.
SAMUELL, Ariaentie and Henryck Symonse, 25 October 1693, New York.
SAMUEL, John and Lucie Wight (widow), 24 October 1652, Boston, Mass.
SANBORN, John and Judith Coffin, 19 November 1674, Hampton, N. H.
SANBORN, Jonathan and Elizabeth Sherburn, 4 February 1692, Dover, N. H.
SANBORN, Richard and Ruth Moulton, 5 December 1678, Hampton, N. H.
SANBORN, Rueben and Hannah Moulton, 25 August 1681, Hampton, N. H.
SANBURN, Nathaniel and Rebecca Prescott, 3 December 1691, Dover, N. H.
SANDERS, Abiel and Thomas Buttolph, 3 December 1689, Boston, Mass.
SANDERS, Ann and James Vanderspiezel, 20 September 1691, New York City.
SANDERS, Elizabeth and Solomon Veasy, 23 November 1680, Braintree, Mass.
SANDERS, James and Sarah Page, 14 January 1669, Haverhill, Mass.
SANDERS, John and Priscilla Grafton, 1636, Salem, Mass.
SANDERS, John and Susanna Tomson, 24 May 1698, Boston, Mass.
SANDERS, Josiah and Rachel Holman, 4 December 1693, Boston, Mass.
SANDERS, Josiah and Rebecka Smith, 7 April 1697, Boston, Mass.
SANDERS, Priscilla and John Gardner, 29 February 1654, Salem, Mass.
SANDERS, Richard and Mary Moss, 17 June 1697, Dover, N. H.
SANDERS, Sarah and John Wood, 26 February 1695, Philadelphia, Penn.

SANDERSON, Lydia and Thomas Jones, 13 October 1654, Boston, Mass.
SANDERSON, Robert and Sarah Crow, 21 December 1693, Boston, Mass.
SANDERSON, Sarah and Andrew White, 4 February 1698, Woburn, Mass.
SANDEY, Winsor and Mehetabel Bull, 12 February 1694, Boston, Mass.
SANFORD, Mary and William Walton, 30 August 1698, New York.
SANDFORD, William and Frances Hummer, 31 March 1684, Bucks Co., Pa.
SANDS, Ann and Joseph Dowding, 21 September 1694, Boston, Mass.
SANDS, Stephen and Jane Cowgill, 25 August 1685, Middletown, Penn.
SANDY, John and Ann Holmes, 7 May 1653, Boston, Mass.
SANDYE, Joseph and Berhia Lucas, 18 October 1682, Bristol, R. I.
SANFORD, Grace and Barne Cosins, 28 April 1697, New York.
SANFORD, Hannah and Abraham Chalker, 16 January 1679, Saybrook, Conn.
SANFORD, James and Elizabeth Smith, December 1656, Boston, Mass.
SANFORD, John and Sarah Potter (widow), 19 December 1656, Boston, Mass.
SANFORD, Mary (dau. of Richard) and Edward Turner, 25 October 1656, Boston, Mass.
SANFORD, Mary and John Webb, 14 July 1673, Richmond Co., Va.
SANFORD, Mary and Thomas Tuttle, 28 June 1692, New Haven, Conn.
SANFORD, Ruth and Samuel Bushnell, 17 April 1684, Saybrook, Conn.
SANGHURST, Elizabeth and Godwin Walter, 2 September 1696, Chester Co., Pa.
SARGEANT, John and Mary Bense, 3 September 1669, Malden, Mass.
SARGENT, Abigail and William Stevens, 15 June 1682, Gloucester, Mass.
SARGENT, Digory and Constance James, 13 October 1693, Boston, Mass.
SARGENT, Edward and Joana Homan, 3 June 1695, Dover, N. H.
SARGENT, Thomas and Rachel Barnes, 2 January 1667, Amesbury, Mass.
SARSON, Samuel and Ann Clay, 3 January 1694, Boston, Mass.
SATTERLEE, Benedict and Rebecca Bemis, 2 August 1682, New London, Conn.
SATTERTHWAITE, William and Ann Bursham, 3 October 1685, Chesterfield, N. J.
SAUNDERS, Edward and Mary Hudnall (widow), May 1660, Northumberland Co., Va.
SAUNDERS, Edward and Elizabeth Teil, May 1685, Middlesex Co., Va.
SAUNDERS, Edward and Mary Brown, 1687, Middlesex Co., Va.
SAUNDERS, Elizabeth and Charles Ceeley, 1697, Elizabeth City Co., Va.
SAUNDERS, John and Mary Mungy, 9 August 1650, Braintree, Mass.
SAUNDERS, Martin and Elizabeth Bancroft, 23 March 1654, Braintree, Mass.
SAUNDERS, Martin, Jr., and Liddia Hardier, 1 February 1651, Braintree, Mass.
SAUNDERS, Paul and Ann Folle, 30 April 1699, Philadelphia, Penn.
SAVAGE, Ephriam and Sarah Hough, 12 April 1688, Charlestown, Mass.
SAVAGE, Habbiah and Hannah Ting, 8 May 1661, Boston, Mass.
SAVAGE, Hannah and Benjamine Gillam, 26 October 1660, Boston, Mass.
SAVAGE, Sarah and Joshue Wells, 25 December 1699, Boston, Mass.
SAVAGE, Thomas (Capt.) and Mary Simmes, 15 July 1652, Boston, Mass.
SAVAGE, Thomas and Mehitable Harwood, 5 February 1690, Boston, Mass.
SAVARY, John and Ann Reeves, 27 June 1699, Harford Co., Md.
SAVELL, William and Deborah Faxon, 1 January 1679, Braintree, Mass.
SAVILL, Benjamin and Lydia Barnes, 30 October 1670, Braintree, Mass.
SAVILL, Hannah and John Needham, March 1669, Braintree, Mass.
SAVILL, John and Mehitable Hands, 20 August 1668, Braintree, Mass.

SAVILL, Samuel and Hannah Adams, 10 February 1673, Braintree, Mass.
SAVILL, Sarah (widow) and Thomas Jackson, 5 July 1670, Braintree, Mass.
SAVILL, William and Sarah Gannitt, 9 June 1655, Braintree, Mass.
SAVORY, Robert and Mary Mitchell, 8 December 1635, Newbury, Mass.
SAVOY, Mary and John Francis, 19 December 1698, Elizabeth City Co., Va.
SAWTELL, Zacharia and Elizabeth Harris, April 1668, Malden, Mass.
SAWYER, Caleb and Sarah Houghton, 28 December 1687, Lancaster, Mass.
SAWYER, Mary and John Emery, 12 June 1683, Newbury, Mass.
SAWYER, Mercy and Anthony Eames, 2 December 1686, Marshfield, Mass.
SAWYER, Ruth and Benjamin Morse, 27 August 1667, Newbury, Mass.
SAWYER, Sarah and Joshua Brown, 15 January 1669, Newbury, Mass.
SAWYER, Samuel and Mary Emery, 13 March 1670, Newbury, Mass.
SAXTON, John and Mary Hill, 30 July 1677, Windsor, Conn.
SAXTON, Joseph and Hannah Wright, 20 November 1690, Lebanon, Conn.
SAXTON, Mary and William Gillett, 14 September 1699, Simsbury, Conn.
SAXTON, Patience and John Roberts, 1688, Windsor, Conn.
SAXTON, Susanna and Thomas Hunt, 21 June 1694, Boston, Mass.
SAXTON, Thomas and Ann Atwood (widow), 10 January 1651, Boston, Mass.
SAYLES, Mary and William Greene, 17 December 1674, Warwick, R.' I.
SAYLES, Phebe and Job Greene, 22 January 1684-5, Warwick, R. I.
SAYWELL, David and Abigail Buttolph, 15 August 1660, Boston, Mass.
SAYWELL, Elizabeth and Joseph Davis, 7 May 1662, Boston, Mass.
SAYRE, Ichabod and Mary Hubbart, 31 March 1697, New London, Conn.
SAYRE, Joshua and Sarah Potter (widow), 2 January 1677, Concord, Mass.
SCAIFE, Mary and John Rumford, 27 July 1699, Middletown, Penn.
SCALES, James and Sarah Curtis, 7 November 1677, Rowley, Mass.
SCAMP, Robert and Joane Collins, 25 December 1661, Gloucester, Mass.
SCANT, Susanna and John Turner, 17 January 1693, Boston, Mass.
SCANT, William and Sarah Browne, 29 January 1654, Braintree, Mass.
SCARLET, Elizabeth and William Gill, 3 May 1692, Boston, Mass.
SCARLET, Sarah and Peter Grant, 25 July 1694, Boston, Mass.
SCATTERGOOD, Hannah and William Pancoast, 1 July 1695, Burlington Co.,
    N. J.
SCHOLEY, Sarah and Caleb Wheatly, 5 September 1696, Chesterfield, N. J.
SCHOLLY, Sarah and Jonathan Eustice, 16 November 1699, Boston, Mass.
SCHOUT, Jan and Marie Farnelie, 10 June 1663, Brooklyn, N. Y.
SCHUYLER, Margaret and Robert Livingston, Jr., 26 July 1696, New York.
SCHUYLER, Meyndert and Rachel Cuyler, 23 October 1693, New York.
SCHUYLER, Peter and Marie Van Ranselaer, 1 October 1691, New York City.
SCHUT, Magdalena and Gerrit Decker, April 1684, Kingston, N. Y.
SCOFIELD, Robert and Mary Lewis, 14 October 1697, Anne Arundel Co., Md.
SCOLLY, John and Lydia Grover, 22 December 1690, Boston, Mass.
SCOT, Benjamin and Mary Daniell, 31 May 1699, Milton, Mass.
SCOT, Peter and Abigail Neale, 22 January 1673, Dorchester, Mass.
SCOTSON, George and Elizabeth Coombes, 24 July 1686, Philadelphia, Penn.
SCOTT, Elizabeth and John Loomis, 6 February 1648, Windsor, Conn.
SCOTT, Hannah and Christopher Webb, 18 January 1656, Braintree, Mass.
SCOTT, Jane and Stephen Kent, Jr., 25 December 1683, Woodbridge, N. J.
SCOTT, Joseph and Elizabeth Winslow, 18 January 1693, Boston, Mass.

SCOTT, Mary and Samuell Emmons, 16 August 1660, Boston, Mass.
SCOTT, William and Hannah Allis, 28 January 1670, Hatfield, Mass.
SCOTTOW, Lydia and Elisha Webb, 18 November 1697, Boston, Mass.
SCOTTOW, Sarah and Benjamin Blackman, 1 April 1675, Malden, Mass.
SCRANTON, Margrett and David Shippe, 15 August 1664, Warwick, R. I.
SCRIBNER, Benjamin and Hannah Crampton, 5 March 1680, Norwalk, Conn.
SCUDDER, Sarah and John Smith, 16 September 1691, Boston, Mass.
SCUDDER, Thomas and Sarah Phillips, 4 November 1689, Boston, Mass.
SEABURY, John and Elizabeth Alden, 1697, New London, Conn.
SEABURY, Samuel and Patience Kemp, 16 November 1660, Duxbury, Mass.
SEAMAN, Elizabeth and Timothy Knapp, 16 March 1699, Greenwich, Conn.
SEAMER, Hannah and Francis Bushnell, 12 October 1675, Norwalk, Conn.
SEARLE, Edward and Ann Lippett (widow), 21 February 1670, Warwick, R. I.
SEARLE, Grace and John Harris, 8 January 1685, Ipswich, Mass.
SEARLE, John and Katherine Warner (widow), 26 November 1661, Boston, Mass.
SEARLE, Robert and Rebeckah Evens, 4 December 1695, Dorchester, Mass.
SEARLE, Susannah and Richard Barnes, 1 February 1672, Somerset Co., Md.
SEARLES, Elizabeth and Jarrett Ingraham, 28 May 1662, Boston, Mass.
SEARLES, John and Ruth Janes, 3 July 1667, Springfield, Mass.
SEARLES, Miriam and William Carpenter, 10 December 1668, Rehoboth, Mass.
SEARS, Bethiah and John Crowell, 27 May 1684, Eastham, Mass.
SEARS, Paul and Deborah Willard, 1658, Yarmouth, Mass.
SEARS, Richard and Dorothy Thacher, 1632, Plymouth, Mass.
SEARS, Thomas and Mary Hilton, 11 December 1656, Newbury, Mass.
SEAVEY, John and Hannah Walker, 29 July 1680, Rye, N. H.
SEDGWICK, Sarah and Joseph Snelling, 8 June 1693, Boston, Mass.
SEGAR, Richard and Abigail Griffin, 21 March 1682, Simsbury, Conn.
SELDON, Joseph and Rebecca Church, 11 February 1677, Hadley, Conn.
SELLERS, Samuel and Anna Gibbons, 13 August 1684, Darby, Penn.
SELLY, Dorcas and George Courtney, 2 June 1698, Boston, Mass.
SELONER, Isaac and Judith Waldron, 16 December 1679, New York City.
SELSBY, John and Sarah Thompson, 1 August 1696, New York.
SENNET, Mary and John Sparke, 26 November 1661, Boston, Mass.
SENTER, John and Mary Muzzy, 27 January 1656, Boston, Mass.
SERGENT, Eliza and William Crow, 10 December 1691, Boston, Mass.
SERGENT, John and Hannah Howard, 24 December 1679, Gloucester, Mass.
SERGENT, William and Mary Duncan, 21 June 1678, Gloucester, Mass.
SERGENT, William and Naomi Stanwood, 26 October 1681, Gloucester, Mass.
SERVANT, Frances and John George, 16 June 1696, Elizabeth City Co., Va.
SERVANT, Mary and Francis Ballard, 25 December 1699, Elizabeth City Co., Va.
SESSIONS, Alexander and Elizabeth Spafford, 24 April 1672, Andover, Mass.
SESSIONS, Elizabeth and Richard Carrier, 18 July 1694, Andover, Mass.
SESSIONS, Hanna and Philip Parker, 10 November 1685, Penn. State License.
SEWARD, Humphry and Sophia Dewitt, 31 May 1687, New York.
SEWARD, Margaret and Jonathan Hall, 21 June 1698, Boston, Mass.
SEWARD, William and Grace Norton, 2 April 1651, Guilford, Conn.
SEWELL, Mary and Samuel Handy, 31 March 1679, Somerset Co., Md.
SEWER, Henry and Mary Huntress, 21 June 1694, Dover, N. H.
SEXTON, Judith and Joshua Burle, 5 September 1698, New York.

SEXTON, Richard and Sara Cook, 16 April 1646, Windsor, Conn.

SEYMOUR, Hannah and Francis Bushnell, 2 October 1675, Norwalk, Conn.

SEYMOUR, John and Elizabeth Webster, 19 December 1693, Hartford, Conn.

SHADDOCK, James and Martha Moon, 25 August 1689, Philadelphia, Penn.

SHALER, Elizabeth and Ebenezer Lowle, 30 January 1694, Boston, Mass.

SHAPLEY, Anna and John Fosdick, 1648, Charlestown, Mass.

SHAPLEY, Sarah and Samuel Gurney, 26 October 1693, Boston, Mass.

SHARMAN, Thomas and Frances Ward, 1 November 1682, Burlington, N. J.

SHARP, Eliza and Nathaniel Beedle, 30 January 1694, Boston, Mass.

SHARP, Elizabeth and Samuel Craft, 25 December 1693, Roxbury, Mass.

SHARP, Hannah and Benjamin Gallop, 1 November 1694, Boston, Mass.

SHARP, John and Mary Brooks, 6 September 1697, Boston, Mass.

SHARPE, Agnes and John Penquite, 14 April 1690, Middletown, Penn.

SHARPE, Mary and Shadrach Walley, 12 January 1688, Middletown, Penn.

SHATLEWORTH, Vincent and Elizabeth Leonard, 18 December 1677, Dedham, Mass.

SHATSWELL, Rebecca and Roger Rindge, 9 June 1684, Ipswich, Mass.

SHATTOCK, Exercise and George Corlies, 10 December 1680, Shrewsbury, N. J.

SHATTOCK, Demaris and Isaac Page, 30 July 1653, Boston, Mass.

SHATTOCK, Hannah and Restore Lippincott, 6 November 1674, Shrewsbury, N. J.

SHATTUCK, William and Hannah Underwood, 19 March 1688, Watertown, Mass.

SHAW, Anne and Samuel Fogg, 12 October 1652, Hampton, N. H.

SHAW, Anthony and Alice Stanare, 8 February 1653, Boston, Mass.

SHAW, Benjamin and Esther Richardson, 25 May 1663, Hampton, N. H.

SHAW, Elizabeth and Peter Ston, 25 June 1696, Warwick, R. I.

SHAW, John and Elizabeth Ramsdel, 12 August 1674, Malden, Mass.

SHAW, Joseph and Mary Sowther, 1 October 1653, Boston, Mass.

SHAW, Joseph and Mercy Cross, 22 February 1699, Boston, Mass.

SHAW, Mary (widow) and John Blake, 16 June 1654, Boston, Mass.

SHAW, Nathaniel and Margaret Jackson, 12 July 1698, Boston, Mass.

SHAW, Susanna and Jonah Perry, 9 June 1698, Boston, Mass.

SHAW, Thomas and Anna Hancock, 20 April 1692, New York City.

SHAW, William and Margaret Holland, 22 November 1680, Richmond Co., Va.

SHEAFE, Jacob and Margaret Webb (dau. of Henry), 1643, Boston, Mass.

SHEAFFE, Elizabeth and Robert Gibbs, 7 September 1660, Boston, Mass.

SHEARER, Thomas and Hannah Bumsteed, 18 April 1659, Boston, Mass.

SHEARS, Mehitable and John Archer, 5 January 1692, Bristol, R. I.

SHEARS, Samuel and Elizabeth Heath, 27 October 1683, Wrentham, Mass.

SHEARS, Samuel and Mary Peacock, 29 July 1663, Dedham, Mass.

SHEATHER, Mary and Robert Chapman, 29 October 1694, Saybrook, Conn.

SHED, Sarah and John Dutton, 20 September 1681, Billerica, Mass.

SHEELD, John and Elizabeth Bunn, 16 January 1696, Harford Co., Md.

SHEERES, Samuel and Ann Grosse (widow), 15 June 1658, Boston, Mass.

SHEFFIELD, Edmond and Sarah Marsh, 5 July 1662, Braintree, Mass.

SHELDON, Isaac and Mary Woodford, 1653, Hartford, Conn.

SHELDON, Mary and John Bridgeman, 11 December 1670, Northampton, Mass.

SHELDON, William and Hannah Armistead, 10 December 1698, Elizabeth City Co., Va.

SHEPARD, Abigail and Thomas Butler, 8 August 1691, Hartford, Conn.

SHEPARD, Deborah and Jacob White, 4 February 1692, Hartford, Conn.
SHEPARD, Hannah and Thomas Ensign, 1 December 1692, Hartford, Conn.
SHEPARD, John and Rebecca Greenhill, 4 October 1649, Cambridge, Mass.
SHEPARD, Margaret (widow) and Jonathan Mitchell, 19 November 1650, Cambridge, Mass.
SHEPARD, Samuel and Alice Mason, 14 July 1698, Boston, Mass.
SHEPARD, Thomas and Hannah Ensign, 19 September 1658, Malden, Mass.
SHEPARD, Trial and Walter Power, 11 January 1660, Malden, Mass.
SHEPARD, Violet and John Stedman, 10 August 1678, Hartford, Conn.
SHEPARDSON, Elidea and Thomas Call, 22 May 1657, Malden, Mass.
SHEPERDSON, Daniel and Elizabeth Tingle, 11 April 1667, Malden, Mass.
SHEPERDSON, Joana and Roger Kenicot, November 1661, Malden, Mass.
SHEPPARD, Elizabeth and William Cofield, 5 January 1694, Elizabeth City Co., Va.
SHEPPARD, Elizabeth (widow) and John Poole, 10 October 1699, Elizabeth City Co., Va.
SHEPPERD, Samuel and Dorothy Flynt, 30 February 1666, Braintree, Mass.
SHEPPERD, Sarah and Samuel Tomson, 25 February 1656, Braintree, Mass.
SHEPPERD, William and Sarah Edey, 20 May 1686, Middlesex Co., Va.
SHERBURN, Elizabeth and Jonathan Sanborn, 4 February 1692, Dover, N. H.
SHERBUTT, John and Mary Fowler, 14 September 1697, Anne Arundel Co., Md.
SHERMAN, Abijah and Sarah Franks, 12 July 1694, Boston, Mass.
SHERMAN, Edmond and Grace Steevens, 8 December 1656, Dedham, Mass.
SHERMAN, Hannah and William Ring, 1693, Plymouth, Mass.
SHERMAN, Priscilla and Martin Garwood, 25 March 1658, Dedham, Mass.
SHERMAN, Samuel, Jr., and Abigail Curtis (nee Thompson), 1 August 1695, Stratford, Conn.
SHERMAN, Sarah and Daniel Hodson, 20 October 1696, Boston, Mass.
SHERMAN, William and Prudence Hill, 23 January 1638, Plymouth, Mass.
SHERRAR, Hannah and Richard Green, 1 June 1692, Boston, Mass.
SHERWOOD, Daniel and Mary Hopkins, 26 December 1689, Talbot Co., Md.
SHERWOOD, Mary and Josiah Tibbals, 13 July 1670, Milford, Conn.
SHERWOOD, Mary and Daniel Fitch, March 1698, Fairfield, Conn.
SHERWOOD, Ruth and Joshua Holcom, 4 June 1663, Windsor, Conn.
SHILETTO, Mary and John Ellis, Jr., September 1686, Somerset Co., Md.
SHINN, Mary and Daniel Wills, Jr., 12 November 1695, Burlington, N. J.
SHIPMAN, Edward and Elizabeth Comstock, 1 January 1651, Saybrook, Conn.
SHIPMAN, John and Martha Humphries, 5 May 1686, Saybrook, Conn.
SHIPMAN, William and Alice Hand, 25 November 1690, Saybrook, Conn.
SHIPPE, David and Margarett Scranton, 15 August 1664, Warwick, R. I.
SHIPTON, Edward and Mary Andrews, July 1663, Saybrook, Conn.
SHOFELD, Tamersen and Jonathan Adams, 1 February 1696-7, Dedham, Mass.
SHOOTER, Hannah and Nathaniel Mott, 25 October 1656, Braintree, Mass.
SHORT, Clement and Faith Munt, 21 November 1660, Boston, Mass.
SHORT, Henry and Sarah Glover, 1648, Newbury, Mass.
SHORT, Luke and Susanna Stewart, 13 June 1692, Weymouth, Mass.
SHORT, Mercy and Joseph Marshall, 29 July 1694, Boston, Mass.
SHORT, Patience and David Copp, 27 December 1694, Boston, Mass.
SHORT, Rachel and Mical Coars, 7 July 1699, Boston, Mass.

SHOVE, Elizabeth and John Mills, Jr., 26 February 1653, Braintree, Mass.
SHRIMPTON, Henry and Mary Fenn (widow), 27 February 1661, Boston, Mass.
SHRIMPTON, Mary and Robert Gibbs, 19 May 1692, Boston, Mass.
SHRIMPTON, Sarah and John Clark, 30 April 1691, Boston, Mass.
SHURAH, Mary and Thomas Smith, 10 March 1696, Boston, Mass.
SHURTLEFF, Abial and Lidia Barnes, 14 January 1695-6, Plymouth, Mass.
SHURTLEFF, Benjamin and Elizabeth Lettice, 18 October 1655, Plymouth, Mass.
SHUTE, William and Martha Budd, 19 May 1690, Boston, Mass.
SHUTT, William and Hopestill Viall, 1 July 1659, Boston, Mass.
SIBBLE, Sarah and Francis Chickering, 11 April 1650, Dedham, Mass.
SIBBORNS, Elizabeth and Thomas Farnum, 8 July 1660, Andover, Mass.
SIBLEY, Mary and Jonathan Walcott, 11 December 1664, Salem, Mass.
SIBLEY, Richard and Susan Follett, 4 February 1684, Salem, Mass.
SIBTHORPE, Christopher and Mary Fincher, 26 February 1689, Philadelphia,
    Penn.
SILL, Anna de and Antje Breyant, 20 December 1691, Bergen Co., N. J.
SILL, Joseph and Jemima Belcher, 5 December 1660, Lyme, Conn.
SILL, Joseph and Sarah Reynold, 12 February 1677, Lyme, Conn.
SILLEY, Thomas and Ann Stanian, 2 July 1697, Dover, N. H.
SILLSBEE, Mary and Zachery Marsh, 15 August 1664, Salem, Mass.
SILSBEE, Samuel and Mary Biscow, 4 July 1676, Lynn, Mass.
SILSBY, Henry and Grace Eaton (widow), 18 November 1680, Lynn, Mass.
SILVER, Anne and Thomas Wilson, 6 July 1693, Burlington, N. J.
SILVERWOOD, Joshua and Mary Hoffmire (widow), 15 March 1679, Rye, N. Y.
SIMES, Elizabeth and Hezekiah Usher, 2 September 1652, Boston, Mass.
SIMKINS, John and Elizabeth Page, 28 December 1698, Boston, Mass.
SIMKINS, Sarah and Christopher Kilbey, 20 May 1691, Boston, Mass.
SIMMES, Mary and Thomas Savage (Capt.), 15 July 1652, Boston, Mass.
SIMMONS, John and Mercy Pabodie, 16 November 1669, Duxbury, Mass.
SIMMONS, Patience and George Barrow, 14 February 1694-5, Plymouth, Mass.
SIMMS, Elizabeth and John Marten, 17 December 1685, Penn. License.
SIMMS, Lancaster and Katharine Larkin, 2 November 1694, New York.
SIMONDS, Juda and John Barker, 9 December 1668, Concord, Mass.
SIMONDS, William and Judith Hayward, 8 January 1644, Woburn, Mass.
SIMONS, Mary and Ambrose Bennet, 15 February 1653, Boston, Mass.
SIMPKINS, Pilgrim and Katherine Richardson, 27 November 1661, Boston, Mass.
SIMPKINS, Rebecca and William Terrill, 29 November 1654, Boston, Mass.
SIMPSON, Elizabeth and Jeremiah Reder, 27 July 1676, New York.
SIMPSON, John and Rely Holmes, 4 June 1695, Boston, Mass.
SINART, Lydia and Thomas Pryor, 28 February 1699, Philadelphia, Penn.
SINGLETON, Jane and Joseph Latham, 7 February 1698, New York.
SINGLY, Margaret and Edward Ryston, 7 December 1698, Anne Arundel Co., Md.
SIP, Jane Arianse and Johanne Van Vorst, 22 April 1684, Bergen Co., N. J.
SIRY, George and Jane Fall, 16 March 1697, Boston, Mass.
SISAM, Thomas and Priscilla Smith, 27 August 1693, Philadelphia, Penn.
SISSON, George and Sarah Lawton, 1 August 1667, Portsmouth, R. I.
SKEATH, Joseph and Hannah Davise, 18 April 1692, Boston, Mass.
SKELTON, Joseph and Deborah How, 25 February 1673, Dorchester, Mass.
SKELTON, Robert and Alse Throgmorton, 30 October 1691, New York City.

SKERRY, Elizabeth and William Randol, 21 December 1699, Boston, Mass.
SKERRY, Hannah and Richard Wale, 21 December 1699, Boston, Mass.
SKIFF, Abigail and Shubal Smith (2nd marriage), 1684, Sandwich, Mass.
SKIFF, Nathan and Mercy Chipman, 13 December 1699, Sandwich, Mass.
SKILLING, Abigail and John Curney, 18 November 1670, Gloucester, Mass.
SKINER, James and Jane Smith, 4 October 1697, Elizabeth City Co., Va.
SKINER, Rebecca and William Davis, 5 April 1698, Elizabeth City Co., Va.
SKINNER, Joseph and Mary Filley, 5 April 1666, Windsor, Conn.
SKINNER, Mary (widow) and Owen Tudor, 13 November 1651, Windsor, Conn.
SKINNER, Mary and Nathaniel Harmon, 19 November 1685, Suffield, Conn.
SKINNER, Richard and Tamozine Taylor, 21 April 1692, Boston, Mass.
SKIPPER, Catharine and John Mavericke, 9 February 1656, Boston, Mass.
SKIPPER, Jane and Abram Browne, 19 June 1653, Boston, Mass.
SKIPPER, Sarah and Walter Fairfield, 28 December 1654, Reading, Mass.
SLADE, Peter and Margery Wislake, 26 December 1694, New York.
SLATER, Edward and Elizabeth Bonham, 9 January 1685, Piscataway, N. J.
SLEADE, Marjory L. and Richard Sackett, 11 May 1699, New York City.
SLECHT, Cornelis and Johana Van De Water, 11 April 1696, Brooklyn, N. Y.
SLEIGH, Charles and Sarah Purrington, 27 June 1693, New York.
SLINGERLAND, Teunis and Geertie Fonda (widow), 9 April 1684, Albany, N. Y.
SLOCUM, Elizabeth and Peter Greene, 12 February 1695-6, Warwick, R. I.
SLOW, Philip and Barbary Hitchil, 24 February 1697, Boston, Mass.
SMALL, Elizabeth and Christopher Slegge, 17 January 1687-8, New York.
SMALL, Elizabeth and William Allen, March 1695, Salem, Mass.
SMALL, John and Ann Walden, 1638, Plymouth, Mass.
SMALLPIECE, John and Olive Furnel, 7 April 1699, Boston, Mass.
SMEAD, William and Elizabeth Lawrence, 31 October 1658, Dorchester, Mass.
SMEDLEY, George and Sarah Gooden, 24 April 1687, Philadelphia, Penn.
SMEDLEY, Sarah and Ebenezer Hartwell, 27 March 1690, Concord, Mass.
SMELT, William and Elizabeth Traverse (widow), 21 October 1697, Elizabeth
    City Co., Va.
SMITH, Abigail and John Adams, 1657, Hartford, Conn.
SMITH, Abigail and George Lilly, 1659, Reading, Mass.
SMITH, Ann and Israel Clifford, 15 March 1680, Hampton, N. H.
SMITH, Ann and Robert Everinden, 11 July 1698, New York.
SMITH, Anna and Moses Barrett, 10 September 1684, Dorchester, Mass.
SMITH, Anne and John Allyn, 19 November 1651, Springfield, Mass.
SMITH, Anne and John Moore, 16 November 1654, Sudbury, Mass.
SMITH, Barbardus and Elsey Meyers, 25 October 1698, New York.
SMITH, Benjamin and Mary Clarke, 10 June 1641, Dedham, Mass.
SMITH, Benjamin and Phebe Arnold, 25 December 1691, Warwick, R. I.
SMITH, Christopher and Mary (or Martha) Metcalfe, 2 June 1654, Dedham, Mass.
SMITH, Daniel and Esther Chickering, 20 October 1659, Dedham, Mass.
SMITH, Daniel and Mary Murfin, 7 April 1695, Chesterfield, N. J.
SMITH, Daniel and Abigail Preston, 23 June 1696, Dorchester, Mass.
SMITH, Dorcas and Ephriam Andrews, 16 November 1671, Barnstable, Mass.
SMITH, Edward and Sarah Allyn, 21 April 1685, Ipswich, Mass.
SMITH, Eliza and Humphrey Horrell, 10 January 1687, Beverly, Mass.
SMITH, Elizabeth and James Sanford, December 1656, Boston, Mass.

SMITH, Elizabeth and John MacDaniell, 17 May 1658, Boston, Mass.
SMITH, Elizabeth and William Lawrence, 4 March 1664, Smithtown, L. I., N. Y.
SMITH, Elizabeth and Samuel Clap, 31 January 1668, Dorchester, Mass.
SMITH, Elizabeth and William Ely, 12 May 1681, Lyme, Conn.
SMITH, Elizabeth and Edward Tuffe, 6 June 1684, Philadelphia, Penn.
SMITH, Elizabeth and John Bacon, 17 October 1688, Salem Co., N. J.
SMITH, Elizabeth and Israel Arnold, 28 February 1698-9, Warwick, R. I.
SMITH, Elizabeth and John Venteman, 13 July 1699, Boston, Mass.
SMITH, Elizabeth and George Morgan, 10 February 1699, Harford Co., Md.
SMITH, Else and William Willkission, 15 November 1697, New York.
SMITH, Ephriam and Mary Ramsdell, 6 September 1694, Boxford, Mass.
SMITH, Esther and Joseph Bosworth, 10 February 1680, Rehoboth, Mass.
SMITH, Hannah and Joseph Hills, November 1653, Malden, Mass.
SMITH, Hannah and Benjamin Chambers, 3 March 1686, Philadelphia, Penn.
SMITH, Hannah and Zachery Bignell, 24 November 1692, Boston, Mass.
SMITH, Hannah and Andrew Gibb, 13 April 1696, New York.
SMITH, Hannah and William Ady, 19 July 1697, Bristol, R. I.
SMITH, Isabella (widow) and John Parker, 12 September 1699, Harford Co., Md.
SMITH, Jane and James Skiner, 4 October 1697, Elizabeth City Co., Va.
SMITH, Jeremiah and Mary Gerreardy, 2 January 1672, Warwick, R. I.
SMITH, Jeremiah and Ann Peather, 21 December 1699, Boston, Mass.
SMITH, John and Susanna Hinkley, 1642, Barnstable, Mass.
SMITH, John and Sarah Hunt, 1647, Lancaster, Mass.
SMITH, John and Abigail Day, 21 October 1677, Dedham, Mass.
SMITH, John and Mary Warner, 17 February 1680, Gloucester Co., Va.
SMITH, John and Elizabeth Ball, 13 August 1685, Burlington, N. J.
SMITH, John and Hannah Phips, 17 September 1697, New York.
SMITH, John and Sarah Scudder, 16 September 1691, Boston, Mass.
SMITH, Jonathan and Martha Bushnell, 1 January 1663, Saybrook, Conn.
SMITH, Jonathan and Alyce Leeke, 25 December 1695, Saybrook, Conn.
SMITH, Joseph and Margaret Barents, 8 July 1695, New York.
SMITH, Joseph and Susannah Fisher, 17 August 1698, Dedham, Mass.
SMITH, Judith, and Richard Tozer, 3 May 1656, Boston, Mass.
SMITH, Lucy and Robert Moulton, 29 May 1689, Hampton, N. H.
SMITH (GOWAN), Margaret and Daniel Emery, 17 March 1695, Berwick, Maine.
SMITH, Margaret and Thomas Parmiter, 14 August 1697, New York.
SMITH, Martha and Caleb Burbank, 6 May 1669, Rowley, Mass.
SMITH, Mary and Samuel Pelton, 16 May 1673, Dorchester, Mass.
SMITH, Mary and Thomas Hopkins, 1 April 1678, Providence, R. I.
SMITH, Mary and John Dunham, 1 March 1680, Barnstable, Mass.
SMITH, Mary and Joseph Chew, 17 November 1685, Herring Creek, Md.
SMITH, Mary and Bellany Bosworth, 11 November 1685, Bristol, R. I.
SMITH, Mary and John Atwood, 27 October 1690, Boston, Mass.
SMITH, Mary and Ebenezer Parker, 3 September 1694, Saybrook, Conn.
SMITH, Mary and Duncan Maycome, 18 April 1695, Boston, Mass.
SMITH, Mary and Joseph Blydenburgh, 8 July 1692, New York City.
SMITH, Meribah and Francis Page, 5 December 1669, Hampton, N. H.
SMITH, Morris and Sarah Millet, 4 November 1681, Gloucester, Mass.
SMITH, Nehemiah and Anne Bourne, 21 January 1639, Mansfield, Mass.

SMITH, Nehemiah and Lydia Winchester, 24 October 1669, Roxbury, Mass.
SMITH, Phoebe and Isaac Platt, 12 March 1640, Milford, Conn.
SMITH, Priscilla and Thomas Sisam, 27 August 1693, Philadelphia, Penn.
SMITH, Rebecca and Thomas Clark, 30 April 1691, Boston, Mass.
SMITH, Rebecca and John Throop, 26 November 1697, Bristol, R. I.
SMITH, Rebecka and Josiah Sanders, 7 April 1697, Boston, Mass.
SMITH, Rebecca and Benjamin Hoar, 10 April 1699, Bristol, R. I.
SMITH, Richard and Mary Kirby, 6 October 1647, Sudbury, Mass.
SMITH, Richard and Joanna Quarlls, 2 June 1654, Boston, Mass.
SMITH, Richard and Hannah Cheney, November 1660, Ipswich, Mass.
SMITH, Richard and Marey Reedman, 13 January 1676, Milton, Mass.
SMITH, Richard and Hannah Johns, 19 October 1669, Warwick, R. I.
SMITH, Richard and Mary Clay, 9 February 1699, Boston, Mass.
SMITH, Robert and Margaret Swillaway, 15 August 1687, Malden, Mass.
SMITH, Robert and Deborah King, 12 July 1694, Boston, Mass.
SMITH, Samuel and Susanna Read, 13 December 1659, Boston, Mass.
SMITH, Samuel and Mary Appleton, 25 November 1685, Burlington, N. J.
SMITH, Samuel (2nd marriage) and Elizabeth Pierce, 8 June 1692, Woodbridge,
    N. J.
SMITH, Samuell and Elizabeth Adams, 14 August 1695, Dedham, Mass.
SMITH, Samuel and Priscilla Hovey, 23 November 1699, Malden, Mass.
SMITH, Sarah and Stephen Arnold, 24 November 1646, Rehoboth, Mass.
SMITH, Sarah and John Pickard, 1 February 1679, Rowley, Mass.
SMITH, Sarah and John Thompson, 1682, Rehoboth, Mass.
SMITH, Sarah and Elias Maverick, 3 February 1695, Boston, Mass.
SMITH, Sarah and Joseph Humphry, 28 October 1697, Boston, Mass.
SMITH, Sarah and Samuel Bridge, 24 December 1696, Boston, Mass.
SMITH, Seth and Mehitable Heath, 10 January 1693, Boston, Mass.
SMITH, Shubael and Mary Swift, 6 February 1677, Sandwich, Mass.
SMITH, Shubael (2nd marriage) and Abigail Skiff, 1684, Sandwich, Mass.
SMITH, Simon and Mary Andrewes, 5 January 1698-9, Warwick, R. I.
SMITH, Stephen and Susanna Hinckley, 1643, Machias, Maine.
SMITH, Stephen and Decline Lamb, 7 December 1663, Charlestown, Mass.
SMITH, Thomas and Priscilla Allen, 9 November 1682, Philadelphia, Penn.
SMITH, Thomas and Mary Richards, 11 October 1687, Milton, Mass.
SMITH, Thomas and Mary Shurah, 10 March 1696, Boston, Mass.
SMITH, William and Priscilla Garwood (widow), 11 September 1683, Dedham,
    Mass.
SMITH, William and Mary Croasdell, 20 September 1690, Middletown, Penn.
SMITH, William and Mary Perry, 8 January 1699, Boston, Mass.
SMITH, William and Alice Gott, 2 February 1696, Anne Arundel Co., Mo.
SMOUT, Edward and Jane Abbott, 16 February 1691, Burlington, N. J.
SMYLOLARY, Unity and Thomas Eaton, 6 January 1658, Andover, Mass.
SMYTH, John and Bethia Snow, 14 May 1694, Eastham, Mass.
SNEDINX, Grietie and Jan Ginom, 12 August 1662, Brooklyn, N. Y.
SNEED, William and Mary Thomas, 28 October 1688, Philadelphia, Penn.
SNELLING, Benjamin and Jamina Andrews, 29 January 1694, Boston, Mass.
SNELLING, Joseph and Sarah Sedgwick, 8 June 1693, Boston, Mass.
SNELLING, Joseph and Rebecca Adams, 19 July 1694, Boston, Mass.

SNOW, Abigail and Michael Ford, 12 December 1667, Marshfield, Mass.

SNOW, Benjamin and Elizabeth Alden, 12 December 1693, Bridgewater, Mass.

SNOW, Bethia and John Smyth, 14 May 1694, Eastham, Mass.

SNOW, Ebenezer and Hopestill Horton, 22 December 1698, Eastham, Mass.

SNOW, Hannah and William Cole, 2 December 1688, Eastham, Mass.

SNOW, Mark and Anna Cook, 18 January 1654, Abington, Mass.

SNOW, Millatiah and Samuell Fisher, 22 January 1659, Dedham, Mass.

SNOW, Sarah and William Walker, 25 January 1654, Eastham, Mass.

SNOWDEN, John and Anne Barrett, 13 April 1682, Burlington, N. J.

SNOWTON, William and Rachel Woodward, 28 June 1699, Boston, Mass.

SOLENDINE, John and Elizabeth Usher, 2 August 1680, Dunstable, Mass.

SOLOMON, Sarah and John Conklin, 2 December 1653, Southold, L. I., N. Y.

SOMERBY, Elizabeth and Daniel Moody, 29 March 1683, Salisbury, Mass.

SOMERS, John and Hannah Hodgkins, 2 January 1685, Somerton, Penn.

SOMES, Mary and John Heman, 17 October 1660, Gloucester, Mass.

SOMES, Sarah and Henry Whitham, 15 June 1665, Gloucester, Mass.

SOMES, Timothy and Jane Stanwood, 2 April 1672, Gloucester, Mass.

SONGHURST, Sarah and Zachary Whitplain, 26 September 1686, Philadelphia. Penn.

SOPER, Joseph and Elizabeth Alcocke, 6 March 1656, Boston, Mass.

SOULE, James and Lidia Tomson, 14 December 1693, Duxborough, Mass.

SOULE, Mary and John Peterson, 1664, Duxbury, Mass.

SOULE, Patience and John Haskell, January 1666, Middleboro, Mass.

SOUTHER, Daniel and Elizabeth Boden, 15 June 1697, Boston, Mass.

SOUTHER, Diana and Henry Mattock, 3 March 1698, Boston, Mass.

SOUTHMAYD, William and Millicent Addis, 28 November 1642, Middletown, Conn.

SOUTHMAYD, William and Esther Hamlin, October 1673, Middletown, Conn.

SOUTHWORTH, Constant and Elizabeth Collier, 2 November 1637, Duxbury, Mass.

SOUTHWORTH, Edward and Mary Pabodie, June 1669, Duxbury, Mass.

SOUTHWORTH, Elizabeth and Samuel Gallup, 12 May 1685, Bristol, R. I.

SOUTHWORTH, Priscilla and Samuel Talbot, 1 March 1689, Bristol, R. I.

SOUTHWORTH, William and Rebecca Pabodie, 1680, Duxbury, Mass.

SOUWARD, Mary and Edmond Thomas, 9 July 1694, New York.

SOWTHER, John and Hannah Read, 11 January 1660, Boston, Mass.

SOWTHER, Joseph and Elizabeth Fairefeild, 22 August 1657, Boston, Mass.

SOWTHER, Mary and Joseph Shaw, 1 October 1653, Boston, Mass.

SOWTHER, Nathaniel and Sarah Hill (widow), 5 November 1653, Boston, Mass.

SPAFFORD, Elizabeth and Alexander Sessions, 24 April 1672, Andover, Mass.

SPAFFORD, Hanna and John Mitchell, 20 May 1680, Newbury, Mass.

SPALDIN, Dorithy and Joseph Ellice, 18 May 1690, Dedham, Mass.

SPALDING, Edward and Margaret Barrett, 22 November 1681, Chelmsford, Mass.

SPARHAWK, John and Elizabeth Pool, 22 June 1699, Boston, Mass.

SPARKE, John and Mary Sennet, 26 November 1661, Boston, Mass.

SPARKS, Henry and Martha Barrett, 10 July 1676, Chelmsford, Mass.

SPARKS, Rebecca (widow) and Robert McKenney, 1 December 1692, Dover, N. H.

SPARROW, Alice (widow) and William Russell, 7 July 1653, Boston, Mass.

SPARROW, Jane and William Rawlinson, 16 September 1660, Charles City Co., Va.

SPARROW, Jonathan and Sarah Lewis Cobb (widow), 23 November 1698, Barnstable, Mass.

SPARRY, Nicholas and Sarah Sams, 20 August 1694, Boston, Mass.

SPAULDING, John and Hannah Hale, May 1658, Concord, Mass.

SPAULDING, John and Ann Ballard, 20 July 1681, Chelmsford, Mass.

SPAULDING, Lydia and Timothy Pierce, 29 May 1696, Plainfield, Conn.

SPAULE, Thomas and Marry Gutteridge, 18 June 1653, Boston, Mass.

SPEAR, Samuel and Elizabeth Daniel, 5 June 1694, Milton, Mass.

SPEED, Mary and Peter Branch, 6 December 1652, Marshfield, Mass.

SPEERE, Ebenezer and Rachel Deering, 16 July 1679, Braintree, Mass.

SPEERE, George and Mary Deering, 27 February 1675, Braintree, Mass.

SPEERE, Sarah and George Witty, 19 April 1672, Braintree, Mass.

SPENCER, Elizabeth and Samuel Colver, 23 December 1663, Farmington, Conn.

SPENCER, James and Mary Carly, 28 May 1695, New York.

SPENCER, Moses and Elizabeth Botts (widow), July 1679, Kittery, Maine.

SPENCER, Sam and Hepzibah Church, 16 August 1696, Hadley, Conn.

SPENCER, Thomas and Sarah Barding, 11 September 1645, Hartford, Conn.

SPERRY, Richard and Martha Mansfield, 16 December 1680, New Haven, Conn.

SPICER, Peeter and Mary Busecott, 15 December 1670, Warwick, R. I.

SPICER, Samuel and Esther Tilton, 25 March 1665, Oyster Bay, N. Y.

SPIKEMAN, Randolph and Mary Cockin, 29 August 1697, Philadelphia, Penn.

SPINKS, Sarah and Robert West, 10 November 1695, Harford Co., Md.

SPINNEY, Hannah and Samuel Fernald, December 1698, Portsmouth, N. H.

SPINNEY, Samuel and Elizabeth Knight, 26 September 1687, York Co., Maine.

SPINNING, Humphrey, Jr., and Abigail Hubbard, 14 October 1657, Guilford, Conn.

SPINNING, John and Deborah Bartlett, 16 March 1687, Guilford, Conn.

SPOFFORD, Samuel and Sarah Burkbie, 5 December 1676, Rowley, Mass.

SPOWEL, Elizabeth and Joshua Wight, 4 October 1699, Boston, Mass.

SPRAGUE, Anthony and Elizabeth Bartlett, 26 December 1661, Hingham, Mass.

SPRAGUE, Edward and Dorothy Lain, 24 November 1693, Malden, Mass.

SPRAGUE, Joana and Caleb Church, 16 December 1667, Hingham, Mass.

SPRAGUE, John and Ruth Bassett, 1655, Duxbury, Mass.

SPRAGUE, John and Lydia Goffee, 2 May 1651, Malden, Mass.

SPRAGUE, Phineas and Mary Carrington, 11 October 1661, Malden, Mass.

SPRAGUE, Phineas and Sarah Hasse, 5 January 1670, Malden, Mass.

SPRAGUE, Rebecca and John Brown, 24 June 1697, Malden, Mass.

SPRAGUE, Samuel and Recuba Crawford, 23 June 1655, Boston, Mass.

SPRAGUE, Samuel and Loise Burrell, 5 June 1695, Boston, Mass.

SPRIGG, Mary and Thomas Stockett (1st marriage), 12 March 1689, Anne Arundel Co., Md.

SPRINGFIELD, Emanuel and Mary Mellowes, 13 July 1655, Boston, Mass.

SPRINGSTEN, Caspar and Jannetie Jacobs, 24 July 1695, New York.

SPUR, Johanna and Nathaniel Wyatt, 8 November 1668, Dorchester, Mass.

SPURR, John and Mercy Hoare, 26 December 1676, Dorchester, Mass.

SPURR, Patience and Jonathan Elmes, 24 May 1693, Milton, Mass.

SPURR, Robert and Elizabeth Tilstone, 24 October 1684, Dorchester, Mass.

SQUIER, Mary and Samuel Whittaker, 5 May 1697, Rehoboth, Mass.

SQUIER, Jonathan and Leah Gould, 29 August 1681, Chelmsford, Mass.

SQUIRE, Mary and John Hascall, Jr., 2 March 1699, Cambridge, Mass.
STAAPLE, John and Jemina Jewit, 6 July 1693, Milton, Mass.
STABBS, Richard and Margaret Read, 3 March 1659, Boston, Mass.
STACE, Thomas and Susannah Wooster, 4 August 1653, Ipswich, Mass.
STACEY, Simon and Sarah Wallis, 19 April 1659, Ipswich, Mass.
STACY, Ann and Daniel Leeds, February 1681, Springfield, N. J.
STACKHOUSE, Thomas and Grace Heaton, 27 July 1688, Middletown, Penn.
STADLEY, Ana and William Jenkins, 25 August 1674, Somerset Co., Md.
STAFFORD, Amos and Mary Burlingam, 19 December 1689, Warwick, R. I.
STAFFORD, Sarah and Amos Westcott, 13 July 1667, Warwick, R. I.
STAFFORD, Thomas, Jr., and Fanne Dodge, 20 December 1671, Warwick, R. I.
STAFORD, Deborah and Amos Westcott, 9 January 1670, Warwick, R. I.
STAIRNS, Nathaniel and Mary Raine, 25 October 1687, Milton, Mass.
STAKE, Rose and Thomas Yates, 1679, Middlesex Co., Va.
STALE, Katherine and Anthony Pintard, 14 May 1692, New York City.
STALLION, Sarah and John Edgecomb, 9 November 1673, New London, Conn.
STANARE, Alice and Anthony Shaw, 8 February 1653, Boston, Mass.
STANBOROUGH, Mary and John Edwards, 1666, East Hampton, L. I., N. Y.
STANBURY, Abigail and Richard Frankin, 29 September 1697, Boston, Mass.
STANBURY, Nathan and Mary Ewer, 31 January 1699, Philadelphia, Penn.
STANDISH, Myles and Sarah Winslow, 19 July 1660, Boston, Mass.
STANDLEY, Abigail and John Hooker, 24 November 1687, Farmington, Conn.
STANFIELD, James and Mary Hutchinson, 27 April 1690, Philadelphia, Penn.
STANHOPE, Jonathan and Susannah Ayers, 16 April 1656, Charlestown, Mass.
STANIAN, Ann and Thomas Silley, 2 July 1697, Dover, N. H.
STANLEY, Abigail and Samuel Cowles, 14 February 1660, Hartford, Conn.
STANLEY, Elizabeth and Thomas Horton, Jr., 26 September 1686, Philadelphia, Penn.
STANNIFORD, Mary and Nicholas Wilton, 20 November 1656, Windsor, Conn.
STANTON, Anne and Charles Reade, 23 July 1690, Middletown, Penn.
STANTON, Dorothy and Nicholas Lynde, 9 May 1696, Stonington, Conn.
STANTON, Elizabeth and Thomas French, 25 July 1696, Philadelphia, Penn.
STANTON, Joana and Robert Denison, 1696, Stonington, Conn.
STANTON, Mary and Robert Lay, 22 January 1679, Saybrook, Conn.
STANTON, Samuel and Borodel Benison, 15 June 1680, Stonington, Conn.
STANTON, Sarah and Henry Tibbits, December 1661, Kingston, R. I.
STANTON, Thomas and Ann Lord, 1637, Hartford, Conn.
STANWOOD, Jane and Timothy Somes, 2 April 1672, Gloucester, Mass.
STANWOOD, Jane and John Pearcy, 17 July 1673, Gloucester, Mass.
STANWOOD, Jonathan and Mary Nichols, 27 December 1688, West Amesbury, Mass.
STANWOOD, John and Lydia Cutler, 9 December 1680, Gloucester, Mass.
STANWOOD, Naomi and William Sergent, 26 October 1681, Gloucester, Mass.
STANWOOD, Phillip and Mary Blackwell, 22 November 1677, Gloucester, Mass.
STAPILS, Benjamin and Mary Cox, 26 May 1699, Boston, Mass.
STAPLE, Sarah and Increase Sumner, 26 January 1667, Dorchester, Mass.
STAPLES, Abraham and Mary Randall, 17 September 1660, Weymouth, Mass.
STAPLES, Samuel and Mary Boles, 30 June 1652, Braintree, Mass.
STAPLES, Samuel and Hannah Lincoln, 9 February 1693, Taunton, Mass.

STAPLES, Rebecca and Thomas Rutter, 11 October 1685, Middletown, Penn.
STARBORD, Thomas and Abigail Dame, 4 January 1687, Dover, N. H.
STAR, Hannah and John Cutt, 30 July 1662, Dover, N. H.
STARKIE, John and Mary Channelhouse, 27 July 1687, Monmouth Co., N. J.
STARR, Comfort and Mary Stone, 14 September 1683, Dedham, Mass.
STARR, Constant and (Dr.) John Morley, 20 February 1647, Braintree, Mass.
STARR, Jonathan and Elizabeth Morgan, 12 January 1699, New London, Conn.
STARR, Joseph and Abigail Baldwin, 24 June 1697, Boston, Mass.
STARR, Mary and John Maynard, 16 May 1640, Duxbury, Mass.
STARR, Ruth and Joseph Moore, 21 March 1656, Boston, Mass.
STEADFORD, Elizabeth and Jeremiah Fenwick, 3 January 1699, Boston, Mass.
STEADMAN, Sarah and James Herring, 16 February 1685, Dedham, Mass.
STEARNES, Mary and Joseph Wight, 22 February 1685, Dedham, Mass.
STEARNS, Elizabeth and Samuel Manning, 13 April 1664, Cambridge, Mass.
STEARNS, Isaac and Sarah Beers, 24 June 1660, Watertown, Mass.
STEARNS, Sarah and Thomas Wheeler, 23 July 1677, Watertown, Mass.
STEBBINS, Benjamin and Abigail Denton, 9 October 1682, Springfield, Mass.
STEBBINS, John and Ann Munson, 14 March 1646, Springfield, Mass.
STEBBINS, Thomas and Hannah Wright, November 1645, Springfield, Mass.
STEDMAN, Elizabeth and Thomas Dunk, 10 July 1677, Saybrook, Conn.
STEDMAN, Elizabeth and Samuel Gibson, 14 June 1679, Roxbury, Mass.
STEDMAN, Hannah and Robert Murdock, 28 April 1692, Roxbury, Mass.
STEDMAN, John and Violet Shepard, 10 August 1678, Wethersfield, Conn.
STEDMAN, Mary and David Stowell, 7 April 1695, Cambridge, Mass.
STEELE, James and Ann Bishop, 18 October 1651, Cambridge, Mass.
STEEVENS, Grace and Edmond Sherman, 8 December 1656, Dedham, Mass.
STEEVINS, Sarah and John Cleavery, 18 January 1664, Braintree, Mass.
STEPHENS, Catherine and Thomas Dean, 5 January 1669, Taunton, Mass.
STEPHENS, Elizabeth and Peter Hoxworth, 27 February 1699, Boston, Mass.
STEPHENS, Margery and John Homer, 13 July 1693, Boston, Mass.
STEPHENS, Thomas and Mary Caswell, 28 September 1699, Taunton, Mass.
STEPHENSON, Bartholomew and Mary Clark, 10 October 1680, Dover, N. H.
STEPHSON, Sarah (widow) and William Blackston, 4 July 1659, Boston, Mass.
STERLING, Sarah and Ralph Farnum, 9 October 1685, Andover, Mass.
STERNS, John and Joana Parker, 22 April 1696, Malden, Mass.
STETSON, Benjamin and Grace Turner, 22 January 1690, Scituate, Mass.
STETSON, Robert and Mary Callomer, 12 January 1692-3, Scituate, Mass.
STEUARD, Alexander and Cornelia Depheyster, 18 August 1699, New York.
STEVENS, Cyprian and Mary Willard, 1671, Lancaster, Mass.
STEVENS, David and Eliza Webster, 29 January 1690, Boston, Mass.
STEVENS, Elizabeth and Joshua Woodman, 22 January 1665, Andover, Mass.
STEVENS, Elizabeth and Charles Baggley, 27 May 1682, Burlington Co., N. J.
STEVENS, Elizabeth and Morris Tucker, 14 October 1661, Salisbury, Mass.
STEVENS, Ephriam and Sarah Abbott, 11 October 1680, Andover, Mass.
STEVENS, Esther and Thomas Tingley, 14 August 1694, Rehoboth, Mass.
STEVENS, John and Hannah Barnard, 13 June 1662, Andover, Mass.
STEVENS, John and Joana Thom, 17 February 1670, Salisbury, Mass.
STEVENS, John and Esther Barker, 10 August 1676, Andover, Mass.
STEVENS, John and Abigail Cole, 28 April 1684, Wallingford, Conn.

STEVENS, John and Ruth Poor, 20 December 1689, Andover, Mass.
STEVENS, John and Grace Gammon, 6 June 1694, Boston, Mass.
STEVENS, Joseph and Mary Ingalls, 28 May 1679, Andover, Mass.
STEVENS, Joseph and Mary Fry, 22 December 1696, Andover, Mass.
STEVENS, Judith and Samuel Buell, 1686, Killingworth, Conn.
STEVENS, Mary and John Whipple, 21 July 1663, Charlestown, Mass.
STEVENS, Mary and John Barker, 6 July 1670, Andover, Mass.
STEVENS, Mary and Samuel Johnson, 20 December 1698, Boston, Mass.
STEVENS, Mary and Jesse Kipp, 30 September 1695, New York.
STEVENS, Nathan and Elizabeth Abbott, 24 October 1692, Andover, Mass.
STEVENS, Obadiah and Rebecca Rose, 18 December 1678, Stamford, Conn.
STEVENS, Rebecca and Edward Rutty, 6 May 1678, Killingworth, Conn.
STEVENS, Ruth and Stephen Glover, 7 October 1663, Gloucester, Mass.
STEVENS, Sarah and Andrew Blake, 14 August 1696, Wrentham, Mass.
STEVENS, Sarah and Stephen Dodd, 18 May 1678, Killingworth, Conn.
STEVENS, Thomas and Mary Fletcher, 1650, Milford, Conn.
STEVENS, Thomas and Hannah Evarts, 9 June 1686, Killingworth, Conn.
STEVENS, Thomas and Sarah Bushnell, 9 November 1688, Killingworth, Conn.
STEVENS, William and Abigail Sargent, 15 June 1682, Gloucester, Mass.
STEVENSON, Elizabeth and George Anderson, 26 June 1693, New York.
STEVENSON, Janetie and Joihn Lawrence, 6 April 1696, Perth Amboy, N. J.
STEVENSON, Mary and Enoch Hutchins, 5 April 1667, Dover, N. H.
STEVENSON, Sarah (widow) and William Blaxton, 1659, Boston, Mass.
STEWARD, Sarah and Thomas Abbot, 15 December 1664, Andover, Mass.
STEWART, Hannah and Barrett Dyer, 29 June 1699, Boston, Mass.
STEWART, Joseph and Ales Wright, 7 December 1694, Chesterfield, N. J.
STEWART, Robert and Bethia Rumball, 13 June 1661, Stratford, Conn.
STEWART, Susanna and Luke Short, 13 June 1692, Weymouth, Mass.
STICKNEY, Benjamin and Sarah Morse, 24 June 1663, Newbury, Mass.
STILER, John and Mary Bull, 9 June 1697, Boston, Mass.
STILES, Henry and Elizabeth Wilcoxen, 16 April 1663, Windsor, Conn.
STILES, Sara and Ephriam Bancroft, 1 May 1681, Windsor, Conn.
STILEMAN, Robert and Elizabeth Fry, 4 October 1660, Andover, Mass.
STILWELL, Alice and Samuel Holmes, 26 October 1665, Long Island, N. Y.
STILWELL, Ann (widow) and William Wilkins, 29 December 1672, Gravesend,
    L. I., N. Y.
STILWELL, Mary and Adam Mott, 1678, New York City.
STILWELL, Nicholas and Catherine Morgan (widow), 6 February 1671, Long
    Island, N. Y.
STILWELL, Rebecca and James Craven, 23 March 1644, Guilford, Conn.
STILWELL, Rebecca and Abraham Emans, 20 October 1693, New York.
STILWELL, Sarah and Richard Crego, 29 June 1696, New York.
STILWELL, Thomas and Martha Balien (widow), 8 January 1670, New York.
STILLWELL, Elizabeth and John Grave, 26 November 1657, Guilford, Conn.
STILLWELL, Mary and Thomas Walton, 23 December 1698, New York.
STIMSON, Andrew and Abigail Sweetzer, 9 March 1678, Charlestown, Mass.
STIMSON, Hannah and William Burgess, 20 May 1684, Cambridge, Mass.
STIMSON, Mary and Thomas Richardson, 5 January 1670, Cambridge, Mass.
STIMSON, Rebecca and James Patterson, 29 May 1662, Cambridge, Mass.

STOCKBRIDGE, Hannah and William Ticknor, 29 August 1656, Boston, Mass.
STOCKBRIDGE, Mary (widow) and Daniell Henricke, 8 April 1660, Boston, Mass.
STOCKER, Martha and Isaac Adams, 4 January 1699, Boston, Mass.
STOCKER, Mary and Benjamin Hallawell, 12 May 1692, Boston, Mass.
STOCKETT, Thomas and Mary Sprigg, 12 March 1689, Anne Arundel Co., Md.
STOCKETT, Thomas and Damaris Welch, April 1699, Anne Arundel Co., Md.
STOCKTON, Richard and Susanna Robinson, 8 September 1691, Chesterfield, N. J.
STODDARD, Elizabeth and Thomas Joy, 6 March 1695, Boston, Mass.
STODDARD, Mary and Robert Wells, 13 October 1698, Boston, Mass.
STODDER, John and Mary Jay, 14 November 1699, Boston, Mass.
STOKES, Deborah and Richard Kenney, 15 August 1687, Dover, N. H.
STOLLARD, Giles and Elizabeth Tuder, 8 July 1695, New York.
STON, Peter and Elizabeth Shaw, 25 June 1696, Warwick, R. I.
STONE, Ann and Samuel Capen, 16 November 1693, Boston, Mass.
STONE, Hugh and Hannah Foster, 15 October 1667, Andover, Mass.
STONE, Joan and Isaac Read, 10 March 1673, Salem, Mass.
STONE, Joanna and Simon Tainter, 9 May 1693, Boston, Mass.
STONE, John and Mary Russ, 14 November 1690, Andover, Mass.
STONE, Martha and Rachell Pond, May 1681, Dedham, Mass.
STONE, Mary (widow) and Roger Wheeler, 23 November 1659, Boston, Mass.
STONE, Mary and Comfort Starr, 14 September 1683, Dedham, Mass.
STONE, Samuel and Mary Treadwell, 28 January 1684, Salem, Mass.
STONE, William and Hannah Walley, 2 June 1686, Bristol, R. I.
STORER, Joseph and Hannah Hill, September 1691, Saco, Maine.
STORRS, Mary and Joseph Jacobs, 6 December 1666, Ipswich, Mass.
STORY, Joshuah and Als Hust, 7 September 1692, Dorchester, Mass.
STORY, Margaret and Gilbert Dallison, 24 October 1661, Boston, Mass.
STORY, William and Susanne Fuller, 25 October 1671, Ipswich, Mass.
STOUGHTON, John and Sarah Fitch, 23 January 1689, Hartford, Conn.
STOUGHTON, Rebecca and William Taylor, 25 June 1664, Dorchester, Mass.
STOUT, Alice and John Throckmorton, 12 December 1670, Middletown, N. J.
STOUT, David and Rebecca Ashton, 1688, Freehold, N. J.
STOUT, John and Elizabeth Crawford, 12 January 1671, Monmouth Co., N. J.
STOUT, Jonathan and Anne Bullen, 27 August 1685, Monmouth Co., N. J.
STOUT, Mary and James Bowne, 31 December 1664, Monmouth Co., N. J.
STOUT, Sarah and John Pike, 2 February 1675, Monmouth Co., N. J.
STOUT, Richard and Penelope Kent or Lent (widow of Von Printzen), 1634-5, Gravesend, L. I., N. Y.
STOW, Thomas and Mary Griggs, 4 December 1639, Roxbury, Mass.
STOWEL, Mary and Nathaniel Hubbert, 31 May 1695, Boston, Mass.
STOWELL, David and Mary Stedman, 7 April 1695, Cambridge, Mass.
STOWELL, Elizabeth and George Lane, 14 December 1699, Hingham, Mass.
STOWELL, Mary (widow) and Joshua Beal, 10 October 1689, Hingham, Mass.
STOWELL, Remember and Thomas Remington, 16 March 1688, Hingham, Mass.
STOWELL, Samuel and Mary Farrow, 25 October 1649, Hingham, Mass.
STOWER, Hannah and Abram Hills, October 1666, Malden, Mass.
STRANGNISH, Katrine and John Hutton, 28 October 1695, New York.
STRATTON, Ann and William Lake, 1661, Salem, Mass.

STRATTON, John and Elizabeth Train, 10 March 1658, Watertown, Mass.
STRATTON, Samuel and Margaret Parker (widow), 27 June 1657, Boston, Mass.
STREARD, Alexander and Cornelia Dishington, 18 August 1699, New York.
STREET, Daniel and Hannah East, 16 January 1687, Philadelphia, Penn.
STREET, John and Sarah Wing, 10 September 1694, Boston, Mass.
STREET, Sarah and James Heaton, 20 November 1662, New Haven, Conn.
STREET, Sarah and Thomas Tomlin, 30 December 1697, Boston, Mass.
STRONG, Elizabeth and John Hill, 16 November 1656, Boston, Mass.
STRONG, Experience and Zerubabel Fyler, 27 May 1669, Windsor, Conn.
STRONG, John, Jr., and Mary Clark, 26 November 1656, Windsor, Conn.
STRONG, Josiah and Joan Gillett, 6 January 1699, Windsor, Conn.
STRONG, Mary and John Clark, 16 March 1679, Northampton, Mass.
STRONG, Return and Sara Warham, 11 May 1664, Windsor, Conn.
STRONG, Thomas and Mary Hewitt, 5 December 1660, Northampton, Mass.
STRONG, Thomas and Rachel Horton, 10 October 1671, Northampton, Mass.
STRYKER, Aeltie and Abraham Brinckerhoff, 20 May 1660, New York City.
STRYKER, Jan and Johannes Nevius, 30 April 1679, New York City.
STUARD, Mary and John Foster, 18 March 1672, Salem, Mass.
STUDSON, James and Susanna Townsend, 26 November 1696, Boston, Mass.
STUKEY, George and Ann Quinby, 28 September 1657, Stamford, Conn.
STURGIS, Edward and Mary Rider (widow), April 1692, Yarmouth, Mass.
STURGIS, Samuel and Mary Hedge, 1667, Yarmouth, Mass.
STURTEVANT, Hannah and John Bass, 21 September 1675, Plymouth, Mass.
STUYVESANT, Elizabeth and George Sydenham, 4 November 1698, New York.
SUDDER, Thomas and Sarah Phillip, 3 November 1699, Boston, Mass.
SUEDEN, Grietje and Jan Genour, 13 August 1664, Harlem, N. Y.
SUEDEN, Jan and Lysbeth Vesschuwr, 1671, Harlem, N. Y.
SUMER, Mary and William Webber, 19 September 1699, Boston, Mass.
SUMMER, William and Rachel Avery, 22 March 1677, Dedham, Mass.
SUMNER, Clement and Margaret Harris, 18 May 1698, Boston, Mass.
SUMNER, Deliverance and Ebenezar Weeks, 8 May 1689, Milton, Mass.
SUMNER, Ebenezer and Elizabeth Clap, 14 March 1699, Dorchester, Mass.
SUMNER, Experience and Eleazer Carver, 11 June 1695, Milton, Mass.
SUMNER, Increase and Sarah Staple, 26 January 1667, Dorchester, Mass.
SUMNER, Mary and Nicholas How, 19 November 1671, Dorchester, Mass.
SUMNER, Mary and Israel Nichols, 10 January 1688, Milton, Mass.
SUMNER, Rebeca and Epherim Wilson, 10 March 1681, Dedham, Mass.
SUMNER, Rebeckah and Aaron Hubbart, 27 January 1697, Milton, Mass.
SUMNER, Waitstil and Manasseh Tucker, 29 December 1679, Milton, Mass.
SUMNER, William and Esther Puffer, 2 June 1697, Milton, Mass.
SUMNER, William and Margaret Harris, 18 May 1698, Boston, Mass.
SUNDERLAND, John and Mary Ujall, 26 January 1658, Boston, Mass.
SUNDERLAND, Mary and Jonathan Ransford, 29 September 1656, Boston, Mass.
SUNDERLAND, Nathananiel and Elizabeth Minott, 7 December 1695, Dorchester, Mass.
SUTTON, Ann and John Cheshire, 14 February 1692, Middletown, N. J.
SUTTON, Anna and John Daggett, Jr., 23 September 1651, Rehoboth, Mass.
SUTTON, William and Damaris Bishop, 11 July 1666, Eastham, Mass.
SUTTON, William and Mary Johnson, 31 January 1694, Boston, Mass.

SWAIN, Deborah and Peter Tyler, 20 November 1671, Branford, Conn.
SWAIN, Hepzibah and James Pearson, 1698, Lynn, Mass.
SWAINE, Daniel and Dorothy Rose, 26 January 1653, Branford, Conn.
SWALDEN, Mary and James Poffer, 14 December 1655, Braintree, Mass.
SWALLOW, Ambrose and Sarah Barrett, 8 December 1696, Chelmsford, Mass.
SWALLOW, John and Anna Barrett, 3 January 1693, Chelmsford, Mass.
SWALLOW, Marah and Samuel Warner, 4 May 1684, Dunstable, Mass.
SWAN, Alex and Judith Hinds, 15 November 1678, Richmond Co., Va.
SWAN, John and Susanna Wood (widow), 1 August 1699, Haverhill, Mass.
SWAN, Mercy and Samuel Warner, 21 October 1662, Ipswich, Mass.
SWAN, Robert and Hanah Ruse, 1 April 1690, Haverhill, Mass.
SWANN, Helena and Daniel Dunscomb, 8 July 1696, New York.
SWANN, Thomas and Elizabeth Thompson, 1692, Nansemond Co., Va.
SWEET, Henry and Elizabeth Walker, 31 March 1687, Swansea, Mass.
SWEETING, John and Elinor Evans, 7 February 1694, Boston, Mass.
SWEETMAN, Sarah and Josiah Treadway, 9 June 1674, Cambridge, Mass.
SWEETSER, Elizabeth and Samuel Howard, 1661, Malden, Mass.
SWEETZER, Abigail and Andrew Stinson, 9 March 1678, Charlestown, Mass.
SWETLAND, Sarah and William Basset, 14 June 1693, Milton, Mass.
SWETMAN, Samuel and Margaret Peard, 26 October 1693, Boston, Mass.
SWETT, Benjamin and Hester Weare, 1 November 1647, Newbury, Mass.
SWETT, Hester (widow of Benjamin) and Stephen Greenleaf, 31 March 1678, Newbury, Mass.
SWETT, Sarah and Norris Hobbs, 13 June 1678, Hampton, N. H.
SWETT, Stephen and Hannah Merrill, 24 May 1647, Newbury, Mass.
SWIFT, Anna and Obadiah Reed, 19 June 1664, Dorchester, Mass.
SWIFT, Jireh and Abigail Gibbs, 26 November 1697, Sandwich, Mass.
SWIFT, Joan and John Baker, 5 September 1657, Boston, Mass.
SWIFT, Mary and John White, 11 November 1663, Dorchester, Mass.
SWIFT, Mary and Shubael Smith, 6 February 1677, Sandwich, Mass.
SWIFT, Obadiah and Abigall Blake, 31 December 1695, Dorchester, Mass.
SWIFT, Ruth and William Greenow, 10 October 1660, Boston, Mass.
SWIFT, Samuel and Ruth Hatch, 9 April 1686, Watertown, Mass.
SWIFT, Susanna and Hopestill Clap, 18 February 1672, Dorchester, Mass.
SWIFT, Thomas and Elizabeth Vose, 10 September 1657, Dorchester, Mass.
SWIFT, Thomas and Sara Clap, 16 October 1676, Milton, Mass.
SWILLAWAY, Margaret and Robert Smith, 15 August 1687, Malden, Mass.
SWILVAN, Joell and William Tosh, 7 December 1660, Braintree, Mass.
SWITSER, Wigleworth and Ussillah Coles, 2 February 1699, Boston, Mass.
SYDENHAM, George and Elizabeth Stuyvesant, 4 November 1698, New York.
SYKES, Joane and John Warin, 7 September 1688, Chesterfield, N. J.
SYKES, Nathaniel and Eleanor Pain, 7 April 1686, Philadelphia, Penn.
SYLVESTER, Mary and Richard Edgerton, 17 April 1653, Saybrook, Conn.
SYLVESTER, Mary and Mathew Carey, 1 August 1693, Bristol, R. I.
SYMMES, Mary and Thomas Savage, 15 September 1652, Charlestown, Mass.
SYAMES, Sarah and Moses Fiske, 7 September 1672, Braintree, Mass.
SYMONDS, John and Hannah Hathaway, 14 December 1697, Taunton, Mass.
SYMONSE, Henryck and Ariaentie Samuell, 25 October 1693, New York.

T

TAINTER, Dorcas (widow) and John Collins, 6 March 1699, Branford, Conn.

TAINTER, Joana and Josiah Gillet, 30 June 1676, Colchester, Conn.

TAINTER, Simon and Joanna Stone, 9 May 1693, Boston, Mass.

TAINTOR Elizabeth and Noah Roger, 8 April 1673, Branford, Conn.

TALBOT, James and Elizabeth Blore, 25 December 1699, Boston, Mass.

TALBOT, Samuel and Priscilla Southworth, 1 March 1689, Bristol, R. I.

TALBURS, John (of Paul) from Portsmouth, Eng., to Sarah Locker (Daughter of Thomas Lockyer of this Parish), 2 February 1696, Prince George Co., Md.

TALBUT, Peter and Mary Wadell, 12 January 1677, Dorchester, Mass.

TALLY, Hannah and David Buckly, 3 June 1697, Boston, Mass.

TALLY, Richard and Elizabeth Gross, 27 January 1697, Boston, Mass.

TALMADGE, Sarah and Samuel Hotchkiss, 18 March 1679, New Haven, Conn.

TALMAGE, Enos and Hannah Yale, 9 May 1682, New Haven, Conn.

TALMAGE, Hannah (widow) and Samuel Bishop, 2 November 1695, New Haven, Conn.

TANEY, Whankey and John Duplonvis, 29 February 1687, Philadelphia, Penn.

TANKEE, Martha and Daniel Medlicott, 2 October 1684, Philadelphia, Penn.

TAPLEY, Patience and Nathaniel Holmes, 27 January 1667, Dorchester, Mass.

TAPPIN, John and Mary Woodmansey, 20 June 1654, Boston, Mass.

TAPRILL, Priscilla and Francis Caswell, 18 August 1699, Boston, Mass.

TARBELL, Abigail and Joshua Whitney, 30 September 1672, Groton, Mass.

TARBOX, Samuel and Experience Look, 16 October 1678, Lynn, Mass.

TARNE, Sarah and Edward Babbitt, 7 September 1654, Boston, Mass.

TASHER, John and Anna Lightfoott, 6 January 1691-2, New York City.

TAY, Eliza and Paul Myham, 17 December 1689, Boston, Mass.

TAY, Jeremiah and Mercy Woodward, 4 March 1683, Boston, Mass.

TAYLOR, Abraham and Mary Whitaker, 16 December 1681, Concord, Mass.

TAYLOR, Edward and Mary Merrill, 19 February 1663, Barnstable, Mass.

TAYLOR, Edward and Hannah Fitch, 5 September 1674, Westfield, Mass.

TAYLOR, Edward and Jane Payn, 4 August 1692, Boston, Mass.

TAYLOR, Francis and Martha Thompson, 23 February 1699, Hanover Co., Va.

TAYLOR, Hannah and Abiel Lamb, 4 December 1699, Framingham, Mass.

TAYLOR, Lawrence and Mary Miles, 5 February 1699, Harford Co., Md.

TAYLOR, Margaret and Alexander Bulman, 22 December 1690, Boston, Mass.

TAYLOR, Martha and Josias Ellsworth, 30 October 1679, Windsor, Conn.

TAYLOR, Martha and Benjamin Nason, 30 June 1687, Hampton, N. H.

TAYLOR, Mary and Stephen Farr, 25 May 1674, Concord, Mass.

TAYLOR, Mary and William Payn, 11 October 1694, Boston, Mass.

TAYLOR, Mary and Thomas Burroughs, 16 November 1695, New York.

TAYLOR, Samuel and Ruth Cogan, 24 June 1675, Springfield, Mass.

TAYLOR, Stephen and Sara Hosford, 1 November 1642, Windsor, Conn.

TAYLOR, Tamozine and Richard Skinner, 21 April 1692, Boston, Mass.

TAYLOR, Walter and Deliverance Graves, 24 September 1697, New York.

TAYLOR, William and Rebecca Stoughton, 25 June 1664, Dorchester, Mass.

TAYLOR, William and Sarah Byfield, 2 March 1699, Boston, Mass.
TECK, Sarah and Samuel Allen, 1660, Beverly, Mass.
TEIL, Elizabeth and Edward Saunders, 1685, Middlesex Co., Va.
TEMPLE, Abigail and Henry Willard, 21 July 1698, Concord, Mass.
TEMPLE, Abraham and Deborah Hadlocke, 4 December 1673, Concord, Mass.
TEMPLE, Alice and Jacob Kendall, 10 January 1694, Woburn, Mass.
TEMPLE, Mary and Isaac Decoster, 2 November 1699, Boston, Mass.
TEMPLE, Richard and Mary Barker, 7 June 1699, Concord, Mass.
TEMPLE, Sarah and Thomas Esterbrook, 11 May 1683, Concord, Mass.
TEMPLE, Thomas and Elinor Loreson, 17 April 1698, Harford Co., Md.
TEN BROECK, Effey and Lodwyck Vander Burgh, 4 August 1699, New York.
TEN BROEKE, Cornelia and Johannus Wynkoop, 9 June 1696, New York.
TENNEY, Sarah and Alexander Chamberlin, 20 April 1699, Boston, Mass.
TERRELL, Thomas and Mary Reeve, 5 September 1665, Southold, L. I., N. Y.
TERRY, John and Elizabeth Wadsworth, 27 November 1662, Windsor, Conn.
TERRY, Rebecca and Abel Wright, 16 September 1691, Springfield, Mass.
TERRY, Samuel and Anna Lobdell, 3 January 1660, Boston, Mass.
TERRY, Samuel and Martha Crane (widow), 4 January 1698, Wethersfield, Conn.
TESDELL, James and Mary Avery, 5 November 1666, Dedham, Mass.
TEWSBERY, Henry and Martha Harvy (widow), 10 November 1659, Boston, Mass.
THACHER, Dorothy and Richard Sears, 1632, Plymouth, Mass.
THACHER, Thomas and Eliza Kemp, 11 May 1643, Duxbury, Mass.
THACKER, Alice and William Gough, 31 May 1688, Middlesex Co., Va.
THACKER, Henry, Jr., and Elizabeth Payne, June 1690, Middlesex Co., Va.
THACKER, Martha and Thomas Hickman, 18 December 1683, Middlesex Co., Va.
THAIR, Thomas and Mary Pool, 28 October 1687, Milton, Mass.
THATCHER, John and Lydia Gorham, 1 January 1683, Yarmouth, Mass.
THATCHER, Mary and Moses Draper, 3 November 1692, Boston, Mass.
THATCHER, Peter and Susanna Bayley, 25 December 1699, Boston, Mass.
THAXTER, Benjamin and Susanna Molton, 4 December 1693, Boston, Mass.
THAXTER, Deborah and Thomas Cushing, 17 October 1687, Boston, Mass.
THAXTER, John and Elizabeth Jacobs, 4 December 1648, Hingham, Mass.
THAXTER, Sarah and Nathaniel Holmes, 1 October 1691, Boston, Mass.
THAXTER, Samuel and Hannah Gridley, 19 April 1671, Hingham, Mass.
THAYER, Deborah and Thomas Faxon, Jr., 11 April 1653, Braintree, Mass.
THAYER, Ebenezer and Martha Tomson, 13 June 1695, Milton, Mass.
THAYER, Elizabeth and Edward Babbitt, 22 December 1698, Taunton, Mass.
THAYER, Ferdinand and Huldah Hayward, 14 January 1653, Braintree, Mass.
THAYER, Joell and John Harbour, Jr., 17 March 1654, Braintree, Mass.
THAYER, Nathaniel and Hannah Heidon, 27 May 1679, Braintree, Mass.
THAYER, Richard and Jane Parker (widow), July 1646, Boston, Mass.
THAYER, Richard and Dorothy Pray, 24 December 1651, Braintree, Mass.
THAYER, Richard and Rebecca Micall, 16 July 1679, Braintree, Mass.
THAYER, Sarah and Samuel Davis, 20 May 1651, Boston, Mass.
THAYER, Shadrack and Mary Barrett, 11 February 1654, Braintree, Mass.
THAYER, Thomas and Abigail Veasy, 25 March 1680, Braintree, Mass.
THAYR, Sarah and Jonathan Hayward, 6 March 1663, Braintree, Mass.
THAYRE, Deborah and Thomas Jackson, 29 January 1654, Braintree, Mass.

THAYRE, Hannah and Samuel Hoidon, 28 August 1664, Braintree, Mass.

THERRELL, William and Rebecca Simpkins, 29 November 1654, Boston, Mass.

THOM, Joana and John Stevens, 17 February 1670, Salisbury, Mass.

THOMAS, David and Elizabeth Kennedy, 1683, Middleboro, Mass.

THOMAS, Dorothy and Joseph Otis, 20 November 1688, Scituate, Mass.

THOMAS, Edmond and Mary Souward, 9 July 1694, New York.

THOMAS, Elizabeth and Thomas Chesley, 22 August 1663, Dover, N. H.

THOMAS, Gwenlin and Micah Thomas, 28 December 1689, Philadelphia, Penn.

THOMAS, James and Ellin Barber, 26 May 1689, Philadelphia, Penn.

THOMAS, James and Mary Tilden, 3 January 1692-3, Duxborough, Mass.

THOMAS, James and Ann Warner, 26 February 1695, Philadelphia, Penn.

THOMAS, Jane and John Jackson, 14 September 1657, Boston, Mass.

THOMAS, Mary and Francis Deane, 21 November 1677, Andover, Mass.

THOMAS, Mary and William Sneed, 28 October 1688, Philadelphia, Penn.

THOMAS, Nathaniel and Elizabeth Dolberry, 5 October 1696, Marshfield, Mass.

THOMAS, Micah and Gwenlin Thomas, 28 December 1689, Philadelphia, Penn.

THOMAS, Richard and Mary Mason, 16 July 1695, Boston, Mass.

THOMAS, Robert and Ellen Jones, 3 November 1693, Merion, Penn.

THOMAS, Robert and Ancoretta Wells, 1679, Warwick Co., Va.

THOMAS, Samuel and Mary Hutchins, 15 May 1688, West River, Md.

THOMAS, Susannah and Philip Brannan, February 1699, Harford Co., Md.

THOMPSON, Abigail and Joseph Alsop, 25 November 1672, New Haven, Conn.

THOMPSON, Abigail and John Pearce, 6 January 1693, Dorchester, Mass.

THOMPSON, Elizabeth and William Plumly, 7 January 1688, Middletown, Penn.

THOMPSON, Elizabeth and Edwin Conway, 1695, Lancaster Co., Va.

THOMPSON, Elizabeth and Thomas Swann, 1692, Nansemond Co., Va.

THOMPSON, John and Ellen Harrison, 25 October 1650, Milford, Conn.

THOMPSON, John and Anne Vicaris, 4 June 1656, Boston, Mass.

THOMPSON, John and Priscilla Powell, 22 May 1667, New Haven, Conn.

THOMPSON, John and Sarah Smith, 1682, Rehoboth, Mass.

THOMPSON, Katherine and Nicholas Camp, 16 July 1652, Milford, Conn.

THOMPSON, Margaret (widow) and Robert Kent, 5 August 1686, Philadelphia, Penn.

THOMPSON, Martha and Francis Taylor, 23 February 1699, Hanover Co., Va.

THOMPSON, Mary and Joseph Wise, 3 December 1641, Braintree, Mass.

THOMPSON, Sarah and Elias Henly, 4 September 1657, Boston, Mass.

THOMPSON, Sarah and John Selsby, 1 August 1696, New York.

THOMPSON, Simon and Mary Converse, 19 December 1643, Woburn, Mass.

THOMPSON, Susanna and John Sanders, 24 May 1698, Charlestown, Mass.

THOMPSON, Thomas and Ann Welles, 14 April 1648, Farmington, Conn.

THOMPSON, Thomas and Elizabeth Hill, 1682, Middlesex Co., Va.

THOMPSON, William and Katherine Treat, 27 November 1655, Boston, Mass.

THOMPSON, William and Grace Elwood, 1680, Middlesex Co., Va.

THOMPSON, William and Ellen Montague, 1684, Lancaster Co., Va.

THOMPSON, William and Bridget Cheseboro, 7 December 1692, Stonington, Conn.

THOMSON, Benjamin and Prudence Pacen, 13 December 1698, Dedham, Mass.

THOMSON, John and Mary Steele, 24 October 1670, Farmington, Conn.

THOMSON, John and Margaret Orton, 2 November 1699, Farmington, Conn.

THONG, Arabella and Thomas Reed, 29 December 1689, Sudbury, Mass.

THOREL, Maria and Daniel Perrin, 12 February 1665, Elizabethtown, N. J.

THORING, Anthony and Sarah Courser, 3 November 1693, Boston, Mass.

THORN, Joana and John Stevens, 17 February 1669, Salisbury, Mass.

THORN, Joseph and Mary Bowne, 1679, Woodbridge, N. J.

THORN, Samuel and Abigail Barber, 17 December 1691, Boston, Mass.

THORNBURY, James and Lydia Curtice, 14 September 1699, Boston, Mass.

THORNE, Elizabeth and Rigebell Mott, 14 October 1696, Hempstead, N. Y.

THORNE, Mary and Benjamin Mills, 1 May 1674, Dedham, Mass.

THORNE, Richard and Phebe Denton, 29 August 1699, New York.

THORNE, Susannah and John Kissam, 10 July 1667, Jamaica, N. Y.

THORNSON, Sarah and Edward Coats, January 1694, New York.

THORNTON, Mehitabel and Thomas White, December 1687, Boston, Mass.

THORNTON, Robert and Mary Merry, 13 September 1657, Boston, Mass.

THORNTON, William and Ann Hanet, 17 August 1697, Boston, Mass.

THORP, Hanna and Samuell Bullard, 14 November 1683, Dedham, Mass.

THORP, James and Hannah Newcomb, 8 November 1657, Dedham, Mass.

THORP, John and Mary Davis, 15 May 1699, Fairfield, Conn.

THORP, Peter and Abigail White, 29 October 1695, Dedham, Mass.

THORP, Rachael and Jonathan Whiting, 3 December 1689, Dedham, Mass.

THORP, Samuell and Elizabeth Whit, 15 February 1699, Dedham, Mass.

THORP, Thomas and Rebecca Milward, 27 March 1656, Boston, Mass.

THORPE, Alice and William Davis, 21 October 1658, Roxbury, Mass.

THORPE, John and Hannah Frost, 1684, Fairfield, Conn.

THORPE, Mary and Edward Fenn, 15 November 1688, Wallingford, Conn.

THORPE, Nathaniel and Mary Ford, 20 November 1662, New Haven, Conn.

THORPE, Nathaniel and Sarah Robbins, 16 December 1692, New Haven, Conn.

THORPE, Samuel and Mary Benton, 6 December 1666, Wallingford, Conn.

THORTES, Mary and Edward Gilling, 25 December 1696, Boston, Mass.

THRALL, Deborah and John Moses, 14 July 1680, Simsbury, Conn.

THRALL, Phillipa and John Hosford, 5 November 1657, Windsor, Conn.

THREDNEEDLE, Mary and Thomas Mellens, 28 September 1693, Boston, Mass.

THRESHER, Francis and Eliza Hicks, 9 August 1694, Boston, Mass.

THROCKMORTON, Gabriel and Frances Cooke, 1690, Gloucester Co., Va.

THROCKMORTON, John and Alice Stout, 12 December 1670, Middletown, N. J.

THROCKMORTON, Sarah and Moses Lippitt, 8 December 1697, Freehold, N. J.

THROGMORTON, Alse and Robert Skelton, 30 October 1691, New York City.

THROOP, Daniel and Dorcas Barney, 23 August 1689, Bristol, R. I.

THROOP, Daniel and Deborah Macey, 5 January 1697, Bristol, R. I.

THROOP, Elizabeth and Jonathan Peck, 31 March 1695, Bristol, R. I.

THROOP, John and Rebecca Smith, 25 November 1697, Bristol, R. I.

THROOP, Mary and John Barney, 4 November 1686, Bristol, R. I.

THROOP, William and Mary Chapman, 4 May 1666, Barnstable, Mass.

THROOP, William and Martha Collye, 20 March 1698, Bristol, R. I.

THURBER, Charity and Robert Miller, 14 February 1690, Swansea, Mass.

THURBER, Thomas and Ruth Buzigut, 23 February 1677, Swansea, Mass.

THUROGOOD, Ann and Joseph Marsh, 2 March 1692, Boston, Mass.

THURSTON, Benjamine and Elisha Walker, 12 December 1660, Boston, Mass.

THURSTON, Hannah and Thomas Love, 23 July 1652, Boston, Mass.

THURSTON, Hannah and Benjamin Pearson, 1680, Newburyport, Mass.

THURSTON, Mahitabell and Eleazer Ellice, 27 May 1690, Dedham, Mass.
THURSTON, Thomas and Mehitable Mayo, 23 July 1695, Wrentham, Mass.
THWING, Rebecca and Samuel Hood, 17 July 1692, Boston, Mass.
TIBBALS, Josiah and Mary Sherwood, 13 July 1670, Milford, Conn.
TIBBETS, Elizabeth and John Bickford, 1 December 1692, Dover, N. H.
TIBBETS, Samuel and Dorothy Tuttle, 2 September 1686, Dover, N. H.
TIBBETTS, William and Judith Dam, 6 July 1684, Dover, N. H.
TIBBITS, Henry and Sarah Stanton, December 1661, Kingston, R. I.
TICHENOR, Martin and Mary Charles, 16 May 1651, New Haven, Conn.
TICKNOR, William and Hannah Stockbridge, 29 August 1656, Boston, Mass.
TIDD, Mary and Francis Kendall, 24 December 1644, Woburn, Mass.
TIDD, Elizabeth and Thomas Fuller, 13 June 1643, Woburn, Mass.
TIDDER, Mary and Richard Ormes, 3 April 1686, Philadelphia, Penn.
TIFFE, Tabitha and George Garner, 13 February 1670, Warwick, R. I.
TILDEN, Joseph and Alice Twisden, 20 November 1649, Marshfield, Mass.
TILDEN, Lydia and Samuel Rider, 14 June 1680, Taunton, Mass.
TILDEN, Mary and James Thomas, 3 January 1692-3, Duxborough, Mass.
TILDEN, Thomas and Hannah Mendall, 20 December 1692, Marshfield, Mass.
TILL, Peter and Elizabeth Nick, 26 December 1651, Boston, Mass.
TILLER, Helena and Philip Wilkison, 11 October 1694, New York.
TILLERY, Henry and Mary Wasscole, 7 November 1675, Richmond Co., Va.
TILLESON, Jane and John Robbins, 23 June 1670, Branford, Conn.
TILLESTON, Ruth and Richard Denton, 10 November 1657, Dorchester, Mass.
TILLESTONE, Sarah and Abraham Christen, 18 January 1699, Boston, Mass.
TILLETSON, John and Mary Morris, 25 November 1680, Saybrook, Conn.
TILLETSON, Jonathan and Mary Jones, 10 January 1683, Saybrook, Conn.
TILLEY, Elizabeth and John Howland, 1624, Yarmouth, Maine.
TILSON, Joan and Giles Rickard, 20 May 1662, Plymouth, Mass.
TILSTONE, Elizabeth and Robert Spur, 24 October 1684, Dorchester, Mass.
TILTON, Esther and Samuel Spicer, 25 March 1665, Oyster Bay, N. Y.
TIMBERLAKE, Mary and Stephen Mumford, 30 August 1697, Boston, Mass.
TINDALE, Mary and James Chilcott, 1698, Anne Arundel Co., Md.
TINDELL, Margaret and John Hopper, 5 July 1698, New York.
TING, Hannah and Habbiah Savage, 8 May 1661, Boston, Mass.
TINGLE, Elizabeth and Daniel Sheperdson, 11 April 1667, Malden, Mass.
TINGLEY, Thomas and Esther Stevens, 14 August 1694, Rehoboth, Mass.
TINKER, Amos and Sarah Blake, 1 June 1682, Lyme, Conn.
TINKHAM, John and Hannah Howland, 6 October 1694, Middleborough, Mass.
TIPLADY, John, Sr., and Rebecca Hathersall, 1687, York Co., Va.
TISDALE, Abigail and William Makepeace, 2 December 1685, Taunton, Mass.
TISDALE, John and Hannah Rogers, 23 November 1664, Duxbury, Mass.
TISDALE, Mary and Nathaniel French, 9 January 1677, Taunton, Mass.
TITCHBORN, John and Sarah Allin, 17 August 1699, Boston, Mass.
TITCOMB, Rebecca and Nathaniel Treadwell, 25 March 1667-8, Ipswich, Mass.
TITCOMB, Sarah and Thomas Treadwell, 16 March 1664-5, Ipswich, Mass.
TITE, Henry and Sarah Walton, 11 December 1656, Boston, Mass.
TITHERTON, Mary and Samuel Sherman, Jr., 19 June 1665, Stratford, Conn.
TITTERY, Joshua and Cecelia Woolly, 4 April 1688, Philadelphia, Penn.
TITUS, Abigail and Jonah Palmer, 11 February 1692, Rehoboth, Mass.

TITUS, John and Sarah Miller, 3 July 1677, Rehoboth, Mass.
TITUS, Silas and Sarah Battelle, 23 August 1679, Dedham, Mass.
TITUS, Theunis and Mary Barre, 20 December 1699, New York.
TOALMAN, Elisabeth and Moses Heirs, 28 October 1692, Dorchester, Mass.
TOALMAN, John and Mary Paul (widow), 15 June 1692, Dorchester, Mass.
TOBEY, Stephen and Hanna Nelson, 29 November 1688, Dover, N. H.
TODD, Benjamin and Lydia Alling, 23 January 1699, New Haven, Conn.
TODD, Samuel and Mary Bradley, 26 November 1688, New Haven, Conn.
TOLEMAN, John and Susannah Breck, February 1696-7, Dorchester, Mass.
TOLEMAN, Mary and Ebenezar Crane, 13 December 1689, Dorchester, Mass.
TOLMAN, Thomas and Elizabeth Johnson, 4 November 1664, Lynn, Mass.
TOMLIN, Thomas and Sarah Street, 30 December 1697, Boston, Mass.
TOMLINE, John and Sarah Barnes, 26 December 1660, Boston, Mass.
TOMLINSON, John and Deborah Booth, 28 September 1691, Middletown, Penn.
TOMPKINS, Elizabeth and William Ladd, 17 February 1696, Newport, R. I.
TOMPKINS, Martha and John Foster, 1648, Salem, Mass.
TOMPKINS, Nathaniel and Elizabeth Allen, 15 January 1670, Newport, R. I.
TOMPKINS, Samuel and Elizabeth Clark, 1680, York Co., Va.
TOMPSON, Samuel, Jr., and Hannah Parmeter, 25 October 1684, Braintree, Mass.
TOMSON, Henry and Mary Keeffe, 8 August 1693, Boston, Mass.
TOMSON, Henry and Mary Vocory, 11 September 1693, Boston, Mass.
TOMSON, John and Mary Cooke, 5 January 1646, Plymouth, Mass.
TOMSON, Lidia and James Soule, 14 December 1693, Duxborough, Mass.
TOMSON, Martha and Ebenezer Thayer, 13 June 1695, Milton, Mass.
TOMSON, Samuel and Sarah Shepperd, 25 February 1656, Braintree, Mass.
TOOTHAKER, Sarah and Jonathan Whitaker, 15 November 1694, Boston, Mass.
TOPLIFFE, Obedience and David Cope, 20 February 1659, Boston, Mass.
TOPLIFFE, Patience and Nathaniel Holmes, 27 March 1667, Roxbury, Mass.
TOPPAN, Isaac and Hannah Kent, 29 September 1669, Haverhill, Mass.
TOPPING, Ann and Thomas Baker, 29 April 1686, East Hampton, N. Y.
TOPPING, Temperance and Richard Woodhull, 20 November 1684, Southampton, N. Y.
TORBET, John and Abigall Case, 17 November 1698, Dedham, Mass.
TORNEL, William and Elizabeth Tyssen (widow), 9 November 1695, Brooklyn, N. Y.
TORREY, Marie and John Davis, 14 January 1673, Dorchester, Mass.
TORREY, Samuel and Mary Rawson, 15 March 1657, Boston, Mass.
TORRY, Samuel and Abigail Bridge, 29 June 1699, Boston, Mass.
TOSH, William and Joel Sullivan, 7 December 1660, Braintree, Mass.
TOUNG, James and Elizabeth Hagborne, 8 July 1654, Boston, Mass.
TOUNSEND, Joseph and Judith Woodman, 9 August 1694, Boston, Mass.
TOURNEUR, Hester and Frederick DeVoe, 24 June 1677, Harlem, N. Y.
TOUT, Benjamin and Mary Winsor, 29 August 1691, Boston, Mass.
TOWER, Hannah and David Whipple, 11 November 1677, Hingham, Mass.
TOWER, Rachel and Joshua Bates, 15 January 1695, Hingham, Mass.
TOWERS, Abigail and Abram Gourden, 5 January 1692, Boston, Mass.
TOWLE, Joseph and Mehitable Hobbs, 14 December 1692, Hampton, N. H.
TOWLE, Joshua and Sarah Reed, 2 December 1686, Hampton, N. H.
TOWLE, Philip and Isabella Austin, 19 November 1657, Hampton, N. H.

TOWNSEND, Ann and Abraham Cole, 30 September 1697, Boston, Mass.
TOWNSEND, Eliza and Joseph Lobdale, 1 September 1692, Boston, Mass.
TOWNSEND, Hannah and Thomas Hull, 3 April 1657, Boston, Mass.
TOWNSEND, James and Mary Lynck, 7 November 1693, Boston, Mass.
TOWNSEND, James and Rebecca Mosely, 22 January 1694, Boston, Mass.
TOWNSEND, John and Mehitable Brown, 23 April 1690, Lynn, Mass.
TOWNSEND, Jonathan and Elizabeth Walton, 22 March 1695, Boston, Mass.
TOWNSEND, Joseph and Elizabeth Berry, 22 May 1690, Boston, Mass.
TOWNSEND, Lydia and Lawrence Copeland, 12 October 1654, Braintree, Mass.
TOWNSEND, Peter and Mary Welcome, 15 November 1694, Boston, Mass.
TOWNSEND, Rose and Joseph Dickinson, 1680, Oyster Bay, N. Y.
TOWNSEND, Susannah and James Studson, 26 November 1696, Boston, Mass.
TOWNSEND, Samuel and Elizabeth, 15 March 1693, Boston, Mass.
TOWNSEND, Sarah and Edmond Wright, 1695, Oyster Bay, N. Y.
TOWNSEND, Solomon and Elizabeth Jarvis, 20 June 1698, Boston, Mass.
TOWNSHEND, Andrew and Abigail Collins, 18 July 1678, Lynn, Mass.
TOWNSHEND, Elizabeth and Samuel Mansfield, 22 December 1669, Lynn, Mass.
TOWNSHEND, Mary and John Washington, 15 March 1692, Stafford Co., Va.
TOZER, Richard and Judith Smith, 3 May 1656, Boston, Mass.
TRACEY, Hannah and Thomas Davison, 28 November 1695, Norwich, Conn.
TRACEY, Legoe and Mary James, 5 November 1694, Anne Arundel Co., Md.
TRACEY, Susannah and James Rogers, 17 February 1697, Eastham, Mass.
TRACY, Jonathan and Mary Griswold, 11 July 1672, Saybrook, Conn.
TRADWAY, Henry and Anne Driver, 8 November 1685, Burlington, N. J.
TRAIN, Elizabeth and John Stratton, 10 March 1658, Watertown, Mass.
TRALL, Timothy and Debro Gunn, 10 November 1659, Windsor, Conn.
TRASK, Sarah and John Williams, Jr., 15 February 1695, Salem, Mass.
TRAVERES, Francis and Mary Burgess, 27 January 1699, Boston, Mass.
TRAVERSE, Elizabeth (widow) and William Smelt, 21 October 1697, Elizabeth
    City Co., Va.
TRAVIS, Bridget and Richard Window, 30 March 1659, Gloucester, Mass.
TRAVIS, James and Mercy Pearce, 8 April 1667, Gloucester, Mass.
TRAVIS, Richard and Grace Clements, 22 October 1657, Boston, Mass.
TRAVISE, Lydia and Roger Earl, 25 October 1694, Boston, Mass.
TRAWELL, Jane and Phillip Johnson, 15 October 1699, Elizabeth City Co., Va.
TREADWAY, Josiah and Sarah Sweetman, 9 June 1674, Cambridge, Mass.
TREADWAY, Josiah and Dorothy Cutler, 3 February 1697, Charlestown, Mass.
TREADWAY, Lydia and Josiah Jones, 2 October 1667, Watertown, Mass.
TREADWELL, Esther and Daniel Hovey, 8 October 1665, Ipswich, Mass.
TREADWELL, Hannah and John Adams, Jr., 22 May 1690, Ipswich, Mass.
TREADWELL, Martha and Robert Cross, 19 February 1665, Ipswich, Mass.
TREADWELL, Mary and John Gaines, 1659, Ipswich, Mass.
TREADWELL, Mary and Samuel Stone, 28 January 1684, Salem, Mass.
TREADWELL, Nathaanial and Abigail Wells, 19 June 1661, Ipswich, Mass.
TREADWELL, Nathanial and Rebecca Titcomb, 25 March 1667-8, Ipswich, Mass.
TREADWELL, Thomas and Sarah Titcomb, 16 March 1665, Ipswich, Mass.
TREAT, Katherine and Rev. William Thompson, 27 November 1655, Boston, Mass.
TREGENNY, Humphrey and Miss Brookesbanck, 12 August 1696, New York.
TRERICE, John and Hannah Lynde, 3 September 1663, Charlestown, Mass.

TREGO, Hannah and Thomas Kinington, 15 June 1695, Harford Co., Md.
TRERICE, Rebecca and Thomas Jenner, 22 May 1655, Charlestown, Mass.
TRERICE, Sarah and John Goose, 10 August 1666, Charlestown, Mass.
TRICKEY, Margaret and Elihu Gullison, 10 November 1674, Dover, N. H.
TRESCOT, Martha and Jacob Huens, 24 February 1680, Dorchester, Mass.
TRESCOTE, Patience and Noah Beaman, 1 January 1684, Dorchester, Mass.
TRESCOTT, Abigail and Amiel Weekes, 2 March 1682, Dorchester, Mass.
TRESCOTT, Mary and John Heneway, 6 August 1665, Dorchester, Mass.
TRIANS, Ananias and Abigail Norton, 6 August 1667, Saybrook, Conn.
TROT, Sarah and Barnard Capen, 2 June 1675, Dorchester, Mass.
TROTT, John and Mehitable Rigby, 3 February 1696, Dorchester, Mass.
TROTT, Mary and Mathew Grosse, 5 August 1652, Boston, Mass.
TROTT, Preserved and John Baker, 11 May 1667, Dorchester, Mass.
TROTTER, Rebecca and Rev. John Drake, 7 July 1677, Elizabethown, N. J.
TROTTER, Sarah and Joseph Martin, 25 November 1679, Middlesex Co., N. J.
TROTTER, William and Catherine Gibbs, 9 December 1652, Newbury, Mass.
TROTTER, William and Alice Ebell, 28 September 1667, New York City.
TRUE, Henry and Jane Bradbury, 15 March 1643, Salisbury, Mass.
TRUSDELL, Richard and Mary Faierbank, 24 February 1696-7, Dedham, Mass.
TUBBS, Benjamin and Elizabeth Kim (widow), 12 January 1699, Dover, N. H.
TUBBS, William and Lydia Roach, 27 September 1698, New London, Conn.
TUCKER, Elizabeth and John Colwell, 5 January 1699, Elizabeth City Co., Va.
TUCKER, Ephriam and Hannah Gouliver, 27 September 1688, Milton, Mass.
TUCKER, Jane (widow) and John Pleasants, 1670, Henrico Co., Va.
TUCKER, John and Sarah Riggs, 9 May 1681, Gloucester, Mass.
TUCKER, John and Ruth Woolly, 25 February 1688, Shrewsbury, N. J.
TUCKER, Joshua and Hannah Cleverly, 2 November 1697, Boston, Mass.
TUCKER, Manasseh and Waitstil Sumner, 29 December 1679, Milton, Mass.
TUCKER, Mary and Samuel Joanes, 25 July 1681, Dorchester, Mass.
TUCKER, Mary and Joseph Church, 13 December 1660, Hingham, Mass.
TUCKER, Mary and Thomas Debell, Jr., 10 October 1676, Windsor, Conn.
TUCKER, Mary and Samuel Perry, 9 May 1690, Sandwich, Mass.
TUCKER, Mary and John Fryby, 5 June 1699, Elizabeth City Co., Va.
TUCKER, Morris and Elizabeth Stevens, 14 October 1661, Salisbury, Mass.
TUCKER, Richard and Jane Batchelor, 1 February 1684, Philadelphia, Penn.
TUCKER, Sarah and Daniel Brown, 9 June 1698, Anne Arundel Co., Md.
TUCKER, Sarah and Peter Warren, 1 August 1660, Boston, Mass.
TUCKERMAN, Abraham and Constance Worster, 15 July 1692, Boston, Mass.
TUCKERMAN, John and Susanna Chamberline, 14 November 1693, Boston, Mass.
TUDER, Elizabeth and Giles Stollard, 8 July 1695, New York.
TUDER, Frances and John Righton, 27 November 1696, New York.
TUDER, John and Affie Van Hoorn, 20 April 1695, New York.
TUDMAN, Sarah and Timothy Batt, 3 August 1699, Boston, Mass.
TUDOR, Owen and Mary Skinner (widow), 13 November 1651, Windsor, Conn.
TUDOR, Sara and James Porter, 15 January 1679, Windsor, Conn.
TUESDALL, Eliza and Andrew Bondman, 16 December 1697, Boston, Mass.
TUFFE, Edward and Elizabeth Smith, 5 June 1684, Philadelphia, Penn.
TUFFE, Jane and Philip Howell, 3 March 1686, Philadelphia, Penn.
TUFFTS, Sarah and Thomas Oaks, 22 May 1689, Malden, Mass.

TUFT, Mercy and Joseph Wayt, 24 October 1688, Malden, Mass.

TULLY, John and Mary Beamont, 3 January 1671, Saybrook, Conn.

TULLY, John and Elizabeth Eldridg, 20 January 1696, Boston, Mass.

TUNE, James and Mary Jackman, 6 September 1680, Richmond Co., Va.

TUPPER, Katherine and Benjamin Nye, 19 October 1640, Sandwich, Mass.

TURBERFEELD, James and Mercy Campball, 6 December 1699, Boston, Mass.

TURELL, Daniel and Mary Barrell (widow), December 1659, Boston, Mass.

TURNER, Benjamin and Elizabeth Hawkins, 14 April 1692, Scituate, Mass.

TURNER, Catherine and John Baldwin, 31 March 1689, Philadelphia, Penn.

TURNER, Charles and Mary Cox, 12 August 1695, New Kent Co., Va.

TURNER, Edward and Mary Sanford, daughter of Richard, 25 October 1656, Boston, Mass.

TURNER, Edward and Katherine Carter, 25 January 1687, Philadelphia, Penn.

TURNER, Eliab and Elnathan Hinksman, 22 November 1694, Scituate, Mass.

TURNER, Elizabeth and Richard Wheeler, 4 March 1644, Dedham, Mass.

TURNER, Elizabeth and Alexander Duncan, 6 July 1698, Boston, Mass.

TURNER, Elizabeth and Robert Harris, October 1699, New Kent Co., Va.

TURNER, Eunice and Isaac Beck, Jr., 24 October 1684, Scituate, Mass.

TURNER, Grace and Benjamin Stetson, 22 January 1690, Scituate, Mass.

TURNER, Grace and Richard Christophers, 3 September 1691, New London, Conn.

TURNER, Hezekiah and Elizabeth Hugell, 8 June 1674, Richmond Co., Va.

TURNER, John and Mary Brewster, 12 November 1645, Scituate, Mass.

TURNER, John, Jr., and Ann James, 24 April 1649, Scituate, Mass.

TURNER, John and Susanna Scant, 17 January 1693, Boston, Mass.

TURNER, John and Susana Kennett, 14 February 1693, Boston, Mass.

TURNER, Jonathan and Martha Bisbee, 1677, Scituate, Mass.

TURNER, Lydia and James Doughty, 15 August 1649, Scituate, Mass.

TURNER, Martha and Edward Hubbard, 2 March 1670, New York.

TURNER, Martha and Francis Rawle, 27 July 1689, Philadelphia, Penn.

TURNER, Mary and Thomas Yale, 1645, New Haven, Conn.

TURNER, Mary and William Parker, 13 November 1651, Scituate, Mass.

TURNER, Mary and Benedict Arnold, 9 March 1671, Newport, R. I.

TURNER, Merriam and Nathan Pickles, 3 August 1687, Scituate, Mass.

TURNER, Nathaniel and Mehitable Rigby, 29 January 1665, Dorchester, Mass.

TURNER, Oseeth and Joseph White, Jr., 16 September 1696, Scituate, Mass.

TURNER, Ruth and Thomas Prince, 23 December 1685, Scituate, Mass.

TURNER, Sarah and John Faireweather, 15 November 1660, Boston, Mass.

TURNER, Sarah and Thomas Pinson, 26 December 1693, Scituate, Mass.

TURNER, Sarah and John Plimton, 28 February 1696, Dedham, Mass.

TURNER, Thomas and Sarah Hiland, 6 January 1652, Scituate, Mass.

TURNER, Thomas and Hannah Jenkins, 9 February 1695, Scituate, Mass.

TURNER, William and Hannah Jacklin, 28 August 1689, Boston, Mass.

TURPIN, Mary and Thomas Beauchamp, 9 October 1692, Somerset Co., Md.

TUTHILL, Abigail and Joseph Conkling, November 1690, Southold, L. I., N. Y.

TUTTLE, Abigail and Jonathan Barret, 8 December 1698, Boston, Mass.

TUTTLE, Dorothy and Samuel Tibbets, 2 September 1686, Dover, N. H.

TUTHILL, John and Deliverance King, 17 February 1657, Southold, L. I., N. Y.

TUTTLE, Mary and John Wallingsford, 6 December 1687, Dover, N. H.

TUTTLE, Sarah and Richard Martine, 1 December 1653, Boston, Mass.
TUTTLE, Sara and Edward Cloutman, 22 April 1698, Dover, N. H.
TUTTLE, Stephen and Ruth FitzRandolph, 12 September 1695, New Haven, Conn.
TUTTLE, Thomas and Hannah Powell, 21 May 1661, New Haven, Conn.
TUTTLE, Thomas and Mary Sanford, 28 June 1692, New Haven, Conn.
TWAMBLY, John and Mary Canney, 18 April 1687, Dover, N. H.
TWAMBLY, John and Rachel Allen, 3 October 1693, Dover, N. H.
TWELLS, Mary and Ebenezer King, 4 September 1676, Braintree, Mass.
TWELLS, Robert and Martha Brackett, 23 September 1655, Braintree, Mass.
TWING, William and Ruth Chapin, 26 January 1698, Boston, Mass.
TWISDEN, Alice and Joseph Tilden, 20 November 1649, Marshfield, Mass.
TWITCHELL, Mary and Samuell Miles, 3 February 1684, Dedham, Mass.
TWOMBLY, John and Rachel Allin, 3 October 1692, Dover, N. H.
TYBOTT, Mary and William Haskell, 6 November 1643, Gloucester, Mass.
TYBOTT, Widow and John Harding, 22 February 1652, Plymouth, Mass.
TYLER, Hannah and Robert Busswell, 9 December 1697, Andover, Mass.
TYLER, John and Hannah Parker, 14 September 1682, Andover, Mass.
TYLER, John and Deborah Leatherland, 2 November 1699, Boston, Mass.
TYLER, Mary and John Farnum, 30 June 1693, Andover, Mass.
TYLER, Moses and Prudence Blake, 6 July 1666, Andover, Mass.
TYLER, Peter and Deborah Swaine, 20 November 1671, Branford, Conn.
TYLER, Peter, Sr., and Hannah Whitehead, 25 December 1688, Branford, Conn.
TYRRELL, 'William and Rebecca Simpkins, 29 January 1654-5, Boston, Mass.
TYSSEN, Elizabeth (widow) and William Tornel, 9 November 1695, Brooklyn, N. Y.

U

UJALL, Mary and John Sunderland, 26 January 1658, Boston, Mass.

UNDERHILL, Sarah and Joseph Budd, 11 October 1695, Rye, N. Y.

UNDERWOOD, Alice and Thomas Warring, 5 October 1673, Richmond Co., Va.

UNDERWOOD, Deborah and Nathaniel Butterfield, 25 December 1668, Chelmsford, Mass.

UNDERWOOD, Hannah and John Gibson, 14 October 1680, Watertown, Mass.

UNDERWOOD, Joseph and Mary How, 29 April 1665, Dorchester, Mass.

UNDERWOOD, William and Anna Kidder (widow), 17 March 1685, Chelmsford, Mass.

UPHAM, John and Abigail Haward, 31 October 1688, Malden, Mass.

UPHAM, Phineas and Ruth Wood, 14 February 1658, Malden, Mass.

UPHAM, Thomas and Elizabeth Hovey, 21 April 1693, Topsfield, Mass.

UPSHALL, Elizabeth and William Greenough, 4 July 1652, Boston, Mass.

UPSHALL, Susanna and Joseph Cocke, 10 November 1659, Boston, Mass.

UPSON, Hannah and Edward Wright, 18 June 1659, Sudbury, Mass.

USHER, Elizabeth and John Solendine, 2 August 1680, Dunstable, Mass.

USHER, Hezekiah and Elizabeth Simes, 2 September 1652, Boston, Mass.

USHER, Jacob and Ruth Wood, 23 December 1699, Philadelphia, Penn.

USHER, Rebecca and Abraham Browne, 1 May 1660, Boston, Mass.

USHER, Robert and Elizabeth Jaggers, 13 May 1659, Middlesex Co., Mass.

UTHUSE, Margaret Symonse and Jan Dehance, 9 October 1697, New York.

UTLEY, Samuel and Sarah Ashby, 9 April 1691, Stonington, Conn.

V

VAIL, Jeremiah and Mary Paine, 24 May 1660, Southampton, N. Y.

VALE, Christopher and Joanna Heiferman, 21 September 1692, Boston, Mass.

VALES, James and Ann Brock, 28 March 1655, Dedham, Mass.

VALLOU, Stephen and Mary Gallais, 19 November 1692, New York.

VAN ALEN, Catherine and Melgert Van Del Poel, 17 May 1696, Albany, N. Y.

VAN BAAL, Margaret and (Capt.) Nicholas Evorste, 13 December 1697, New York.

VAN BURSUM, Margaret and Cornelius Low, 1 July 1695, New York.

VAN BURSUM, Mary Anne and Lewis Bougeaud, 8 November 1695, New York.

VAN BRUGEN, Johannes and Margaret Provoost, 6 July 1696, New York.

VAN BRUGHEN, Mary and Stephen Richard, 20 July 1696, New York.

VANCE, John and Elizabeth Calloway, June 1697, Middlesex Co., Va.

VAN CLYFF, Cornelia and Benjamin Norwood, 20 February 1693, New York.

VAN CLYFF, Elizabeth and John Bentie, 1 August 1696, New York.

VAN CLYFF, Katherine and John Loring, 16 April 1694, New York.

VAN COURTLAND, Jacobus and Evah Phillips, 7 May 1691, New York City.

VANDE LINDE, Machteld and Albrecht Zabriske, 17 December 1676, Hackensack, N. J.

VANDERBERGH, Hendrick Jansen and Mary Ann Burton, 11 October 1694, New York.

VAN DERBECK, Paulus and Mary Thomas (widow), 9 October 1644, Flatbush, N. Y.

VAN DERBECK, Paulus and Sara Schouten, 13 June 1677, Gowanus, N. Y.

VANDER BURGH, Cornelia and John White, 29 September 1699, New York.

VANDER BURGH, Lodwyck and Effey Ten Broeck, 4 August 1699, New York.

VAN DER HEYDEN, Antie and Paul Miller, 31 January 1695, New York.

VAN DER HEYDEN, Johannes and Mary Wooden, 9 January 1697, New York.

VANDERHUEL, Johannus and Janitje Rosevest, 9 November 1699, New York.

VANDERHULE, Ffemmie and Benjamin Wyncoop, 20 October 1697, New York.

VAN DER POEL, Melgert, Jr., and Catherine Van Alen, 17 May 1696, Albany, N. Y.

VANDERPOOL, Gerrijt and Deborah Warm, 11 February 1697, New York.

VANDERSPIEGEL, James and Ann Sanders, 20 September 1691, New York City.

VAN DEUSEN, Elizabeth and John Benson, 26 July 1676, Albany, N. Y.

VANDEVEER, Neeltje and Daniel Polhemus, 13 August 1685, Flatbush, L. I., N. Y.

VANDEWATER, Hendrycke and Anthony Rutherse, 23 December 1698, New York.

VANDEWATER, Johana and Cornelius Slecht, 11 April 1696, Brooklyn, N. Y.

VAN DYKE, Mary and Hans Harmensen, 14 February 1699, New York.

VAN ELMENDORP, Jacob and Grietie Aerstsen, 28 January 1668, Esopus, N. Y.

VAN GELDER, Hester and Peter W. Roome, 26 November 1684, New York City.

VAN HEYNINGE, Janitye and Matthis Low, 22 August 1698, New York.

VAN HOLST, Anna and Stephen Buckenhoven, 7 May 1696, New York.

VAN HOORN, Affie and John Tuder, 20 April 1695, New York.
VAN HOORN, John and Cathrina Meybi, 20 March 1693, New York.
VAN HOORN, Gerry and Altie Provoost, 14 June 1693, New York City.
VAN HORNE, Janike and Reyneir Van Sickland, 26 March 1687, New York.
VAN NUWENHUYSEN, Catrina and Martinus Lamberts, 19 June 1695, New York.
VAN PRINCESS, Penelope (widow) and Richard Stout, 1663, New York City.
VAN QUACKENBOSH, Reynier and Elizabeth Masten, 2 March 1674, New York City.
VAN RANSELAER, Marie and Peter Schuyler, 1 October 1691, New York City.
VAN SCHAICK, Anna Mary and John Cortlandt, 20 June 1695, New York.
VAN SCHAICK, Catherine and Mathew Clarkson, 19 January 1692, Albany, N. Y.
VAN SICKLAND, Reynier and Janike Van Horne, 26 March 1687, New York.
VAN SLYKE, Teunis and Jannetje Van Wie, 5 February 1696, Coeymans, N. Y.
VAN STRYDT, John and Johanna Lewis, 22 June 1694, New York.
VAN SWEARINGEN, Genett and Barbara de Barrette, 1659, New Castle, Del.
VAN TEUYL, Elizabeth and William Pell, 23 November 1694, New York.
VAN VLECQ, Kathalina and Abraham Kip, 26 January 1697, New York.
VAN VLECQUE, Magdalen and Henricus Kip, 8 June 1696, New York.
VAN VORST, Johanne and Jan Arianse Sip, 22 April 1684, Bergen Co., N. J.
VAN VREDENBURG, William and Apolloma Barents, 19 October 1664, New York.
VAN WINKLE, Jacob and Cather Michelson, 15 March 1671, Hudson Co., N. J.
VARNEY, Mary and John Flack, 23 December 1693, Boston, Mass.
VASEY, Elizabeth and James Allison, 28 May 1674, Dorchester, Mass.
VASSALL, Judith and Resolved White, 5 November 1640, Scituate, Mass.
VAUGHN, George and Mary Belcher, 8 December 1698, Boston, Mass.
VAUGHTON, Michaell and Susannah Leislaer, 24 June 1687, New York.
VEASY, Abigail and Thomas Thayer, 25 March 1680, Braintree, Mass.
VEASY, Ellen and Steven Paine, 20 February 1681, Braintree, Mass.
VEASY, Hanna and John Greenlief, 26 August 1665, Braintree, Mass.
VEASY, Solomon and Elizabeth Sanders, 23 November 1680, Braintree, Mass.
VEAZEY, Samuel and Mary Virgoose, 25 November 1691, Boston, Mass.
VEDDER, Albert and Maria Glen, 17 December 1699, Schenectady, N. Y.
VENTEMAN, John and Elizabeth Smith, 13 July 1699, Boston, Mass.
VERAY, Mehitabel and Thomas Hammond, 15 June 1693, Boston, Mass.
VEREN, John and Mary Wiseman, 12 June 1660, Boston, Mass.
VERIN, John and Penelope Cooke, 30 August 1683, Seaconnet, R. I.
VERPLANK, Susanna and John Garland, 20 April 1669, New York.
VERY, Abigail and Ralph Andrews, 12 December 1682, Gloucester, Mass.
VERY, Hannah and Barthe Foster, 9 November 1669, Gloucester, Mass.
VESEY, William and Mary Reade, 1 March 1698, New York.
VESSCHUWR, Lysbeth and Jan Sueden, 1671, Harlem, N. Y.
VIAL, John and Mary Adams, 27 December 1694, Boston, Mass.
VIALL, Hopestill and William Shutt, 1 July 1659, Boston, Mass.
VIELLE, Cornelius and Catharine Bogardus, 10 April 1693, New York.
VICARIS, Anne and John Thompson, 4 June 1656, Boston, Mass.
VICKARS, Jane and Richard Borden, 12 April 1677, Shrewsbury, N. J.
VILLAROCK, Phillip and Eliza Wilcot, 3 May 1694, Boston, Mass.

VINCENT, Francis and Ann Lynch, 14 February 1699, New York.
VINSON, Elizabeth and James Gardner, 19 January 1662, Gloucester, Mass.
VINSON, Hannah and William Ellery, 8 October 1664, Gloucester, Mass.
VINSON, Sarah and Jeffrey Parsons, 11 November 1657, Gloucester, Mass.
VINSON, William and Rachel Cook, 17 October 1660, Gloucester, Mass.
VINTEN, John and Hannah Greene, 16 August 1677, Malden, Mass.
VIRGOOSE, Isaac and Elizabeth Foster, 5 July 1692, Boston, Mass.
VIRGOOSE, Mary and Samuel Veazey, 25 November 1691, Boston, Mass.
VIRGUE, Peter and Sarah Johnson, 21 January 1690, Boston, Mass.
VISSCHER, Nanning and Alida Vinhagen, June 1686, Albany, N. Y.
VITTERELL, Sarah and William Owen, 28 April 1693, Boston, Mass.
VOCARY, Mary and Henry Tomson, 11 September 1693, Boston, Mass.
VODEN, Abigail and Isaac Jarvis, 19 January 1698, Boston, Mass.
VODEN, Philip and Abigail Kemball, 22 December 1692, Boston, Mass.
VORE, Abigail and Timothy Buckland, 27 March 1662, Windsor, Conn.
VORE, Lydia and Nathaniel Cook, 29 June 1649, Windsor, Conn.
VORE, Mary and Elexander Alvord, 29 October 1646, Windsor, Conn.
VOSE, Elizabeth and Thomas Swift, 10 September 1657, Dorchester, Mass.
VOSE, Elizabeth and Henry Cran, Jr., 18 October 1683, Milton, Mass.
VOSE, Elizabeth and John Wadsworth, 28 December 1698, Milton, Mass.
VOSE, Jane and Joseph Haughton, 31 October 1693, Milton, Mass.
VOSE, Nathaniell and Mary Belsher, 16 December 1696, Milton, Mass.
VOSE, Thomas, Jr., and Hannah Badcock, 28 May 1695, Milton, Mass.
VOYSEEN, Francis and Mary Mears, 28 September 1699, Anne Arundel Co., Md.
VRINGE, Sarah and Francis Burns, 26 January 1699, Boston, Mass.
VYLAND, David and Elizth Henry 17 February 1696, New York.

W

WADDELL, John`and Mary Gould, 25 December 1665, Braintree, Mass.

WADE, Benjamin and Ann Looken, April 1670, Long Island, N. Y.

WADE, Elizabeth and Elihu Wardwell, 27 May 1665, Hampton, N. H.

WADE, Jonathan and Dorothy Buckley, 9 December 1660, Ipswich, Mass.

WADE, John and Elizabeth Gerrish, 3 September 1696, Dover, N. H.

WADE, Nathaniel and Merry Bradstreet, 31 October 1672, Andover, Mass.

WADE, Prudence and Anthony Crosby, 28 December 1659, Rowley, Mass.

WADE, Rebecca and John Owen, 3 October 1650, Windsor, Conn.

WADE, Robert and Abigail Royce, 11 March 1691, Norwich, Conn.

WADE, Sarah and Nathaniel Rogers, 13 November 1661, Ipswich, Mass.

WADELL, Mary and Peter Talbut, 12 January 1677, Dorchester, Mass.

WADKINS, Margeret and Richard Hixon, 14 September 1686, Milton, Mass.

WADLE, William and Abigail Belcher, 29 April 1697, Milton, Mass.

WADLEIGH, Mary and John Cram, 1690, Exeter, N. H.

WADSWORTH, Abigail and Thomas Davis, 25 November 1689, Milton, Mass.

WADSWORTH, Abigail and Jacob Tomson, 28 December 1693, Middleborough, Mass.

WADSWORTH, Elisha and Elizabeth Wiswell, 9 December 1694, Duxborough, Mass.

WADSWORTH, Elizabeth and John Terry, 27 November 1662, Windsor, Conn.

WADSWORTH, Hannah and Benjamin Peterson, 9 February 1698, Duxbury, Mass.

WADSWORTH, John and Elizabeth Vose, 28 December 1698, Milton, Mass.

WAINWRIGHT, Sarah and Charles Frost, 7 February 1698-9, Haverhill, Mass.

WAITE, Grace and Richard Price, 6 May 1662, Boston, Mass.

WAITE, Mary and Joseph Bartlett, Sr., 27 October 1668, Newton, Mass.

WAKEFIELD, John and Eliza Walker, 23 November 1693, Boston, Mass.

WAKEFIELD, Elizabeth and Jasper Frost, 20 August 1660, Boston, Mass.

WAKEFIELD, Mary and Eben Dibble, 27 October 1663, Windsor, Conn .

WAKEMAN, Elizabeth and Samuel Kitchell, 11 March 1657, Piscataway, N. J.

WAKER, Andrew and Elizabeth Allen, 8 August 1689, Boston, Mass.

WALBRIDGE, Henry and Anna Amos, 25 December 1688, Preston, Conn.

WALCOM, James and Elizabeth Hopkins, 27 May 1695, Boston, Mass.

WALCOTT, Jonathan and Mary Sibley, 11 December 1664, Salem, Mass.

WALDEN, Ann and John Small, 1638, Plymouth, Mass.

WALDEN, John and Dorcas Rice, 22 July 1680, Wenham, Mass.

WALDO, Debohar and Joseph Ford, 6 December 1683, Bristol, R. I.

WALDO, Jonathan and Hannah Mason, 28 November 1692, Boston, Mass.

WALDRON, John and Mary Horn (widow), 29 August 1698, Dover, N. H.

WALDRON, Judith and Isaac Seloner, 16 December 1679, New York City.

WALDRON, Sarah and Thomas Cocker, 3 May 1697, Boston, Mass.

WALES, Content and John Mason, 15 October 1679, Dorchester, Mass.

WALES, Mary and Nicholas George, 4 June 1684, Dorchester, Mass.

WALES, Nathaneel and Susanah Black, 30 August 1688, Milton, Mass.

WALE, Richard and Hannah Skerry, 21 December 1699, Boston, Mass.
WALKER, Elisha and Benjamine Thurston, 12 December 1660, Boston, Mass.
WALKER, Eliza and John Wakefield, 23 November 1693, Boston, Mass.
WALKER, Elizabeth and Henry Sweet, 31 March 1687, Swansea, Mass.
WALKER, Emanuel and Margaret Matthews, 30 April 1699, Philadelphia, Penn.
WALKER, George and Mary Jackson, 25 December 1689, Dover, N. H.
WALKER, George and Rebecca Davenport, 5 October 1699, Boston, Mass.
WALKER, Hannah and John Seavey, 29 July 1680, Rye, N. Y.
WALKER, Hannah and Andrew Belcher, 13 February 1689, Boston, Mass.
WALKER, Henry and Mary Brown (widow), 26 September 1662, Gloucester, Mass.
WALKER, Israel and Hannah Leffingwell, 10 December 1696, Woburn, Mass.
WALKER, Jane (widow) and John Polly, 2 June 1684, Roxbury, Mass.
WALKER, Jane and Edward Day, April 1681, Somerset Co., Md.
WALKER, John and Mary Pierce, 14 October 1672, Woburn, Mass.
WALKER, Joseph and Margaret Cutler, 27 January 1691, Philadelphia, Penn.
WALKER, Mary and John Wilkinson, 10 August 1690, Middletown, Penn.
WALKER, Mary E. and Ralph King, March 1663, Lynn, Mass.
WALKER, Patience and Francis Drake, Jr., 10 November 1698, Piscataway, N. J.
WALKER, Philip and Jane Metcalf, 1654, Rehoboth, Mass.
WALKER, Philip and Martha Ide, 11 November 1681, Rehoboth, Mass.
WALKER, Samuel and Sarah Reed, 10 September 1662, Woburn, Mass.
WALKER, Samuel and Judith Howard, 1 June 1688, Concord, Mass.
WALKER, Sarah and Nathaniel Warren, November 1645, Plymouth, Mass.
WALKER, Sarah and Jeremiah Holmes, 22 September 1689, Dover, N. H.
WALKER, Sarah and Abraham Perrin, 27 December 1677, Rehoboth, Mass.
WALKER, Sarah and Benjamin Lombard, 19 November 1685, Barnstable, Mass.
WALKER, Solomon and Elizabeth Howell, 29 October 1699, Philadelphia, Penn.
WALKER, Susanna and Matthew Pauling, 15 June 1698, Boston, Mass.
WALKER, Thomas and Susanna Collins, 25 March 1662, Boston, Mass.
WALKER, Thomas and Elizabeth Johnson, 1695, Elizabeth City Co., Va.
WALKER, William and Sarah Snow, 25 January 1654, Eastham, Mass.
WALKER, William and Elizabeth Morgan, 25 August 1689, Philadelphia, Penn.
WALKINGTON, Mary and Roger Baker, 4 September 1693, New York.
WALLACE, James and Enne Wythe, 11 July 1695, Elizabeth City Co., Va.
WALLAR, Elizabeth and John Harris, June 1687, Berkeley, N. Car.
WALLER, Marjorie and Arnold Elzey, October 1682, Somerset Co., Md.
WALLEY, Elizabeth and Edward Adams, 19 May 1692, Bristol, R. I.
WALLEY, Hannah and William Stone, 2 June 1686, Bristol, R. I.
WALLEY, John and Elizabeth Wing, 3 April 1661, Boston, Mass.
WALLEY, Naomy and William Beny, 9 July 1686, Middletown, Penn.
WALLEY, Shadrach and Mary Sharpe, 12 January 1688, Middletown, Penn.
WALLEY, Thomas and Christian Johnson, 22 September 1692, Boston, Mass.
WALLINGSFORD, John and Mary Tuttle, 6 December 1687, Dover, N. H.
WALLIS, Samuel and Sarah Watson, 10 December 1690, Ipswich, Mass.
WALLIS, Sarah and Simon Stacy, 19 April 1659, Ipswich, Mass.
WALLY, Sarah and Charles Channey, 19 October 1699, Boston, Mass.
WALN, Jane and Samuel Allen, Jr., 27 March 1691, Middletown, Penn.
WALNER, Rachel and Henry Jones, 25 December 1686, Philadelphia, Penn.
WALSBEE, David and Ruth Ball, 24 July 1656, Braintree, Mass.

WALSTONE, John and Anna Wright, 26 February 1677, Guilford, Conn.
WALTER, Godwin and Elizabeth Sanghurst, 2 September 1696, Chester Co., Pa.
WALTERS, Elizabeth and John Gardner, 3 April 1684, Philadelphia, Penn.
WALTHALL, Elizabeth and Hugh Ligon, May 1689, Cumberland Co., Va.
WALTON, Daniel and Mary Lamb, 21 June 1688, Byberry, Pa.
WALTON, Elizabeth and Jonathan Townsend, 22 March 1695, Boston, Mass.
WALTON, Nathaniel and Martha Bowling, 1 December 1685, Philadelphia, Penn.
WALTON, Rebecca (widow of William) and Thomas Carroll, Jr., 19 October 1686, Somerset Co., Md.
WALTON, Sarah and Henry Tite, 11 December 1656, Boston, Mass.
WALTON, Thomas and Mary Stilwell, 23 December 1698, New York.
WALTON, Thomas and Priscilla Hun, 28 December 1689, Philadelphia, Penn.
WALTON, William and Sarah Howell, 20 April 1689, Byberry, Pa.
WALTON, William and Mary Sandford, 30 August 1698, New York.
WALTON, William and Bridget Bingham, 3 September 1687, Chesterfield, N. J.
WAMPONY, John (an Indian) and Anne Praske, 21 May 1661, Boston, Mass.
WANTON, Persis and John Bonner, 23 September 1699, Boston, Mass.
WARD, Alce and Nathaniel Dougherty, 14 September 1679, Somerset Co., Md.
WARD, Charity and Jonathan Rose, 5 January 1669, Branford, Conn.
WARD, Esther (widow) and Ebenezer Hawley, 1678, Stratford, Conn.
WARD, Esther and William Cornwall, 22 January 1692, Middletown, Conn.
WARD, Frances and Thomas Sharman, 1 November 1682, Burlington, N. J.
WARD, Israel and Hannah Hutson, 29 October 1697, New York.
WARD, John and Mary Harris, 18 April 1664, Middletown, Conn.
WARD, Lucy and Thomas Merritt, 12 September 1695, Boston, Mass.
WARD, Margaret and James Hildreth, 1 June 1659, Chelmsford, Mass.
WARD, Maria and Jonathan Betts, 4 November 1662, Branford, Conn.
WARD, Martha and George Cleare, 26 November 1648, Dedham, Mass.
WARD, Richard and Mary Gusteen, 22 October 1697, Boston, Mass.
WARD, Samuel and Maria Carter, 1 January 1658, Branford, Conn.
WARD, Samuel and Mary Sale, 10 December 1691, Boston, Mass.
WARD, Sarah and Henry Gould, 30 September 1675, Ipswich, Mass.
WARDELL, Alice and John Gladding, 31 October 1693, Bristol, R. I.
WARDELL, Elther and Robert Bonell, 4 August 1699, Shrewsbury, N. J.
WARDELL, Lydia and William Biddle, 1691, Shrewsbury, N. J.
WARDELL, Margaret and Ephriam Allen, 28 August 1687, Shrewsbury, N. J.
WARDELL, William and Elizabeth Jellet (widow), 5 October 1656, Boston, Mass.
WARDLE, Samuel and Sarah Hawker, 9 January 1672, Andover, Mass.
WARDWELL, Elihu and Elizabeth Wade, 27 May 1665, Hampton, N. H.
WARDWELL, Mercie and John Wright, 31 August 1697, Andover, Mass.
WARE, Ebenezer and Martha Herring, 18 March 1689-90, Dedham, Mass.
WARE, Epherim and Hannah Herring, 13 May 1685, Dedham, Mass.
WARE, Esther and (Rev.) Samuel Man, 13 May 1673, Dedham, Mass.
WARE, Jacob and Elizabeth Osburne, 3 October 1692, New York City.
WARE, John and Mary Metcalfe, 10 December 1668, Dedham, Mass.
WARE, John and Mehitable Chapin, 14 January 1696, Wrenthan, Mass.
WARE, Nathaniel and Mary Wheelock, 12 October 1696, Wrentham, Mass.
WARE, Robert and Margaret Huntings, 24 March 1644-5, Dedham, Mass.
WARE, Robert and Sarah Metcalf, 4 June 1677, Dedham, Mass.

WARE, Samuell and Elizabeth Rice, 21 July 1690, Dedham, Mass.
WAREHAM, Abigail and Thomas Allyn, October 1658, Windsor, Conn.
WARFIELD, John and Hannah Randall, 26 December 1671, Taunton, Mass.
WARFIELD, John and Ruth Gaither, 16 February 1690, South River, Md.
WARHAM, Sara and Return Strong, 11 May 1664, Windsor, Conn.
WARING, Edward and Elizabeth Bouton, 6 October 1698, Norwalk, Conn.
WARING, Thomas and Alice Underwood, 5 October 1673, Richmond Co., Va.
WARM, Deborah and Gerritjt Vanderpool, 11 February 1697, New York.
WARMAL, Mary and Nathaniel Emmons, 15 September 1698, Boston, Mass.
WARNE, Bridgett and Samuell Judson, 2 February 1644, Dedham, Mass.
WARNER, Abigail and John Dane, 27 December 1671, Essex Co., Mass.
WARNER, Ann and James Thomas, 26 February 1695, Philadelphia, Penn.
WARNER, Daniel and Faith Broune, 1 June 1660, Ipswich, Mass.
WARNER, Daniel and Sarah Dane, 23 September 1668, Essex Co., Mass.
WARNER, Elizabeth and Edmond Heard, 26 September 1672, Essex Co., Mass.
WARNER, Ephriam and Esther Richards, 16 August 1692, Waterbury, Conn.
WARNER, Isaac and Ann Craven, 30 October 1692, Philadelphia, Penn.
WARNER, John and Ann Norton, 28 June 1649, Guilford, Conn.
WARNER, John and Sarah Bachelour, 20 April 1665, Essex Co., Mass.
WARNER, John and Sarah Wood, 12 June 1677, Woburn, Mass.
WARNER, John and Anna Gorton, 4 August 1670, Warwick, R. I.
WARNER, John, Jr., and Elizabeth Coggshall, 27 November 1694, Warwick, R. I.
WARNER, Katherine (widow) and John Searle, 26 November 1661, Boston, Mass.
WARNER, Mark and Abigail Montague, 8 December 1671, Hadley, Mass.
WARNER, Mary and John Smith, 17 February 1680, Gloucester Co., Va.
WARNER, Mercy and John Steele, June 1645, Farmington, Conn.
WARNER, Nathaniel and Hannah Boynton, 29 November 1673, Essex Co., Mass.
WARNER, Priscilla and Thomas Cummings, 19 December 1688, Ipswich, Mass.
WARNER, Rachel and Henry Jones, 8 March 1687, Philadelphia, Penn.
WARNER, Rachell and Abell Potter, 16 November 1669, Warwick, R. I.
WARNER, Samuel and Mercy Swan, 20 October 1662, Ipswich, Mass.
WARNER, Samuel and Marah Swallow (widow), 4 May 1685, Dunstable, Mass.
WARNER, Susanna and John Bremer, Jr., January 1674, Ipswich, Mass.
WARNER, William and Hannah Robbins, 1 November 1667, Essex Co., Mass.
WARNER, William and Ellen Jewett, 1 June 1686, Rowley, Mass.
WARREN, Abigail and Richard Lord, 14 January 1672, Hartford, Conn.
WARREN, Amey and John Edwards, 2 March 1693, Boston, Mass.
WARREN, Ebenezer and Mary Ryder, 2 June 1697, Milton, Mass.
WARREN, Jane and Benjamin Lombard, 19 September 1672, Barnstable, Mass.
WARREN, Jane and William Grant, 4 August 1690, Dover, N. H.
WARREN, Jane and Peter Mills, 10 December 1691, Hartford, Conn.
WARREN, John and Deborah Wilson, 21 October 1650, Exeter, Mass.
WARREN, Mary and John Bigelow, 30 October 1642, Watertown, Mass.
WARREN, Mercy and John Bradford, 6 January 1674, Plymouth, Mass.
WARREN, Nathaniel and Sarah Walker, November 1645, Plymouth, Mass.
WARREN, Peter and Sarah Tucker, 1 August 1660, Dorchester, Mass.
WARREN, Samuel and Mehitable Sabin, 2 January 1694-5, Woodstock, Conn.
WARREN, Thomas and Sarah Fitch, 14 December 1694, Boston, Mass.
WARREN, William and Abiel Rogers, 1 November 1690, Boston, Mass.

WASHBOURNE, Sarah and Isaac Arnold, 30 October 1691, New York City.
WASHBURN, James and Mary Bowden, 20 December 1693, Bridgewater, Mass.
WASHBURN, John and Elizabeth Mitchell, 6 December 1645, Plymouth, Mass.
WASHINGTON, John and Mary Townshend, 15 March 1692, Stafford Co., Va.
WASTE, Richard and Mary Samson, 26 October 1693, Duxborough, Mass.
WATERMAN, Elizabeth and (Capt.) John Fitch, 10 July 1695, Windham, Conn.
WATERMAN, Samuel and Mercy Ransom, 26 July 1692, Taunton, Mass.
WATERMAN, Wait and John Roades, 12 February 1684-5, Warwick, R. I.
WATERS, Grace and Obedience Robins, 1634, Accomac Co., Va.
WATERS, Joseph and Martha Mellowes, 13 July 1655, Boston, Mass.
WATERS, Penelopee and James Jarvise, 18 July 1694, Boston, Mass.
WATERUS, Rebekah and Steven Whittlesey, 14 October 1696, Saybrook, Conn.
WATKINS, Bridget and John Davenport, 1 September 1667, Dorchester, Mass.
WATKINS, Anne and Fenwick Adams, 18 August 1687, Salem Co., N. J.
WATKINS, Elizabeth (widow) and Lackeford Brewster, April 1655, Surry Co., Va.
WATKINS, Thomas and Mary Wells, 8 September 1698, Anne Arundel Co., Md.
WATSON, Ann and Thomas Drincall, 17 April 1699, New York.
WATSON, Benjamin and Ann Drue, 15 September 1694, Boston, Mass.
WATSON, Hanna and James Birg, 28 March 1678, Windsor, Conn.
WATSON, Mary and Thomas Leonard, 21 August 1662, Plymouth, Mass.
WATSON, Robard and Mary Rockwell, 10 December 1646, Windsor, Conn.
WATSON, Robert and Susanna Prior, 13 February 1690, Boston, Mass.
WATSON, Sarah and John Merrill, July 1658, Hartford, Conn.
WATSON, Sarah and Samuel Wallis, 10 December 1690, Ipswich, Mass.
WATSON, Sarah (widow) and Samuel Dunham, 15 January 1693-4, Plymouth,
    Mass.
WATTS, Lydia and John Gerrish, 19 April 1692, Boston, Mass.
WATTS, Mercy and Joshua Finney, 31 May 1688, Bristol, R. I.
WATTS, Sarah and Archibald Michael, 25 December 1686, Philadelphia, Penn.
WATTEL, Rose and John Bruce (1st. M.), 31 January 1693, Woburn, Mass.
WAY, Agnes and Samuel Harris, 14 May 1689, New London, Conn.
WAY, Elizabeth and William Osborn, 12 December 1698, New York.
WAY, Martha and Edward Allen, 7 May 1652, Boston, Mass.
WAY, Richard and Hannah Knight, 13 August 1689, Boston, Mass.
WAYE, Alice and George Chappell, 3 October 1676, New London, Conn.
WAYES, Ann and William Hudson, 12 August 1686, Philadelphia, Penn.
WAYTE, Hannah and William Buckman, 11 October 1676, Malden, Mass.
WAYTE, Joseph and Mercy Tuft, 24 October 1688, Malden, Mass.
WAYTE, John and Sarah Muzzy, 12 June 1674, Malden, Mass.
WAYTE, John and Sarah Parker, 4 August 1675, Malden, Mass.
WAYTE, Joseph and Hannah Oakes, 7 August 1672, Malden, Mass.
WEAR, Daniel and Lydia Hillier, 31 October 1698, Boston, Mass.
WEAR, Peter and Eliza Wilson, 6 January 1692, Dover, N. H.
WEARE, Hester and Benjamin Swett, 1 November 1647, Newbury, Mass.
WEARE, John and Joana Whiteing, 24 January 1678-9, Dedham, Mass.
WEARE, Robert and Hannah Jones, 3 March 1676, Dedham, Mass.
WEAVER, Clement and Mary Weeborn, 1657, Newport, R. I.
WEAVER, Martha and Robert Dummer, 22 June 1699, Burlington, N. J.
WEAVER, William and Elizabeth Harris, 27 December 1693, East Greenwich,
    R. I.

WEBB, Benjamin and Mercy Buckman, 7 December 1669, Malden, Mass.
WEBB, Benjamin and Susana Ballintine, 21 November 1692, Boston, Mass.
WEBB, Christopher and Hanna Scott, 18 November 1654, Braintree, Mass.
WEBB, Elizabeth and Thomas Greene, 19 August 1667, Malden, Mass.
WEBB, Elizabeth and John Hurd, 16 March 1691, Boston, Mass.
WEBB, Elisha and Lydia Scottow, 18 November 1697, Boston, Mass.
WEBB, Isaac and Mary Bedwell, 16 April 1678, Richmond Co., Va.
WEBB, John and Mary Sanford, 14 July 1673, Richmond Co., Va.
WEBB, John and Bethia Adams, May 1680, Braintree, Mass.
WEBB, Joseph and Deborah Bass, 29 November 1699, Boston, Mass.
WEBB, Margaret (dau. of Henry) and Jacob Sheafe, 1643, Boston, Mass.
WEBB, Samuel and Marah Adams, 16 December 1686, Braintree, Mass.
WEBB, Sarah and Zachariah Buckmaster, 7 January 1655, Boston, Mass.
WEBB, Sarah and John Withered, 3 October 1695, Anne Arundel Co., Md.
WEBB, Sarah and John Marshall, 26 May 1699, Boston, Mass.
WEBBER, Benedict and Sarah Rice, 14 May 1694, Boston, Msas.
WEBBER, William and Mary Sumer, 19 September 1699, Boston, Mass.
WEBSTER, Abigail and James Marden, 23 October 1695, New Castle, Maine.
WEBSTER, Eliza and David Stevens, 29 January 1690, Boston, Mass.
WEBSTER, Elizabeth and John Worth, 17 March 1686, Newbury, Mass.
WEBSTER, Elizabeth and John Seymour, 19 December 1693, Hartford, Conn.
WEBSTER, Esther and Richard Henchman, 24 December 1697, Boston, Mass.
WEBSTER, James and Mary Hay, 14 February 1658, Boston, Mass.
WEBSTER, Jonathan and Dorcas Hopkins, 11 May 1681, Hartford, Conn.
WEBSTER, Mary and John Emery, 2 October 1648, Newbury, Mass.
WEBSTER, Peter and Mary Gilkinson, 30 November 1695, Middletown, Penn.
WEBSTER, Sarah and Joseph Mygant, 15 November 1677, Hartford, Conn.
WEBSTER, Sarah and William Lane, 21 June 1680, Boston, Mass.
WEBSTER, Thomas and Sarah Bremer, 29 November 1657, Hampton, N. H.
WEBSTER, Thomas and Abigail Alexander, 16 June 1663, Northampton, Mass.
WEBSTER, William and Mary Mosely, 25 November 1696, Boston, Mass.
WEEBORN, Mary and Clement Weaver, 1657, Newport, R. I.
WEED, Hannah and Benjamin Hoyt, 5 January 1670, Stamford, Conn.
WEEK, Joshua and Comfort Hubberd, 7 November 1699, Boston, Mass.
WEEKS, Ebenezer and Deliverance Sumner, 8 May 1689, Milton, Mass.
WEEKS, Elizabeth and John Robinson, 1 May 1667, Falmouth, Mass.
WEEKS, Elizabeth and Terrence Henley, 2 April 1694, Boston, Mass.
WEEKS, Joseph and Mary Atherton, 9 February 1667, Dorchester, Mass.
WEEKS, Joshua and Comfort Hubbard, 7 November 1699, Greenland, N. H.
WEEKS, Mary and Thomas Greene, 22 March 1676, Malden, Mass.
WEEKS, Samuel and Eleanor Haines, 23 August 1695, Greenland, N. H.
WEEKS, Submit and Robert Cook, 26 October 1693, Boston, Mass.
WEEKS, Zachariah and Katherine Meyer, 8 August 1696, New York.
WEEKES, Amiel and Abigail Trescott, 2 March 1682, Dorchester, Mass.
WEEKES, Elizabeth and Timothy Mather, 20 March 1678, Dorchester, Mass.
WEEKES, Jane and John Blackeman, 26 March 1685, Dorchester, Mass.
WEEKES, John and Sarah Hamon, 4 November 1674, Dorchester, Mass.
WEELER, William and Ann Phippen, 16 May 1686, Boston, Mass.
WELCH, Mary and James Dudley, 1679, Gloucester Co., Va.

WELCH, Philip and Hannah Haggert, 20 February 1666, Wenham, Mass.
WELCOME, Mary and Peter Townsend, 15 November 1694, Boston, Mass.
WELD, Daniel and Ann Hide, 30 May 1647, Braintree, Mass.
WELD, John and Margaret Bowen, 24 December 1647, Roxbury, Mass.
WELD, Joseph and Elizabeth Devotion, 2 September 1674, Roxbury, Mass.
WELDE, Joseph and Barbara Clapp, 20 October 1639, Sudbury, Mass.
WELLER, Joshua and Asubaty Lamson, May 1670, Windsor, Conn.
WELLER, Richard and Ann Wilson, 17 September 1640, Windsor, Conn.
WELLES, Ann and Thomas Thompson, 14 April 1648, Farmington, Conn.
WELLES, Ann and Anthony Hawkins, 16 July 1656, Farmington, Conn.
WELLES, John and Mary Allison, 6 May 1667, Hatfield, Mass.
WELLES, John and Elizabeth Bourne, 1647, Stratford, Conn.
WELLES, Joshua and Hanna Buckland, 14 August 1681, Windsor, Conn.
WELLS, Abigail and Nathaniel Treadwell, 19 June 1661, Ipswich, Mass.
WELLS, Ancoretta and Robert Thomas, 1679, Warwick Co., Va.
WELLS, Elizabeth and John Wheeler, 25 June 1684, Marlboro, Mass.
WELLS, Jane and John Hancock, 8 December 1698, New York.
WELLS, John and Eliza Bickford, 31 October 1698, Boston, Mass.
WELLS, John and Mary Peck, 18 February 1697, Boston, Mass.
WELLS, Joshua and Sarah Savage, 25 December 1699, Boston, Mass.
WELLS, Mary and Thomas Watkins, 8 September 1698, Anne Arundel Co., Md.
WELLS, Robert and Mary Stoddard, 13 October 1698, Boston, Mass.
WELLS, Sarah and Joseph Clark, 11 December 1693, Boston, Mass.
WELLS, Stephen and Alice Howard, 3 December 1677, Richmond Co., Va.
WELLS, Thomas and Naomi Marshall, 1655, Boston, Mass.
WELSH, Sarah and John Giles, 1 October 1695, Anne Arundel Co., Md.
WENTWORTH, Samuel and Eliza Hopson, 12 November 1691, Boston, Mass.
WENTWORTH, Samuel and Abigail Goffe, 28 October 1699, Boston, Mass.
WEST, Ann and Robert Wharton, 25 January 1694, New York.
WEST, Francis and Margaret Reeves, 27 February 1639, Duxbury, Mass.
WEST, Francis and Sarah Harry, 10 November 1696, Anne Arundel Co., Md.
WEST, Joan and Joshua Coggshall, 22 December 1652, Shrewsbury, N. J.
WEST, John and Judah Armistead, 15 October 1695, Elizabeth City Co., Va.
WEST, Robert and Sarah Spinks, 10 November 1695, Harford Co., Md.
WEST, William and Mary Bingham, 17 November 1697, New York.
WESTCOAT, Stuckly and Prosilah Bennit, 21 December 1693, Warwick, R. I.
WESTCOTE, Rebecca and Benjamin Brown, 16 August 1695, Bristol, R. I.
WESTCOTT, Abigail and Moses Knapp, 1669, Stamford, Conn.
WESTCOTT, Amos and Sarah Stafford, 13 July 1667, Warwick, R. I.
WESTCOTT, Amos and Deborah Staford, 9 January 1670, Warwick, R. I.
WESTCOTT, Jeremy and Ellen England, 27 February 1665, Warwick, R. I.
WESTKOT, Katherin (widow of Robert) and John Hazleton, 10 April 1678, War-
    wick, R. I.
WESTOE, Susanna and Robert Higgins, 2 September 1654, Boston, Mass.
WESTON, Abigail and Jonathan Barrett, 26 June 1696, Woburn, Mass.
WESTOVER, Hannah and Josiah Alford, 22 May 1693, Simsbury, Conn.
WESTBROKE, Sara and John Woodcock, 5 September 1682, Dedham, Mass.
WESTWOOD, Sarah and Aaron Cooke, Jr., 20 May 1661, Hadley, Mass.
WETHERILL, Christopher and Mary Fothergill, 8 April 1687, Burlington Co.,
    N. J.

WETHERILL, Christopher and Elizabeth Pope, 10 November 1690, Burlington Co., N. J.

WHALY, Sarah and William Marlton, 1 January 1696, Boston, Mass.

WHARFE, Rebecca and Francis Holmes, 15 February 1693, Boston, Mass.

WHARTON, John and Sarah Ballentine, 14 October 1698, Boston, Mass.

WHARTON, Robert and Ann West, 25 January 1694, New York.

WHARTON, Sarah and John Cotta, 4 May 1698, Boston, Mass.

WHEATLY, Caleb and Sarah Scholey, 5 September 1696, Chesterfield, N. J.

WHEATLEY, Leah and Robert Permetter, 13 February 1648, Braintree, Mass.

WHEDON, Jane and Thomas Edgerly, 3 December 1691, Oyster River, N. H.

WHEELER, Abigail and Samuel Hills, 20 May 1679, Newbury, Mass.

WHEELER, Abigail and Ebenezer Barker, 25 May 1686, Andover, Mass.

WHEELER, David and Sarah Wise, 11 May 1650, Newbury, Mass.

WHEELER, Elizabeth and Francis Fletcher, 11 October 1656, Concord, Mass.

WHEELER, Elizabeth and William Green, 13 July 1659, Malden, Mass.

WHEELER, Elizabeth and Jonathan Rice, 12 February 1691, Sudbury, Mass.

WHEELER, Esther and Samuel Prescott, 5 May 1698, Acton, Mass.

WHEELER, James and Elizabeth Meek, 13 January 1696, New York.

WHEELER, John and Elizabeth Wells, 25 June 1684, Marlboro, Mass.

WHEELER, Joseph and Jane Hodges, 1 July 1695, Boston, Mass.

WHEELER, Joseph and Elizabeth Pell, 14 December 1697, Boston, Mass.

WHEELER, Lydia and Daniel Ennes, 25 April 1683, Andover, Mass.

WHEELER, Mary and Eliphalet Fox, 26 October 1665, Concord, Mass.

WHEELER, Mary and Samuel Greene, 4 May 1694, Malden, Mass.

WHEELER, Nathaniel and Mary Bridges, 9 November 1697, Boston, Mass.

WHEELER, Obadiah and Elizabeth White, 17 July 1672, Concord, Mass.

WHEELER, Rebecca and John Pierce, 10 June 1654, Boston, Mass.

WHEELER, Rebecca and John Curtis, 26 December 1661, Boston, Mass.

WHEELER, Richard and Elizabeth Turner, 4 March 1644, Dedham, Mass.

WHEELER, Richard and Sarah Prescott, 2 August 1658, Lancaster, Mass.

WHEELER, Roger and Mary Stone (widow), 23 November 1659, Boston, Mass.

WHEELER, Ruth and Ephriam Jones, 7 May 1673, Concord, Mass.

WHEELER, Samuel and Mary Perry, 10 November 1673, Stratford, Conn.

WHEELER, Sarah and John Greene, 18 October 1660, Malden, Mass.

WHEELER, Sarah and Francis Dudley, 26 October 1665, Concord, Mass.

WHEELER, Sarah and Joseph Rice, 22 December 1677, Dedham, Mass.

WHEELER, Thankful and Jonas Prescott, 15 October 1699, Concord, Mass.

WHEELER, Thomas and Sarah Beers Stearns (widow), 23 July 1677, Concord, Mass.

WHEELER, Timothy and Lydia Wheeler, 19 May 1692, Concord, N. H.

WHEELER, William and Hannah Buss, 30 October 1659, Concord, Mass.

WHEELEWRIGHT, Mary and Edward Loyd, 4 December 1660, Boston, Mass.

WHEELEWRIGHT, Rebecca and Samuell Mavericke, December 1660, Boston, Mass.

WHEELOCK, Mary and Nathaniel Ware, 12 October 1696, Wrentham, Mass.

WHETMORE, Elizabeth and Josiah Atkins, 8 October 1673, Middletown, Conn.

WHETSTONE, Hannah (widow) and Benjamin Lombard, 24 May 1694, Barnstable, Mass.

WHIDDEN, Michael and Elizabeth Meservey, 6 June 1694, Dover, N. H.

WHIPPLE, David and Hannah Tower, 11 November 1677, Hingham, Mass.
WHIPPLE, David and Sarah Hernden, 15 May 1675, Hingham, Mass.
WHIPPLE, John and Elizabeth Woodman, 5 May 1659, Ipswich, Mass.
WHIPPLE, John and Mary Stevens, 21 July 1663, Charlestown, Mass.
WHIPPLE, Mathew and Mary Bartholomew, 24 December 1657, Gloucester, Mass.
WHIT, Elizabeth and Samuell Thorp, 15 February 1699, Dedham, Mass.
WHITE, Abigail and Peter Thorp, 29 October 1695, Dedham, Mass.
WHITE, Andrew and Sarah Sanderson, 4 February 1698, Woburn, Mass.
WHITE, Anna and John Baxter, 24 September 1659, Braintree, Mass.
WHITE, Daniel and Susannah Mould, March 1683, New London, Conn.
WHITE, Ebenezer and Hannah Phillips, 1671, Weymouth, Mass.
WHITE, Elizabeth and Henry Kerley, 2 November 1654, Sudbury, Mass.
WHITE, Elizabeth and Thomas Pincin, 1662, Scituate, Mass.
WHITE, Elizabeth and Obadiah Wheeler, 17 July 1672, Concord, Mass.
WHITE, Elizabeth and William Avery, 29 June 1682, Dedham, Mass.
WHITE, Jacob and Deborah Shepard, 4 February 1692, Hartford, Conn.
WHITE, James and Sarah Baker, 22 December 1664, Dorchester, Mass.
WHITE, James and Mary Kitchen, 28 August 1698, Philadelphia, Penn.
WHITE, James and Elizabeth Withenton, 13 February 1695-6, Dorchester, Mass.
WHITE, Jane and Thomas Garwood, Jr., 28 July 1693, Shrewsbury, N. J.
WHITE, John and Cornelia Vander Burgh, 29 September 1699, New York.
WHITE, John and Mary Swift, 11 November 1663, Dorchester, Mass.
WHITE, Joseph and Lydia Rogers, 19 September 1660, Mendon, Mass.
WHITE, Joseph, Jr., and Oseeth Turner, 16 September 1696, Scituate, Mass.
WHITE, Martha and Samuel Workman, 3 August 1693, Boston, Mass.
WHITE, Mary and Samuel Hooper, 16 February 1693, Boston, Mass.
WHITE, Mary and John French, 21 October 1694, New York.
WHITE, Mary and Richard Lippincott, 12 October 1695, Shrewsbury, N. J.
WHITE, Mary and Solomon Clark, 24 October 1698, Dedham, Mass.
WHITE, Paul and Ann Jones, 14 March 1665, Newbury, Mass.
WHITE, Phillippe and John Carter, 6 November 1699, Boston, Mass.
WHITE, Resolved and Judith Vassall, 5 November 1640, Scituate, Mass.
WHITE, Richard and Elizabeth Rust, 4 January 1699, Boston, Mass.
WHITE, Samuel and Anna Bingley, 6 December 1687, Milton, Mass.
WHITE, Sarah and Thomas Young, January 1689, Scituate, Mass.
WHITE, Sarah and William Adkinson, 31 August 1698, Boston, Mass.
WHITE, Sarah and John Bailey, 25 January 1672, Scituate, Mass.
WHITE, Stephen and Sarah Harris, 25 September 1695, Boston, Mass.
WHITE, Thankful and James Humphryes, 4 November 1697, Boston, Mass.
WHITE, Thomas and Mehitabel Thornton, December 1687, Boston, Mass
WHITE, William and Ann Baker (widow), 12 August 1699, Harford Co., Md.
WHITE, William and Phillip Wood, 4 June 1653, Boston, Mass.
WHITEACHE, Sarah and William Young, 11 October 1694, Boston, Mass.
WHITAKER, Jonathan and Sarah Toothaker, 15 November 1694, Boston, Mass.
WHITAKER, Mary and Abraham Taylor, 16 December 1681, Concord, Mass.
WHITEHART, John and Martha Ladd, 6 June 1695, Boston, Mass.
WHITEHEAD, Esther and John Beasor, 21 December 1694, Philadelphia, Penn.
WHITEHEAD, Hannah and Peter Tyiler, Sr., 21 December 1688, Branford, Conn.
WHITEHEAD, John and Martha Bradfield, 9 March 1661, Branford, Conn.

WHITEHEAD, Jonathan and Sarah Ffield, 23 July 1696, New York.
WHITEHEAD, Mary and William Luddington, June 1690, Branford, Conn.
WHITEHEAD, Susan and Nathaniel Bunnell, 8 June 1665, New Haven, Conn.
WHITEMORE, John and Ruth Bassett, 22 December 1692, Bridgewater, Mass.
WHITFIELD, Abigail and John Fitch, 1 October 1648, Saybrook, Conn.
WHITHAM, Henry and Sarah Somes, 15 June 1665, Gloucester, Mass.
WHITIMORE, Elizabeth and Benhemoth Humphris, 11 March 1699, Dedham, Mass.
WHITING, Joana and John Weare, 24 January 1678-9, Dedham, Mass.
WHITING, Joana and John Blake, 6 February 1689, Wrentham, Mass.
WHITING, John and Mary Billing, 25 December 1688, Milton, Mass.
WHITING, Jonathan and Rachael Thorp, 3 December 1689, Dedham, Mass.
WHITING, Mary and John Fairbanks, 1 January 1672, Dedham, Mass.
WHITING, Nathaniell and Hanah Dwight, 4 September 1643, Dedham, Mass.
WHITING, Nathaniel and Johanna Gay, 29 March 1664, Dedham, Mass.
WHITING, Samuel and Sarah Metcalf, 23 September 1676, Dedham, Mass.
WHITLOCK, Rose and Abraham Parker, 18 November 1644, Woburn, Mass.
WHITMARSH, Ezra and Bathsheba Richards, 20 January 1693, Boston, Mass.
WHITMORE, Abigail and Samuel Wilcox, 9 May 1683, Middletown, Conn.
WHITMORE, Ann and George Farrar, 16 November 1643, Ipswich, Mass.
WHITMORE, Francis and Ann Peirce, 7 December 1699, Boston, Mass.
WHITMORE, Mary and John Brewer, 23 August 1647, Ipswich, Mass.
WHITNEY, Benjamin and Mary Poor, 11 April 1695, York, Maine.
WHITNEY, John and Judith Clement, 29 September 1659, Watertown, Mass.
WHITNEY, Joshua and Abigail Tarbell, 30 September 1672, Groton, Mass.
WHITNEY, Moses and Sarah Knight, 30 September 1686, Stow, Mass.
WHITNEY, Richard and Martha Coldam, 19 March 1650, Watertown, Mass.
WHITPAIN, Jachary and Sarah Songhurst, 26 September 1686, Philadelphia, Penn.
WHITAKER, Samuel and Mary Squier, 5 May 1697, Rehoboth, Mass.
WHITTEMORE, Elizabeth and Jacob Winslow, 26 May 1690, Malden, Mass.
WHITTEMORE, Hannah and John Nicholls, 18 November 1686, Malden, Mass.
WHITTEMORE, Hannah (widow) and Benjamin Butterfield, 6 June 1663, Chelmsford, Mass.
WHITTEN, Grace and Nathan Cripps, 9 January 1694, Burlington, N. J.
WHITTIER, Hannah and Edward Young, 30 May 1683, Haverhill, Mass.
WHITTLESEY, John and Ruth Dudley, 20 June 1664, Saybrook, Conn.
WHITTLESEY, Steven and Rebekah Waterus, 14 October 1696, Saybrook, Conn.
WHITTREDGE, Sylvester and Mary Buckley, 17 November 1684, Essex Co., Mass.
WYPPOL, Dorothy and Malichy Roades, 8 March 1699, Warwick, R. I.
WHYPPOLL, Elnathan and John Rice, 25 July 1695, Warwick, R. I.
WHYPPOLL, Mary and James Carder, 6 January 1686-7, Warwick, R. I.
WIAT, John and Hannah Garret, 7 February 1694, Boston, Mass.
WIBORN, James and Mary Graford, 11 January 1699, Boston, Mass.
WIBORN, John and Esther Ripple, 10 May 1694, Boston, Mass.
WIBORNE, Thomas and Abigail Eliot, 16 October 1657, Boston, Mass.
WICKEN, John and Kathrine Fredricksen, 28 April 1693, New York.
WICKES, John and Sarah Groton, 15 December 1698, Warwick, R. I.

WICKES, Joseph and Marie Hartwell, 7 May 1656, Kent Co., Md.
WICKES, Mary and Francis Gilbourne, 9 June 1671, Warwick, R. I.
WICKHAM, Samuel and Barbara Holden, 4 June 1691, Warwick, R. I.
WICKS, Richard and Mercy Lee, 2 December 1686, Malden, Mass.
WIET, Nathaniel and Mary Corbin, 13 December 1688, Milton, Mass.
WIGGIN, Andrew and Hannah Bradstreet, 3 June 1659, Andover, Mass.
WIGGIN, Andrew and Abigail Follett, 2 September 1697, Dover, N. H.
WIGGLESWORTH, Michael and Lydia Avery, 23 June 1691, Braintree, Mass.
WIGHT, Abiel and Samuel Manning, 6 May 1673, Billerica, Mass.
WIGHT, An and Isaac Bullard, 11 February 1655, Dedham, Mass.
WIGHT, Daniel and Annah Dueing, 17 December 1686, Dedham, Mass.
WIGHT, Jonathan and Elizabeth Fisher, 19 April 1687, Suffolk Co., Mass.
WIGHT, Jonathan and Elizabeth Hawes, 19 August 1687, Wrentham, Mass.
WIGHT, Joseph and Mary Stearnes, 22 February 1685, Dedham, Mass.
WIGHT, Joshua and Abigaell Rockwood, 30 November 1696, Dedham, Mass.
WIGHT, Joshua and Elizabeth Spowel, 4 October 1699, Boston, Mass.
WIGHT, Mary and Thomas Elice, 21 May 1657, Medfield, Mass.
WIGHT, Lydia and Samuel Cook, 27 April 1681, Medfield, Mass.
WIGHT, Lydia and Nathaniel Partridge, 24 November 1686, Medfield, Mass.
WIGHT, Lucie (widow) and John Samuell, 24 October 1652, Boston, Mass.
WILBORNE, Elizabeth (widow) and Henry Bishop, 20 December 1656, Boston, Mass.
WILCOCK, Mary (widow) and Jacob Elliott, 9 November 1654, Boston, Mass.
WILCOCKSON, Elizabeth and Henry Stiles, 16 April 1663, Windsor, Conn.
WILCOT, Eliza and Philip Villarock, 3 May 1694, Boston, Mass.
WILCOT, Josiah and Mary Freek, 1 May 1694, Boston, Mass.
WILCOX, Daniel and Elizabeth Cook, 28 November 1661, Portsmouth, R. I.
WILCOX, Samuel and Abigail Whitmore, 9 May 1683, Middletown, Conn.
WILCOXEN, John and Elizabeth Bourne, March 1663, Stratford, Conn.
WILDE, Edey and John Yeates, 5 July 1699, New York.
WILDE, John and Sarah Hayden, 1 June 1689, Braintree, Mass.
WILDS, Priscilla and Henry Lake, 9 March 1681, Topsfield, Mass.
WILDER, Thomas and Anna Eames, April 1640, Charlestown, Mass.
WILFORD, Mary and John Corliss, 17 December 1684, Haverhill, Mass.
WILKINS, Helena and Benjamin Cooper, 7 April 1694, New York.
WILKINS, John and Elizabeth How, 27 April 1697, Boston, Mass.
WILKINS, William and Ann Stilwell (widow), 29 December 1672, Gravesend, L. I., N. Y.
WILKINSEN, Philip and Mary Brazier, 16 September 1697, New York.
WILKINSON, John and Mary Walker, 10 August 1690, Middletown, Penn.
WILKINSON, Susanna and Samuel Howard, March 1671, Malden, Mass.
WILKINSON, Philip and Helena Tiller, 11 October 1694, New York.
WILL, Martha and John Moon, 23 May 1686, Philadelphia, Penn.
WILLAKE, Edward and Margery Cergoe, 28 April 1692, New York City.
WILLIAMS, Greetjie and Francois DuPuis, 26 December 1661, Brooklyn, N. Y.
WILLAMS, Janette and Huybert Clomp, 25 June 1662, Brooklyn, N. Y.
WILLARD, Abigail and Benjamen Easterbrook, 29 November 1694, Boston, Mass.
WILLARD, Daniel and Mary Mills, 19 June 1691, Milton, Mass.
WILLARD, Deborah and Paul Sears, 1658, Yarmouth, Mass.

WILLARD, Hannah and Janna Meigs, 18 May 1696, Wethersfield, Conn.
WILLARD, Henry and Mary Lakin, 18 July 1674, Groton, Mass.
WILLARD, Henry and Abigail Temple, 21 July 1698, Concord, Mass.
WILLARD, Mary and Cyprian Stevens, 1671, Lancaster, Mass.
WILLARD, Mercy and Joseph Belden, 1693, Wethersfield, Conn.
WILLARD, Samuel and Sarah Clark, 6 June 1683, Saybrook, Conn.
WILLBORNE, Michael and Mary Beamsley, 17 August 1656, Boston, Mass.
WILLCOX, Hannah and John Rhoads, 28 August 1692, Philadelphia, Penn.
WILLCOX, Joseph and Ann Powell, 25 January 1687, Philadelphia, Penn.
WILLEMKE, Ann and George Harwood, 19 August 1695, New York.
WILLES, Joshua and Azubwh Lamson, 5 May 1670, Windsor, Conn.
WILLES, Joshua and Hannah Buckland, 14 August 1681, Windsor, Conn.
WILLES, Joshua and Abigail Rix (widow), 1696, Wethersfield, Conn.
WILLES, Joshua and Elizabeth Grant (widow), 12 May 1697, Tolland, Conn.
WILLET, Sarah and Jacobus Dekey, 9 May 1694, New York.
WILLETT, Hezekiah and Anna Brown, 7 January 1675, Rehoboth, Mass.
WILLETT, Mary and Richard Willett, 22 December 1697, New York.
WILLET, Richard and Mary Willett, 22 December 1697, New York.
WILLETT, Sarah (widow) and Charles Bridges, 2 November 1647, New York City.
WILLETT, Thomas and Sara Cornell, 1 September 1643, New York City.
WILLETT, Thomas and Sarah Hinchman, 24 August 1695, Jamaica, N. Y.
WILLEY, Alice and John Garretson, 5 December 1659, Boston, Mass.
WILLEY, Frances and Joseph Howe, 16 May 1652, Boston, Mass.
WILLEY, Frances and Clement Minor, 1662, New London, Conn.
WILLEY, Isaac and Rose Bennet, 14 December 1697, New Lyme, Conn.
WILLEY, John and Miriam Moore, 18 March 1668, New London, Conn.
WILLIAMS, Bethyah and Ebenezer Rice, 17 May 1698, Dorchester, Mass.
WILLIAMS, Catherine and William Brown, 26 March 1699, Philadelphia, Penn.
WILLIAMS, Ebenezer and Martha Hall, 18 September 1674, Dorchester, Mass.
WILLIAMS, Ebenezer and Sarah Beaman, 28 December 1680, Dorchester, Mass.
WILLIAMS, Eleanor and Nicholas de Morris, 20 January 1686-7, New York.
WILLIAMS, Eliza and Joseph Cowell, 6 August 1676, Boston, Mass.
WILLIAMS, George and Kathrine Lloyd, 30 December 1697, New York.
WILLIAMS, Hanna and Nathaniel Bancroft, 26 December 1677, Windsor, Conn.
WILLIAMS, Hannah and John Morss, 10 May 1697, Woodstock, Conn.
WILLIAMS, James and Sarah Salsbury, 7 August 1694, Boston, Mass.
WILLIAMS, Joanna and James Jones, 2 April 1697, Boston, Mass.
WILLIAMS, John and Sarah May, 14 February 1679, Roxbury, Mass.
WILLIAMS, John, Jr., and Sarah Trask, 15 February 1695, Salem, Mass.
WILLIAMS, Jonathan and Mary Hunlock, 12 July 1697, Boston, Mass.
WILLIAMS, Joseph and Sarah Layton, 9 December 1698, Boston, Mass.
WILLIAMS, Mehitable and Increase Robinson, 11 February 1695, Taunton, Mass.
WILLIAMS, Nathaniel and Elizabeth Rogers, 17 November 1668, Duxbury, Mass.
WILLIAMS, Rachel and Samuel Lowel, 22 July 1698, Boston, Mass.
WILLIAMS, Rachel and Thomas Puddington, 20 September 1689, Dover, N. H.
WILLIAMS, Rebecca and Samuel Ingham, 3 November 1686, Saybrook, Conn.
WILLIAMS, Samuel and Theoda Holgrave, 2 March 1653, Roxbury, Mass.
WILLIAMS, William and Johanna Linn, 19 July 1660, Boston, Mass.

WILLING, Mary and William Cannon, 18 February 1695, Harford Co., Md.
WILLIS, Experience and Elizabeth Bolton, 25 October 1676, Dorchester, Mass.
WILLIS, John and Hannah Elsse, 11 November 1654, Boston, Mass.
WILLIS, Lawrence and Mary Makepeace, 5 July 1656, Boston, Mass.
WILLIS, Mary and William Peacock, 12 April 1653, Roxbury, Mass.
WILLIS, Roger and Ruth Hill, 19 May 1664, Dorchester, Mass.
WILLIS, Stephen and Hannah Elliott, 3 June 1670, Braintree, Mass.
WILLISTON, John and Abrgal Salsbury, 9 June 1676, Milton, Mass.
WILLISTON, Joseph and Mary Ashley (widow), 2 March 1699, Springfield, Mass.
WILLWISSION, William and Else Smith, 15 November 1697, New York.
WILLS, Ann and James Fox, Jr., 31 January 1699, Philadelphia, Penn.
WILLS, Daniel, Jr., and Mary Shinn, 12 November 1695, Burlington, N. J.
WILLS, Samuel and Mary Love (widow of Thomas), 28 November 1688, Salmon Falls, Maine.
WILLY, Isaac and Francis Burcham, 8 June 1660, Boston, Mass.
WILLMARTH, Mary and Joseph Rockett, 5 January 1681, Behoboth, Mass.
WILMARTH, Thomas and Mary Robinson, 7 June 1674, Rehoboth, Mass.
WILMOT, Mary and Miles Oakley, 1669 Great Neck, L. I., N. Y.
WILSFORD, John and Rebekah Baker, 4 February 1695, Chesterfield, N. J.
WILSON, Abigail and Joseph Hildreth, 25 February 1683, Chelmsford Mass.
WILSON, Ann and Richard Weller, 17 September 1640, Windsor, Conn.
WILSON, Anna and Thomas Peart, 2 February 1688, Philadelphia, Penn.
WILSON, Deborah and John Warren, 21 October 1650, Exeter, Mass.
WILSON, Ebenezer and Marjary Dudley, 17 September 1687, New York.
WILSON, Eliza and Peter Wear, 6 January 1692, Dover, N. H.
WILSON, Elizabeth and John Rice, 4 October 1684, Dedham, Mass.
WILSON, Epherim and Rebecca Sumner, 10 March 1681, Dedham, Mass.
WILSON, Henry and Mary Metcalf, 24 September 1642, Dedham, Mass.
WILSON, Jacob and Susan Ross, 20 May 1696, Malden, Mass.
WILSON, Jane and Francis Jordon, 6 September 1635, Ipswich, Mass.
WILSON, Jane and John Furs, 21 September 1698, Boston, Mass.
WILSON, Joseph and Mary Lovejoy, 4 July 1670, Andover, Mass.
WILSON, Joseph and Sarah Lord, 24 April 1678, Andover, Mass.
WILSON, Katherine and Richard Barnerd, 3 April 1690, Boston, Mass.
WILSON, Mary and Samuel Marshall, 6 May 1652, Windsor, Conn.
WILSON, Richard and Sarah Hurst, 7 February 1654, Boston, Mass.
WILSON, Rihard and Kathrine Pugsley, 27 April 1698, New York.
WILSON, Samuel and Mary Griffen, 1 May 1672, Windsor, Conn.
WILSON, Sarah and Anthony Hanoke, 17 April 1678, Dorchester, Mass.
WILSON, Sarah and Cornelius Empson, 1 April 1693, Chesterfield, N. J.
WILSON, Seaborn and David Fiske, Jr., 6 September 1655, Ipswich, Mass.
WILSON, Stephen and Sarah Baker, 13 August 1692, Middletown, Penn.
WILSON, Thomas and Anna Silver, 6 July 1693, Burlington, N. J.
WILSON, William and Jane Davis, 16 September 1698, Elizabeth City Co., Va.
WILTON, Niholas and Mary Staumford, 20 November 1656, Windsor, Conn.
WINANS, John and Susannah Melyn, 1664, New Haven, Conn.
WINBOURNE, John and Elizabeth Hart, 11 April 1667, Malden, Mass.
WINCHELL, David and Elizabeth Filly, 17 November 1669, Windsor, Conn.

WINCHELL, Jonathan and Abigail Brunson, 16 May 1666, Windsor, Conn.
WINCHELL, Nathaniel and Sarah Porter, 8 April 1664, Windsor, Conn.
WINCHESTER, Elizabeth (widow) and John Card, 16 January 1683, York, Maine.
WINCHESTER, Josiah and Mary Lyon, 10 December 1678, Dorchester, Mass.
WINCHESTER, Lydia and Nehemiah Smith, 24 October 1669, Roxbury, Mass.
WINCHESTER, Mary and John Aldis, 23 May 1682, Wrentham, Mass.
WINCHESTER, Mary and Thomas Card, 26 July 1694, York, Maine.
WINDEBANK, Elizabeth and James Graham, 18 July 1684, Staten Island, N. Y.
WINDOW, Richard and Bridget Trains, 30 March 1659, Gloucester, Mass.
WINFIELD, Richard and Magdalen Becker, 12 January 1696, Albany, N. Y.
WINFREY, Jacob and Elizabeth Alford, 1698, New Kent Co., Va.
WING, Eliza and James Dowell, 27 April 1693, Boston, Mass.
WING, Elizabeth and John Walley, 3 April 1661, Boston, Mass.
WING, Sarah and John Street, 10 September 1694, Boston, Mass.
WINES, Ann and Francis Nichols, December 1645, Southold, N. Y.
WING, Hannah and Jededia Lombard, 20 May 1668, Barnstable, Mass.
WINN, Ann and Moses Cleveland, 26 September 1648, Woburn, Mass.
WINN, Edward and Sarah Beal, 10 August 1649, Woburn, Mass.
WINSLOW, Edward and Elizabeth Hutchinson, 8 February 1668, Plymouth, Mass.
WINSLOW, Elizabeth and Stephen Burton, 4 September 1684, Bristol, R. I.
WINSLOW, Eliza and Joseph Scott, 18 January 1693, Boston, Mass.
WINSLOW, Isaac and Mary Nowell, 14 August 1666, Plymouth, Mass.
WINSLOW, Jacob and Elizabeth Whittemore, 26 May 1690, Malden, Mass.
WINSLOW, John and Sarah Moulton, 5 May 1652, Malden, Mass.
WINSLOW, Judith and John Packard, 12 April 1688, Taunton, Mass.
WINSLOW, Kenelm and Mercy Worden, 23 September 1667, Yarmouth, Mass.
WINSLOW, Margaret and John Miller, 24 December 1659, Marshfield, Mass.
WINSLOW, Mary and Jonathan Pollard, 26 December 1693, Boston, Mass.
WINSLOW, Parnell and Richard Foster, 4 May 1686, Plymouth, Mass.
WINSLOW, Sarah and Myles Standish, 19 July 1660, Boston, Mass.
WINSLOW, Thomas and Anne Parker, 15 August 1694, Essex Co., Va.
WINSOR, Mary and Benjamin Tout, 29 August 1691, Boston, Mass.
WINTER, Hannah and Robert Burditt, November 1653, Malden, Mass.
WINTER, John and Ann Phenix, 2 April 1697, Boston, Mass.
WINTER, Timothy and Hester Plumley, 16 October 1670, Braintree, Mass.
WINTHROP, Elizabeth (widow) and John Richards, 3 March 1654, Boston, Mass.
WINTHROP, Martha and John Coggan, 10 January 1651, Boston, Mass.
WINTHROP, Mercy and Atherton Haugh, 11 July 1699, Boston, Mass.
WISE, Joseph and Mary Thompson, 3 December 1641, Braintree, Mass.
WISE, Katharine and Richard Mather, 1 July 1680, Dorchester, Mass.
WISE, Sarah and David Wheeler, 11 May 1650, Newbury, Mass.
WISE, Susanah (widow) and Samuel Greenfield, 26 March 1639, Ipswich, Mass.
WISEMAN, Mary and John Veren, 12 June 1660, Boston, Mass.
WISLAKE, Margery and Peter Slade, 26 December 1694, New York.
WISWALL, Heaster and Silence Allin, 20 January 1692, Dorchester, Mass.
WISWALL, Oliver and Sarah Baker, 1 January 1690, Dorchester, Mass.

WISWALL, Susanna and Edward Breck, 1 April 1698, Dorchester, Mass.

WISWEL, Ebenezer and Sarah Foster, 26 March 1685, Dorchester, Mass.

WISWEL, Elizabeth and Elisha Wadsworth, 9 December 1694, Duxborough, Mass.

WISWELL, John and Hanah Baker, 5 May 1685, Dorchester, Mass.

WISWELL, Enoch and Elizabeth Oliver, 25 September 1657, Dorchester, Mass.

WISWELL, Ichabod and Priscilla Pabodie, 1677, Duxbury, Mass.

WIT, Bethia and Solomon Ridgeway, 25 April 1698, Boston, Mass.

WITE, Joseph and Deboarh Colborne, 15 November 1679, Dedham, Mass.

WITHAM, Susana and Thomas Robison, 1 March 1690, Chesterfield, N. J.

WITHENTON, Elizabeth and James White, 13 February 1695-6, Dorchester, Mass.

WITHERED, John and Sarah Webb, 3 October 1695, Anne Arundel Co., Md.

WITHERLY, Nathaniel and Sarah Burgis, 10 December 1699, Boston, Mass.

WITHERSPOON, Isabel and Abraham Pringle, 11 March 1687, Watertown, Mass.

WITHINGTON, Ann and James Bird, 13 November 1679, Dorchester, Mass.

WITHINGTON, Henery and Sarah Leadbetter, 29 May 1684, Dorchester, Mass.

WITHINGTON, Joseph and Deliverance Leadbetter, 29 March 1693, Boston, Mass.

WITHINGTON, Philip and Thankfull Pond, 17 November 1682, Dorchester, Mass.

WITHINGTON, Sarah (widow) and Ebenezer Holms, 2 February 1692, Dorchester, Mass.

WITT, Thomas and Bethiah Potter, 26 February 1685, Salem, Mass.

WITTOMS, Peter and Redgon Clarke, 17 April 1652, Boston, Mass.

WITTUM, Ruth and Moses Boudey, 29 November 1697, Dover, N. H.

WITTY, George and Sarah Speere, 19 April 1672, Braintree, Mass.

WOERTMAN, Jan and Ann Andries, 17 January 1691, Brooklyn, N. Y.

WOLCOT, Henry and Sarah Newberry, 8 November 1640, Windsor, Conn.

WOLCOT, Simon and Martha Pitken, 17 October 1661, Windsor, Conn.

WOLCOTT, Henry, Jr., and Abia Goffe, 12 October 1664, Windsor, Conn.

WOLCOTT, Mary and Job Drake, 25 June 1646, Windsor, Conn.

WOLDERSON, Frances and Thomas Barrett, 14 July 1655, Braintree, Mass.

WOLF, Sarah and Abraham Cox, 26 October 1686, Bucks Co., Penn.

WOOD, Ann and Theodore Price, 1 August 1667, Salem, Mass.

WOOD, Anne and Thomas Everton, April 1686, Somerset Co., Md.

WOOD, Dorothy and Hooker Osgood, 26 April 1692, Andover, Mass.

WOOD, Ebenezer and Rachel Nichols, 5 April 1695, Rowley, Mass.

WOOD, Elizabeth and Moses Mudge, 17 December 1668, Warwick, R. I.

WOOD, Hanna and John Harding, 28 November 1665, Watertown, Mass.

WOOD, James and Experience Fuller, 12 April 1693, Middleborough, Mass.

WOOD, John and Isabel Hazen, 26 January 1680, Rowley, Mass.

WOOD, John and Bethiah Mason, 23 May 1688, Swansea, Mass.

WOOD, John and Sarah Sanders, 26 February 1695, Philadelphia, Penn.

WOOD, Jonathan and Mary Daniel, 26 May 1674, Milton, Mass.

WOOD, Joseph and Judieth Hely, 20 October 1697, Boston, Mass.

WOOD, Josiah and Lydia Bacon, 28 October 1657, Charlestown, Mass.

WOOD, Judith and Thomas Dorman, 16 March 1662, Topsfield, Mass.

WOOD, Margaret and James Grant, 5 October 1676, Dedham, Mass.

WOOD, Mary and James Chute, 10 November 1673, Ipswich, Mass.
WOOD, Mary and Thomas Reed, 7 March 1678, Sudbury, Mass.
WOOD, Mehitable and William Dean, 13 October 1677, Dedham, Mass.
WOOD, Phillipy and William White, 4 June 1653, Boston, Mass.
WOOD, Ruth and Phineas Upham, 14 February 1658, Malden, Mass.
WOOD, Ruth (widow of Richard) and Thomas Duckett, 28 January 1687, Philadelphia, Penn.
WOOD, Ruth and Jacob Usher, 23 December 1699, Philadelphia, Penn.
WOOD, Sarah and John Warner, 12 June 1677, Woburn, Mass.
WOOD, Sarah and Thomas Bass, 4 October 1660, Medford, Mass.
WOOD, Sarah and Francis Baleman, 18 April 1699, Elizabeth City Co., Va.
WOOD, Thomas and Susanna Eastman, 16 May 1693, Haverhill, Mass.
WOOD, Thomas, Jr., and Hannah Rider, 1 May 1690, Swansea, Mass.
WOODBRIDGE, Lucy and (Rev.) Simon Bradstreet, 2 October 1667, Newbury, Mass.
WOODBURY, Abigail and John Sampson, 9 August 1694, Beverly, Mass.
WOODBURY, John and Mary Reynolds, 18 May 1694, Bristol, R. I.
WOODBURY, Nicholas and Anna Paulsgrave, 1657, Charlestown, Mass.
WOODCOCK, Debora and Benjamin Onian, 24 March 1683, Dedham, Mass.
WOODCOCK, Israel and Elizabeth Gatchel, 5 September 1682, Dedham, Mass.
WOODCOCK, Jeremiah and Mary Metcalfe, 5 January 1698-9, Dedham, Mass.
WOODCOCK, John and Sara Westbroke, 5 September 1682, Dedham, Mass.
WOODCOCK, Mary and Samuel Guild, 29 September 1676, Dedham, Mass.
WOODEN, Andrew and Elizabeth Fitz Randolph, 22 August 1676, Piscataway, N. J.
WOODEN, Mary and Johannes Vanderheyden, 9 January 1697, New York.
WOODEY, Mary (widow) and Thomas Robinson, 10 November 1652, Boston, Mass.
WOODFORD, Mary and Isaac Sheldon, 1653, Windsor, Conn.
WOODFORD, Mary and Thomas Bird, 8 July 1693, Farmington, Conn.
WOODFORD, Thomas and Mary Blott, 4 March 1634, Roxbury, Mass.
WOODHOUSE, Mary and George Pearse, September 1659, Boston, Mass.
WOODHOUSE, Mary and William Remington, 13 April 1693, Salem Co., N. J.
WOODHOUSE, Samuel and Ann Hudson, 22 January 1694, Salem Co., N. J.
WOODHULL, Richard and Temperance Topping, 20 November 1684, Southampton, N. Y.
WOODIN, Dorcas and Anthony Coombs, 5 September 1688, York Co., Maine.
WOODMAN, Edward and Mary Goodridge, 20 December 1653, Newbury, Mass.
WOODMAN, John and Mary Field, 15 July 1656, Oyster River, N. H .
WOODMAN, Jonathan and Hannah Hilton, 2 July 1668, Newbury, Mass.
WOODMAN, Joshua and Elizabeth Stevens, 22 January 1665, Andover, Mass.
WOODMAN, Judith and Joseph Townsend, 9 August 1694, Boston, Mass.
WOODMAN, Remember and Thomas Perkins, 26 July 1694, Boston, Mass.
WOODMANSEY, John and Elizabeth Carr, 1 May 1662, Boston, Mass.
WOODMANSEY, Margaret and John Richardson, 22 June 1699, Boston, Mass.
WOODMANSEY, Mary and John Tappin, 20 June 1654, Boston, Mass.
WOODROFE, Elizabeth and Henry Jordani, 20 October 1691, New York City.
WOODRUFF, Hannah and John Broughton, 29 October 1678, Northampton, Mass.
WOODRUFF, Hannah and Israel Richardson, 5 December 1697, Farmington, Conn.

WOODRUFF, John and Mary Platt, 22 December 1698, Milford, Conn.

WOODRUFF, Matthew and Mary Plum, 16 June 1668, Milford Conn.

WOODRUFF, Matthew and Elizabeth Balding, 16 September 1694, Farmington, Conn.

WOODS, Samuel and Alice Rushton, 28 September 1659, Cambridge, Mass.

WOODS, Samuel and Hannah Forwell, 30 December 1685, Chelmsford, Mass.

WOODWARD, Anthony and Hannah Folkes, 3 December 1686, Chesterfield, N. J.

WOODWARD, Daniel and Elizabeth Dana, 14 January 1679, Watertown, Mass.

WOODWARD, Experience and Medad Pomeroy, 21 November 1661, Dorchester, Mass.

WOODWARD, Israel and Bennet Eddy, 28 December 1698, Taunton, Mass.

WOODWARD, John and Sarah Crossman, 11 November 1675, Rehoboth, Mass.

WOODWARD, John and Hannah Hide, 11 April 1698, Boston, Mass.

WOODWARD, Margaret and William Andrews, 21 October 1672, Chebacco, Mass.

WOODWARD, Mary and John Russel, 5 December 1683, Philadelphia, Penn.

WOODWARD, Mary and John Bull, 21 April 1692, Boston, Mass.

WOODWARD, Mercy and Jeremiah Tay, 4 March 1683, Boston, Mass.

WOODWARD, Prudence and Christopher Mosse, 1 July 1661, Boston, Mass.

WOODWARD, Rachel (widow) and Thomas Harwood, 7 May 1654, Boston, Mass.

WOODWARD, Rachel and William Snowton, 28 June 1699, Boston, Mass.

WOODWARD, Rebecca and Thomas Fisher, 11 December 1666, Dedham, Mass.

WOODWARD, Smith and Thankfull Poop, 29 July 1691, Dorchester, Mass.

WOODWARD, Thomas and Mary Guns, 7 March 1659, Boston, Mass.

WOODWORTH, Benjamin and Mary Swift, 19 July 1699, Lebanon, Conn.

WOODY, Isaac and Dorcas Harper, 20 January 1656, Boston, Mass.

WOOLLY, Cecelia and Joshua Tittery, 4 April 1688, Philadelphia, Penn.

WOOLLY, Ruth and John Tucker, 25 February 1688, Shrewsbury, N. J.

WOOSTER, Susannah and Thomas Stace, 4 August 1653, Ipswich, Mass.

WOOTON, Elizabeth and (Rev.) William Perkins, 30 August 1636, Roxbury, Mass.

WOOTEN, Margrett and John Gorton, 20 January 1668, Warwick, R. I.

WORCESTER, Samuel and Elizabeth Parrott, 29 November 1659, Rowley, Mass.

WORCESTER, William and Martha Cheney, 29 January 1690, Rowley, Mass.

WORDEN, Mary and John Burgess, 8 September 1657, Yarmouth, Mass.

WORDEN, Mehitabel and William Avery, 25 August 1698, Boston, Mass.

WORDEN, Mercy and Kenelm Winslow, 23 September 1667, Yarmouth, Mass.

WORKMAN, Samuel and Martha White, 3 August 1693, Boston, Mass.

WORMWOOD, Lidia and Richard Holt, 10 May 1693, Bridgewater, Mass.

WORMWOOD, Mary and Edward Belcher, 8 November 1655, Boston, Mass.

WORRAL, Martha and Samuel Dark, 6 December 1685, Middletown, Penn.

WORRILOE, Elizabeth and William Benks, 28 January 1690, Philadelphia, Penn.

WORRILOW, Jane and Daniel Hoops, 10 October 1696, Middletown, Penn.

WORSTER, Constance and Abraham Tuckerman, 15 July 1692, Boston, Mass.

WORTH, John and Elizabeth Webster, 17 March 1686, Newbury, Mass.

WORTH, Judith and Joses Buckman, 1 May 1673, Malden, Mass.

WORTH, Richard and Mary Pike, 11 September 1667, Newbury, Mass.

WORTH, Sarah and Samuel Gill, 5 November 1678, Salisbury, Mass.

WORTH, Susanna and Moses Pillsbury, March 1668, Newbury, Mass.

WORTHEN, Ezekial and Hannah Martin, 4 December 1661, Amesbury, Mass.

WORTHILAKE, Sarah and John Plaisted, 25 March 1698, Boston, Mass.

WORTHILEG, Susanna and Robert Fletcher, 13 January 1697, Boston, Mass.
WORTHLY, John and Elizabeth Hance, 12 January 1676, Shrewsbury, N. J.
WORTHYLAKE, Eliza and Henry Champney, 8 December 1693, Boston, Mass.
WORTMAN, Dirck J. and Annetje Aukes, 9 April 1691, New York City.
WRIGHT, Abel and Martha Kitcherel, 1 December 1659, Hartford, Conn.
WRIGHT, Abel and Rebecca Terry, 16 September 1691, Springfield, Mass.
WRIGHT, Ales and Joseph Stewart, 7 December 1694, Chesterfield, N. J.
WRIGHT, Ann and Samuel Gaines, 7 April 1665, Lynn, Mass.
WRIGHT, Anna and John Walstone, 26 February 1677, Guilford, Conn.
WRIGHT, Anna and Peter Talman, 7 November 1683, Guilford, Conn.
WRIGHT, Benjamin and Mary Chapin, 24 January 1694, Springfield, Mass.
WRIGHT, Benjamin and Barbara Peppiatt, 23 December 1699, Philadelphia, Penn.
WRIGHT, Darkis and Obediah Alyn, 29 November 1699, Middletown, Conn.
WRIGHT, Edmond and Sarah Townsend, 1695, Oyster Bay, N. Y.
WRIGHT, Edward and Hannah Upson, 18 June 1659, Sudbury, Mass.
WRIGHT, Edward and Mary Powell, 27 March 1657, Boston, Mass.
WRIGHT, Elizabeth and Edward Lees, 7 November 1676, Saybrook, Conn.
WRIGHT, Elizabeth and Better Fretwell, 6 September 1687, Chesterfield, N. J.
WRIGHT, Hannah and Thomas Stebbins, 14 November 1645, Springfield, Mass.
WRIGHT, Hannah and Joseph Saxton, 20 November 1690, Lebanon, Conn.
WRIGHT, Hannah and John Coleman, 24 April 1695, Wethersfield, Conn.
WRIGHT, Jane and Joseph Hand, 1664, Guilford, Conn.
WRIGHT, John and Mercy Wardwell, 31 August 1697, Andover, Mass.
WRIGHT, Jone and John Copestaffe, 26 January 1680, New York.
WRIGHT, Joseph and Elizabeth Hassell, 1 November 1661, Charlestown, Mass.
WRIGHT, Joseph and Elizabeth Bateman, 7 July 1692, Charlestown, Mass.
WRIGHT, Joseph and Ann Henry, 1 January 1694, New York.
WRIGHT, Judah and Mercy Burt, 17 January 1667, Deerfield, Mass.
WRIGHT, Lydia and Isaac Horner, 1684, Oyster Bay, N. Y.
WRIGHT, Martha and Thomas Morley, 8 December 1681, Springfield, Mass.
WRIGHT, Mary and Gideon Allen, 1698, Guilford, Conn.
WRIGHT, Maudlin and Matthias Bellows, 29 November 1696, Philadelphia, Penn.
WRIGHT, Mercy and Samuel Allen, 15 December 1692, Northampton, Mass.
WRIGHT, Priscilla and John Hartwell, 1 June 1664, Bedford, Mass.
WRIGHT, Rachel and David Curtis, 2 July 1697, Chesterfield, N. J.
WRIGHT, Ruth and Jonathan Butterfield, 20 March 1693, Woburn, Mass.
WRIGHT, Sarah and Samuel Potter, 8 January 1673, Woburn, Mass.
WRIGHT, Sarah and Thomas Chapin, 15 February 1694, Lebanon, Conn.
WRIGHT, Thomas and Sarah Benton, 9 December 1673, Guilford, Conn.
WRIGHT, Thomas and Lydia Cobbitt, 28 August 1696, New York.
WRIGHT, Walter and Susanna Johnson, 26 February 1667, Andover, Mass.
WRIGHT, Walter and Elizabeth Sadir, 9 September 1684, Andover, Mass.
WROTHAM, Susana and Samuel Hough, 25 November 1679, Farmington, Conn.
WYATT, Nathaniel and Johanna Spur, 8 November 1668, Dorchester, Mass.
WYBORNE, Elizabeth and John Merick, 3 February 1655, Boston, Mass.
WYER, Edward and Elizabeth Johnson, 5 January 1659, Charlestown, Mass.
WYER, Edward and Abigail Lawrence, 1 September 1684, Charlestown, Mass.
WYER, Nathaniel and Elizabeth Swain, 3 December 1636, Newbury, Mass.
WYETH, Rebecca and Thomas Fox, 16 December 1685, Cambridge, Mass.

WYLLYS, Samuel and Mary Love, 28 November 1688, Berwick, Maine.
WYMAN, Benjamin and Elizabeth Hancock, 25 August 1674, Cambridge, Mass.
WYMAN, Francis and Judith Pierce, 30 January 1645, Woburn, Mass.
WYMAN, Francis and Abigail Read, 2 October 1650, Woburn, Mass.
WYMAN, Sarah and Thomas Fuller, 25 August 1684, Woburn, Mass.
WYMAN, Thomas and Mary Richardson, 5 May 1696, Yarmouth, Maine.
WYNANS, Aeltje and Jan Bennit, 12 April 1690, Brooklyn, N. Y.
WYNCOOP, Benjamin and Ffemmie Vanderhule, 20 October 1697, New York.
WYNKOOP, Evert and Gertrude Elmendorf, 26 August 1688, Kingston, N. Y.
WYNKOOP, Johannes and Judith Bloodgood, January 1687, Kingston, N. Y.
WYNKOOP, Johannus and Cornelia Ten Broeke, 9 June 1696, New York.
WYNNE, Hester and Jellis A. Fonda, 1695, Albany, N. Y.
WYTHE, Anne and James Wallace, 11 July 1695, Elizabeth City Co., Va.

Y

YALE, Elizabeth and Joseph Pardee, 31 July 1688, New Haven, Conn.
YALE, Hannah and Enos Talmage, 9 May 1682, New Haven, Conn.
YALE, Mary and Joseph Ives, 3 January 1672, New Haven, Conn.
YALE, Thomas and Mary Turner, 1645, New Haven, Conn.
YALE, Thomas and Rebecca Gibbards, March 1667, Wallingford, Conn.
YARDLEY, Francis and Sarah Gookin, 20 November 1647, Norfolk Co., Va.
YARESLY, Richard and Dorothy Gore, 23 October 1694, New York.
YARNALL, Francis and Hannah Baker, February 1686, Chester Co., Penn.
YARNALL, Philip and Dorothy Baker, 20 April 1694, Chester Co., Penn.
YATES, Mary and Richard Higgins, October 1651, Eastham, Mass.
YATES, Thomas and Rose Stake, June 1679, Middlesex Co., Va.
YEATES, John and Edey Wilde, 5 July 1699, New York.
YELLING, Triphena and William Francis, 29 April 1699, Boston, Mass.
YEOMANS, Edward and Elizabeth Joslyn, 12 June 1652, Boston, Mass.
YEOMANS, Edward and Mary Button, 2 December 1652, Haverhill, Mass.
YEOMANS, Elizabeth (widow) and Edward Kilby, 9 May 1662, Boston, Mass.
YORK, James and Deborah Bell, 19 January 1669, Boston, Mass.
YORKE, Abigail and John Beebe, May 1659, Stonington, Conn.
YOUNG, Daniel and Judith Frink, 12 January 1699, New London, Conn.
YOUNG, David and Anne Doane, 20 January, 1687, Eastham, Mass.
YOUNG, Edward and Hannah Whittier, 30 May 1683, Haverhill, Mass.
YOUNG, John and Sarah Runnals, 16 March 1698, Northwood, N. H.
YOUNG, Robert and Lydia Hicks, 22 March 1694, Eastham, Mass.
YOUNG, Sarah and John Marsh, 22 March 1662, Salem, Mass.
YOUNG, Sarah and Isaac Loreing, 5 August 1691, Boston, Mass.
YOUNG, Sarah and William Codner, 21 November 1697, Boston, Mass.
YOUNG, Simon and Ann Elum, 10 May 1695, New York.
YOUNG, Thomas and Sarah White, January 1689, Scituate, Mass.
YOUNG, William and Sarah Whiteache, 11 October 1694, Boston, Mass.
YOUNGER, Francis and Anna Heath (widow), 2 December 1685, Dedham, Mass.

Z

ZABRISKIE, Albrecht and Machteldt Van de Linde, 17 December 1676, Hackensack, N. J.

ZACHARY, Daniel and Elizabeth Lloyd, 29 January 1699, Philadelphia, Penn.

ZANE, Nathaniel and Grace Rakestraw, 27 June 1697, Philadelphia, Penn.

ADDENDA

ALLEN, John and Eleanor Beardsley, 11 September 1653, Weymouth, Mass.

ANDREWS, Mary and Isaac Cowles, 2 January 1697, New Haven, Conn.

ANDRIES, Anna and Dirck Van Vliet, 23 April 1685, Kingston, N. Y.

BEARDSLEY, Eleanor and John Allen, 11 September 1653, Weymouth, Mass.

BIRDLEY, Andrew and Mary Conant, 14 March 1682, Ipswich, Mass.

BLISS, John and Patience Burt, 7 October 1667, Taunton, Mass.

BOWMAN, Mary and John Eveleth, January 1692, Manchester, Mass.

BRADLEY, Abraham and Hannah Thompson, 25 December 1673, New Haven, Conn.

BRADLEY, William and Abigail Pritchard, 18 February 1645, Saybrook, Conn.

BRADSTREET, John and Sarah Perkins, 11 June 1677, Topsfield, Mass.

BRADSTREET, Moses and Elizabeth Harris, 11 March 1661, Rowley, Mass.

BRADSTREET, Simon and Ann Gardiner (widow), 2 May 1676, Andover, Mass.

BRAINERD, James and Deborah Dudley, 1 April 1696, Haddam, Conn.

BRANCH, John and Mary Speed, 5 December 1652, Marshfield, Mass.

BULL, Thomas and Esther Cowles, 25 April 1669, Hadley, Mass.

BURGE, John and Jane Garney, 6 September 1677, Dorchester, Mass.

BURGESS, Thomas and Sarah Storrs, 26 February 1696, Barnstable, Mass.

BURNET, Lot and Phoebe Mills, 20 October 1675, Elizabethtown, N. J.

BURNHAM, Richard and Sarah Humphries, 11 June 1680, East Hartford, Conn.

BURRITT, William and Sarah Nichols, 8 November 1673, Stratford, Conn.

BURROUGHS, Thomas and Mary Taylor, 16 November 1695, New York City.

BURROWS, Robert and Mary Ireland (widow), December 1672, Groton, Conn.

BURT, Patience and John Bliss, 7 October 1667, Taunton, Mass.

BUSHNELL, Elizabeth and William Johnson, 2 July 1651, Guilford, Conn.

BUSHNELL, John and Sarah Scranton, 15 May 1665, Saybrook, Conn.

BUSHNELL, Samuel and Ruth Sanford, 17 April 1684, Saybrook, Conn.

CHAUNCEY, Charles (Rev.) and Sarah Burr, 29 June 1692, Fairfield, Conn.

CLARKE, Carew and Ann Dyre, 4 February 1693, Tiverton, R. I.

CONANT, Mary and Andrew Birdley, 14 March 1682, Ipswich, Mass.

COWLES, Elizabeth and Richard Lyman, 26 May 1675, Hadley, Mass.

COWLES, Esther and Thomas Bull, 25 April 1669, Hadley, Mass.

COWLES, Isaac and Mary Andrews, 2 January 1697, New Haven, Conn.

COWLES, Samuel and Rachel Porter, 12 May 1685, Farmington, Conn.

COWLES, Sarah and Stephen Hart, 18 December 1689, Avon, Conn.

COWLES, Timothy and Hannah Pitkin, 1 January 1690, East Hartford, Conn.

CUSHMAN, Sarah and William Hoskins, 2 November 1636, Plymouth, Mass.

DEWEY, Josiah and Hepzibah Lyman, 6 November 1662, Windsor, Conn.

DEWEY, Josiah, Jr., and Mehitable Miller, 24 December 1666, Lebanon, Conn.

DYRE, Ann and Carew Clarke, 4 February 1692, Tiverton, R. I.

EVELETH, John and Mary Bowman, January 1692, Manchester, Mass.

FITCH, James and Abigail Whitfield, 1 October 1648, Guilford, Conn.

FITCH, James and Priscilla Mason, 3 October 1664, Saybrook, Conn.

GLOVER, Abigail and Daniel Burr, 11 December 1678, Fairfield, Conn.

GURNEY, Jane and John Burge, 6 September 1677, Dorchester, Mass.

HARRIS, John and Elizabeth Wells, 27 October 1677, Rowley, Mass.

HART, Stephen and Sarah Cowles, 18 December 1689, Avon, Conn.

HIGBY, John and Rebecca Treadwell, 1 May 1679, Middletown, Conn.

HINDS, Ann and William Hoskins, 21 December 1638, Plymouth, Mass.

HOSKINS, William and Sarah Cushman, 2 November 1636, Plymouth, Mass.

HOSKINS, William and Ann Hinds, 21 December 1638, Plymouth, Mass.

HOSSEY, Judith and Jan Van Vliet, 4 October 1684, Kingston, N. Y.

HUMPHRIES, Sarah and Richard Burnham, 11 June 1680, East Hartford, Conn.

IRELAND, Mary and Robert Burrows, December 1672, Groton, Conn.

JOHNSON, William and Elizabeth Bushnell, 2 July 1651, Guilford, Conn.

JORDAN, Mary and John Kimball, 8 October 1666, Ipswich, Mass.

KIMBALL, John and Mary Jordan, 8 October 1666, Ipswich, Mass.

LYMAN, Hepzibah and Josiah Dewey, 6 November 1662, Windsor, Conn.

LYMAN, Richard and Elizabeth Cowles, 26 May 1675, Hadley, Mass.

MASON, Priscilla and James Fitch, 3 October 1664, Saybrook, Conn.

MILLER, Mehitable and Josiah Dewey, Jr., 24 December 1666, Lebanon, Conn.

NICHOLS, Sarah and William Burritt, 8 November 1673, Stratford, Conn.

PERKINS, Sarah and John Bradstreet, 11 June 1677, Topsfield, Mass.

PITKIN, Hannah and Timothy Cowles, 1 January 1690, East Hartford, Conn.

PORTER, Rachel and Samuel Cowles, 12 May 1685, Farmington, Conn.

PRITCHARD, Abigail and William Bradley, 18 February 1645, Saybrook, Conn.

SANFORD, Ruth and Samuel Bushnell, 17 April 1684, Saybrook, Conn.

SCRANTON, Sarah and John Bushnell, 15 May 1665, Saybrook, Conn.

SHELTON, Daniel and Elizabeth Wells, 4 April 1692, Stratford, Conn.

SPEED, Mary and John Branch, 5 December 1652, Marshfield, Mass.

STOL, Jan Jacob and Machtel Van Vliet, 18 September 1684, Kingston, N. Y.

STORRS, Sarah and Thomas Burgess, 26 February 1696, Barnstable, Mass.

THOMPSON, Hannah and Abraham Bradley, 25 December 1673, New Haven, Conn.

TREADWELL, Rebecca and John Higby, 1 May 1679, Middletown, Conn.

VAN DAM, Rip and Sarah Van der Spiegel, 14 September 1684, New York.

VAN DER SPIEGEL, Laurens and Sarah Webbers, 1 April 1661, New York.

VAN DER SPIEGEL, Sarah and Rip Van Dam, 14 September 1684, New York.

VAN VLIET, Dirck and Anna Andries, 23 April 1685, Kingston, N. Y.

VAN VLIET, Jan and Judith Hossey, 4 October 1684, Kingston, N. Y.

VAN VLIET, Machtel and Jan Jacob Stol, 18 September 1684, Kingston, N. Y.

WEBBERS, Sarah and Laurens Van der Spiegel, 1 April 1661, New York.

WELLS, Elizabeth and John Harris, 27 October 1677, Rowley, Mass.

WELLS, Elizabeth and Daniel Shelton, 4 April 1692, Stratford, Conn.

Finis

Genealogy Magazine

Vol. XIV   JULY, 1929   No. 4

MARRIAGES BEFORE 1699.

(Being a Supplement to "American Marriages Before 1699", by William Montgomery Clemens, published in 1926.)

A.

ADAMS, HANNAH and JOHN HAYDEN, 6 April 1660, Braintree, Mass.

ADAMS, MEHITABLE and THOMAS WHITE JR., 21 July, 1697, Braintree, Mass.

ADAMS, PETER and MARY WEBB, 12 February, 1695, Braintree Mass.

ADAMS, ROBERT and SARAH SHORT, (widow)9 February, 1678, Ipswich, Mass.

ADDAMS, PHILLIP and ANNE CREW, 7 July, 1670, Somerset Co., Md.

ADOLPH, DIRCK and ARIENTJIE KIERSTEAD, 27 Sept., 1693, New York.

ALDEN, MERCY and JOHN BURRILL, June, 1688, Taunton, Mass.

ALLEN, ANNE and FRANCIS ELMORE, 2 December, 1677, Richmond Co., Va.

ALLEN, ANNIE and WILLIAM CRESSWELL, 18 June, 1697, Richmond Co., Va.

ALLEN, ELIZABETH and JOHN PUCKETT, 18 Nov., 1691, Henrico Co., Va.

ALLEN, John and ELIZABETH EDWARDS, 22 July, 1697, Boston, Mass.

ALLEN, MARY and NATHANIEL GREENWOOD, 24 Jan., 1656, Weymouth, Mass.

ANDERSON, KATHERINE and JASPER HOOD, 2 June, 1696, New York.

ANDRIES, ANNA and DIRCK VAN VLEET, 23 April, 1685, Kingston, N. Y.

ANDRIESSEN, BARBARA and TJERK DE WITT, 24 April, 1656, New York.

ANNABLE, HANNAH and THOMAS BORMAN, 1 March, 1645, Barnstable, Mass.

ANNABLE, SAMUEL and PATIENCE DAGGETT, 11 April, 1695, Rehoboth, Mass.

ANTRUM, HANNAH and ISAAC BURNAP, 8 Sept., 1658, Salem, Mass.

ATKINSON, THEODORE and SARAH MYRICK, 27 April, 1664, Newbury, Mass.

AUSTIN, ANTHONY and ESTER HAGGINS, 19 Oct., 1664, Charleston, Mass.

AVERILL, WILLIAM and HANNAH JACKSON, 31 July, 1661, Ipswich, Mass.

AXTELL, ELIZABETH and H. JOSEPH BLAKE, 1 Dec., 1698, Paulets, S. Car.

B.

BACON, JOHN and REBECCA HALL, 17 Dec., 1651, Dedham, Mass.

BADCOCK, RUTH and JOHN DOWN, 30 August, 1690, Boston, Mass.

BADSON, ELIZA and JOHN FAIRFIELD, 18 April, 1693, Boston, Mass.

BAGNALL, FRANSES and WILLIAM BURTON, 20 Dec., 1699, Accomac Co., Va.

BALCH, SAMUEL and MARTHA NEWMARCH, 27 October, 1675, Beverly, Mass.

BALDING, ELIZABETH and MATTHEW WOODRUFF, 16 Sept., 1694, Farmington, Conn.

BARDWELL, ROBERT and MARY GULL, 29 Nov, 1676, Hatfield, Mass.

BARENTZ, APOLLOMA and WILLIAM VREDENBURG, 19 October, 1664, New York.

BARKER, WILLIAM and DOROTHY HAYWARD, 12 March, 1695, Boston, Mass.

BARSTOW, JOHN, JR. and LYDIA HATCH, 16 Jan., 1678, Watertown, Mass.

BARTLETT, DEBORAH and JOHN COLE, 22 Nov., 1668, Hadley, Mass.

BASS, JOHN and REBECCA SAVILL, 17 May, 1698, Plymouth, Mass.

BASS, JOSEPH and MARY BELCHER, 5 June, 1688, Plymouth, Mass.

BASS, MARY and CHRISTOPHER WEBB, JR., 24 May, 1686, Plymouth, Mass.

BASS, SAMUEL and MERCY MARSH, 29 Nov., 1689, Braintree, Mass.

BASS, SARAH and EPHRIAM THAYER, 7 June, 1692, Plymouth, Mass.

BASSETT, MARY and JOHN READING, 22 Oct., 1676, Bridgewater, Mass.

BASSETT, WILLIAM and SARAH SWETLAND, 14 June, 1693, Milton, Mass.

BASSETT, WILLIAM and SARA HOOD, 25 October, 1675, Lynn, Mass.

BATTALL, THOMAS and MARY FISHER, 5 July, 1648, Dedham, Mass.

BAYER, MARY and MOSES LEUWIS, 16 Sept., 1695, New York.

BEAKS, STEPHEN and ELIZABETH BILES, 31 Aug., 1688, Middletown, Penn.

BEAN, MARY and JOEL JUDKINS, 25 June, 1674, Exeter, Mass.

BEARDSLEY, SARAH and OBADIAH DICKINSON, 8 Jan., 1669, Hatfield, Mass.

BECKER, MAGDALEN and RICHARD WINFIELD, 12 Jan., 1696, Albany, N. Y.

BEEKMAN, WILLIAM and CATHERINE DE BOW, 5 Sept., 1649, New York City.

BEDFORD, STEPHEN and NAOMI GAGE, 15 Feb., 1693, Bristol, R. I.

BELCHER, MARY and JOSEPH BASS, 5 Jan., 1688, Plymouth, Mass.

BELDEN, JOHN and LYDIA STANDISH, 27 June, 1677, Wethersfield, Conn.

BELDEN, SAMUEL and HANNAH ELDERKIN, 14 Jan., 1685, Wethersfield, Conn.

BELVERE, MONSIEUR and LADY FRANCES HOPKINS, 9 April, 1656, Boston, Mass.

BEMAN, JONAH and LYDIA WARNER, 29 April, 1696, Springfield, Mass.

BEMAN, SIMON and ALICE YOUNG, 15 October, 1654, Springfield, Mass.

BENJAMIN, DOROTHY and JOHN GREEN, 24 Aug., 1673, Richmond Co., Va.

BENNITT, PROSILAH and STUCKLEY WESTCOAT, 27 Dec., 1693, Warwick, R. I.

BENTON, DANIEL and RACHEL GUTTREDGE, 23 Nov., 1658, Guilford, Conn.

BENTON, EBENEZER and ABIGAIL GRAVES, 14 June, 1694, Guilford, Conn.

BERCK, CATALINA and HARMEN HUN, 1 June, 1661, Albany, N. Y.

BERR, WILLIAM and NAOMY WALLEY, 9 July, 1686, Middletown, Penn.

BERRY, SAMUEL and CATALYNA RYERSON, 3 Feb., 1691, Pompton, N. J.

BIGELOW, SARAH and ISAAC LARNARD, 23 July, 1679, Sherborne, Mass.

BILES, ELIZABETH and STEPHEN BEAKS, 31 Aug., 1688, Middletown, Penn.

BIRD, MARGARET and EDMOND COUSSINS, 1 Nov., 1656, Boston, Mass.

BLAKE, JOSEPH and ELIZABETH AXTELL, 1 Dec., 1698, Paulets, S. Car.

BLANCON, CATHERINE and LOUIS DE BOIS, 10 Oct., 1655, New Paltz, N. Y.

BLOSSOM, PETER and SARAH BODFISH, 21 June, 1663, Plymouth, Mass.

Genealogy Magazine

Vol. XIV   OCTOBER, 1929   No. 5

MARRIAGES BEFORE 1699.

(Being a Supplement to "American Marriages Before 1699", by William Montgomery Clemens, published in 1926.)

BOARDMAN, JOANNA and ISAAC FELLOWS, 24 January, 1672, Ipswich, Mass.

BOARDMAN, OFFIN and SARAH HEARD, 28 February, 1698, Ipswich, Mass.

BOARDMAN, SAMUEL and SARAH STEELE, 8 February, 1682, Wethersfield, Conn.

BOARDMAN, THOMAS and ELIZABETH PERKINS, 1 January, 1667, Ipswich, Mass.

BODFISH, SARAH and PETER BLOSSOM, 21 June, 1663, Plymouth, Mass.

BOGART, JACOB and JENNETJE QUACKENBUSH, 1 January, 1679, Albany, N. Y.

BONHAM, RUTH and RICHARD SMYTHE, 27 March, 1646, Taunton, Mass.

BORDEN, AMY and BENJAMIN CHASE, 21 September, 1696, Cumberland, R. I.

BORDEN, BENJAMIN and ABIGAIL GROVER, 22 January, 1670, Shrewsbury, Mass.

BORDEN, RICHARD and INNOCENCE WARDELL, 1 September, 1692, Portsmouth, R. I.

BORMAN, MARTHA and THOMAS LOW, 4 July, 1660, Ipswich, Mass.

BORMAN, THOMAS and HANNAH ANNABLE, 1 March, 1645, Barnstable, Mass.

BOSWORTH, ANN (widow) and THOMAS COOPER, 17 August, 1656, Boston, Mass.

BOSWORTH, BELLAMY and MARY SMITH, 11 November, 1685, Bristol, R. I.

BOSWORTH, ELIZABETH and NICHOLAS PEARE, 28 October, 1686, Ipswich, Mass.

BOZWORTH, ELIZABETH and PETER BRACKETT, 6 July, 1661, Braintree, Mass.

BOUGLAND, LEWIS and MARY ANN VAN BURSOM, 8
November, 1695, New York.
BOWEN, ELIZABETH and EDWARD MORRIS, 24 May,
1683, Roxbury, Mass.
BOWLES, MARY and CHARLES FROST, January, 1666,
Wells, Maine.
BOWMAN, MARY and REV. JOHN EVELETH, January,
1692, Lexington, Mass.
BOYCE, JOSEPH and SARAH MEACHAM, 4 February,
1668, Salem, Mass.
BOYNTON, HANNAH and NATHANIEL WARNER, 29
November, 1673, Essex Co., Mass.
BRACKETT, RACHEL and SIMON CROSBY, 15 May, 1659,
Braintree, Mass.
BRACKETT, PETER snd ELIZABETH BOSWORTH, 6 July,
1661, Braintree, Mass.
BRADBURY, JANE and HENRY TRUE, 15 March, 1643,
Salisbury, Mass.
BRADBURY, JUDITH and CALEB MOODY, 9 November,
1665, Newbury, Mass.
BRADFIELD, WIDOW and GEORGE ADAMS, 5 September,
1651, Branford, Conn.
BRADSTREET, SARAH and NICHOLAS WALLIS, 13 Sep-
tember, 1657, Rowley, Mass.
BRAMHALL, MARTHA (widow) and GERSHAM GALL, 9
December, 1698, Harwich, Mass.
BRECK, ISABEL and ANTHONY FISHER, 14 November,
1663, Dorchester, Mass.
BREED, SAMUEL and ANNE HOOD, 5 February, 1692,
Lynn, Mass.
BREWSTER, HANNAH and SAMUEL STARR, 23 December,
1664, New London, Conn.
BREWSTER, JONATHAN and LUCRETIA OLDHAM, 10
April, 1634, Plymouth, Mass.
BREWSTER, MARY and JOHN TURNER, 12 November,
1645, Scituate, Mass.
BRIDGER, SARAH and JOHN AINSWORTH, 15 July, 1678,
Richmond Co., Va.
BRIDGES, SARAH and JOHN LAURENCE, 20 November,
1682, Jamaica, N. Y.
BRIGGS, RICHARD and REBECCA HOSKINS, 15 August,
1662, Taunton, Mass.
BRONSON, ELZABETH and SAMUEL GREENWOOD, 1687,
Roxbury, Mass.

BRONSON, REBECCA and ELIPHALET DICKINSON, 4 November, 1697, Wethersfield, Conn.

BROOKE, ROBERT and MARY MANWARING, 11 May, 1635, Calvert, Co., Md.

BROOKESBANCK, MISS and HUMPHREY TREGENNY, 12 August, 1696, New York.

BROOKS, ABIGAIL and LEVI PRESTON, 16 October, 1695, Swansea, Mass.

BROOKS, ELIZABETH and THOMAS LEWIS, 10 April, 1689, Swansea, Mass.

BROOKS, HEPSIBAH and PELETIAH MASON, 22 May, 1694, Swansea, Mass.

BROOKS, GILBERT and SARAH CARPENTER, 17 January, 1687, Marshfield, Mass.

BROOKS, JOSHUA and HANNAH MASON, 17 October, 1653, Concord, Mass.

BROOKS, MARY and NATHANIEL COLEBOURNE, 19 November, 1669, Dedham, Mass.

BROOKS, TIMOTHY and HANNAH BOWEN, 10 November, 1685, Swansea, Mass.

BROWN, BENJAMIN and REBECCA WESTCOTE, 16 August, 1695, Bristol, R. I.

BROWN, JOHN and SARAH MAYNARD, 16 September, 1668, Somerset Co., Md.

BROWN, SARAH and ANDREW GREELEY, 12 June, 1673, Salisbury, Mass.

BRYANT, JOHN and MARY BATTELLEX, 20 January, 1677, Dedham, Mass.

BUCK, RACHEL and JOHN BRONSON, January, 1697, Wethersfield, Conn.

BUCKENHOVEN, STEPHEN and ANNA VAN HOLST, 7 May, 1696, New York.

BUCKLAN, ELIZABETH and DANIEL MILLER, 11 December, 1699, East Hampton, N. Y.

BUCKLEY, DOROTHY and JONATHAN WADE, 9 December, 1660, Ipswich, Mass.

BUCKMAN, SARAH and RICHARD DEXTER, 23 February, 1698, Malden, Mass.

BULL, THOMAS and ESTHER COLE, 25 April, 1669, Hadley, Mass.

BULLARD, ELIZABETH and BENJAMIN MORSE, 8 November, 1648, Dedham, Mass.

BUNNELL, REBECCA and SAMUEL BURWELL, 1684, New Haven, Conn.

BURCH, MARY and JOHN COLLINS, 3 December, 1688, Salem, Mass.

BURCHSTEAD, HENRY and MARY KIRKLAND, 24 April, 1690, Lynn, Mass.

BURGESS, MARY and MATHIAS ELLIA, 1678, Sandwich, Mass.

BURNET, ISABELL and WILLIAM MONTGOMERY, 8 January, 1684, Eglinton, N. J.

BURNET, LOT and PHEBE MILLS, 20 October, 1675, Easthampton, N. Y.

BURRITT, STEPHEN and SARAH NICHOLS, 8 November, 1673, Stratford, Conn.

BURTON, WILLIAM and FRANCES BAGNALL, 20 December, 1699, Accomac Co., Va.

BURWELL, SAMUEL and REBECCA BUNNELL, 1684, New Haven, Conn.

BUSHNELL, JOSEPH and MARY LEFFINGWELL, 10 October, 1654, Norwich, Mass.

BUTLER, MARY and EBENEZER HOPKINS, 21 January, 1691, Hartford, Conn.

Genealogy Magazine

Vol. XV   JANUARY, 1930   No. 1

MARRIAGE RECORDS BEFORE 1699.
(Being a Supplement to "American Marriages
Before 1699," by William Montgomery
Clemens, published in 1926.)

(Continued from October Issue.)

CALLENDER, ELIZABETH and BANFIELD CAP-
RON, 1 December, 1680, Rehoboth, Mass.

CANTRILL, JOSEPH and ANNIE GARDNER, 13
December, 1697, Boston, Mass.

CAREY, MARY and JOHN JACOBS, 8 November,
1680, Richmond County, Virginia.

CARHART, THOMAS and MARY LORD, 22 November, 1691, New York City.

CARRIONTON, MISS and WILLIAM PERSON, 21
October, 1692, Simsbury, Conn.

CHAPMAN, MARAH and JOHN CROASDILL, 28
February, 1697, Middletown, Penn.

CHASE, SARAH and CHARLES ANNIS, 15 May,
1666, Newbury, Mass.

CHAUNCY, (Rev.) CHARLES and SARAH BURR,
(daughter of JOHN), 29 June, 1692, Fairfield,
Conn.

CHESEBORO, BRIDGET and WILLIAM THOMP-
SON, 7 December, 1692, Stonington, Conn.

CHICKERING, NATHANIEL and LYDIA FISHER,
3 October, 1673, Dedham, Mass.

CHRISTOPHERS, RICHARD and GRACE TUR-
NER, 3 September, 1691, New London, Conn.

CLARK, DEBORAH and ISAAC JONES, 21
November, 1692, New Haven, Conn.

CLARK, WILLIAM and HANNAH GRISWOLD,
7 March, 1678, Saybrook, Conn.

CLARKE, ELIZABETH and JOHN LORD, 9 December, 1695, Ipswich, Mass.

CLEMENCE, ABRAHAM and HANNAH GOVE,
10 May, 1684, Newbury, Mass.

CLEMENT, JOB and MARGARET DUMMER, 25 December, 1644, Haverhill, Mass.

CLEMENTS, GRACE and RICHARD TRAVIS, 22 October, 1657, Boston, Mass.

CLEVERLY, SARAH and WILLIAM JOYCE, 24 September, 1691, Boston, Mass.

COCK, HENRY and MARY FEKE, 28 August, 1699, Killingsworth, N. Y.

COCKE, JAMES and ELIZABETH PLEASANTS, 11 January, 1681, Henrico County, Virginia.

COLDHAM, MARTHA and RICHARD WHITNEY, 19 March, 1650, Watertown, Mass.

COLE, ELIZABETH and RICHARD LYMAN, Jr., 26 May, 1675, Hadley, Mass.

COLE, ESTHER and THOMAS BULL, 25 April, 1669, Hadley, Mass.

COLE, HUGH and MARY MORTON (widow), 30 January, 1693-4, Plymouth, Mass.

COLE, JOHN and DEBORAH BARTLETT, 22 November, 1668, Hadley, Mass.

COLLAR, NATHANIEL and MARY BARRETT, 10 October, 1693, Chelmsford, Mass.

COLLINS, JOHN and MARY BURCH, 3 December, 1688, Salem, Mass.

COOK, HANNA and JOHN BAKER, 30 January, 1676, Windsor, Conn.

COOKE, FRANCES and GABRIEL THROCK-MORTON, 1690, Gloucester County, Virginia.

COOLEY, DEBORAH and NICHOLAS FIELDING, 9 August, 1694, New York City.

COOPER, MARY and JOHN MERRIAM, 1663, Concord, Mass.

COPELAND, WILLIAM and MARY BASS WEBB (widow), 13 April, 1694, Plymouth, Mass.

COPESTAFF, JOHN and JOAN WRIGHT, 26 January, 1680, New York.

CORSON, WILLIAM and MARY ELLIS, 27 June, 1699, Boston, Mass.

COTTA, JOHN and SARAH WHARTON, 4 May, 1698, Boston, Mass.

COWES, GILES and AGNES BERRY, 27 February, 1672, Ipswich, Mass.

COWLES, ISAAC and MARY ANDREWS, 2 January, 1697, East Hartford, Conn.

COWLES, JOSEPH and ABIGAIL ROYS, 13 July, 1697, Farmington, Conn.

COWLES, SAMUEL and RACHEL PORTER, 12 May, 1685, Farmington, Conn.

COWLES, SARAH and STEPHEN HART, 18 December, 1689, East Hartford, Conn.

COWLES, TIMOTHY and HANNAH PITKIN, 1 January, 1690, Farmington, Conn.

COX, WILLIAM and JUDA MARTINS, 30 March, 1687, New York.

CRAGIN, JOHN and SARAH DAWES (born in England), 4 November, 1661, Woburn, Mass.

CREWE, ANNE and PHILLIP ADDAMS, 9 May, 1670, Somerset County, Maryland.

CROFUT, MARY H. and ABNER FELLOWS, 16 July, 1667, Berlin, Conn.

CURRIER, WILLIAM C. and ELIZABETH ELLIS, 1 June, 1683, Somerset County, Maryland.

CURTIS, DANIEL and MARY GREENE, 1 July, 1666, Somerset County, Maryland.

Genealogy Magazine

Vol. XV   APRIL, 1930   No. 2

MARRIAGE RECORDS BEFORE 1699
(Being a Supplement to "American Marriages Before 1699," by William Montgomery Clemens, published in 1926)

(Continued from January issue.)

DAGGETT, PATIENCE and SAMUEL ANNABEL, 11 April, 1695, Rehoboth, Mass.

DALTON, PHILEMON and MEHITABLE GOVE, daughter of Edward, 25 September, 1690, Hampton, N. .H.

DALTON, SAMUEL and MEHITABLE PALMER, 6 February, 1650, Haverhill, Mass.

DAM, MARY and THOMAS TITCOMB, 30 November, 1693, Newbury, Mass.

DANFORTH, JONATHAN and REBECCA PARKER, daughter of Jacob, 27 June, 1682, Billerica, Mass.

DANIEL, SARAH and JAMES JOHNSON, 26 March, 1675, Hampton, N. H.

DANN, MARY and PHILIP CONNARD, 17 December, 1677, Somerset Co., Md.

DARLING, DENNIS and HANNAH FRANCIS, 3 November, 1662, Braintree, Mass.

DAVENPORT, JOHN and MARTHA GOULD SELLECK, 18 April, 1695, Stamford, Conn.

DAVIDSON, PETER and ANN PRESTON, 6 March, 1695, Charlestown, Mass.

DAVIS, HANNAH and JOSEPH GRIGGS, 8 November, 1654, Roxbury, Mass.

DAVIS, JACOB, JR., and MARY HASKELL, 1 September, 1687, Gloucester, Mass.

DAWES, SARAH and JOHN CRAGIN (born in England), 4 November, 1661, Woburn, Mass.

DAWES, WILLIAM and SUSANNA MILLS, January, 1641, Braintree, Mass.

DAY, JOHN and SARAH PENGRY, 20 April, 1664, Ipswich, Mass.

DAY, SAMUEL and MARY DUMBLETON, 22 July, 1697, West Springfield, Mass.

DEARE, EDWARD and ELIZABETH GRIFFIN, 3 March, 1660, Ipswich, Mass.

DEMMING, THOMAS and MARY WILLIAMS, 2 June, 1698, Wethersfield, Conn.

DENISON, MARGARET and JAMES BROWN, JR., 5 June, 1678. Rehoboth, Mass.

DENNETT, MOSES and LYDIA FERNALD, 18 February, 1674, York Co., Maine.

DE WITT, EMERENTZE and MARTINUS HOFF-MAN, May, 1664, Hoffmantown, N. Y.

DICKINSON, ELIPHALET and REBECCA BRON-SON, 4 November, 1697, Wethersfield, Conn.

DICKINSON, OBADIAH and SARAH BEARDS-
· LEY, 8 January, 1669, Hatfield, Mass.

DICKINSON, SAMUEL and ELIZABETH WRIGHT, 16 September, 1684, Wethersby, Conn.

DIXON, ANTHONY and ELIZABETH CAM-MELL, 8 January, 1684, Salem Co., N. J.

DODGE, ANNA and JOHN EDWARDS, 1 April, 1698, Wenham, Mass.

DORCHESTER, JAMES and SARAH PARSONS, 1 March, 1677, Hartford, Conn.

DOUGLASS, ANN and NATHANIEL GARY, 14 October, 1658, Roxbury, Mass.

DOWNING, JANE and NICHOLAS CARNABY, 12 December, 1694, New York.

DUDLEY, KATHERINE (Mrs.) and JOHN ALLIN, 8 September, 1653, Dedham, Mass.

DUDLEY, MARY and JOSEPH FLETCHER, 17 June, 1688, Concord, Mass.

DUMBLETON, MARY and Samuel DAY, 22 July, 1697, Springfield, Mass.

DUMMIN, JANE and JOHN PLIMPTON, 13 January, 1644, Dedham, Mass.

DUYTS, CATHERINE and JOHN PAULDING, 16 March, 1688, Westchester Co., N. Y.

Genealogy Magazine

Vol. XV   JULY, 1930   No. 3

MARRIAGE RECORDS BEFORE 1699

(Being a Supplement to "American Marriages
Before 1699," by William Montgomery
Clemens, published in 1926.)

(Continued from April Issue.)

AMES, ANNA and THOMAS WILDER, 1 April,
1640, Charleston, Mass.

EARL, ROGER and LIDIA TRAVISE, 25 October,
1694, Boston, Mass.

EASTERBROOK, BENJAMIN and ABIGAL WIL-
LARD, 29 November, 1694, Boston, Mass.

EASTMAN, SUSANNA and THOMAS WOOD, 16
May, 1693, Haverhill, Mass.

EATON, BENJAMIN and SARAH HOSKINS, 4
December, 1660, Plymouth, Mass.

EBREW, GRACE and ROBERT ONION, 3 October, 1643, Dedham, Mass.

EDMUNDS, MARY and WILLIAM HUTCHINS,
1 September, 1657, Bradford, Mass.

ELLIOTT, HANNAH and STEPHEN WILLIS, 3
June, 1670, Braintree, Mass.

ELDERKIN, JOHN and ELIZABETH GAYLORD,
1 March, 1660, Wethersfield, Conn.

ELLIS, WILLIAM and MARY MITCHELL, 1675,
Charlestown, Mass.

ELMENDORF, GERTRUDE and EVERT WYN-
KOOP, 26 August, 1688, Kingston, N. Y.

EMERY, ZACHARIAH and ELIZABETH GOOD-
WIN, 9 December, 1686, Kittany, Maine.

EMES, HANNAH and SAMUEL BABCOCK, 1 July,
1674, Milton, Mass.

EVERETT, JOHN and MARY BOWMAN, 1 January, 1692, Lexington, Mass.

EXETER, ELIZABETH and SAMUEL NEALE, 29
June, 1699, Elizabeth City County, Va.

EYERS, SIMON and ELIZABETH ALLERTON, 22
July, 1679, New Haven, Conn.

www.ingramcontent.com/pod-product-compliance
Lightning Source LLC
Chambersburg PA
CBHW070357270326
41926CB00014B/2588